CONTEMPORARY READINGS IN BIOMEDICAL ETHICS

Harcourt College Publishers

Where Learning Comes to Life

TECHNOLOGY

Technology is changing the learning experience, by increasing the power of your textbook and other learning materials; by allowing you to access more information, more quickly; and by bringing a wider array of choices in your course and content information sources.

Harcourt College Publishers has developed the most comprehensive Web sites, e-books, and electronic learning materials on the market to help you use technology to achieve your goals.

PARTNERS IN LEARNING

Harcourt partners with other companies to make technology work for you and to supply the learning resources you want and need. More importantly, Harcourt and its partners provide avenues to help you reduce your research time of numerous information sources.

Harcourt College Publishers and its partners offer increased opportunities to enhance your learning resources and address your learning style. With quick access to chapter-specific Web sites and e-books . . . from interactive study materials to quizzing, testing, and career advice . . . Harcourt and its partners bring learning to life.

Harcourt's partnership with Digital:Convergence™ brings :CRQ™ technology and the :CueCat™ reader to you and allows Harcourt to provide you with a complete and dynamic list of resources designed to help you achieve your learning goals. Just swipe the cue to view a list of Harcourt's partners and Harcourt's print and electronic learning solutions.

http://www.harcourtcollege.com/partners/

CONTEMPORARY READINGS IN BIOMEDICAL ETHICS

Walter Glannon

HARCOURT COLLEGE PUBLISHERS

Fort Worth   Philadelphia   San Diego   New York   Orlando   Austin   San Antonio
Toronto   Montreal   London   Sydney   Tokyo

Publisher	Earl McPeek
Executive Editor	David Tatom
Market Strategist	Adrienne Krysiuk
Project Manager	Andrea Archer

[Photo credits/Cover credit: Bibliothèque nationale de France/Sheirazada Herring]

ISBN: 0-15-507544-6
Library of Congress Catalog Card Number: 2001090945

Address for Domestic Orders
Harcourt College Publishers, 6277 Sea Harbor Drive, Orlando, FL 32887-6777
800-782-4479

Address for International Orders
International Customer Service
Harcourt, Inc., 6277 Sea Harbor Drive, Orlando, FL 32887-6777
407-345-3800
(fax) 407-345-4060
(e-mail) hbintl@harcourt.com

Address for Editorial Correspondence
Harcourt College Publishers, 301 Commerce Street, Suite 3700, Fort Worth, TX 76102

Web Site Address
http://www.harcourtcollege.com

Printed in the United States of America

1 2 3 4 5 6 7 8 9 0   202   9 8 7 6 5 4 3 2 1

Harcourt College Publishers

CONTENTS

PREFACE

This book is designed to engage students in thinking about the main ethical issues in medical practice, biomedical research, and health policy that have been of perennial and contemporary interest and debate. The articles capture these issues in six general areas of biomedical ethics. They include the patient-physician relationship, research involving human subjects, reproductive rights and technologies, death and dying, human genetics, and allocation of scarce medical resources. There are other related areas that deserve attention, such as psychiatric ethics, privacy and confidentiality of medical information, especially in the light of the AIDS epidemic, and genetic modification of crops and food. But these go beyond the aim and limits of this book. With only a few exceptions, the articles were originally published after 1990, and many of these have appeared since 1995. This gives the book a contemporary flavor, especially with respect to developments in research involving human subjects, genetics, and cross-cultural aspects of the patient-physician relationship.

The structure of the book is as follows. In Part I, the main historical developments in medicine and the parallel evolution of biomedical ethics are sketched. In addition, the main ethical theories from philosophy are presented and analyzed to elucidate ethical problems in medical practice and research. A framework for justifying decisions and actions in these contexts is also presented. Different methods of reasoning about particular cases are then examined. In Parts II through VII, a brief introduction to each of the general themes and a brief summary of each of the seven articles are given. The articles are followed by questions for discussion, cases illustrating legal aspects of biomedical ethics corresponding to the general topic in each Part, and then suggestions for further reading. Although many of the cases cited were decided in court, not all of them were. But all have had important legal implications. The structure of each of the book's parts and the contents of the articles they contain are designed to present both the theoretical and practical aspects of biomedical ethics and to reflect the interdisciplinary nature of the subject. The article summaries are guides intended to assist students in interpreting and critically evaluating the claims and arguments of the authors. Accordingly, they are not substitutes for the articles but rather supplements to them. Moreover, the discussion questions, cases, and bibliography are intended to assist in stimulating and refining students' own ethical reflections on the material.

ACKNOWLEDGMENTS

I thank the five readers commissioned by Harcourt for their constructive comments and suggestions regarding the structure and contents of the book. Drake Bush, the advisory editor for Harcourt, wisely and patiently guided me at every step along the way to the book's completion. His help is greatly appreciated. I also thank David Tatom, Executive Editor for Harcourt, for allowing me to do the book, John Martin Fischer, who encouraged and supported me in this project, and Lainie Friedman Ross, who first got me interested in biomedical ethics. I am most grateful to my wife, Teresa Yee-Wah Yu, for her inspiration and unconditional love and support.

PART I:

INTRODUCTION TO THE HISTORY, THEORIES, AND METHODS OF BIOMEDICAL ETHICS

Walter Glannon

✝

HISTORY

Biomedical ethics is a species of practical normative ethics. It is the study of issues pertaining to what ought to or ought not to be done in biotechnology, medical research, and medical practice. It involves the formulation of theoretical and methodological frameworks within which to analyze ethical questions and provide justification for actions and policies in such areas as research involving human subjects, treatment of patients, and allocation of scarce medical resources. Whereas philosophy has provided most of the theory behind biomedical ethics, religion, law, anthropology, and sociology also have played a major role in shaping its evolution. Thus, biomedical ethics is very much an interdisciplinary field.

Although, in many respects, biomedical ethics had its origins in the fifth century B.C. in the school of thought associated with the physician Hippocrates (460–377), developments within the last 30 years have made biomedical ethics emerge as a discipline in its own right. These developments include the abuse of human subjects in research, the repudiation of physician paternalism, and technological advances in hemodialysis, organ transplantation, mechanical life-support, assisted reproduction, and prenatal genetic testing and diagnosis. Insofar as these developments entail questions of

1

considerable ethical import, biotechnology, medicine, and ethics are inextricably intertwined [1].

The School of Hippocrates emphasized the qualities of the good physician, especially the sort of behavior the physician should exhibit toward patients on the way to healing them. Thus, the doctor-patient relationship was the first area of ethical concern in medicine. Unlike the contemporary emphasis on curing, the concern with healing in the earliest days of Western medicine reflected the aim of restoring and reintegrating the sick into harmony with the natural order [2]. Indeed, this aim has not been restricted to Western medicine alone but has been the essence of both ancient and contemporary Chinese medicine as well, to cite just one example. 'Cure' derives from the Latin 'curare,' to get rid of disease, while 'heal' derives from the Old English 'haelen,' to become whole or sound. Generally, curing is associated with disease, whereas healing is associated with illness. The first pertains to treating a dysfunction of physiological processes. The second pertains to addressing a person's subjective experience of and response to such dysfunction. Healing patients, then, consists in helping them cope with the diseases that afflict them. It is not surprising that the emphasis in ancient medicine was on healing, because there were so few diseases that could be cured. Still today, many maintain that although more diseases now can be cured or at least controlled with appropriate therapeutic interventions, healing and curing should be seen as complementary goals of medicine.

The ethical principles of the School of Hippocrates defined the duty of the physician, which specified benefiting the sick and doing them no harm. These are captured in the Hippocratic Oath, attributed to Hippocrates but more likely derived from the Pythagoreans, which requires that the physician "follow the method of treatment which, according to my ability and judgments, I consider for the benefit of my patients, and abstain from whatever is deleterious and mischievous . . . " [3]. This was the first articulation of the principles of beneficence and nonmaleficence, the duty to benefit and not harm patients, which are strictly adhered to today as two essential components of the doctor-patient relationship. However, the Hippocratic model is very much a paternalistic one, whereby the good doctor gives orders for the good patient to follow. The idea that the patient, after being informed of his or her medical condition, could make decisions about treatment in accord with his or her own best interests was at this time anathema and took more than two thousand years to be accepted and respected in the form of patient autonomy or self-determination [4]. Respect for autonomy, together with beneficence and nonmaleficence, is now one of the core principles of biomedical ethics. In fact, many now maintain that patient autonomy is the most important of these principles.

It is worth repeating that the Hippocratic tradition was focused on healing rather than curing, largely or most likely because of the limited efficacy of the available medicines at that time to treat disease. Understanding the etiology of disease was very primitive. In the early Common Era, however, the philosopher and physician Galen (131–201?) wrote extensively on anatomy, physiology, pathology, and, indeed, every branch of medicine known at that time. The dominant belief from Galen was that disease resulted from an imbalance of the four humours of the body— blood, phlegm, yellow bile, and black bile. But this mode of classification did little to improve medical care, and for most people, acute infectious diseases made life relatively short. Later, the Jewish philosopher and physician Moses Maimonides (1135–1204) most notably carried on the Hippocratic ethical tradition of his Greek predecessor, focusing on the doctor-patient relationship in his writings, specifying the doctor's duties to his patients. Maimonides' work displayed a general estimation of the Greek tradition of medical practice, which leaned on the ethical teachings of Hippocrates and the physiological teachings of Galen.

Surprisingly, Galen's views remained virtually unchallenged until the sixteenth century, when they were rectified by Andreas Vesalius in his work on human anatomy, *De humani corporus fabrius libri septem* (1543). Less than 100 years after Vesalius, William Harvey (1578–1657), an English physician and physiologist, established that the blood circulates within a closed system, with the heart understood as a pump. Together, the works of Vesalius and Harvey provided the underpinning for many advances in human anatomy, physiology, clinical medicine, and surgery that would take place in the remainder of the millennium.

The next important work on medical ethics, and the first to bear the term explicitly, was *Medical Ethics*, written by the English physician Thomas Percival in 1803. It expanded the ethics of Hippocrates and Maimonides to a broader social ethics of medicine, emphasizing, in particular, the professional responsibility of physicians. This idea of professional responsibility later was incorporated into the first version of the American Medical Association's Code of Medical Ethics in 1847, which subsequently was revised under the new title, *Principles of Medical Ethics*, in 1903 and 1912. After many transformations, the 1966 version of the Code embodied a number of principles that, very much in the spirit of Percival, emphasized not only beneficence and nonmaleficence to patients, but also professional responsibility and responsibility to the social community at large. The ideas of fiduciary responsibility, of the physicians' duty to serve the interests of their patients rather than their own, may be taken as a modern version of the Hippocratic injunction to help and do no harm to patients. In this respect, there is a common ethical thread extending from the School of Hippocrates to the current AMA Code, a thread consisting fundamentally of the principles of beneficence and nonmaleficence [5].

Developments in the 1960s and 1970s, however, showed that there were additional ethical dimensions to medical practice and medical research beyond the ideas of benefit and harm to patients. What became increasingly evident was a paternalism implicit in beneficence that effectively left the patient out of any decision-making about treatment. Furthermore, patients were entered as research subjects in various forms of medical experimentation without knowledge of the risks this experimentation entailed.

In an influential article published in the *New England Journal of Medicine* in 1966, the distinguished Harvard Professor of Anesthesiology, Henry Beecher, exposed twenty-two clinical investigations involving human subjects that he deemed unethical [6]. This generated widespread concern about the ethics of clinical research involving human subjects. Beecher's work followed in the wake of the Nuremberg Trials of 1947, which redressed the inhumane horrors of medical experimentation in the ostensibly scientific research done by Nazi doctors in the concentration camps of

World War II. The Nuremberg Tribunal formulated ten basic principles that have become known as the Nuremberg Code of 1947, which specifies certain types of medical experimentation that "conform to the ethics of the medical profession generally" and that "must be observed in order to satisfy moral, ethical, and legal concepts" [7]. Albert Jonsen notes that the public attention to Nuremberg marked "a new beginning in the moral traditions of medicine, a beginning that would become bioethics" [8]. Also, around the time Beecher's article was published, it was revealed that, from 1931 onward, the United States Public Health Service had sponsored a study in which poor African Americans living in Tuskegee, Alabama, were unknowingly deprived of treatment for syphilis so that the course of untreated disease could be studied [9].

All of these revelations showed that there were widespread violations of the autonomy, interests, and rights of human subjects in medical research who, thus, were being harmed by it. For these reasons, in 1964, the World Medical Association formulated the Declaration of Helsinki, which distinguished between clinical research that is essentially therapeutic for a patient, and clinical research that is essentially scientific and without therapeutic intent. Subsequently, in the early 1970s, the United States Congress established the National Commission for the Protection of Human Subjects of Biomedical and Behavioral Research. The Commission's *Belmont Report* of 1979 formulated respect for persons as autonomous agents, beneficence, and justice as the ethical principles that should govern research. These principles led to the respective requirements of informed consent, an appropriate risk-benefit ratio, and equitable selection of subjects for research. The Commission defended respect for autonomy in giving "weight to autonomous persons' considered opinions and choices while refraining from obstructing their actions unless they are clearly detrimental to others" [10]. The significance of this point is underscored by the fact that such preeminent bioethicists as H.Tristram Engelhardt, Robert Veatch, Tom Beauchamp, and James Childress all have emphasized autonomy, and the respect for persons that it entails, as the core principle of biomedical ethics [11]. Significantly, the concept of autonomy (from the Greek *auto* = 'self' + *nomos* = 'law'), or self-determination, combines two fundamental principles from two distinct traditions of ethical theory: the Kantian notion of respect for persons as ends in themselves; and the Millian notion of liberty, of individual persons pursuing their own interests provided that doing so does not interfere with the interests of or result in harm to others.

For many in the field, respect for autonomy has replaced beneficence (and correspondingly nonmaleficence) as the most important ethical principle grounding biomedical ethics. At least, autonomy has become equal in ethical importance to these other more traditional principles. It must be emphasized, however, that it was not just research on human subjects that motivated the need to give pride of place to patient autonomy, but also certain aspects of the patient-physician relationship. I have pointed out already that many have taken the Hippocratic Oath to be excessively paternalistic, showing little, if any, concern for patients' self-determination in making decisions about treatment that they judged to be in their own best interests. The emphasis on autonomy has accorded special status to the doctrine of informed consent.

The doctrine of informed consent was articulated by Justice Cardozo in the case of *Schloendorff v. Society of New York Hospitals* (1914). Cardozo states that to be informed a patient must receive adequate medical information on which to base his or her choice about treatment. To consent freely, the patient must be of sound mind, which gives him or her the right to determine what shall be done to his or her body. Furthermore, the patient must not be subject to any coercion or undue influence. Still, informed consent did not become firmly established until the legal case of *Salgo v. Stanford* in 1957, which ruled that the physician must disclose to the patient the nature of the illness, the risks and benefits of the proposed procedure and its alternatives, as well as the consequences of refusing treatment.

Informed consent consists of two components: the professional duty of the physician to disclose all relevant medical information, including diagnosis, prognosis, and available treatments; and the right of the competent patient to make his or her own decision about treatment in the light of this information. It forges a special link between doctor and patient, a link which, unlike the paternalistic Hippocratic model, puts physician and patient on equal footing. Ideally, it is a model of shared decision-making between informing physicians and competent patients, who weigh the benefits and risks and voluntarily choose whether to be treated or to enter a clinical trial in a way that is consistent with their own beliefs, interests, and values. This exercise of self-determination is what makes the patient's choice autonomous [12]. As the articles in Part II show, however, the interaction between patient and physician is a complex one, and in many instances it may be difficult to claim that there is a clear transition from physician paternalism to patient autonomy.

One reason for this is that competence is not always an all-or-nothing fact but often comes in degrees. And when a patient's decision about whether to have or forego a treatment entails a significant risk of harm to the patient or others, the threshold of competence necessary to uphold patient autonomy will be set quite high. In these cases, if a patient fails to meet that threshold, then physician paternalism may outweigh patient autonomy. Generally, the less competent a patient is and the greater the risk of harm, the stronger reasons there are to override patient autonomy regarding the decision to have or forego treatment. On the other hand, the more competent a patient is and the lower the risk of harm in having or foregoing a given treatment, the stronger the reasons are for upholding his or her autonomy [13]. For example, if a schizophrenic patient has not been taking the prescribed medication, is deluded and threatening to burn down an apartment building, then there would be reasons for physician paternalism to override patient autonomy. If, however, the patient has been taking the medication and his or her delusions are under control, the possibility that the patient may burn down an apartment building would not be a sufficient reason to override his or her autonomy. In the first scenario, the combination of the degree of competence and risk of harm gives more weight to paternalism; in the second scenario, the combination of the same factors gives more weight to autonomy.

Veatch and others have argued that deontological principles such as respect for autonomy, not killing, justice, and fairness in meeting different patients' needs have assumed priority over consequentialist principles such as beneficence and nonmaleficence.

In this regard, contemporary biomedical ethics has, in Jonsen's words, "turned the Hippocratic tradition, based in medical beneficence, on its head" [14]. Still, it is more appropriate to say, not that autonomy and justice have usurped the position of beneficence and nonmaleficence, but rather that the first two complement the latter two. All four of these principles constitute necessary and sufficient conditions of explanation and justification for decisions and actions in all areas of medicine and biomedical research. Indeed, these four principles constitute the core framework of medical ethics according to the most widely read and respected text in the field, Beauchamp and Childress' *Principles of Biomedical Ethics*. It is equally important to point out that, insofar as the first three of the principles of biomedical ethics pertain to the patient-physician relationship, the focus of the discipline has remained fundamentally unchanged since the time of the School of Hippocrates.

There are more ethical dimensions in medicine and medical research than the physician-patient relationship, however. In 1961, thanks to the inventive work of Dr. Belding H. Scribner, hemodialysis became a reality for people with renal failure. This made it possible to purify the blood of patients who otherwise would have died. In this regard, it was one of the first life-saving technologies in modern medicine. Yet dialysis was expensive and not available on a large scale, which meant that not all patients who needed it could receive it. This marked one of the first instances of allocating scarce medical resources, the ethical aspects of which arose with respect to the question of how patients would be selected. It was here, as distinct from cases involving the doctor-patient relationship, that justice or fairness began to figure prominently and take on as much ethical significance as the other three principles we have discussed. Justice is concerned generally with the proper distribution of benefits and burdens. Fairness is concerned generally with meeting people's claims of need in proportion to their strength, where claims of greater need have greater strength. But how do we adjudicate between or among equal claims of need to a scarce resource when its very scarcity means that not everyone's needs can be met? The articles in Part VII address this question.

As dialysis became more common, the problem of treating people in renal failure became more tractable. What helped ameliorate the situation even more was the advent of organ transplantation, not only of kidneys, but also of hearts, livers, and other organs. Moreover, the development of immunosuppressive drugs to reduce the likelihood of rejection by recipients' immune systems has made organ transplantation largely successful. Nevertheless, there are many more people who need hearts and livers than are available, thus giving rise to the question of how criteria of prioritizing patients can be done justly and fairly. What distinguishes this issue, and the principle of justice or fairness with which it is associated, from the principles of beneficence and nonmaleficence, is that questions about how to allocate scarce medical resources arise on macro or policy levels, quite unlike the microlevel of bedside decision-making. And while the principle of beneficence and the theory of consequentialism (or utilitarianism) are what underlie the idea of cost-effectiveness in the allocation of scarce resources, this issue cannot be discussed without some appeal to contractarian theory and the idea of public agreement on principles that all follow for the sake of mutually beneficial cooperation and which no one can reasonably reject. Contractarianism, along with other ethical theories, will be discussed later in this chapter.

Some have argued that the importance of autonomy has been exaggerated. For example, Edmund Pellegrino and David Thomasma assert that "the patient autonomy model does not give sufficient attention to the impact of disease on the patient's capacity for autonomy. . . . Ill persons often become so anxious, guilty, unreasonable, fearful, or hostile that they make judgments they would not make in calmer times" [15]. On this view, illness, not a paternalistic physician, is the main obstacle to autonomy, which arguably should be the goal rather than the starting point of treatment. In times of illness, what some patients want is not so much the ability or opportunity to make their own decisions about treatment. Rather, they want a physician who, while respecting the patient's interests and values, takes control of the situation and acts on his or her best professional judgment, which the patient implicitly trusts. The patient's trust in the physician can in some cases be critical to the patient's response to treatment, and this is not a phenomenon that can be accommodated within the autonomy model. These considerations suggest that beneficence should be construed broadly enough to include trust, compassion, empathy, and other virtues of the physician that work to the patient's benefit. Despite any shortcomings of the principle of autonomy, this broad interpretation of the principle of beneficence should not be seen as competing with autonomy but instead as complementing it.

Many of the pioneers in bioethics in the 1970s were theologians or people with a background in religious ethics. Joseph Fletcher, Paul Ramsey, and Richard McCormick are the most prominent names that come to mind [16]. Their role in the debate was motivated largely by the ethical, religious, and legal questions raised by the diametrically opposed issues of prolonging lives of patients with terminal illnesses, on the one hand, and allowing them to die, on the other. These questions arose only because of new life-extending technology, such as mechanical life-support in the form of ventilators to maintain respiration and brain function when patients had become unable to do these on their own. Twenty years earlier, such patients would have died because the technology sustaining their lives did not exist. Particularly significant in this regard was the case of Karen Ann Quinlan, a patient who had been in a prolonged persistent vegetative state. It came to public attention in 1976 when the New Jersey Superior Court granted her father the right to have her life-support disconnected, [17]. This landmark case raised for the first time such legal questions as a state's interest in protecting life. At a deeper level, it forced many religious ethicists to reflect on these cases in the light of the Sanctity-of-Life Doctrine and whether it would be permissible, or whether it would be a violation of this Doctrine, to withdraw or withhold treatment.

At the other end of human life, the Florida case of "Baby Theresa" in 1992 forced many to consider whether it was permissible on religious grounds to withhold treatment from an anencephalic infant, one with only a brain stem and basic autonomic nervous system functioning and with a very short life expectancy [18]. This issue was addressed against the secular view that treating such an infant with life-sustaining technology was not permissible because it served no therapeutic purpose.

Christian, Jewish, and other religious as well as secular ethicists all have contributed to fruitful ethical debate about medical decisions at the margins of life. Some of the main religious-based principles motivating much of this debate are examined later in this chapter.

Another area where religion has influenced biomedical ethics is reproduction in general and assisted reproductive technologies such as in vitro fertilization (IVF), artificial insemination, preimplantation genetic diagnosis of embryos, and embryo selection in particular. Much of the ethical debate over these technologies stems from the debate over abortion. Questions such as whether a fetus has a moral status and right to life, and how this status and right weigh against a pregnant woman's right to make autonomous reproductive choices, extend into further questions of whether embryos have any moral status and right to be allowed to develop into fetuses and persons, regardless of the sort of life they would have once they are born. Moreover, multiple births resulting from the use of fertility drugs and IVF have raised the question of how to weigh the sanctity of life in, for example, bringing septuplets to term, against the quality of life each would have after birth, and whether such qualitative judgments could justify terminating some of them at an early fetal stage. Secular ethical views have had as much force in this debate as religious ones.

Advances in the same molecular biology that made IVF possible have made possible presymptomatic testing and diagnosis of genetically based diseases in adults. The information yielded by these tests can have a significant psychological impact on individuals and their families, and depending on how they are used, can be either beneficial or harmful. The most recent of these advances, at once fascinating and worrisome, is the prospect of cloning human beings. All of these technologies raise vexing ethical questions about what our responsibilities are to the people we bring into existence. Are there some lives with so much protracted pain and suffering that they would not be worth living? Does the idea of testing for genetic predisposition to disease cause undue psychological harm and, thus, constitute a reason against it? Would the availability of genetic information indicating that one had a genetic predisposition to a disease make one vulnerable to discrimination by potential employers and insurers? Does the idea of testing and selectively terminating embryos with genetic mutations that would result in severe disease and disability discriminate against people with disabilities? Does cloning represent the height of genetic determinism and genetic reductionism and thereby violate fundamental features of our humanity?

In this first part, the main developments in medical practice and medical research since antiquity have been outlined, and parallel developments in medical ethics have been sketched briefly. Roughly, biomedical ethics can be divided into research and clinical ethics, on the one hand, and policy issues, on the other. In more precise terms, it falls into six categories, corresponding to the six subsequent parts of this book: Part II The Patient-Physician Relationship; Part III Research Involving Human Subjects; Part IV Reproductive Rights and Technologies; Part V Genetics; Part VI Death and Dying; and Part VII Allocation of Scarce Medical Resources [19].

Analysis of ethical questions in these different categories requires a theoretical framework of principles and theories to inform and justify our judgments about the rightness or wrongness of actions in different cases or of different policies. There are at least seven ethical theories that are relevant to decision-making and justification in biomedical ethics; some of them have been alluded to already. But a more sustained analysis of them and their relevance to bioethics is in order. Each of them will be considered in turn.

ETHICAL THEORIES

The history of Western ethics begins with Socrates, and the central question of ethics is traceable to Socrates' question in one of Plato's early dialogues: 'How should one live?' [20]. The injunction in the Hippocratic Oath that physicians should comport themselves in a certain way toward their patients may be taken as a restricted application of Socrates' much broader question. For Hippocrates, as well as for Socrates and his successors in Greek philosophy, there was no substantive distinction between the actions of a physician or any other person and their disposition to act in a certain way. One was the natural expression of the other. Nevertheless, it is necessary to distinguish the substantive question 'How should one live?' or 'How should medical professionals act toward their patients?' from the formal question of the point or nature of ethics and biomedical ethics. These two types of question are to be distinguished in turn from how people actually behave.

Descriptive ethics is concerned with the way things are, with how people do in fact act and live. *Normative ethics* is concerned with the way things ought to be, with how people ought to act or what sort of person one ought to be. It is 'normative' in the sense that it specifies norms or standards of right action and right behavior. The enterprise of employing the principles of normative ethics to inform our judgments about actions in such areas as biomedical ethics is practical normative ethics. While normative ethics seeks to articulate and defend principles that prescribe which actions are right or wrong, good or bad, permissible or impermissible, *meta-ethics* focuses on the meaning of terms like 'right' and 'wrong,' and on the forms of arguments employed to justify ethical principles. Meta-ethics also is concerned with the properties of ethics, as for instance whether there are moral or ethical facts independent of our judgments or social conventions that we may or may not come to know, as well as what sorts of moral facts there are. Put another way, normative ethics focuses on the *content* of morality, whereas meta-ethics focuses on the *nature* of morality [21].

With respect to normative ethical theories, there are two criteria that most of them have in common: (1) *objectivity*, where the morally right course of action will be the one that is based on the best reasons for doing it, and where these reasons can be recognized universally by anyone and thus cannot be reduced to any particular point of view; and (2) *impartiality*, where the reasons for or against actions assume that each person's interests and needs are equally important. Together, these criteria effectively are proscriptions against arbitrariness and personal or group bias in the ethical justification of behavior.

Although biomedical ethics is a normative enterprise, it cannot be totally divorced from meta-ethics because we need to justify our claims and judgments about the right or wrong course of action in a given case or class of cases. These claims presuppose an implicit understanding of the meaning of terms such as 'right' and 'wrong.' This is especially significant in the light of the challenge that cultural relativism poses to the presumed objectivity and impartiality of all ethical theories. That is, on the view that there are no universally valid judgments about what constitutes right or wrong action across all cultures, judgments about right and wrong actions in general, and about medical treatments or interventions in particular, will always be relative to and thus a function of different belief systems in different cultures. The challenge of cultural relativism, among other things, illustrates the importance of meta-ethical considerations in biomedical ethics.

The first normative ethical theory that has influenced biomedical ethics is *Divine Command Theory* [22]. This derives mainly from the Judeo-Christian tradition and roughly says that what is right is what is commanded by God, and that what is wrong is forbidden by God. This also has been called *Natural Law Theory*, whereby God endows all creatures with certain potentialities intended to serve a natural purpose in accord with laws of nature created by God. Human behavior is deemed right or wrong to the extent that it conforms or fails to conform to natural law. Perhaps the most common instance of this theory in biomedical ethics is something already mentioned, the Sanctity-of-Life Doctrine (SLD) [23]. Life is sacred and has infinite value precisely because it has been created by God. From this religious perspective, abortion, voluntary active (and perhaps also passive) euthanasia, infanticide, and some cases of withdrawing life support are wrong because they undermine the intrinsic value of all human life. Taken literally, SLD says that life should be prolonged regardless of quality of life considerations involving the condition of a patient. But many have objected that prolonging the life of a patient in a persistent vegetative state (PVS), for example, on sanctity-of-life grounds would be indefensible because it would be futile both in terms of medical treatment and the dignity and value of life for that person. Still another objection is that strictly following SLD would result in the pointless overuse of life-prolonging technologies and, thus, strain already scarce medical resources.

In fairness to Divine Command Theory and religious ethics, however, it should be pointed out that the interpretation and application of these principles are more subtle and nuanced than what might appear at first glance. For example, the Jewish *Halachic* tradition follows the Torah's teaching that every moment of life is intrinsically valuable, which suggests that no life-sustaining treatment ever can be futile [24]. But when principles of this tradition are invoked in cases involving patients with life-threatening conditions in an intensive care unit (ICU), they are based on the balance of the obligation to save and the prohibition against actively shortening life, versus not prolonging unnecessary suffering when there is no hope for recovery. This important qualification does not alter the sanctity or infinite value of a patient's life, but it can direct us in deliberating about what to do given the patient's condition, especially the nature and degree of pain and suffering and whether death is considered imminent.

The Doctrine of Double Effect (DDE) has a religious ancestry in the Catholic tradition. It was first formulated by Thomas Aquinas in his analysis of justifiable homicide and stated that any action that necessarily causes two inextricably linked effects, one good the other evil (or bad), is morally justified if and only if the good effect is intended, the evil effect is foreseen but unintended, and the good is proportional to the bad [25]. 'Proportional' simply means that the good effect morally outweighs the bad effect. This doctrine distinguishes between intended ends and necessary means, on the one hand, and foreseen but unintended side effects of intended actions, on the other. To illustrate its significance in medical ethics, a physician gives morphine to a patient in extreme pain with the intention of relieving the pain, but knows or foresees that morphine can depress respiration and thus might hasten the patient's death. The physician would be morally justified in acting in this way. The patient's death in this case would be a foreseen but unintended consequence of an act intended to do good—relieve pain and suffering—and would be proportional to, in the sense of morally outweighing, the bad outcome. In contrast, if the physician gave potassium chloride to the patient to kill that patient so that his or her organs could be harvested for transplantation to other patients, then the physician's action would be prohibited because the patient would be used as a means and the physician would intentionally be causing the bad effect of death.

One of the most common examples used to illustrate the DDE involves the distinction between craniotomy and hysterectomy in cases where a fetus must be killed to save the mother's life. There may be instances in which a woman may die because of complications at birth unless the head of the fetus she is trying to deliver is crushed. Strict adherents of the DDE might argue that there is an absolute prohibition against killing the fetus, and thus that a craniotomy should not be performed even if the woman will die. But these same adherents also might argue that if the pregnant woman has cancer of the uterus and must have a hysterectomy to remove the cancer, then it might be permissible. The end result in either case is the same—the death of the fetus. But there are important differences between them, and the defense of this distinction hinges on the fact that, in the craniotomy, the crushing of the fetus' head is an intended consequence of the procedure, whereas in the hysterectomy the death of the fetus is merely a foreseen but unintended side effect of the hysterectomy. Moreover, whereas in the second case the good effect is proportional to the bad one, the same does not hold in the first case.

It is precisely because religion-based principles like SLD and DDE are concerned almost exclusively with the intrinsic value of life and pay little if any attention to quality-of-life considerations bearing on benefit and harm that they are inadequate for many problem areas of biomedical ethics. Moreover, religious views are limited in offering helpful ways of interpreting the justice principle and how scarce medical resources or how expensive life-extending medical technology should be used. Nor can religious principles help interpret and apply the principle of autonomy to actual cases. These issues can be adequately addressed only by appeal to secular ethical theories.

Deontology and *consequentialism* are the two ethical theories most commonly invoked to justify medical decisions and determine whether actions in a medical context are right or wrong. They are invoked for guidance and justification of what are highlighted as the four main principles of biomedical ethics. Beneficence and nonmaleficence are at bottom consequentialist principles, concerned with treating patients in such a way as to bring about outcomes that will be beneficial and not harmful to them. Autonomy and justice are deontological principles concerned with such things as individuals' rights and freedom to engage in the process of rational decision-making and ensuring that procedures involved in distributing benefits and burdens give equal consideration to the claims of all persons. Of course, how scarce resources are to be distributed will be determined in part by estimation of outcomes and thus will involve consequentialist considerations as well as considerations of fairness.

For example, when there are more patients needing a liver transplant than there are available livers, we should follow the deontological principle of giving equal weight to the claims of all who have an equal need for the transplant. At the same time, though, one might be a better donor match than the others and be less likely to reject the transplant. For this reason, this individual may be given priority over the others to receive a transplant. The fact that some people would be more likely to have a better outcome than others with a transplant, plus the fact that livers are scarce, would constitute justifiable reasons for giving more weight to consequentialist considerations over deontological ones in such a case. Ignoring the differences among potential recipients in compatibility of tissue and blood type with the donor to give all an equal chance of receiving a transplant would be untenable. This is merely one illustration of the fact that most problems in biomedical ethics require consideration of the comparative weights of different principles. In most cases, practical ethical problems cannot be addressed adequately by the application of one overriding principle alone.

Deontology (from the Greek *deon* = 'duty') specifies that the rightness or wrongness of actions is a function not of the consequences of actions but instead of our duty or obligation to act in a way that respects the rights, interests, and claims of persons. These, in turn, are functions of persons' intrinsic dignity or worth. Deontology prescribes constraints on what we can or cannot do to other persons given their inviolable moral status. It is a backward-looking ethical theory in the sense that it is concerned with the motivation for and the reasoning process leading to action. Consequentialism, on the other hand, determines that the rightness or wrongness of an action is solely a function of its consequences. It is a forward-looking ethical theory in the sense that it looks beyond the action itself. Deontology defines the concept of 'right' in terms of such notions as respect for persons and fairness and takes these to be prior to the outcome-oriented concept of 'good.' Consequentialism defines the right as that which derives from the good. It first specifies what good is in nonmoral terms—pleasure, well-being, etc. Then it defines the right act as the one that produces the greatest balance of good over bad. Despite their differences, deontology and consequentialism prescribe rules that tell us which actions are obligated, prohibited, or permitted. Thus, both theories consist of moral requirements: in the first case, the requirement to respect the rights, interests, and claims of individuals; in the second, the requirement to bring about good outcomes that benefit others and prevent them from being harmed. It will be helpful to give a more detailed analysis of the defining features of each of these theories and then go on to assess their comparative strengths and weaknesses.

The most well-known deontologist is Immanuel Kant (1724–1804). Kant held that there is one fundamental or supreme principle of morality, the categorical imperative. This principle is based on and justified by rational considerations alone, given that the essence of our humanity is that we are beings with the capacity for reason. Indeed, for Kant, any emotions should be ruled out of the motivation and justification for action because they are too unstable a basis for ethical behavior. The categorical imperative consists of two main formulations: (1) Act only on that maxim by which you can at the same time will that it should become a universal law of nature; (2) Act so that you treat humanity, whether in your own person or in that of any other, always as an end and never as a means only [26]. This imperative is categorical in the sense that it is unconditional and, thus, admits no exceptions. It applies to us regardless of our personal desires, plans, or projects. And it is based on reason alone, which always tells us which action is right in every situation. This is distinct from a hypothetical imperative, which is conditional upon obtaining certain conditions of one's desires or emotions. A hypothetical imperative has the form: 'If you want x, then do y.' A categorical imperative has the form: 'Do not kill!' 'Always keep your promises!' and 'Always tell the truth!' For Kant, an action is right to the extent that it accords with the moral law, which is self-legislated by rational human beings and embodies the categorical imperative.

These examples of the categorical imperative specify what Kant calls perfect duties, or duties to follow the moral law without exception and without options with respect to how they are discharged. Imperfect duties allow options with respect to how we discharge them in following the moral law. In a triage situation in an ICU where there are fewer beds than there are patients who need them, the scarcity of the resource would give medical staff at most an imperfect duty to meet the claims of need of as many patients as possible. In choosing to give beds to those with a better chance of surviving, they would be defensibly discharging their imperfect duty to all the patients [27].

A maxim for Kant is a subjective principle or rule that guides one's action. To be universalizable, the maxim must pass two related tests. It must be both conceived and willed as a universal law without exceptions. For example, regarding the maxim to keep one's promises, the test would go as follows: 'What if everyone, without exception, acted on the principle that when I am in need, I should make promises that I have no intention of keeping.' The point here is a subtle one. Kant is not concerned so much with the consequences of everyone lying, but rather with the idea that doing so would be self-contradictory and hence irrational, a blatant violation of our rational humanity.

Still, the second formulation of the categorical imperative is more pertinent to biomedical ethics. For this formulation, not the first, specifies constraints on what we do to or for others, especially in cases where we may be strongly inclined to bring about a certain outcome by acting. Recall the example of the physician who intends to kill one patient with a lethal injection to remove the patient's organs and transplant them into others who need them. Although the physician may have been motivated to bring about the best outcome of saving the lives of four by killing one, the act of killing would be wrong because the physician would not be treating the patient as a locus of intrinsic dignity and worth, not as an end in itself, but only as a means to some end. Recall that a core notion in deontology is that there are certain prohibitions against performing some actions (killing) and requirements to perform other actions (telling the truth), which hold regardless of their outcome. Another example illustrating this point is the case of a competent patient who refuses to undergo a certain treatment for some condition despite knowing that it involves minimal risk and can correct the disorder. Although the physician would be strongly inclined to persuade the patient that the treatment should be performed on grounds of beneficence and nonmaleficence, if the patient knows the medical facts of his or her condition as well as the risks of not having treatment, then the physician would be obligated to uphold the patient's decision. The physician would have to respect the patient's autonomy and the exercise of the patient's right to informed consent. The physician would be treating the patient as an end in itself.

Perhaps the best example of the relevance of the second formulation of the categorical imperative to biomedical ethics involves research on human subjects. Those conducting clinical trials enlist subjects who may be randomized into control or study groups (see Part III). Because the purpose of a study is to determine the safety and efficacy of a given drug, and whether it is more effective than the standard treatment or a placebo, the researcher effectively is using the subjects as means. But insofar as the subjects give voluntary informed consent acknowledging their awareness of the risks and potential benefits of the clinical trial and of the randomization process, they are being treated as ends in themselves capable of autonomous decision-making. These subjects are being used as means, yet not merely as means but also as ends in themselves. Using human subjects in clinical trials who have given informed consent to participate and who are treated as ends in themselves can be justified as morally right action on deontological grounds.

The core idea in *consequentialism* is that what makes an action or policy right is that it brings about better consequences than any of its alternatives. Utilitarianism is the most well-known version of consequentialism, where the good is defined in terms of the principle of utility, or Greatest Happiness Principle, which directs us to act in such a way as to maximize pleasure, happiness, or welfare. Jeremy Bentham (1748–1832) first formulated this principle, which John Stuart Mill (1806–1873) later claimed "holds that actions are right in proportion as they tend to promote happiness, wrong as they tend to produce the reverse of happiness" [28]. Mill emphasized a condition of equality. That is, in applying the principle of utility we are to act such that each person counts for one, and nobody counts for more than one. In addition, Mill defended a principle of liberty, which says that people ought to be allowed to act freely, without interference from others, provided that they do not harm others [29].

As noted earlier, despite the differences in the ethical theories they defend, Kant's principle of respect for persons and Mill's principle of liberty together form a basis of autonomy and informed consent in biomedical ethics. But it is important not to confuse Mill's principle of liberty with his principle of utility, which conflicts with the concept of autonomy by not recognizing the uniqueness and inviolability of each person. Mill's two principles should be treated separately because they address different ethical issues.

Because consequentialism does not define the good solely in terms of utility, it is broader than and, accordingly, should not be identified with utilitarianism. And because the good in biomedical research and medical practice involves much more than pleasure or happiness, it is more appropriate to use consequentialism as the theory concerned with bringing about the best outcomes of actions in these contexts.

There are two types of consequentialism, act-consequentialism and rule-consequentialism (these correspond on a narrower scale to act- and rule-utilitarianism). Act-consequentialism says that an act is obligatory insofar as it promotes better consequences than any of its alternatives, and permissible insofar as it promotes consequences that are at least as good as any of its alternatives [30]. The earlier example of triage in the ICU can be justified on act-utilitarian grounds. As we have seen, it also can be justified on Kantian deontological grounds in terms of the imperfect duties of the medical staff to patients in this setting.

But another example of act-consequentialism is more problematic. If a doctor breaches confidentiality by divulging medical information about a patient with AIDS to a third party to prevent harm to other potential sexual partners, then this could deter other patients from being tested and come to distrust the medical profession. In this case, an act done to prevent harm and thereby bring about what seems to be a good consequence could have more harmful consequences in the long term.

Rule-consequentialism often is invoked to avoid this sort of problem with act-consequentialism. Whereas the latter asks 'Which action will promote the best consequences in this one situation?' the former asks 'What general rules will promote the best consequences in the long run, assuming that everyone accepts and complies with them?' Following the sort of guidance implicit in this question would tell the doctor of the AIDS patient to uphold confidentiality, for the reasons given. Nevertheless, some might claim that rule-consequentialism always collapses into act-consequentialism because there is no reason why long-term considerations cannot be factored into one's deliberations before performing a particular act. They might also contend that rule-consequentialism leads to a type of rule-worship, where agents are more concerned with following rules than with acting. But deontology is no better off in this respect if one rigidly adheres to the rules of action specified in the categorical imperative.

The most serious objection to consequentialism (in both 'act' and 'rule' forms) is that doing what promotes or brings about the best consequences may lead to actions that violate individuals' rights. This was evident in the forced transplantation case. A second and perhaps less serious objection is that consequentialism fails to take seriously the uniqueness and separateness of persons, being fundamentally an impersonal principle more concerned with *how much* of some good there is than with *who* has it. In other words, consequentialism, unlike deontology, is more concerned with the aggregate amount of some good than with the people who have this good, whether it be defined in terms of health or something else. Although consequentialism may appear to be superior in terms of grounding considerations of how to allocate scarce medical resources, it fails to pay sufficient attention to the claims of each patient who stands to benefit from or be burdened by a particular distribution. Because consequentialism fails to seriously consider such things as fairness or the autonomy of individual decision-makers, deontology would appear to be a superior ethical theory. But each of these theories has appealing features as well as shortcomings.

The main objection to deontology is that it does not offer a satisfactory explanation of and justification for actions. For the deontologist concerned with rights, fairness, and the process of ethical decision-making rather than its product, the number of people who stand to benefit or be harmed in situations of scarcity presumably is not a factor in ethical deliberation. But this suggests that it does not matter morally how many are treated or saved in these situations. Deontology does not offer much guidance about how to best meet the claims of need of many in such a way as to minimize harm to all those who may be affected by an action or set of actions. Consequentialism can provide the necessary justification for certain actions by appealing to the fairly simple idea that we should act in such a way as to promote the best consequences, while appealing to the notion that each person who stands to be affected counts for one and therefore that more people count for more.

It is important to emphasize, however, that in most ethical problems arising within biomedical ethics, deontological and consequentialist principles will have varying weight depending on the issues at hand. Thus, neither theory, nor the principles that are shorthand for them, should be taken as absolute but rather as prima facie. Each has considerable ethical weight, but each may be overridden by the other. In the transplant case, it is fairly obvious that the deontological principle of respect for the patient's right not to be harmed would override any consequentialist considerations of promoting the better outcome of saving the other four patients by transplanting the first patient's organs into them. On the other hand, the example of triage in the ICU shows rather straightforwardly that consequentialist considerations would have more weight than the deontological idea of flipping a coin and treating each patient equally, regardless of their prospects for survival and recovery. Other cases are more subtle and require careful weighing or balancing of the two theories and their corresponding principles.

A physician has received lab tests indicating a grim diagnosis and prognosis for a patient. The physician believes that the patient would become seriously depressed upon hearing this information, given a history of clinical depression. So, rather than telling the patient that he or she has a stage-four cancer that, with treatment, has only a 20% chance of five-year survival, the doctor says that the patient has a serious condition that can be treated. The physician intentionally leaves the meaning of 'treated' ambiguous. A deontologist would consider this action to be wrong because it fails to respect the patient as an end in itself and prevents the patient from giving informed consent about treatment. Any patient would reasonably want to know the whole truth. Truth-telling is an absolute, perfect, duty and, therefore, not telling the patient the whole truth would be wrong. But this seems to be too hasty a judgment. The physician is concerned with not harming the patient, and given the patient's psychiatric history as well as the traumatic nature of the information, there may be defensible grounds for not telling that patient every medical fact about his or her condition. After all, the patient here is not the typical "reasonable person."

In most cases, though, the physician has a duty to disclose all pertinent medical information to the patient. The doctrine of informed consent and the principle of fidelity require this. The point here is that, in *some* (admittedly rare) cases, pre-existing conditions may constitute exceptions to the rule that the whole truth always be told to patients. In these circumstances, although physicians must not lie to patients, *how much* information is given to patients, as well as *how* it is given, will depend on the physician's professional judgment in interpreting the concept of "therapeutic privilege" (to be addressed in Part II). Again, deontological considerations involving autonomy and informed consent must be balanced against consequentialist considerations involving beneficence and nonmaleficence in acting in the best interests of patients.

Suppose that a competent patient with an irreversible, terminal condition demands aggressive treatment to prolong his life. If the treatment will not yield any physiological benefit to the patient and will only prolong his suffering, then the physician would be obligated to explain to the patient that any possible benefits of the treatment would be outweighed by the likely burdens. Acceding to the patient's demand would compromise the physician's professional integrity by making the physician offer a treatment that he knows will not benefit the patient. The physician could appeal to nonmaleficence and professional integrity to justify not giving the treatment. Patient autonomy need not and indeed should not be upheld in such a case.

The doctor-patient relationship is even more nuanced than what has been suggested thus far. How we interpret such notions as respecting patient autonomy or doctors acting in patients' best interests is always influenced by certain attitudes of both doctors and patients toward each other. These include empathy, sympathy, and trust, all of which fall under the heading of virtue ethics. By capturing these nuances, this theory is a necessary supplement to deontology and consequentialism in understanding all the relevant ethical aspects of the interactions between patients and physicians.

In the general debate on ethical theory, *Virtue Ethics* is often seen as an antidote to the inadequacies of both deontology and consequentialism. These last two theories emphasize deontic terms such as 'ought,' 'duty,' 'obligation,' 'right,' and 'wrong.' In contrast, virtue ethics focuses more on such aretaic (*arete* = 'virtue,' 'excellence') terms as 'good,' 'bad,' 'admirable,' 'praiseworthy,' and 'reprehensible.' This was the dominant ethical theory for the ancient Greeks, especially Aristotle, and it has made a comeback in contemporary moral debate in response to what philosophers such as Elizabeth Anscombe and Alasdair MacIntyre have called the "bankruptcy" of modern moral philosophy [31]. Some believe that a virtue-based approach is at least as relevant to biomedical ethics as duty-based approaches because virtue ethics more adequately captures the humane aspects of medicine, particularly in the doctor-patient relationship. A physician is presumed to be compassionate, conscientious, courteous, and empathetic to patients. Correspondingly, patients are presumed to display such traits as self-control and moderation toward their health and reasonableness toward their physicians in terms of what they expect from them. Together, these traits engender the virtue of trust in the relationship.

Virtue ethics is agent-based rather than action-based. It is concerned with the agent's motivation for action, the disposition or character from which the action issues, rather than with features of the action itself. On this view, an action is evaluated as an expression of an agent's disposition or character. A person is compassionate, then, not so much because of the compassionate acts that are performed, but instead because these actions derive from a compassionate disposition. The disposition is fundamental; the properties of the action are derivative. And our moral evaluations of agents and their actions follow in this same order.

In terms of the emphasis on the motivation for action, there are parallels between virtue ethics and Kantian deontology. But they differ in at least one crucial respect. Unlike deontology, virtue ethics maintains that it is no part of the motivation of the virtuous agent that the physician morally *ought* to adopt this course of action or be a certain sort of person. Acting from duty is not the mark of excellence. The distinguishing feature of the virtuous person is a virtuous disposition with the belief that it is intrinsically good to be virtuous, and the person's actions reflect this in general. The person does not feel compelled to act from duty or a sense of obligation.

For Aristotle, a virtue is a mean between the extremes of excess and deficiency [32]. Courage, for example, is a mean between the extremes of cowardice and foolhardiness. It is cowardly to run away from all danger, but it is foolhardy to risk too much in the face of danger. Furthermore, generosity is a virtue between the extremes of stinginess and extravagance. But what about honesty or veracity? Earlier, we used an example to test the idea that a physician must always tell the truth to a patient, even when this might involve a grim diagnosis that would cause the patient psychological harm. When the issue was raised, it was done in the context of Kantian deontology and the absolute duty to always tell the truth out of respect for both patient autonomy and for the patient as an end in itself. But some might understand truth-telling in general as a virtue. If so, and if one must always tell the truth regardless of the consequences of doing so, then it seems that veracity is not a mean between extremes but instead is itself an extreme. Alternatively, some might argue that, although lying is always forbidden, not telling a patient every piece of information about the condition may be permissible in some cases. For instance, it is permissible for doctors not to tell a patient or their family about cardiopulmonary resuscitation when the patient's condition is terminal and death is imminent. Yet even if this is plausible, it is difficult to know which medical facts a patient needs to know to be sufficiently informed and which facts can be permissibly withheld. This is a delicate form of medical judgment requiring careful weighing of probable benefits and harms for which the idea of veracity as a virtue offers little help.

This case shows the main shortcoming of virtue ethics: it cannot handle instances of moral conflict. The physician wants to be honest with the patient in giving information. At the same time, the physician wants to be kind. Honesty and kindness are both virtues, yet they are not always compatible, and nothing in virtue ethics provides a principle to which we could appeal to adjudicate between these competing virtues and yield a solution to such a dilemma. A more general shortcoming of virtue ethics is that it does not have much relevance in biomedical ethics beyond the doctor-patient relationship. Ethical problems in research on human subjects, death and dying, and allocation of scarce medical resources are not amenable to analysis based on virtue ethics.

Feminist ethics is an extension of virtue ethics in the sense that it emphasizes an ethic of care involving human connectedness and the importance of human relationships [33]. "Feminine" virtues like kindness, generosity, helpfulness, and the emotions of empathy and sympathy on which they are based, serve as an antidote, or at least a necessary supplement, to the "masculine" emphasis on cool, impartial reason in addressing ethical issues. But feminist ethics is much more than this. Although there is no one definition of the enterprise, generally feminist ethics can be characterized as a concern for the rights and welfare of all women. Moreover, it is meant to be a corrective to the oppression, discrimination, and exclusion of women that have occurred in patriarchal societies and institutions. Feminist ethics seeks to redress the balance of power between men and women and put them on an equal scale with an equal voice on all ethical issues affecting them and their lives.

Exclusion of and discrimination against women have occurred all too often in the domain of health care. The most important gain in women's status in this domain has been in reproductive technology where, ever since the landmark *Roe v. Wade* decision on abortion in 1973, a woman's reproductive rights have assumed priority over the putative rights of the fetus. This is especially significant in the context of genetic testing and the right of a woman who is pregnant or is contemplating pregnancy to decide whether to be tested or not tested when there is a genetic risk to offspring. It also entails the right to decide whether she wants to share that information with other family members. Feminist ethics has contributed to the correction of wrongs in other areas of health care as well. For years, women were underrepresented in clinical trials for such conditions as heart disease, the result of which was a reprehensible ignorance of the prevalence of this disease in postmenopausal women. The right to be included in such trials has been one of the important advances in health care for which feminist ethics can take at least some of the credit. In addition, the doctor-patient relationship was a patriarchal one in which most doctors were male. Physician paternalism was, to a large extent, a function of this patriarchal way of thinking. With the emphasis on the informed consent of patients (male and female) and with many more women practicing as physicians, there is much less of this in medicine in general, though it by no means has been eradicated altogether. There is still a long way to go in this regard.

Some feminist philosophers have warned that an emphasis on emotion over reason may lead to the absence of any standards that would show the wrongness of men's oppression of women. As Martha Nussbaum points out, "on the whole, the rationalist idea of a fixed human essence, far from promoting women's oppression, helped to advance their equality. For if we are not more than what we are made to be by society, and women appear to be different, then they are different; but if we all have an inalienable rational core, then that core may be seen to exert moral claims even on those who would deny its presence" [34]. Moreover, Virginia Held insists that, "an absence of principles can be an invitation to capriciousness." Issues such as justice and equal treatment "cry out for relevant principles. Although caring may be needed to motivate us to act on such principles, the principles are not dispensable" [35]. Whereas these comments underscore some of its limitations, feminist ethics has influenced many areas of medical ethics to varying degrees.

Social contract theory, or *contractarianism*, derives from Thomas Hobbes (1588–1679), who believed that people are basically self-interested individuals but who realize that pursuing unconstrained self-interest in a state of nature would make life "nasty, brutish, and short" [36]. Hobbes maintained that if people were to live decent lives at all, their interactions must be regulated by social rules that all would accept on the assumption that doing so would be mutually advantageous. Furthermore, Hobbes believed that a sovereign government is necessary to enforce agreement to rules and thus ensure social cooperation. Morality for Hobbes, as indeed for all contractarians after him, consists in a set of rules that people come to accept for mutual benefit, on the condition that others follow them as well. This view of morality is captured in the idea of a social contract.

Hobbes' conception of contractarianism is basically negative, focusing on the idea of enforcement to ensure compliance with rules rather than on positive incentives. More positive conceptions of contractarianism can be found in the recent theories of John Rawls and T. M. Scanlon. These two conceptions are related to Hobbes' in that they understand morality as consisting in a framework of impartial principles or rules that people agree to follow for mutually beneficial social cooperation. The similarities end there, however.

Rawls' version of contractarianism is the theoretical foundation of his conception of justice, which he develops in great detail in A *Theory of Justice* [37]. Generally, justice is concerned with what people's rights are, what we owe to others, and the proper distribution of benefits and burdens. Reversing the order in consequentialism, Rawls emphasizes the idea of right over the idea of good. For him, justice is more about the process through which people's rights or claims are met than it is about actions performed or policies designed to maximize outcomes. Rawls is interested in establishing principles that govern the legal, political, and economic institutions of a just society. These principles are such that anyone would have a rational self-interest in committing themselves to them if they acted in ignorance of all distinguishing facts about themselves. They would choose principles under a "veil of ignorance" with no knowledge of their economic or social status, race, gender, or even health.

The two principles Rawls maintains rational agents would choose are the principle of liberty and the principle of equality, which he also calls the "difference principle." The latter comes in two parts, the first of which says that social goods should be distributed equally across social groups, where the only admissible inequalities in distribution would be those that worked to the benefit of the least advantaged groups or members of society. Rawls' "veil" is a compelling notion, because if one did not know one's social position or health status, it would be irrational to choose a distribution where some have more than others. For one may be among those on the short side of things and end up with less liberty or social goods than what one had bargained for. The second part of the second principle of justice is a principle of equality of opportunity to have access to various roles and offices in society. The idea of universal access to a decent minimum of health care (antibiotics, immunizations, prenatal care, insulin for diabetes, emergency care, and general continuity of care with an overseeing primary care physician) may be taken as an application of this principle of equal opportunity [38]. It is one way of trying to equalize opportunities for people in general and especially for those who have not fared well in the "natural lottery." In terms of health, this class would include people with genetic diseases, disabilities, or those so poor or otherwise disadvantaged that they cannot afford to have a decent basic minimum of health care. In all of these instances, people have conditions that befall them through no fault of their own. The difference principle gives priority to these worst-off groups in having their basic health and other needs met.

The hypothetical veil of ignorance could be criticized on the ground that it seems implausible that people could act prudentially without knowing anything about their particular interests. A related criticism is that different people have different orders of priority regarding social goods. Some might value housing or even education over health care and therefore their choices of which principles to accept will reflect different valuations of different social goods. Nevertheless, Rawls' principles provide the most convincing framework for a theory of justice in general and for deciding what constitutes a just health care system in particular.

One respect in which Rawls departs quite radically from Hobbes is in his interpretation of contractarianism as a Kantian enterprise. What he calls "Kantian constructivism" follows from the two formulations of the categorical imperative in the sense that such concepts as equal consideration and equal opportunity follow from the Kantian principles of universalizability and respect for persons [39]. Where contractarianism and Kantian deontology differ, however, is that whereas the point of departure in the former is self-interested individuals accepting principles for mutual benefit, in the latter it is duty and respect for the moral law, which is not concerned with self-interest or mutual benefit at all. Accordingly, these two theories will be kept separate.

An intuitively more attractive version of contractarianism, especially with a view to health care, is Scanlon's, which is inspired by Rawls' account but is different in important respects [40]. Whereas Rawls' principles of justice are principles that people would choose if they lacked knowledge of their social and economic situation, Scanlon's idea is that ethical principles are such that no one could reasonably reject them, given an interest in finding impartial and mutually agreeable standards of conduct. Scanlon's focus is on what would make an action or policy morally wrong, and wrongness is defined in terms of what would be unreasonable to any individual with an interest in accepting and abiding by ethical principles. A policy would be unreasonable to one if it imposed a significant burden on one for the sake of benefitting others. By the same token, however, it would be unreasonable for one to reject a rule or principle because it imposed a small burden on one when it was the only way to benefit others.

There are two problems with Scanlon's account. First, it is not always clear when a burden could be objectively determined as small or large, reasonable or unreasonable. This would be a function largely of subjective points of view of different people, reflecting their varying needs and interests and different ideas about when a burden to themselves could be outweighed by a benefit to others. Second, contractarian principles are such that people could not reasonably reject them, but *only* on the assumption that everyone is motivated to live by principles that are mutually agreeable. And yet it is quite possible that not everyone will have the same motivation.

Nevertheless, what makes Scanlon's contractarianism attractive for health care is that it can serve as a framework within which to discuss such macroallocation issues as: How much of Gross Domestic Product (GDP) should be spent on health care, as opposed to education, housing, or environmental protection? What sorts of services should people have access to in a health care system with universal coverage? Should priority be given to less expensive basic preventive public health programs that benefit more people or to more sophisticated but more expensive programs of genetic testing and therapy or assisted forms of reproduction that benefit fewer people? All of these questions hinge on the more basic question of which principles and policies people generally could reasonably accept or reject, assuming a common understanding of the balance between benefits and burdens to people in the distribution of limited health resources. This model has been employed by Norman Daniels and James Sabin in their account of how to achieve a fair process of medical rationing [41]. They claim that this should be determined by a democratic process of deliberation, where all parties with a stake in health care allocation are given a fair hearing, all points of view are considered, and each is entitled to a veto if they would be unreasonably burdened by some allocation decision. The democratic flavor of this process is what makes contractarianism distinctive from the other ethical theories we have considered. Specifically, it can be applied to help sort out the main issues in the recent conflict between patients and the Health Maintenance Organizations (HMOs)—or Managed Care Organizations (MCOs)—with whom they or their employers contract for medical services. Whether cost-cutting measures in these organizations result in an unreasonable burden or even harm to patients is just one issue that can be addressed constructively within a contractarian framework.

Communitarianism can be said to derive from Aristotle's claim that each person is essentially a social being (*zoion politikon*) [42]. Rather than seeing them as a collection of isolated self-interested individuals, each with their own conception of the good, communitarianism takes persons to be members of communities with shared values, ideals, and goals. Exponents of this view, including Michael Sandel, Alasdair MacIntyre, and Charles Taylor, maintain that the ethical norms that govern our behavior and by which we live are not to be found in the universal tenets of rationality, but in different historical and religious traditions [43]. Communitarianism thus rejects the liberal individualism that many of the ethical theories we have examined thus far at bottom have in common, despite their other differences. Liberal individualism, or simply *liberalism,* focuses on the rights, dignity, interests, and reasoning capacity of individual moral agents. It says that people have the right to live in accordance with their own conception of a good life, and in this regard it is consistent with autonomy, or self-determination. Yet it is important to distinguish liberalism from the *libertarianism* of Robert Nozick and (in health care ethics) Englehardt [44]. Whereas liberalism affirms the importance of government to ensure that procedures are in place to allow individuals to pursue their own conception of a good life, libertarianism advocates only a minimal security role for government to protect citizens from harm. More important for present purposes, liberalism takes access to health care to be a right, which is necessary for individuals to have equal opportunity for a decent minimum level of well-being. Libertarianism does not take health care as a social good to which individuals have a right but, instead, as a commodity that can be bought or sold on the free market or else received as a form of charity.

Liberalism differs from communitarianism in two main respects: (1) There is no one conception of the good or one overarching moral value that all individuals share and live by; (2) the rights and interests of individuals should never be sacrificed for the interests of the larger society. Because different individuals have different values and different conceptions of what a good life consists of, it would be wrong to try to adopt a particular conception of the good. Therefore, society should remain neutral on these normative issues [45].

Communitarians reject this view because of their commitment to the idea that individual conceptions of the good cannot be divorced from the values of the community in which individuals live. What is good for one is a reflection of the common good. Because we are social beings, any question about right or wrong, good or bad actions or policies always must be raised within a common social framework and will be equivalent to the question 'Which actions or policies will promote the kind of community in which we want to live?'

Communitarianism has become quite influential recently in the bioethics debate. Daniel Callahan, for example, maintains that questions such as what the goals of medicine should be in the last stages of life, specifically whether we should try to cure and extend life or focus on dignified palliative care, must be framed by the larger question of what kind of life our society wants [46]. These questions require a shared common understanding of our goals and values to be fruitfully discussed and resolved. Questions about rights to medical services and responsibility for health outcomes are to be raised and determined not individually but socially. Moreover, Ezekiel Emanuel contends that questions about how we should allocate scarce medical resources are not ultimately about economics but instead about the values of the society or polity in which we all live [47]. Today's medical ethical dilemmas are not created by advances in medical technology but instead are the consequences of liberal political values. He proposes that these values be replaced by a federation of political communities committed to democratic deliberations to guide the formulation of laws and policies in the domain of medicine and health care. Although this may appear to be like Scanlon's contractarianism, its point of departure is significantly different. It specifies a social community with shared values and goals rather than self-interested individuals agreeing on a set of principles for mutual benefit.

One objection to Callahan's adoption of communitarianism to discuss questions about medical treatment at the end of life is that it is extremely difficult to arrive at a consensus on common goals of treatment at this stage. Some patients and their families adhere to the Sanctity-of-Life Doctrine, in which case prolonging life is a value that cannot be overridden by any considerations of dignity or quality of life. Palliation might relieve a patient's suffering but may not be the most important goal for everyone. Others may want to preserve patients' dignity and quality of life and not violate these by extending life. Different people have different understandings of what constitutes "futile" treatment. The point here is that patient and family wishes should be respected, and because not all patients and families have the same values about end-of-life care, liberal individualism seems to serve as a more helpful ethical framework for these questions than communitarianism. More generally, communitarianism is suspect because it can limit the freedom of individuals to act in accord with their self-determined needs and interests. Among other things, this conflicts with the important principle of respect for autonomy. Accordingly, rather than try to find or impose one conception of the good on all people, we should adopt principles that encourage us to appreciate and respect cultural and religious diversity. These principles should be able to accommodate different conceptions of a good life as well as how health care fits in with these conceptions.

In sum, no one of the theories we have considered can serve as a satisfactory framework for discussion of all of the questions that arise within biomedical ethics. As the shortcomings that have been outlined indicate, some theories offer more plausible responses to these questions than others. Each of them has its own strengths and weaknesses. Which theory will better or best serve a particular issue will depend on the sorts of questions the issue entails. In most cases, one theory and its representative principles will have to be weighed against another to give the most perspicuous ethical evaluation of the issue at hand.

The last ethical "theory" to be considered is really not a theory in the strict sense of the term but, instead, a challenge to the properties of objectivity (or universality) and impartiality that characterize ethical theories. According to *cultural relativism*, there are no objective universal truths in ethics; there are only cultural codes that vary from one culture to the next [48]. No code has any special status; each code is merely one among many, and each has its own sense of right and wrong. From this it follows that there is no absolute or universal sense of right and wrong. On the contrary, these concepts are determined by and within particular cultures. As noted earlier, cultural relativism is really about meta-ethics, about the nature or point of ethics rather than its content. If cultural relativism is correct, then it deals a decisive blow to the claim that ethical theory is necessary to justify behavior because there would not be any objective basis for such justification.

One can challenge cultural relativism on both formal (logical) and substantive grounds. As James Rachels has argued, just because people from different cultures disagree about some phenomenon, it does not follow that there is no objective truth of the matter [49]. To illustrate this formal point, Rachels uses the example of infanticide among Eskimos as their way of surviving in a situation of scarce resources. Infanticide is practiced, not because infants have no rights or moral status, but instead because there is only enough food to support a certain number of people. And when this is the case, priority is given to those who are able to gather and prepare food—adults. It is important to emphasize that the issue here is not about infanticide as such but rather about survival given scarcity. The objective truth is that all people in all cultures have different justifiable ways of dealing with scarce resources that often involve harming some to benefit others. Just because different cultures have different ways of allocating scarce resources does not mean that there is no objective way to justify the very idea of allocating under scarcity. Substantively, although customs or practices differ from culture to culture, this does not mean that there are no rules or values common to all cultures. Most cultures have some moral rules in common because such rules are necessary for societies and cultures themselves to exist and remain stable. Rules against lying and murder are two examples.

Still, not all cultures outside our own Western culture perceive the physician-patient relationship, research involving human subjects, or the role of informed consent in either of these areas in the same way we do. Different belief systems may not accord the same status to individual patient autonomy as ours does. But this does not necessarily imply that there is fundamental disagreement on values in hard cases or that the ethical principles at stake are completely different for people from different cultures. In one culture, it may be the case that the oldest male in the family makes decisions about medical treatment for other family members, even if they are competent and capable of giving informed consent on their own. Although this is different in many respects from our Western principle and practice of informed consent, it could plausibly be interpreted as a different form of informed consent, where decisions by individuals cannot be separated from the families to which these individuals belong. One family member may be designated to make all such decisions on behalf of the rest of the family. The best interests of each are defined in terms of the best interests of the family as a whole.

With respect to cultural practices that should be prohibited, most people draw the line at female genital mutilation, clitoridectomy. This practice violates the universal right not to be harmed, a right that any culture with any sort of normative code must uphold. It also violates principles of equality and justice, given the fact that women are persons with the same basic rights as males and are free and equal members of society. Clitoridectomy is incompatible with these principles and only contributes to the continued oppression of women.

As Ruth Macklin argues in her article in Part II, ethical *universals* exist across all cultures, but these are not equivalent to ethical *absolutes* [50]. This is an important distinction that underscores the idea that an acceptance of universal ethical truths does not commit one to ethical absolutism, the view that there is one theory or set of principles that applies to all cultures in the same way. Ethical universalism is compatible with a variety of culturally relative interpretations of principles. Nevertheless, it would be difficult to deny that the basic human right not to be harmed by others is not only a universal but also an absolute truth more fundamental than any theory and that must apply across all cultures and societies.

As has been pointed out, no one ethical theory will be applicable to all cases of ethical conflicts in biomedical research or medical practice. Instead, different issues may lend themselves to one theory over another. Generally, the theories and their representative principles will have to be weighed against each other to offer the most illuminating analysis of the problems as well as a possible resolution of them. A note of caution is in order, however. We cannot expect more from theories than what they can offer us, given the particular facts of a given case. Simply applying theories to cases without careful assessment of the medical, psychological, social, or religious features that make each case unique runs the risk of being an artificial analysis of a practical problem. Still, theories are necessary to test and refine our ethical intuitions about biomedical issues and, more importantly, to explain and justify decision-making about them. In addition, the different methods in which theories and principles are employed to address practical ethical problems need to be considered. Methodology is discussed in the next section.

METHODS

Whereas ethical theories are necessary to explain and justify certain courses of action in medical research, biotechnology, and medical practice, there are various methods of using these theories that serve to guide health professionals and researchers in addressing ethical problems in these areas. Methodology is especially important in clinical ethics, where it can help health care professionals identify, analyze, and resolve ethical problems in cases as they arise in the clinical setting [51].

One method is *deductivism* and is "top-down" in the sense that it moves from a general theory abstracted from experience down to the particular medical and other relevant features of a case [52]. The method consists of a three-step process of reasoning from an ethical theory to a deduction of the relevant ethical principle or rule and then an application of the principle or rule to the case at hand. The main criticism of deductivism is that beginning with theories or principles and simply imposing them on cases is insensitive to particular features of the case that generate ethical intuitions in us and influence our deliberation about it. The deontological principle that doctors should always tell the truth to their patients regardless of their mental state is a case in point. By ignoring this and other important facts in a patient's medical and life history, deductivism is lacking in important respects. This is a function of applying principles to cases in such a strict a priori fashion.

An alternative method is *inductivism,* which holds that experience and objective features of cases provide the premises of ethical arguments. Inductivism is a three-step "bottom-up" approach in the sense that one begins by responding to the particular facts of a case, forming intuitive normative judgments about it. Then one finds general principles that are relevant to the case and our intuitions about it. Finally, one attempts to balance general principles with particular facts. The aim in inductivism is not to derive a theory on the basis of which to make a final ethical judgment on a case, but instead to find principles that can support our intuitions about its empirical features. The particular facts of the case, which may include psychological, social, and religious aspects as well as medical ones, remain the focus of attention. This method also has been labeled "contextualism."

The most well-known inductivist approach in biomedical ethics is casuistry, case-based ethical reasoning [53]. Writings on the casuistic method flourished in the sixteenth and seventeenth centuries, though it derives from the ancient discipline of rhetoric expounded in Aristotle's *Rhetoric* and (to a lesser degree) *Nicomachean Ethics* and Cicero's *De Inventione*. Casuistry focuses on practical decision-making in particular cases, moving from cases to principles rather than the other way around. It rejects the "tyranny of principles" and instead consists of analogical reasoning, relying on precedents and existing paradigms to yield insight into and achieve shared agreement about new cases [54]. As Beauchamp and Childress aptly put it, "[T]he process is similar to that of a physician in clinical diagnosis and recommendations.

Paradigms of accurate diagnosis and proper treatment function as sources of comparison when new problem cases arise" [55]. There also are parallels with law in the sense of reasoning about new cases on the basis of legal precedent.

This is not to say that principles and theories have no role in casuistry in shaping our intuitions about cases. Albert Jonsen maintains that "the work of casuistry is to determine which maxims should rule the case and to what extent" [56]. In addition, Baruch Brody claims that in case-based reasoning, "the goal is to find a theory that systematizes these intuitions, explains them, and provides help in dealing with cases about which we have no intuitions. In the course of this systematization, it may be necessary to reject some of the initial intuitions on the grounds that they cannot be systematized into the theory" [57]. To quote Jonsen once more, "casuistry bridges the gap between the speculative domain of philosophy and theology and the practical demands of decision-making in particular circumstances" [58]. So, far from rejecting principles or theories, casuistry presupposes them as having a role in analyzing cases.

One criticism of casuistry and the inductive method it embodies is that, because of its reliance on precedent, it is not forward-looking enough to analyze insightfully new cases that have little in common with preceding ones. Furthermore, the same case may generate different and competing intuitive ethical judgments from different parties. Some may pay attention to certain features of a case, while others may ignore them or judge them as being less important. In such a scenario, it is unclear how appeal to a given paradigm or preceding cases could result in a generalization on which all parties could agree. The aim of achieving a shared consensus on the relevant ethical issues of a case or how to resolve it cannot simply be assumed from the outset in a casuist model. Recognizing this problem, Beauchamp and Childress point out that "perhaps cases will evolve in the wrong way because they were wrongly treated from the outset. Casuists have no clear methodological resource to prevent a biased development of cases and a neglect of relevant features of cases" [59]. This raises the more general question of how justification can occur in a casuistic model. If principles are not objective, impartial standards outside our intuitive judgments but only instruments or rules of thumb on the way to an ideal of consensus or shared agreement, and if different parties addressing a case have different judgments about it, then it is difficult to see how there can be any adjudication between these judgments.

Arguably, the most promising method for analyzing ethical problems in biomedical ethics is *coherentism* [60]. This is a hybrid of deductivism and inductivism and consists in a dialectical process of moving back and forth between principles and cases to find a coherent fit between them. This idea derives from the theory of coherentism in epistemology, according to which a belief is justified to the extent that it is a member of, or coheres with, a consistent set of beliefs. In the words of Beauchamp and Childress, coherentism in biomedical ethics is "neither top-down nor bottom-up; it moves in both directions" [61]. The point of this method is to find the appropriate fit between the four main ethical principles we have discussed (respect for autonomy, beneficence, nonmaleficence and justice) and particular empirical facts about cases, adjusting each in the light of the other until we reach a state of "reflective equilibrium" between the theoretical and the practical.

This idea of a reflective equilibrium is due to Rawls, who introduced it in a political framework as one element of his theory of justice [62]. The two elements in the dialectic are what Rawls calls "considered judgments," which are intuitions that have undergone a process of reflective scrutiny, and political principles. We seek a state in which our considered judgments are in alignment (equilibrium) with political principles. There is a constant process of adjustment between these two elements. Principles serve as curbs and stabilizers on our considered judgments, which in turn give substance to principles. Similarly, in biomedical ethics, cases generate intuitions about the right or wrong course of action to take in them. These intuitions become refined by being tested against principles, which are necessary to justify whichever decision or course of action is taken. In fact, we should think of the coherentist method as consisting of three components: (1) our ethical intuitions generated by cases; (2) principles or theories against which intuitions are tested and refined, and in terms of which our decisions and actions are justified; and (3) the cases themselves, which serve as hinges around which intuitions and principles turn as they constantly adjust to each other. Cases are the solid ground on which the adjustment between intuitions and principles takes place, which is why the point of departure in bioethical discussion generally should be the case itself.

There are three features of coherentism that make it a more attractive method than the casuistry typical of inductivism. First, by emphasizing the idea of constant adjustment between intuitions and principles, it offers a more effective framework for addressing new cases that may be disanalogous to previous ones and thus recalcitrant to analogical reasoning. By not being limited to backward-looking paradigms and being open to adjustment, it can yield more insightful analyses of ethical issues. Second, it places more emphasis on principles than inductivism in general and casuistry in particular. This is significant given that it is not enough to presuppose principles when reasoning about cases. It is also necessary to appeal to them to adjudicate between conflicting judgments about cases as well as to justify a given course of action. Cases and precedent are important, but only principles can provide the requisite adjudication of conflicting judgments about cases and justification for what is done or not done in them. Third, the idea of constant adjustment of intuitions to principles, and vice versa, accords with the idea of balancing, of comparing the different weights of ethical principles depending on the relevant features of a given case.

The "four-principle" approach that Beauchamp and Childress have developed and defended, and that has been adopted as a framework for bioethical analysis, has been criticized on different fronts. Some have written disparagingly of the "mantra" of invoking principles in any practical normative context. The strongest criticism has been made by K. Danner Clauser and Bernard Gert, who maintain that the principles of respect for autonomy, beneficence, nonmaleficence and justice do not provide a guide for practical decision-making or action but only "a checklist of considerations that should be kept in mind when reflecting on moral problems" [63]. Furthermore, they claim that, unlike Rawls' two principles of justice, or Mill's utilitarian principle, the four principles in question are not shorthand for theories, which calls their theoretical backing into question. There is no well-developed unified theory that can link principles with theories in a helpful way. "Indeed, some of the 'principles'—for example, the 'principle' of justice—contain within themselves several competing theories" [64].

Although these criticisms may at first glance seem compelling, they lose much of their force when we restrict their application to a biomedical context. Contrary to what Clauser and Gert maintain, there is no reason why principles cannot serve as shorthand for ethical theories. Indeed, it has already been explained how autonomy and justice are most plausibly understood as deontological principles, while beneficence and nonmaleficence are most plausibly understood as consequentialist principles. Moreover, unless we adopt a "top-down" deductive method and run the risk of ignoring relevant practical features of cases by making them artificially fit our theories, principlism is a more satisfactory way of achieving reflective equilibrium. For principles, and their comparative strengths, are sensitive to and can be adjusted in accord with the practical features of cases. Also, the four principles have a sound motivation. They are so frequently invoked precisely because they capture the main issues of most ethical problems in medicine and biotechnology, and do so better than any methodological or theoretical alternatives.

Regarding Clauser and Gert's criticism about the principle of justice, it is important to point out that although there are utilitarian and libertarian interpretations of justice, the deontological interpretation arguably is the most relevant for assessing the question of allocating scarce medical resources. For the most prominent issue here is fairness in meeting the claims of all those who need the resources. And even if one insisted that outcomes and thus utilitarian considerations were at least as important in this regard as deontological ones, we could say that this serves to illustrate that in most biomedical ethical problems at least two principles will figure and that each has to be weighed against the other in deciding upon the proper course of action. This in no way suggests that the principles are without adequate theoretical backing for explanation and justification, assuming that they are representative of ethical theories and, therefore, have the same explanatory and justificatory force. So the charges against principlism largely can be defused.

As a final note, we need to be reminded that we should not expect more from principles and theories than they can deliver, which is a function of particular features of a given case. Determining which facts are medically relevant will require medical expertise that cannot be separated from cases as they arise in the clinical setting. Similarly, identifying, analyzing, and resolving the ethical issues surrounding these facts will require not only philosophical expertise in reasoning but also attention to relevant medical and nonmedical features of the case. Although theory is essential for explanation and justification, especially on policy and macroallocation issues, we cannot abstract too much from practical matters in doing biomedical ethics.

REFERENCES

[1] Albert Jonsen, *A Short History of Medical Ethics* (New York: Oxford University Press, 2000), and *The Birth of Bioethics* (New York: Oxford University Press, 1998), Chapter 1; Van Rensselaer Potter, *Bioethics: Bridge to the Future* (Englewood Cliffs, NJ: Prentice-Hall, 1971).

[2] Ludwig Edelstein, *Ancient Medicine,* O. Temkin and C. L. Temkin, eds. (Baltimore: The Johns Hopkins University Press, 1967); Roy Porter, ed., *Medicine: A History of Healing—Ancient Traditions to Modern Practices* (New York: Marlowe & Company, 1997); Albert Jonsen, *The Birth of Bioethics,* Chapter 1.

[3] From W. H. S. Jones, *The Loeb Classical Library* (Cambridge, MA: Harvard University Press, 1923), Volume 1: 164-165. Ludwig Edelstein offers a different translation in *Ancient Medicine.*

[4] Albert Jonsen, *The Birth of Bioethics,* Chapters 1–5; David J. Rothman, *Strangers at the Bedside: How Law and Bioethics Transformed Medical Decision Making* (New York: Basic Books, 1991); H. Tristram Engelhardt, Jr., *The Foundations of Bioethics,* Second Edition (New York: Oxford University Press, 1996).

[5] *Code of Medical Ethics: Current Opinions,* Council on Ethical and Judicial Affairs (Chicago: American Medical Association, 1999-2000 Edition); Chauncey Leake, ed., *Percival's Medical Ethics* (Baltimore: Williams & Wilkins, 1927).

[6] Henry K. Beecher, "Ethics and Clinical Research," *New England Journal of Medicine* 274 (1966): 1354–1360; Beecher, "Experimentation in Man," *Journal of the American Medical Association* 169 (1959): 461–478; Jay Katz, Alexander Morgan Capron, and Eleanor Swift, *Experimentation with Human Beings* (New York: Russell Sage, 1972); Albert Jonsen, *The Birth of Bioethics,* Chapter 5.

[7] *Trials of War Criminals before the Nuremberg Military Tribunal under Control Council Law No. 10* (Washington, D.C.: U.S. Government Printing Office, 1949), Volume 2), 181.

[8] Albert Jonsen, *The Birth of Bioethics,* 134. Here Jonsen spells out the ten principles of the Nuremberg Code.

[9] James H. Jones, *Bad Blood* (New York: Free Press, 1981); Alan Brandt, "Racism and Research: The Case of the Tuskegee Study," *Hastings Center Report* 8 (1978): 21–29; *Final Report of the Tuskegee Syphilis Study, Ad Hoc Advisory Panel* (Washington, D.C.: U.S. Government Printing Office, 1973).

[10] *The Belmont Report: Ethical Principles and Guidelines for the Protection of Human Subjects of Research* (Washington, D.C.: U.S. Government Printing Office, 1979), 4.

[11] H. Tristram Engelhardt, Jr., *The Foundations of Bioethics,* Second Edition; Robert M. Veatch, *A Theory of Medical Ethics* (New York: Basic Books, 1981); Tom L. Beauchamp and James Childress, *Principles of Biomedical Ethics* Fourth Edition (New York: Oxford University Press, 1994).

[12] Jay Katz, *The Silent World of Doctor and Patient* (New York: Free Press, 1984); Ruth R. Faden and Tom L. Beauchamp, *A History and Theory of Informed Consent* (New York: Oxford University Press, 1986); Dan Brock, "Informed Consent," and "The Ideal of Shared Decision Making Between Physicians and Patients," in Brock, *Life and Death* (New York: Cambridge University Press, 1993): 21–79.

[13] Such a "sliding-scale" conception of competence, where the degree of competence required in a given case is a function of the risk entailed by having or foregoing a given treatment, is developed and defended by Allen Buchanan and Dan Brock in *Deciding for Others: The Ethics of Surrogate Decision Making* (New York: Cambridge University Press, 1989), Chapter 1.

[14] Albert Jonsen, *The Birth of Bioethics,* 331.

[15] Edmund Pellegrino and David Thomasma, *For the Patient's Good: The Restoration of Beneficence in Health Care* (New York; Oxford University Press, 1988), 14–15.

[16] Joseph Fletcher, *Morals and Medicine: The Moral Problems of: The Patient's Right to Know the Truth, Contraception, Artificial Insemination, Sterilization, and Euthanasia* (Princeton:

Princeton University Press, 1954), and *Humanhood: Essays in Biomedical Ethics* (Buffalo: Prometheus Books, 1979); Paul Ramsey, *The Patient as Person: Explorations in Medical Ethics* (New Haven: Yale University Press, 1970), and *Ethics at the Edges of Life: Medical and Legal Intersections* (New Haven: Yale University Press, 1978); Richard McCormick, *How Brave a New World: Dilemmas in Bioethics* (Garden City: Doubleday, 1981), and *Ambiguity in Moral Choice* (Milwaukee: Marquette University Press, 1973).

[17] *In re Quinlan*, Supreme Court of New Jersey, 1976.

[18] *In re T.A.C.P.*, Supreme Court of Florida, 1992.

[19] This is not meant to be an exhaustive list. Psychiatric ethics, privacy and confidentiality of medical information, the different dimensions of the AIDS epidemic, and genetically modified crops and food are other important areas of bioethics. There is not enough space to address them adequately in this book.

[20] Socrates, in Plato's dialogue *Gorgias* 500c2-4, from *The Complete Dialogues of Plato*, M. Atherton and H. Cairns, eds. (Princeton: Princeton University Press, 1969).

[21] Peter Singer, ed., *A Companion to Ethics* (Oxford: Blackwell, 1991); Stephen Darwall, *Philosophical Ethics* (Boulder, CO: Westview, 1997); Shelly Kagan, *Normative Ethics* (Boulder, CO: Westview, 1997).

[22] Paul Helm, ed., *Divine Commands and Human Morality* (Oxford: Oxford University Press, 1978); Thomas Aquinas, *Summa Theologiae* (London: Blackfriars, 1980–84), Books I-II, Question 71, Article 2; John Finnis, *Natural Law and Natural Rights* (Oxford: Oxford University Press, 1980).

[23] Thomas Aquinas, *Summa Theologiae*, Book II, Question 64, Article 5; Paul Ramsey, *Ethics at the Edges of Life*, 147 ff; Helga Kuhse, *The Sanctity-of-Life Doctrine in Medicine: A Critique* (Oxford: Clarendon Press, 1987). Jeremiah 1: 5: "Before I formed thee in the womb, I knew thee . . . I sanctified thee."

[24] J. David Bleich and Fred Rosner, *Jewish Bioethics* (New York: Hebrew Publishing, 1979); Rosner, *Modern Medicine and Jewish Ethics* (New York: Yeshiva University Press, 1986).

[25] Thomas Aquinas, *Summa Theologiae*, Book II, Question 64, Article 7; Warren Quinn, "Actions, Intentions, and Consequences: The Doctrine of Double Effect," *Philosophy & Public Affairs* 18 (1989): 334–351; special issue of the *Journal of Medicine and Philosophy* 16 (October 1991) on the Doctrine of Double Effect.

[26] Immanuel Kant, *Groundwork of the Metaphysics of Morals*, trans. H. J. Paton (New York: Harper and Row, 1964), 75 ff; Nancy Davis, "Contemporary Deontology," in *A Companion to Ethics*: 205–218; F. M. Kamm, "Non-Consequentialism, the Person as an End-in-Itself, and the Significance of Status," *Philosophy & Public Affairs* 21 (1992): 354–389.

[27] Immanuel Kant, *Groundwork*, 89 ff.

[28] John Stuart Mill, *Utilitarianism*, ed. George Sher (Indianapolis: Hackett, 1979), 7. Jeremy Bentham, *The Principles of Morals and Legislation* (New York: Hafner, 1948).

[29] John Stuart Mill, *On Liberty* (1859), Elizabeth Rapaport, ed. (Indianapolis: Hackett, 1978).

[30] Marcia Baron, Philip Pettit, and Michael Slote, *Three Methods of Ethics* (Oxford: Blackwell, 1996), especially Pettit's section on consequentialism.

[31] Elizabeth Anscombe, "Modern Moral Philosophy," *Philosophy* 33 (1958): 1–19; Alasdair MacIntyre, *After Virtue*, Second Edition (Notre Dame, IN: University of Notre Dame Press, 1984) Michael Slote, in *Three Methods of Ethics*.

[32] *Nicomachean Ethics*, Book II, in Volume II of *The Complete Works of Aristotle*, ed. and trans. Jonathan Barnes (Princeton: Princeton University Press, 1984).

[33] Nel Noddings, *Caring: A Feminine Approach to Ethics and Moral Education* (Berkeley: University of California Press, 1984); Susan Wolf, ed., *Feminism and Bioethics: Beyond Reproduction* (New York: Oxford University Press, 1995); Rosemarie Tong, *Feminist Approaches to Bioethics*, Second Edition (Boulder, CO: Westview Press, 1999).

[34] Review of Louise Antony and Charlotte Witt, eds., *A Mind of One's Own: Feminist Essays on Reason and Objectivity* (Boulder: Westview, 1992), *New York Review of Books*, October 20, 1994: 59–63, at 62.

[35] "Feminism and Moral Theory," in James E. White, ed., *Contemporary Moral Problems*, Fourth Edition (St. Paul, MN: West Publishing Co., 1994): 75.

[36] Thomas Hobbes, *Leviathan*, Herbert Schneder, ed. (Indianapolis: Bobbs-Merrill, 1958), 107.

[37] John Rawls, *A Theory of Justice* (Cambridge, MA: Belknap Harvard University Press, 1971): 136–142 (on the "veil of ignorance"), 75–83 (on the "difference principle").

[38] Allen Buchanan, "The Right to a Decent Minimum of Health Care," *Philosophy & Public Affairs* 13 (1984): 55–78; Norman Daniels, *Just Health Care* (New York: Cambridge University Press, 1985).

[39] John Rawls, "Kantian Constructivism in Moral Theory: The Dewey Lectures 1980," *Journal of Philosophy* 77 (1980): 515–572.

[40] "Contractualism and Utilitarianism," in B. Williams and A. Sen, eds., *Utilitarianism and Beyond* (Cambridge: Cambridge University Press, 1982): 103–128, and *What We Owe to Each Other* (Cambridge, MA: Harvard University Press, 1999).

[41] Norman Daniels and James Sabin, "Limits to Health Care: Fair Procedures, Democratic Deliberation, and the Legitimacy Problem for Insurers," *Philosophy & Public Affairs* 26 (1997): 303–350.

[42] *Politics*, in Volume II of *The Complete Works of Aristotle*.

[43] Michael Sandel, *Liberalism and the Limits of Justice* (Cambridge: Cambridge University Press, 1982); Alasdair MacIntyre, *After Virtue*, and *Whose Justice? Which Rationality?* (Notre Dame, IN: University of Notre Dame Press, 1988); Charles Taylor, "Cross-Purposes: The Liberal-Communitarian Debate," in N. Rosenblum, ed., *Liberalism and the Moral Life* (Cambridge, MA: Harvard University Press, 1988): 53–68; Stephen Mulhall and Adam Swift, *Liberals and Communitarians* (Oxford: Blackwell, 1992).

[44] Robert Nozick, *Anarchy, State, Utopia* (New York: Basic Books, 1975); H. Tristram Englehardt, Jr., *The Foundations of Bioethics*

[45] Ronald Dworkin, "Liberalism," in *A Matter of Principle* (Cambridge, MA: Harvard University Press, 1985): 181–204. Rawls, Scanlon, Kant, and Mill all may be considered defenders of liberalism.

[46] Daniel Callahan, *Setting Limits: Medical Goals in an Aging Society* (New York: Simon & Schuster, 1987), and *What Kind of Life?* (New York: Simon & Schuster, 1990).

[47] Ezekiel Emanuel, *The Ends of Human Life: Medical Ethics in a Liberal Polity* (Cambridge, MA: Harvard University Press, 1991).

[48] James Rachels, *The Elements of Moral Philosophy*, Third Edition (New York: McGraw-Hill, 1999), Chapter 2, "The Challenge of Cultural Relativism."

[49] *Ibid.*, 30.

[50] Ruth Macklin, *Against Relativism: Cultural Diversity and the Search for Ethical Universals in Medicine* (New York: Oxford University Press, 1999), Chapters 1 and 4.

[51] Albert Jonsen, Mark Siegler, and William Winslade, *Clinical Ethics: A Practical Approach to Ethical Decisions in Clinical Medicine*, Fourth Edition (New York: McGraw-Hill, 1998).

[52] Tom L. Beauchamp and James Childress, *Principles of Biomedical Ethics*, 14–20.

[53] *Ibid.*, 92–100; Albert Jonsen and Stephen Toulmin, *The Abuse of Casuistry: A History of Moral Reasoning* (Berkeley: University of California Press, 1988); Albert Jonsen, *The Birth of Bioethics*, 82 ff.

[54] Stephen Toulmin, "The Tyranny of Principles," *Hastings Center Report* 11 (1981): 31–39.

[55] Tom L. Beauchamp and James Childress, *Principles of Biomedical Ethics*, 96.

[56] Albert Jonsen, "Casuistry as Methodology in Clinical Ethics," *Theoretical Medicine* 12 (1991): 299–302.

[57] Baruch Brody, *Life and Death Decision Making* (New York: Oxford University Press, 1988), 13.

[58] Albert Jonsen, *The Birth of Bioethics*, 82.

[59] Tom L. Beauchamp and James Childress, *Principles of Biomedical Ethics*, 97.

[60] *Ibid.*, 20–28.

[61] *Ibid.*, 20.

[62] John Rawls, *A Theory of Justice*, 48–51.

[63] K. Danner Clouser and Bernard Gert, "A Critique of Principlism," *Journal of Medicine and Philosophy* 15 (1990): 219–236, at 221.

[64] *Ibid.*, 218; Richard B. Davis, "The Principlism Debate: A Critical Overview," *Journal of Medicine and Philosophy* 20 (1995): 85–105. See also the articles in a special issue on principlism in this same journal, Volume 17 (1992).

PART II:

THE PATIENT-PHYSICIAN RELATIONSHIP

The articles in this part explore different ethical dimensions of the relationship between patients and physicians (or nurses) in different clinical and cultural settings. To a large extent, analysis of this relationship is framed by the doctrine of informed consent, as articulated in Part I. It is often difficult, however, to determine when true voluntary informed consent has been obtained. What makes it so difficult is that interaction between a physician and a patient is complicated by factors such as the authority of the physician, which can influence the way the patient perceives, interprets, and makes a decision on the basis of the medical information conveyed by the physician. The patient's response, in turn, may be influenced by values and interests that may be a function of cultural factors different from those of the Western liberal tradition. Patients might not fully understand the medical information that is being conveyed to them. Informed consent may be complicated further by the fact that competence is rarely an all-or-nothing mental capacity but usually comes in degrees. Also, patients from different cultures may not share the same concept of informed consent as we do, or they may base it on something other than the autonomous decision-making of separate individuals. All of this suggests that informed consent itself is a matter of degree that comes in different forms, falling somewhere between pure physician paternalism and pure patient self-determination.

In the first selection, Ezekiel and Linda Emanuel outline and discuss four models of the patient-physician relationship. The paternalistic model corresponds to the Hippocratic tradition of the physician acting in the best interests of the patient, who plays mainly a passive role in decisions about treatment. The informative model gives the patient ultimate responsibility for decisions about treatment, where the physician is simply an expert giving necessary medical information. The interpretive model sees the physician as taking the patient's values and preferences into account in determining which treatment will best serve the patient's needs. The deliberative model, the one that the Emanuels defend, describes the physician as engaged not only in presenting information to the patient but also in making recommendations about treatment in accord with the patient's values and preferences. Their analysis is a significant contribution to debate on the physician-patient relationship because it offers a richer and more nuanced picture of the relationship and steers clear of simple distinctions between physician paternalism and patient autonomy.

Marc Rodwin outlines and discusses some ethical conflicts for physicians in the present era of managed care that can adversely affect the patient-physician relationship. Designed to control rising health care costs and improve quality of patient care, Managed Care Organizations (MCOs) have employed certain practices that have dramatically changed the way in which health care is delivered by physicians and providers. Two conflicts generated by these practices are especially pertinent to the patient-physician relationship. First, by limiting expensive diagnostic tests and referrals to specialists because of financial incentives, physicians may not be acting in the best interests of their patients and thus may be failing to fulfill their fiduciary responsibility to them. Second, by not fully disclosing to the patient what services the MCO does *not* cover, the physician may be undermining the patient's voluntary informed consent to various treatments. In both cases, the physician may act as a "double agent" with conflicting obligations to his or her own interests or to the MCO, on the one hand, and to the patients, on the other. Rodwin argues that public policy measures should be implemented to minimize the physician's role as double agent so that patient care would not be compromised. Rodwin's article is important because the ethical issues he raises will continue to be addressed by health care professionals in the ongoing public debate on health care reform.

Robert Veatch discusses the concept of therapeutic privilege in the third piece. This principle gives physicians considerable latitude in disclosing or withholding medical information to patients on grounds of potential harm and thus emphasizes beneficence and nonmaleficence over patient autonomy. Therapeutic privilege is controversial because it seems to undermine the advances in patient autonomy over the last thirty years and to shift the physician-patient relationship back toward the paternalistic Hippocratic model. Veatch refers to legal cases from the 1960s and 1970s to shed light on the tension between physician therapeutic privilege and patient autonomy. He also demonstrates how therapeutic privilege can lead to various forms of deception and self-deception. Veatch argues that, even in cases of severe illness, unless they have explicitly waived their right to be informed, most patients would want to know everything about their condition and not have any of it withheld for reasons of putative psychological harm. A strong burden of proof is on the proponents of therapeutic privilege to justify overriding patient autonomy and informed consent on grounds of potential harm.

Jennifer Jackson presents an argument for the doctor's duty to tell patients the truth, which is not motivated by concerns about patient autonomy and informed consent. Rejecting utilitarian reasons for telling the truth, she argues for doctors' duty to care for patients, and that truth-telling is an essential component of this duty of care. Interestingly, the duty in question is not a Kantian deontological one but rather something necessary for engendering trust between patients and doctors. The link between truth-telling and trust suggests that virtue ethics is the appropriate framework within which to discuss the patient-physician relationship.

The papers by Lawrence Gostin, Nancy Jecker et al., and Ruth Macklin force us to reassess and broaden our Western concepts of autonomy and informed consent. To the extent that non-Western cultures embody values about life and the goals of medicine that are different from our own, the very meaning of such terms as 'autonomy' and 'benefit' are thrown into question. Gostin points out that our concept of informed consent may seem alienating and dehumanizing to patients from cultures that value family and community over individuals. He proposes that independent ethical review be established to resolve conflicts between physicians and patients with different cultural expectations of the therapeutic relationship. Perhaps most important is Gostin's claim that the universality of human rights is the foundation for resolving such conflicts. This suggests that there is an objective court of appeal that can settle differences between physicians and patients in cross-cultural settings.

Jecker et al. propose a more specific model for resolution of conflicts between physicians and patients when there is a lack of shared standards and values in cross-cultural health care settings. They present two cases of cross-cultural conflict, which they argue can be resolved by appeal to a broad notion of integrity. This consists in the (Western) professional health care worker being open to the different values of their patients and critically examining his or her own values, coming to change or adjust them in the light of the patient's needs, interests, and values. Such openness and engagement with the patient can help generate discussion of treatment options in such a way as to facilitate the goal of healing. In this way, there can be a convergence of the goals of both the physician and the patient. It allows for a fair procedure for resolving cultural differences that reflects the equal validity of both sides' views.

Macklin essentially concurs with Gostin in maintaining that just because different cultures have different conceptual frameworks for bioethics from the American model does not mean that the ethical principles constituting these frameworks are culturally relative. Respect for human dignity and the right not to be harmed are two universal principles that should underlie all patient-physician relationships. Bioethical principles can be objective and universal even though they may be interpreted and practiced differently across different cultures. Macklin's article is a compelling refutation of bioethical relativism and suggests that the concept of informed consent can be broadened to accommodate different cultural points of view.

Ꙩ

Four Models of the Physician-Patient Relationship

Ezekiel J. Emanuel MD, PhD, and Linda L. Emanuel MD, PhD

During the last two decades or so, there has been a struggle over the patient's role in medical decision-making that is often characterized as a conflict between autonomy and health, between the values of the patient and the values of the physician. Seeking to curtail physician dominance, many have advocated an ideal of greater patient control.[1,2] Others question this ideal because it fails to acknowledge the potentially imbalanced nature of this interaction when one party is sick and searching for security, and when judgments entail the interpretation of technical information.[3,4] Still others are trying to delineate a more mutual relationship.[5,6] This struggle shapes the expectations of physicians and patients as well as the ethical and legal standards for the physician's duties, informed consent, and medical malpractice. This struggle forces us to ask, What should be the ideal physician-patient relationship?

We shall outline four models of the physician-patient interaction, emphasizing the different understandings of (1) the goals of the physician-patient interaction, (2) the physician's obligations, (3) the role of patient values, and (4) the conception of patient autonomy. To elaborate the abstract description of these four models, we shall indicate the types of response the models might suggest in a clinical situation. Third, we shall also indicate how these models inform the current debate about the ideal physician-patient relationship. Finally, we shall evaluate these models and recommend one as the preferred model.

As outlined, the models are Weberian ideal types. They may not describe any particular physician-patient interactions but highlight, free from complicating details, different visions of the essential characteristics of the physician-patient interaction.[7] Consequently, they do not embody

minimum ethical or legal standards, but rather constitute regulative ideals that are "higher than the law" but not "above the law."[8]

THE PATERNALISTIC MODEL

First is the *paternalistic* model, sometimes called the parental[9] or priestly[10] model. In this model, the physician-patient interaction ensures that patients receive the interventions that best promote their health and well-being. To this end, physicians use their skills to determine the patient's medical condition and his or her stage in the disease process and to identify the medical tests and treatments most likely to restore the patient's health or ameliorate pain. Then the physician presents the patient with selected information that will encourage the patient to consent to the intervention the physician considers best. At the extreme, the physician authoritatively informs the patient when the intervention will be initiated.

The paternalistic model assumes that there are shared objective criteria for determining what is best. Hence the physician can discern what is in the patient's best interest with limited patient participation. Ultimately, it is assumed that the patient will be thankful for decisions made by the physician even if he or she would not agree to them at the time.[11] In the tension between the patient's autonomy and well-being, between choice and health, the paternalistic physician's main emphasis is toward the latter.

In the paternalistic model, the physician acts as the patient's guardian, articulating and implementing what is best for the patient. As such, the physician has obligations, including that of placing the patient's interest above his or her own and soliciting the views of others when lacking adequate

From JAMA, 267:2221–2226–1992.

knowledge. The conception of patient autonomy is patient assent, either at the time or later, to the physician's determinations of what is best.

THE INFORMATIVE MODEL

Second is the *informative* model, sometimes called the scientific,[9] engineering,[10] or consumer model. In this model, the objective of the physician-patient interaction is for the physician to provide the patient with all relevant information, for the patient to select the medical interventions he or she wants, and for the physician to execute the selected interventions. To this end, the physician informs the patient of his or her disease state, the nature of possible diagnostic and therapeutic interventions, the nature and probability of risks and benefits associated with the interventions, and any uncertainties of knowledge. At the extreme, patients could come to know all medical information relevant to their disease and available interventions and select the interventions that best realize their values.

The informative model assumes a fairly clear distinction between facts and values. The patient's values are well defined and known; what the patient lacks is facts. It is the physician's obligation to provide all the available facts, and the patient's values then determine what treatments are to be given. There is no role for the physician's values, the physician's understanding of the patient's values, or his or her judgment of the worth of the patient's values. In the informative model, the physician is a purveyor of technical expertise, providing the patient with the means to exercise control. As technical experts, physicians have important obligations to provide truthful information, to maintain competence in their area of expertise, and to consult others when their knowledge or skills are lacking. The conception of patient autonomy is patient control over medical decision-making.

THE INTERPRETIVE MODEL

The third model is the *interpretive* model. The aim of the physician-patient interaction is to elucidate

Comparing the Four Models

	Informative	Interpretive	Deliberative	Paternalistic
Patient values	Defined, fixed, and known to the patient	Inchoate and conflicting, requiring elucidation	Open to development and revision through moral discussion	Objective and shared by physician and patient
Physician's obligation	Providing relevant factual information and implementing patient's selected intervention	Elucidating and interpreting relevant patient values as well as informing the patient and implementing the patient's selected intervention	Articulating and persuading the patient of the most admirable values as well as informing the patient and implementing the patient's selected intervention	Promoting the patient's well-being independent of the patient's current preferences
Conception of patient's autonomy	Choice of, and control over, medical care	Self-understanding relevant to medical care	Moral self-development relevant to medical care	Assenting to objective values
Conception of physician's role	Competent technical expert	Counselor or adviser	Friend or teacher	Guardian

the patient's values and what he or she actually wants, and to help the patient select the available medical interventions that realize these values. Like the informative physician, the interpretive physician provides the patient with information on the nature of the condition and the risks and benefits of possible interventions. Beyond this, however, the interpretive physician assists the patient in elucidating and articulating his or her values and in determining what medical interventions best realize the specified values, thus helping to interpret the patient's values for the patient.

According to the interpretive model, the patient's values are not necessarily fixed and known to the patient. They are often inchoate, and the patient may only partially understand them; they may conflict when applied to specific situations. Consequently, the physician working with the patient must elucidate and make coherent these values. To do this, the physician works with the patient to reconstruct the patient's goals and aspirations, commitments and character. At the extreme, the physician must conceive the patient's life as a narrative whole, and from this specify the patient's values and their priority.[12,13] Then the physician determines which tests and treatments best realize these values. Importantly, the physician does not dictate to the patient; it is the patient who ultimately decides which values and course of action best fit who he or she is. Neither is the physician judging the patient's values; he or she helps the patient to understand and use them in the medical situation.

In the interpretive model, the physician is a counselor, analogous to a cabinet minister's advisory role to a head of state, supplying relevant information, helping to elucidate values and suggesting what medical interventions realize these values. Thus the physician's obligations include those enumerated in the informative model but also require engaging the patient in a joint process of understanding. Accordingly, the conception of patient autonomy is self-understanding; the patient comes to know more clearly who

he or she is and how the various medical options bear on his or her identity.

THE DELIBERATIVE MODEL

Fourth is the *deliberative* model. The aim of the physician-patient interaction is to help the patient determine and choose the best health-related values that can be realized in the clinical situation. To this end, the physician must delineate information on the patient's clinical situation and then help elucidate the types of values embodied in the available options. The physician's objectives include suggesting why certain health-related values are more worthy and should be aspired to. At the extreme, the physician and patient engage in deliberation about what kind of health-related values the patient could and ultimately should pursue. The physician discusses only health-related values, that is, values that affect or are affected by the patient's disease and treatments; he or she recognizes that many elements of morality are unrelated to the patient's disease or treatment and beyond the scope of their professional relationship. Further, the physician aims at no more than moral persuasion; ultimately, coercion is avoided, and the patient must define his or her life and select the ordering of values to be espoused. By engaging in moral deliberation, the physician and patient judge the worthiness and importance of the health-related values.

In the deliberative model, the physician acts as a teacher or friend,[14] engaging the patient in dialogue on what course of action would be best. Not only does the physician indicate what the patient could do, but, knowing the patient and wishing what is best, the physician indicates what the patient should do, what decision regarding medical therapy would be admirable. The conception of patient autonomy is moral self-development; the patient is empowered not simply to follow unexamined preferences or examined values, but to consider, through dialogue, alternative health-related values, their worthiness, and their implications for treatment.

COMPARING THE FOUR MODELS

The Table compares the four models on essential points. Importantly, all models have a role for patient autonomy; a main factor that differentiates the models is their particular conceptions of patient autonomy. Therefore, no single model can be endorsed because it alone promotes patient autonomy. Instead the models must be compared and evaluated, at least in part, by evaluating the adequacy of their particular conceptions of patient autonomy.

The four models are not exhaustive. At a minimum there might be added a fifth: the *instrumental* model. In this model, the patient's values are irrelevant; the physician aims for some goal independent of the patient, such as the good of society or furtherance of scientific knowledge. The Tuskegee syphilis experiment[15-17] and the Willowbrook hepatitis study[18,19] are examples of this model. As the moral condemnation of these cases reveals, this model is not an ideal but an aberration. Thus we have not elaborated it herein.

A CLINICAL CASE

To make tangible these abstract descriptions and to crystallize essential differences among the models, we will illustrate the responses they suggest in a clinical situation, that of a 43-year-old premenopausal woman who has recently discovered a breast mass. Surgery reveals a 3.5-cm ductal carcinoma with no lymph node involvement that is estrogen receptor positive. Chest roentgenogram, bone scan, and liver function tests reveal no evidence of metastatic disease. The patient was recently divorced and has gone back to work as a legal aide to support herself. What should the physician say to this patient?

In the paternalistic model a physician might say, "There are two alternative therapies to protect against recurrence of cancer in your breast: mastectomy or radiation. We now know that the survival with lumpectomy combined with radiation therapy is equal to that with mastectomy. Because lumpectomy and radiation offers the best survival and the best cosmetic result, it is to be preferred. I have asked the radiation therapist to come and discuss radiation treatment with you. We also need to protect you against the spread of the cancer to other parts of your body. Even though the chance of recurrence is low, you are young, and we should not leave any therapeutic possibilities untried. Recent studies involving chemotherapy suggest improvements in survival without recurrence of breast cancer. Indeed, the National Cancer Institute recommends chemotherapy for women with your type of breast cancer. Chemotherapy has side effects. Nevertheless, a few months of hardship now are worth the potential added years of life without cancer."

In the informative model a physician might say, "With node-negative breast cancer there are two issues before you: local control and systemic control. For local control, the options are mastectomy or lumpectomy with or without radiation. From many studies we know that mastectomy and lumpectomy with radiation result in identical overall survival, about 80% 10-year survival. Lumpectomy without radiation results in a 30% to 40% chance of tumor recurrence in the breast. The second issue relates to systemic control. We know that chemotherapy prolongs survival for premenopausal women who have axillary nodes involved with tumor. The role for women with node-negative breast cancer is less clear. Individual studies suggest that chemotherapy is of no benefit in terms of improving overall survival, but a comprehensive review of all studies suggests that there is a survival benefit. Several years ago, the NCI suggested that for women like yourself, chemotherapy can have a positive therapeutic impact. Finally, let me inform you that there are clinical trials, for which you are eligible, to evaluate the benefits of chemotherapy for patients with node-negative breast cancer. I can enroll you in a study if you want. I will be happy to give you any further information you feel you need."

The interpretive physician might outline much of the same information as the informative physician, then engage in discussion to elucidate the patient's wishes, and conclude, "It sounds to me as if you have conflicting wishes. Understandably, you seem uncertain how to balance the demands required for receiving additional treatment, rejuvenating your personal affairs, and maintaining your psychological equilibrium. Let me try to express a perspective that fits your position. Fighting your cancer is important, but it must leave you with a healthy self-image and quality time outside the hospital. This view seems compatible with undergoing radiation therapy but not chemotherapy. A lumpectomy with radiation maximizes your chance of surviving while preserving your breast. Radiotherapy fights your breast cancer without disfigurement. Conversely, chemotherapy would prolong the duration of therapy by many months. Further, the benefits of chemotherapy in terms of survival are smaller and more controversial. Given the recent changes in your life, you have too many new preoccupations to undergo months of chemotherapy for a questionable benefit. Do I understand you? We can talk again in a few days."

The deliberative physician might begin by outlining the same factual information, engage in a conversation to elucidate the patient's values, but continue, "It seems clear that you should undergo radiation therapy. It offers maximal survival with minimal risk, disfigurement, and disruption of your life. The issue of chemotherapy is different, fraught with conflicting data. Balancing all the options, I think the best one for you is to enter a trial that is investigating the potential benefit of chemotherapy for women with node-negative breast cancer. First, it ensures that you receive excellent medical care. At this point, we do not know which therapy maximizes survival. In a clinical study the schedule of follow-up visits, tests, and decisions is specified by leading breast cancer experts to ensure that all the women receive care that is the best available anywhere. A second reason to participate in a trial is altruistic; it allows you to contribute something to women with breast cancer in the future

who will face difficult choices. Over decades, thousands of women have participated in studies that inform our current treatment practices. Without those women, and the knowledge they made possible, we would probably still be giving you and all other women with breast cancer mastectomies. By enrolling in a trial you participate in a tradition in which women of one generation receive the highest standard of care available but also enhance the care of women in future generations because medicine has learned something about which interventions are better. I must tell you that I am not involved in the study; if you elect to enroll in this trial, you will initially see another breast cancer expert to plan your therapy. I have sought to explain our current knowledge and offer my recommendation so you can make the best possible decision."

Lacking the normal interchange with patients, these statements may seem contrived, even caricatures. Nevertheless, they highlight the essence of each model and suggest how the objectives and assumptions of each inform a physician's approach to his or her patients. Similar statements can be imagined for other clinical situations such as an obstetrician discussing prenatal testing or a cardiologist discussing cholesterol-reducing interventions.

THE CURRENT DEBATE AND THE FOUR MODELS

In recent decades there has been a call for greater patient autonomy or, as some have called it, "patient sovereignty,"[20] conceived as patient *choice* and *control* over medical decisions. This shift toward the informative model is embodied in the adoption of business terms for medicine, as when physicians are described as health care providers and patients as consumers. It can also be found in the propagation of patient rights statements,[21] in the promotion of living will laws, and in rules regarding human experimentation. For instance, the opening sentences of one law state: "The Rights of the Terminally Ill Act authorizes an adult person to *control* decisions regarding administration of life-sustaining treatment. . . . The Act merely provides one way by which a terminally-ill patient's *desires* regarding the use of life-sustaining procedures can be legally implemented" (emphasis added).[22] Indeed, living will laws do not require or encourage patients to discuss the issue of terminating care with their physicians before signing such documents. Similarly, decisions in "right-to-die" cases emphasize patient control over medical decisions. As one court put it[23]:

> The right to refuse medical treatment is basic and fundamental. . . . Its exercise requires no one's approval. . . . [T]he controlling decision belongs to a competent informed patient. . . . It is not a medical decision for her physicians to make. . . . *It is a moral and philosophical decision that, being a competent adult, is [the patient's] alone.* (emphasis added)

Probably the most forceful endorsement of the informative model as the ideal inheres in informed consent standards. Prior to the 1970s, the standard for informed consent was "physician based."[24–26] Since 1972 and the *Canterbury* case, however, the emphasis has been on a "patient-oriented" standard of informed consent in which the physician has a "duty" to provide appropriate medical facts to empower the patient to use his or her values to determine what interventions should be implemented.[25–27]

> True consent to what happens to one's self is the informed exercise of a choice, and that entails an opportunity to evaluate knowledgeably the options available and the risks attendant upon each. . . . *[I]t is the prerogative of the patient, not the physician, to determine for himself the direction in which his interests seem to lie.* To enable the patient to chart his course understandably, some familiarity with the therapeutic alternatives and their hazards becomes essential.[27] (emphasis added)

SHARED DECISION MAKING

Despite its dominance, many have found the informative model "arid."[20] The President's Commission and others contend that the ideal rela-

tionship does not vest moral authority and medical decision-making power exclusively in the patient but must be a process of shared decision making constructed around "mutual participation and respect."[20,28] The President's Commission argues that the physician's role is "to help the patient understand the medical situation and available courses of action, and the patient conveys his or her concerns and wishes."[20] Brock and Wartman[29] stress this fact-value "division of labor"—having the physician provide information while the patient makes value decisions—by describing "shared decision making" as a collaborative process

> in which both physicians and patients make active and essential contributions. Physicians bring their medical training, knowledge, and expertise—including an understanding of the available treatment alternatives—to the diagnosis and management of patients' condition. Patients bring knowledge of their own subjective aims and values, through which risks and benefits of various treatment options can be evaluated. With this approach, selecting the best treatment for a particular patient requires the contribution of both parties.

Similarly, in discussing ideal medical decision making, Eddy[30] argues for this fact-value division of labor between the physician and patient as the ideal:

> It is important to separate the decision process into these two steps. . . . The first step is a question of facts. The anchor is empirical evidence. . . . [T]he second step is a question not of facts but of personal values or preferences. The thought process is not analytic but personal and subjective. . . . [I]t is the patient's preferences that should determine the decision. . . . Ideally, you and I [the physicians] are not in the picture. What matters is what Mrs. Smith thinks.

This view of shared decision making seems to vest the medical decision-making authority with the patient while relegating physicians to technicians "transmitting medical information and using their technical skills as the patient directs."[20] Thus, while the advocates of "shared decision making" may aspire toward a mutual dialogue between physician and patient, the substantive view informing their ideal reembodies the informative model under a different label.

Other commentators have articulated more mutual models of the physician-patient interaction.[5,6,25] Prominent among these efforts is Katz'[31] *The Silent World of the Doctor and Patient*. Relying on a Freudian view in which self-knowledge and self-determination are inherently limited because of unconscious influences, Katz views dialogue as a mechanism for greater self-understanding of one's values and objectives. According to Katz, this view places a duty on physicians and patients to reflect and communicate so that patients can gain a greater self-understanding and self-determination. Katz' insight is also available on grounds other than Freudian psychological theory and is consistent with the interpretive model.[13]

OBJECTIONS TO THE PATERNALISTIC MODEL

It is widely recognized that the paternalistic model is justified during emergencies when the time taken to obtain informed consent might irreversibly harm the patient.[1,2,20] Beyond such limited circumstances, however, it is no longer tenable to assume that the physician and patient espouse similar values and views of what constitutes a benefit. Consequently, even physicians rarely advocate the paternalistic model as an ideal for routine physician-patient interactions.[32]

OBJECTIONS TO THE INFORMATIVE MODEL

The informative model seems both descriptively and prescriptively inaccurate. First, this model seems to have no place for essential qualities of the ideal physician-patient relationship. The informative physician cares for the patient in the sense of competently implementing the patient's selected interventions. However, the informative physician lacks a caring approach that requires understanding what the patient values or should value and how his or her illness impinges on these values. Patients seem to expect their physician to have a caring approach; they deem a technically proficient but detached physician as deficient, and properly condemned. Further, the informative physician is proscribed from giving a recommendation for fear of imposing his or her will on the patient and thereby competing for the decision-making control that has been given to the patient.[25] Yet, if one of the essential qualities of the ideal physician is the ability to assimilate medical facts, prior experience of similar situations, and intimate knowledge of the patient's view into a recommendation designed for the patient's specific medical and personal condition,[3-5,25] then the informative physician cannot be ideal.

Second, in the informative model the ideal physician is a highly trained subspecialist who provides detailed factual information and competently implements the patient's preferred medical intervention. Hence, the informative model perpetuates and accentuates the trend toward specialization and impersonalization within the medical profession.

Most importantly, the informative model's conception of patient autonomy seems philosophically untenable. The informative model presupposes that persons possess known and fixed values, but this is inaccurate. People are often uncertain about what they actually want. Further, unlike animals, people have what philosophers call "second order desires,"[33-35] that is, the capacity to reflect on their wishes and to revise their own desires and preferences. In fact, freedom of the will and autonomy inhere in having "second order desires" and being able to change our preferences and modify our identity. Self-reflection and the capacity to change what we want often require a "process" of moral deliberation in which we assess the value of what we want. And this is a process that occurs with other people who know us well and can articulate a vision of who we ought to be that we can assent to.[13] Even though changes in health or implementation of alternative interventions can have profound effects on what we desire and how we realize our desires, self-reflection and deliberation play no essential role in the informative physician-patient interaction. The informative model's conception of autonomy is incompatible with a vision of autonomy that incorporates second-order desires.

OBJECTIONS TO THE INTERPRETIVE MODEL

The interpretive model rectifies this deficiency by recognizing that persons have second-order desires and dynamic value structures and placing the elucidation of values in the context of the patient's medical condition at the center of the physician-patient interaction. Nevertheless, there are objections to the interpretive model.

Technical specialization militates against physicians cultivating the skills necessary to the interpretive model. With limited interpretive talents and limited time, physicians may unwittingly impose their own values under the guise of articulating the patient's values. And patients, overwhelmed by their medical condition and uncertain of their own views, may too easily accept this imposition. Such circumstances may push the interpretive model toward the paternalistic model in actual practice.

Further, autonomy viewed as self-understanding excludes evaluative judgment of the patient's values or attempts to persuade the patient to adopt other values. This constrains the guidance and recommendations the physician can offer. Yet in practice, especially in preventive medicine and risk-reduction interventions, physicians often attempt to persuade patients to adopt particular health-related values. Physicians frequently urge patients with high cholesterol levels who smoke to change their dietary habits, quit smoking, and begin exercise programs before initiating drug therapy. The justification given for these changes is that patients should value their health more than they do. Similarly, physicians are encouraged to persuade their human immunodeficiency virus (HIV)–infected patients who might be engaging in unsafe sexual practices either to abstain or, realistically, to adopt "safer sex" practices. Such appeals are not made to promote the HIV-infected patient's own health, but are grounded on an appeal for the patient to assume responsibility for the good of others. Consequently, by excluding evaluative judgments, the interpretive model seems to characterize inaccurately ideal physician-patient interactions.

OBJECTIONS TO THE DELIBERATIVE MODEL

The fundamental objections to the deliberative model focus on whether it is proper for physicians to judge patients' values and promote particular health-related values. First, physicians do not possess privileged knowledge of the priority of health-related values relative to other values. Indeed, since ours is a pluralistic society in which people espouse incommensurable values, it is likely that a physician's values and view of which values are higher will conflict with those of other physicians and those of his or her patients.

Second, the nature of the moral deliberation between physician and patient, the physician's recommended interventions, and the actual treatments used will depend on the values of the particular physician treating the patient. However, recommendations and care provided to patients should not depend on the physician's judgment of the worthiness of the patient's values or on the physician's particular values. As one bioethicist put it[36]:

> The hand is broken; the physician can repair the hand; therefore the physician must repair the hand—as well as possible—without regard to personal values that might lead the physician to think ill of the patient or of the patient's values. . . . [A]t the level of clinical practice, medicine should be value-free in the sense that the personal values of the physician should not distort the making of medical decisions.

Third, it may be argued that the deliberative model misconstrues the purpose of the physician-patient interaction. Patients see their physicians to receive health care, not to engage in moral deliberation or to revise their values. Finally, like the interpretive model, the deliberative model may easily metamorphose into unintended paternalism, the very practice that generated the public debate over the proper physician-patient interaction.

THE PREFERRED MODEL AND THE PRACTICAL IMPLICATIONS

Clearly, under different clinical circumstances different models may be appropriate. Indeed, at different times all four models may justifiably guide physicians and patients. Nevertheless, it is important to specify one model as the shared, paradigmatic reference; exceptions to use other models would not be automatically condemned, but would require justification based on the circumstances of a particular situation. Thus, it is widely agreed that in an emergency where delays in treatment to obtain informed consent might irreversibly harm the patient, the paternalistic model correctly guides physician-patient interactions. Conversely, for patients who have clear but conflicting values, the interpretive model is probably justified. For instance, a 65-year-old woman who has been treated for acute leukemia may have clearly decided against reinduction chemotherapy if she relapses. Several months before the anticipated birth of her first grandchild, the patient relapses. The patient becomes torn about whether to endure the risks of reinduction chemotherapy in order to live to see her first grandchild or whether to refuse therapy, resigning herself to not seeing her grandchild. In such cases, the physician may justifiably adopt the interpretive approach. In other circumstances, where there is only a one-time physician-patient interaction without an ongoing relationship in which the patient's values can be elucidated and compared with ideals, such as in a walk-in center, the informative model may be justified.

Descriptively and prescriptively, we claim that the ideal physician-patient relationship is the deliberative model. We will adduce six points to justify this claim. First, the deliberative model more nearly embodies our ideal of autonomy. It is an oversimplification and distortion of the Western tradition to view respecting autonomy as simply permitting a person to select, unrestricted by coercion, ignorance, physical interference, and the like, his or her preferred course of action from a comprehensive list of available options.[34,35] Freedom and control over medical decisions alone do not constitute patient autonomy. Autonomy requires that individuals critically assess their own values and preferences; determine whether they are desirable; affirm, upon reflection, these values as ones that should justify their actions; and then be free to initiate action to realize the values. The process of deliberation integral to the deliberative model is essential for realizing patient autonomy understood in this way.

Second, our society's image of an ideal physician is not limited to one who knows and communicates to the patient relevant factual information and competently implements medical interventions. The ideal physician—often embodied in literature, art, and popular culture—is a caring physician who integrates the information and relevant values to make a recommendation and, through discussion, attempts to persuade the patient to accept this recommendation as the intervention that best promotes his or her overall well-being. Thus, we expect the best physicians to engage their patients in evaluative discussions of health issues and related values. The physician's discussion does not invoke values that are unrelated or tangentially related to the patient's illness and potential therapies. Importantly, these efforts are not restricted to situations in which patients might make "irrational and harmful" choices[29] but extend to all health care decisions.

Third, the deliberative model is not a disguised form of paternalism. Previously there may have been category mistakes in which instances of the deliberative model have been erroneously identified as physician paternalism. And no doubt, in practice, the deliberative physician may occasionally lapse into paternalism. However, like the ideal teacher, the deliberative physician attempts to *persuade* the patient of the worthiness of certain values, not to *impose* those values paternalistically; the physician's aim is not to subject the patient to his or her will, but to persuade the patient of a course of action as desirable. In the *Laws*, Plato[37] characterizes this fundamental distinction between persuasion and imposition for medical practice that distinguishes the deliberative from the paternalistic model:

> A physician to slaves never gives his patient any account of his illness . . . the physician offers some orders gleaned from experience with an air of infallible knowledge, in the brusque fashion of a dictator. . . . The free physician, who usually cares for free men, treats their diseases first by thoroughly discussing with the patient and his friends his ailment. This way he learns something from the sufferer and simultaneously instructs him. Then the physician does not give his medications until he has persuaded the patient; the physician aims at complete restoration of health by persuading the patient to comply with his therapy.

Fourth, physician values are relevant to patients and do inform their choice of a physician. When a pregnant woman chooses an obstetrician who does not routinely perform a battery of prenatal tests or, alternatively, one who strongly favors them; when a patient seeks an aggressive cardiologist who favors procedural interventions or one who concentrates therapy on dietary changes, stress reduction, and life-style modifications, they are, consciously or not, selecting a physician based on the values that guide his or her medical decisions. And, when disagreements between physicians and patients arise, there are discussions over which values are more important and should be realized in medical care. Occasionally, when such disagreements undermine the physician-patient relationship and a caring attitude, a patient's care is transferred to another

physician. Indeed, in the informative model the grounds for transferring care to a new physician is either the physician's ignorance or incompetence. But patients seem to switch physicians because they do not "like" a particular physician or that physician's attitude or approach.

Fifth, we seem to believe that physicians should not only help fit therapies to the patients' elucidated values, but should also promote health-related values. As noted, we expect physicians to promote certain values, such as "safer sex" for patients with HIV or abstaining from or limiting alcohol use. Similarly, patients are willing to adjust their values and actions to be more compatible with health-promoting values.[38] This is in the nature of seeking a caring medical recommendation.

Finally, it may well be that many physicians currently lack the training and capacity to articulate the values underlying their recommendations and persuade patients that these values are worthy. But, in part, this deficiency is a consequence of the tendencies toward specialization and the avoidance of discussions of values by physicians that are perpetuated and justified by the dominant informative model. Therefore, if the deliberative model seems most appropriate, then we need to implement changes in medical care and education to encourage a more caring approach. We must stress understanding rather than mere provisions of factual information in keeping with the legal standards of informed consent and medical malpractice; we must educate physicians not just to spend more time in physician-patient communication but to elucidate and articulate the values underlying their medical care decisions, including routine ones; we must shift the publicly assumed conception of patient autonomy that shapes both the physician's and the patient's expectations from patient control to moral development. Most important, we must recognize that developing a deliberative physician-patient relationship requires a considerable amount of time. We must develop a health care financing system that properly reimburses—rather than penalizes—physicians for taking the time to discuss values with their patients.

CONCLUSION

Over the last few decades, the discourse regarding the physician-patient relationship has focused on two extremes: autonomy and paternalism. Many have attacked physicians as paternalistic, urging the empowerment of patients to control their own care. This view, the informative model, has become dominant in bioethics and legal standards. This model embodies a defective conception of patient autonomy, and it reduces the physician's role to that of a technologist. The essence of doctoring is a fabric of knowledge, understanding, teaching, and action, in which the caring physician integrates the patient's medical condition and health-related values, makes a recommendation on the appropriate course of action, and tries to persuade the patient of the worthiness of this approach and the values it realizes. The physician with a caring attitude is the ideal embodied in the deliberative model, the ideal that should inform laws and policies that regulate the physician-patient interaction.

Finally, it may be worth noting that the four models outlined herein are not limited to the medical realm; they may inform the public conception of other professional interactions as well. We suggest that the ideal relationships between lawyer and client,[14] religious mentor and laity, and educator and student are well described by the deliberative model, at least in some of their essential aspects.

References

1. Veatch RM. *A Theory of Medical Ethics*. New York, NY: Basic Books Inc Publishers; 1981.

2. Macklin R. *Mortal Choices*. New York, NY: Pantheon Books Inc; 1987.

3. Ingelfinger FJ. Arrogance. *N Engl J Med.* 1980;304:1507.

4. Marzuk PM. The right kind of paternalism. *N Engl J Med.* 1985;313:1474–1476.

5. Siegler M. The progression of medicine: from physician paternalism to patient autonomy to bureaucratic parsimony. *Arch Intern Med.* 1985;145:713–715.

6. Szasz TS, Hollender MH. The basic models of the doctor-patient relationship. *Arch Intern Med.* 1956; 97:585–592.

7. Weber M; Parsons T, ed. *The Theory of Social and Economic Organization*. New York, NY: The Free Press; 1947.

8. Ballantine HT. Annual discourse—the crisis in ethics, anno domini 1979. *N Engl J Med.* 1979;301: 634–638.

9. Burke G. Ethics and medical decision-making. *Prim Care.* 1980;7:615–624.

10. Veatch RM. Models for ethical medicine in a revolutionary age. *Hastings Cent Rep.* 1975; 2:3–5.

11. Stone AA. *Mental Health and Law: A System in Transition*. New York, NY: Jason Aronson Inc; 1976.

12. MacIntyre A. *After Virtue*. South Bend, Ind: University of Notre Dame Press; 1981.

13. Sandel MJ. *Liberalism and the Limits of Justice*. New York, NY: Cambridge University Press; 1982.

14. Fried C. The lawyer as friend: the moral foundations of the lawyer client relationship. *Yale Law J.* 1976;85:1060–1089.

15. Jones JH. *Bad Blood*. New York, NY: Free Press; 1981.

16. *Final Report of the Tuskegee Syphilis Study Ad Hoc Advisory Panel*. Washington, DC: Public Health Service; 1973.

17. Brandt AM. Racism and research: the case of the Tuskegee Syphilis Study. *Hastings Cent Rep.* 1978; 8:21–29.

18. Krugman S, Giles JP. Viral hepatitis: new light on an old disease. *JAMA.* 1970; 212:1019–1029.

19. Ingelfinger FJ. Ethics of experiments on children. *N Engl J Med.* 1973; 288:791–792.

20. President's Commission for the Study of Ethical Problems in Medicine and Biomedical and Behavioral Research. *Making Health Care Decision*. Washington, DC: US Government Printing Office; 1982.

21. *Statement on a Patient's Bill of Rights*. Chicago, Ill: American Hospital Association; November 17, 1972.

22. Uniform Rights of the Terminally Ill Act. In: *Handbook of Living Will Laws*. New York, NY: Society for the Right to Die; 1987:135–147.

23. *Bouvia v Superior Court*, 225 Cal Rptr 297 (1986).

24. *Natanson v Kline*, 350 P2d 1093 (Kan 1960).

25. Appelbaum PS, Lidz CW, Meisel A. *Informed Consent: Legal Theory and Clinical Practice*. New York, NY: Oxford University Press Inc; 1987:chap 3.

26. Faden RR, Beauchamp TL. *A History and Theory of Informed Consent*. New York, NY: Oxford University Press Inc; 1986.

27. *Canterbury v Spence*, 464 F2d 772 (DC Cir 1972).

28. Brock D. The ideal of shared decision-making between physicians and patients. *Kennedy Institute J Ethics*. 1991;1:28–47.

29. Brock DW, Wartman SA. When competent patients make irrational choices. *N Engl J Med*. 1990;322:1595–1599.

30. Eddy DM. Anatomy of a decision. *JAMA*. 1990;263:441–443.

31. Katz J. *The Silent World of Doctor and Patient*. New York, NY: Free Press; 1984.

32. Tannock IF, Boyer M. When is a cancer treatment worthwhile? *N Engl J Med*. 1990;322:989–990.

33. Frankfurt H. Freedom of the will and the concept of a person. *J Philosophy*. 1971;68:5–20.

34. Taylor C. *Human Agency and Language*. New York, NY: Cambridge University Press; 1985:15–44.

35. Dworkin G. *The Theory and Practice of Autonomy*. New York, NY: Cambridge University Press; 1988:chap 1.

36. Gorovitz S. *Doctors' Dilemmas: Moral Conflict and Medical Care*. New York, NY: Oxford University Press Inc; 1982:chap 6.

37. Plato; Hamilton E, Cairns H, eds; Emanuel EJ, trans. *Plato: The Collected Dialogues*. Princeton, NJ: Princeton University Press; 1961:720 c-e.

38. Walsh DC, Hingson RW, Merrigan DM, et al. The impact of a physician's warning on recovery after alcoholism treatment. *JAMA*. 1992;267:663–667.

Conflicts in Managed Care

Marc A. Rodwin JD, PhD

Managed care changes traditional indemnity insurance and fee-for-service practice by integrating the financing and delivery of medical services, with the aim of controlling costs and improving quality. Both the patient and the physician are managed through policies that restrict the patient's choice of providers and medical options and that limit the clinical autonomy of doctors.

Managed-care organizations use a variety of approaches to change the decisions of doctors and providers.[1] They may use case managers to coordinate medical care in expensive cases, financial incentives to encourage physicians to make medical decisions that conserve resources, gatekeepers to control referrals for specialty services, and administrative rules or protocols to guide the delivery of medical services. Managers may review medical records and deny physicians payment for unnecessary medical care and explicitly or implicitly ration certain services. The common element is the control by organizations and institutional arrangements of choices traditionally made exclusively within the patient–physician relationship.

TWO MODELS OF MANAGED CARE

One can distinguish a consensus from a conflict model of managed care. In the consensus model, goals of managed care are mutually reinforcing and the interests of the actors—that is, the patients, physicians, managers, providers, and third-party payers—are always compatible.

From *N Engl J Med* 332: 604–607, 1995.

Here I focus primarily on the conflict model of managed care. According to this model, managed-care organizations have multiple goals that can diverge and multiple actors with distinct interests—only some of which are compatible. Furthermore, each actor may have several conflicting interests.[2-4]

CONFLICTS IN MANAGED CARE

Managed care may promote several goals that can conflict: reducing expenditures and the use of services, increasing efficiency, eliminating unnecessary and potentially harmful treatments, providing better or more desirable treatment for patients, expanding the range of services offered, and improving patients' quality of life.

Often these diverse objectives are mutually reinforcing. Eliminating inappropriate medical services can reduce expenditures and improve the quality of life for patients. Coordinating activity can lead to greater efficiency and expand the use of services. Using protocols can eliminate some clinical errors and enable physicians to spend more time with patients for nonroutine matters.

However, there are also tensions among these objectives. Reducing expenditures can limit desirable services and decrease the quality of life for patients. Relying strictly on protocols can lead to poorer medicine, particularly in complex or uncertain cases. Increasing efficiency may result in patients' receiving less individual attention. Sometimes measures to promote one objective require trade-offs with another.

Within each managed-care organization are multiple actors who may have incompatible interests, including patients, physicians, case managers, administrators, and third-party payers. Furthermore, each of these groups may have several interests that are in conflict with one another. For example, physicians are agents for their patients. But they are often also employees of managed-care organizations or enter into contracts with them and have obligations to serve these firms as well. Administrators of managed-care or-

ganizations have legal obligations to the financial interests of owners or shareholders as well as to the care of patients. When doctors are partners or shareholders in closely held medical care organizations, they too have legal obligations to act in a way that does not jeopardize the financial interests of other partners or shareholders.[5-7] For their part, patients have an interest in receiving good—perhaps "the best"—medical care, which can increase spending. Patients also pay premiums and deductibles, however, and so have an interest in lowering medical costs. The patients' interests as both payers and recipients of medical care may conflict.

Parties with diverse goals and differing interests frequently cooperate. Buyers and sellers, for example, have different interests—recall the legal maxim, "Let the buyer beware"—yet through bargaining, negotiating, contracting, and trading, they further their respective interests. Economic and negotiation theory suggests that voluntary market transactions can increase the collective welfare.[8-10] Still, markets can fail and vulnerable parties may be taken advantage of, especially when there is a disparity in information or power. Because society finds this unacceptable, the law sometimes prevents certain people—whom it calls fiduciaries—from acting in an arm's-length competitive relationship.

FIDUCIARY RELATIONS AND CONFLICTS OF INTEREST

A fiduciary is a person who has power over the affairs of another party and who is required by law to act on that person's behalf. The law holds fiduciaries to the highest standards of conduct.[11-15] Fiduciaries are expected to be loyal to those for whom they act and, in exercising discretion and independent judgment, to act for their exclusive benefit. The law explicitly defines some relations as fiduciary, including the trustee–beneficiary relation, the lawyer–client relation, the corporate officer–shareholder relation, relations among partners, and the public servant in relation to the public. The law has held that physicians, nurses, and medical care institutions are fiduciaries for patients, but only in limited contexts.[16–20] Still, it is generally believed that medical personnel should act as fiduciaries for patients.[21,22]

Anything that compromises the fiduciary's loyalty to the person whose affairs he or she controls or the exercise of independent judgment on that person's behalf creates a conflict of interest. There are two major types of conflict: those stemming from financial and other personal interests, and those stemming from divided loyalties because of competing obligations.[23] Conflicts of interest exist even before any breach of trust. They involve an increased risk that the fiduciary may not act as expected. Thus, conflicts of interest of health care providers place patients at risk. Once conflicts of interest are identified, policy makers can inquire into the kinds of problems that may result, the probability of their occurrence, and the seriousness of their consequences. With this information, managed-care systems can be designed with fewer conflicts, or remedies can be devised to mitigate conflicts.

DEALING WITH CONFLICTS OF INTEREST IN MANAGED CARE

Financial Incentives for Physicians to Reduce Spending

Many financial incentives for physicians to control costs create conflicts of interest that compromise the interests of patients. Most health maintenance organizations and a few preferred-provider organizations increase or decrease a physician's compensation depending on the cost implications of his or her clinical choices or the organization's profitability.[24–31] For example, they may reduce a physician's income if the number of referrals, tests ordered, or other medical choices cost more than the threshold the organization sets. A physician's income may also be reduced on the basis of the organization's financial per-

formance.[27–31] In addition, managed-care organizations simply may not renew a contract with physicians who practice medicine in a manner they consider unnecessarily costly.[32,33] Typically, managed-care organizations use primary care physicians as gatekeepers and provide incentives for them to limit referrals to specialists. Such compensation arrangements create a direct incentive to limit the use of resources. Some managed-care organizations spread the financial risk among groups of doctors. All such incentives, however, create conflicts of interest: physicians have an incentive to reduce services even when it is in the patient's interest to receive them and their responsibility as fiduciaries to provide them.[30] Public policy should restrict physician risk-sharing and manage care in other ways.

Patient Choice and Informed Consent

The legal doctrine of informed consent requires that physicians explain to patients the choices available, the risks and benefits of any proposed treatment, and any alternatives. They must also obtain the patient's consent before performing any medical procedure or therapy. Under traditional fee-for-service practice, patients have a broad choice of providers, therapies, and procedures. Managed-care organizations structure the delivery of medical care to limit patients' choices and control. They restrict choices by implicitly excluding medical services through management decisions that limit the resources available to physicians (such as reducing budgets for equipment), by imposing rules and incentives that encourage physicians to practice more frugally and thus not consider or recommend certain medical options,[34] and by explicitly excluding certain medical services from the benefits package.

Only the last-mentioned method is obvious to patients. Implicit methods of restricting services—by resource management or rules and incentives—hide from patients their limited choices. Such practices compromise the values underlying informed consent because doctors and providers do not inform patients that their clinical choices are restricted. If managed-care providers explicitly exclude clearly defined broad categories of medical care from the beginning, consumers—in theory—will be able to inform themselves about policy limits and choose among different managed-care plans. Such a choice, some people argue, preserves the values underlying informed consent.[35]

Unless they are already ill, however, most people are unable to predict what services they will need—a fact that undermines meaningful choice among policies with different exclusions. Informed choice is further reduced if only particular therapies are excluded, since most people will not understand the implications of these exclusions until they seek the advice of a doctor.[36]

If managed-care organizations do not fully disclose their policies of limiting services, should physicians? Should physicians, as fiduciaries, also inform patients of medical options that managed-care organizations exclude? And should doctors inform patients of their own financial incentives to reduce services?

Malpractice law imposes liability on physicians for "failure to disclose" in obtaining consent.[17,37,38] Courts have not yet made clear whether limitations on services in managed care need to be disclosed.[39-44] But this will be a major issue in the future, especially if physicians who fail to disclose have financial incentives to reduce services. Physicians working in managed-care organizations are under pressure to pass over some options silently or to emphasize their risks and minimize their benefits. In some cases primary care physicians are prohibited from informing their patients that they are seeking a referral until they have received authorization.[45] Thus, physicians may have difficulty reconciling their dual obligations: on the one hand, their fiduciary obligation to inform patients of clinical options and risks and allow them to choose from among them; on the other, to follow the organizational policies that limit patient choice. Public policy needs to preserve meaningful choice for patients. This will require that physicians disclose restrictions on choice at the point of service, but even more important it will require policies that minimize the physician's role as "double agent."[46,47] Disclosing organizational policies is not a panacea for the limitation of services in managed care, but it may reduce the risk of legal liability.[48]

For Whom Does the Case Manager Work?

Case managers are usually nonphysicians who are employed by managed-care organizations to coordinate medical care and benefits in cases that have potentially high costs; for example, when a person receives a head injury or is partially paralyzed.[49,50] Case managers are supposed to improve the quality of medical care, but how well they do so depends on many variables.[51] They can question physicians about their clinical choices and limit the provision of medical services, inform physicians and patients of alternatives, and authorize the use of funds for purchases and treatment that are not allowed in the standard benefits packages. Supplemental benefits (such as refurbishing a home to enable a person using a wheelchair to recuperate or receive treatment) make possible treatment in a setting less expensive than a hospital. Such benefits can save money for providers and may improve quality for patients.[52,53]

Case managers are paid by managed-care organizations and can be expected to be loyal to their employers. As case managers supervise medical care, however, patients should be able to expect that they will not take actions that are contrary to their interests. But at present there is no organized way for patients to monitor case managers or to hold them accountable to the patients' interests.

There are ways to address this problem. Public policy could encourage the development of professional norms for case managers as well as codes of conduct. Such norms and codes would be a countervailing force to interests that favor managed-care organizations over patients. Faced with pressure from employers to make decisions that are not in the patients' interests, case managers could point to these codes as their basis of refusal.

Public policy could also create legal obligations for case managers as well as means to enforce them. Independent review organizations could monitor the conduct of case managers to ensure that their decisions followed norms. If the decisions of case managers were monitored, it might also be possible to deny payment to case managers who abuse their discretion.

Another approach would be to allow patients to share in the choice of case manager. A case manager could have the status of an independent contractor and neutral party—something like an arbitrator—and could be chosen jointly by the patient and the managed-care organization. Associations of case managers could provide lists of members to choose from.

Records of case managers' decisions could be made public (with provisions to preserve patient confidentiality) so that patients and managed-care organizations could assess their performance. Patients could interview prospective case managers. Even if patients were unable to evaluate case managers, patient advocacy groups could do so and publish their findings. Such procedures would provide greater accountability to patients and decrease the chance that case managers would skew decisions to favor managed-care organizations over patients.

References

1. Hurley RE, Freund DA. Managed care in Medicaid: lessons for policy and program design. Ann Arbor, Mich.: Health Administration Press, 1993.

2. Balbus I. The concept of interest in pluralist and Marxist analysis. Polit Soc 1971;1:151–77.

3. Connolly W. On 'interests' in politics. Polit Soc 1972;2:459–77.

4. Stone DA. Policy paradox and political reason. Glenview, Ill.: Scott, Foresman/Little, Brown College Division, 1988.

5. National conference on uniform state laws. Vol. 6. The uniform partnership act. St. Paul, Minn.: West, 1969.

6. Clark RC. Corporate law. Boston: Little, Brown, 1986.

7. Model business corporation act annotated. 2nd ed. New York: American Bar Association, 1985.

8. Raiffa H. The art and science of negotiation. Cambridge, Mass.: Harvard University Press, 1982.

9. Fisher R, Urey W. Getting to yes. Boston: Houghton Miffin, 1981.

10. Susskind L, Cruikshank J. Breaking the impasse: consensual approaches to resolving public disputes. New York: Basic Books, 1987.

11. Finn PD. Fiduciary obligations. Sydney, Australia: Law Book, 1977.

12. Frankel T. Fiduciary law. Calif Law Rev 1983;71:795–836.

13. Scott AW. The fiduciary principle. Calif Law Rev 1949;37:539–55.

14. Sealy LS. Some principles of fiduciary relationships. Cambridge Law J 1963; 119–40.

15. Weinrib EJ. The fiduciary obligation. U Toronto Law J 1975;25:1–22.

16. Miller v. Kennedy, 522 P.2d 852 (Wash. App. 1974).

17. Canterbury v. Spence, 464 F.2d 772 (D.C. 1972).

18. Cobbs v. Grant, 104 Cal. Rptr. 505 (1972).

19. Lockett v. Goodill, 430 P.2d 589 (Wash. 1967).

20. Hammonds v. Aetna Casualty & Surety Co., 243 F. Supp. 793 (Ohio 1965).

21. Council on Ethical and Judicial Affairs, American Medical Association. Report A (I-86): conflicts of interest. Chicago: American Medical Association, 1986.

22. Fiduciary duty and conflicts of interest. In: Darr K. Ethics in health services management. New York: Praeger, 1987:87–103.

23. The Random House dictionary of the English language. 2nd ed. New York: Random House, 1987.

24. Gold M, Hurley R, Berenson R. Results from a 1994 managed care survey: preliminary results and partial sample: Mathematica Policy Research/Medical College

of Virginia Survey. Testimony presented to Physician Payment Review Commission, October 27, 1994.

25. Gold M, Hurley R, Lake T, Ensor T, Berenson R. Arrangements between managed care plans and physicians: results from a 1994 survey of managed care plans. Washington, D.C.: Physician Payment Review Commission (in press).

26. Gold M, Reeves I. Preliminary results of the Group Health Association of America Blue Cross/Blue Shield survey of physician incentives in health maintenance organizations. Research briefs. Vol. 1. Washington, D.C.: Group Health Association of America, 1987:1–15.

27. Hillman AL. Welch WP, Pauly MV. Contractual arrangements between HMOs and primary care physicians: three-tiered HMOs and risk pools. Med Care 1992;30:136–48.

28. Sullivan L. Incentive arrangements offered by health maintenance organizations and competitive medical plans to physicians. Washington, D.C.: Department of Health and Human Services, 1990. (DHHS publication no. 90-202646/AS.)

29. Hillman AL. Financial incentives for physicians in HMOs: is there a conflict of interest? N Engl J Med 1987;317:1743–8.

30. Rodwin MA. Medicine, money and morals: physicians' conflicts of interest. New York: Oxford University Press, 1993.

31. Welch WP, Hillman AL, Pauly MV. Toward new typologies for HMOs. Milbank Q 1990;68:221–43.

32. Johnsson J. 'Deselection' suit dismissed in Texas. American Medical News. September 12, 1994:3, 31.

33. Johnson J, Mitka M. Managed care maelstrom. American Medical News. July 25. 1994:1.

34. Hillman AL. Managing the physician: rules versus incentives. Health Aff (Millwood) 1991;10(4):138–46.

35. Hall MA. Informed consent to rationing decisions. Milbank Q 1993;71:645–68.

36. Appelbaum PS. Must we forgo informed consent to control health care costs? A response to Mark A. Hall. Milbank Q 1993;71:669–76.

37. Katz J. The silent world of doctor and patient. New York: Free Press, 1984.

38. Appelbaum PS, Lidz CW, Meisel A. Informed consent: legal theory and clinical practice. New York: Oxford University Press, 1987.

39. Anthony Tetti Sr. v. U.S. Healthcare, Inc., C.A. 89-9808 U.S. District Court, Eastern District, Pennsylvania (Dec. 27, 1988).

40. Kelly Anne Swedo v. CIGNA Health Plan of Delaware, Third Amended Complaint, C.A. No. 87C-SE-171-1-CV, Superior Court, New Castle County, Del. (Sept. 1988).

41. Boyde v. Albert Einstein Medical Center, C.A. No. 4887, Court of Common Pleas, Civil Division, Philadelphia, Pa. (July 1983).

42. Wickline v. California, 228 Cal. Reptr. 661, 183 Cal. App. 3d 1175 (1986). Review granted 231 Cal. Reptr. 560, 727 P.2d 753 (1986); review dismissed 239 Cal. Reptr. 805, 741 P.2d 613 (1987).

43. Boyde v. Albert Einstein Medical Center, 547 A. 2d 1229 (1988).

44. Levinson DF. Toward full disclosure of referral restrictions and financial incentives by prepaid health plans. N Engl J Med 1987;317:1729–31.

45. Molina Medical Care Center provider care manual. Knox-Keene license application. Sacramento, Calif.: Department of Corporations, 1993. (Ex. 1–6P: 0284–7.)

46. Angell M. The doctor as double agent. Kennedy Inst Ethics J 1993;3:279–86.

47. Mechanic D. From advocacy to allocation: the evolving American health care system. New York: Free Press, 1986.

48. Rodwin MA. Physicians' conflicts of interest: the limitations of disclosure. N Engl J Med 1989;321: 1405–8.

49. Franklin JL, Solovitz B, Mason M, Clemons JR, Miller GE. An evaluation of case management. Am J Public Health 1987;77:674–8.

50. Henderson MG, Wallack SS. Evaluating case management for catastrophic illness. Business and Health. January 1987:7–10.

51. Henderson MG, Collard A. Measuring quality in medical case management programs. Qual Rev Bull 1988;14:33–9.

52. Merrill JC. Defining case management. Business and Health. 1985;2: July/Aug:5–9.

53. Henderson MG, Souder BA, Bergman A, Collard AF. Private sector initiatives in case management. Health Care Financ Rev 1988; Annu Suppl:89–95.

⟨ΤΙΙΙΙΟ⟩

When Should the Patient Know? The Death of the Therapeutic Privilege

Robert M. Veatch PhD

Case 5: Lying to Serve the Patient

Mrs. Anna Domingues, a fifty-four-year-old woman, was born in Puerto Rico but lived most of her adult life in New York City. She came to the hospital with a complaint of severe abdominal pain and went to surgery on a Wednesday morning.

The medical student assigned to her case was unsure about what she should be told. He spoke to the resident responsible for the patient, telling him that Mrs. Domingues had stage-four cancer of the cervix, the most advanced stage. They had cleaned out all of the tumor they could see, but since it had spread to the pelvic wall, all they now could do was try chemotherapy and radiation. The five-year survival rate of stage-four cancer is 0-20 percent—bleak news for the woman.

The medical student was tempted to keep the information to himself, at least for the time being. He thought it could produce a severe depression, and maybe Mrs. Domingues would not cooperate as well in chemotherapy and radiation. On the other hand, he felt that it would not be fair to her to withhold the potent prognosis: somehow, she had a right to know her fate.

The student discussed the problem in turn with the resident, the attending physician, the staff psychiatrist, the hospital chaplain, and a social worker. An enormous dispute emerged. The attending physician was adamant that such bad news should not be disclosed, at least not with the full force of its meaning. The hospital chaplain was equally adamant in the other direction. The social worker seemed to side with the chaplain, stressing the need to prepare for the care Mrs. Domingues's three adolescent children were going to need. The resident was confused himself but reflected the consensus of the majority of his profession; he reluctantly concluded that it would

be inhumane to let the woman know her poor prognosis.

Why are there disagreements about telling patients such as Mrs. Dominques about their medical conditions? When is it appropriate not to tell patients, and what are the ethical, legal, and clinical bases for making such decisions?

HAVING DIFFERING VIEWS OF THE SAME PATIENT

Looking at Different Facts

Different ethical perspectives support the various stances taken by the student's advisors. First, his mentors were examining different data. The attending physician was afraid that there would be a bad medical outcome if the patient knew; he was afraid she would become uncooperative in the treatment regimen. The psychiatrist emphasized the psychological impact on the woman; to him the enemy was anxiety, fear, and depression, for which withholding the negative information was a powerful preventive.

The chaplain looked at very different facts. He knew that the woman was a devout Catholic and had an obligation to prepare spiritually for an impending death. For him, the religious or spiritual consequences dominated. The social worker, on the other hand, emphasized the social, economic, and familial consequences. She was concerned about the effect on the woman's family—the three children who needed care, and the enormous financial impact on this family of modest means.

Each of the consulting professionals, then, brought to bear very different information.

From *The Patient-Physician Relation: The Patient as Partner*, Part 2, Bloomington: Indiana University Press, 1991.

Moreover, they seemed to be weighing the facts differently. The psychiatrist saw the psychological impact as very harmful. The chaplain was not at all convinced that disclosures need be so devastating. Physicians have a uniquely high fear of death, at least according to one study of the problem, and that fear may cause them systematically to overemphasize the bad psychological impact of disclosures about terminal illness. Yet even if all consultants had agreed upon what kind of facts were relevant, they might have assessed the benefits and harms quite differently.

Appealing to Different Principles: The Therapeutic Privilege

There may well have been another, even more fundamental reason for the disagreement. The people involved in the dispute may have disagreed about the underlying moral principles that would influence the decision. The physicians probably applied the traditional Hippocratic principle of benefiting the patient when trying to decide whether to disclose a diagnosis to someone who is terminally ill. They were apparently working in the older, paternalistic, priestly model. The law calls the physician's argument "the therapeutic privilege." The idea has been with us since at least 1946, when Dr. Hubert Smith published an article in the *Tennessee Law Review* entitled "Therapeutic Privilege to Withhold Specific Diagnosis from Patient Sick with Serious or Fatal Illness." In spite of the fact that Smith recognized that there is no legal authority for such a privilege, there have been hints of its legitimacy in court cases ever since. According to this concept, the doctor is privileged to use his or her judgment to determine whether the patient would be hurt by disclosure, and if so, to withhold the information.

Cases Implying Support for a Therapeutic Privilege

The therapeutic privilege argument has arisen in both research and therapy settings. For example, it was used by Dr. Chester M. Southam of the Sloan-Kettering Cancer Research Institute in defense of his now-infamous study at the Brooklyn Jewish Chronic Disease Hospital in July 1963.

Case 6: The Brooklyn Jewish Chronic Disease Case

Dr. Southam injected cancer cells into terminally ill patients for experimental purposes. He admitted readily that no consent had been obtained, arguing that the physician has the right or even the obligation to withhold information that could be distressing to the patient, and pointing out that such information might indeed have been distressing to his research subjects.

He was charged by the New York State Board of Regents with a violation of his professional obligation to obtain consent from research subjects. The board concluded, "it is not uncommon for a doctor to refrain from telling his patient that he has cancer when the physician concludes in his professional judgment that such a disclosure would be harmful to the patient. The respondent overlooked the key fact that so far as this particular experiment was concerned, there was not the usual doctor-patient relationship and, therefore, no basis for the exercise of their usual professional judgment applicable to patient care."

The implication was clear: the Board of Regents thought that the therapeutic privilege argument is legitimate, but only in a therapeutic setting. One cannot argue that withholding the information would have been the most beneficial course to Dr. Southam's research subjects, because they simply could have been left out of the research entirely, thus avoiding the problem. Can we accept, however, the implication that it is morally permissible for a physician who is in a therapeutic relation to withhold information that he or she feels will be upsetting to the patient? May a physician ethically exercise the so-called therapeutic privilege?

In 1977, the same Board of Regents incorporated a limited therapeutic privilege argument in its policy on patient access to medical records. Acknowledging the general existence of such a right, the policy permits physicians to withhold access when they think the information would be seriously harmful to patients. While that policy has never been tested in the courts, it does represent the current thinking of an important state regulatory body, and apparently acknowledges the legitimacy of therapeutic privilege in cases where the physician believes disclosure to the patient would be harmful.

We shall see how the therapeutic privilege argument is applied in other state policies regarding the patient's right of access to medical records.

A case in Hawaii seems to accept the same idea. In *Nishi versus Hartwell* the court concluded, "the doctrine [of informed consent] recognizes that the primary duty of the physician is to do what is best for his patient. The physician may withhold disclosure of information regarding any untoward consequences of a treatment, where full disclosure would be detrimental to the patient's total care and best interest."

According to the *Nishi* opinion, the law accepts the principle that physicians should use their judgment to do what they think will benefit their patients. Other early court cases defending the therapeutic privilege operate on the same principle. I think that is a mistake. The model is one where medical therapy becomes the ultimate goal. The physician Bernard Meyer conveys this therapeutic metaphor when he argues, "What is imparted to the patient about his illness should be planned with the same care and executed with the same skill that are demanded by any potentially therapeutic measure. Like the transfusion of blood, the dispensing of certain information must be distinctly indicated, the amount given consonant with the needs of the recipient, and the type chosen with the view of avoiding untoward reactions."

Cases Challenging the Therapeutic Privilege

A careful reading of some of the earlier court cases reveals that even then there were limits placed on professional judgment. The important 1960

case of *Natanson versus Kline*, for example, often is cited as a justification for the use of professional judgment in placing limits on disclosure. The case involved a woman who suffered injury from cobalt therapy and successfully claimed lack of informed consent. The court said that "the physician's choice of plausible courses should not be called into question if it appears, all circumstances considered, that the physician was motivated only by the patient's best therapeutic interests and he proceeded as competent medical men would have done in a similar situation." That seems to be a blunt justification of therapeutic privilege based on professional consensus. However, an introductory clause in the opinion says that the physician's judgment is justifiable "so long as the disclosure is sufficient to assure an informed consent by the patient." Thus even in earlier decisions, the information had to be full enough for the patient to exercise an informed judgment.

The therapeutic privilege argument recently has come upon hard times. Opinion in the last fifteen years has moved in the other direction. Challenges have increased among lawyers, philosophers, and even physicians.

There are two objections to therapeutic privilege. First, there is often a high error rate in assessing benefits and harm of disclosure. Physicians may give undue emphasis to medical or psychological consequences. They may incorporate their own uniquely high fear of death. They may overlook values dear to the patient. Predicting the psychological impact of bad news on someone whom the physician may not know very well is an enormously complicated task. The result is sometimes a rule or guideline at the level of the second contract that says that in order to do the most good in the long run, one should disclose all reasonable information to the patient, even if it appears the patient might be upset. The physician who decides that it would do more harm than good to disclose may be mistaken.

A second objection to the therapeutic privilege argument is far more fundamental. This view holds that all the arguments about benefit and harm miss the point: what is at stake is a basic right of the patient or a basic obligation on the part of the health care provider derived from nonconsequentialist principles of the first social contract—principles of veracity, fidelity, and autonomy. If the patient is to be an active partner in the process of medical treatment working with the clinician insofar as the two can agree on mutually acceptable goals, then he or she has to know what would reasonably be relevant to any decisions.

Disclosure of a diagnosis and prognosis is at the very least a necessary part of any informed consent. Consent might be omitted only if the goal were merely maximum benefit to the patient. A physician may conclude that a prognosis should be withheld on this basis, but those who criticize the therapeutic privilege argument reject this logic in principle. They say that maximizing benefit is not the goal at all; rather, the objective is protecting the patient's autonomy. No exception is offered for withholding information necessary for an informed consent on the grounds that it would be disturbing to the patient. This excludes the therapeutic privilege argument.

While mere appeals to harm to the patient, psychological distress, or physical risks are not adequate morally or legally, an important legal case raises a problem that gives rise to what some are calling a therapeutic privilege "stringently formulated." In *Canterbury v. Spence,* one of the cases of the early 1970s that helped establish the reasonable person standard for consent, the problem of therapeutic privilege was addressed. The case, involving a nineteen-year-old left paraplegic after an exploratory laminectomy, presented two exceptions to the consent requirement. The first was ethically obvious and consistent with the partnership model. It is often referred to as the emergency exception. When patients are unconscious or otherwise incapable of consenting, and harm from a failure to treat is imminent, we may presume the consent of the patient (unless previous objection has been recorded). In the language of the triple contract, reasonable patients and professionals would agree at the level of the second contract that clinicians are authorized to make such a presumption in these circumstances.

The second is the therapeutic privilege. It obtains "when risk-disclosure poses such a threat of detriment to the patient as to become unfeasible or contraindicated from a medical point of view." The language is provocative and potentially offensive. It sounds as though the court was preparing to grant physicians the right to withhold information whenever they determined that it was potentially harmful to the patient. The court even uses the traditional medicalizing language of Bernard Meyer, suggesting that information can be "contraindicated from a medical point of view." That implies that it might be possible "based in pure medical science" to determine that it was medically wrong to disclose certain information. The notions of "medical indications" and "contraindications" were analyzed elsewhere. We saw that such expressions are usually simply jargon for the evaluative conclusion that based on the clinician's values, some action is appropriate or inappropriate. It should be clear that medical science alone can never disclose that an action is right or wrong; only value judgments about the outcome of the action can.

The *Canterbury* court backtracks somewhat from these implications when it spells out what it means by "unfeasible or contraindicated." It goes on to say:

> It is recognized that patients occasionally become so ill or emotionally distraught on disclosure as to foreclose a rational decision, or complicate or hinder the treatment, or perhaps even pose psychological damage to the patient. Where that is so, the cases have generally held that the physician is armed with a privilege to keep the information from the patient, and we think it clear that portents of that type may justify the physician in action he deems medically warranted.

It is critical to distinguish those cases where disclosure will literally render the patient so ill or distraught as to foreclose a rational decision from those where it will simply hinder treatment or pose psychological damage. If information is withheld because it will hinder treatment or pose psychological damage without rendering the patient incapable of rational decisionmaking, it is withheld on purely paternalistic grounds. Especially when one realizes the enormous difficulty in predicting such harm and when the autonomy of the patient to participate fully in the decision is given proper priority, there seems to be no justifiable ground for authorizing withholding on this basis. The *Canterbury* court, in fact, makes clear that it "does not accept the paternalistic notion that the physician may remain silent simply because divulgence might prompt the patient to forgo therapy the physician feels the patient really needs."

The cases in which disclosure would actually make the patient so ill as to foreclose a rational decision are nother matter, however. In such a case a partnership with full sharing of decisionmaking is literally impossible. The patient will be rendered incompetent by the very action that is required to make him or her a partner in the decision. Appeals to autonomy to attack the therapeutic privilege become impossible. If the prediction of foreclosure of rationality is accurate, there can be no partnership. Such a patient is, de facto, incompetent to give an adequately informed consent.

This does not justify straightforward therapeutic privilege, however. If a clinician suspects the patient will be rendered incompetent by a disclosure, the proper course is to treat the patient as potentially incompetent. For incompetents, some surrogate must assume decisionmaking authority. If the patient refuses to yield this authority to a next of kin or other designated agent, the only avenue open is a competency determination. The clinician's argument that the patient is incompetent to offer a consent (because the informing process will render the patient irrational) should be presented to a court, which can determine whether the clinician's case is plausible.

If this sounds harsh or cumbersome, that is as it should be. The burden of proof needs to be on the one who claims that information alone will have such a devastating and unpredictable effect. Even if the case is made, the clinician is not hereby given license to treat without consent. Rather, the partnership is expanded. A full, active agreement will now have to be reached between the clinician and a surrogate acting on behalf of the patient. The surrogate will, as usual, be expected to act based on substituted judgment insofar as that is possible, that is, based on the patient's beliefs and values insofar as they can be determined. If they cannot be, then the surrogate will have to pursue the best interest of the patient. The surrogate judgment can be overturned only if the clinician can convince a court that it is beyond reason.

If patients have the right of self-determination and the right of access to information so they can participate in decisions about their care, then the doctrine of therapeutic privilege is dead. This seems to be the conclusion one must reach from the law on informed consent and the principle of autonomy. It is even more clearly the ethical conclusion one must reach. Even so, sometimes the therapeutic privilege argument gets through the back door; other rationalizations that are really therapeutic privilege arguments in disguise are offered for withholding information.

RATIONALIZATIONS FOR THE THERAPEUTIC PRIVILEGE

One such self-deception might be called the "you can't tell them everything" argument. Like the attending physician in Mrs. Domingues's case, some people justifiably point out that it really is impossible to tell patients everything about their conditions, and thus "fully informed" consent is impossible—adding, no one would be foolish enough to want full information even if it were somehow possible to define it. But that still leaves open the question whether the patient should be told reasonably significant or meaningful information regardless of a possibly negative psychological impact. While we cannot tell patients everything, we might still tell them the information that a reasonable person would find significant, meaningful, or interesting.

A second kind of self-deception is expressed in what might be called "truthful jargon." The patient had leiomyo-sarcoma with disseminated meta-static tissue growth. Dr. Charles C. Lund, who was then in Harvard Medical School's Department of Surgery, captured the technique's usefulness when he advised fellow physicians to proceed cautiously with blunt disclosure. He said, "certainly at the start of the interview [the physician] should avoid the words carcinoma or cancer. He should use cyst, nodule, tumor, lesion, or some loosely descriptive word that has not so many frightening connotations." In other words, jargon may be truthful and still not communicate. Physicians using jargon such as this should not kid themselves into thinking they have fulfilled their moral obligation to convey to patients what reasonably would be useful or meaningful in deciding about therapy.

Another type of self-deception might be called the "we'll never know for sure" argument. It begins with the profound clinical insight that medical prognosis is extremely subtle and complicated. At best, physicians are able to estimate the likely outcome with some degree of probability. But they can say truthfully, "we'll never know for sure." The deception comes when they use this as a rationalization for failure to disclose what they do know—that the prognosis is bleak and the likelihood of long-term survival is small.

Still another kind of self-deception occurs when the physician attempts to make a sharp separation between lying and withholding information. There may well be a moral difference between some omissions and commissions. For instance, in the related area of euthanasia, many believe that there is an enormous moral difference between actively killing a patient and simply letting him or her die. The law seems to make a clear separation.

The critical factor in omission, however, is whether the physician had an obligation to act. It seems clear that there is no obligation to act if the patient has withdrawn or withheld consent; in fact, continuing treatment on a terminally ill patient in such a case might be a battery. Withdrawal of consent for continued treatment is radically different from an instruction to actively kill a patient. Even the giving of consent does not necessarily justify any intervention that actively would hasten a patient's death.

With information disclosure, however, the physician is in a very different situation. He or she has not been instructed by the patient to refrain from acting; in fact, the patient has not given a signal one way or another. In disclosure, the physician can be seen as in the process of negotiating consent for possible further treatment. Withholding information in a way that deceives the patient into thinking that he or she is going to recover is not lying, but it is a violation of the principle of fidelity, a failure to live up to the implied covenant with the patient to disclose what the patient would reasonably want to know.

A final kind of self-deception is what might be called the "indirect communication" argument. Sometimes physicians and other health professionals convince themselves that they are able to read signals from patients about their desire for further information or lack thereof. The patient in the midst of a cancer diagnosis workup may talk about long-term plans for building an addition to his home. Physicians have been known to take that as a signal that the patient does not want to discuss imminent death. It is conceivable that some communication between patient and physician may take place using such indirect signals or even body language, but there is great danger that the signals may be misread. It probably is safer to avoid the use of indirect communication arguments whenever possible.

In summary, all of these arguments are really self-deceptions. They do not justify withholding information or deceiving the patient. If that is justifiable at all, it will have to be established on some other grounds.

SOME SPECIAL CASES

There are a number of special cases requiring additional comment. These tend to be brought out in defense of therapeutic privilege. One special case occurs when the family requests that the patient not be told of the diagnosis. But how does the family know about the situation in the first place? Physicians have a well-recognized obligation to maintain confidentiality. In many jurisdictions, this is elevated to the level of law. If confidentiality is to be broken, it is the patient's right to authorize breaking it and not the family's. Whenever physicians disclose to family members first, without the patient's permission, they have violated confidence. Except in cases where the patient has specifically authorized a family member to advise the physician about the nature of the disclosure, the family seems to have no legitimate or justifiable role in deciding to withhold bad news. The partnership is between physician and patient, not physician and family.

That suggests a second special case in which the patient waives the right to information. Normally, patients should not make such requests. They have not only the right but the responsibility to be actively involved in decisions about their own care; but as we saw in the previous chapter, from the point of view of the law as well as of the medical professional, it really is not our business to force patients to have information against their wishes. If a request comes from a patient that such information be withheld, I see no problem ethically with honoring it. At the level of a special individual contract between physician and patient, an agreement for the patient to waive access to traumatic news is tolerable.

There is one final special case that may ease the burden on health professionals faced with the enormous task of telling patients about their medical conditions and futures. If patients have a right to all information that they would find

meaningful in making a decision about the future of their care, might it still be possible that in some situations there is nothing a reasonable person would want to know?

In research medicine, this question arises when researchers want to make use of the waste products of routine clinical care, when a physician wants to use remainder blood, body waste, or the materials removed during surgery. Do such researchers have to get explicit consent from patients who would be unwittingly contributing to the research if they were not told, or would it suffice to obtain, upon hospital admission, a general consent statement that such waste may be used for research?

It seems that the proper test would be to ask whether reasonable patients would want to have information about a specific study. Normally, they probably would not, although if there were risks of confidentiality violation, or if the purpose of the study were unusually controversial, they might want more detail. Barring special circumstances, many have concluded that there is simply nothing the reasonable person would want to know. In that case, a general blanket consent statement might prove adequate.

Likewise, in therapeutic settings there may be some procedures so trivial or commonplace that patients would not want to know anything about them. Normally there is not a long explanation before routine blood samples are drawn in a laboratory, in spite of the fact that there is always a very small but real risk of infection and blood clots from the procedure. If reasonable people would not find such details meaningful in deciding to participate, then the current practice is reasonable and justified.

It seems unlikely, however, that people faced with serious illness—with a lump that looks suspiciously like a malignant tumor, for example—would be as indifferent to the information relevant to their case. The burden of proof is going to be on the medical professional to demonstrate that reasonable people would not want the information, unless a patient has explicitly waived the right to know. And the burden of proof ought to be very high.

It thus appears that the cases that seem to justify the therapeutic privilege may not make an exception to the general rule of telling patients what they would find meaningful. In some cases reasonable people would not want to know anything; in others patients are literally incapable of giving consent because of their condition or the traumatic nature of the information, and in still other cases patients explicitly waive their right to the information.

Our public policy is and should remain that competent individuals have the right to self-determination regarding participation in medical treatment, and that information necessary to make a decision about participation must be presented for a consent to be adequately informed. In cases where the patient is not competent to make such decisions, the legal agent for the patient must give permission for the medical treatment. The apparent exceptions to the requirement are really not therapeutic privilege arguments at all. Ethics and law both require that if patients are capable of understanding their conditions, they should be told about them. Many physicians have come to agree, but a consensus of professional opinion cannot be decisive. The ethical and legal mandate remains independent of professional medical opinion. The therapeutic privilege is dead if the patient is to be a true partner in the medical enterprise.

Telling the Truth

Jennifer Jackson MA

Roger Higgs, in his thoughtful article, On telling patients the truth (1), raises the question whether honesty is as much a duty for doctors and nurses as it is for everyone else. He argues that lying is defensible in medical practice only at either end of the scale of importance: 'It may finally be decided that in a crisis there is no acceptable alternative, as when life is ebbing and truthfulness would bring certain disaster. Alternatively, the moral issue may appear so trivial as not to be worth considering (as, for example, when a doctor is called out at night by a patient who apologises by saying, "I hope you don't mind me calling you at this time, doctor", and the doctor replies, "No, not at all")' (2). But 'given the two ends of the spectrum of crisis and triviality, the vast middle range of communication', Higgs maintains, 'requires honesty' (3). Within the 'middle range' lack of candour does more harm than candour, Higgs maintains. But, to minimise the harm done through telling the truth, doctors and nurses must study *how* to tell it (at the right time, in the right way, and if the news is distressing, with proper follow-up).

All this is surely both sound good sense and important. But Roger Higgs also argues that there is no important difference between outright lying and other forms of intentional deception; 'that it does not matter morally whether a deception is achieved with an outright lie, or by an

From *J Medical Ethics* 17:5–9, 1991.

equivocation, evasion, by being "economical with the truth", or merely by refraining from correcting a misunderstanding'. Thus, he says: 'Surely it is the *intention* that is all important. We may be silent, tactful or reserved, but if we intend to deceive, what we are doing is tantamount to lying' (4). And later on, he observes: 'It is hard, but vital, to see one's own evasion, duplicity or equivocation for what it is, a lie' (5).

Yet in general it is obviously *not* the intention alone that counts: we may aim to improve our bank balance—by thrift or by theft: it surely matters which. And we should not confuse the virtue of plain speaking with the vice of breezy error. It is false, rather than frank, to say that an evasion is the same as a lie. (To be sure, someone who lies may pretend to himself he is guilty only of equivocation or evasion: that is quite another story. We need, of course, to see our behaviour for what it really is, but *also* not to confuse categories.) The assimilation of lying to other forms of intentional deception makes sense if one is adopting a utilitarian approach to the issue of truth-telling. Otherwise not, as I hope to show.

It should also be noted that if you share with Roger Higgs the view that doctors and nurses do not enjoy a general dispensation from the duty everyone else is under not to lie and if you also share his view that intentional deception is tantamount to lying, you must take a pretty dim view of the reputability of medical practice past and present. Has not benevolent deception always been part and parcel of accepted medical practice—'he who cannot dissimulate cannot cure'(6)?

If doctors did think they had a special duty not to deceive intentionally we should expect it to get a mention in their codes and declarations. But it does not: not until 1980 (7) and then there is only the bland pronouncement that doctors should 'deal honestly'—no guidance is provided as to whether that means 'Tell no lies' or 'Don't hide the truth' or 'Tell all'. Current practice suggests that doctors do not interpret it as prohibiting benevolent deception.

Admittedly, many doctors past and present are sceptical about the therapeutic value of benevolent deception though perhaps none deny that there are some occasions when it is plainly in a patient's interests to be deceived. What these situations are and how common are not questions we need pursue here. We are addressing a prior question: whether the benevolent deception of a patient by his doctor is, like lying, generally contrary to duty. If it is, then the question whether or not benevolent deception is therapeutic in certain circumstances, though perhaps fascinating from the point of view of cause and effect, ceases to have any bearing on the question of right and wrong.

Here I hope to establish the importance of differentiating lying from intentional deception and to point up some of the practical implications for good medical practice of the differences to which I draw attention. My discussion is divided into three parts. In Part I, I distinguish lying from intentional deception. In Part II, I enquire how far everyone is obliged 1) to tell the truth and 2) to refrain from deliberate deception. In Part III, I enquire whether doctors are obliged 1) to tell the truth and 2) to refrain from deliberate deception when others, in general, are not.

PART I—SOME DISTINCTIONS

Deception in General

A deceives B if and only if A causes B to be misled. My doctor's dour expression gives me the (false) impression that the symptoms which I am relating to him are sinister: I am misled.

Deceiving may be voluntary or involuntary. In the former case, my doctor maybe means to frighten me a little so that he can persuade me to adopt healthier habits. In the latter case, where his deception of me is involuntary, he is not putting on that expression for my benefit, still less to mislead me. He is perhaps simply following the advice of Securis that a doctor's 'countenance must be lyke one that is given to studye and sadde' (8)—

advice which Securis offers to counter the risk run by the doctor who is always laughing, who is in danger of being 'taken for a lewde person' (9).

A sub-species of voluntary deception is: *Intentional deception:* Voluntary deception is intentional if and only if A aims to mislead B: that is, if A acts as he does *in order* to mislead B. Perhaps my doctor's dour expression initially has nothing to do with me—it is directed not at me but at the clouds gathering outside the window. He is half-listening to me while fretting over whether it will be raining by the time the surgery ends and whether he will have to postpone his game of golf yet agains. If he notices my misapprehension, recognises its cause, and does nothing to correct it then his deception of me which was initially involuntary becomes voluntary. If he does nothing to correct it because he realises how it might help him to bring me to my senses, then his deception of me becomes intentional as well as voluntary.

Lying

A lies to B if and only if A, in order to mislead B, informs B that something is the case although A believes that it is not the case. Lying is not a subspecies of intentional deception, on the account given above, since B need not be 'taken in' by A's lies. I ask my doctor, 'Have you been talking to my husband?' and he replies 'No' although he has and I already know it. I was just putting my doctor's honesty to the test. He lies to me but I am not deceived.

Whereas all liers intend to deceive not all who intentionally deceive tell lies. One way in which the discrepancy emerges is this—intentional deception like lying, does not require that A be communicating with B. Thus, for example if I, noticing that you are eavesdropping on my private conversation with someone else, say something false in order to mislead you, I am intentionally deceiving you but I am not lying to you. Intentional deception need not, of course, involve assertion of any kind.

Moreover, intentional deception, unlike lying, does not require that A believes what he imparts to B to be false. Suppose, for example, that B thinks that A is going to lie to him and suppose that A is aware of B's suspicion. A might proceed to tell B the truth in order to mislead B who will take what A says to be false. In this case A is not lying to B though plainly he is intentionally deceiving him. I am alarmed by my symptoms and suspect as I relate them to my doctor that he is going to play down their gravity to spare me anguish. My doctor, realising my suspicions, decides to take advantage of it to persuade me into adopting a healthier diet. Thus he proceeds truthfully to make light of my symptoms but he is at the same time intentionally deceiving me.

Notice that what we might call the conventional falsehoods of polite conversation, as in the exchange of greetings, are not lies by the above definition. Dennis Potter during a hospital stay overheard a nurse saying to a patient who was dying of throat cancer, 'How are you?' to which the patient managed to croak the reply 'In the pink': plainly a false assertion but hardly intended to deceive (10).

PART II—TELLING THE TRUTH AS A GENERAL OBLIGATION

Does Everyone Have a Duty Not To Tell Lies?

Do people have a duty, at least a *prima facie* duty, not to tell lies—and if so, what is its source? To some people, the very notion of a moral duty or obligation might be problematic—they might wonder how there *could* be constraints on our conduct which are neither a mere matter of custom nor set up by some authority celestial or secular. Such misgivings should be respected. Necessities, moral or otherwise, must have an explanation—there must always be a reason *why* we must. . . . But what kind of explanation we should be looking for in regard to 'moral' necessities and what counts as sufficient explanation are questions we cannot hope to dispose of adequately in a few incidental remarks.

One kind of explanation of the wrongness of lying, though, that is, I think, manifestly inadequate locates its wrongness in the harm suffered by those to whom we lie: as if a person taken in by a lie is *ipso facto* harmed thereby. Suppose my doctor asks if I have taken my medicine and I lyingly reply that I have. The doctor wanted to know—but not for his own good: his remaining in ignorance does not damage him. Yet it is still the case that I have lied to him.

In seeking an explanation of the wrongness of lying we need rather to reflect on the necessity for any community to preserve trust and the crucial role upholding a rule against lying plays here. Just how strict a rule against lying it is necessary to uphold is not so easy to establish—although in view of the importance of preserving trust as the basis of fellowship and the extreme difficulty of restoring it in a community if once it is lost, it would seem that a pretty firm teaching is called for.

At least it would seem so if we can also assume that people would lie unless they were subjected to a firm teaching to check the tendency: only if we are prone to lie in the first place do we need to arm ourselves against the tendency with an appropriate teaching. Such an assumption about human nature might be challenged. Common sense, I suggest, endorses it despite the elementary familiar fact that simple prudence provides us with a natural restraint against lying (teachings aside): we do not want to risk being found out and forfeiting other people's trust. But we are not always prudent and anyway prudence does not always rule out lying. There are, I suggest, enough circumstances in which lying would appear to us an altogether convenient way to help our friends or hurt our enemies, to render a firm moral teaching against lying necessary. At any rate, if we are prepared to recognise any duties at all, we will surely include at least a *prima facie* duty not to tell lies.

Does Everyone Have a Duty Not Intentionally To Deceive?

In contrast to the case with lying the answer appears to be no. We all intentionally deceive one another daily without a second thought. Women wear make-up, men cover their incipient balding with strategic combings, we smile at each other's feeble witticisms even though we are not amused and we feign delight over gifts which fail to please. To be sure the fact that we all behave in a certain way without scruple is no proof that our behaviour is in fact innocent. But in this particular instance, I submit, there is no good reason to fault our behaviour. Are we not quite able to enjoy fellowship as a community despite a public tolerance of the many tricks of deceit we continually practise on one another, for example in casual conversation?

But when we enter a special relationship in which there is an understanding, explicit or implicit, between the parties the situation can change. The understanding may itself impose special duties and corresponding rights. Where such a special relationship exists, intentional deception in regard to certain matters may involve a betrayal of trust. Only then is it *prima facie* unjust. But B does not suffer such a betrayal unless 1) B has put trust in A and 2) B was entitled to do so.

PART III—TELLING THE TRUTH AS A SPECIAL OBLIGATION OF DOCTORS

When Is Lying To Patients Morally Defensible?

Even doctors who would defend lying as an acceptable feature of normal medical practice may agree with the rather feeble-sounding conclusion I have drawn in Part II, that everyone has at least a *prima facie* duty not to tell lies. They simply argue that often they are obliged to set aside this merely *prima facie* duty in order to fulfil their first duty as doctors—to care for their patients.

Two points deserve comment here. This defence of lying assumes (i) the patient's deception is often necessary (ii) where deception is justified, lying is justified.

(i) Is it true that doctors often have no alternative in fulfilling their caring duties—that deliberate deception is often therapeutically necessary? Perhaps doctors would want this question to be made more specific if it is to be sensibly discussed—is deception of child-patients or dying patients, or depressed patients often necessary? Be that as it may, the question does need to be made more specific in another way—in view of the inherent vagueness of the notion of necessity. A particular treatment, for example, may be said to be necessary in order to cure a patient—or to do so without enormous expense, or trouble, or distress to the patient. Thus, when it is said that lying is therapeutically necessary, we may need further clarification as to how, in what way, it is necessary.

There is, moreover, a lack of precision about a duty of care as opposed say to a duty not to commit adultery or a duty to pay one's debts. The duty of care is open-ended. There being virtually no end to what you can do in accordance with the duty of care it is far from clear what you must do in order to fulfil this duty. Legally, a doctor's duty of care is measured against the yardstick of normal practice. But morally?

In view of the vagueness about the notion of necessity and the imprecision about requirements imposed by a duty of care, we should not be surprised to find that doctors who agree that they have a duty not to lie and a duty of care may still disagree when presented with the same case history whether the one duty is overridden by the other.

Suppose, for example, that while doing a locum for a colleague away on holiday, you are called to attend a patient who is dying of cancer and whose relatives tell you that she does not know and must not be told: the truth, they insist, would kill her more swiftly than the disease. But what if when you meet her, she asks you point blank: 'Have I got cancer?' Could you be justified in lying?

In anticipation of finding yourself in such a situation let us suppose that you consult with some colleagues—they do not agree in their advice: Dr Noteller agrees with the relatives. He cites cases he has encountered in which patients upon being told the truth have died with unexpected suddenness as if, indeed, the news precipitated their demise. Why risk that for patients whose diseases might otherwise allow them weeks, even months, of tolerable existence? Thus, does Dr Noteller counsel you to withhold the truth and, if necessary, lie rather than shatter the patient's hopes. Dr Teller disagrees with the relatives. He dismisses the tales of patients dying because allegedly 'they could not live with the truth'. This happens only where the doctors concerned botch the telling, he insists, and do not follow it up with proper counselling. It is not necessary to lie or even to deceive in such a case. On the contrary, the patient and the relatives should be told the truth so that they can be freed from the isolating trap of deception that makes dying an unnecessarily lonely experience for both parties. But the patient and the relatives need help and support to come to terms with reality. Thus does Dr Teller counsel you *not* to lie. Indeed he urges that the patient be told the truth.

(ii) Supposing that there is often (seen to be) a therapeutic justification for doctors deliberately deceiving their patients, it does not follow that lying to them is thereby justified. Even if, as in the above case, you are asked point blank, 'Have I got cancer?' you are not forced either to lie or tell. Suppose you agree with Dr Teller but think that it would be better for her to be told by her own doctor than by a relative stranger—you mean to persuade him to talk to her as soon as he returns. Meanwhile you can evade even a direct question without actually lying. You could say, perhaps: 'I don't know your case fully . . . I have not talked about your case in depth with your specialist. You should talk to him.'

Many people fall in with a utilitarian approach to ethics—for them, our question as to when lying to patients is morally defensible turns on the overall harm/benefit of lying—whether it would be for the best to lie, bearing in mind all relevant interests (which would doubtless, include the interests of other people, for example, family, nursing staff). Once it is established as it surely would be, that in some cases deliberate deception *is* for the best, the further question of whether to accomplish it by a lie, or an equivocation, evasion or whatever becomes a mere technicality of no particular moral significance, to be decided again by applying the same procedure of weighing costs against benefits. Those who adopt this approach are understandably impatient with fine distinctions such as I have attempted—to them these are a practical irrelevance—certainly not to be inflicted on doctors addressing questions of medical ethics.

But this utilitarian approach to the ethics of lying seems to me to be radically misguided. The distinctions to which I drew attention in Part I were not proffered merely as an example of minute philosophising but as of *practical* relevance to the issues before us, for example, whether lying to patients is morally defensible.

As I argued in Part II the wrongness of lying is not to be located in the harm suffered by the person lied to—nor, I now would add, by the harm suffered generally, bearing in mind, for example, its effect on observers. It is to be explained rather in terms of the need a community (any community) has to maintain a firm rule against lying—a rule the function of which is to preclude lying as a practical option, as a possible method for achieving whatever aims we happen to have. And if as a community we need the rule we cannot allow ourselves the freedom to set aside the rule whenever an occasion presents where it appears that so doing would be for the best: that would be to abandon the rule—it would lose its essential function.

Yet the very question I have posed: 'When is lying to patients morally defensible?' rather invites us to adopt a utilitarian approach—it invites us to review the plight of patients in various situations to see whether lying is never, sometimes, or often, justified. On my account of the wrongness of lying maybe we should not allow ourselves to be drawn into a discussion of what harm there is in setting this rule aside in regard to patient A or patient B.

Now some utilitarians would actually share my misgivings about what I have been calling the utilitarian approach and which they would call, rather, an act utilitarian approach. They too, as rule utilitarians, argue that there are certain rules which a community needs to uphold and which we should be learning to follow as a matter of course in our day-to-day activities without stopping to calculate consequences though meanwhile, they say, in our less active more reflective moments, we should be reviewing and revising our rules in the light of our day-to-day experience—seeking always to develop our rules so as to improve them (11).

How does the position I am advocating in regard to lying differ from that of the rule utilitarians? If the rule against lying is, as I have allowed, *prima facie,* it may on occasion be morally defensible for doctors to lie to their patients. How else then are we to decide on what occasion except by considering, as rule utilitarians do, what departures from the rule would be for the best?

But I have not defended a rule against lying on the grounds that we need to live by this rule so that we may achieve what is for the best. Why suppose it is *necessary* to aim for the best? We may doubt anyway whether that aim is even intelligible. Rather, I have maintained that we need the rule just so as to get by—whatever particular further aims we happen to have in life. If the rule would still allow us to get by if certain departures were generally allowed, then the departures *can* be allowed. If the rule would only allow us to get by if certain departures were allowed, then the departures *must* be allowed.

When Is Intentional Deception of Patients Morally Defensible?

Suppose that many people think, as does Roger Higgs, that, morally speaking, deliberate deception and lying are on the same footing. In their view then the one practice poses just as much of a threat to trust as does the other. Such a supposition, if it comes to be widely shared is self-fulfilling.

But I do not think that this view *is* widely shared. It is not shared, at any rate, outside the medical context: as I have argued, we practise deliberate deception on one another in a variety of ways that we believe pose no significant threat to trust: for example, by putting someone off the scent so as to keep a planned treat a surprise: a stratagem, it may be noted, which we play on our friends with whom we care most to preserve trust.

Perhaps, though, it can be shown that doctors have a special duty not to deceive their patients, a duty which derives from another duty universally acknowledged by doctors, *viz* their duty of care. While some might protest that it is this very duty of care which makes benevolent deception on occasion not just permissible but obligatory, it might be argued that on the contrary from the duty of care may be derived a duty to maintain trust (without which a patient cannot be got to follow advice) and, from that duty derives another, to refrain from deception. Thus Roger Higgs remarks: 'If truth is the first casualty, trust is the second' (12).

This pronouncement has a certain force and simplicity about it. On examination it is not so clear, though, what is being asserted. Firstly, should we go along with the assertion that the absence of truth is a casualty? A casualty for whom? After all, truth can be withheld without recourse to deception—and without any injury to those shielded from it: there are many things that we are better off not knowing (the result of a match if we are about to watch the replay) or that we ought not to be told (a doctor has many

confidences to keep). Secondly, non-deceptive withholding of truth aside, it remains unclear whether the truth which is being said to underpin trust is a matter of not telling lies (my view) or also a matter of not deliberately deceiving (the Higgs view)? In other words, the saying could be cited in support of either view; it does not tell in favour of one against the other.

I conclude that while doctors generally speaking should have no truck with lying, deliberate deception need not in general pose a significant threat to trust.

References

1. Higgs R. On telling patients the truth. In: Lockwood M, ed. *Moral dilemmas in modern medicine.* Oxford: Oxford University Press, 1985.

2. See reference (1): 194–195.

3. See reference (1): 201.

4. See reference (1): 189–190.

5. See reference (1): 200.

6. Hoffman F. *Medicus politicus,* part 3, ch 4, vol 5: 24: 'qui enim nescit simulare, nescit curare'. The *Medicus politicus* (separately paginated) is in the 'second part' of a two-volume *Operum omnium physico-medicorum supplementum,* Geneva, 1749. These two volumes are a supplement to Hoffman's *Opera omnia physico-medico* (6 vols). Geneva, 1748.

7. See reference (1): 190–191.

8. Securis J. *A detection and querimonie of the daily enormitites and abuses committed in physick.* London: 1566. SIG A iv recto. (This was the way pages were numbered at that time: by signature, by letter and number, and by right-hand [recto] or left-hand [verso] page.)

9. See reference (8): SIG A iv verso.

10. As reported by Sampson P. People who don't give stock responses the time of day. *The Sunday Times* 1990 Aug 19: 5–11 (cols 2–8).

11. For recent discussion of rule utilitarian, or as some would now prefer, indirect utilitarian, ethics see the ongoing debate between R M Hare and his critics in: Seanor D, Fotion N, eds. *Hare and critics.* Oxford: Oxford University Press, 1988.

12. See reference (1): 188.

Informed Consent, Cultural Sensitivity, and Respect for Persons

Lawrence O. Gostin JD

The doctrine of informed consent to medical treatment or research is grounded in the ethical principle of respect for persons that regards individuals as autonomous agents "capable of deliberation about personal goals and of acting under the direction of such deliberation."[1] International ethical codes and human rights law appear to accept informed consent as a universal expression of respect for persons. The Nuremberg Code, Helsinki IV, and the Council of International Organizations of Medical Sciences' ethical guidelines focus on the need for full disclosure to enable individuals to make free and informed decisions. Informed consent is also thought to be incorporated into the right to security of the person recognized in the International Bill of Human Rights. The right to autonomy or self-determination, then, is broadly perceived to be a morally necessary method of demonstrating genuine respect for human integrity.

But is the kind of rugged individualism inherent in informed consent truly respectful of all people in all cultures? Two articles[2,3] in this issue of JAMA suggest that the formalistic requirements of informed consent in pluralistic America may be inconsistent with the belief systems of cultural and ethnic minorities. Blackhall and colleagues[2] find that Korean Americans and Mexican Americans are less likely than European Americans and African Americans to believe that the patient should be truthfully informed about the diagnosis and prognosis of a serious illness and are less likely to believe that the patient should make decisions about the use of life support. Carrese and Rhodes[3] observe that the belief system in traditional Navajo culture emphasizes the importance of positive thinking (expressing the culturally meaningful concepts of beauty, goodness, order, and harmony). Physician conformance with the cultural expectations of these and other ethnic minorities may run afoul of informed consent requirements to make full and truthful disclosures and to allow autonomous patient decision making.

These findings, moreover, are consistent with a growing body of national and cross-national literature[4] suggesting that moral values, including human rights, are culturally relative[5]; family and community decision making should be taken more seriously[6]; and autonomy must be balanced against other morally important concepts in the physician-patient relationship, such as loyalty, integrity, solidarity, and compassion.[7] In some cultures, the very concept of respect for persons as individuals may be at variance "with more relational definitions of the person found in other societies . . . which stress the embeddedness of the individual within society and define persons by their relations to others."[8]

The formalistic requirements of informed consent are particularly rigid in the United States where the judiciary has subjected the medical profession to intense scrutiny. American informed consent characteristically requires full information presented to the person of the material benefits, adverse effects, and risks of the treatment or research protocol; the person must be legally competent and understand the information provided; and he or she must make a voluntary choice free from undue influence or coercion. Each element of informed consent poses potential difficulties in US subcultures: full, truthful disclosure may be at variance with cultural beliefs about hope, wellness, and thriving of individuals; autonomous decision making may counter family-centered values and the social meanings of competency; and

From JAMA, 274:844–845, 1995.

uncoerced choices may contradict cultural norms about, for example, obedience to the wishes of spouses or family elders.[9]

Would US tort law compel physicians to press information on patients despite their culturally based desire not to be informed? Since the boundaries of the duty to reveal are shaped by the patient's right of self-determination,[10] it follows logically that the patient can decide whether to receive full information or whether disclosure should be made to the family. Courts have expressly determined that physicians should not be liable for failure to disclose resulting from the patient's specific request not to be informed.[11,12] Furthermore, it has long been recognized that the physician can decline to disclose relevant information if necessary to avert a significant clinical harm to the patient, such as serious depression or suicide.[13] So too must the law rationally permit a standard of disclosure guided by the patient's desire not to receive information. Whether that choice is wise—whether having the information is beneficial or burdensome—depends on the patient's own values.

The cultural contexts and clinical settings in which physicians and patients interact are so multifarious, the informational needs and expectations so various, and the professional relationships so intimate and judgment laden that legally imposed information is suspect.[12] Genuine respect for human dignity requires deeper understanding of the patient's values, culture, family, and community. The formal specifications of informed consent—eg, fixed disclosure requirements, isolated individual decision making, and signed, written consent forms—may faithfully advance individual autonomy and human dignity for many patients in dominant Western cultures. But this same formalism may be alienating and dehumanizing to those who view caring and healing not as a bilateral contractual relationship with a physician, but within a mutually supportive, loving environment in the family and community.

Cultural sensitivity in the application of ethical norms or human rights, to be sure, is complex and full of risk. Does such an approach suggest the absence of core standards of humanity that must be honored universally? The international community has painstakingly built up norms of compelling universality that recognize the unique worth of all human beings. Ethical norms or human rights are universal not because they are recognized by certain countries or cultures, but because the human dignity in which they are grounded is universal. It is respect for that human dignity that compels health care professionals to obtain the consent of patients in ways that are comprehensible and consistent with the person's language, custom, and culture. The fact that individuals give deference to the views of family and community, and even prefer the therapeutic discourse to occur with family members, does not negate their individual assent to medical treatment or research.

Straying from the standard formula for informed consent also runs the risk of a return to medical paternalism; physicians may use cultural arguments as justifications for withholding or manipulating truthful information to assure decisions consistent with their own clinical judgment. Ethical or legal rules, however, cannot guarantee uniformly beneficent outcomes. Formalistic consent requirements can become a way of delegating the entire burden of medical decisions to the patient, thus isolating him or her from physician and familial support and limiting medical responsibility.[14]

To facilitate deeper understanding of and respect for cultural variation and to avoid inappropriately paternalistic judgments, physicians should seek an independent ethical review when there is reason to believe that the patient has different cultural expectations of the therapeutic relationship. The ethical review should include persons with experience and understanding of the patient's culture, customs, and language. Deviation from the usual formal standards of informed consent would be justified only by reference to patient-centered values.

Ethical review can enrich therapeutic relationships within a multiplicity of cultural contexts:

by providing an opportunity for examining the values, languages, and cultures of patients, it can educate health care professionals; by providing a forum for the physician, patient, and family, it can facilitate meaningful dialogue; and by assuring a thoughtful and respectful decision-making process, it can increase cultural sensitivity and reduce the potential for legal liability.

Vast personal, cultural, and social differences will perennially pose challenges to meaningful dialogue among physician, patient, and family; it is the regard, consideration, and deference shown to the patient that remains the hallmark of respect for persons. Respecting persons may mean assuring their decisions are informed and made in isolation, free from influence or conflict of interest; or it may mean that individuals remain free to act in ways that demonstrate the embeddedness of collective interdependence in their families, communities, and society.

References

1. National Commission for the Protection of Human Subjects of Biomedical and Behavioral Research. *The Belmont Report: Ethical Principles and Guidelines for the Protection of Human Subjects of Research.* Washington, DC: Public Health Service; 1979.

2. Blackhall LJ, Murphy ST, Frank G, Michel V, Azen S. Ethnicity and attitudes toward patient autonomy. JAMA. 1995;274:820–825.

3. Carrese JA, Rhodes LA. Western bioethies on the Navajo reservation: benefit or harm? JAMA. 1995;274:826–829.

4. Ankrah EM, Gostin LO. Ethical and legal considerations of the HIV epidemic in Africa. In: Essex M, Mboup S, Kanki PJ, Nbowa KR, eds. *AIDS in Africa.* New York, NY: Raven Press; 1994:547–558.

5. Donoho DL. Relativism versus universalism in human rights: the search for meaningful standards. *Stanford J Int Law.* 1991:27:345–391.

6. Nelson JL. Taking families seriously. *Hastings Cent Rep,* 1992;22:6–12.

7. Murray T. Individualism and community: the contested terrain of autonomy. *Hastings Cent Rep.* 1994;24:32–35.

8. Christakis NA: The ethical design of an AIDS vaccine trial in Africa. *Hastings Cent Rep.* 1988;18:31–37.

9. Levine RJ. Informed consent: some challenges to the universal validity of the Western model. *J Law Med Ethics.* 1991;19:207–213.

10. *Canterbury v Spence,* 464 F2d 772, 786 (DC Cir 1972).

11. *Putensen v Clay Adams Inc,* 91 Cal Rptr 319, 333 (1970).

12. *Arato v Avedon,* 858 P2d 598, 609 (Cal SCt 1993).

13. Meisel A. The 'exceptions' to the informed consent doctrine: striking a balance between competing values in medical decision making. *Wis Law Rev.* 1979:413–488.

14. Surbone A. Truth telling to the patient. JAMA. 1992;268:1661–1662.

Caring for Patients in Cross-Cultural Settings

Nancy S. Jecker PhD, Joseph A. Carrese MD and Robert A. Pearlman MD

In our multicultural society, cross-cultural encounters are becoming increasingly common in the health care setting, often leading to distinct ethical and interpersonal tensions. Members of different cultures cannot take for granted a common catalog of recognized diseases; a shared understanding of their ascribed causes and usual treatments; or similar attitudes toward sickness,

From *Hastings Center Report* 25:6–14, 1995.

health, death, particular illnesses, and accidents. Although value differences also exist among different groups within a "shared" culture—across class, caste, gender, age, religious, and political lines—cross-cultural conflicts may be more deeply rooted, for such differences embody not just different opinions or beliefs, but different ways of everyday living and different systems of meaning.[1]

The difference between intra- and intercultural disagreements in health care may fall along a continuum, with intercultural tensions often appearing more striking and all encompassing. To illustrate this, consider the case of a Western patient diagnosed with carcinoma of the breast who disagrees with a Western physician's recommendation to undergo a mastectomy. The patient prefers instead to preserve the breast and treat the cancer with lumpectomy. In reaching her conclusion, the patient may stress the value she places on bodily integrity, physical wholeness, social attractiveness, and sexuality. Although the physician shares the patient's goal of preserving quality of life, the physician may place greater stress on curing disease. The physician may therefore reach a decision after consulting survival rates for the two procedures for patients at a similar stage of the disease. Despite the different concerns the patient and physician entertain, they are likely to share many of the same ethical concepts and principles. Thus they may articulate their differences in terms of a common moral vocabulary, for example, in terms of a tension between competing values of autonomy and beneficence. Or their discussion may refer to the relative priority of maximizing the quality versus the duration of the patient's life. This shared conceptual repertoire is likely to assist in reaching a treatment decision.

By contrast, intercultural disagreements in health care often involve the clash of different dominant social understandings. For example, consider the case of a Navajo patient who expresses to a Western physician a preference for a traditional healing ceremony to cure disease.

Both the patient's and the physician's ideas about healing seem ordinary and "natural" within the context of their respective cultures. In attempting to communicate their respective orientations to each other, however, each will refer to practices and traditions, concepts and values, and systems and methods of knowledge that appear unusual from the other's perspective. Thus, cross-cultural debates often seem to introduce moral anarchy because people lack shared cultural standards or vantage points from which to communicate and resolve value differences.

There are at least two distinct ways in which cross-cultural differences may become especially striking in the clinical setting. First, a health provider may come from a dominant cultural group and the patient may be a representative of an immigrant or refugee group or of a historical ethnic minority. Alternatively, health professionals themselves may be members of immigrant, refugee, or ethnic minorities and patients may be from the mainstream of society. In this paper, we address the first sort of paradigm case.

BACKGROUND AND CONTEXT

Although individuals with culturally distinct identities exist across many different subgroups in society, cultural differences among dominant and minority ethnic groups have become especially pronounced in recent years. The influx of immigrant and refugee populations has meant that today physicians are more likely than ever before to encounter patients from diverse cultures in their daily practice, and the need for ethical analyses has increased.[2]

Despite the fact that the United States has long been "a nation of nations"—a mix of different cultural groups—American bioethicists have paid relatively little attention to the distinctive ethical challenges this poses. Some have charged that American bioethics "considers its principles, its style of reasoning, and its perceptions to be objective, unbiased, and reasonable to a degree that not only makes them socially and culturally neutral but also endows them with a kind of universality."[3] Others find bioethical analyses "entangled in asocial, acultural, and de-contextualized philosophical, moral, and legal discourses" and therefore lacking tools to "investigate comprehensively the social and cultural realities that matter to diverse patient populaces."[4] Reflecting these concerns, standard bioethics textbooks often frame principles of ethics in health care to represent Western ethical traditions, while omitting discussion of pertinent and potentially conflicting values held by patients from non-Western cultures. When textbooks do address cross-cultural conflicts, they denounce ethical relativism and proceed to enumerate Western ethical standards,[5] or note cultural diversity on a case-by-case basis, without formulating general strategies for resolving differences.[6]

The dearth of coverage of cross-cultural issues in bioethics itself reflects the general paucity of scholarship in this area. Although a growing number of articles address specific cross-cultural problems,[7] only a few cover a full range of topics in a systematic fashion.[8] Reports of health care ethics in other countries have been forthcoming yet fail to touch upon the problems that arise when cultures collide.[9] Undoubtedly, such analyses can benefit from the contribution of diverse disciplines,[10] yet social science contributions to cross-cultural health care ethics have only recently begun to appear.[11]

A PRACTICAL ETHICAL APPROACH

We propose addressing the ethical predicaments cross-cultural medical encounters raise by means of an approach consisting of three distinct steps: identifying goals; identifying mutually agreeable strategies; and meeting ethical constraints.

Identifying Goals

The first step in this process asks the health practitioner to identify the central aims that health professional and patient bring to the medical encounter. This requires the health professional

to solicit information about the patient's ethical values and cultural orientation. Like an ethnographer, the clinician in a cross-cultural setting must try

> to get things right from the native's point of view . . . he practices an intensive, systematic, and imaginative empathy with the experiences and modes of thought of persons who may be foreign to him but whose foreignness he comes to appreciate and to humanly engage.[12]

Like the ethnographer, providers in cross-cultural settings should function as observational scientists, attending carefully to particular details, gathering information not only by communicating directly with the patient, but also by speaking with important persons in the patient's life. In clarifying their own goals, health providers must be self-reflective, distinguishing the purpose they bring to a patient encounter from the practices typically employed to realize this purpose.

Identifying Mutually Agreeable Strategies

Once the provider in a cross-cultural encounter has clarified provider and patient goals, the provider should take the initiative in identifying alternative mutually agreeable strategies to meet these goals. For example, signing informed consent forms represents but one method, among others, of realizing health providers' goal of ensuring that patients receive the treatment they truly want. Other ways of realizing informed consent include communicating with family members who then speak directly with patients, or postponing discussion of treatment options until the patient begins to know and trust the provider. The general point is that the goals of the medical encounter serve only as general guideposts, indicating a direction without charting a specific course; providers should search for alternative paths to realize the aims that patient and provider hold.[13]

Ideally, health professionals caring for patients in cross-cultural settings have access to consultants familiar with the patient's cultural circumstances, fluent in the patient's native language, and trained in medical interpreting. Health care institutions that regularly serve non-Western patient groups have special responsibilities to make such resources available, and new tools have become available to hospitals in many areas. For example, the AT&T Language Line provides a twenty-four-hour service that guarantees access to interpreters who speak 147 different languages. Health care institutions also have developed "language banks" (that is, computerized lists of bilingual staff members), utilized flash cards containing common phrases written in different languages, and provided intensive language training to staff to assist them in interactions with clients from commonly served non-English-speaking populations.[14]

Meeting Ethical Constraints

The final step of our approach engages the health professional in ethical deliberation about the acceptability of alternative means of realizing goals. At an initial stage, the provider brings two central ethical criteria to bear (figure 1). First, the means chosen to achieve the goals of the medical encounter should be compatible with the health care provider's own conscientiously held values as well as with the ethics of the health care profession to which the provider belongs. As the American College of Physicians notes, "The physician [in a cross-cultural setting] cannot be required to violate fundamental personal values, standards of scientific or ethical practice, or the law."[15] A second criterion holds that the means employed should be compatible with the patient's values and the values of the culture with which the patient identifies. This constraint is necessary to ensure that relationships between providers and patients remain mutually respectful and to safeguard patients against abuses of power and authority by health professionals. Health professionals generally have greater authority and power than patients, and patients are frequently confused, upset, and compromised by their illness. When these power dynamics are compounded by cultural differences, with the health care provider representing the dominant culture and the patient coming from a "different" culture, the risk of unjustly coercing the patient is heightened.

Both constraints gain justification from the concept of ethical integrity. Integrity refers to the disposition to act in accordance with one's own moral beliefs and character.[16] It presupposes having the self-knowledge and moral commitment necessary to know and honor one's moral convictions. Understood in this light, integrity cannot be identified with any particular set of moral virtues or principles, but is instead compatible with diverse moral perspectives. For example, two persons with different positions on the morality

---

FIGURE 1.   **First Level of Ethical Analysis.**

Requirements

The means chosen should be

- consistent with the health care provider's conscientiously held beliefs
- compatible with the patient's values and the values of the culture with which the patient identifies

Justification

Integrity requires acting in accordance with ethical convictions and beliefs that are one's own

of assisted suicide may show integrity by acting in opposite ways. Someone who believes that the sanctity of human life prohibits assisting with suicide may display integrity by refusing to meet a friend's request for aid in dying. By contrast, someone in the same situation who maintains that compassion for human suffering permits assisting with suicide may show integrity by assisting with suicide. Thus, if it can be called a virtue, integrity is a higher-order virtue. It does not presuppose any specific lower-order virtues to which a person's actions must conform.[17]

Within the limits set by integrity, alternative practical means for resolving culturally based conflicts may emerge, as people are frequently able to agree about particular cases without ever agreeing at all about the basic ethical tenets underlying them. A particularly impressive illustration of this phenomenon is the work of the National Commission for the Protection of Human Subjects of Biomedical and Behavioral Research. In describing the development of the commission's guidelines, one member notes that although the eleven commissioners had different ethical, religious, and professional orientations, "so long as the Commission stayed on the taxonomic or casuistical level, they usually agreed in their practical conclusions."[18]

When examination of more basic ethical goals is necessary, the health professional proceeds to a second stage of ethical analysis (figure 2). At this stage, integrity again furnishes guidance.

Properly understood, integrity does not manifest itself merely as exceptional resoluteness. Rather, persons of true integrity make convictions and principles their own through critically examining and questioning them. By contrast, someone who acts blindly or stubbornly, holding fast to principles for their own sake, does not evince genuine integrity. Nor does the individual who accepts on faith whatever moral principles she or he receives from others. Instead, persons with integrity scrutinize their moral principles and commitments carefully to interpret and apply them to new situations. They regard their moral convictions as potentially mistaken and as continuously open to criticism and improvement in the wake of new circumstances and challenges. Whereas an ideologue claims "a monopoly of truth and justice," a person of integrity shows the qualities of a reasonable person, including "a disposition to find reasons for and against the possible lines of conduct . . . open to him, . . . to consider [viewpoints] . . . in the light of further evidence and reasons which may be presented, . . . [and] to know his own emotional, intellectual, and moral predilection."[19]

Understood in this light, integrity directs health professionals to examine critically the values they bring to the medical encounter. Similarly, the patient with integrity is "empowered not simply to follow unexamined preferences . . . but to consider, through dialogue, alternative

---

FIGURE 2.   Second Level of Ethical Analysis.

Requirements

Reexamine personal values and consider reinterpreting, reordering, or changing them in light of the case

Justification

Integrity requires scrutinizing one's values and regarding them as open to criticism and improvement

health-related values, their worthiness, and their implications for treatment."[20] Providers and patients who show integrity may continue to assume that their own views are correct; however, they will also recognize that they could be mistaken. As Martin Benjamin notes, the give and take of conversation may lead thoughtful persons to alter their positions, replacing an initial viewpoint with a different viewpoint that comes to be regarded as superior.[21] This process of amending ethical beliefs does not necessarily show that persons have betrayed their principles; instead, it may show that ethical belifs have been changed in light of new evidence and circumstances. Therefore, although the idea of integrity may conjure up images of people who hold tenaciously to principles in the face of enticements to give them up, many instances of integrity do not conform to this model. Persons manifest integrity by reexamining existing values and changing their course of action to conform to new or more fully enunciated values. Thus, integrity is able to survive changes in basic allegiances over time.[22]

The interpretation of integrity as nondogmatic is supported by the observation that context influences the weight ethical principles bring to bear. In the health care setting, for example, the force of ethical principles depends upon circumstances of context, such as the values of patients, family members, and relevant social groups; personal and professional values of health care providers; and the institutional setting in which ethical situations arise.[23] In addition, a nondogmatic reading of integrity is persuasive when one considers the myriad ways in which context shapes the actual meaning ethical principles hold.[24] Thus, in health care the very generality of bioethical principles to "do good" and "avoid harm" renders interpretation inescapable, and health professionals cannot get along on a diet of general principles alone.[25]

CASE ANALYSES

To illustrate the strategy outlined above we now turn to two cases drawn from the clinical setting.

Each reveals ethical tensions that arise between Western physicians and Navajo patients. The first case is relatively straightforward and is intended primarily to illustrate the approach we have described. It bears some resemblance to the intracultural example described at the outset of the paper, in which a patient and provider share common goals but place different emphases on curing disease versus preserving quality of life. Unlike the intracultural case, however, the Western physician and Navajo patient we describe below do not share a common moral vocabulary and framework, nor do they function with similar systems of meaning and modes of interacting. These cultural differences make the resolution of even a relatively straightforward ethical conflict more challenging. In the second cross-cultural encounter we describe, the provider and patient bring different goals to the medical encounter, and have different ethical frameworks, meaning systems, and ways of interacting.

Case 1   A fifty-five-year-old Navajo man, Mr. Begay, presented with hypertension for a routine clinic appointment. On this visit, as on previous visits, the patient's blood pressure was elevated. In the past, the physician had devoted considerable energy to educating Mr. Begay about high blood pressure: its etiology, natural history if untreated, and the benefits of controlling it. In addition, he had stressed the importance of nonpharmacologic measures, such as restricting salt, moderating alcohol use, exercising appropriately and losing weight. At the time of this visit Mr. Begay was being treated with two drugs. The physician considered adding a third drug; however, he was concerned that Mr. Begay would not adhere to a new medical regimen. Mr. Begay had not followed the physician's recommendations pertaining to diet and exercise in the past, and the physician suspected that he had not taken medication with prescribed frequency. Despite the physician's efforts, Mr. Begay's blood pressure was elevated and he was at risk for stroke, renal injury, and coronary artery disease.

Complicating the situation was the fact that the physician's ordinary manner of relating to patients involved disclosing negative possibilities and risks in order to inform and educate patients. In this situation, his inclination was to stress to Mr. Begay the negative risks associated with his refusal to follow medical advice. Mr. Begay, however, was a traditional Navajo and his expectations reflected his culture's ideas about healing as a process of moving the patient from a negative state of illness or "imbalance" to a positive state of harmony and health. Hopefulness and positive thinking are perceived as integral to healing, while negative thinking is regarded as potentially deleterious. Thus, "Navajos emphasize that if one thinks of good things and good fortune, good things will happen. If one thinks of bad things, bad fortune will be one's lot."[26] According to traditional Navajos, people can acquire disease through a process of "witching." Witching involves manipulating agents that produce disease, and can occur through explicit discussion of potential morbid events.[27]

In view of how explicit disclosure of possible bad outcomes may adversely affect traditional Navajo patients, how should the physician proceed? The strategy proposed in the previous section instructs the physician to begin by identifying the underlying goals at stake in the situation for both Mr. Begay and himself. Through eliciting the patient's values and engaging others who know the patient well, the physician may learn that Mr. Begay's central goals include staying healthy, existing in harmony with nature, thinking in a positive and hopeful manner about the future, and living long enough to see his grandchildren's children. The physician may identify his own objectives to include minimizing Mr. Begay's risks of morbidity and mortality from hypertension and persuading Mr. Begay to adhere to treatment. These objectives of the physician are themselves instrumental to a more fundamental and, namely, keeping Mr. Begay healthy. The physician's aims also may include keeping Mr. Begay informed and educated about the purpose and importance of treatments.

Our second step directs the physician to determine mutually acceptable means to realize the goals patient and provider bring to the medical encounter. Stating goals explicitly helps to show that although the goal of achieving health is shared, there is not a shared conception of the appropriate means to achieve this goal. The physician's means of ensuring Mr. Begay's health are educating Mr. Begay; Mr. Begay's means of ensuring his health are avoiding witching by thinking only in positive and hopeful terms about the future. How can the physician accomplish both his and the patient's objectives and act in accordance with the values that both he and Mr. Begay hold? One approach that traditional Navajos use is to communicate information about possible bad outcomes by making reference to a hypothetical third party. This approach would avoid direct reference to Mr. Begay and avert his concern about being witched. Another option consists of reframing the interaction with the patient to focus on the positive benefits that Mr. Begay would gain if he abides by treatment. Thus, the physician might begin by affirming that he shares with Mr. Begay the goal that Mr. Begay stay healthy or "move to a state of harmony." The physician might then make the case that taking medication facilitates these positive ends. Similarly, the physician may explain to Mr. Begay that taking medication furthers his positive aim of seeing his grandchildren's children. This approach contrasts with the alternative, to which the physician was initially drawn, namely, focusing on his perception of the negative risks of nonadherence. The physician's goal of educating the patient is still achieved, but the means used accommodate the patient's concern not to be witched and to think affirmatively about the future.

Applying our approach to case 1 makes evident the central importance of integrity in cross-cultural conflicts. In the case resolutions we develop, the physician makes adjustments in his ordinary manner of communicating with patients, but does this without violating the standards he or the patient holds. In the actual resolution of the case, the physician caring for Mr. Begay had learned through experience with

Navajo patients to devise innovative strategies that accomplish both his and the patient's goals. On previous occasions, however, the physician had taken the opposite tack and discussed explicit risks, thereby offending patients and discouraging them from returning to Western physicians.

Case 2 A sixty-five-year-old widowed Navajo woman, Mrs. Tsosie, presented to the hospital with her two adult daughters following nearly two months of lethargy, impaired memory, confusion, possible visual hallucinations, anorexia, and fever. These symptoms had progressed in the two weeks prior to admission, but the patient had refused to come to the hospital for treatment. She had instead sought a healing ceremony from a traditional Navajo medicine man, but the medicine man had refused to perform the ceremony, claiming that she was too sick to participate. When Mrs. Tsosie had become too weak and confused to protest going to the hospital, her daughters brought her there.

The patient had a history of rheumatic heart disease. Despite two admissions over the past three years for congestive heart failure, Mrs. Tsosie had refused an echocardiogram and cardiac catheterization to evaluate the severity of her disease. The patient, a weaver and shepherd, conceived of illness and healing in terms of the traditional Navajo worldview. Since childhood, cross-cultural tensions had rendered her relationship with Western physicians tentative.

Medical evaluation of Mrs. Tsosie's change in mental status included electroencephalogram, computerized axial tomography scan, and blood workup to rule out metabolic causes. When these tests were unrevealing, Mrs. Tsosie's daughters refused to consent to a lumbar puncture to rule out meningitis as a possible basis for delirium. The daughters explained that their mother had consistently refused surgical or invasive procedures. They believed this was due to their mother's skepticism about Western medicine. Especially when the perceived harm was great, Mrs. Tsosie was reluctant to put her trust in Western doctors.

Following one week in the hospital, the two daughters requested that their mother be discharged to participate in a healing ceremony. Mrs. Tsosie had apparently communicated to her daughters that she wished to have a healing ceremony performed. The patient's daughters insisted that they must honor their mother's wishes. As they perceived their mother's condition to be slightly improved, they hoped that the medicine man who had previously refused to perform a healing ceremony would now agree to do so.

In contrast to case 1, case 2 shows that sometimes there may seem to be no mutually agreeable means available to meet both the patient's and the health care provider's goals. How does the approach we endorse fare in light of this more challenging case? As before, the first step involves stating explicitly the goals of both physician and patient. The physician's primary goals might be diagnosing the patient and prescribing beneficial treatment. The alternative the physician sees is postponing diagnosis indefinitely with the expectation that the patient's status would deteriorate. Empirically based treatments for acute bacterial meningitis, such as broad spectrum antibiotics, had been tried without significant improvement in the patient's condition. Pursuing other treatment options was potentially hazardous without the more definitive diagnosis that the lumbar puncture would provide. Thus, the physician regarded the risks associated with acceding to the family's wishes as extremely high: an undiagnosed and inappropriately treated central nervous system infection was potentially fatal. The patient's goals, as conveyed by her daughters, included leaving the hospital to participate in a healing ceremony. The daughters' goals included abiding by their mother's wishes and returning her to an active and healthy state. The alternative for them was to violate their filial duties and perpetuate their mother in her current unhealthy state. There appeared to be no mutually acceptable means that respected the concerns of both sides. To the physician, performing the lumbar puncture seemed to be the only way to make an accurate diagnosis and identify appropriate treatments; to the patient and family, leaving the hospital to participate in a healing ceremony appeared to be the sole path to restoring harmony.

In applying our approach to case 2, the requirements of integrity indicate that the physician should engage in a critical process of examining, and possibly reconfiguring, her values. Earlier, we noted that altering one's values is possible without compromising personal integrity. How might the physician in case 2 weigh her values differently in view of the circumstances of the case? Although the physician perceives her primary responsibility to be minimizing Mrs. Tsosie's risks of morbidity and mortality, she also subscribes to values other than preservation of life and avoidance of harm. Among the physician's other values are respect for patient autonomy and self-determination. Thus, the contemporary Western ethics that this physician endorses pays homage to the idea that all persons possess a right to liberty and to freedom from interference by outside parties. Evaluating these commitments in the context of the case, the physician might decide, on balance, to assign greater weight to the value of freedom from outside interference, represented by having the family pursue other (non-Western) modes of healing. This would entail assigning comparatively less weight to saving life and avoiding harm in situations where the patient or a valid surrogate prefers to incur risks. On this analysis, the physician does not sever her attachment to prior values. Instead, she casts these values in a different light by considering them in the context of other values that apply to the case. Needless to say, from the patient's perspective the Western ethics the physician endorses would appear unfamiliar, and perhaps unappealing. Yet despite disparate value frameworks, the physician and patient may be able to agree about how the medical encounter should proceed.

A different, and more demanding, strategy would be for the physician not only to reinterpret her present values but to make fundamental changes in them. Individuals compelled to reexamine their values in new situations generally resist making more than the minimal changes necessary to resolve the immediate problem. This avoids constant and disruptive upheavals in value

frameworks. Had an examination of basic values been necessary in case 2, it might have taken the following form. The physician might have initially placed considerable emphasis on benefitting the patient, and interpreted benefitting her to mean performing the lumbar puncture. She might have reasoned at the outset that any disappointment resulting from omitting a healing ceremony was far outweighed by the benefit of accurately diagnosing and treating Mrs. Tsosie's illness. Yet the meaning the physician assigned to beneficence might have undergone a profound change had the physician exerted a genuine effort to understand Mrs. Tsosie's perspective. Mrs. Tsosie, like other traditional Navajos, viewed herself primarily in the context of her relationships with others and with the physical and spiritual universe. She held in high regard the values of connectedness and solidarity with others and with nature. In keeping with traditional Navajo practice, Mrs. Tsosie might have regularly included her family members in medical decisions, or deferred to them entirely. Thus, from her perspective it would be comforting and right to know that her daughters were looking out for her interests. Similarly, the healing ceremony is intended to establish in Mrs. Tsosie a state of harmony and balance. Whereas "in the hospital a Navajo is lonely and homesick, living by a strange routine and eating unfamiliar foods . . . during the chant [of a traditional ceremony] the patient feels himself personally . . . being succored and loved, for his relatives are . . . rallying round to aid in the ceremonial."[28]

These considerations might have led the physician to think empathically about the meaning of benefit from the patient's perspective and the perspective of her traditional Navajo culture. For example, the physician might ask herself, Do the benefits of competent diagnosis and treatment fit into the broader view of what the patient conceives as the good life? This question may lead the physician to see the paradox of applying the word *benefit* to an outcome that the person in question does not appreciate. Although the physician does not subscribe to traditional Navajo medicine, she may come to appreciate that the patient would benefit by participating in a healing ceremony. Although the physician does not concur with the daughters' wish to refuse the lumbar puncture, she may nevertheless recognize that Mrs. Tsosie stands to benefit by placing matters in her daughters' hands. Understood in this light, the subject of medicine becomes the suffering patient, and the injunction to benefit the patient does not necessarily require producing certain physiolgical effects on the body, but requires instead caring for the patient and producing outcomes that patients themselves can appreciate.

In the actual resolution of the case, Mrs. Tsosie's daughters took her out of the hospital to participate in a healing ceremony. In reflecting on the case, the physician felt she had acted in accordance with her sense of professional integrity. The patient's daughters also felt a sense of closure about the case, as they had abided by their mother's wishes and met their filial duties toward her.

As our framework and case analyses attest, health professionals who treat patients from cultures different from their own should expect to devise alternative ways of interacting with patients. But this need not entail giving up the fundamental values the provider holds. Instead, our approach advises health professionals to step back from their ordinary manner of relating to patients to distill the underlying purposes and goals of the medical encounter. This enables the provider to find a manner of coping with differences that respects the integrity of both provider and patient. We acknowledge the likelihood that disparate values will at times require reexamination in light of the context and relationships at stake in the case. In such instances, no practical measure may be available that is consistent with the values espoused by both parties. Faced with an intractable conflict of values, health care providers must interpret and weigh their values with sensitivity to context. Reaching a resolution may not

be possible unless one or more parties reshape their values in light of the circumstances of the case. We underscore the point that genuine integrity requires humility and openness to change.

Although we have pressed the idea of integrity throughout, we also recognize its potential limits. Hence, we recognize that on some occasions it may not be possible to preserve the integrity of both sides and reach a resolution to the case. There will be occasions where a provider or patient regards the other's values as not only different but wrong or extremely offensive and therefore is unable to accommodate them. Although we are not aware of Navajo medical practices that Westerners would view in this extreme manner, there are many examples from other non-Western cultures. For example, most Western providers find wrong and offensive the practice of clitoridectomy, or excision of the clitoris, that is practiced in parts of Africa, and would refuse to meet an African patient's request for this procedure.

We submit that under circumstances where Western eyes see non-Western health care decisions as wrong, preference should not automatically be given to Western medicine and its representatives. Instead, a "negotiated settlement" of conflict should occur (figure 3).[29] This requires both sides to agree upon a fair procedure for resolving differences. Although the specific details of such a procedure can be developed to address the concerns at hand, the core idea is that intercultural disagreement should be publicly argued and negotiated. Beyond agreement on procedural standards of adjudication, it may be exceedingly difficult in cross-cultural situations to resolve ethical disagreements by finding substantive cross-cultural ethical generalizations to apply to the situation. As others have noted,

> What has made objectifying representations and universalist claims [in ethics] particularly offensive . . . are . . . the asymmetries of power that have prevented [people from nondominant cultures] . . . from participating in the conversation on equal footing.[30]

FIGURE 3.   Third Level of Ethical Analysis.

Requirements

Adjudicate differences through a fair procedure that reflects a nonjudgmental stance

Justification

Inequalities of power in the provider-patient relationship must be recognized and patients protected against abuses

To avoid imposing foreign values on either patient or physician, both parties should refrain from assuming that their own ethical standards and cultural traditions represent universally valid truths. Rather, a fair adjudicative process will call initially for a nonjudgmental stance, in which both provider and patient are regarded as having equally important ethical concerns.

One basis for requiring an equal starting point is the presumption that diverse cultures possess worth and dignity. This presumption may be defended on the ground that

> it is reasonable to suppose that cultures that have provided the horizon of meaning for large numbers of human beings of diverse characters and temperaments, over a long period of time . . . are almost certain to have something that deserves our admiration and respect . . . it would take a supreme arrogance to discount this possibility *a priori*.[31]

Alternatively, requiring an equal starting point may be justified by appealing, not to the worth or truth of different cultural beliefs and practices, but to the assumption that both provider and patient are equally invested in their cultures. For example, when providers feel strongly that Western medical practices are valid, a nonjudgmental stance is called for because patients feel just as strongly that their cultural beliefs and practices are valid.

In light of these considerations, we propose that a fair procedure for resolving cultural differ-

ences reflects a presumption of the equal validity of both sides' views. This requires a process involving a balanced representation of individuals from both Western medicine and the patient's culture. Initially, adjudication might proceed through a process of discovery, analogous to what occurs in legal proceedings. In the cross-cultural setting, discovery entails gathering further information about the patient's culture and way of life as well as the professional and personal values of the health care worker. The specific details of the case can then guide the adjudicative process toward a resolution.

In response to our proposal it might be objected that in fact we have not avoided the errors of arrogance and cultural imperialism. Instead, we have proposed applying Western democratic standards of adjudication upon people from non-Western cultures. Worse, we have defended and elaborated this approach by appealing to concepts such as integrity and procedural justice as interpreted and developed by Western moral philosophers. Perhaps our model for resolving cross-cultural differences would persuade Western readers, but how might we rationally defend our position to persons who have no ethical concept corresponding to our idea of "integrity"?

Our reply to this objection can only be to admit that our ethical approach reflects Western meanings and values. Rather than presuming to "step outside" our own cultural traditions, or presuming to represent all cultural perspectives, we have sought to find within our own ethical traditions a meaningful way for Western providers to understand and help to resolve intercultural differences. We fully expect that members of non-Western cultures will appeal to concepts and ideas quite different from the ones we have developed. If diverse cultural justifications can be given for the kind of intercultural adjudication we propose, this only strengthens the practical usefulness of the approach.

In closing, although we have suggested a philosophical grounding for our proposal in the concept of ethical integrity, its ultimate validity turns on its practical usefulness. We therefore welcome the application of our approach to diverse cross-cultural settings, including those in which health care providers belong to a cultural minority and patients come from a dominant cultural group. The varied contexts and circumstances in which our approach is deployed should direct its further refinement.

References

1. Norma C. Ware and Arthur R. Kleinman, "Culture and Somatic Experience," *Psychosomatic Medicine* 54 (1992):546–60.

2. Judith Barker, "Cultural Diversity—Changing the Context of Medical Practice," *Western Journal of Medicine* 157, no. 3, (1992): 248–54; Alan M. Kraut, "Healers and Strangers: Immigrant Attitudes toward the Physician in America—A Relationship in Historical Perspective," *JAMA* 263 (1990): 1807–11.

3. Renée C. Fox and Judith P. Swazey, "Medical Morality Is Not Bioethics—Medical Ethics in China and the United States," *Perspectives in Biology and Medicine* 27, no. 3 (1984): 336–60, at 356.

4. Barker, "Cultural Diversity," p. 251.

5. C. E. Harris, *Applying Moral Theories*, 2nd ed. (Belmont, Calif.: Wadsworth Publishing Company, 1992).

6. Howard Brody, *Ethical Decisions in Medicine*, 2nd ed. (Boston: Little, Brown and Company, 1981).

7. John F. Kilner, "Who Shall Be Saved: An African Answer," *Hastings Center Report* 14, no. 3 (1984): 19–22; Peter Lurie et al., "Ethical, Behavioral, and Social Aspects of HIV Vaccine Trails in Developing Countries," *JAMA* 271 (1994): 295–301; John Klessig, "The Effect of Values and Culture on Life Support Decisions." *Western Journal of Medicine* 157, no. 3 (1992): 316–21.

8. Peter Kunstadter, "Medical Ethics in Cross-Cultural Perspectives," *Social Science and Medicine* 14B (1980): 289–96; Geri-Ann Galanti, *Caring for Patients from Different Cultures* (Philadelphia: University of Pennsylvania Press, 1991); Robert Veath, *Cross Cultural Perspectives in Medical Ethics* (Boston: Jones and Bartlett, 1989).

9. Azim A. Nanji, "Medical Ethics and the Islamic Tradition," *Journal of Medicine and Philosophy* 13 (1988): 257–75; Zbigniew Szawarski, "Poland: Biomedical Ethics in a Socialist State," Special Supplement, *Hastings Center Report* 17, no. 3 (1987): 27–29; Bertha Mo, "Modesty, Sexuality, and Breast Health in Chinese-American Women," *Western Journal of Medicine* 157, no. 3 (1992): 260–64.

10. D. F. Philip, "New Voices Ask to Be Heard in Bioethics," *Cambridge Quarterly of Healthcare Ethics* 2 (1992): 169–77.

11. Arthur R. Kleinman, "Anthropology of Bioethics," in *Encyclopedia of Bioethics*, 2nd ed., ed. Warren T. Reich (New York: Macmillan, forthcoming); George Weisz, ed., *Social Science Perspectives on Medical. Ethics* (Philadelphia: University of Pennsylvania Press, 1990); Patricia A. Marshall, "Anthropology and Bioethics," *Medical Anthropology Quarterly* 6, no. 1 (1992): 49–73.

12. Arthur R. Kleinman, *The Illness Narratives* (New York: Basic Books, 1988).

13. Lawrence R. Churchill and J. J. Siman, "Principles and the Search for Moral Certainty," *Social Science and Medicine* 23 (1986): 461–68.

14. Lisa Belkin, "Patients Say 'Ah' in Many Languages," *New York Times*, 31 December 1992.

15. American College of Physicians, Ethics Committee, American College of Physicians Ethics Manual, 3rd ed., *Annals of Internal Medicine* 117, no. 11 (1992): 947–60.

16. Gabriele Taylor and Raimond Gaita, "Integrity," *Proceedings of the Aristotelian Society Supplement* 55 (1981): 143–59; Lynn McFall, "Integrity," *Ethics* 98, no. 1 (1987): 5–20.

17. Bernard Williams, *Moral Luck* (Cambridge: Cambridge University Press, 1981), pp. 40–53.

18. Albert R. Jonsen and Stephen Toulmin. *The Abuse of Casuistry* (Berkeley and Los Angeles: University of California Press, 1988), p. 17.

19. John Rawls, "An Outline for a Decision Procedure for Ethics," *Philosophical Review* 60, no. 2 (1950): 177–97.

20. Linda L. Emanuel and Ezekiel J. Emanuel, "Four Models of the Physician-Patient Relationship," *JAMA* 267 (1992): 2221–26, at 2222.

21. Martin Benjamin, *Splitting the Difference: Compromise and Integrity in Ethics and Politics* (Lawrence: University Press of Kansas, 1990).

22. Jeffrey Blustein, *Care and Commitment* (New York: Oxford University Press, 1992).

23. David C. Thomasma, "The Context as a Moral Rule in Medicine," *Journal of Bioethics* 5, no. 1 (1984): 63–79.

24. Thomas H. Murray, "Medical Ethics, Moral Philosophy and Moral Tradition," *Social Science and Medicine* 25, no. 6 (1987): 637–44.

25. Stephen Toulmin, "The Tyranny of Principles," *Hastings Center Report* 11, no. 6 (1981): 31–39.

26. Gary Witherspoon, *Language and Art in the Navajo Universe* (Ann Arbor: University of Michigan Press, 1977).

27. S.J. Kunitz and J. E. Lety, "Navajos," in *Ethnicity and Medical Case*, ed. Allen Hardwood (Cambridge: Harvard University Press, 1981), pp. 337–95.

28. Clyde Kluckhohn and D. Leighton, *The Navajo* (Cambridge, Mass.: Harvard University Press, 1974).

29. Nicholas A. Christakis and Morris J. Panner, "Existing International Guidelines for Human Subjects Research," *Law, Medicine & Health Care* 19, no. 3-4 (1991): 214–21.

30. Thomas McCarthy, "Doing the Right Thing in Cross-Cultural Representation," *Ethics* 102, no. 3 (1992): 635–49.

31. Charles Taylor, *Multiculturalism and the Politics of Recognition* (Princeton, N.J.: Princeton University Press. 1992), pp. 25–74, at 72–73.

The Doctor–Patient Relationship in Different Cultures

Ruth Macklin PhD

When bioethicists from the United States call for recognition of the rights of patients, are they simply expressing their unique American adherence to individualism? The familiar charge of "ethical imperialism" is leveled against proposals that patients in other countries, where individualism is not a prominent value, should nevertheless be granted a similar right to informed consent. While it is true that the doctrine of informed consent focuses on the rights of individual patients, it is not rooted solely in the cultural value of individualism. Rather, it stems from a value many cultures recognize, especially those that aspire to democracy and a just social order: the notion that powerful agents, be they from governmental or nongovernmental organizations, may not invade the personal lives, and especially the bodies, of ordinary citizens.

The prominent American sociologist Renée Fox accurately describes the early focus of

From *Against Relativism: Cultural Diversity and The Search for Universals in Medicine*, New York: Oxford University Press, 1999.

American bioethics: "From the outset, the conceptual framework of bioethics has accorded paramount status to the value-complex of individualism, underscoring the principles of individual rights, autonomy, self-determination, and their legal expression in the jurisprudential notion of privacy."[1] Critics of mainstream bioethics within the United States and abroad have complained about the narrow focus on autonomy and the concept of individual rights. Such critics argue that much—if not most—of the world embraces a value system that places the family, the community, or the society as a whole above that of the individual person. But we need to ask: What follows from value systems that accord the individual a lower priority than the group? It hardly follows that individual patients should not be granted a right to full participation in medical decisions. Nor does it follow that individual doctors need not be obligated to disclose information or obtain their patients' voluntary, informed consent. It surely does not follow that the needs of society or the community for organs, bone marrow, or blood should permit those bodily parts or products to be taken from individuals without their permission. What might follow, however, is that patients' families may be fuller participants in decision-making than the patient autonomy model ordinarily requires.

Perhaps we need to be reminded just why American bioethics began with such a vigorous defense of autonomy. It is because patients traditionally had few, if any rights of self-determination: Doctors neither informed patients nor obtained their consent for treatment or for research. In a country founded on conceptions of liberty and freedom, it was at least odd that the self-determination Americans so highly prized in other areas of life was largely absent from the sphere of medical practice. An evolution took place in the United States over a period of many years, from an early court ruling in 1914 that required surgeons to obtain the consent of patients through a series of informed consent cases in the 1950s and 1970s. By the time bioethics became an international field of study, paternalistic medicine had been largely transformed in the United States and patients' rights had been solidly established. The same developments are occurring today in the many developing countries where bioethics has more recently become a topic of interest and study. Although most of these countries lack the tradition of individualism that marks North American culture, the legal guarantee of certain rights of the individual has in the past few decades been one of the goals of social and political reformers.

Cross-cultural misunderstandings can affect the way people in one country perceive a situation in another. Participating in a workshop in the Philippines,[2] I encountered an example of a common cross-cultural misunderstanding about informed consent. The discussion focused on the ethical principle of respect for persons and its role in justifying the need to inform patients and obtain their permission to carry out therapeutic or research procedures. A Filipino physician in the audience objected that informed consent may be needed in the United States, where people do not trust their doctors, but, he said, in the Philippines patients place great trust in their physicians. Doctors do not need to protect themselves against lawsuits by having patients sign a consent form.

Throughout the world (and even at times in the United States), people confuse informed consent with the informed consent document. The Filipino physician misunderstood two things: first, the ethical basis for informed consent; and second, the difference between the *process* of informing and obtaining permission and the piece of paper (the documentation) attesting that the process took place. The ethical judgment that patients should be full participants in their treatment decisions is the ethical justification for the doctrine of informed consent. It is not the protection of the doctor, as the Filipino physician believed, that serves as an ethical basis for the practice. Although it is true that the number of medical malpractice lawsuits in the United States far exceeds that in other countries, especially in the developing world, that phenomenon bears little relation to whether patients lack trust in their doctors.

"PHYSICIANS TREAT PATIENTS BADLY"

"Physicians treat patients badly" was a constant theme in virtually all of the developing countries I visited. Unfortunately, many of the shortcomings in the physician–patient relationship that are all too common in many countries continue to exist in the United States, as well. A major difference is that patients in this country are more aware of their legal and moral rights and are consequently more assertive. An Egyptian physician said that in Egypt there is no process by which consent is obtained in clinical practice. She complained that there is no physician–patient communication, in part because doctors do not have the time. Patients are not told about complications, about medical errors, or anything that transpires in the course of treatment. Patients can get no information whatsoever from doctors about their diagnosis, prognosis, or proposed treatment. Before surgical procedures, papers are signed. But those papers say nothing at all. Patients who ask questions are viewed by the doctors as "impolite," and in any case doctors do not like to answer questions posed by patients.

This Egyptian physician did not seek to defend the customary practices of doctors in her country or to argue that they were reflections of cultural values in Egypt. On the contrary, she was attempting in her work to introduce reforms into medical practice in order to bring about better treatment of patients. When I asked what possible remedies there could be for all these ethical shortcomings, she replied by describing two broad strategies. The first is to document abuses—violations of patients' rights, failures to obtain proper informed consent, and the like; the second is to mount a campaign by lobbying, bringing these issues before the public, and putting cases into court. I asked whether these steps are likely to be effective, and she replied that they can succeed in raising consciousness and awareness and further that people have received some compensa-

tion when their cases have reached the courts. Gathering cases and making them public can be used to mount campaigns. By this means reforms might be accomplished. The Egyptian physician's criticism of practices in her own country, and the specific reforms she sought to introduce, show that however different in other ways the culture of Egypt may be from that of Western nations, the ethical ideal that requires physicians to treat their patients with respect is widely acknowledged, if not always honored.

A colleague in Mexico gave a similar account of the lack of recognition of patients' rights in her country.[3] One example was a story told to her by the doorman of her building. His wife was in labor and went to the public hospital. She remained in labor for 2 days, during which time neither the woman nor her husband were told anything about her condition. Eventually she gave birth and was discharged from the hospital while the baby had to remain there for a while longer. Still the couple was told nothing. My colleague expressed her outrage at this situation, blaming the doctors in public hospitals for their unwillingness to disclose information to patients, much less to obtain properly informed consent.

While I agreed that this was an outrage, I noted that things were not so very different years ago in the United States. It is a mere 40 years since the concept of informed consent to treatment was introduced into the legal domain and probably only about 25 years since the practice of obtaining informed consent took root. Still, my Mexican colleague insisted, there are cultural differences. As an example, she cited the pervasive corruption in Latin America as a difference between that region and the North. "What, no corruption in the United States or in Europe?" was my surprised reaction. Of course there is, but we have a much lower tolerance for official corruption, we make strenuous efforts to root it out, and we probably succeed more often in punishing instances that are discovered.

In India I heard more stories about how doctors treat patients badly. One physician described the efforts he and others have been making to inform and enlist the public in opposing unethical medical practices.[4] He recounted a long list of horrors: incompetent doctors practicing poorly or negligently; untrained and unlicensed doctors practicing medicine; physicians overcharging patients; and more. The array of unethical behavior ranged from genuine malpractice to arrogance and indifference to patients. I asked about legal recourse, and here the situation is just as bleak. There exists a body called the Medical Council of India, which is supposed to be responsible for monitoring and dealing with the standard of care delivered by physicians. But this is a peer review system in which doctors protect other doctors. When cases of blatant malpractice are brought before this council, they fail to find the physician at fault. As a result, nothing is done to remedy instances of actual malpractice or the behavior of incompetent physicians. Patients can, in principle, bring suits against doctors. However, doctors win most of the cases brought to court in spite of their having committed actual malpractice, and judicial appeals take many years.

A different group of doctors repeated the same list of horror stories that I had heard from the first Indian physician, and more. When they mentioned the "kickback" system, I naively thought they were referring only to money paid to the referring doctor by the surgeon or specialist to whom the referral was made. But they meant much more by "kickbacks," including demands by the referring doctor that the surgeon perform unnecessary procedures, charge the patient for them, and then give a percentage of the take to the referring doctor. Surgeons and other specialists who rely on referrals for their practice have to play the game or else they are not sent a single patient. Thus even doctors who begin by being ethical and idealistic end up getting caught up in a system in which they must play or fail to make a living.

All these accounts of bad behavior of physicians toward patients have little to do with cultural differences or with ethical relativism. They simply remind us that arrogance, corruption, greed, and indifference are universal character flaws that can be found in human beings throughout the world, wherever they live and whatever their profession. The chief difference between these countries and the United States lies not in a divergence in the cultural acceptance of such behavior by physicians but, rather, in the existence of laws and other forms of social control to root out and punish doctors who violate universally acknowledged ethical norms and standards of good clinical practice. The efforts of the Egyptian physician and the Indian doctors to bring about reforms in their countries are evidence of a widespread cross-cultural identification of the same ethical values that ought to govern the doctor–patient relationship everywhere. Respect for persons—in this case, individual patients—was the principle invoked implicitly or explicitly by people from Latin America, Asia, and North Africa in my visits to those regions.

SIMILARITIES AND DIFFERENCES

Even in those parts of the world where the cultural traditions differ radically from those in the West, certain values in the doctor–patient relationship are overarching. I participated in a meeting in Nigeria that included several non-English speaking tribal chiefs and native healers. One chief was asked for his views about helping a woman to have an abortion. (Abortion is illegal in Nigeria as in many other countries, but legal prohibitions have never succeeded anywhere in eliminating requests for or performance of the procedure.) Suppose a woman came to him, a traditional healer, asking for an abortion. What would he do? His reply was translated from his native tongue as follows: "If a client comes to me, as a professional, I will help the woman because I have the knowledge to do so." He added, however, that "the community would not be happy."

Here was a medical person—a traditional healer—referring to his "professional" obligation to his patient. He invoked precisely the same consideration most Western physicians would appeal to as a reason why they should help a woman to have an abortion despite the community's disapproval of abortion. Although the cultures may differ in significant ways, the obligations of healers to those who come to them for help remain a cultural universal, one that exists in virtually all societies.

Not every customary practice is properly termed a *tradition*. Values inherent in a social institution such as medical practice may be a reflection of a value in the culture at large, or they may be specific to that particular institution. Lack of recognition and respect for the decision-making autonomy of patients has been a feature of Western medicine throughout most of history and even today remains prominent in other parts of the world. There is a difference, however, between the professional norm in which doctors decide for their patients and a cultural norm that gives family members complete control of another's freedom of decision and action.

Similarly, not every set of norms deserves to be called a *culture*. Although phrases like "the culture of Western medicine" are tossed around, medicine is not a culture in the genuine sense of the term, as anthropologists define it. To refer to "the culture of medicine" is to speak metaphorically rather than anthropologically. As one commentator observes: "Used metaphorically, *culture* is everywhere these days. . . . Today the press is full of stories about the 'culture' of the Defense Department, the Central Intelligence Agency . . ., Congress . . ., and any large corporation that happens to be in the news. GQ even describes opera as being characterized by 'the culture of booing.' "[5]

Rural areas in many parts of the world still maintain many features of traditional culture in the true sense of the term. Women's health advocates in Mexico reported that in some areas the husband or mother-in-law of a woman decides whether she may visit a physician or whether she may use a method of birth control.[6] This behavior prevails today in rural areas and among indigenous groups and is sanctioned by certain beliefs and values regarding women. For example, women are believed incapable of making their own decisions; or, even if they are capable, they must remain subordinate to men; or the role of women is to reproduce and therefore they should not be permitted to choose to control their own fertility. Control by husbands and mothers-in-law of a woman's fertility is based on the traditional culture and has little to do with the social institution of medicine. Although these sorts of beliefs and values have deep cultural roots they, too, may change over time, as women's health advocates work at the grassroots level and expose women in rural and indigenous communities to the ideas of the global women's movement. Defenders of traditional culture condemn these activists in Mexico and elsewhere as intrusive purveyors of Western feminism who seek to destroy traditional cultural values.

Interestingly, some women's health advocates worry about the effect of introducing values such as autonomy and independence to the women they work with. One social scientist used the example of women with whom they work in a traditional Mexican setting. These women have to ask permission from their mothers-in-law to visit a physician. A mother-in-law may question that decision or refuse to grant permission. The woman then asks the researcher for help. This poses a problem for the researcher: Can the researcher provide some assistance without causing the research subject further psychological damage or harm to her interests? The woman might actually be expelled from her home if the mother-in-law finds out she has gone to a physician without her permission.

While it is no doubt true that some customary practices are rooted in cultural traditions, others may simply have been passed down from one generation to the next as ways of behaving that no one questioned or sought to change. The medical profession has a long history of customary practices, but few qualify as "cultural" traditions. The custom of physicians withholding information from patients and talking, instead, to family members is probably a good example. Everyone from Western anthropologists to physicians in non-Western cultures remark on the difference between the nature of communications between doctors and patients in North America and other parts of the world as if this represents a deep-seated difference in cultural traditions. These commentators probably do not realize, or may have forgotten, that it is only a few decades since physicians in the United States began disclosing diagnoses of fatal illnesses directly to patients. One may call these norms of truth-telling a "tradition," but that would be to distort the more prevalent meaning of "tradition." That meaning is related to the concerns of the ethical relativist—that different societies have distinct and possibly incommensurate ethical values stemming from their cultural diversity.

One commentator suggests that cross-cultural differences in the physician–patient relationship are attributable to different systems of biomedical ethics. Diego Gracia, a professor of public health and history of science in Spain, distinguishes between Mediterranean biomedical ethics and the Anglo-American variety. Gracia notes that patients in Southern European nations are generally less concerned with matters related to informed consent and respect for autonomy than with trust in their physician. Mediterranean bioethics emphasizes virtues rather than rights. Accordingly, the virtue of trustworthiness is more crucial to patients than the right to information.[7]

But Gracia also points to a recent trend in Mediterranean countries, a trend that once again shows the evolution of the physician–patient relationship and the introduction of new ethical values. Gracia notes that in all Mediterranean countries, respect for patients' autonomy and the right of patients to participate in medical decisions have grown extensively in the last decades. Coming some decades after the patients' rights movement began in the United States, this new trend in the Mediterranean countries also includes complaints about health care workers' failure to provide information and for nonconsensual touching.

This phenomenon is one of historical evolution of the doctor–patient relationship rather than a cross-cultural difference between individualistic American culture and the more communitarian or virtue-based value systems in other countries. If the "culture" of medicine has evolved in this way first in the United States and shortly thereafter in some European countries, it is reasonable to suppose that the wider culture—society as a whole—may undergo other changes. No country today is so isolated from the rest of the world that it can remain aloof from and immune to cross-cultural influences.

CONCEPTIONS OF AUTONOMY: EAST AND WEST

A Japanese physician, Noritoshi Tanida, describes sharp differences between features of Japanese and Western culture related to the role of the individual.[8] Tanida says that tradition has left little room for the individual or for individualism in Japan; yet he acknowledges that since the opening of Japan to the West about 130 years ago, Western individualism was introduced into the country. Nevertheless, most Japanese are much less individualistic than are Westerners, a feature that is evident in the decision-making process. In general, Tanida notes, there is no open discussion or clear responsibility, but rather a process of mutual dependency. As a result, the person most affected by a decision may not be informed of what is happening and is not always a part of the decision-making process. The clearest example of this, Tanida holds, is concealing the truth from cancer patients in the practice of clinical medicine.

Another East Asian, Ruiping Fan, puts forth an even stronger view of the difference between East and West with regard to the individual's role in medical decision-making.[9] Fan argues that the Western concept of autonomy, which demands self-determination on the part of the individual, is incommensurable with the East Asian principle of autonomy, which requires family determination. In contending that these two notions of autonomy are incommensurable, Fan insists that there is no shared abstract content between the Western and Eastern principles of autonomy; the two are separate and distinct.

One conclusion that can be drawn from the contrast between East and West is that there simply is no universal ethic regarding disclosure of information, informed consent, and decision-making in medical practice. Not only do these practices differ as a matter of fact in different societies, but they are incompatible. This conclusion is obviously true for the descriptive thesis of ethical relativism: Truth-telling, informed consent, and decision-making about medical treatment vary in different cultures. Furthermore, if we accept Fan's account, a conceptual variation exists as well; autonomy means something different in East Asia from what it signifies in the West.

The East Asian principle of autonomy holds that "Every agent should be able to make his or her decisions and actions harmoniously in cooperation with other relevant persons."[10] Thus when patients and family are in harmony, they decide together. That situation probably prevails most of the time in Western medical practice as well. However, it is the family who has the final authority to make clinical decisions in accordance with the East Asian principle. According to Ruiping Fan, if a patient requests or refuses a treatment while a relevant family member disagrees with that decision, the doctor should not simply follow the patient's wish but should urge the patient and the family to negotiate and come to an agreement before the physician will act. It is the family that constitutes the autonomous social unit, and the physician may not act contrary to their decision.

This example of cultural diversity raises the enduring question of normative ethical relativism: Has Western bioethics arrived at the ethically right position with regard to respecting the individual autonomy of the patient? Is the practice in other cultures of deferring to the patient's family, or leaving the decision in the hands of the physician, right in those cultures although it would be wrong in the United States?

The emphasis on autonomy, at least in the early days of bioethics in the United States, was never intended to cut patients off from their families by insisting on an obsessive focus on the patient. Rather, it was intended to counteract the predominant mode of paternalism on the part of the medical profession. In fact, there was little discussion of where the family entered in and no presumption that a family-centered approach to sick patients was somehow a violation of the patient's autonomy. Most patients want and need the support of their families whether or not they seek to be autonomous agents regarding their own care. Respect for autonomy is perfectly consistent with recognition of the important role that families play when a loved one is ill. Autonomy has fallen into such disfavor among some ethicists in the United States that the pendulum has begun to swing in the direction of families, with urgings to "take families seriously"[11] and even to consider the interests of family members equal to those of the competent patient.[12]

Fan says that some people may deny that what he refers to as the "East Asian principle of autonomy" can even be characterized as a principle of autonomy. He nevertheless defends his use of the term, noting that the word for autonomy in the Chinese language is often used not only for individuals, but also for units like a family or a community. The same is true in the English language: In its political sense, *autonomy* means "self-rule" and can therefore apply to communities, countries, and, as in Mexico, universities.

Fan demonstrates that the East Asian principle of autonomy has significant implications for truth-telling, informed consent, and advance directives in the East Asian clinical setting. If a physician directly informs a patient about a diagnosis of a terminal disease instead of first telling a member of the family, that would be extremely rude and inappropriate. Interestingly, however, while East Asian custom allows the family to choose a treatment on behalf of a competent patient, the family may not readily refuse a treatment on behalf of a competent patient. This is evidently because of the underlying assumption that a treatment recommended by a physician will be beneficial to the patient, whereas it is at least questionable whether a withholding or withdrawing of treatment is in the interests of a competent patient.

So when it comes to actually making medical decisions, who should decide? Should it be patients themselves in the West, in accordance with the principle of autonomy as "self-determination," and families of patients in the East, in accordance with the "family-determination-oriented" principle? There is little doubt at this point that in the United States the patient with decisional capacity holds the moral and legal right to decide, with very rate exceptions. Those exceptions include some cases in which a pregnant woman's refusal of an intervention is deemed harmful to the life or health of the fetus (forced cesarean sections are the clearest example of this) and the situation in which physicians judge a treatment to be "medically futile" and take the decision-making out of the patient's hands. But these exceptions are contested by those who contend that pregnant women should have all the rights of other competent patients and that a physician's assessment that a treatment is "medically futile" should not replace the patient's wish for the treatment, which may have psychological value.

So we are left with ethical relativism. As Ruiping Fan puts it: "Which principle is more true: the Western principle of autonomy or the East Asian principle of autonomy? Who should give up their own principle and turn to the principle held by the other side?"[13] Fan's own solution is to adopt the procedural principle of freedom, allowing both Western and East Asian people to follow their respective and incommensurable principles of autonomy. Interestingly,

Fan's solution appeals to a higher principle, that of freedom or liberty. He acknowledges as much and articulates the principle of freedom commonly associated with Western philosophical and political thought: "Every group of people as well as every single individual has freedom to act as they see appropriate, insofar as their action does not harm other people."[14] That sounds remarkably like something John Stuart Mill might have written.

Application of this principle appears to grant to an individual patient the right to reject the cultural custom of family autonomy in favor of individual decision-making. But would it really? If East Asian patients insisted on their freedom to act as they deem appropriate, doing so might damage family harmony, so perhaps other people would be harmed after all. Ruiping Fan does not raise the explicit question of what individual patients or physicians might do, but refers only to "Western and East Asian people" being free to follow their respective principles of autonomy. It leaves ambiguous the status of the individual patient in East Asia and possibly also the role of a family in the West that seeks to follow the family-determination notion of autonomy.

Is this a relativist solution? Fan says no, it is not to surrender to ethical relativism, "but to secure the most reasonable in a peaceful way in this pluralist world."[15] This reply embraces tolerance and is a practical accommodation to cross-cultural diversity. If not a surrender to relativism, how can we characterize Fan's position? Fan himself describes this type of thought as a "transcendental argument for a content-less principle that ought to be employed in a secular pluralist society."[16] This merely replaces the puzzling with the obscure. Philosophy should seek to explain and clarify, not to obfuscate and muddy. We have to do better.

TRUTH-TELLING

In the Western world the custom of withholding information from patients goes back at least as far as Hippocrates. Hippocrates admonished physicians to perform their duties

> calmly and adroitly, concealing most things from the patient while you are attending to him. Give necessary orders with cheerfulness and sincerity, turning his attention away from what is being done to him; sometimes reprove sharply and emphatically, and sometimes comfort with solicitude and attention, revealing nothing of the patient's future or present condition.[17]

Does this ancient practice represent a tradition of some cultural group? If so, which one? Ancient Greek tradition, carried down through the Greco-Roman empire? That would not have been a likely influence on Asian medical practice. If it is part of any "culture" at all, it is that of the medical profession (speaking metaphorically), renowned throughout the ages for its paternalism. Medical paternalism remains the rule rather than the exception in Asian and Latin America, and it persists to a somewhat lesser extent in some parts of Western Europe, as well.

The shift in attitude toward disclosing the diagnosis to cancer patients began to occur in the United States in the late 1960s, a millennial moment since the time of Hippocrates. Although often portrayed as a cultural tradition, one in which many countries diverge from the preeminence accorded to the individual in the United States, nondisclosure by physicians to patients appears rather to have been a nearly universal customary practice dictated by medical professionals throughout the world.

But things change. Attitudes and practices of physicians in the United States have undergone a striking reversal in the past three decades. A study conducted in 1961 revealed that 90% of physicians did not inform their patients of the diagnosis of cancer.[18] When that study was redone in 1977, it revealed that 98% of doctors usually informed patients of the diagnosis of cancer.[19] It is entirely possible that such changes will begin to occur in other countries as well. Evidence suggests that this has already begun to happen.

These changes do not require us to impugn the motives of physicians who have thought it best not to tell patients they have cancer, nor is it to condemn the benevolence that undergirds medical paternalism in general. Now, as in the past, most justifications for withholding information from patients have rested implicitly or explicitly on an appeal to the principle of beneficence. If the behavior of doctors in the United States has changed in the past three decades or so, it is not because the principle of beneficence no longer serves as a justification or that physicians no longer act from benevolent motives. It is simply that the competing ethical principle of respect for autonomy has taken priority over the principle of beneficence in motivating and justifying physicians' behavior. Once it became evident that patients wished to know their diagnoses (or already knew they had cancer in spite of families and physicians conspiring to keep the news from them), and once physicians came to realize that disclosing a diagnosis of cancer did not typically cast the patient into a deep depression and very rarely, if ever, led to documented cases of patients committing suicide, then benevolent paternalism could no longer be sustained on ethical grounds.

From the earliest moments of modern bioethics, some people worried about the alleged requirement always to "tell the truth." In response to the claim that patients have "a right to know" their diagnosis and prognosis, challengers replied: what about "the right not to know?" Of course, there is no inconsistency here. People have a right to receive information, if they want it, and also the right to refuse to receive that information. That is precisely what "respect for persons" supports: respect for the wishes and values of the individual patient.

This is the point at which the philosophical distinction between ultimate moral principles and specific rules of conduct becomes critical. "Respect for persons" is a fundamental, or ultimate, ethical principle. The imperative "tell patients the truth about their condition" is a specific rule of conduct. Moreover, respecting a particular patient's wish not to know is perfectly consistent with the general obligation to disclose to patients their diagnosis. This also demonstrates the distinction between ethical universals and moral absolutes. "Always tell patients the truth about their condition" would be the moral absolute in this case, clearly a different imperative from one that mandates respect for the wishes of patients.

On this analysis, the answer to the question of how the case of truth telling to patients fits into the debates over ethical relativism is simple (relatively speaking). No universal ethical mandate exists to tell patients the truth about their terminal illness. Nor is it the case that telling the patients the truth is right in some countries or cultures and wrong in others. Moreover, to contend that the principle of autonomy mandates disclosure misinterprets how that ethical principle should be applied. Respect for autonomy means, among other things, acting in a way that respects the values of individuals. Individuals' values often mirror the predominant values of their country or culture, but they do not always do so. When they do, we must be sensitive to those values and respectful of the people who hold them.

A lingering problem, however, is that doctors often do not know or do not take the time or trouble to find out the patient's values. They take the family's word for whether the patient "can handle" the information. Or they simply honor the family's wish not to tell the patient. Here is where the practice in the United States is most likely to diverge from that in other countries. Because respect for the patient's autonomy has become entrenched in American medical practice, most physicians will probably not automatically comply with the family's wish not to reveal a diagnosis of cancer or other fatal or terminal illness.

It is clear from published reports in the medical and bioethical literature that doctors in other countries do readily honor a family's request not

to tell the patient a diagnosis of cancer or other terminal illness. I believe that behavior is as much a reflection of the still dominant paternalism of physicians as it is an expression of a cultural value. When respect for autonomy is not recognized as an ethical principle in medical practice, physicians see no need to find out whether a patient wants to know the diagnosis of cancer or terminal illness. Medicine has always been paternalistic and hierarchical. In some ways, the culture of medicine remains paternalistic in the United States, as anyone can attest who has heard physicians urge the omission of "scary" items from consent forms.

A medical oncologist from Italy, who had practiced for a while in the United States, reported what she had learned in medical school.[20] The Italian Deontology Code, written by the Italian Medical Association, included the following statement: "A serious or lethal prognosis can be hidden from the patient, but not from the family."[21] That was in the late 1970s. The Deontology Code was revised in 1989, with this statement: "The physician has the duty to provide the patient—according to his cultural level and abilities to understand—the most serene information about the diagnosis, the prognosis and the therapeutic perspectives and their consequences. . . . Each question asked by the patient has to be accepted and answered clearly." The code goes on to grant to physicians the well-known "therapeutic privilege" of withholding information if disclosure would be harmful to the patient, and in that case the information must be communicated to the family. But the revised code still represents a sharp reversal from the presumption of nondisclosure in the code of a mere decade earlier.

The Italian oncologist who wrote about this shift stated her belief that ethics is connected to cultural values and varies in different societies. She rejected a belief in "absolute values" in favor of respecting the pluralism of different cultures. This was by way of background to her contention that "the Italian society is not prepared for the

American way." She explained further, saying that even today Italians believe that patients will never acquire enough knowledge to enable them to understand what physicians tell them and therefore to participate in their own care. Italians still believe that protecting an ill family member from painful information prevents the sick person from suffering alone, from isolation, and is essential for keeping the family together.

Is it reasonable to expect that these attitudes will gradually be transformed, just as similar attitudes were in the United States several decades ago? The Italian oncologist waffled a bit on this point. On the one hand, she stated her belief that "Italians should not borrow the American way." On the other hand, she urged Italians to learn from Americans and "try to find a better Italian way." As examples of changes taking place within the medical profession, she noted courses in bioethics in universities and medical meetings on truth telling and communicating with patients. In the end, she reached the conclusion that "the only way to respect both Italian ethical principles and the patient's autonomy and dignity is to let the patient know that there are no barriers to communication and to the truth."[22] What is most peculiar is the reference to "Italian ethical principles." Withholding information from patients is not a function of ethnic traditions but rather of how the medical profession has historically conducted its practice in most places in the world. It is also a class phenomenon, since doctors are typically better educated than most of their patients and question the ability of patients to fully understand what they have been told.

A mere 5 years after its 1989 revision, the Italian code of medical ethics was revised once again. The revision reflected the "constantly changing relationship between the medical profession and society, and between physicians and patients."[23] In the newly revised code, the "Italian way" has come very close to the "American way." Article three of the new code adds to the physician's obligation expressed in the 1989 code "to respect the dignity of the human being" the

additional obligation to respect the patient's freedom of choice. Article four of the new code adds the physician's obligation to respect the rights of the individual, and extensive revisions of the doctrine of informed consent are in conformity with other modern codes of ethics. The code mandates respect for the decisional autonomy of the patient, even in cases in which the life of the patient is threatened.[24]

Equally striking are revisions on the topic of confidentiality. Whereas the earlier Italian code permitted doctors to conceal the truth from the patient and disclose it to the next of kin, the new code essentially prohibits nondisclosure to the patient and disclosure to a third party. Two exceptions to this rule are, first, when the patient specifically authorizes disclosure to others and, second, when there is potential for harm to a third party.[25] It would be absurd to conclude that "Italian ethical principles" have changed in this brief interlude between the 1989 code and the more recent revisions. Instead, as the authors of an article describing the new code observe, "from a paternalistic attitude in which the physician, for the good of the patient, felt authorised and justified to set aside the personal requests of the patient and even to violate his wishes, a therapeutic alliance has evolved, in which the two partners together try to decide on the clinical choices that best promote the patient's wellbeing."[26]

Changes are also occurring in Asia, a region of the world often cited as adhering to family and group values almost to the exclusion of recognizing the importance of the individual. A Japanese physician observes that the concept of informed consent has recently been recognized in his country, yet he acknowledges that most Japanese physicians withhold information about diagnosis and prognosis from their patients who have cancer.[27] It is reasonable to wonder whether "informed consent" means the same thing in Japan as it does in the West. One report notes that the Bioethics Council of the Japanese Medical Association introduced the idea of "Japanese informed consent," which was to be carried out in accordance with the prevailing medical paternalism in that country.[28] A survey in Japan showed that 67% of physicians would disclose the diagnosis to patients with early cancer, but only 16% would tell those with advanced cancer. Studies from other countries show that many patients do want to be informed of a diagnosis of cancer, but a discrepancy exists between patients' preferences and physicians' attitudes.[29]

A physician speaking at an international conference about truth-telling in Japanese medicine[30] described a number of cultural features that help to explain physicians' reluctance to disclose a bad prognosis. That reluctance stems from patients' unwillingness to receive such information, which in turn is based on deeper cultural roots. Patients want to have an "edited" version of the truth. They enter a tacit conspiracy with their family and the physician to avoid a difficult subject. This results in the family taking over all responsibility and decisions for the patient's illness. Although many patients will guess and come to know the truth eventually, they still will not ask directly. This behavior is rooted in the Japanese ethos in which silent endurance is a virtue. The aim is to make dying easier, not to invoke a dogma of telling patients the truth. Patients want to die as calmly and peacefully as possible, and that goal is more readily achieved if they remain ignorant of their prognosis. Relatives assume the burden of making an intuitive judgment of whether the patient wants to know the diagnosis and can handle it. Not to accept one's death gallantly is worse than death itself. Physicians, patients, and families all want to avoid a "disgraceful upset" that conveying bad new could produce. the physician who explained all this echoed what others discussing medicine in Japan have said: Despite powerful influences from Western countries, Japan is not totally Westernized, yet the Japanese do not want to stick to their old traditions completely. The physician ended by saying that the Japanese people must achieve a new type of death education,

with more ethical emphasis, closer to the Western style of dealing with death.

But let us assume that a cultural gap does exist between North American practices of disclosing bad news to patients and different customs in other parts of the world. What should we conclude about whether one cultural practice is "right" and the other "wrong"? How does this example fit into the debates over ethical relativism? The answer depends entirely on how the question is framed and how the situation is described. Consider the following alternative descriptions.

1. Doctors and patients in the United States believe that patients should be told the truth about a diagnosis of terminal illness. Doctors and patients in other countries believe that doctors should tell the family but not the patient. The ethical principle of "respect for autonomy" mandates that doctors treat patients as autonomous individuals and so must inform them about their illness. The truth-telling practice in the United States conforms to this principle and is ethically right, whereas the nondisclosure practice in other countries violates this practice and is ethically wrong.

2. Autonomy is the predominant value in North American culture. Doctors and patients in the United States adhere to an autonomy model of disclosure in medical practice. Family-centered values are more prominent than individual autonomy in other cultures. Doctors and patients in these cultures adhere to a family-centered practice of disclosure of terminal illness. Therefore, it is right to disclose to a patient a diagnosis of terminal cancer in the United States and wrong to make that same disclosure in the other countries.

3. Autonomy is the predominant value in North American culture, but disclosure of terminal illness by doctors to patients is nevertheless a fairly recent practice. The

U.S. population comprises many recent immigrants, and some cultural groups adhere to family-centered values from their country of origin, especially in specific matters such as disclosure of terminal illness. Family-centered values predominate in other countries, but practices such as disclosure of a diagnosis of terminal illness have begun to change in those places. "Respect for persons" requires that in any country or culture, doctors should discuss with their patients whether they want to receive information and make decisions about their medical care or whether they want the physician to discuss these matters only with the family.

The third description is obviously the "right" answer. What is wrong with the other two descriptions shows what is frequently amiss in debates over ethical relativism. Description 1 has two main flaws. The first is the common failing of distorting or misusing the principle of respect for autonomy. The principle does not require inflicting unwanted information on people; rather, it requires first finding out how much and what kind of information they want to know and then respecting that expressed wish. When the principle of autonomy is interpreted in that way, nothing automatically follows regarding whether patients should be told the truth about their diagnosis. The second flaw is the assumption that all people in a country or culture have the same attitudes and beliefs toward the values that predominate in that culture. In a Los Angeles study of senior citizens' attitudes toward disclosure of terminal illness, in no ethnic group did 100% of its members favor disclosure or nondisclosure to the patient. Forty-seven percent of Korean-Americans believed that a patient with metastatic cancer should be told the truth about the diagnosis, 65% of Mexican-Americans held that belief, 87% of European-Americans believed patients should be told the truth, and 89% of African-Americans held that belief. If physicians automatically withheld the diagnosis from Korean-Americans because the majority of people in that ethnic group did not want to be told, they would be making a mistake almost 50% of the time.[31]

Description 2 is flawed for one of the same reasons that description 1 is flawed: It presupposes that all people in a country or culture have the same attitudes and beliefs toward the values that predominate in that culture. That assumption is clearly false, as the Los Angeles study just cited demonstrates. In a multicultural society such as the United States, ethical relativism poses an array of problems not likely to arise in countries that enjoy a common cultural heritage (if any such countries still remain). "Multiculturalism is good," its proponents contend.[32] Whether or not that is true, it surely causes difficulties for doctors and patients.

References

1. Renée C. Fox, "The Evolution of American Bioethics: A Sociological Perspective," (ed.) George Weisz, *Social Science Perspectives on Medical Ethics* (Philadelphia: University of Pennsylvania Press, 1990), p. 206.

2. The workshop, part of my Ford Foundation project, took place in Davao, Mindanao, in December 1995.

3. This interview took place in February 1996 during my second Ford Foundation project.

4. This interview took place in April 1994 in Bombay.

5. Christopher Clausen, "Welcome to Postculturalism," *The Key Reporter*, Vol. 62, No. 1 (1996), p. 2.

6. This meeting took place during my Ford Foundation visit to Mexico in February 1993.

7. Diego Gracia, "The Intellectual Basis of Bioethics in Southern European Countries," *Bioethics*, Vol. 7, No. 2/3 (1993), pp. 100–101.

8. Noritoshi Tanida, "Bioethics Is Subordinate to Morality in Japan," *Bioethics*, Vol. 10 (1996), pp. 202–211.

9. Ruiping Fan, "Self-Determination vs. Family-Determination: Two Incommensurable Principles of Autonomy," *Bioethics*, Vol. 11 (1997), pp. 309–322.

10. Fan, p. 316.

11. James Lindemann Nelson, "Taking Families Seriously," *Hastings Center Report*, Vol. 22 (1992), pp. 6–12.

12. John Hardwig, "What About the Family?" *Hastings Center Report*, Vol. 20 (1990), pp. 5–10.

13. Fan, p. 322.

14. Fan, p. 322.

15. Fan, p. 322.

16. Fan quotes this phrase from H. Tristram Engelhardt, Jr., *The Foundations of Bioethics*, 2nd edition (New York: Oxford University Press, 1996).

17. Citation from President's Commission for the Study of Ethical Problems in Medicine and Biomedical and Behavioral Research, *Making Health Care Decisions* (Washington, DC: Government Printing Office, 1982), Vol. 1, p. 32.

18. D. Oken, "What To Tell Cancer Patients: A Study of Medical Attitudes," *Journal of the American Medical Association*, Vol. 175 (1961), pp. 1120–1128.

19. Dennis H. Novack, Robin Plumer, Raymond L. Smith, Herbert Ochitill, Gary R. Morrow, and John M. Bennett, "Changes in Physicians' Attitudes Toward Telling the Cancer Patient," *Journal of the American Medical Association*, Vol. 341 (1979), pp. 897–900.

20. Antonella Surbone, "Truth-Telling to the Patient," *Journal of the American Medical Association*, Vol. 268 (1992), pp. 1661–1662.

21. Surbone, p. 1661.

22. Surbone, p. 1662.

23. Vittorio Fineschi, Emanuela Turillazzi, and Cecilia Cateni, "The New Italian Code of Medical Ethics," *Journal of Medical Ethics*, Vol. 23 (1997), p. 238.

24. Fineschi, Turillazzi, and Cateni, pp. 241–242.

25. Fineschi, Turillazzi, and Cateni, p. 243.

26. Fineschi, Turillazzi, and Cateni, p. 241.

27. Atsushi Asai, "Should Physicians Tell Patients the Truth?" *Western Journal of Medicine*, Vol. 163 (1995), pp. 36–39.

28. Tanida, p. 208.

29. Asai, p. 36.

30. Shin Ohara, "Truth-Telling and We-Consciousness in Japan: Some Biomedical Reflections on Japanese Civil Religion," unpublished paper presented at the conference, "Ethics Codes in Medicine and Biotechnology," Freiburg, Germany, October 12–15, 1997.

31. Leslie J. Blackhall, Sheila T. Murphy, Gelya Frank, Vicki Michel, and Stanley Azen, "Ethnicity and Attitudes Toward Patient Autonomy," *Journal of the American Medical Association*, Vol. 274, No. 10 (1995), pp. 820–825.

32. Blaine J. Fowers and Frank C. Richardson, "Why Is Multiculturalism Good?" *American Psychologist*, Vol. 51, No. 6 (1996), pp. 609–621.

QUESTIONS FOR DISCUSSION

1. Some might claim that the physician's recommendation to the patient in the deliberative model may be value-laden and perhaps even subtly coercive, reflecting the physician's own views on treatment. How might this be avoided so that the patient's decisions are truly his or her own?

2. Granting the importance of full disclosure of medical information for informed consent, are there factors in the patient's medical history or current health status that might justify invoking therapeutic privilege?

3. What is the significance of trust in the doctor–patient relationship and how does it compare with autonomy, beneficence and nonmaleficence in terms of its importance in this relationship?

4. Even after coming to appreciate the values of a patient from a different culture, suppose that a patient asks a physician for a treatment that the physician believes will be harmful to the patient and in conflict with his or her professional integrity as a physician. If you were the physician, how would you deal with this matter?

5. When a physician is employed by a Managed Care Organization and has a duty to control costs by limiting expensive diagnostic tests or referrals to specialists, does this necessarily compromise care for the patients? Can a patient receive adequate care within these limits? Are there more effective ways of controlling health care costs?

CASES

Schloerndorff v. Society of New York Hospitals 211 N.Y. 125, 105 N.E. 92 (1914). In this case, Justice Cardozo formulated the doctrine of informed consent, although the term 'informed consent' often is attributed to Justice Bray in *Salgo v. Leland Stanford etc. Bd. Trustees* (1957) 154 Cal. App. 2d 560, 578, 317 P.2d 170.

Natanson v. Kline 186 Kan. 393, 350 P. 2d 1093 (1960). Citing negligence, Mrs. Kline sued her radiologist for failing to inform her of the risk of serious burns from cobalt therapy. This case marked a major shift of emphasis in the patient–physician relationship from therapeutic privilege to informed consent.

Canterbury v. Spence 464 F 2d 772 DC Cir (1972). After undergoing a laminectomy, Mr. Canterbury fell from his hospital bed and, as a result, suffered paralysis. He sued his surgeon for failing to inform him of the risk of paralysis. This case expanded the legal requirement for the physician's duty to disclose and established the "reasonable person" standard of informed consent.

Cobbs v. Grant 8 Cal. 3d 229, 502 P.2d 1, 104 Cal. reptr. 505 (1972). This case further broadened the scope and character of the physician's duty of disclosure pertaining to proposed therapy and the risks thereby entailed in obtaining the patient's consent to treatment.

Arato v. Avedon 5 Cal. 4th 1172, 23 Cal Rptr. 2d 131, 858 P. 2d 589 (1993). The lawsuit in this case, filed by a family on behalf of their deceased father, attempted to expand physicians' duty of disclosure to include not only relevant prognostic information but also medical information that might be relevant to a patient's nonmedical interests (e.g., financial affairs). The California Court of Appeal sided with Mr. Arato's family, but the state Supreme Court reversed the decision, siding with the jury in holding that it was unreasonable to impose additional informational requirements on physicians.

SUGGESTED FURTHER READING

Angel, Marcia. "The Doctor as Double Agent." *Kennedy Institute of Ethics Journal* 3 (September 1993): 279–286.

Archives of Internal Medicine 156 (1996). Special Issue on Managed Care.

Blustein, Jeffrey. "Doing What the Patient Orders: Maintaining Integrity in the Doctor–Patient Relationship." *Bioethics* 7 (1993): 289–314.

Brock, Dan. "Informed Consent," "The Ideal of Shared Decision Making Between Physicians and Patients," and "When Competent Patients Make Irrational Choices," in *Life and Death: Philosophical Essays in Biomedical Ethics*. New York: Cambridge University Press, 1993: 21–94.

Brody, Baruch. "A New Model for the Patient–Physician Relationship," in *Life and Death Decision Making*, Chapter 4. New York: Oxford University Press, 1988.

Faden, Ruth, and Beauchamp, Tom. *A History and Theory of Informed Consent*. New York: Oxford University Press, 1986.

Katz, Jay. *The Silent World of Doctor and Patient*. New York: Free Press, 1984.

Morreim, E. Haavi. *The New Medical Ethics of Medicine's New Economics*. Washington, D.C.: Georgetown University Press, 1996.

Orentlicher, David. "Health Care Reform and the Patient-Physician Relationship," *Health Matrix: Journal of Law-Medicine* 5 (1995): 141–180.

Pellegrino, Edmund, and Thomasma, David. *For the Patient's Good: The Restoration of Beneficence in Health Care*. New York: Oxford University Press, 1988.

Rodwin, Marc. *Medicine, Money, and Morals: Physicians' Conflicts of Interests* (New York: Oxford University Press, 1993).

Schneider, Carl. *The Practice of Autonomy: Patients, Doctors, and Medical Decisions*. New York: Oxford University Press, 1998.

Wolf, Susan. "Health Care Reform and the Future of Physician Ethics." *Hastings Center Report* 24 (March-April 1994): 28–41.

PART III:

RESEARCH INVOLVING HUMAN SUBJECTS

As discussed in Part I, many of the issues that gave rise to biomedical ethics as an inter-disciplinary field resulted from the inappropriate use of human subjects in medical research. In all of these instances, full voluntary informed consent was not obtained from the subjects participating in the research. Nor were adequate protections in place to minimize the risk of harm from experimentation or to preclude exploitation of vulnerable subjects such as children, the mentally retarded, the institutionalized, and the destitute. To the extent that the principles of respect for autonomy, nonmaleficence, and beneficence have been invoked to correct these abuses, there is considerable overlap of ethical issues between medical research involving human subjects and the patient-physician relationship. Yet research in general and clinical trials in particular present an additional complicating factor in the patient-physician relationship, which becomes scientific as well as therapeutic. The patient is also a subject in a study whose aim is to further scientific or medical knowledge, which may or may not benefit him directly or even indirectly. The physician is also a researcher whose aim in encouraging the patient to participate in a study is to gain knowledge, which is not motivated solely by acting in the patient's best interests. This dual role presents a potential ethical conflict for the physician between duty to individual patients and duty as a researcher to future patients, the medical community, or society at large.

Generally, five conditions must be met for research protocols to be ethically acceptable: first, informed voluntary consent of the subjects must be obtained; second, the research must minimize risks and involve a favorable risk-benefit ratio; third, there must be an equitable selection of subjects that rules out any form of exploitation or discrimination and adequately represents both sexes and all social groups; fourth, the privacy of the subjects must be protected; and fifth, the confidentiality of the data yielded by the research must be protected. Independent review groups such as institutional review boards (IRBs) have the authority and responsibility to monitor research protocols from the time they are proposed until their completion to ensure that the five conditions just specified are upheld.

Much of medical research consists of clinical trials designed to test the safety and efficacy of a drug or surgical procedure before it is used for patients in a clinical setting. These will follow tests using animal models. All clinical trials involving human subjects follow the same four-phase approval process.

In a Phase I drug trial, researchers aim to determine the toxicity of the drug, or the highest dose human subjects can tolerate. Subjects in noncancer Phase I studies are usually healthy volunteers. However, volunteers in Phase I cancer trials are never healthy because of DNA damage and other carcinogenic consequences of the drugs used. These subjects must have exhausted all therapeutic options and have a life expectancy of at least three to four months. They may enter these trials for altruistic reasons, knowing that they will benefit only future patients. In most cases however, patients enroll because it is their only hope of physical benefit. In Phase II trials, researchers try to establish an optimal dosing regimen and aim to find the experimental conditions that will allow the third phase of the trial to yield a definitive result. Here also the end points of the trial are specified, such as the five-year survival rate with a drug for patients with a certain type of cancer. In Phase III trials, which involve the largest number of subjects, the aim is to learn whether the treatment is effective and what its side effects are. Phase IV trials take place once the drug already has been marketed. They are used to collect additional information about the drug's effects or to study additional uses.

The design of the clinical trial becomes especially important in Phase II, where the control group is introduced as a point of comparison with the intervention group receiving the new experimental treatment. The control group may receive a placebo, in which case it is a placebo-controlled trial, or the standard proven treatment, in which case it is an active-controlled trial. Many trials are randomized in the sense that subjects are assigned randomly to either the control group or the intervention group. Moreover, many trials are "blind" in the sense that neither the subject nor the researcher knows into which group the patient has been assigned. Blinding is essential for eliminating bias on the part of the researcher. These are called double-blind (placebo-controlled or active-controlled) clinical trials. Most clinical trials are prospective in the sense that subjects give consent and are assigned to the control or intervention group in advance of the trial. But in some cases consent can be obtained only retrospectively, as in testing new treatments in emergency situations. Furthermore, for certain reasons, not all trials can be blind. And whereas it is often unethical to use placebos rather than proven treatment in trials because it puts the subjects in the control group under a risk of harm, in some cases it may be ethical to use placebos. There also are ethical implications for when a trial is stopped, because subjects in the control group can benefit from a new treatment if it has been shown to be of therapeutic value to subjects in the active group.

In the first selection, Jay Katz, one of the pioneers in the ethical debate on human experimentation, reviews the impact of Henry Beecher's seminal work revealing the many abuses of human subjects in research. Citing the tension between the dual roles of the physician-researcher and the patient-subject, as well as the potential problem of using subjects as means for the ends of others, Katz emphasizes that respect for persons is the core principle necessary for any research to be ethical. This, in turn, entails respect for individual autonomy of subjects and their right to give voluntary informed consent to medical procedures.

Benjamin Freedman's influential article addresses the important concept of equipoise in clinical trials. The term 'equipoise' was introduced by Charles Fried in 1974 to define a state of uncertainty among researchers that must exist for a concurrently controlled trial to be justified. This means that the available evidence must offer no reason for preferring one arm (active or control) of a trial over the other. Freedman argues that the equipoise required for a scientifically and ethically justified trial is clinical equipoise, a genuine disagreement in the clinical community about the comparative merits of the two arms of the trial. When there is disagreement among researchers, despite the evidence, the conditions justify starting the trial. There is clinical equipoise when the scientific evidence is suggestive but not sufficient for a definitive answer to the question of the efficacy of the treatment in question.

P. P. De Deyn and R. D'Hoog take up the question of when it might be permissible, if not required, to use placebos in controlled randomized clinical trials. Citing examples from neuropsychiatry, they argue that, in schizophrenia, double-blind placebo-controlled trials provide the most reliable evaluation of antipsychotic agents. Furthermore, they argue that, in depression, the difference in improvement rates between drug-treated and placebo-treated patients is not significant enough to make the placebo control unethical. And in trials involving drugs for Alzheimer's disease, placebo-controlled trials are preferable to active controls. The authors emphasize four provisos with the use of placebos: no adequate therapy for the disease should exist; the trial must not last too long; the placebo should not subject patients to unacceptable risk; and they must be adequately informed about and give full voluntary consent to the procedure.

Robert Truog et al. differentiate the therapeutic aim of clinical care from the scientific aim of clinical trials. They further distinguish between general informed consent, which a patient gives in any fiduciary relationship with a physician, and specific informed consent, which is necessary whenever the proposed intervention involves considerable risk relative to benefit, or whenever the preferences and values of the patient are relevant. Provided that certain conditions are met, there are some clinical trials in which specific consent should not be required. Yet, citing the imbalance between consent requirements in clinical trials and clinical care, they argue that many therapeutic interventions are objectionable because they do not adequately protect patients from physicians who want to experiment with new treatments in the name of therapeutic innovation. To ensure such protection, they urge that IRBs exercise careful oversight of this form of experimentation.

Baruch Brody discusses three classes of vulnerable subjects in research: patients in emergency settings; HIV-positive patients; and advanced cancer patients in Phase I trials. All of these subjects are vulnerable because they have life-threatening conditions with few, if any, therapeutic options. Brody proposes a balancing concept of justice as an ethical guideline for these cases, where the balance is between access to the benefits of research and protection from unconsented use and exploitation. He emphasizes that this balance can be difficult to achieve. For when patients are severely ill, their illness requires certain paternalistic forms of protection that limit personal autonomy and, hence, full informed consent.

Alexander Capron focuses on patients in psychiatric research who are mentally incapacitated and, thus, unable to make informed voluntary decisions about their participation in such research. Noting that research allows subjects to be exposed to minimal risk, Capron argues that the very notion of 'minimal risk' is inherently vague and might allow incremental increases in risk above this rough threshold that could be harmful to mentally incapacitated subjects. This threat of harm is made real by the fact that most protocols involving more than minimal risk fail to assess subjects' decision-making capacity. He insists that mentally impaired people need special protection because they fall outside the "reasonable person" standard of informed consent. To ensure that patients with mental disorders are adequately protected, Capron urges that IRBs carefully scrutinize all aspects of the study design, as well as the selection of subjects, the reliance on surrogate decision-making, and the presumed infeasibility of obtaining the subjects' consent.

In the last piece, Lainie Friedman Ross focuses on children as research subjects. She introduces two principles that serve to justify when parents are permitted to enter a child in research. The first is the modified principle of respect, which pertains to parents' treatment of their child in accord with the child's potential to become a fully autonomous person capable of giving full voluntary informed consent and which assumes that the child already has actualized some of this potential. The second is the principle of constrained parental autonomy. This gives parents the authority to override their child's dissent in minimal risk research if they believe that it will guide the child's development according to their vision of a good life. But it must not be abusive, neglectful, or exploitative, consistent with the modified principle of respect. Ross draws important distinctions between therapeutic and non-therapeutic research, direct and indirect therapeutic benefit, and competent and incompetent children in arguing when children can or should not be subjects in research.

"Ethics and Clinical Research" Revisited
A Tribute to Henry K. Beecher

Jay Katz MD

I want to pay tribute to Henry Knowles Beecher by reflecting upon the ethics of human experimentation, past and present. He, and I somewhat later, became absorbed in this topic years prior to the flowering of bioethics. By June 1966, when he published his courageous article "Ethics and Clinical Research,"[1] we had met and talked often about our hopes and fears. We knew that we were exploring uncharted territory, discovering a world whose ethical dilemmas were there to be seen but had largely been ignored. We hoped that our inquiries would persuade our colleagues to examine in depth physician-investigators' responsibilities to medicine, medical science, and patient-subjects in the enterprise of extending the frontiers of medical knowledge. At the same time, we were concerned about the reception our work would receive from the medical community.

I had become interested in human experimentation in late 1964 or early 1965. Many reasons of the heart and mind had sparked my interest. As I reflect upon these origins and my work during the subsequent thirty years, I realize that it has always been my heart that led the way. Only later did my mind begin to impose some order on intense feelings that I can trace back to a number of personal experiences.

First, while on the faculty of the Yale Medical School I had conducted research with "volunteer" subjects. I was then largely oblivious of my responsibilities to disclose to them fully the risks that their participation might entail. My colleagues and I were aware of potential risks. We had taken precautions to minimize them and, should they materialize, to repair any damage. It did not occur to us, however, to share our concerns with our subjects so that they could decide whether or not to take these risks. The unique responsibilities physicians confront in the conduct of research had not been discussed in my medical education, even though we were encouraged to do research.

Second, when I joined the faculty of Yale Law School it was my custom to attend one course or seminar each year in order to learn more about law. One afternoon in the early 1960s I witnessed an intense debate between students and their teacher about how best to protect an accused from the powerful array of forces that the State can so inexorably align against him or her. I was struck by the students' zeal to safeguard the rights of the accused. Their sense of justice and fairness made quite an impression on me. Suddenly I realized that I had stopped listening. Instead, my thoughts had taken me back to my research, and I remembered how little attention I had given to the rights of my research subjects. In subsequent months I often recalled that afternoon and the memories it had evoked. The idea of studying what transpires in human experimentation increasingly captured my imagination.

A third chance encounter reinforced my intention to study the human research process. While perusing a casebook on criminal law, I ran across the trial transcripts of the Nuremberg proceedings against the Nazi physicians. The history of the medical experiments conducted at Auschwitz, Dachau, and other concentration camps had also not been part of my medical school education. The transcripts recounted in

From *Hastings Center Report*, 23: 31–39, 1993.

sickening detail these medical experiments, carried out "with unnecessary suffering and injury, and . . . very little if any [protection of subjects from] injury, disability, or death."[2] I had lost many of my cousins, aunts, and uncles in the Holocaust. How many of them, I wondered, had been condemned to participation in these experiments?

I began to immerse myself in the then scant literature on human experimentation conducted in the Western World. I soon realized that the moral, medical and legal dilemmas posed by such research could not be adequately resolved, as generations of doctors had assumed, by a pledge of allegiance to such undefined principles as *primum non nocere* or to vague aspirational codes. Better safeguards had to be provided, and whatever they might turn out to be, required sustained reflection.

MY FIRST CONVERSATIONS WITH BEECHER

Thus in January 1966 and for the first year with my late colleague Richard Donnelly, I began to teach at Yale Law School a semester-long seminar on the control of human experimentation. The seminar, probably the first of its kind, was announced in the 1965–66 Yale Law School Bulletin rather tersely:

> EXPERIMENTATION ON PEOPLE 2 *Units*. An examination of the variety of "therapeutic" and "experimental" medical procedures which have been carried out on patients and normal volunteers. Central to this exploration will be a detailed study of consent and the role of the state in the supervision of medical experimentation.

While preparing teaching materials for the seminar, I ran across Henry Beecher's monograph *Experimentation in Man*, published in 1958. He had been my teacher at Harvard Medical School and his lectures on anesthesia had made quite an impression on me. I decided to call him. He told me that he had become even more absorbed in

the study of the ethics of clinical research. When I invited him to one of my classes, he accepted eagerly, and during the spring semester of 1966, he returned often to New Haven. We talked and talked. He also made me drink more martinis than I had ever been accustomed to. Remember, these were the months prior to the publication of his 1966 article, and he was quite worried. My students cheered him up. He had made a profound impression on them, not only by what he taught them, but by the moral passion that punctuated his every word.

Those were the days prior to the birth of bioethics. Neither Beecher nor I was interested in creating a new discipline. We came to the study of human experimentation out of a newly acquired conviction that research subjects deserved to be treated with greater respect and that our colleagues had paid too little attention to an increasingly widespread dimension of modern medical practice. As Beecher wrote in the introduction to his 1958 monograph: "The breaches of ethical conduct which have come to [my] personal attention are [the result of] ignorance or thoughtlessness. They were not willful or unscrupulous in origin. It is hoped that the material included here will help those who would do so to protect themselves from the errors of inexperience."[3]

He wanted to teach, not to indict. I too intended to sensitize physicians to the many tensions inherent in the conduct of human research and urge them to study these problems in greater depth. In my first public lecture on human experimentation at Yale Medical School, one and one-half years prior to the publication of Beecher's article, I pleaded that medical schools must become centers for the study of the problems posed by human experimentation. The lecture was not well received. I was criticized for speaking about matters that should not be aired in public.

I realized then that regulation would be inevitable and my exposure to the world of law had begun to teach me a great deal about regulation.

Thus, my students and I began to explore such questions as: Who should define the rights and duties of the parties involved in human experimentation, and who should supervise their implementation? The common law doctrine of informed consent,[4] barely five years old, loomed large in our deliberations. I thought then that it showed considerable promise in providing greater protection to subjects of research. Even though as early as 1947 the Allied Military Tribunal had made "voluntary consent" the cornerstone of its Nuremberg Code, that prescription had made little impact on the conduct of research. Perhaps informed consent would fare better.

After revising draft after draft of my class materials over seven years, I finally, in 1972, published a casebook called *Experimentation with Human Beings*. In its later stages, Eleanor Swift Glass and Alexander Morgan Capron joined me as research assistants. Alex made major and significant contributions to its final version, and once again I want to acknowledge my great debt to him. Extensive sections of the book explored the functions that informed consent could serve for the human experimentation process. That analysis was embedded in a more general examination of the extent and limits of a subject's ability and authority to make decisions on his or her behalf. Equally prominent were materials that sought to explore problems of regulation. Here the overall question was this: "What persons and institutions should have the authority to formulate, administer, and review the human experimentation process?"[5]

As it had been Beecher's hope for his writings, so it was my hope that the book would encourage and facilitate an intensive study of human experimentation and provide better protection for the subjects of research. I believe that my book made a contribution, albeit a limited one, toward that objective. From the perspective of history it will always remain unclear whether the gains I achieved were the result of the book or the public reaction to the Tuskegee syphilis study, both of which date to 1972. I served on the ad hoc advisory panel convened by the Department of Health, Education, and Welfare to investigate the Tuskegee affair, and I wrote the section on our third charge, to make recommendations about necessary changes in "existing policies to protect the rights of patients participating in health research." Our eventual recommendations were largely based on what I had learned over many years.

THE PENCHANT FOR THEORIZING AND ABSTRACTING

Before addressing my misgivings about the contemporary protections afforded to subjects of research, I want to go back once again to Beecher's and my early work, and to the birth of bioethics. Our initial explorations were not influenced by theoretical considerations but by concerns that human beings were not being treated with the respect they deserved. In my case this work was also influenced by an ever increasing sense that the conduct of research was often at odds with fundamental democratic values. In short, we were primarily interested in customary medical practices that eventually might call for theoretical formulations.

Leon Kass in his wonderful address at the Twentieth Anniversary Meeting of The Hastings Center illuminated what I here wish to convey. He deplored the penchant of bioethicists, soon after bioethics' birth, for theorizing and abstraction, their emphasis on extreme examples rather than on "the morality of ordinary practice."[6] He pleaded that "we must think less about doctrine and principles [and more] about how to encourage and enhance the formulation of certain sentiments and attitudes. We must return to what animated the [bioethics] enterprise: the fears and hopes, the repugnancies, the moral concerns, and, above all," he asked us to remember "that beneath the distinctive issues of bioethics lie the deepest matters of our humanity" (p. 12). These were Beecher's and my objectives—Beecher's more than mine perhaps. I have engaged in some

"ETHICS AND CLINICAL RESEARCH"

Henry K. Beecher

Human experimentation since World War II has created some difficult problems with the increasing employment of patients as experimental subjects when it must be apparent that they would not have been available if they had been truly aware of the uses that would be made of them. Evidence is at hand that many of the patients in the examples to follow never had the risk satisfactorily explained to them, and it seems obvious that further hundreds have not known that they were the subjects of an experiment although grave consequences have been suffered as a direct result of experiments described here. There is a belief prevalent in some sophisticated circles that attention to these matters would "block progress." But according to Pope Pius XII, ". . . science is not the highest value to which all other orders of values . . . should be subordinated."

I am aware that these are troubling charges. They have grown out of troubling practices. They can be documented, as I propose to do, by examples from leading medical schools, university hospitals, private hospitals, governmental military departments (the Army, the Navy and the Air Force), governmental institutes (the National Institutes of Health), Veterans Administration hospitals and industry. The basis for the charges is broad.

I should like to affirm that American medicine is sound, and most progress in it soundly attained. There is, however, a reason for concern in certain areas, and I believe the type of activities to be mentioned will do great harm to medicine unless soon corrected. It will certainly be charged that any mention of these matters does a disservice to medicine, but not one so great, I believe, as a continuation of the practices to be cited.

"theorizing," though I think not with the same penchant for abstraction that Leon Kass deplored.

Our work was grounded in cases. We came to the study of human experimentation out of deeply felt "moral concerns" about medical prac-

tices. We felt, to quote Kass again, that there was a "need to think about how to encourage and enhance the formation of certain sentiments and attitudes; [a need to think about] respect, reverence, and gravity [and] what fosters them and undermines them" (p. 11). We believed our inquiries addressed "the deepest matters of our [medical] humanity": the interactions between physicians and patients in medical practice that since World War II had become increasingly infiltrated by the claims of science and its use of patients for the sake of future patients.

From the perspective of hindsight, Beecher and I were not entirely correct in what we emphasized and neglected to stress. In his 1966 article, "Ethics and Clinical Research," Beecher found that twelve "of 100 consecutive human studies published in 1964 in an excellent journal" had been "unethical" (p. 1355). It led him to make these "troubling charges": "that many . . . patients . . . never had the risks satisfactorily explained to them [and that many] have not known that they were the subjects of an experiment although grave consequences have been suffered as a direct result of [these] experiments" (p. 1354). His startling allegations, of course, raise doubts about his accompanying assertion "that American medicine is sound, and most progress in it soundly attained." I pointed this out to him, and he was of two minds about what he had said. Yet he had needed to put it that way in order to support his ultimate conclusion as to remedies: "The ethical approach to experimentation in man has several components . . . the first being informed consent [and the second] the more reliable safeguard provided by the presence of an intelligent, informed, conscientious, compassionate, responsible investigator" (p. 1360). Beecher had greater faith in the second than the first prescription. However, there are intertwined problems with his second prescription. It requires first a thoroughgoing reappraisal of the values that should govern the human experimentation process. Only then can physician-investigators begin to learn how to conduct themselves conscientiously and responsibly to fulfill their new moral responsibilities toward patient-subjects and the claims of science.

TURNING TO MY WORK

I want to describe briefly the impact of theory on my primary objective of sensitizing physician-investigators to their moral responsibilities toward subjects of research. I believe that my theoretical formulations always stayed close to concerns about the realities of practice. Unlike Beecher, however, I realized that a "conscientious, compassionate [and] responsible investigator" could only come into being, as I have just suggested, after the value conflicts inherent in research are clarified and choices are made about the priorities to be given to competing values. Early in my work I did not appreciate the primacy I now wish to assign to respect for persons.

In the introduction to my book *Experimentation with Human Beings* I wrote: "When human beings become the subjects of experimentation . . . tensions arise between two values basic to Western society: freedom of scientific inquiry and protection of individual inviolability. . . . At the heart of this [value] conflict lies an age-old question: When may a society, actively or by acquiescence, expose some of its members to harm in order to seek benefits for them, for others, or for society as a whole?" (p. 1). My question assumed, at least implicitly, both the necessity of conducting human research and the inevitability of harm; it asked only when society may "expose some of its members to harm."

Today, I want to put this question more pointedly. When, if ever, is it justified to use human beings as subjects for research, considering that they also serve as means for the ends of others? My new question seeks to emphasize that the oft-invoked moral right to engage in human experimentation is itself in need of a thoroughgoing examination, for that right which finds its justification in the need to advance the frontiers of knowledge can all too readily obliterate "the

deepest matters of our morality" by the ways in which we use human beings for our own purposes. In pursuing the question of a right to engage in human experimentation, I shall touch on only two issues: (1) the nature and quality of the initial encounter between physician-investigators and patient-subjects; and (2) the necessity for an explicit societal mandate to conduct research.

THE INVITATION TO PARTICIPATE IN RESEARCH

Whenever human subjects of research serve the ends of others, the morality of protecting their physical integrity, which continues to preoccupy the thinking of physician-investigators, is not the central issue. It is, first of all, *the morality with which the invitation to participation in research is extended so that the rights of subjects to be secure in their person and body remain sacrosanct.* That fundamental requirement is viewed too dismissively as an impediment to the conduct of research. In 1972 I believed that the requirement of informed consent could serve as "the primary means for implementing the abstract notion of self-determination" and that it expressed "society's desire to respect each individual's autonomy and his right to make choices concerning his life."[7] I was then all too hopeful that the sentiments contained in both assertions would soon guide the conduct of human experimentation. This has not happened.

Let me begin with informed consent and briefly go back first to 1947, when the requirement of consent for participation in research was for the first time (some exceptions to the contrary notwithstanding)[8] compellingly argued by the Allied Military Tribunal. In promulgating the Nuremberg Code, the tribunal set forth as its first principle that in the conduct of research "the voluntary consent of the human subject is absolutely essential."[9] Beecher demurred. Even though his comments on the code in his 1958 *Experimentation in Man* disclaimed any "attack on the principle of consent," he concluded that "the 'obvious' matter of consent is not so easy to live up to as it sounds" and that it is, therefore, far better to rely on the compassion of the investigator (p. 58). In his 1966 article he modified his position somewhat: While consent in any fully informed sense may not be obtainable, "it is absolutely essential to *strive* for it" (p. 1360). Other physician-investigators remained much more adamant in their assertion that adherence to the Nuremberg Code's first principle is too inhospitable to the conduct of research. Of course, the critics were correct in pointing out that the Nuremberg Code made no provisions for research with children or the mentally disabled. The Nuremberg Code is limited, *as are my comments throughout this article,* to research with persons who have the capacity to consent. Clearly, special provisions need to be drafted for those incapable of giving consent.

Disclosure practices changed, at least in form, when consent was replaced by informed consent. Yet, as I have repeatedly argued elsewhere, this doctrine, borrowed from the law of torts, cannot readily be transplanted into therapeutic settings, and surely not into research settings, without a prior thoroughgoing reappraisal as to whether the functions it is to serve should be the same for purposes of law, therapy, and research.[10]

The common law judges who promulgated the doctrine limited their task to articulating new and more stringent standards of liability whenever physicians withheld information that the judges believed was owed to patients in light of the harm that the spectacular advances in medical technology could inflict. Shaped and circumscribed by legal assumptions about the objectives of the laws of evidence and negligence, and by economic philosophies as to who should assume the financial burdens for medical injuries sustained by patients, the doctrine was most limited in scope, designed to specify those minimal disclosure obligations that physicians must fulfill to escape *legal* liability for alleged nondisclosures. The legal doctrine of informed consent was not designed to serve as a *medical* blueprint for the interaction between physicians and patients or investigators and subjects.

There are a number of reasons why serious attention to the general problem is urgent.

Of transcendent importance is the enormous and continuing increase in available funds. . . .

Taking into account the sound and increasing emphasis of recent years that experimentation in man must precede general application of new procedures in therapy, plus the great sums of money available, there is reason to fear that these requirements and these resources may be greater than the supply of responsible investigators. All this heightens the problems under discussion.

Medical schools and university hospitals are increasingly dominated by investigators. Every young man knows that he will never be promoted to a tenure post, to a professorship in a major medical school, unless he has proved himself as an investigator. . . .

In addition to the foregoing three practical points there are others that Sir Robert Platt has pointed out: a general awakening of social conscience; greater power for good or harm in new remedies, new operations and new investigative procedures than was formerly the case; new methods of preventive treatment with their advantages and dangers that are now applied to communities as a whole as well as to individuals, with multiplication of the possibilities for injury; medical science has shown how valuable human experimentation can be in solving problems of disease and its treatment; one can therefore anticipate an increase in experimentation; and the newly developed concept of clinical research as a profession (for example, clinical pharmacology)—and this, of course, can lead to unfortunate separation between the interests of science and the interests of the patient.

A broader, insufficiently recognized, and surely contested assumption, however, underlies the doctrine: the *idea* of informed consent.[11] It suggests that physicians and patients, investigators and subjects must make decisions jointly, with patients' and subjects' choices ultimately receiving utmost respect. To translate that idea into reality is a difficult undertaking requiring careful study and explication that has barely begun. Without implementation of this idea, informed consent in the sense it is now being adhered to will remain a charade.

The informed consent requirements set forth in the federal regulations on human research[12] do not adequately address the moral issues that deserve consideration whenever human beings serve as means for the ends of others. The drafters of the regulations should have been aware that physician-investigators would view the informed consent requirements, despite their greater specificity, as similar in intent to what they were used to complying with in clinical practice. This problem becomes even more acute in light of the radical transformation of medical practice since World War II. The astronomical increase in clinical research has, in practice, not led to a clear demarcation between therapy and research, bioethical theories notwithstanding. This vital distinction remains blurred when physician-investigators view subjects as patients, and then believe that patients' interests and not science's are being served by participation in the randomized clinical trials that are so commonly conducted in today's world; or when subjects are insufficiently apprised that attention to their individual needs is compromised by the need to comply with the rigid and impersonal methodology of a research protocol.

The drafters should have explicitly warned investigators that taking informed consent seriously in research negotiations requires them to spend considerable time with prospective patient-subjects. They should have provided explicit instructions on the length to which investigators must go in explaining themselves and their intentions so that patient-subjects will know what is being asked of them. Respect for subjects' human rights dictates that they appreciate that the decision to participate in research entails making a gift for the sake of others.

The drafters of the federal regulations needed to be more punctilious in their promulgations because they conferred on physicians a societal mandate to engage in clinical research on a scale that Hippocratic commandments never envisioned

when they instructed doctors to "follow that system of regimen which, according to my ability and judgment, I consider for the benefit of my patients."

I now believe that meaningful informed consent doctrine for clinical research cannot be formulated without committing oneself to a theoretical position, Kass's warning about the snares of abstraction notwithstanding. Mine is this: whenever we use human subjects for the sake of others, using them as means for our ends, the principle of autonomy alone must guide such practices. I hasten to add that I have always used autonomy in James Childress's sense of "respect for autonomy" that "obligates us to respect the autonomous choices and actions of others."[13]

I argued that point in my book *The Silent World of Doctor and Patient*:

> Respect for psychological autonomy requires that both parties pay caring attention to their capacities and incapacities for self-determination by supporting and enhancing their real, though precarious, endowment for reflective thought. In conversation with one another, patients may uncover mistaken notions [and] physicians may uncover [some of] their unconscious preferences and biases. . . . Without conversation, individual self-determination can become compromised by condemning physicians and patients to the isolation of solitary decision making, which can only contribute to abandoning patients prematurely to an ill-considered fate.
>
> Even though choices are influenced by psychological considerations, it is one thing to appreciate that fact and quite another to interfere with choice on the basis of speculations, or even evidence, about underlying psychological reasons. . . . Short of substantial evidence of incompetence, choices deserve to be honored.[14]

Childress qualified his position somewhat when he wrote that "respect for autonomy [as] guiding science, medicine, and health care . . . cannot be assigned unqualified preeminence." A careful reading, however, makes it clear that he only meant to convey that "other important moral considerations . . . must be met prior to soliciting the potential subject's consent to participate—e.g., research design, probability of success, risk-benefit ratio, and selection of subjects." Ultimately he stated unequivocally that "if researchers do not receive the potential subject's voluntary, informed consent, they may not enlist that subject."[15]

I hope that Daniel Callahan will accept my views on autonomy as a moral good, not a moral obsession. What I have talked about so far does not undermine the importance he ascribes to fostering altruism or obligations to the community; for he cautioned his readers that his remarks on obligations toward others should not

> be construed as a plea to either jettison or sharply devaluate autonomy as a value and an ideal. That is not my purpose. We live in a world too prone to tyranny, and in the company of a medicine too prone to forget that patients are persons, to want that outcome. The drive for autonomy that was the major moral mark of the 1960s and 1970s in medical ethics was indispensable. It brought patients into a full partnership with physicians in their medical care. There can be no return to those good old days that understood doctors to be good old boys who could work out moral problems among themselves in the locker room.[16]

Yet, that "full partnership" is a precarious one, as Callahan recognized in the same article: "[W]e may well grant that the notion of autonomy, especially patient autonomy, has hardly become triumphant in the daily life of medicine" (p. 40).

My plea for respect for autonomy, or better, for respect for persons, is based on three premises: that it is absolutely essential in situations where patient-subjects are asked to serve as means for others' ends; that it has never been truly tried out; and, since it is "good as a bodyguard against moral bullies,"[17] that it can protect patient-subjects from the moral bullying of investigators too invested in the morality of their scientific pursuits.

THE SOCIETAL MANDATE

Of course, society may decide to grant scientists a mandate to compromise individual autonomy by permitting them to balance it against the need to advance science for the benefit of mankind. Indeed, the federal regulations confer such a mandate on physician-investigators. This mandate, however, has not been subjected to an intense scrutiny and public debate about the limits to be imposed on the prerogatives of scientists to use human beings for society's sake. Such a debate deserves to be carried on with the same intensity as the one that has repeatedly taken place on the question whether it is preferable to rely on a military draft or a volunteer army to protect citizens' and society's interests.

My reading of the *Congressional Record*, whenever either proposed regulations of research or budgetary allocations for research are debated, leaves me with the impression that Congress is confused about the boundaries between research

> All so-called codes are based on the bland assumption that meaningful or informed consent is readily available for the asking. As pointed out elsewhere, this is very often not the case. Consent in any fully informed sense may not be obtainable. Nevertheless, except, possibly, in the most trivial situations, it remains a goal toward which one must strive for sociologic, ethical and clear-cut legal reasons. There is no choice in the matter.
>
> If suitably approached, patients will accede, on the basis of trust, to about any request their physician may make. At the same time, every experienced clinician investigator knows that patients will often submit to inconvenience and some discomfort, if they do not last very long; but the usual patient will never agree to jeopardize seriously his health or his life for the sake of "science."
>
> In only 2 of the 50 examples originally compiled for this study was consent mentioned. Actually, it should be emphasized in all cases for obvious moral and legal reasons, but it would be unrealistic to place much dependence on it. In any precise sense statements regarding consent are meaningless unless one knows how fully the patient was informed of all risks, and if these are not known, that fact should also be made clear. A far more dependable safeguard than consent is the presence of a truly responsible investigator.

and practice; that it has, therefore, insufficiently faced up to the fact that the practice of medicine and the conduct of research are different enterprises. The mandate conferred on physicians at the beginning of this century to practice medicine with few constraints cannot be readily transported into research settings. Policymakers must confront their responsibility to formulate a distinctly separate societal mandate for the conduct of research that specifies the lengths to which a democratic society like ours can go in compromising citizen-subjects' rights to autonomy and physical integrity for the sake of medical science. We have been all too willing in our longing to conquer disease and death, as Edmond Cahn once put it, "to possess the end and yet not be responsible for the means, to grasp the fruit while disavowing the tree, to escape being told the cost, until someone else has paid it irrevocably."[18]

Twenty years ago I urged that we resist such a resolution. In the final report of the ad hoc advisory panel of the Tuskegee syphilis study I recommended, and the panel concurred, that Congress establish a permanent body, a National Human Investigation Board (NHIB), with the authority to regulate at least all federally supported research involving human subjects.[19] Among its functions would be the responsibility to formulate research policies, to promulgate procedures for the review of research decisions and their consequences, and to publish important IRB and NHIB decisions.

Senator Edward Kennedy incorporated that proposal in a bill submitted to the Senate. A major reason why his bill was never enacted may have been the Senate's reluctance to expose to public view the value conflicts inherent in the conduct of research. Had the Senate seriously debated the bill, it would have been forced to consider when, if ever, inadequately informed subjects can serve as means to society's and science's ends.

I believed then, as I do now, that the rejection of an NHIB was not just a mistake but a subterfuge to avoid giving greater public visibility to the decisions made in the conduct of human experimentation. Current practices do not provide for in-

The ethical approach to experimentation in man has several components; two are more important than the others, the first being informed consent. The difficulty of obtaining this is discussed in detail. But it is absolutely essential to strive for it for moral, sociologic and legal reasons. The statement that consent has been obtained has little meaning unless the subject or his guardian is capable of understanding what is to be undertaken and unless all hazards are made clear. If these are not known this, too, should be stated. In such a situation the subject at least knows that he is to be a participant in an experiment. Secondly, there is the more reliable safeguard provided by the presence of an intelligent, informed, conscientious, compassionate, responsible investigator.

Ordinary patients will not knowingly risk their health or their life for the sake of "science." Every experienced clinician investigator knows this. When such risks are taken and a considerable number of patients are involved, it may be assumed that informed consent has not been obtained in all cases.

The gain anticipated from an experiment must be commensurate with the risk involved.

An experiment is ethical or not at its inception; it does not become ethical post hoc—ends do not justify means. There is no ethical distinction between ends and means.

In the publication of experimental results it must be made unmistakably clear that the proprieties have been observed. It is debatable whether data obtained unethically should be published even with stern editorial comment.

"Ethics and Clinical Research"
by Henry K. Beecher
NEJM 274 (1966): 1354–60
Excerpted with permission from NEJM

stitutional review committees' publication of, or unencumbered access to, such decisions. A low level of visibility not only hampers efforts to evaluate and learn from attempts to resolve the complex problems of human research but also precludes the public at large from reacting to what is being done for the sake of the advancement of science.

Local IRBs cannot assume the functions that a National Human Investigation Board should serve. Existing federal regulations, as is true for many statutory enactments, are too vague and broad in scope; they require constant interpretation, refinement, and revision. Such tasks are beyond the capacity and perhaps authority of IRBs. Moreover, as George Annas has observed, "IRBs as currently constituted do not protect research subjects but rather protect the institution and the institution's investigator."[20] While this is perhaps too sweeping an indictment, there is considerable truth to his allegation. The majority of IRB members are on the faculty of the institutions to which investigators belong, and they share similar interests and objectives. Thus, particularly in the murky area of informed consent, it is unlikely that members of IRBs will hold investigators to a standard of disclosure and consent that would protect the subjects of research if doing so would place impediments on the conduct of research and, in turn, affect the professional and personal pursuits of their colleagues in decisive ways.

RESPECT FOR PERSONS

Throughout this essay I have tried to make it clear that in the pursuit of scientific progress we have not taken the human rights of research subjects as seriously as they deserve to be taken. The idea that human beings possess human rights is of such recent origin that the contours of such rights remain ill defined. It is an idea, however, that since World War II has captured the imagination of the world community, as the many United Nations' resolutions on human rights attest.

It is important to remember that at the dawn of bioethics, respect for human rights, autonomy, self-determination was foremost in the minds of the philosophers, theologians, and the many others who created this new discipline. Their contributions remain an important legacy. Like the judges who promulgated the informed consent doctrine, these philosophers and theologians, when they entered the scene, were astonished by the low priority physicians accorded to autonomy. Twenty years later respect for the principle of autonomy is once

again going out of favor, and it is time to be astonished once again about the principle's short life.

To conclude, my initial interest in the study of human experimentation was shaped by my own practices and what I had read about the practices of others. Beecher's work, even more, was shaped by what he had observed about his research and that of his colleagues. After reflecting about where we began and where we now are, I want to argue more uncompromisingly then I ever have done that respect for autonomy and self-determination in clinical research, whenever human beings serve as means to others' ends, should be a binding commitment, except under the most exceptional and well-defined circumstances, and then only with societal approval.

Perhaps I would put this somewhat differently if I could share David Rothman's optimism that "the record since 1966 . . . makes a convincing case for a fundamental transformation [of medical decision making in] the conduct of research. [T]he experiments that Henry Beecher described could not now occur."[21] They do occur now, though Rothman is correct that a Tuskegee syphilis study would not now pass IRB scrutiny. Tuskegees, however, have always been rare events in the annals of medical research; mini-Tuskegees are still all too prevalent. John Fletcher's concerns in one of the earliest volumes of The Hastings Center remain concerns in 1993. His conclusion then continues to ring true today: "Now that the period of concern about the principle of informed consent has crested, and lest this concern be found to be mere sentimentality, more thorough steps to institutionalize and embody the value of personhood in medical research are required."[22]

Henry Beecher's vision of the ethics that should govern research still eludes us. Kass put it perhaps too pessimistically when, in reflecting on the contemporary state of bioethics, he observed that "though originally intended to improve our deeds, the reigning practice of ethics, if truth be told, has, at best, improved our speech."[23] Yet he is correct that improving speech alone does not suffice. We must remember that concerns over conduct brought us into bioethics, and improving conduct remains our ethical task. This task was Beecher's intent, and that is why he wrote "Ethics and Clinical Research," even though he knew that in doing so he would infuriate many of his colleagues. The greatest tribute we can pay to this man of remarkable moral courage is to build on the legacy he has left us.

References

1. Henry K. Beecher, "Ethics and Clinical Research," *NEJM* 274 (1966): 1354–60.

2. *Trials of War Criminals before the Nuremberg Military Tribunal*, volume 2, *The Medical Case* (Washington, D.C.: U.S. Government Printing Office, 1948), p. 183.

3. Henry K. Beecher, *Experimentation in Man* (Springfield, Ill.: Charles C. Thomas, 1958), p. 4.

4. Natanson v. Kline, 350 P. 2d 1093 (Kan. 1960).

5. Jay Katz (with the assistance of Alexander M. Capron and Eleanor S. Glass), *Experimentation with Human Beings* (New York: The Free Press, 1972), p. 4.

6. Leon Kass, "Practicing Ethics: Where's the Action?" *Hastings Center Report* 20, no. 1 (1990): 5–12, at 7.

7. Katz, *Experimentation with Human Beings*, pp. 521, 524.

8. See Michael A. Grodin, "Historical Origins of the Nuremberg Code," in *The Nazi Doctors and the Nuremberg Code*, ed. George J. Annas and Michael A. Grodin (New York: Oxford University Press, 1992), pp. 127–32.

9. *Trials of War Criminals before the Nuremberg Military Tribunal*, vol. 2, p. 181.

10. Jay Katz, "Duty and Caring in the Age of Informed Consent: Unlocking Peabody's Secret," *Humane Medicine* 8 (1992): 187–97.

11. Katz, "Duty and Caring," pp. 188–89.

12. Department of Health and Human Services, *Rules and Regulations* 45 CFR 46, § 14.116, 1983.

13. James F. Childress, "The Place of Autonomy in Bioethics," *Hastings Center Report* 20, no. 1 (1990): 12–17.

14. Jay Katz, *The Silent World of Doctor and Patient* (New York: The Free Press, 1984), pp. 128, 112–13.

15. Childress, "The Place of Autonomy in Bioethics," p. 16.

16. Daniel Callahan, "Autonomy: A Moral Good, Not a Moral Obsession," *Hastings Center Report* 14, no. 5 (1984): 40–42, at 42.

17. Callahan, "Autonomy," p. 42.

18. Edmond Cahn, "Drug Experiments and the Public Conscience," in *Drugs in Our Society*, ed. Paul Talalay (Baltimore: The Johns Hopkins Press, 1964), p. 260.

19. *Tuskegee Syphilis Study Ad Hoc Advisory Panel Final Report* (Washington, D.C.: U.S. Government Printing Office, 1973).

20. George J. Annas, *Judging Medicine* (Clifton, N.J.: Humana Press, 1988), p. 331.

21. David Rothman, *Strangers at the Bedside* (New York: Basic Books, 1991), p. 251.

22. John Fletcher, "Realities of Patient Consent to Medical Research," *Hastings Center Studies* 1, no. 1 (1973): 39–49 at 49.

23. Kass, "Where Is the Action?" p. 8.

Equipoise and the Ethics of Clinical Research

Benjamin Freedman Ph.D.

There is widespread agreement that ethics requires that each clinical trial begin with an honest null hypothesis.[1,2] In the simplest model, testing a new treatment B on a defined patient population P for which the current accepted treatment is A, it is necessary that the clinical investigator be in a state

From *N Engl J Med*, 317: 141–145, 1987.

of genuine uncertainty regarding the comparative merits of treatments A and B for population P. If a physician knows that these treatments are not equivalent, ethics requires that the superior treatment be recommended. Following Fried, I call this state of uncertainty about the relative merits of A and B "equipoise."[3]

Equipoise is an ethically necessary condition in all cases of clinical research. In trials with several arms, equipoise must exist between all arms of the trial; otherwise the trial design should be modified to exclude the inferior treatment. If equipoise is disturbed during the course of a trial, the trial may need to be terminated and all subjects previously enrolled (as well as other patients within the relevant population) may have to be offered the superior treatment. It has been rigorously argued that a trial with a placebo is ethical only in investigating conditions for which there is no known treatment[2]; this argument reflects a special application of the requirement for equipoise. Although equipoise has commonly been discussed in the special context of the ethics of randomized clinical trials,[4,5] it is important to recognize it as an ethical condition of all controlled clinical trials, whether or not they are randomized, placebo-controlled, or blinded.

The recent increase in attention to the ethics of research with human subjects has highlighted problems associated with equipoise. Yet, as I shall attempt to show, contemporary literature, if anything, minimizes those difficulties. Moreover, there is evidence that concern on the part of investigators about failure to satisfy the requirements for equipoise can doom a trial as a result of the consequent failure to enroll a sufficient number of subjects.

The solutions that have been offered to date fail to resolve these problems in a way that would permit clinical trials to proceed. This paper argues that these problems are predicated on a faulty concept of equipoise itself. An alternative understanding of equipoise as an ethical requirement of clinical trials is proposed, and its implications are explored.

Many of the problems raised by the requirement for equipoise are familiar. Shaw and Chalmers have written that a clinician who "knows, or has good reason to believe," that one arm of the trial is superior may not ethically participate.[6] But the reasoning or preliminary results that prompt the trial (and that may themselves be ethically mandatory)[7] may jolt the investigator (if not his or her colleagues) out of equipoise before the trial begins. Even if the investigator is undecided between A and B in terms of gross measures such as mortality and morbidity, equipoise may be disturbed because evident differences in the quality of life (as in the case of two surgical approaches) tip the balance.[3–5,8] In either case, in saying "we do not know" whether A or B is better, the investigator may create a false impression in prospective subjects, who hear him or her as saying "no evidence leans either way," when the investigator means "no controlled study has yet had results that reach statistical significance."

Late in the study—when P values are between 0.05 and 0.06—the moral issue of equipoise is most readily apparent,[9,10] but the same problem arises when the earliest comparative results are analyzed.[11] Within the closed statistical universe of the clinical trial, each result that demonstrates a difference between the arms of the trial contributes exactly as much to the statistical conclusion that a difference exists as does any other. The contribution of the last pair of cases in the trial is no greater than that of the first. If, therefore, equipoise is a condition that reflects equivalent evidence for alternative hypotheses, it is jeopardized by the first pair of cases as much as by the last. The investigator who is concerned about the ethics of recruitment after the penultimate pair must logically be concerned after the first pair as well.

Finally, these issues are more than a philosopher's nightmare. Considerable interest has been generated by a paper in which Taylor et al.[12] describe the termination of a trial of alternative treatments for breast cancer. The trial foundered on the problem of patient recruitment, and the investigators trace much of the difficulty in enrolling patients to the fact that the investigators were not in a state of equipoise regarding the arms of the trial. With the increase in concern about the ethics of research and with the increasing presence of this topic in the curricula of medical and graduate schools, instances of the type that Taylor and her colleagues describe are likely to become more common. The requirement for equipoise thus poses a practical threat to clinical research.

RESPONSES TO THE PROBLEMS OF EQUIPOISE

The problems described above apply to a broad class of clinical trials, at all stages of their development. Their resolution will need to be similarly comprehensive. However, the solutions that have so far been proposed address a portion of the difficulties, at best, and cannot be considered fully satisfactory.

Chalmers' approach to problems at the onset of a trial is to recommend that randomization begin with the very first subject.[11] If there are no preliminary, uncontrolled data in support of the experimental treatment B, equipoise regarding treatments A and B for the patient population P is not disturbed. There are several difficulties with this approach. Practically speaking, it is often necessary to establish details of administration, dosage, and so on, before a controlled trial begins, by means of uncontrolled trials in human subjects. In addition, as I have argued above, equipoise from the investigator's point of view is likely to be disturbed when the hypothesis is being formulated and a protocol is being prepared. It is then, before any subjects have been enrolled, that the information that the investigator has assembled makes the experimental treatment appear to be a reasonable gamble. Apart from these problems, initial randomization will not, as Chalmers recognizes, address disturbances of equipoise that occur in the course of a trial.

Data-monitoring committees have been proposed as a solution to problems arising in the course of the trial.[13] Such committees, operating independently of the investigators, are the only bodies with information concerning the trial's ongoing results. Since this knowledge is not available to the investigators, their equipoise is not disturbed. Although committees are useful in keeping the conduct of a trial free of bias, they cannot resolve the investigators' ethical difficulties. A clinician is not merely obliged to treat a patient on the basis of the information that he or she currently has, but is also required to discover information that would be relevant to treatment decisions. If interim results would disturb equipoise, the investigators are obliged to gather and use that information. Their agreement to remain in ignorance of preliminary results would, by definition, be an unethical agreement, just as a failure to call up the laboratory to find out a patient's test results is unethical. Moreover, the use of a monitoring committee does not solve problems of equipoise that arise before and at the beginning of a trial.

Recognizing the broad problems with equipoise, three authors have proposed radical solutions. All three think that there is an irresolvable conflict between the requirement that a patient be offered the best treatment known (the principle underlying the requirement for equipoise) and the conduct of clinical trials; they therefore suggest that the "best treatment" requirement be weakened.

Schafer has argued that the concept of equipoise, and the associated notion of the best medical treatment, depends on the judgment of patients rather than of clinical investigators.[14] Although the equipoise of an investigator may be disturbed if he or she favors B over A, the ultimate choice of treatment is the patient's. Because the patient's values may restore equipoise, Schafer argues, it is ethical for the investigator to proceed with a trial when the patient consents. Schafer's strategy is directed toward trials that test treatments with known and divergent side effects and will probably not be useful in trials conducted to test efficacy or unknown side effects. This approach, moreover, confuses the ethics of competent medical practice with those of consent. If we assume that the investigator is a competent clinician, by saying that the investigator is out of equipoise, we have by Schafer's account said that in the investigator's professional judgment one treatment is therapeutically inferior—for that patient, in that condition, given the quality of life that can be achieved. Even if a patient would consent to an inferior treatment, it seems to me a violation of competent medical practice, and hence of ethics, to make the offer. Of course, complex issues may arise when a patient refuses what the physician considers the best treatment and demands instead an inferior treatment. Without settling that problem, however, we can reject Schafer's position. For Schafer claims that in order to continue to conduct clinical trials, it is ethical for the physician to offer (not merely accede to) inferior treatment.

Meier suggests that "most of us would be quite willing to forego a modest expected gain in the general interest of learning something of value."[15] He argues that we accept risks in everyday life to achieve a variety of benefits, including convenience and economy. In the same way, Meier states, it is acceptable to enroll subjects in clinical trials even though they may not receive the best treatment throughout the course of the trial. Schafer suggests an essentially similar approach.[5,14] According to this view, continued progress in medical knowledge through clinical trials requires an explicit abandonment of the doctor's fully patient-centered ethic.

These proposals seem to be frank counsels of desperation. They resolve the ethical problems of equipoise by abandoning the need for equipoise. In any event, would their approach allow clinical trials to be conducted? I think this may fairly be doubted. Although many people are presumably altruistic enough to forgo the best medical treatment in the interest of the progress of science, many are not. The numbers and propor-

tions required to sustain the statistical validity of trial results suggest that in the absence of overwhelming altruism, the enrollment of satisfactory numbers of patients will not be possible. In particular, very ill patients, toward whom many of the most important clinical trials are directed, may be disinclined to be altruistic. Finally, as the study by Taylor et al.[12] reminds us, the problems of equipoise trouble investigators as well as patients. Even if patients are prepared to dispense with the best treatment, their physicians, for reasons of ethics and professionalism, may well not be willing to do so.

Marquis has suggested a third approach. "Perhaps what is needed is an ethics that will justify the conscription of subjects for medical research," he has written. "Nothing less seems to justify present practice."[4] Yet, although conscription might enable us to continue present practice, it would scarcely justify it. Moreover, the conscription of physician investigators, as well as subjects, would be necessary, because, as has been repeatedly argued, the problems of equipoise are as disturbing to clinicians as they are to subjects. Is any less radical and more plausible approach possible?

THEORETICAL EQUIPOISE VERSUS CLINICAL EQUIPOISE

The problems of equipoise examined above arise from a particular understanding of that concept, which I will term "theoretical equipoise." It is an understanding that is both conceptually odd and ethically irrelevant. Theoretical equipoise exists when, overall, the evidence on behalf of two alternative treatment regimens is exactly balanced. This evidence may be derived from a variety of sources, including data from the literature, uncontrolled experience, considerations of basic science and fundamental physiologic processes, and perhaps a "gut feeling" or "instinct" resulting from (or superimposed on) other considerations. The problems examined above arise from the principle that if theoretical equipoise is disturbed, the physician has, in Schafer's words, a "treatment preference"—let us say, favoring experimental treatment B. A trial testing A against B requires that some patients be enrolled in violation of this treatment preference.

Theoretical equipoise is overwhelmingly fragile; that is, it is disturbed by a slight accretion of evidence favoring one arm of the trial. In Chalmers' view, equipoise is disturbed when the odds that A will be more successful than B are anything other than 50 percent. It is therefore necessary, to randomize treatment assignments beginning with the very first patient, lest equipoise be disturbed. We may say that theoretical equipoise is balanced on a knife's edge.

Theoretical equipoise is most appropriate to one-dimensional hypotheses and causes us to think in those terms. The null hypothesis must be sufficiently simple and "clean" to be finely balanced: Will A or B be superior in reducing mortality or shrinking tumors or lowering fevers in population P? Clinical choice is commonly more complex. The choice of A or B depends on some combination of effectiveness, consistency, minimal or relievable side effects, and other factors. On close examination, for example, it sometimes appears that even trials that purport to test a single hypothesis in fact involve a more complicated, portmanteau measure—e.g., the "therapeutic index" of A versus B. The formulation of the conditions of theoretical equipoise for such complex, multidimensional clinical hypotheses is tantamount to the formulation of a rigorous calculus of apples and oranges.

Theoretical equipoise is also highly sensitive to the vagaries of the investigator's attention and perception. Because of its fragility, theoretical equipoise is disturbed as soon as the investigator perceives a difference between the alternatives— whether or not any genuine difference exists. Prescott writes, for example, "It will be common at some stage in most trials for the survival curves to show visually different survivals," short of significance but "sufficient to raise ethical difficulties for the participants."[16] A visual difference, however, is purely an artifact of the research

methods employed: when and by what means data are assembled and analyzed and what scale is adopted for the graphic presentation of data. Similarly, it is common for researchers to employ interval scales for phenomena that are recognized to be continuous by nature—e.g., five-point scales of pain or stages of tumor progression. These interval scales, which represent an arbitrary distortion of the available evidence to simplify research, may magnify the differences actually found, with a resulting disturbance of theoretical equipoise.

Finally, as described by several authors, theoretical equipoise is personal and idiosyncratic. It is disturbed when the clinician has, in Schafer's words, what "might even be labeled a bias or a hunch," a preference of a "merely intuitive nature."[14] The investigator who ignores such a hunch, by failing to advise the patient that because of it the investigator prefers B to A or by recommending A (or a chance of random assignment to A) to the patient, has violated the requirement for equipoise and its companion requirement to recommend the best medical treatment.

The problems with this concept of equipoise should be evident. To understand the alternative, preferable interpretation of equipoise, we need to recall the basic reason for conducting clinical trials: there is a current or imminent conflict in the clinical community over what treatment is preferred for patients in a defined population P. The standard treatment is A, but some evidence suggests that B will be superior (because of its effectiveness or its reduction of undesirable side effects, or for some other reason). (In the rare case when the first evidence of a novel therapy's superiority would be entirely convincing to the clinical community, equipoise is already disturbed.) Or there is a split in the clinical community, with some clinicians favoring A and others favoring B. Each side recognizes that the opposing side has evidence to support its position, yet each still thinks that overall its own view is correct. There exists (or, in the case of a novel therapy, there may soon exist) an honest, professional disagreement among expert clinicians about the preferred treatment. A clinical trial is instituted with the aim of resolving this dispute.

At this point, a state of "clinical equipoise" exists. There is no consensus within the expert clinical community about the comparative merits of the alternatives to be tested. We may state the formal conditions under which such a trial would be ethical as follows: at the start of the trial, there must be a state of clinical equipoise regarding the merits of the regimens to be tested, and the trial must be designed in such a way as to make it reasonable to expect that, if it is successfully concluded, clinical equipoise will be disturbed. In other words, the results of a successful clinical trial should be convincing enough to resolve the dispute among clinicians.

A state of clinical equipoise is consistent with a decided treatment preference on the part of the investigators. They must simply recognize that their less-favored treatment is preferred by colleagues whom they consider to be responsible and competent. Even if the interim results favor the preference of the investigators, treatment B, clinical equipoise persists as long as those results are too weak to influence the judgment of the community of clinicians, because of limited sample size, unresolved possibilities of side effects, or other factors. (This judgment can necessarily be made only by those who know the interim results—whether a data-monitoring committee or the investigators.)

At the point when the accumulated evidence in favor of B is so strong that the committee or investigators believe no open-minded clinician informed of the results would still favor A, clinical equipoise has been disturbed. This may occur well short of the original schedule for the termination of the trial, for unexpected reasons. (Therapeutic effects or side effects may be much stronger than anticipated, for example, or a definable subgroup within population P may be recognized for which the results demonstrably disturb clinical equipoise.) Because of the arbitrary

character of human judgment and persuasion, some ethical problems regarding the termination of a trial will remain. Clinical equipoise will confine these problems to unusual or extreme cases, however, and will allow us to cast persistent problems in the proper terms. For example, in the face of a strong established trend, must we continue the trial because of others' blind fealty to an arbitrary statistical bench mark?

Clearly, clinical equipoise is a far weaker—and more common—condition than theoretical equipoise. Is it ethical to conduct a trial on the basis of clinical equipoise, when theoretical equipoise is disturbed? Or, as Schafer and others have argued, is doing so a violation of the physician's obligation to provide patients with the best medical treatment?[4,5,14] Let us assume that the investigators have a decided preference for B but wish to conduct a trial on the grounds that clinical (not theoretical) equipoise exists. The ethics committee asks the investigators whether, if they or members of their families were within population P, they would not want to be treated with their preference, B? An affirmative answer is often thought to be fatal to the prospects for such a trial, yet the investigators answer in the affirmative. Would a trial satisfying this weaker form of equipoise be ethical?

I believe that it clearly is ethical. As Fried has emphasized,[3] competent (hence, ethical) medicine is social rather than individual in nature. Progress in medicine relies on progressive consensus within the medical and research communities. The ethics of medical practice grants no ethical or normative meaning to a treatment preference, however powerful, that is based on a hunch or on anything less than evidence publicly presented and convincing to the clinical community. Persons are licensed as physicians after they demonstrate the acquisition of this professionally validated knowledge, not after they reveal a superior capacity for guessing. Normative judgments of their behavior—e.g., malpractice actions—rely on a comparison with what is done by the community of medical practitioners. Failure to follow a "treatment preference" not shared by this community and not based on information that would convince it could not be the basis for an allegation of legal or ethical malpractice. As Fried states: "[T]he conception of what is good medicine is the product of a professional consensus." By definition, in a state of clinical equipoise, "good medicine" finds the choice between A and B indifferent.

In contrast to theoretical equipoise, clinical equipoise is robust. The ethical difficulties at the beginning and end of a trial are therefore largely alleviated. There remain difficulties about consent, but these too may be diminished. Instead of emphasizing the lack of evidence favoring one arm over another that is required by theoretical equipoise, clinical equipoise places the emphasis in informing the patient on the honest disagreement among expert clinicians. The fact that the investigator has a "treatment preference," if he or she does, could be disclosed; indeed, if the preference is a decided one, and based on something more than a hunch, it could be ethically mandatory to disclose it. At the same time, it would be emphasized that this preference is not shared by others. It is likely to be a matter of chance that the patient is being seen by a clinician with a preference for B over A, rather than by an equally competent clinician with the opposite preference.

Clinical equipoise does not depend on concealing relevant information from researchers and subjects, as does the use of independent data-monitoring committees. Rather, it allows investigators, in informing subjects, to distinguish appropriately among validated knowledge accepted by the clinical community, data on treatments that are promising but are not (or, for novel therapies, would not be) generally convincing, and mere hunches. Should informed patients decline to participate because they have chosen a specific clinician and trust his or her judgment—over and above the consensus in the professional community—that is no more than the patients' right.

We do not conscript patients to serve as subjects in clinical trials.

THE IMPLICATIONS OF CLINICAL EQUIPOISE

The theory of clinical equipoise has been formulated as an alternative to some current views on the ethics of human research. At the same time, it corresponds closely to a preanalytic concept held by many in the research and regulatory communities. Clinical equipoise serves, then, as a rational formulation of the approach of many toward research ethics; it does not so much change things as explain why they are the way they are.

Nevertheless, the precision afforded by the theory of clinical equipoise does help to clarify or reformulate some aspects of research ethics; I will mention only two.

First, there is a recurrent debate about the ethical propriety of conducting clinical trials of discredited treatments, such as Laetrile.[17] Often, substantial political pressure to conduct such tests is brought to bear by adherents of quack therapies. The theory of clinical equipoise suggests that when there is no support for a treatment regimen within the expert clinical community, the first ethical requirement of a trial—clinical equipoise—is lacking; it would therefore be unethical to conduct such a trial.

Second, Feinstein has criticized the tendency of clinical investigators to narrow excessively the conditions and hypotheses of a trial in order to ensure the validity of its results.[18] This "fastidious" approach purchases scientific manageability at the expense of an inability to apply the results to the "messy" conditions of clinical practice. The theory of clinical equipoise adds some strength to this criticism. Overly "fastidious" trials, designed to resolve some theoretical question, fail to satisfy the second ethical requirement of clinical research, since the special conditions of the trial will render it useless for influencing clinical decisions, even if it is successfully completed.

The most important result of the concept of clinical equipoise, however, might be to relieve the current crisis of confidence in the ethics of clinical trials. Equipoise, properly understood, remains an ethical condition for clinical trials. It is consistent with much current practice. Clinicians and philosophers alike have been premature in calling for desperate measures to resolve problems of equipoise.

References

1. Levine RJ. Ethics and regulation of clinical research. 2nd ed. Baltimore: Urban & Schwarzenberg, 1986.

2. *Idem.* The use of placebos in randomized clinical trials. IRB: Rev Hum Subj Res 1985; 7(2):1–4.

3. Fried C. Medical experimentation: personal integrity and social policy. Amsterdam: North-Holland Publishing, 1974.

4. Marquis D. Leaving therapy to chance. Hastings Cent Rep 1983; 13(4):40–7.

5. Schafer A. The ethics of the randomized clinical trial. N Engl J Med 1982; 307:719–24.

6. Shaw L W, Chalmers TC. Ethics in cooperative clinical trials. Ann NY Acad Sci 1970; 169:487–95.

7. Hollenberg NK, Dzau VJ, Williams GH. Are uncontrolled clinical studies ever justified? N Engl J Med 1980; 303:1067.

8. Levine RJ, Lebacqz K. Some ethical considerations in clinical trials. Clin Pharmacol Ther 1979; 25:728–41.

9. Klimt CR, Canner PL. Terminating a long-term clinical trial. Clin Pharmacol Ther 1979; 25:641–6.

10. Veatch RM. Longitudinal studies, sequential designs and grant renewals: what to do with preliminary data. IRB: Rev Hum Subj Res 1979; 1(4):1–3.

11. Chalmers T. The ethics of randomization as a decision-making technique and the problem of informed consent. In: Beauchamp TL, Walters L, eds. Contemporary issues in bioethics. Encino, Calif.: Dickenson, 1978:426–9.

12. Taylor KM, Margolese RG. Soskolne CL. Physicians' reasons for not entering eligible patients in a randomized clinical trial of surgery for breast cancer. N Engl J Med 1984; 310:1363–7.

13. Chalmers TC. Invited remarks. Clin Pharmacol Ther 1979; 25:649–50.

14. Schafer A. The randomized clinical trial: for whose benefit? IRB: Rev Hum Subj Res 1985; 7(2):4–6.

15. Meier P. Terminating a trial—the ethical problem. Clin Pharmacol Ther 1979; 25:633–40.

16. Prescott RJ. Feedback of data to participants during clinical trials. In: Tagnon HJ, Staquet MJ, eds. Controversies in cancer: design of trials and treatment. New York: Masson Publishing, 1979:55–61.

17. Cowan DH. The ethics of clinical trials of ineffective therapy. IRB: Rev Hum Subj Res 1981; 3(5):10–1.

18. Feinstein AR. An additional basic science for clinical medicine. II. The limitations of randomized trials. Ann Intern Med 1983; 99:544–50.

Placebos in Clinical Practice and Research

Peter P. De Deyn MD, PhD, MMPR, and Rudi D'Hooge MA, MSc, PhD

PLACEBO-CONTROLLED RANDOMISED CLINICAL TRIALS

Shapiro[1] defined placebo as "any therapeutic procedure (or that component of any therapeutic procedure) which is given deliberately to have an effect, or unknowingly has an effect on a patient, symptom, syndrome, or disease, but which is objectively without specific activity for the condition being treated". Since the earliest days of medical science, and certainly since the

From *J Medical Ethics,* 22:140–146, 1996.

advent of chemotherapy, placebo effects have been considered more often a nuisance than a therapeutic tool. Both inert and active therapies were observed to produce effects beyond their predicted physiological properties. These rather surprising observations on the clinical consequences of the administration of placebos became known as "the placebo effect", comprising the total of unexplained consequences of administering placebos as well as active treatments. Due to, amongst other things, the unpredictability of placebo effects in individuals and patient groups, placebos came to play an irreplaceable role as "inactive" controls in randomised clinical trials (RCTs).

The first rather isolated placebo-controlled clinical trial took place in 1916 and was conducted by Macht who compared the analgesic action of morphine with that of physiological saline.[2] It was only in the 1940s and 1950s that the large-scale use of placebos in clinical research emerged, simultaneously with scientific knowledge pertaining to the placebo effect. The unabated need for placebo-controlled clinical trials is illustrated by several anecdotes in the development of presumedly therapeutic procedures. Surgical ligation of the internal mammary artery, once proclaimed to be efficacious for treatment of angina pectoris, might serve as an example. In the 1950s, considerable relief of symptoms was reported for patients with angina pectoris subjected to bilateral ligation of the internal mammary artery. In the early '50s, Italian clinicians Battezzati and colleagues[3] were the first to apply this technique, and the Reader's Digest published an enthusiastic report.[4] A year later promising results were also reported by American researchers who based their enthusiasm upon data from non-controlled trials.[5-7] It only took two double-blind placebo-controlled studies, involving 35 subjects, to disprove the presumed efficacy of this putative treatment. Fourteen subjects were placebo-treated (sham-operated) and 21 underwent a ligation of the internal mammary arteries under local anaes-

thesia.[8,9] The placebo procedure consisted of parasternal skin incisions without ligation, while the "active" treatment consisted of parasternal skin incisions followed by ligation of the internal mammary artery. It was demonstrated that internal mammary artery ligation did not increase cardiac muscle perfusion and had no effect on the pathophysiology of coronary artery disease. Although deception was obvious in these two placebo-controlled trials (patients were not informed about the possibility of sham operation), the double-blind evaluation of the procedure's effect in 35 patients prevented wide-spread introduction of this non-efficacious surgical procedure.

Demonstration of safety and effectiveness of a drug is a legal requirement for marketing drugs in many countries. In the USA, evidence submitted to the Food and Drug Administration (FDA) to meet this requirement has to include results of "adequate and well-controlled investigations" capable of distinguishing "the effect of a drug from other influences, such as spontaneous change in the course of the disease, placebo effect, or biased observation". According to FDA regulation this usually implies standard clinical trial features such as (inactive) control groups, randomised assignment to treatment, and blinded outcome assessment. Difference in outcome among patients, concurrently randomised to therapy, should not be due to personal beliefs, secondary interests, and/or prejudices of patients, investigators or sponsors. FDA official Leber[10] stresses the necessity of RCTs. Even though Leber states that "[t]here is no alternative to the randomised controlled design—no ifs, ands, or buts!", he certainly does not take the RCT device as infallible. In any case, open studies, case series and studies relying on external or historical controls do not allow sound conclusions. Historical controls are highly unreliable, especially in regard to diseases with poorly known or highly variable natural courses such as insomnia, anxiety, depression and pain syndromes.[11-13] As Leber[10] argues, it is often impossible to show improvement to be unrelated to pharmacological effects of the administered agents without the inclusion of a placebo arm.

DECEPTIVE USE OF PLACEBO

The two major ethical problems in the use of placebo involve deception when used either therapeutically or in research without adequate patient information and consent, and the potential conflict between the Hippocratic and scientific obligations of the therapist-researcher. Even though it remains inadmissible to use placebo for therapeutic or diagnostic purposes, most therapists do occasionally apply placebo in a deceptive but rather benevolent way. Use of placebo for therapeutic and diagnostic use is inadmissible since the patient may be withheld from an active treatment, may be denied his or her right to self-determination and finally, because there is no scientific ground for the application of placebo in diagnosis. Deception is certainly unacceptable when applying placebo as an inactive control in clinical research.

Park and Covi[14] demonstrated that deceit may not be necessary in therapeutic application. They showed that in neurotic patients presenting signs of anxiety, placebo could be used openly as a therapeutic agent. Virtually all patients accepted the placebo and improved over a one-week treatment. Park and Covi[14] found that a number of patients even refused to believe they had received placebo. Alternatively, in discussing placebo use with patients, one might consider another ethically acceptable or preferable description of placebo: "Placebo is a medicine which does not act directly through known bodily mechanisms but which may work through the mind".

Although many authors[15] vividly defend consequentialist or utilitarian strategies and deceptive use of placebo, others point to the important unethical and non-scientific use of placebo in so-called therapeutic or diagnostic contexts. Goodwin et al.[16] surveyed the knowledge of placebo action in 60 house officers and 39 registered nurses, and their patterns of placebo use. Most respondents underestimated or were unaware of the power of placebo effects, and the following unfortunate patterns of placebo use emerged: (a) to prove the patient "wrong" (ie, to expose a patient thought to be exaggerating, imagining or faking symptoms); (b) in disliked or "undeserving" patients (for example, alcoholic, psychotic or manipulative and demanding patients); (c) in situations where standard treatments either fail or make patients worse, (d) as a group activity to act out staff annoyance towards "difficult" patients.

Deception in the therapeutic use of placebo might be ethically acceptable in a few well-defined cases, for example, when the physician is dealing with subjects with a history of substance abuse or when subjects have to be withdrawn from certain addictive agents. Indeed, in these cases, giving placebo without obtaining consent of the patient, will almost invariably contribute to the patient's well-being, and in addition does not imply that one withholds a possibly beneficial medical treatment. Other therapeutic usage of placebo in noninformed patients is regrettable, ethically unacceptable and illustrative of ignorance and prejudice. It needs to be stressed, however, that malingerers or drug addicts are not relieved more efficiently by placebo. Quite on the contrary, most studies suggest that such patients are less likely placebo responders. Also, complaining or "manipulative" patients are no more likely to respond to placebo than patients who are well liked by the hospital staff.[17]

In the scientific application of placebo, however, informed consent should be mandatory, implying that thorough information with regard to the rationale, the design, the eventual standard therapeutic procedures for the given disease, the randomisation procedure as well as the chance of being randomised to placebo should be communicated and discussed. Moreover, informed consent procedures require subjects to be informed about all risks and benefits associated with the trial and their right to withdraw at any time. Some authors disagree with this and oppose compulsory informed consent. Brewin[18] argues that "too much information may be as bad as too little." This author also suggests that some investigators, once in possession of written informed consent, might become less concerned than they should about their ethical responsibilities. Still other authors perceive an incompatibility between informed consent and placebo control. Levine[19] warns us about subjects who are *thoroughly informed* of the expected therapeutic and adverse effects of pharmacologically active agents in placebo-controlled trials. In several clinical trials, subjects unblinded the study by correctly guessing their treatment assignment. Levine[19] proposes a modification in consent procedures that would eliminate or at least reduce this possibility without defeating the ethical purpose of informed consent. Levine suggests adding irrelevant side-effects in the provided information that are of the same order of importance as the actual expected side-effects. This is consistent with the ethical purposes of informed consent in that it entails disclosure of material risks.

Another poignant issue concerns the patient's ability to understand placebo-controlled trials. Do the patients really know what placebo means, do they realise that they have a certain chance of receiving placebo and why they will be on it? Stanley[20] reviewed the literature and concluded that irrespective of their condition and whether or not they were psychiatric patients, patients were fairly able to understand the risks and benefits of a proposed treatment and the purpose of a particular treatment or procedure.

CONFLICT BETWEEN HIPPOCRATIC AND SCIENTIFIC OBLIGATIONS

The therapist-researcher is subject to two fundamental ethical obligations, a Hippocratic one and a scientific one. The therapist's Hippocratic obligation obliges him/her to apply all existing knowledge for the best possible treatment of individual patients. On the other hand, in agreement with the researcher's scientific obligations it is unethical to produce unsound scientific data. Thus, it is the duty of the researcher to acquire new knowledge so that future patients might benefit, and to communicate accurately this knowledge to the scientific community in order to contribute to the collective benefit. However, these two obligations may on certain occasions be in contradiction to the execution and design of placebo-controlled RCTs. According to certain people, randomisation by itself means that patients are no longer treated purely for their own good but are used at best for the benefit of future sufferers from their condition, at worst merely to satisfy scientific curiosity, and that they risk being treated inappropriately. It is thought that some kind of sacrifice is being demanded of them and that they should either be given a full explanation or else not randomised.

The primary question is whether it can be ethically justified to deprive a certain percentage of patients in placebo-controlled trials of their "right to receive" treatment of acknowledged efficacy merely in order to verify whether or not other active treatments exist. Withholding treatment of proven efficacy clearly violates the therapist's commitment to individual patient welfare. However, the conflict between therapist and researcher more often is emotionally, rather than scientifically, based. Patients can be allocated to standard therapy control groups, or to placebo groups when no standard therapy exists, without violation of Hippocratic commitment; developing new treatments of an already (partially) treatable disease need not necessarily be dangerous to the subject. Some therapists stress the pragmatic viewpoint of the RCT: only the application of an accepted treatment as control arm can answer the question whether the new treatment improves on a standard method. The use of placebo-controlled RCT designs is the only way to minimise the number of ineffective drugs and therapeutic procedures. The conviction that ignorance may cause patient harm may not only be used as a justification for research but in addition renders research an ethical obligation. The important ethical difficulties associated with the widespread application of a new treatment without a trial, and consequently potentially without specific effects but with varying degrees of side-effects, is far greater than those associated with the trial itself. The optimal and therefore often placebo-controlled and ethically founded RCT meets the duties of benefiting society and increasing knowledge without jeopardising the well-being of the experimental subjects.

There are many examples of marketed compounds without scientifically demonstrated efficacy and, in addition, several companies market so-called alternative medicines without needing to meet rigorous drug regulatory requirements for proof of efficacy. Recently, Pope[21] correctly stated that forty different compounds for treatment of Alzheimer's disease are available in Europe without any proven efficacy. The Ginkgo biloba case is an example where rigorous scientific standards of efficacy are not met.[21-25] In 1988, 5.24 million prescriptions for Ginkgo biloba extract involved a cost of DM 370 million to former West German health insurance. In 1992, sales were comparable with total costs of approximately DM 368 million. The drug, licensed under the 1986 drug law which does not require scientific evidence from controlled trials but merely positive therapeutic "experiences", is promoted for treatment of disorders as diverse as peripheral arterial disease, memory impairment, vertigo and impotence. Kimbel,[25] writes that "[t]he obvious discrepancy that Ginkgo biloba extracts are among the most prescribed medicines in France and Germany but not licensed in Anglo-American and Scandinavian countries suggests widely differing standards of acceptance. Would it not be advisable to base any therapeutic conclusions on the criteria of leading regulatory agencies—ie, evaluation of all published and unpublished studies and use of established standards for clinically relevant efficacy?"

ACCEPTABILITY OF PLACEBO-CONTROLLED RANDOMISED CLINICAL TRIALS

One definitely needs to be fully informed about current biomedical knowledge with regard to the disease at hand in order to be able to make ethical decisions correctly. Some examples pertaining to the development of new agents against depression, schizophrenia, epilepsy and dementia will illustrate this necessity.

Depression

With the advent of a variety of potent anti-depressive agents, one might be tempted to conclude that placebo-controlled trials should be considered ethically unacceptable. However, we believe that the difference in improvement rates between drug-treated and placebo-treated non-endogenous patients is not big enough to make placebo control unethical.

Endogenous depressions have placebo response rates around 30 per cent, while neurotic or reactive depressions have rates approaching 70 per cent.[26] The more severe depressions (Hamilton Depression score above 20) have placebo response between 30 and 40 per cent, whereas those with less severe illness (Hamilton score below 14) have placebo response rates greater than 50 per cent. Brown et al[26] found no difference between baseline clinical and demographic characteristics of placebo responders and non-placebo responders in a large group of patients with major depression, illustrating the limited predictability of placebo response. Quitkin et al[27] analysed the heterogeneity of placebo responses in 144 depressive patients (DSM-III criteria) randomly assigned to placebo medication in four double-blind antidepressant drug trials. Half of the patients were rated as improved for at least one week: 23 per cent with abrupt improvement; 27 per cent with gradual improvement. Gradual improvement was observed later in the course of treatment, more resembled drug response, and was more likely to persist than abrupt improvement. The authors attributed gradual improvement to spontaneous remission.

Although placebo use may not always be advisable (for example, in depressed patients at significant risk of suicide, with psychotic features, or with severe functional impairment), Brown's[28] suggestion to apply placebo in an open manner in mild to moderate depression might hold some merit. He proposes to inform the patients about the fact that their condition tends to respond to placebo (he defines placebo adequately), and that in an attempt to treat them, they will receive placebo for a period of six weeks after which the need for other treatment will be evaluated. The authors provide, of course, possibilities for escape in case of deterioration of the symptomatology and/or increased risk for complications such as suicide.

Schizophrenia

Several authors have questioned the ethical acceptability of short-term placebo treatment of chronic schizophrenics.[29] Even though double-blind placebo-controlled trials provide the most reliable evaluation of antipsychotic agents, some clinicians fear that subjects exposed to placebo or inactive new agents might suffer lasting *harm* when the trial leads to relapse. Sixty-six per cent of patients given placebo and only eight per cent of those given fluphenzine decanoate relapsed during a trial that showed no differences between groups—neither in any clinical or social variable measured at the end of seven years follow-up, nor in the number of relapses after the trial.[29] Placebo-controlled clinical trials of antipsychotic agents can still be acceptable on condition that escape treatment is provided by applying well thought-through exit criteria within reasonable time after relapse.

Epilepsy

The first guidelines of the *International League Against Epilepsy* on the development of anti-epileptic agents state that new agents cannot be introduced unless it has been proved that patients with intractable epilepsy become seizure-free or experience an appreciable (for example, 25 or 50 per cent) reduction in seizure frequency.[30] The placebo-controlled add-on design is the appropriate clinical trial to identify such agents. In this type of clinical trial, the patient's baseline medication is maintained but in addition, either placebo or the new investigational drug is introduced. However, research on new antiepileptic drugs with similar efficacy as drugs already marketed but with fewer or no side-effects should also find a place. The placebo-controlled add-on design is obviously not the best approach in this latter case. Equally active antiepileptic agents with fewer side-effects might be missed since side-effects are difficult to assess in add-on designs due to drug interactions and difficulties in analysing individual drug actions. Determination of the activity of a compound may also be impossible in add-on designs when the agent tested influences the blood levels of concomitant agents.[31] Add-on trials may overestimate the toxicity of the test compound, especially if toxicity of the new compound is similar and additive to that of concomitant drugs. Finally, placebo-controlled add-on trials are often expected to yield an unlikely 50 per cent reduction in subject seizure frequency, whereas Schmidt[32] found only 15 per cent reduction with co-administration of a marketed drug.

Since epileptic seizures can result in serious discomfort or lasting disability, the sometimes more appropriate placebo-controlled, single-drug designs face adverse ethical judgment. (Of course, certain seizure types such as primary generalised tonic-clonic seizures are imminently more dangerous than, for example, simple focal seizures without secondary generalisation; also, patients who only present seizures during sleep are less likely to develop complications). We argue that placebo application in clinical epilepsy research can be considered ethically acceptable under certain conditions and in the following trial designs: (a) placebo-controlled add-on designs in intractable epilepsy; (b) developmental drug monotherapy versus placebo in presurgical video-EEG or video-invasive neuroelectrophysiological monitoring (in order to be able optimally to observe epileptic seizures in this patient population, the baseline medication is withdrawn in the presurgical workup; following this short observation period, the efficacy of the new developmental drug can be compared against that of placebo); (c) active control designs with attenuated form of the active control (in this design, an active control group is used but the administered dosage of the classical antiepileptic agent is too low to be really effective); (d) placebo-controlled design in *de novo* patients presenting with a first-ever epileptic seizure.

We suggest that monotherapy designs b and c should always be preceded by more than one placebo-controlled add-on design indicating probable antiepileptic efficacy of the test compound. Monotherapy trials were proposed to overcome the deadlock of no-difference outcome,[33] and have actually been used in the recent development of the antiepileptic agents vigabatrin and felbamate. The acceptability of the designs rests upon a variety of factors such as type, frequency and onset time of seizures, investigational circumstances (for example, pre-surgery investigation of patients), preset safeguards such as escape criteria, duration of treatment, and (tentative) antiepileptic efficacy of the test drug. Preset escape criteria are mandatory in design (b) trials. Bourgeois *et al*[34] used as primary efficacy parameter the time required to reach either a certain number of seizures or a fixed number of seizure-free days, whichever first. After a predetermined number of seizures or, for example, one (secondarily) generalised seizure, patients returned to the preregistration treatment schedule. This protocol was considered justified in the case of felbamate because of its promising clinical profile and strong interaction with other antiepilep-

tics. In favour of a placebo-controlled design instead of an active-controlled design was the lack of sensitivity of the latter.[35]

In design (c), the test compound is compared against attenuated active control. The active control (a marketed anti-epileptic) can be administered in different doses (the lowest dose is not considered efficacious and such doses should be seen as pseudoplacebos) or at one fixed low dose. Patients with sufficient seizure control but side-effects can be enrolled in this type of trial. Although the exact percentage of seizure-free patients suffering side-effects is unknown, one could still find it unethical to run the risk of losing seizure control only in the hope that an adverse effect would disappear. Therefore, inclusion criteria eliminating patients with severe epilepsy and escape criteria are again mandatory. Treatment failure, the primary efficacy variable in these trials, is defined by specific exit criteria relating to either seizure frequency or seizure severity.

Placebo-controlled designs could be considered in *de novo* patients presenting with a first-ever seizure, provided that development of epilepsy is not too imminent as it might be in patients with epileptiform electroencephalographic elements or in those with predisposing structural lesions. As early as 1881, Gowers noted that seizures apparently beget seizures, an observation that remains controversial up to the present.[36] According to some authors but not to others, one of the most decisive factors in long-term seizure remission might be the number of pretreatment seizures.[37, 38] This consideration also holds for non-*de novo* patients in whom additional seizures could change the prognosis of the disease. Only a trial with a placebo arm and an active antiepileptic arm would be reliable in helping to resolve the issue of the risk of epileptogenesis after a firstever epileptic seizure.

Alzheimer's Disease

With recent FDA approval of tacrine as a drug against Alzheimer's disease, one might question the acceptability of placebo-controlled clinical trials. For several reasons we argue that placebo-controlled clinical trials in dementia are not only acceptable but ethically and scientifically preferable: (a) cholinesterase inhibitors such as tacrine cannot nearly be called standard therapy as only 23 per cent of Alzheimer patients benefit from tacrine treatment[39]; the clinical relevance of the therapeutic efficacy, at best only symptomatic and very limited, could even be doubted; (b) cholinesterase inhibitors are not devoid of side-effects since some 30 per cent of patients develop transaminitis, a reversible increase in liver transaminases, and some 15 per cent develop gastrointestinal complaints[39 40]; (c) placebo treatment does not inflict unacceptable risk on the patient suffering from this slowly progressing neurodegenerative disorder; (d) investigating new anti-dementic agents in cholinesterase inhibitor-controlled designs could lead to false positive findings (type II errors) when applying equipotency or no-difference outcome criteria; (e) cholinesterase inhibitor-controlled designs would require larger patient populations in order to reach sound conclusions: (f) cholinesterase inhibitor treatment as an active control arm would definitely unblind the study because of the high frequency of transaminitis.

CONCLUSION

Since it is inadmissible to perform ill-designed clinical trials and to market compounds or employ treatments without specific effect (efficacy not exceeding that of placebo) and/or with serious side-effects, properly controlled RCTs form the only scientifically valid tool. Nature of the disease process, duration of the study period, therapeutic-toxic ratio of the agent tested, availability and appropriateness of alternative therapy, and many other considerations all play a role in clinical trial design. Even though the placebo-controlled RCT remains the gold standard in therapy development, the need for and acceptability of placebo control has to be evaluated case by case, considering and reconciling both scientific and ethical issues. Often, placebo control might even be considered an ethical obligation but some provisos should be kept in mind: (a) no adequate therapy for the disease should exist and/or the (presumed) active therapy should have serious side-effects; (b) placebo treatment should not last too long; (c) placebo treatment should not inflict unacceptable risks on the patients, and (d) the experimental subject should be adequately informed and informed consent given.

References

1. Shapiro AK. Factors contributing to the placebo effect. Their implications for psychotherapy. *American Journal of Psychotherapy* 1961; **18:** 73–88.

2. Delay J, Pichot P. *Medizinische Psychologie*. Stuttgart: Thieme, 1973.

3. Battezzati M, Tagliaferro A, de Marchi G. La legatura delle due arterie mammarie interne nei disturbi di vascolarizzazione del miocardio: nota preventiva relativa de primi dati sperimentali e clinici. *Minerva Medica* 1995; **46:** 1178–88.

4. Ratcliff JD. New surgery for ailing hearts. *Reader's Digest* 1957; **71:** 70–3.

5. Brill IC, Rosenbaum WM, Rosenbaum EE, Flanery JR. Internal mammary artery ligation. *Northwest Medicine* 1958; **57:** 483–6.

6. Harken DE. Clinical conference: long-term management of patients with coronary artery disease. *Circulation* 1958; **17:** 945–52.

7. Kitchell JR, Glover RP, Kyle RH. Bilateral internal mammary artery ligation for angina pectoris. *American Journal of Cardiology* 1958; **1:** 46–50.

8. Cobb LA, Thomas GI, Dillard DH, *et al.* An evaluation of internal-mammary-artery ligation by a double-blind technique. *New England Journal of Medicine* 1959; **260:** 1115–8.

9. Diamond EG, Kittle CF, Crockett JE. Evaluation of internal mammary artery ligation and sham procedure in angina pectoris. *Circulation* 1958; **18:** 712–3.

10. Leber P. Is there an alternative to the randomized controlled trial? *Psychopharmacology Bulletin* 1991; **27:** 3–8.

11. Lasagna L. Testimony given at Hearings before the Subcommittee on Antitrust and Monopoly of the Committee on the Judiciary, United States Senate,

87th Congress, Ist Session S. Res 52 on S. 1961; 1552: Part 1: 282–3.

12. Leber PD. The implicit assumptions of active control trials (a critical examination). *Controlled Clinical Trials* 1983; **14**: 133.

13. Leber PD. Hazards of inference: the active control investigation. *Epilepsia* 1989; **30**: S1: 57–63.

14. Park LC, Covi L. Nonblind placebo trial. An exploration of neurotic patients' responses to placebo when its inert content is disclosed. *Archives of General Psychiatry* 1965; **12**: 336–45.

15. Elander G. Ethical conflicts in placebo treatment. *Journal of Advanced Nursing* 1991; **16**: 947–51.

16. Goodwin JS, Goodwin JM, Vogel AV. Knowledge and use of placebos by house officers and nurses. *Annals of Internal Medicine* 1979; **91**: 106–10.

17. Lasagna L, Masteller F, von Felsinger JM, Beecher HK. A study of the placebo response. *American Journal of Medicine* 1954; **16**: 770–9.

18. Brewin TB. Consent to randomised treatment. *Lancet* 1982; **ii**: 919–21.

19. Levine RJ. The apparent incompatibility between informed consent and placebo-controlled clinical trials. *Clinical Pharmacology and Therapy* 1987; **42**: 247–9.

20. Stanley B. Informed consent in treatment and research. In: Weiner JB, Hess AK, eds. *Handbook of Forensic Psychology*. New York: John Wiley & Sons, 1987: 63–85.

21. Pope K. FDA chief answers critics. *Academic Focus* 1992; **28**: 28a–d.

22. Schönhöfer PS, Schulte-Sasse H, Manhold C, Werner B. Sind Extracte aus den Blattern des Ginkgobaumes bei peripheren Durchblutungs- und Hirnleistungsstörungen im Alter wirksam? Beurteilung von Tebonin und Rökan. *Internal Praxis* 1989; **29**: 585–601.

23. Schönhöfer PS. Ginkgo biloba extracts. *Lancet* 1990; **1**: 788.

24. Kleijnen J, Knipschild P. Ginkgo biloba. *Lancet* 1992; **340**: 1136–9.

25. Kimbel KH. Ginkgo biloba. *Lancet* 1992; **340**: 1474.

26. Brown WA. Predictors of placebo response in depression. *Psychopharmacology Bulletin* 1988; **24**: 14–7.

27. Quitkin FM, Rabkin JG, Stewart JW, *et al.* Heterogeneity of clinical response during placebo treatment. *American Journal of Psychiatry* 1991; **148**: 193–6.

28. Brown WA. Placebo as a treatment for depression. *Neuropsychopharmacology* 1994; **10**: 265–9.

29. Curson DA, Hirsch SR, Platt SD, *et al.* Does short term placebo treatment of chronic schizophrenia produce long term harm? *British Medical Journal* 1986; **293**: 726–8.

30. Meinardi H. Clinical evaluation of antiepileptic drugs: Guidelines of the International League Against Epilepsy. In: De Deyn PP, D'Hooge R, Schafer A, eds. *The ethics of animal and human experimentation*. London: John Libbey, 1994: 279–85.

31. Theodore WH, Rauberras RF, Porter RJ. Felbamate: a clinical trial for complex partial seizures. *Epilepsia* 1991; **32**: 392–7.

32. Schmidt D. Two antiepileptic drugs for intractable epilepsy with complex partial seizures. *Journal of Neurology, Neurosurgery and Psychiatry* 1982; **45**: 1119–24.

33. Gram L, Schmidt D. Innovative designs of controlled clinical trials in epilepsy. *Epilepsia* 1993; 34 S7: 1–6.

34. Bourgeois B, Leppik JF, Sackellares JC. Felbamate: a double-blind controlled trial in patients undergoing presurgical evaluation of partial seizures. *Neurology* 1993; **43**: 693–6.

35. Pledger GW, Kramer LD. Clinical trials of investigational antiepileptic drugs: monotherapy designs. *Epilepsia* 1991; **32**: 716–21.

36. Elwes RDC, Johnson AL, Reynolds EM. The course of untreatable epilepsy. *British Medical Journal* 1988; **297**: 948–50.

37. Beghi L, Tognoni G. Prognosis of epilepsy in newly referred patients: a multicentre prospective study. *Epilepsia* 1988; **29**: 236–43.

38. Reynolds EH. The influence of antiepileptic drugs on the natural history of epilepsy. *Epilepsy Research* 1991; **S3**: 15–20.

39. Knapp MJ, Knopman DS, Solomon PR, *et al.* A 30-week randomised controlled trial of high-dose tacrine in patients with Alzheimer's disease. *Journal of the American Medical Association* 1994; **271**: 985–91.

40. Watkins PB, Zimmerman HJ, Knapp MJ, *et al.* Hepatotoxic effects of tacrine administration in patients with Alzheimer's disease. *Journal of the American Medical Association* 1994; **271**: 992–8.

Is Informed Consent Always Necessary for Randomized, Controlled Trials?

Robert D. Truog MD, Walter Robinson MD, Adrienne Randolph MD, Alan Morris MD

CONSIDER this paradox: if a physician reads a case report about a novel method of ventilation for critically ill patients and wants to try it in the next several patients with respiratory failure he or she treats, the physician may do so provided the patients have given general consent for treatment. On the other hand, if a physician is interested in performing a randomized, controlled trial to determine rigorously which of two widely used antibiotics is more effective at treating bronchitis, he or she must prepare a formal protocol, obtain approval from the institutional review board, and seek written informed consent from potential participants. In each case, the physician is performing an experiment. In each case, there is uncertainty about the best way to treat the patient. Yet in the context of clinical care, the experiment can be done with virtually no external scrutiny, whereas in the context of a clinical trial, the experiment is prohibited unless substantial hurdles are overcome. This is true even when the experimental therapy (e.g., a promising but risky method of ventilation) involves risks that are unknown or substantially different from those of the alternatives.

To put it another way, physicians can do almost anything they want in the name of therapeutic innovation, but only if there is no attempt to gain systematic knowledge from the intervention. Or, to paraphrase Smithells, "I need permission to give a new drug to half my patients but not to give it to all of them."[1] In this article we argue that the current approach to informed consent is at least partially off target, in that patients are often "protected" from clinical trials under circumstances in which the risks associated with participation in the trial are virtually nil, but they receive no protection from physicians who want to experiment with new treatments in the name of therapeutic innovation.

The reasons for the current approach are not mysterious. In a simplistic sense, all medical interventions may be characterized as either therapy or research. Research differs from therapy in many important ways. The goal of research is to gain new knowledge, and any benefits from the research are reaped primarily by future patients. The aim of therapy is to benefit the patient at hand. These differences have predictably led to an elaborate process designed to protect patients involved in clinical trials, whereas minimal constraints are placed on physicians providing clinical care.

This emphasis on protecting subjects during research should not be surprising. Since the Nuremberg trials, society has been wary of the conflict of interest that is present in all research—that the interests of the current patient may be sacrificed to other interests, such as those of future patients or even those of the investigators. Indeed, the distrust of society seems justified, because even after the adoption of the Nuremberg Code[2] and the Declaration of Helsinki,[3,4] examples of abuse in the conduct of research have been documented throughout the world.[5]

An analysis of the goals of informed consent can provide insight into the paradox described above. Informed consent is either general or specific. A patient gives general informed consent for treatment as part of the process of establishing a fiduciary relationship with a physician. Specific informed consent is necessary whenever the proposed intervention involves a high risk–benefit ratio, either in an absolute sense or in comparison with the alternatives, or whenever the preferences or values of the patient are relevant to the decision

From *N Engl J Med*, 340: 804–806, 1999.

at hand. The distinction between these two tiers of informed consent is illustrated by the fact that physicians typically order routine tests and prescribe standard medications under the general consent for treatment but obtain specific consent before undertaking a major diagnostic or therapeutic procedure, before prescribing a potentially toxic medication, or whenever a patient's values and preferences would be expected to have a substantial influence on the clinical course chosen.

We suggest that the obligation to seek specific consent for research should likewise depend on the risk–benefit ratios of the intervention and the alternatives as well as the degree to which the patient would be expected to have preferences about the various options for diagnosis or treatment that are under investigation. We believe that as with clinical care, in the case of many randomized, controlled trials, the patient's participation can and should be considered to be authorized by his or her general consent for treatment and that specific consent should not be required.

Consider, for example, a hypothetical trial comparing two similar cephalosporins for preoperative prophylaxis. Both are widely used, but they differ markedly in cost, and their comparative efficacy in preventing wound infections is unknown. If both drugs have been in use long enough that their side-effect profiles are known to be similar, patients are unlikely to prefer one medication over another; it is also unlikely that the process of obtaining specific consent would serve the patient in any meaningful way. Other examples of this type of study are a randomized trial to assess whether low-dose heparin increases the longevity of intra-arterial catheters in the intensive care unit, a randomized trial of two brands of antacid to control gastric acidity, and a randomized comparison of two methods of mechanical ventilation to determine which method results in more rapid resumption of spontaneous, unassisted breathing. These hypothetical trials share several characteristics, which we have integrated into the following proposed criteria for determining whether the requirement of informed consent for a randomized, controlled trial can be waived.

First, informed consent should not be waived unless all the treatments offered in the trial could be offered outside the trial without the specific informed consent of the patient. This is often the case when a trial is comparing two therapies that are already in use or when an existing therapy or drug is being used for a new indication. In the hypothetical trials described above, the specific informed consent of the patient would thus not be required for any of the options being offered.

Second, the treatments should not involve more than minimal additional risk in comparison with any of the alternatives.[6] When the risks associated with each of the options are assumed to be similar, the patient could be treated outside the trial with any one of the interventions under study. Again, the examples we cited could meet this requirement. Of course, physicians would exclude a patient for a justifiable medical reason— for example, if the patient were known to be allergic to one of the medications being studied.

Third, genuine clinical equipoise must exist among the treatments. This state of balance is, of course, a general ethical requirement before a randomized, controlled study can be undertaken. There should be honest uncertainty about which treatment is superior.[7] If the informed consent of the patient is judged unnecessary, investigators have an even greater burden of proof to ensure clinical equipoise.

Fourth, no reasonable person should have a preference for one treatment over any other, regardless of the differences between the treatments being compared. This standard would cover not only the direct effects of the intervention being studied but also the indirect effects associated with research, such as whether the study would require extra visits to the clinic or other inconveniences.

Although the reasonable-person standard is widely used in the law, it is far from perfect.[8] For example, there is always the possibility that a patient may be unusual in ways that cannot be anticipated and that would lead the patient to have an unanticipated preference for one treatment over another. This problem arises with both general and specific informed consent, however, and cannot be addressed solely by demanding more rigorous standards for research.

The validity of the reasonable-person standard depends in large part on how it is implemented. We propose that studies for which a waiver of informed consent is requested should, like all other studies, be submitted to an institutional review board for review and approval. The institutional review board would therefore assume responsibility for applying the standard. Because an important function of the institutional review board is to ensure the involvement of the community through the representation of people without medical backgrounds, the board would be in the best position to apply the reasonable-person standard and to determine whether the informed-consent requirement could be waived.

How should the reasonable-person standard be applied with reference to the community in which the research is being performed? Since the abuses of the Tuskegee syphilis study, members of racial minority groups have been particularly sensitive to the implications of being involved in research without their consent.[9] Although we believe that exemptions to informed consent should be considered only when potential subjects would have no reason to decline participation, we recognize that for some the refusal to participate in research may not be related to the pertinent facts of a particular study but, rather, may be based on important historical and cultural issues of concern. Depending on the community and the context of the research, these issues may be grounds for insisting on specific informed consent for participation in the research.

Fifth, patients should be informed that the institution or clinical setting in which they are being treated uses the standards that we have described as guidelines for determining the need for specific instead of general informed consent. Thus, patients would have the opportunity to obtain additional information about the policy or to seek care elsewhere.

These criteria for the waiver of informed consent should be interpreted narrowly and applied conservatively. For example, a trial comparing a beta-blocker with an angiotensin-converting–enzyme inhibitor for treatment of hypertension should not be approved for a waiver of informed consent, because of the substantially different side effects of the two classes of drugs. Similarly, comparisons of medical treatments and surgical interventions should always require specific informed consent, even if the outcomes are presumed to be similar, because of the probable relevance of patients' preferences to the decision. Finally, specific informed consent should be required whenever a study compares therapies that involve a trade-off between efficacy and safety, as would be the case in a trial of the use of an anticoagulant to reduce the morbidity associated with strokes. This decision requires the balancing of benefits against qualitatively dissimilar risks, necessitating the involvement and specific consent of the patient.

Our arguments may also have important implications for studies that fall under the heading of quality improvement.[10] Consider, for example, a study that seeks to identify the more effective disinfectant hand soap by using one brand for patients in one hospital ward and a different brand for patients in another, with nosocomial infection rates as the outcome measure. The patients are to be randomly assigned to the wards. Should specific informed consent be sought from the patients enrolled in the study? If so, then what should be done if a patient chooses not to participate? (Should he or she be transferred to another ward, or should data not be collected on that patient?) Our criteria may be useful in determining the need for specific informed consent in a context such as this one.

Our arguments pull in two different directions. Greater respect for the autonomy of patients means that many experiments that are currently undertaken in the context of clinical care under the guise of therapeutic innovation should be subject to much greater scrutiny. Such a shift in thinking would have far-reaching consequences, from changing the way that surgeons approach consent for the use of new techniques in the operating room to altering the way that physicians prescribe drugs for indications for which they have not been approved by the Food and Drug Administration (FDA).

Yet we have argued that specific informed consent should not be mandatory for all randomized, controlled trials. Although this idea has been proposed before,[11–14] many will nevertheless find it objectionable. They may argue that it backtracks from crucial elements of human rights at a time when we need to be as vigilant as possible and that essential principles enunciated at Nuremberg and Helsinki must not be compromised under any circumstances. Furthermore, they may claim that informed consent is an essential protection against the exploitation of patients by research investigators. These are important objections.

In response, our proposal should serve as a reminder that the process of informed consent is not a goal or ideal in itself. Rather, informed consent is important because it is frequently essential for ensuring that the patient's right to self-determination is respected. Our proposal not only supports this important objective but also provides grounds for criticizing the inappropriate use of what are termed therapeutic innovations without the specific informed consent of the patient.

There is little evidence to support the claim that informed consent, as currently practiced, provides protection against the exploitation of patients in research. Studies have shown that patients rarely demonstrate an adequate understanding of consent forms[15–17] and often do not even understand the meaning or implications of randomization.[18,19] The most effective protection against exploitation comes not from the process of informed consent but, rather, from the careful oversight and scrutiny of conscientious institutional review boards. Boards that approve questionable studies on the assumption that the informed-consent process will protect research subjects against abuse abrogate their responsibility to defend patients against unethical research. Our proposal recognizes and emphasizes the essential role of institutional review boards in this regard.

In addition, there is a price that is paid when one insists on specific informed consent for all randomized, controlled trials. Many worthwhile studies will not be conducted if investigators are required to obtain specific informed consent. Many small but meaningful improvements in the quality of care will not occur if clinicians are forced to engage every patient in a dialogue about informed consent, especially when there is no reason to believe that the patient would have any preference regarding participation in the research. When unnecessary roadblocks prevent the easy evaluation of the comparative efficacy of new forms of technology and new interventions, these innovations tend to be adopted uncritically into practice.[20] And this result is unfortunate, given that many of them would probably be found worthless or even harmful if subjected to formal evaluation in a clinical trial.

These clinical and practical realities were recently acknowledged in the United States with regard to research under emergency conditions. For many years, research on emergency treatments was virtually paralyzed by the impossibility of obtaining informed consent from the subjects. For new therapies, such as the administration of hemoglobin substitutes in severe trauma and of thrombolytic agents in acute myocardial infarction, or new methods of performing cardiopulmonary resuscitation, systematic clinical trials could not be undertaken. In 1996, the FDA and the Department of Health and Human Services endorsed a waiver of informed consent for this type of research under certain clearly defined conditions. Although they acknowledged the importance of informed consent to medical practice, these agencies endorsed the waiver on the grounds that it would allow desperately ill patients access to new therapies and would result in important benefits to future patients.[21] The agencies recognized that without the waiver, this important work would never be done.[22]

We believe that the same rationale supports our proposal against the anticipated objections of those who prefer to see no exceptions made to the doctrine of informed consent. When benefits to society and to future patients can be gained without meaningfully compromising respect for patients' autonomy and without any serious increase in risk to those involved, blind insistence on informed consent is not only unnecessary, but also harmful.

References

1. Smithells R. Iatrogenic hazards and their effects. Postgrad Med J 1975; 51:Suppl 2:39–52.

2. Shuster E. Fifty years later: the significance of the Nuremberg Code. N Engl J Med 1997; 337:1436–40.

3. World Medical Association. Declaration of Helsinki: recommendations guiding physicians in biomedical research involving human subjects. JAMA 1997; 277:925–6.

4. WMA's Declaration of Helsinki serves as a guide to physicians. JAMA 1964; 189:33–4.

5. Beecher HK. Ethics and clinical research. N Engl J Med 1966; 274: 1354–60.

6. Levine RJ. Research in emergency situations: the role of deferred consent. JAMA 1995; 273:1300–2.

7. Freedman B. Equipoise and the ethics of clinical research. N Engl J Med 1987; 317:141–5.

8. Beauchamp TL, Childress JF. Principles of biomedical ethics. 4th ed. New York: Oxford University Press, 1994:148–9.

9. Curran WJ. The Tuskegee syphilis study. N Engl J Med 1973; 289:730–1.

10. Goldberg HI, McGough H. The ethics of ongoing randomization trials: investigation among intimates. Med Care 1991; 29: Suppl: JS41–JS48.

11. Lantos J. Informed consent: the whole truth for patients? Cancer 1993; 72: Suppl:2811–5.

12. Brewin TB. Consent to randomised treatment. Lancet 1982; 2:919–21.

13. Tobias JD. BMJ's present policy (sometimes approving research in which patients have not given fully informed consent) is wholly correct. BMJ 1997; 314:1111–4.

14. Modi N. Informed consent difficult in paediatric intensive care. BMJ 1993;307:1495.

15. Jubelirer SJ. Level of reading difficulty in educational pamphlets and informed consent documents for cancer patients. W V Med J 1991;87:554–7.

16. Lavelle-Jones C, Byrne DJ, Rice P, Cuschieri A. Factors affecting quality of informed consent. BMJ 1993;306:885–90.

17. Tarnowski KJ, Allen DM, Mayhall C, Kelly PA. Readability of pediatric biomedical research informed consent forms. Pediatrics 1990;85:58–62.

18. Snowdon C, Garcia J, Elbourne D. Making sense of randomization: responses of parents of critically ill babies to random allocation of treatment in a clinical trial. Soc Sci Med 1997;45:1337–55.

19. Appelbaum PS, Lidz CW, Meisel A. Informed consent: legal theory and clinical practice. New York: Oxford University Press, 1987.

20. Sackett DL, Haynes RB, Guyatt GH, Tugwell P. Clinical epidemiology: a basic science for clinical medicine. 2nd ed. Boston: Little, Brown, 1991.

21. Final Rule. Fed Regist 1996;61:51498–533.

22. Ellenberg SS. Informed consent: protection or obstacle? Some emerging issues. Control Clin Trials 1997;18:628–36.

Research on the Vulnerable Sick

Baruch A. Brody PhD

We are in the midst of a reconceptualization of the concept of justice in research. The older conceptualization, the protective conception, emphasized the protection of vulnerable subjects from being used without their consent and from being exploited in excessively risky research. The newer

From *Beyond Consent: Seeking Justice in Research*, JP Kahn, AC Mastroianni, J Sugarman, eds. New York: Oxford University Press, 1998.

conceptualization, the balancing conception, incorporates access to the benefits of research as an additional demand of justice. As a result, justice in research is now seen as demanding a proper balance of access to the benefits of research with protection from unconsented use and from exploitation.

This chapter includes a number of examples of this reconceptualization involving patients for whom established therapies are unavailable or unsatisfactory. The emergence of new experimental therapies that are both promising and risky, is also involved in each case. It is this combination of need, promise, and risk that makes these patients different from other patients and makes them both vulnerable to exploitation and in need of access to better therapies. The initial response in each example was to emphasize justice as protection. Each example raises questions about how protection and access should be integrated to provide us with a balanced theory of justice in research.

The first example, research on patients upon their initial presentation in the emergency room, also requires us to look at the impact of the balancing conception of justice on such fundamental commitments as informed consent. The second example, research involving new treatments for HIV-positive patients, also requires us to examine the ways in which the balancing conception of justice has to be integrated with the social need for adequate evidence before new drugs are approved for general use. The third example, Phase I oncology trials, also requires us to consider how new research designs can improve implementation of the balancing conception of justice.

JUSTICE ACROSS TIME

Research on Patients in the Emergency Room

Past and Present

Medical research in emergency situations where there is no time to obtain consent from a competent patient or his surrogate poses unique concerns. Under what conditions, if any, can this type of research be carried out legitimately without obtaining informed consent? Does it make a difference that there are no available adequate treatments for these patients?

A protective approach was advocated for some years by the Office for Protection from Research Risks (OPRR) of the NIH.[1] According to this approach, research without valid prospective consent in the emergency setting is acceptable only if (1) it involves no more than minimal risks, (2) does not adversely affect the rights and welfare of the subject, and (3) cannot otherwise be carried out practically. With this approach, both therapeutic and nontherapeutic research could be approved without consent, because of its minimal risk. However, research could not be carried out without prospective consent, no matter what the possible benefit to the patient, if the risks were more than minimal or if other subjects (e.g., those who can consent or who are accompanied by someone who could consent for them) could be found.

Consider, as one example, the NIH trial of tissue plasminogen activator (TPA), a clot-dissolving drug, for the treatment of patients with ischemic strokes produced by clots in the arteries leading to the brain.[2] There is a desperate need to find better treatments for that often devastating emergency. TPA offered great promise (in light of both theoretical plausibility and the results of two small unblinded studies of escalating doses of TPA), but it involved considerable risks (especially the risk of bleeding). The trial was conducted on patient-subjects treated within the first 3 hours from the onset of symptoms, with half of them being treated within the first 90 minutes. While the authors report that informed consent was obtained for each patient-subject, the very narrow time frame makes it difficult to believe that most of those who consented really understood the complex issues relevant to participating when they consented. Moreover, their obvious anxieties and fears raise serious questions about whether their consent was due to desperation rather than a voluntary choice. Nevertheless, the trial was a great scientific and medical success, and

TPA is now[3] recommended for such patients. Given the realities of the consent process and the risks from bleeding, it is doubtful that this trial included meaningful informed consent or that it was acceptable by the standards of the protective conception of justice advocated by the OPRR.

A number of points emerge clearly from this example. First, there is no doubt that prior independent review of such research protocols, required under all regulatory proposals, must be undergone; there is, after all, no reason not to have such research protocols reviewed in advance. This provides some measure of protection against exploitation of vulnerable subjects. Second, if meaningful prospective consent from the patient or a surrogate can be obtained, it should be, both to provide further protection against exploitation and to protect subjects from being enrolled in research without their consent or the consent of a surrogate. The question is what to do about planned risky but important emergency research that has been independently reviewed and approved but for which truly meaningful informed consent cannot be obtained.

One approach, favored by some of the researchers in emergency medicine,[4] attempted to justify the research by obtaining retrospective consent (often called "deferred consent") from the patient-subjects or from their surrogates. These researchers appealed to studies[5] that showed overwhelming approval of this approach, but doubts can be cast both upon those studies and upon the rationale of using retrospective consent to justify earlier enrollment. In what sense is the patient's deferred consent relevant to justifying the earlier research given that a refusal would be irrelevant since the research has already been done?

A second approach, advocated by a coalition of critical care researchers, proposed[6] that emergency research without consent should be acceptable even if the incremental risks (those greater than the risks of receiving the standard treatment for the condition in question) are more than minimal as long as these incremental risks

are still likely in the judgment of the independent review board to be acceptable to the vast majority of potential patients. They called this approach the appropriate incremental risk approach. Even this proposed liberalization might have difficulty justifying the stroke research since the intervention in question posed substantial incremental risks from bleeding.

A third approach, adopted by the Council of Europe,[7] emphasized that such research can proceed without consent provided that it is "intended for the direct health benefit of the patient." On this account, it is the benefits to the patient-subject that justifies research without consent. But this account fails to balance these possible benefits with the need to protect vulnerable subjects.

It makes sense to balance all of these factors (the vulnerability of the subjects, the possible benefits to them, the need to protect them from the risks of the research, the possibility of getting some degree of consent beforehand, and the possibility of finding other subjects) in deciding whether or not to approve the research protocol. Just such an approach has recently been adopted by the FDA.

On October 2, 1996, the FDA issued final regulations allowing for a waiver (in certain cases of emergency research) of the requirement of obtaining informed consent from research subjects or their surrogates.[8] Many of the commentators on the earlier proposed version of these regulations saw them as a major retreat from the fundamental moral requirement of obtaining informed consent before research can be conducted. But it is more appropriate to view them as a recognition of the existence of multiple values surrounding the research effort that need to be balanced in particular cases.

What are these values? They include:

1. the social need for research in an emergency to test treatments for patients presenting with acute crises such as strokes for which there are few valuable treatments that limit the resulting disabilities;

2. the potential benefit to some patient-subjects (those in the treatment group) who receive new therapies if those therapies are successful;
3. the need to protect these individuals from being exploited by researchers and harmed by new therapies that turn out to be harmful;
4. the right of all individuals to not be used as research subjects without consent.

In the nonemergency setting, all four of these values can be respected. Needed research takes place after informed consent from those subjects who decide that the potential benefits outweigh the potential risks. But in the emergency setting, this joint realization of all four values may not be possible. The subjects or surrogates may not be able to give informed consent. Even if consent is obtained, the pressure of time, fear, and anxiety raises serious questions about whether that consent is meaningfully informed or truly voluntary.

The FDA's regulations offer a new balancing of the related values. They accept the possibility that conducting the research may be morally licit even if informed consent is not obtained. Instead, the research is justified when the other three values are present to a significant extent. This becomes clear by examining the requirements that must be satisfied before the waiver is authorized.

Under the regulations, waivers may only be issued when "the human subjects are in a life-threatening situation, available treatments are unproven or unsatisfactory, and the collection of valid scientific evidence . . . is necessary to determine the safety and effectiveness of particular interventions." (21 CFR 50.24 (a1)) This requirement ensures that the value of social need is significantly present. The significant presence of the value of potential benefit to the patient-subjects in the treatment group is ensured by the requirement that "appropriate animal and other preclinical studies have been conducted, and the information derived from those studies and related evidence support the potential for the intervention to provide a direct benefit to the individual subjects." (21 CFR 50.24 (a3ii)) The significant presence of the third value of protecting vulnerable subjects from being harmed is ensured by a number of special mechanisms. These include, in addition to the usual IRB review, community consultation (21 CFR 50.24 (a7i)), supervision of the research by a data and safety monitoring board (21 CFR 50.24 (a7iv)), and FDA approval through its Investigational New Drug approval mechanism even when the drug being tested is already approved for other indications (21 CFR 50.24 (d)).

If prospective informed consent is seen, as it was in the OPRR's earlier protective conception of justice in the research setting, as an absolute demand of justice, then none of this makes a difference. The research is still using people as subjects without their consent, and that is unjust. The injustice is heightened by the fact that their vulnerability may be exploited as there are serious risks associated with their involvement. But whatever the risk, it is unjust to use people this way.

The FDA regulations make sense only when one stops seeing the moral world as governed by the protective conception of justice. Justice consists of balancing many independent values, none of which are absolute. These values may in some cases be jointly satisfiable. When they are not, their respective significance in different cases leads to different values being given different priorities in different cases. It is this balancing conception of justice that justifies the approach found in the FDA regulations.

Future Trends

This is not to say that all is in order with the regulations. There are two issues that deserve further thought. One is in cases where informed consent is obtainable if we are willing to accept a slower enrollment rate. The other concerns the control group.

Suppose that the time available for using the experimental therapy is longer than 3 hours from the onset of symptoms. This allows for finding more surrogate decision makers to give consent if the patient-subjects cannot, although there will still be many surrogates who cannot be found in the time in question. It also gives the potential consenters more time to understand the issues and to give a more meaningful consent. Shall we then require that only those for whom consent may be obtained be enrolled? What if this means a significant delay in enrolling the needed number of patient-subjects to complete the study? Moreover, is this fair to those who lose the potential benefits of participation because they cannot consent and their surrogates cannot be found? How shall the values be balanced in such a case?

This is not a purely theoretical question. A recent trial[9] of free radical scavengers for patients with severe closed-head injury illustrates these difficult questions. Treatment was provided within 8 hours of the time of injury. Of the 463 patients enrolled, consent was obtained from surrogates of 408. The other 55 were enrolled without surrogate consent, using the concept of deferred consent. What should be done in such cases under these FDA regulations? Shall we enroll such subjects, enabling them to receive the potential benefit and enabling society to answer the crucial research question more quickly? Or shall we give a higher priority to informed consent, only enrolling those for whom meaningful consent is obtainable, and extending the time needed to answer the research question?

The FDA regulations are not sufficiently clear on this point. They do provide (21 CFR 50.24 (a5–a6)) for seeking consent where possible even when the waiver has been issued. But the waiver can be issued as long as "the clinical investigation could not practicably be carried out without the waiver." (21 CFR 50.24 (a4)) This leaves the question open: how much of a delay in completing enrollment makes waiting for those for whom consent can be obtained impractical?

IRBs and the FDA, both of whom have to approve such waivers, will have to engage in delicate casuistic balancings, deciding this question on a case by case basis; the balancing conception of justice is not mechanically applicable.

The other issue relates to the control group. The FDA regulations specifically allow for emergency research using a placebo-controlled design (21 CFR 50.24 (a1)). The scientific advantages of such a study are familiar. But is it ethically justifiable in such a case? I am not raising here the general question of the ethics of placebo-controlled research, an issue I have extensively addressed elsewhere.[10] What I am raising is the issue of its justification in the situations in which a waiver of the requirement for informed consent can be issued. Under the regulations, the condition being studied must be life-threatening, available treatments must be unproven or unsatisfactory, and there must be evidence supporting the potential for a direct benefit as well as a favorable risk-benefit ratio. These are precisely the conditions under which, on many accounts,[11] it is hardest to justify placebo-controlled trials even with consent. But here, those who are getting the placebo have not even consented to being in the trial, so justifying a placebo-control group is harder.

I am not claiming that such placebo-controlled trials can never be justified in cases where a waiver has been issued. The best cases will be those in which the evidence supporting the potential for benefit is modest. But, of course, the more modest that evidence, the harder to justify the waiver on the grounds that it benefits the patient-subjects who receive the experimental treatment. Therefore, placebo-controlled trials run under a waiver will be justified only when there is some, but not enough, evidence supporting the treatment as beneficial. IRBs and the FDA, both of whom have to approve such waivers, will again have to engage in delicate casuistic balancings on a case by case basis as they decide whether a placebo-control group is justifiable when a waiver has been issued. In doing so, they will have to consider the possibility of alternative trial designs. Once more, the balancing conception of justice is not mechanically applicable.

Neither of these issues is intended as criticism of the basic thrust of the new regulations. They are intended rather as clarifications of the balancings of values that will have to be made on a case by case basis as the new regulations are employed. We will learn a lot about the abilities of IRBs and the FDA to deal with delicate moral deliberations as we study their response to protocols submitted under the new regulations. For now, however, I conclude that the FDA regulations represent the triumph of the balancing conception of justice in research over the earlier protective conceptions of justice.

Research on HIV-Positive Patients

Past and Present

A considerable portion of clinical research is designed to support claims of the safety and effectiveness of new drugs or devices so that they can be approved for general use by the FDA and other national regulatory agencies. This has significant implications for the balancing conception of justice. It means, among other things, that we cannot just balance protecting vulnerable subjects with assuring their access to the newest therapeutic agents. We also need to consider the rights of other patients who are not subjects in the research protocol both to protection against inefficacious and/or dangerous drugs and to quick access to these therapeutic agents if, and as soon as, the benefits of their use have been adequately established. This additional consideration played a role in our discussion of emergency research, when we factored in the issue of completing the study as soon as possible. But it was not the central issue in that discussion, which primarily focused on the research subjects themselves. It will be the central issue in our discussion of our second example of the emergence of the balancing conception of justice: research on HIV positive patients.

Since the reforms of the 1960s in response to the thalidomide tragedy described in Chapter 2, new drugs are approved for use by national regulatory agencies only after their safety and efficacy have been demonstrated with great scientific precision.[12] Because the protective conception of justice was very influential, approval has been a lengthy process, even when the new drugs are desperately needed. This emphasis on the protective conception came under challenge by AIDS activists in the 1980s who demanded quicker access to new drugs. As a result, two major programs have been adopted by the FDA for research on such patients and others like them. One is the Treatment Investigational New Drug (IND) program[13] and the other is the Accelerated Approval (Subpart H) program.[14] I will begin by reviewing these two programs, and I will then discuss the issues of justice raised by them.

The Treatment IND regulations apply to immediately life-threatening ("a stage of a disease in which there is a reasonable likelihood that death will occur within a matter of months or in which premature death is likely without early treatment") or serious (not defined in the regulations) diseases. It allows drugs to be used outside of clinical trials in treating such illnesses providing that "there is no comparable or satisfactory alternative drug or treatment available" and providing that the drug is being investigated in controlled trials or all trials have been completed and the sponsor is actively pursuing marketing approval. In the case of serious illnesses, the FDA may deny a request for a Treatment IND "if there is insufficient evidence of safety and effectiveness to support such use." In the case of an immediately life-threatening illness, the FDA may deny a request for a Treatment IND only if "the available scientific evidence, taken as a whole, fails to provide a reasonable basis for concluding that the drug (A) may be effective for its intended use in its intended population or (B) would not expose the patients to whom the drug is to be administered to an unreasonable and significant additional risk of illness or injury." The latter requirements are far less demanding than the former. In a very important passage in its discussion of these regulations when they were issued,[15] the FDA had the following to say in support of this new standard against some of its critics who emphasized a more protective approach:

> Because of the different risk–benefit considerations involved in treating such diseases, FDA continues to believe there needs to be a separate standard for drugs intended to treat immediately life-threatening diseases . . . the level of evidence needed is well short of that needed for new drug approval—and may be less than what would be needed to support treatment use in diseases that are serious but not immediately life-threatening.[16]

Like the Treatment IND program, the Subpart H Accelerated Approval Program applies to all life-threatening or serious illnesses. Unlike the Treatment IND program, however, it constitutes final approval of the use of the drug, not just access while approval is being considered. The program applies to new treatments which "provide meaningful therapeutic benefit to patients over existing treatment," either because particular patients are unresponsive to or intolerant of the existing treatment or because the general response to the new treatment is an improvement over the response to the existing treatment. Most crucially, the Subpart H program explicitly authorizes approval based on surrogate endpoints (e.g., tumor shrinkage for cancer patients and improvements in CD4 counts for AIDS patients), endpoints that are thought to be predictive of clinical benefit. It is this provision that produces the acceleration of the approval, since it is often possible to get data on surrogate endpoints quicker than data on clinical benefits (length of survival or decreased morbidity).

The spirit behind this new program is well illustrated in the following statement in the 1990 Final Report of the National Committee to Review Current Procedures for Approval of New Drugs for Cancer and AIDS (the "Lasagna Report"):

The committee recognizes that, by making new drugs available for marketing at this early stage, when there is substantial evidence but not yet definitive evidence of effectiveness, there is an attendant greater risk of serious adverse reactions that have not yet been discovered. Cancer and AIDS patients have made it clear to the committee, however, that in light of the seriousness of the diseases involved, they are willing to accept this greater risk. Earlier approval of new drugs will mean that the patient will bear greater responsibility, along with the physician, for understanding and accepting the risks involved.[17]

The spirit behind these two programs, the Treatment IND Program and the Accelerated Approval Program, is clear. While sick patients who are not research subjects will continue to be offered protection against inappropriate approval of unsafe and/or inefficacious new drugs, there will also be an emphasis on assuring quicker access to drugs whose promise is supported but not fully established by research data when the patients are very sick and when existing treatments are not that helpful. The actual choice to use these new drugs will be made by patients with the advice of their doctors, and society will not stand in their way once some promising evidence becomes available. Is this new approach appropriate?

It would seem that it is. As in the case of emergency research, justice demands that we balance values rather than treat any single value as absolute. The very need for official approval by such agencies as the FDA before promising drugs can be used by patients who want to use them constitutes a commitment to protecting the vulnerably ill from exploitation. But it is at the same time a limitation of personal autonomy. There are those who treat personal autonomy as an absolute value. They would abolish the need for official approval and would at most allow official agencies to serve as clearinghouses for information that patients and clinicians might consider.[18] They are wrong in making personal autonomy such an absolute value. When people are desperately ill, their illness makes them vulnerable and in need of some paternalistic protection, even if this means limiting personal autonomy. There are also those who treat protecting the vulnerably ill as an absolute value. Until the scientific evidence is complete, they would not allow patients to use promising new therapies. That is why they object to these new programs. They are also wrong. When there is promising evidence from trials, even from trials using surrogate endpoints, those who do not have other good treatments available should be free to take their chances with these promising new treatments, even while further clinical trials continue. The new programs constitute an appropriate attempt to balance respecting personal autonomy and protecting the vulnerable. By balancing these two fundamental values, they constitute an important addition to the balancing conception of justice in research.

Future Trends

This does not mean that all is in order with these new programs. Most crucially, it is important to ensure that both patients and clinicians better understand the ways in which the approval of drugs under these programs differ from the approval of drugs under the conventional system. It is important to ensure that they understand the detriments as well as the benefits of Treatment INDs and of accelerated approval. The current regulations contain no provisions explicitly addressing this issue. While there are extra Subpart H provisions (21 CFR 314.550) relating to promotional materials, they are purely procedural provisions. These new programs may therefore need to be modified. But their existence is a welcome further triumph for the balancing conception of justice over the protective conception of justice in research.

Phase I Trials in Adults with Cancer

Past and Present

Traditionally, the first step in the clinical testing of new cancer drugs is the conducting of Phase I trials. The primary goal of a Phase I trial is to identify the maximum tolerated dose of a new drug. The traditional approach is to administer the drug at a very low dose to an initial cohort of cancer patients who have failed traditional therapy and then to give increasing doses to later cohorts of subjects. Eventually, a dose is reached at which the level of toxicities is sufficiently severe so that it is treated as the maximum tolerated dose. The previous dose level becomes the recommended dose that is tested for efficacy in a subsequent Phase II trial. This is a very protective approach, emphasizing the safety of the early cohorts rather than the likelihood of their receiving a clinical benefit. This represents a protective approach to justice in research regarding these vulnerable subjects.

A recent report[19] from the M.D. Anderson Hospital, gives a good picture of how these trials are run and of their results. The report surveyed all 23 published Phase I trials conducted at that institution during the period 1991–1993. For the trials of drugs not previously tested in humans, a median of 10 dose levels were required before the maximum tolerated dose was reached, and the median resulting recommended dose was 40 times the initial dose given. For the trials of drugs or biologic agents previously tested in humans, a median of 5–6 dose levels were required, and the median resulting recommended dose was less than three times the initial dose given, except for the trials of some of the biologic agents. Of the 610 patients enrolled, 29% got less than 70% of the recommended dose. As can be seen, the conservative protective approach resulted in many subjects getting suboptimal doses of the drugs being tested. There was some response in 19 patients (3%), with four being complete responses and 15 being only partial responses. This is at the lower end of what is usually reported. In reviews[20] of both adult and pediatric Phase I oncology trials from the early 1990s, the response rate was 4%–6%, with more than half coming only at the end of the Phase I trials, where the doses are higher. As can be seen, the conservative protective approach resulted in few subjects receiving any clinical benefit.

In light of these data, two related ethical issues can be raised. They relate to the fact that the subjects in question are both vulnerable and needy because they have life threatening illnesses and few, if any, therapeutic options. The first concerns informed consent for phase I trials. Are the patient-subjects adequately informed about the realities (toxicities and likelihood of benefit) of these trials? Even if they are, do they agree based upon an understanding of the information, or is their agreement based upon a failure of understanding, perhaps related to their vulnerability, that undercuts the validity of the consent? The second concerns the risk/benefit ratio for these trials. Given the substantial toxicities experienced by the subjects, especially those that are close to the end of the trial, and given the low response rate, even near the end of the trial, is there an acceptable risk/benefit ratio? Or is that ratio unacceptable and reflective of exploitation of these vulnerable subjects? Is that ratio improved by the social benefits of these trials, especially if subjects were to consent because of a sense of altruistic concern about future patients? In thinking about both of these issues, we will, of course, need to keep in mind this chapter's fundamental theme of the need to balance protection and access.

Future Trends

Two recent studies support the above mentioned concerns about the informed consent process. One[21] studied 30 patient-subjects in Phase I trials to find out why they participated. The predominant reasons were the possibility of benefit (100%), lack of a better option (89%), and trust in the oncologist (70%). Only 33% talked about helping future patients, the benefit that is most likely to occur. It is certainly possible to interpret these data as at least suggesting that these desperate and therefore vulnerable subjects were exploited by the oncologists they trusted to participate in a trial in the hopes of securing a benefit that they were very unlikely to attain. This troubling possibility is not the only interpretation of the data; an alternative interpretation is that the

patient-subjects clearly understood the situation and knowingly and freely chose to participate with the hope that they might be one of the lucky few who responded. The troubling interpretation is, however, supported by the facts that only one-third clearly understood the purpose of Phase I trials and that only 30% acknowledged that the no-treatment-except-for-palliation option had been discussed as an alternative to participation in the Phase I trial (although it was mentioned in the consent forms they signed).

A 1996 report from the ACHRE also highlighted these issues. As part of its work, it conducted a project called the Research Proposal Review Project (RPRP) and concluded on the basis of it as follows:

> . . . we reviewed consent forms that appeared to overpromise what research could likely offer the ill patient and underplay the effect of the research on the patient's quality of life. . . . Not surprisingly, this problem was the most acute in the RPRP among Phase 1 trials that, while not being nontherapeutic in the strict sense, appeared to offer only a remote possibility of benefit to the patient-subject . . . desperate hopes are easily manipulated.[22]

These concerns about informed consent are obviously very serious. They cannot be overcome by the balancing of values that allowed for research without informed consent in the emergency situation, because here one cannot, among other things, appeal to the potential therapeutic benefits of participation. But these concerns are manageable if we can find better consent processes for Phase I trials. Among the suggestions that can be offered,[23] even without the modifications in the trial designs discussed below, are the following:

1. patients need to be told very explicitly that the likelihood of any response is very low and that the few responses are not particularly significant;
2. patients need to be told very explicitly that the purpose of the trial is to learn about

toxicities so that better trials can be run for future patients that might help them;

3. patients need to be told very explicitly that the trial is designed to keep on escalating the doses until significant toxicities are reached so that they are at risk of suffering those toxicities;

4. patients need to be told explicitly which cohort they are in and what is the significance of that fact both for the slim likelihood of benefit and the much larger risks of suffering toxicities;

5. patients need to be told very clearly about good palliative care as a legitimate alternative;

6. finally, patients need to be encouraged to think about the relative importance to them at this point near the end of their life of altruistic motives, even if that is not their major reason for enrolling.

If all of this information could be conveyed so that it was understood, then the ethical concerns about informed consent would be alleviated. It remains to be seen what the enrollment rate would be in Phase I trials for which such consent was obtained.

I now turn to the more difficult issues about the acceptability of the risk/benefit ratio. It needs to be remembered that even if subjects consent to participation in a research protocol, that protocol is illegitimate and against all the international standards for research ethics if the risk/benefit ratio is sufficiently unfavorable. Even when informed consent is necessary for legitimate research, it is not sufficient. Are then the risk/benefit ratios in Phase I trials acceptable?

It seems to me that this issue of risk/benefit ratio is directly related both to current debates about the design of Phase I trials and to our discussion in this chapter about the balancing conception of justice.

The traditional design of Phase I trials is quite conservative, emphasizing the protection of the research subjects from excessive toxicities. For example, the starting dose is chosen, based on animal toxicology data, to be at a level considered to be minimally toxic. As a result of that policy and similarly conservative policies governing the escalation of dosages, many subjects receive dosages that are significantly below the dosage ultimately recommended for study in the succeeding Phase II trial. While these dosages are safer, they are also more likely to be nontherapeutic. With this approach, an acceptable risk/benefit ratio is achieved for many subjects by protecting them from toxicities, but at the cost of lowering an already low likelihood of therapeutic benefit. Given what we know about why these subjects are enrolling in the Phase I trial, is that much protection appropriate? Is this approach downplaying the desired access to dosages that are more likely to be therapeutic?

Several alternative approaches to the design of Phase I trials have recently been advocated. I am particularly interested in variations on the continual reassessment method (CRM).[24] The basic ideas behind that method are to treat the subjects from the very beginning at the dosage anticipated to be recommended for study in the Phase II trial and to adjust that anticipation as toxicity data becomes available. This Bayesian approach (an approach relying upon initial estimates of likely results) offers the hope of more responses, but at the price of more experienced toxicities. The resulting risk/benefit ratio is acceptable because of the greater chance of benefit, the very chance that motivates enrollment. Access to potential benefit is emphasized more than protection from toxicities.

It is important to keep in mind that the information conveyed in the informed consent process will have to be modified if such a design is adopted. Points (3) and (4), about how dosages are modified from one cohort to another and about the meaning of being in a particular cohort, will certainly have to be modified. But there may also be a need to modify what is said about the likelihood of responses and of toxicities.

There is obviously balancing to be done here. We want to protect these vulnerable subjects from excessive toxicities. At the same time, we want to give them a better chance of access to dosages that are more likely to be effective. We also want to complete the Phase I trial as soon as possible so that trials of efficacy can begin. How to best balance these three goals in a proper trial design is unclear. However, there is good reason to take a less conservative approach than the traditional approach, given what motivates these adult subjects to volunteer. This would be more in keeping with the balancing conception of justice.

The traditional design of Phase I trials saw dying patients as vulnerable and as requiring protection. That is why its approach, to the choice both of the initial dose and of the successive doses, is so conservative. It represents the protective conception of justice in research. Perhaps it is too conservative. We need to better balance protection with assuring access to promising therapies, both for those in the Phase I trials and for those who will be enrolled in the succeeding Phase II and Phase III trials. Newly proposed Bayesian designs may be more successful in achieving this needed balance. Developing better versions of these designs, and shaping an informed consent process that conveys what is involved in Phase I trials with these new designs, is a major challenge for the balancing conception of justice in research.

CONCLUSIONS

Reconceptualizations are often best assessed by their products. This chapter demonstrates the success of the recent reconceptualization of justice in research from justice as protection to justice as balancing. In this new balancing conception, justice in research involves balancing the values of protecting vulnerable research subjects, of promoting their access to new needed therapies, and of meeting the social need for research to validate new needed therapies.

Adopting this balancing conception of justice has led to better standards for emergency research by emphasizing the value of meeting the

social need for research as well as the value of protecting vulnerable subjects. Adopting this balancing conception of justice has led to valuable programs such as the Treatment IND Program and the Subpart H Accelerated Access Program by emphasizing the value of promoting access to needed therapies as well as the value of protecting vulnerable subjects. Adopting this balancing approach has led to the search for better designs of Phase I trials by emphasizing all three values.

Few other reconceptualizations have been so productive.

Notes

1. *OPRR Reports* 91–01; May 15, 1991.

2. National Institute of Neurological Disorders and Stroke rt-PA Stroke Study Group, "Tissue Plasminogen Activator for Acute Ischemic Stroke," *NEJM* 333(24):1581–1587; December 14, 1995.

3. Michael McCarthy, "New Guidelines Recommend rt-PA for Ischaemic Stroke," *Lancet* 348:741; September 14, 1996.

4. N. S. Abramson, *et al.*, "Deferred Consent," *JAMA* 255:2466–2471; 1986.

5. N. S. Abramson, *et al.*, "Deferred Consent: Use in Clinical Resuscitation Research," *Annals of Emergency Medicine* 19:781–784; 1990.

6. M. Biros, *et al.*, "Informed Consent in Emergency Research," *JAMA* 273:1283–1287; 1995.

7. Recommendation R(90)3, Principle 8.

8. *Federal Register* 61(192):51497–51531; October 2, 1996.

9. B. Young, et al., "Effects of Pegorgotein on Neurologic Outcome of Patients with Severe Head Injury," *JAMA* 276(7):538–543; August 21, 1996.

10. Baruch Brody, *Ethical Issues in Drug Testing, Approval, and Pricing* (New York: Oxford University Press, 1995), pp. 112–131.

11. AMA Council on Ethical and Judicial Affairs, *Ethical Use of Placebo Controls in Clinical Trials*, CEJA Report 2-A-96.

12. Brody, *supra* note 10, chapter III.

13. The regulations governing Treatment INDs are found in 21 *Code of Federal Regulations* 312.34.

14. 21 *Code of Federal Regulations* 314.500–314.560.

15. *Federal Register* 52(99):19468; May 22, 1987.

16. The views of the critics, including Representative Waxman and Senator Kennedy, are nicely summarized in Eaglstein, M.D., "Overview of the Reproposed and Final IND Regulations Concerned with the Treatment Use and Sale of Investigational New Drugs: The Congressional Perspective," *Food Drug Cosmetic Law Journal* Vol.43, pp. 435–442, 1988.

17. National Committee *Final Report* (August 15, 1990) p. 3.

18. Two versions of this position are advocated in H. G. Grabowski and J. M. Vernon, *The Regulation of Pharmaceuticals* (Washington: The American Enterprise Institute, 1983); and D. G. Green, *Medicines in the Marketplace* (London: IEA Health Unit, 1987).

19. T. Smith et al., "Design and Results of Phase I Cancer Clinical Trials," *Journal of Clinical Oncology* 14:287–295; 1996.

20. These surveys are summarized in C. Daugherty et al., "Perceptions of Cancer Patients and their Physicians Involved in Phase I Trials," *Journal of Clinical Oncology* 13:1062–1072; 1995.

21. *Ibid.*

22. Advisory Committee on Human Radiation Experiments, "Research Ethics and the Medical Profession," *JAMA* 276:403–409; 1996.

23. Useful discussions are found in E. Emanuel, "A Phase I Trial on the Ethics of Phase I Trials," *Journal of Clinical Oncology* 13:1049–1051; 1995; B. Freedman, "Cohort-Specific Consent" *IRB*, [12]:5–7; Jan./Feb., 1990; and Y. Willems, C. Sessa, "Informing Patients about Phase I Trials," *Acta Oncologica* 28: 106–107; 1989.

24. J. O'Quigley et al., "Continual Reassessment Method: A Practical Design for Phase I Clinical Trials in Cancer," *Biometrics* 46:33–48; 1990.

Ethical and Human-Rights Issues in Research on Mental Disorders That May Affect Decision-Making Capacity

Alexander M. Capron LLB

FOR research with human subjects, the more things change, the more they remain the same. In the 50-odd years since the 10 principles of the Nuremberg Code were set forth by the U.S. judges who convicted the Nazi concentration-camp physicians of crimes against humanity, the tensions inherent in using human beings as a means to advance biomedical knowledge have surfaced repeatedly. Ever more detailed codes and regulations from governments as well as professional bodies, such as the World Medical Association in its oft-revised Declaration of Helsinki,[1] have not put the subject to rest. Indeed, the lesson of the past half-century is that suffering, death, and violation of human rights can arise not only when dictators give inhumane scientists free rein to treat human beings as guinea pigs,[2,3] but also when well-meaning physicians conduct research in a free and enlightened society.[4–6]

The most recent evidence of this phenomenon can be seen in two sets of problems: those associated with local supervision of research with human subjects in general and those that arise in psychiatric research, particularly that involving children and patients who are unable to make informed, voluntary decisions about their participation in such research. The two types of problems have come together in a number of instances, as investigators and institutions conducting research on mental disorders have been found by courts and federal bureaus, such as the Office for Protection from Research Risks at the National Institutes of Health, to have violated applicable statutes and regulations.

From *N Engl J Med* 340: 1430–1434, 1999.

In a series of reports released in June 1998, the inspector general of the Department of Health and Human Services concluded that reforms were needed in the system of review by institutional review boards (IRBs) at both the local and the national level.[7] Since the passage of the 1974 National Research Act, universities and other research centers have been required to use IRBs to protect the rights and welfare of human subjects. Research institutions provide the Department of Health and Human Services with single- or multiproject assurances that their IRBs will apply the federal rules to all federally funded research conducted at the institution or by its employees; many assurances encompass all research with human subjects regardless of sponsorship. The inspector general concluded that the IRB system is in jeopardy because the local boards are overworked, they fail to oversee approved studies, their members lack sufficient training, and they face inherent conflicts of interest.[7] These problems persist because the Office for Protection from Research Risks and its counterparts in other departments have neither the resources nor the independence to provide adequate guidance to IRBs, much less to monitor their activities.

Nowhere have the problems with this delegation of federal authority been more apparent in recent times than in research on mental disorders. There have been press accounts of abuses at major institutions—particularly a series in the *Boston Globe* in November 1998[8] that concluded with an editorial calling on the Justice Department to conduct a criminal investigation—as well as congressional hearings on studies in which mental symptoms were provoked through either the withdrawal of medication or the administration of drug challenges to psychiatric patients or children.

The difficulties run deeper than inept review by IRBs or inadequate consent forms.[9] They involve not only the actions of individual researchers or the failings of their institutions but also conflicts over principles and objectives in the entire enterprise of medical research. These conflicts have not been—and may never be—resolved. Developing knowledge about human diseases and their treatment ultimately depends on using people as experimental animals. As articulated in the Nuremberg Code and reaffirmed since then, exposing people to risk in the name of science becomes licit only with their informed, voluntary consent. Today we add to that requirement the prior review of research protocols by IRBs to weed out projects whose scientific merit does not justify their risks and to ensure that accurate and understandable descriptions of the research will be conveyed to subjects. Yet even if IRBs did their job perfectly, their approval was never intended to substitute for consent freely provided by potential research subjects.

What, then, should happen when research focuses on conditions that interfere with a person's capacity to provide informed consent? Not too long ago, the prevailing view was that when consent could not be obtained (because of the mental incapacity of a child or a person with a mental disorder) "procedures which are of no direct benefit and which might carry risk of harm to the subject should not be undertaken."[10] Over the past 30 years, however, two exceptions have seriously eroded the prohibition against enrolling incapacitated subjects in research protocols. First, it now seems widely accepted that research would be unnecessarily impeded if such subjects could not be enrolled with the permission of their guardians when the research presents no more than minimal risk. Second, guardians may also enroll patients who lack decision-making capacity in riskier research that can reasonably be predicted to provide the patient with direct benefits that would otherwise be unattainable. Many of the problematic situations regarding research with mentally impaired subjects are connected to the second exception. It is the first, however, that actually raises graver issues.

THE PROBLEMS OF THERAPEUTIC RESEARCH

The Nuremberg Code—framed, as it was, in the context of research in concentration camps on unconsenting prisoners—made no exception for therapeutic intent in its consent requirements. The World Medical Association, however, reflected the prevailing medical view when it framed the 1964 Declaration of Helsinki around the "fundamental distinction . . . between clinical research in which the aim is essentially therapeutic for a patient, and clinical research the essential object of which is purely scientific and without therapeutic intent."[1] Although this articulation of the categories is seriously flawed,[11] the conclusion that "therapeutic research" should be subject to more relaxed standards of consent was incorporated into U.S. policies by the National Commission for the Protection of Human Subjects of Biomedical and Behavioral Research—for example, in its 1977 report on research involving children,[12] which led to federal regulations, and its 1978 report on institutionalized mentally infirm patients,[13] which never became part of the regulations regarding research on human subjects.

Yet the conventional formulation has it backwards. As a general rule, as I have written elsewhere, we should "set higher requirements for consent" and "impose additional safeguards on therapy combined with experimentation [than on research with normal volunteers], lest investigators even unwittingly expose 'consenting' patient-subjects to unreasonable risks."[14] The risk is not simply that patients who are recruited for research will become victims of what is called the therapeutic misconception—that is, construing research interventions as advantageous (especially when no other proven intervention exists) even when the prospect of benefit is in truth nonexistent or at best extremely remote.

The greater risk is that everyone involved, from the investigator to the members of the IRB to society at large, will allow this misconception to blind them to the reality that the entire rationale for supporting and pursuing research is that even the careful accumulation of observations derived from treatment interventions (in which choices are framed in terms of what is best for a particular patient) is not an adequate way

to produce reliable, generalizable medical knowledge. Rather, the achievement of such knowledge requires a scientific approach in which, as Hans Jonas cogently observed, the subject of research is not an agent any longer but a "mere token or 'sample' . . . acted upon for an extraneous end without being engaged in a real relation."[15] Indeed, a collective therapeutic misconception may lie behind the shift in the paradigm over the past decade: today, many investigators, IRB members, and commentators alike apparently think the primary ethical requirement is no longer to protect research subjects from harm (especially in the case of those least able to protect themselves) but to avoid the perceived injustice of excluding potential subjects from studies.

There may be no medical field in which the limited effectiveness of available treatments generates more persistent despair among patients, their families, and physicians than mental illness. This despair is particularly evident with respect to conditions that radically compromise their victims' ability to function successfully in the world, to be themselves, and to enjoy the sense of safety and stability that most people take for granted. That sense of desperation has led to a willingness to permit research in which the potential for harm would lead any rational person to decline to participate. IRBs have, for example, approved "washout" studies, in which medications that successfully prevent symptoms in patients with schizophrenia are withdrawn, apparently on the basis of the investigators' suggestion that such studies offer the prospect of benefit because antipsychotic medication can have harmful side effects and some patients successfully stop medication after a while. But if the real purpose of the study is to develop criteria for predicting which patients are most likely to relapse, and if the manner and timing of the washout are dictated by the protocol rather than by the needs or preferences of individual patients, it is wrong to characterize the study as aiming to provide subjects with benefit, which will occur adventitiously if at all.[9]

ASSESSING THE CAPACITY TO CONSENT TO PARTICIPATE IN RESEARCH

The dangers in lowering standards of protection in therapeutic research are exacerbated for patients whose disorder may impair their capacity to make decisions. For this reason, the National Bioethics Advisory Commission, of which I am a member, recently recommended that IRBs "should require that an independent, qualified professional assess the potential subject's capacity to consent" to any protocol presenting more than minimal risk, unless the investigator provides good reasons for using less formal assessment procedures (recommendation 8).[16] This recommendation was criticized on the grounds that such assessments would stigmatize patients with mental disorders insofar as they are not routine for research on the medically ill. However, it would not stigmatize potential subjects in the world's eyes to tell them that the research design requires that their capacity to consent be evaluated, since that information would remain entirely within the confidential relationship between the potential subjects and those carrying out the research project. As any competent patient should quickly realize, such a requirement reflects no disrespect for potential subjects, though it may indicate some concern about the conflicting motives of researchers.

Nor are the norms of fairness violated by imposing such a requirement when none exists for research in other areas. Even if empirical investigation showed that decision-making capacity is just as likely to be as compromised among patients suffering from other medical conditions as among those with mental illness, it is not prejudicial to insist that investigators take reasonable steps to make sure that subjects whose condition directly affects the brain can actually provide voluntary, informed consent. The objection based on unequal treatment would seem much more fitting if researchers on mental disorders already routinely used appropriate means to assess their subjects' decision-making capacity and were simply urging that investigators in other areas be held to the same standard. The National Bioethics Advisory Commission reviewed protocols for a number of recently published studies of mental disorders, all of which involved more than minimal risk to participants. Many involved patients with serious psychiatric conditions. Not a single protocol gave evidence of any effort on the part of the researchers to assess subjects' decision-making capacity. Nor was such a requirement apparently imposed by any IRB in approving these protocols.

The failures, if any, of researchers in other fields do not excuse the lack of attention on the part of psychiatric researchers to one of the basic prerequisites for ethical research. Insisting that the capacity to consent be appropriately assessed does not contradict the presumption, which applies to patients with mental disorders as to every other potential research subject, that all adults are competent. Ignoring the prima facie need for some evaluation of the ability to consent makes a mockery of that presumption by rendering it nothing more than a convenient rationale for ignoring the fact that the consent obtained from some subjects may not be valid.

The National Bioethics Advisory Commission further concluded that, whether or not the research offers the prospect of direct medical benefit to subjects, the enrollment of a subject depends on one of three procedures: informed consent, if the subject has decision-making capacity; "prospective authorization" for a particular class of research, given when the subject was still competent; or permission from a legally authorized representative chosen by the subject or from a concerned relative or friend who is available to monitor the subject's involvement in the research and who will base decisions about participation on "a best estimation of what the subject would have chosen if [still] capable of making a decision" (recommendations 11 through 14).[16] Moreover, even when research is intended to benefit subjects, objection by any subject (even one who lacks decision-making capacity) to enrolling or continuing in a protocol "must be heeded" (recommendation 7).[16]

THE USE OF PATIENTS IN RESEARCH TO BENEFIT OTHER PATIENTS

As compared with the harm that has arisen from the more lenient standards for therapeutic research, the other exception to the requirement of personal consent—namely, allowing guardians to enroll incapacitated subjects when the research presents no more than minimal risk of harm to the patient—may seem not to be problematic. Any difficulties this exception creates would seem to center around the vagueness of the term "minimal risk." Yet this exception has far-reaching, troubling effects.

The exception arose initially in the context of research with children. A flat prohibition against using children in research that provides them no direct benefit was seen as a barrier not only to conducting medical examinations and similar procedures to accumulate data on normal functioning, but also to using standard psychological tests or observational tools. Some theorists argued that guardians' permission should be honored as vicarious consent in such situations (on the presumption that, were they capable of deciding, children as reasonable people would recognize their obligation to aid the community) and as an exercise of appropriate paternalism (that is, a guardian by volunteering a child's participation is teaching the child the importance of sacrifice for the sake of others).[17] Even more important was the idea that parents' choice to expose their children to the risks of everyday life encompasses children's enrollment in research studies posing minimal risk. The same reasoning was then applied to other potential subjects who lacked the capacity to make decisions for themselves, including adults with various illnesses and injuries.

The exception for studies posing no more than minimal risk establishes the principle that it is acceptable to expose unconsenting people to some risk—not for their own direct good, but for the good of some larger group. But if minimal risk is acceptable, what about permitting participation when there is a minor increase over minimal risk? That is precisely what the National Commission for the Protection of Human Subjects recommended in 1977[12] and the Department of Health and Human Services adopted for research with children in 1983.[18] Furthermore, the regulations link the allowable interventions to those inherent in subjects' "actual or expected medical, dental, psychological, social, or educational situation," meaning that greater risks and burdens may be imposed on sick children than on healthy ones.

Psychiatric researchers urged the National Bioethics Advisory Commission to adopt a similar approach for people whose mental disorders prevented them from consenting to participate in research. This is what an advisory group in New York did when it recommended allowing surrogate decision makers to permit persons incapacitated with respect to decision making to participate in nonbeneficial research that presented a minor increase in risk over the minimal level.[19] The commission, however, rejected the creation of this intermediate category, whose nebulous nature only compounds the vagueness of minimal risk.

"Minor increase" is just the camel's head and neck following the nose of "minimal risk" into the tent. The flexible nature of these categories invites a relativist view, in which the addition of a little burden or risk to the lives of patients with chronic mental illnesses can easily be justified by the prospect of substantially advancing medical knowledge. Once IRBs become used to this way of thinking, it is easily applied not just to federally funded basic research but also to clinical trials of new drugs, which are less likely to advance scientific knowledge than to offer financial rewards to the pharmaceutical manufacturers that sponsor the trials and the clinicians who are paid to conduct them.

The Need to Confront Problems Openly and Solve Them

Occasionally, research may offer the prospect of developing critical knowledge about a disease or ways of treating it that cannot be obtained in any other way than by studying subjects who have the disease. If all who suffer from the condition are permanently unable to decide for themselves whether to participate in the research, and if it would be impossible for them to agree in advance to become subjects and to appoint a representative to make decisions on their behalf, then society may wish to ask whether this might be the rare case in which researchers may add the risk of injury to the insult of the illness that already burdens the patients.

An affirmative response to that question amounts to placing some especially vulnerable people in a role that, however worthy, is not one that they have chosen. If such a step is to receive the thoughtful attention it deserves, it should be confronted openly, not behind the doors of a local IRB but in a much more public forum. And the group that considers it must do what IRBs seldom do—namely, look at every aspect of the study design (has everything possible been done to reduce the chance of injury and to ameliorate any adverse event that does occur?), the selection of subjects (among all who suffer from the disease, why was this group chosen, and are no others available who are more able to assent or object to their participation?), the reliance on surrogate decision making (are the people asked to provide permission for these subjects actually able to do so in an informed, voluntary fashion?), and the claimed infeasibility of obtaining the subjects' consent (is the condition one in which prospective authorization is truly impossible, or is it merely inconvenient for the researchers?).

It seems likely that a body will be established to consider just such issues. Steven Hyman, the director of the National Institute of Mental Health (NIMH), has announced plans to create a new review panel to screen high-risk intramural and extramural studies funded by the institute.

He also plans to eliminate "some of the repetitious 'me-too' studies in the intramural portfolio," in a separate initiative that is linked to the creation of the new review body "by a desire to make sure that the science in NIMH studies is good enough to justify the use of human subjects."[20]

Dr. Hyman may hope his move will blunt the effect of the recommendation by the National Bioethics Advisory Commission that the secretary of the Department of Health and Human Services appoint a special standing panel to review protocols that IRBs would be unable to approve on their own under the commission's proposed regulations (recommendation 2). The reason to assign this task to a national panel is to provide a process that is more visible, more knowledgeable, and more independent than can be expected from many IRBs. The special standing panel would review principally protocols that expose subjects to greater than minimal risk yet are not intended to benefit them directly and for which the subjects are not able to give informed consent and have not previously provided prospective authorization (recommendation 12). Besides approving studies employing methods that an IRB regards as posing more than minimal risk to participants, the special standing panel could in time reclassify some of these methods as ones that IRBs could approve for particular types of research with specified groups, without further review and approval by the panel. The guiding principle, as the commission puts it, is that the special standing panel should never "approve a protocol that reasonable, competent persons would decline to enter."[16] That principle does not resolve the tension inherent in research involving incapacitated persons, but at least it does not hide it.

Experience over the past two decades has made clear the need for special protection for patients with mental disorders. The regulations and official actions—as well as the recommendations for IRBs—of the National Bioethics Advisory Commission are the minimum needed. The federal government should adopt them without further delay.

References

1. World Medical Association. Declaration of Helsinki. N Engl J Med 1964;271:473–4.

2. Alexander L. Medical science under dictatorship. N Engl J Med 1949;241:39–47.

3. Annas GJ, Grodin MA. The Nazi doctors and the Nuremberg Codes: human rights in human experimentation. New York: Oxford University Press, 1992.

4. Jones JH. Bad blood: the Tuskegee syphilis experiment. Rev. ed. New York: Free Press, 1993.

5. United States Advisory Committee on Human Radiation Experiments. Final report on human radiation experiments. New York: Oxford University Press, 1996.

6. Hornblum AM. Acres of skin: human experiments at Holmesburg Prison: a true story of abuse and exploitation in the name of medical science. New York: Routledge, 1998.

7. Department of Health and Human Services, Inspector General. Institutional review boards: a time for reform. Washington, D.C.: Department of Health and Human Services, 1998.

8. Kong D, Whitaker R. Doing harm: research on the mentally ill. Boston Globe. November 15–18, 1998: A1.

9. Katz J. Human experimentation and human rights. St Louis Univ Law J 1993;38:7–54.

10. British Medical Research Council. Responsibility in investigations on human subjects. In: Report of the British Medical Research Council for 1962–63. London: Her Majesty's Stationery Office (Cmnd. 2382), 1963:23–4.

11. Levine RJ. Ethics and regulation of clinical research. 2nd ed. Baltimore: Urban & Schwarzenberg, 1986:8–10.

12. National Commission for the Protection of Human Subjects of Biomedical and Behavioral Research. Report and recommendations: research involving children. Washington, D.C.: Government Printing Office, 1977.

13. *Idem*, Report and recommendations: research involving those institutionalized as mentally infirm. Washington, D.C.: Government Printing Office, 1978.

14. Capron AM. The law of genetic therapy. In: Hamilton MP, ed. The new genetics and the future of man. Grand Rapids, Mich.: Eerdmans, 1972:133–56.

15. Jonas H. Philosophical reflections on experimenting with human subjects. In: Freund PA, ed. Experimentation with human subjects. New York: George Braziller, 1970:1–31.

16. Research involving persons with mental disorders that may affect decisionmaking capacity. Rockville, Md.: National Bioethics Advisory Commission, November 12, 1998.

17. McCormick RA. Proxy consent in the experimental situation. Perspect Bio Med 1974;18(1):2–20.

18. 48 Fed Reg 9818, March 8, 1983, codified at 45 CFR §§ 46.406–46.408, 1998.

19. New York State Advisory Work Group on Human Subject Research Involving the Protected Classes. Recommendation on the oversight of human subject research involving the protected classes. Albany: State of New York Department of Health, 1998. (App. D, Proposed regulations, p. D-56, §20 (b) & §20 (d).)

20. Marshall E. NIMH to screen studies for science and human risks. Science 1999; 283:464–5.

The Child as Research Subject

Lainie Friedman Ross MD, PhD

1. PROXY CONSENT

The Nuremberg Code was adopted in 1946 in response to the documented abuse of human beings as research subjects by the Nazis. The Code was quite explicit that '[t]he voluntary consent of the human subject is absolutely essential'.[1] There was no mention of proxy consent; the subject had to be able to consent to participation. Later codes

From Lainie Friedman Ross, *Children, Families, and Health Care Decision-Making*. New York: Oxford University Press, 1998.

of ethics included the possibility of participation by incompetent subjects by permitting proxy consent.[2] Whether such consent is morally adequate, particularly when the incompetent subjects are children, was the topic of a series of articles between two American Christian theologians, Paul Ramsey and Richard McCormick, in the early 1970s. Despite contributions by many other ethicists, there remains vigorous disagreement within the medical ethics community as to the morality of a child's participation as a research subject.

Here I address the moral question of whether and when children can serve as subjects of human experimentation. My goals are to show that (1) children *can* participate morally as human subjects; (2) the present regulations are overbroad in the scope of research in which children can participate; and (3) the present regulations place too much emphasis on the young child's dissent.

2. CAN CHILDREN MORALLY PARTICIPATE AS HUMAN SUBJECTS?

In the early 1970s, Ramsey argued that children should never participate as research subjects in 'non-therapeutic research'[3] (that is, research which offers no direct therapeutic benefit to the children subjects). His first argument is that for research to be moral it requires the informed consent of the subject. Because the child cannot give informed consent, his parents must act as his surrogate. However, parental responsibility to their child is fiduciary, and to authorize their child's participation is a breach of this duty.[4]

McCormick rejected Ramsey's argument, using a natural law approach that states that parental consent 'is morally valid precisely insofar as it is a reasonable presumption of the child's wishes'.[5] McCormick held that there are 'certain identifiable valuables that we *ought* to support, attempt to realize, and never directly suppress because they are definitive of our flourishing and well-being'.[6] The child, then, would want to participate as a research subject because he ought to

do so.[7] That is, the child would choose to participate because

> [t]o pursue the good that is human life means not only to choose and support this value in one's own case, but also in the case of others when the opportunity arises. In other words, the individual *ought* also to take into account, realize, make efforts in behalf of the lives of others also, for we are social beings and the goods that define our growth and invite to it are goods that reside also in others.[8]

Ramsey rebutted McCormick's argument on the grounds that it was too broad and would justify compulsory altruism.[9] At the extreme, if McCormick's arguments are valid, 'then anyone—and not only children—may legitimately be entered into human experimentation without his will [consent]'.[10]

Ramsey's second argument against using children as research subjects is based on the Kantian principle that persons should never be treated solely as a means, but always simultaneously as an end.[11] Ramsey argued that the use of a child as a research subject in research which offers no direct therapeutic benefit treats the child solely as a means. While it may serve useful societal goals, it fails to serve the child subject's interests and thus cannot be performed morally.

McCormick objected to this argument on the grounds that it presumes an atomistic view of humans. Humans are social beings whose good transcends their individual good. Participation as a research subject is consistent with treating the child as an end understood to mean a social being.[12] The problem with this argument, as McCormick realized, is that it can require the participation of adults in research projects to which they do not give their consent,[13] and while McCormick tolerates this enforced Good Samaritanism, most ethicists and legal scholars do not.

The debate initiated by McCormick and Ramsey continues. The primary consequentialistic motivation for refuting Ramsey's position is that excluding children from research will have long-term negative consequences on the well-being of children in general. Ramsey realized the danger of prohibiting children from participating in all non-therapeutic research because it would leave children 'therapeutic orphans'.[14] His solution was to exhort researchers to 'sin bravely': the trustworthy researcher was the one who did 'not deny the moral force of the imperative he violates'.[15]

Ramsey's arguments are powerful and they remind us of the problems that researchers face when dealing with incompetent subjects. One promising line of argument to justify the participation of children is to refute Ramsey on the grounds that his perspective regarding parental responsibility is too narrow. Henry Beecher argues that parents can authorize a child's participation to promote the child's moral development: 'Parents have the obligation to inculcate into their children attitudes of unselfish service. One could hope that this might be extended to include participation in research for the public welfare, when it is important and there is no discernible risk.'[16]

William Bartholome also argues that parents have the moral authority to permit their children to participate in human experimentation in order to promote their children's moral education.[17] Taking this position further, Terrence Ackerman contends that parents have a *moral duty* to guide the activities of their children because children rely upon adults for guidance. Respect for a child, then, requires that parents 'carefully direct his "choices"'.[18]

Nevertheless, neither Beecher nor Bartholome believed that parental consent was sufficient. Beecher argued for both the child's and the parents' informed consent and given this, only permitted children over the age of fourteen to serve as research subjects.[19] Bartholome took a more liberal view and allowed for the participation of children with their parents' consent if the children could give assent, even if not effective consent.[20] The problem with both of these positions is the practical one that children are usually ill prepared to refuse requests by their physicians and parents.[21]

Ackerman, in contrast, argues that requiring the child's assent makes a mockery both of our duties to children and of their limited present-day capabilities to act autonomously: 'We cannot decide how to intervene in a child's life by projecting what he will come to approve or accept. For what he will come to accept is partly a product of the interventions we make.'[22] Rather, Ackerman argues, parents alone can and must decide whether their children should participate as research subjects.[23]

Although I agree with Ackerman's assessment, he does not offer adequate guidance regarding the limits of parental authority, and whether the child's assent is ever relevant, particularly when the risks are more than minimal. In section 6, I will use the model of constrained parental autonomy to refute Ramsey's arguments. This model will also allow me to formulate guidelines that impose limits on parental autonomy and that delineate the proper role for the child's developing competency and autonomy. These guidelines will be suitably different from those that presently regulate the child's role in human experimentation.

3. RESEARCH GUIDELINES FOR CHILDREN

The first guidelines that specifically addressed the role of children in research were produced by the German Ministry of the Interior in 1931.[24] In the United States, recommendations for the participation of children in research were first developed in the 1970s by the National Commission for the Protection of Human Subjects of Biomedical and Behavioral Research.[25] Based on the National Commission's report, the Department of Health, Education, and Welfare (DHEW) circulated preliminary regulations in 1978.[26] In 1983, the newly overhauled Department of Health and Human Services (DHHS) published the revised Federal Regulations regarding the participation of children in human experimentation.[27] In the United Kingdom, in contrast, four distinct guidelines existed regarding the participation of children by 1980.[28] In 1986, the Institute of Medical Ethics working group on the ethics of clinical research investigations proposed new recommendations based on moral theory.[29] Since then, the Medical Research Council and the British Paediatric Association have updated their guidelines.[30] These guidelines are quite similar to (and refer frequently to) the report by the National Commission unless noted otherwise.

The report by the National Commission begins by justifying its decisions to allow children to participate in human experimentation:

> The Commission recognizes the importance of safeguarding and improving the health and well-being of children, because they deserve the best care that society can reasonably provide. It is necessary to learn more about normal development as well as disease states. . . . Accepted practices must be studied as well, for although infants cannot survive without continual support, the effects of many routine practices are unknown and some have been shown to be harmful.[31]

Although the Commission acknowledged the need to do research on children, it also realized that 'the vulnerability of children, which arises out of their dependence and immaturity raises questions about the ethical acceptability of involving them in research'.[32] To minimize these problems, the Commission established strict criteria that research would need to satisfy. The Commission's report sets them out as follows:

a. The research is scientifically sound and significant;

b. Where appropriate, studies have been conducted first on animals and adult humans, then on older children, prior to involving infants;

c. Risks are minimized by using the safest procedures consistent with sound research design and by using procedures performed for diagnostic or treatment purposes whenever feasible;

d. Adequate provisions are made to protect the privacy of children and their parents and to maintain confidentiality of data;

e. Subjects will be selected in an equitable manner;

f. The conditions of all applicable subsequent conditions are met, and adequate provisions are made for the assent of the child and permission of their parents or guardians.[33]

The Commission recommended additional criteria depending upon the level of risk and harm that the research entailed, the risk/benefit of the proposed project, and the comparative risk/benefit of the alternatives. Local institutional review boards (IRBs) would be created to ensure that these safeguards were fulfilled.[34]

The National Commission classified risk into three categories: minimal risk, a minor increase over minimal risk, and more than a minor increase over minimal risk.[35] The Commission defined minimal risk as 'the probability and magnitude of physical or psychological harm that is normally encountered in the daily lives, or in the routine medical or psychological examination, of healthy children'.[36] The Commission gave several examples including routine immunizations, modest changes in diet or schedule, physical examinations, obtaining blood and urine specimens, and developmental assessments.

When research entails no more than minimal risk, the Commission's recommendations permit the participation of a child as a subject of human experimentation.[37] If the research involves more than minimal risk, the Regulations require the local IRB to determine whether the research presents the prospect of direct therapeutic benefit to the individual patient subject.[38] If the IRB determines that it does, and that the benefits are as favourable to the subjects as those offered by non-experimental alternatives, then the child can serve as a research subject.[39]

However, if the research does not offer the prospect of direct therapeutic benefit, then the IRB can approve the project *only* if the research is likely to yield generalizable knowledge 'of vital importance'.[40] The risks involved in this research may entail only 'a minor increase over minimal risk'.[41] Research that involves greater risk without the prospect of direct benefit (or with the prospect of benefit that is inadequate to justify the risk) may be permitted *only* if it presents 'a reasonable opportunity to further the understanding, prevention, or alleviation of a serious problem affecting the health or welfare of children'.[42] As an additional safeguard, this research requires approval by national review.[43]

Provisions for the solicitation of consent are also under the supervision of the IRBs. For most research, both parental permission and the child's assent are necessary. The Commission explicitly stated that 'assent of the children should be required when they are seven years of age or order'.[44] The Commission emphasized that the child's dissent should be binding except when the research offers the potential of direct therapeutic benefit to the child, in which case the parents can override the child's dissent. The Commission maintained that the decision to override a child's dissent 'becomes heavier in relation to the maturity of the particular child'.[45] The Regulations also require that consent includes parental permission and the child's assent but leave unspecified the age when assent should be sought. Rather, they leave it to individual IRBs to take into account 'the age, maturity and psychological state of the children involved'.[46]

Nevertheless, the National Commission's report and the Federal Regulations do allow for waivers to the consent process. For example, parental permission is not necessary if the research is related to conditions for which adolescents may receive treatment without parental consent,[47] or if the research is designed to understand and meet the needs of neglected or abused children.[48] Alternatively, the child's assent is not necessary if the research offers the prospect of direct therapeutic benefit, and/or if the child is determined to be unable to give assent (e.g. newborns).

4. RISK

A central feature of the Regulations is the classification of the research activity according to the degree of risk. As previously stated, the Commission defines minimal risk as 'the probability and magnitude of physical or psychological harm that is normally encountered in the daily lives, or in the routine medical or psychological examination, of healthy children'.[49]

There are several drawbacks to using a standard which compares research activities with typical or routine activities. Ross Thompson argues that a standard based on 'the normative daily experiences of children at different ages fails because . . . it potentially permits researchers to act in ways that undermine the child, even though these experiences may be familiar to the child'.[50] Thompson argues that children commonly encounter experiences at school that threaten their self-image, but this does not justify similar threats in the research setting. Investigators should be hesitant to violate basic ethics principles, although these principles may be regularly violated by others in their everyday life.[51]

The Commission's use of a comparative definition also threatens to increase the vulnerability of children with chronic illnesses, because a child who has been treated for cancer and has received intrathecal medications[52] would find a non-therapeutic lumbar puncture more commensurate with his life experiences than would a healthy child. To use his previous experience to justify additional lumbar punctures for non-therapeutic purposes is highly problematic.[53]

Ackerman suggests that one way to improve the Commission's definition of risk is to understand activities which are 'normally encountered by a child' not to mean any activity which a child may have previously experienced, but rather an activity with which the child is familiar and with which he is able to cope well: 'The fact that a sick child has undergone a particular procedure, such as a lumbar puncture, during treatment does not guarantee that he or she will not be subjected to considerable stress or anxiety.'[54] He has offered the following standard of minimal risk as an alternative: 'A research procedure involving minimal risk is one in which the probability of physical and psychological harm is no more than that to which it is appropriate to intentionally expose a child for educational purposes in family life situations.'[55] I adopt this standard because it allows parents to balance the responsibility of protecting their child from harm and promoting their child's moral development.

The Commission's guidelines are more vague when research involves more than minimal risk. The Commission does not offer a working definition for either 'a minor increase over minimal risk' or 'more than a minor increase over minimal risk'. Rather, it states that in its determination of degree of risk and harm, the IRB should

> consider the degree of risk presented by the research from at least the following four perspectives: a common sense estimation of risk, an estimation based upon the investigators' experience with similar interventions or procedures, statistical information that is available regarding such interventions or procedures, and the situation of the proposed subject.[56]

The Commission assumed that there would be agreement within the medical community as to what constitutes different degrees of risk. Jeffery Janofsky and Barbara Starfield distributed a questionnaire to paediatric investigators to assess their perception of the degree of risk associated with a variety of paediatric procedures that are typically used in clinical research, and found few procedures for which there was consensus.[57] Although it had been suggested that the American Academy of Pediatrics create a special task force to develop consensus opinions about the risks of paediatric procedures and interventions to avoid such problems,[58] no such task force was created.

Not only is there disagreement as to which procedures impose what degree of risk, but there are also reasons to suspect that researchers and IRBs underestimate risk. Peter Williams explored three reasons why IRBs tend to underestimate risk.[59] First, most members of an IRB are members of the research community and are inherently biased in support of the value of research and may overestimate the importance of research projects in general. Second, IRBs tend to suffer from group think. Citing James Stoner, Williams explains: '[G]roups confronted with choices involving risks were willing to take more chances than the average of individuals in the groups.'[60]

Third, IRBs have two purposes, which are often in tension: to protect the rights of subjects and to promote their welfare. To respect the subject's right to make an autonomous choice is to allow her to gather all the information regarding a potential trial and decide whether or not to participate. When the subject is a child, her rights are protected by promoting the autonomy of her parents. Institutional protection of the subject's welfare, on the other hand, entails promotion of the subjects' well-being. As such, it might require the universal proscription of certain research projects (e.g. research involving deception), regardless of whether the subject himself or his guardians might consent to participate. Given IRB committee members' own biases in favour of research and self-determination, they tend to do a better job promoting the subjects' right to act autonomously than they do in protecting the subjects' welfare.

Assuming that consensus could be obtained regarding the amount of risk and harm of different procedures, consensus also would be needed to define '*direct* therapeutic benefit'. Too rigid a distinction between research that offers '*direct* therapeutic benefit' and other research creates a false dichotomy. Sometimes, it is not known initially whether the project will offer *direct* therapeutic benefit. At other times, a project may be undertaken for a purely scientific purpose, and yet may offer the subjects some *indirect* therapeutic benefit. As the Regulations now stand, such *indirect* therapeutic benefit must either be ignored and the research classified solely by its degree of risk, or the research must be classified as offering a *direct* therapeutic benefit which overstates its expected clinical value. The distinction is important as it determines the level of risk that the Regulations permit and whether the child's dissent is binding. The following example illustrates concerns about indirect therapeutic benefits.

In the United States, pharmaceutical tests of new chemotherapeutic compounds are done in four stages. The first phase determines the drug's ability to kill cancer cells in relationship to its potential to kill healthy cells. Even if a drug has been shown to be effective in killing cancer cells in a test tube, questions remain as to whether the compound can kill cancer cells in patients and whether its toxicity will interfere with its potential usefulness. To characterize these trials as offering the prospect of *direct* therapeutic benefit is very misleading. The distinction is critical, because it changes the level of risk that the Regulations permit and whether the child's dissent is binding. If the trials offer the prospect of *direct* therapeutic benefit, parents can authorize their child's participation over the child's dissent, regardless of the level of risk. However, if these trials do not offer any direct therapeutic benefit, children can participate only if the risk entails no more than a minor increase over minimal risk *and* the child assents. I propose the inclusion of another category to accommodate phase I tests which would offer the potential for 'indirect therapeutic benefit',[61] the potential for generalizable knowledge, and would entail no more than a minor increase over minimal risk. I label this category of research §46.406β to emphasize that it is a subset of section 46.406 of the Federal Regulations.

This may be overstating a difference. Research which offers only the potential for indirect benefit may be coercive to families of critically ill children, particularly since there may be no research which does not offer the potential for indirect benefit. The healthy child who participates as a normal control for a research protocol may become critically ill in the future and benefit from the research. To that extent, all research has potential indirect benefit for all subjects. A crucial difference is that the indirect benefits from research in category 46.406β are needed by the subjects immediately.

I propose one further modification to the classification scheme of the Federal Regulations. The Regulations presently classify all minimal risk research under section 46.404. Minimal risk research which offers a direct therapeutic benefit should be classified under section 46.405.

5. INFORMED CONSENT

The Federal Regulations require that a research protocol has adequate provisions for the procurement of informed consent. The informed consent standard and process were first described by the courts in *Salgo v. Stanford*.[62] The ruling stated that physicians must disclose to the patient the nature of the illness, the harms, risks, and benefits of the proposed procedure and its alternatives as well as the consequences of refusing treatment. The patient, in turn, must give voluntary consent or refusal. Nine years after *Salgo*, the surgeon general proposed similar guidelines for obtaining informed consent in all research that was federally funded.[63]

Despite these standards, most studies show that patients do not give informed consent for proposed therapies,[64] and subjects give inadequate consent for their participation in research protocols.[65] Many explanations exist why patients and subjects do not give informed consent including the failure of physician-scientists to disclose fully the risks, benefits and alternatives,[66] the tendency of ill persons to conflate the roles of patient and subject and physician and scientist,[67] and the overreliance by physicians on informed consent forms which are unreadable to most patients and subjects.[68]

Failures in the informed consent process lead to serious inequities in research as the process serves as a social filter: better-educated and wealthier individuals are more likely to refuse to participate and are underrepresented in most research.[69] The problem is perpetuated in paediatrics because parents who volunteer their children are less educated and underrepresented in the professional and managerial occupations compared to their non-volunteering counterparts.[70]

The National Commission chose seven years as the age at which children should be included in the consent process. The Commission cited empirical evidence that by seven years, most children have some understanding of the research project and the procedures that they entail. The Commission's guidelines require investigators to explain the procedures to children older than seven years in language which they can understand and then to seek their assent. The Commission held that the child's dissent should be binding unless the research offered direct therapeutic benefit in which case parents could override their child's dissent.[71] Although the Regulations did not adopt strict age limits, it retained the spirit of the Commission's report.[72]

Although the Regulations seek increasing respect for children's decisions as they mature,[73] they do not offer specific guidelines that distinguish between the decisions made by competent and incompetent children. In contrast, I propose a three-tiered classification scheme which can adequately account for children's developing maturity and their evolving role in the consent process. The three categories are (1) the category in which the child is incapable of giving assent (e.g. infants); (2) the category in which the child is capable of giving assent, but is incompetent to give full and effective voluntary consent (e.g. school-aged children); and (3) the category in which the child is capable of giving effective and voluntary consent (e.g. the child in mid- to late adolescence). The value of this three-tiered classification scheme will become clearer when I discuss the distinction between research categorized under section 46.406 and the revision I propose, 46.406β, below.

6. Constrained Parental Autonomy as a Moral Framework that can be Used to Justify Minimal-Risk Research (section 46.404)

The Regulations permit some research on children which offers no prospect of direct therapeutic benefit to the children subjects. Ramsey argued that a child can never morally participate as a research subject when the research does not offer the prospect of direct therapeutic benefit.[74] His arguments can be refuted using the model of constrained parental autonomy.

Ramsey argues that parents cannot give informed consent for their child's participation in activities which do not directly benefit the child. The argument that parents can consent only to activities which directly benefit their child holds parents to a best interest standard. Two problems with this standard are that it permits too much state intervention and does not allow for parents to balance the needs of the child with the needs of other family members. In reality, parents are not held to a best interest standard because it would be too intrusive into the daily routine of most families. For example, parents often take their children on self-serving errands and excursions and no one suggests that they should not be allowed to do so. Similarly, parents rear their children according to their own religious and cultural beliefs even when they know that the inculcation of minority beliefs and values may reduce or restrict their child's opportunities. I argue that parents should have presumptive decision-making authority for their children and that parental autonomy should be questioned only if their decision is disrespectful of the child's developing personhood. This does not mean that the parents' decision is best, only that giving parents wide discretion promotes the child's well-being while respecting both parental autonomy and family autonomy.

Ramsey's second objection that the child's participation does not treat the child as a Kantian person is correct. But children are not full Kantian persons and whether their participation is morally permissible must be based on a modified principle of respect. Parental authorization of their child's participation in research of minimal risk and harm does not necessarily treat the child solely as a means. Rather, parents who value participation in social projects will try to inculcate similar values into their child. It is likely that their child will come to share in some, if not most, of their values. To the extent that the child can be expected to share in such social goals, his participation promotes his life plans even if his assent is unattainable at the time. Even if he never shares in these goals, they are goals which responsible parents may try to inculcate into their child.

To justify a child's participation as a research subject, I must refute Ramsey's arguments and show that the child's participation is consistent with the modified principle of respect. Consider, again, minimal-risk non-therapeutic research. This research presents no more risk than that which a child typically experiences, or using Terrence Ackerman's standard, such research presents no more risk than that which is encountered in many activities to which parents typically expose their children for educational purposes. Many activities in a typical child's life present greater risks, including such routine activities as the participation in contact sports and travelling in the family car. Not only is it impossible to live in a risk-free world, but also it is contrary to the pursuit of a meaningful life plan. The development of autonomy requires that children be allowed to take some risks. Parents are morally and legally authorized to decide which risks their child may take and in what settings. Parental authorization or prohibition of their child's participation in minimal-risk research is not abusive or neglectful, even if the child is forced to participate against his will. Rather, it is one way in which parents can attempt to steer their child's

development into a socially responsible adult. They may or may not succeed, but it is reasonable for them to try to guide his development in this way.

This conclusion is at odds with the recommendations of the National Commission and the guidelines of the Federal Regulations.[75] Both recommend that the child's assent or dissent be binding in minimal-risk non-therapeutic research. I am arguing that this recommendation does not pay enough deference to parental autonomy. The model of constrained parental autonomy permits parents to override their child's dissent in minimal risk research if they believe that it will serve to guide his development according to their vision of the good life, realizing that their child may ultimately reject this conception of the good. This may not be the best way for parents to guide their child's development, but the goal is not to define the ideal parent-child relationship. Given a liberal community's tolerance of a wide range of conceptions of the good, state intervention is only justified if the parents' decision is abusive, neglectful, or exploitative, not if an alternative is better.

The arguments presented so far only justify the child's participation in research which entails minimal risk. In the next sections, I consider the impact that the probabilities and degrees of risks and benefits should have on the child's participation and on the child's role in the decision-making process.

7. WHETHER UTILITARIAN ARGUMENTS CAN JUSTIFY THE CHILD SUBJECT'S PARTICIPATION AS A RESEARCH SUBJECT

Ramsey sought to prohibit all research that failed to offer direct benefit to the child subject, even if the risks were minimal. I have argued that this position fails to respect parental autonomy. Parents can authorize their child's participation in research which entails minimal risk, even over their child's dissent, without disrespecting the child's personhood. At the other end of the spectrum is section 46.407 of the Federal Regulations, which states that if the risks are more than a minor increase over minimal risk and the research does not offer the prospect of direct benefit (or offers the prospect of benefit that is inadequate to justify the amount of risk), then the research can be justified only if it offers the 'opportunity to understand, prevent, or alleviate a serious problem affecting the health or welfare of children'.[76]

The moral justification for the child's participation in such research is utilitarian; it permits the enrolment of a child as a research subject if the costs (harms and risks) to the child are significantly outweighed by the potential benefit to society at large. This suggests that when the stakes are high enough, the ends may justify the means. Beecher, one of the earliest critics of the morality of human experimentation in the United States wrote: 'An experiment is ethical or not at its inception. It does not become ethical *post hoc*—ends do not justify means.'[77] Like Beecher, I do not believe that a utilitarian argument can justify a child's participation as a research subject. Although the Regulations require strict national review of such research, this protection is inadequate because such research is inconsistent with the modified principle of respect. The U.K. working group on ethics also concluded that the participation of children in this type of research was immoral and emphasized that this was the one substantive disagreement that they had with the Commission's recommendations.[78]

Imagine that a competent child who can give informed consent, consents to participate in such a research project. If a competent child identifies her good with the research goals and willingly sacrifices her own well-being for society at large, then why not permit her participation as we would permit the participation of a competent adult? Empirical data show that consent to serve as a subject of human experimentation is not a random phenomenon. Rather, subjects tend to be less educated, have less-sophisticated medical knowledge, and less frequently hold professional positions compared to those who refuse.[79] Competent children are at a distinct disadvantage in giving an informed refusal in comparison with better-educated adults. As such, competent children can benefit from extra protection, even if they do not want it. Their consent is insufficient. Incompetent children are in need of even greater protection, and so their assent is also inadequate.

Nor can parents authorize their child's participation in this category of research. Although constrained parental autonomy permits parents to balance the risks to one child against the benefits to other family members, the model does not permit such a balance when the risks threaten one child and the benefits are beyond the intimate family. Parents are given wide latitude in balancing the risks and benefits among family members because of the importance of the family's well-being to the parents' and the child(ren)'s well-being. But once parents seek to balance the child's well-being beyond the boundaries of the family, their autonomy ought to be limited. Their focus must be on the individual child's self-regarding interests and developing personhood which are threatened by such research. As such, the potential knowledge to be gained from such research cannot be obtained morally.

Ramsey argued that all non-therapeutic research on children is immoral. He did not prohibit all such research, but concluded that physicians must 'sin bravely'.[80] I argued in section 6 that minimal-risk non-therapeutic research can be performed morally. In contrast, when non-therapeutic research entails more than a minor increase over minimal risk, the participation of children subjects is always immoral and must be prohibited. Review by a national committee is inadequate; the decision to balance the well-being of a particular child against the possibility of large societal benefit is a utilitarian calculus which fails to respect the developing personhood of the child. *All* children should be prohibited from such research, regardless of their competency and despite the utility of the research.

Notes

1. Nuremberg Code, 1946, Principle 1, reprinted in W. T. Reich (ed.), *Encyclopedia of Bioethics*, iv (New York: Free Press, 1978), 1764.

2. See, for example, 18th World Medical Association, 'Declaration of Helsinki: Recommendations Guiding Medical Doctors in Biomedical Research Involving Human Subjects', Helsinki, Finland, 1964 (revised most recently by the 41st World Medical Association in Hong Kong, September 1989). Both the British Medical Association (BMA) and the American Medical Association (AMA) have published ethical guidelines as well. 'Experimental Research on Human Beings' was drafted by the BMA in 1963 and 'Ethical Guidelines for Clinical Investigation' was published by the AMA in 1966. Both have since been revised and expanded to address other ethical concerns of medical practice.

3. The phrase 'non-therapeutic research' implies that the research has a purely scientific purpose and offers no therapeutic (clinical) function in contrast with 'therapeutic research', which implies that the research has both scientific and clinical goals. In practice, the distinction is not clear-cut. Although there are research projects which offer no therapeutic benefits to the subjects (e.g. when a healthy volunteer is paid to participate in a study to determine the metabolism and excretion rate of a new compound), many research projects offer therapeutic benefits, even if only indirectly. In addition, activities commonly referred to as 'therapeutic research' often entail procedures which do not directly benefit the subject (e.g. the process of randomization in clinical trials). The National Commission for the Protection of Human Subjects of Biomedical and Behavioral Research sought to be more precise by using the notion of research which does or does not offer the prospect of direct benefit. The U.K. Institute of Medical Ethics working group on the ethics of clinical research investigations on children found the National Commission's phrases unwieldy and chose to use the terms 'therapeutic' and 'non-therapeutic' for their simplicity and utility. R. H. Nicholson (ed.), *Medical Research with Children: Ethics, Law, and Practice* (Oxford: Oxford University Press, 1986), 26–31. I use the National Commission's phrasing except in response to Ramsey.

4. P. Ramsey, *The Patient as Person* (New Haven, Conn.: Yale University Press, 1970), esp. 11–19.

5. R. A. McCormick, 'Proxy Consent in the Experimentation Situation', *Perspectives in Biology and Medicine*, 18 (1974), 11.

6. McCormick, 'Proxy Consent', 9.

7. McCormick, 'Proxy Consent', 11–12.

8. McCormick, 'Proxy Consent', 12. Of note, McCormick was willing to impose a minimal positive sociability upon competent adults as well (McCormick, 'Proxy Consent', 12–13).

9. P. Ramsey, 'Children as Research Subject: A Reply', *Hastings Center Report*, 7 (1977), 40.

10. P. Ramsey, 'The Enforcement of Morals: Non-Therapeutic Research on Children', *Hastings Center Report*, 6 (1976), 24.

11. I. Kant, *Grounding for the Metaphysics of Morals* (1785) trans. J. W. Ellington (Indianapolis, Ind.: Hackett Publishing, 1981), paragraph 429.

12. R. A. McCormick, 'Experimentation in Children: Sharing in Sociality', *Hastings Center Report*, 6 (1976), 43.

13. McCormick, 'Experimentation', 42.

14. The phrase was coined by H. Shirkey in 1963, according to J. D. Lockhart, 'Pediatric Drug Testing: Is it at Risk?' *Hastings Center Report*, 7 (1977), 8. It refers to those persons with rare conditions that do not receive adequate clinical study and understanding. The result is that clinicians treat these subject-patients using unproven therapies. So, for example, if new medicines could not be tested on children, then paediatricians would have to rely on adult data which may or may not be appropriate for children, who metabolize drugs differently.

15. Ramsey, 'The Enforcement of Morals', 21, citing 'Medical Progress and Canons of Loyalty to Experimental Subjects', *Proceedings of Conference on Biological Revolution/Theological Impact*, sponsored by the Institute for Theological Encounter with Science and Technology, Fordyce House, St. Louis, Missouri (6–8 April 1973), 51–77.

16. H. K. Beecher, *Research and the Individual* (Boston: Little, Brown, 1970), 63.

17. W. G. Bartholome, 'Parents, Children, and the Moral Benefits of Research', *Hastings Center Report*, 6 (1976), 44–5.

18. T. F. Ackerman, 'Fooling Ourselves with Child Autonomy and Assent in Nontherapeutic Clinical Research', *Clinical Research*, 27 (1979), 345.

19. W. J. Curran and H. K. Beecher, 'Experimentation in Children: A Reexamination of Legal Ethical Principles', *Journal of the American Medical Association*, 210 (1969), 77–83.

20. Bartholome, 'Moral Benefits', 44–5. The term 'assent' can be used to refer to both the incompetent and competent child's agreement to participate in his health care plans. In contrast, the term 'consent' refers *only* to an agreement given by a competent person. Consent meets legal standards whereas assent does not. However, by saying that a (competent) child gave his consent, I do not mean to imply that the competent child's consent or refusal needs to be legally binding, only that it meets legal standards.

21. Ackerman, 'Fooling Ourselves', 346–7. Two empirical studies which validate his arguments are A. H. Schwartz, 'Children's Concepts of Research Hospitalization', *New England Journal of Medicine*, 287 (1972), 589–92; and R. Abramovitch, J. L. Freedman, K. Thoden, and C. Nikolich, 'Children's Capacity to Consent to Participation in Psychological Research: Empirical Findings', *Child Development*, 62 (1991), 1100–9.

22. Ackerman, 'Fooling Ourselves', 345.

23. However, Ackerman challenges his own position later in the article when he writes, '[W]e should respect an intractable objection by the child particularly if it is based upon anxiety or fear which cannot be allayed regarding an experimental procedure.' 'Fooling Ourselves', 348.

24. German Reich, 'Circular of the Ministry of the Interior on Directives Concerning New Medical Treatments and Scientific Experiments on Man', (1931) translated in *International Digest of Health Legislation* (Geneva), 31 (1980), 408–11.

25. National Commission for the Protection of Human Subjects, *Report and Recommendations: Research Involving Children* (Washington, DC: U.S. Government Printing Office, 1977), 2–3.

26. Department of Health, Education, and Welfare (45 C.F.R., part 46), 'Protection of Human Subjects: Proposed Regulations on Research Involving Children', *Federal Register*, 43 (July 21, 1978), 31,786–94. Cites to the *Federal Register* will hereinafter be abbreviated in the form 43 Fed. Reg. 31,786–94 (1978).

27. Department of Health and Human Services (45 C.F.R., part 46), 'Additional Protections for Children Involved as Subjects in Research', 48 Fed. Reg. 9814–20 (1983). The guidelines for human experimentation were

revised again in 1991, although the only change with respect to children concerned exemptions which I do not discuss in this book. See 56 Fed. Reg. 28,032 (1991).

28. Medical Research Council, 'Responsibility in Investigations on Human Subjects', *Report of the Medical Research Council for the year 1962–3* (London: Her Majesty's Stationery Office, 1964), 21–5; Royal College of Physicians, *Supervision of the Ethics of Clinical Research Investigations in Institutions* (London: Royal College of Physicians, 1973); Department of Health and Social Security (DHSS), *Supervision of the Ethics of Clinical Research Investigations and Fetal Research*, HSC(IS) 153 (London: DHHS, 1975); British Paediatric Association (BPA), 'Guidelines to Aid Ethical Committees Considering Research Involving Children', *Archives of Diseases of Childhood*, 55 (1980), 75–7.

29. Nicholson, *Medical Research with Children*.

30. Medical Research Council, Working Party on Research on Children, *The Ethical Conduct of Research on Children* (London: Medical Research Council, 1991); British Paediatric Association, *Guidelines for the Ethical Conduct of Medical Research Involving Children* (London: BPA, 1992).

31. National Commission, *Research Involving Children*, 1–2. The report of the working group on ethics offers a similar argument: '[R]esearch on children is desirable and necessary in order to promote the health and well-being of children.' Nicholson, *Medical Research with Children*, 231.

32. National Commission, *Research Involving Children*, 2.

33. National Commission, *Research Involving Children*, 2–3. See also 46 Fed. Reg. 404 (1983).

34. Institutional review boards (IRBs) serve the primary purpose of protecting the rights and welfare of human research subjects. The first federal document to propose committee review of research procedures was dated 17 November 1953 and 'applied only to intramural research at the newly opened clinical center at the NIH [National Institutes of Health]'. Subcommittee on Health of the Committee on Labor and Public Welfare, U.S. Senate, 'Federal Regulation of Human Experimentation', No. 45-273-0 (Washington DC: U.S. Government Printing Office, 1975), as cited by R. J. Levine, *Ethics and Regulation of Clinical Research*, 2nd ed. (New Haven, Conn.: Yale University Press, 1986), 322. The first federal policy was not issued for another decade. On 8 February 1966, the surgeon general issued a memorandum requiring prior review of all research

involving human subjects funded by U.S. Public Health Service Grants. W.H. Steward, 'Clinical Investigations Using Human Subjects' memorandum dated 8 February 1966, cited by Levine, *Ethics and Regulation*, 323.

Initially most IRB committees were composed of scientists and physicians. Revisions in U.S. Public Health Service policy and DHEW and DHHS regulations have evolved to *require* a more diverse composition. The duties of the IRBs have also expanded. The history of IRBs is given in Levine, *Ethics and Regulation*, Chap. 14.

35. The British Paediatric Association used the terms 'negligible', 'minimal', and 'more than minimal' [risk] in its 1980 document (British Paediatric Association, 'Guidelines to Aid Ethical Committees Considering Research Involving Children'). In 1992, it changed the terms to read 'minimal', 'low', and 'high' (British Paediatric Association, *Guidelines* [1992], 9) despite the recommendations of the working group on ethics to use the terminology used by the U.S. National Commission (Nicholson, *Medical Research with Children*, 105 ff.).

36. National Commission, *Research Involving Children*, p. xx.

37. 46 Fed. Reg. 404 (1983).

38. As the regulations are written, research which entails minimal risk and offers a direct therapeutic benefit is classified as minimal risk research (46 Fed. Reg. 404). I argue in section 5 that by the National Commission's own standards, such research should be classified under research that presents the prospect of direct therapeutic benefit (46 Fed. Reg. 405).

39. 46 Fed. Reg. 405.

40. 46 Fed. Reg. 406.

41. 46 Fed. Reg. 406.

42. 46 Fed. Reg. 407a.

43. 46 Fed. Reg. 407b.

44. National Commission, *Research Involving Children*, 13. The working group on ethics recommends the same age. (Nicholson, *Medical Research with Children*, 149–51.)

45. National Commission, *Research Involving Children*, 16.

46. 46 Fed. Reg. 408.

47. 46 Fed. Reg. 408c. The classic example is if the condition falls under the specialized consent statutes. I argue in Chapter 8 that the specialized consent statutes inappropriately exclude parental involvement.

Likewise, I reject the exclusion of parental consent for research done on these conditions.

48. 46 Fed. Reg. 408c.

49. National Commission, *Research Involving Children*, p. xx.

50. R. Thompson, 'Vulnerability in Research: A Developmental Perspective on Research Risk', *Child Development*, 61 (1990), 7.

51. Thompson, 'Vulnerability', 7.

52. Intrathecal medication is drug delivered directly into the cerebrospinal fluid (the fluid around the brain and spinal cord). This is achieved by performing a spinal tap (lumbar puncture) and injecting the medicine through the needle. This creates a high concentration of the drug in the cerebrospinal fluid, which is the intended target.

53. This does not mean that the child who has been treated for cancer can never participate as a research subject. In fact, his cancer treatment was most likely part of an experimental protocol. In addition, his parents may want to encourage his participation if the research is being done to advance knowledge which may be to the child's own benefit, albeit indirectly. My point is only to remind us of this child's increased vulnerability due to his previous illness. He and his family may feel compelled to help the physician in his own research out of a sense of debt.

54. T. F. Ackerman, 'Moral Duties of Investigators Toward Sick Children', *IRB: A Review of Human Subjects Research*, 3 (June/July 1981), 4.

55. T. F. Ackerman, 'Moral Duties of Parents and Non-Therapeutic Research Procedures Involving Children', *Bioethics Quarterly*, 2 (1980), 94–111, as cited in S. L. Leikin, 'An Ethical Issue in Biomedical Research: The Involvement of Minors in Informed and Third Party Consent', *Clinical Research*, 31 (1983), 38.

56. National Commission, *Research Involving Children*, 8–9.

57. J. Janofsky and B. Starfield, 'Assessment of Risk in Research on Children', *Journal of Pediatrics*, 98 (1981), 842–6.

58. A. Lascari, 'Risks of Research in Children', *Journal of Pediatrics*, 98 (1981), 759–60.

59. P. Williams, 'Success in Spite of Failure: Why IRBs Falter in Reviewing Risks and Benefits', *IRB: A Review of Human Subjects Research*, 6 (May/June 1984), 1–4.

60. Williams, 'Why IRBs Falter', 3, citing J.A.F. Stoner, 'A Comparison of Individual and Group Decisions Involving Risk', M.S. thesis, School of Industrial Management, Massachusetts Institute of Technology, 1961.

61. By 'indirect therapeutic benefit' I mean that the intent of the research is not to offer therapeutic benefit, although the conditions of the research make such a benefit possible.

62. Salgo v. Leland Stanford Jr., University Board of Trustees, 317 P.2d 170 (Cal. Dist. Ct. App., 1957).

63. Surgeon general, memorandum, 'Clinical Investigations.'

64. W. A. Silverman, 'The Myth of Informed Consent in Daily Practice and in Clinical Trials', *Journal of Medical Ethics*, 15 (1989), 6–11; and J. Katz, *The Silent World of Doctor and Patient* (New York: Free Press, 1984).

65. See Silverman, 'The Myth', and A.L. Schultz, G. P. Pardee, and J. W. Ensinck, 'Are Research Subjects Really Informed?' *Western Journal of Medicine*, 123 (1975), 76–80.

66. J. Katz, 'Why Doctors Don't Disclose Uncertainty', *Hastings Center Report*, 14 (February 1984), 35–44.

67. Katz, *The Silent World*.

68. See, for example, M. T. Baker and H. A. Taub, 'Readability of Informed Consent Forms for Research in a Veterans Administration Medical Center', *JAMA*, 250 (1983), 2646–8; T. M. Grunder, 'On the Readability of Surgical Consent Forms', *New England Journal of Medicine*, 302 (1980), 900–2; and K. J. Tarnowski, D. M. Allen, C. Mayhall, and P. A. Kelly, 'Readability of Pediatric Biomedical Research Informed Consent Forms', *Pediatrics*, 85 (1990), 58–62.

69. Silverman, 'The Myth'.

70. S. C. Harth, R. R. Johnstone, and Y. H. Thong, 'The Psychological Profile of Parents Who Volunteer Their Children for Clinical Research: A Controlled Study', *Journal of Medical Ethics*, 18 (1992), 86–93.

71. This is why I believe that minimal risk research which offers the potential for direct therapeutic benefit should be classified under 46 Fed. Reg. 405 (1983). The Commission recommended that parents *always* be allowed to override their child's dissent when the research has therapeutic potential (i.e. when research falls under section 46.405). In contrast, the Commission held that the child's dissent in minimal risk research should be binding (i.e. when research falls under section 46.404). Because parents can override their child's dissent in research which entails minimal risk but which also has the prospect of direct therapeutic benefit, it would be better to classify it under section 46.405.

72. The working group on ethics also recommended seven years of age (Nicholson, *Medical Research with Children*, 235), although the new BPA and Medical Research Council (MRC) guidelines do not offer a specific age.

73. National Commission, *Research Involving Children*, 16.

74. In the terms of the classification scheme proposed in table 5.3, Ramsey's claim is that children should participate in research only if it offers the potential for direct benefit (46 Fed. Reg. 405), and that their participation in all other research is immoral. Specifically, Ramsey denies that children can morally participate in minimal-risk research that does not offer the prospect of direct therapeutic benefit (46 Fed. Reg. 404).

75. It is also against the conclusions of the working group on ethics, the BPA, and the MRC.

76. 46 Fed. Reg. 407.

77. H. K. Beecher, 'Ethics and Clinical Research', *New England Journal of Medicine*, 274 (1966), 1360.

78. Nicholson, *Medical Research with Children*, 14.

79. Silverman, 'The Myth'.

80. P. Ramsey, 'The Enforcement of Morals: Nontherapeutic Research on Children', *Hastings Center Report*, 6 (1976), 21.

QUESTIONS FOR DISCUSSION

1. Physicians who conduct clinical trials may persuade their own patients to enter these trials. Is there any conflict of interest or duty in the physician's dual role of giving therapeutic treatment to patients and using them to gain scientific knowledge? Could the clinical trial itself be considered as another treatment option for the patient?

2. Patients in clinical trials are used as means for the advancement of scientific knowledge and the benefit of future patients. How is it possible for patients in these trials to be treated also as ends in themselves?

3. Many argue that using a placebo rather than an active proven treatment as a control in a research protocol fails to serve the best interests of patients and unnecessarily exposes them to the risk of harm. But others argue that a placebo control yields more definitive results for the experimental treatment being tested. Explain why placebo controls can or cannot be justified.

4. Is it ethical to stop a clinical trial before the safety and efficacy of a given drug definitively have been established? On what grounds could stopping a trial prematurely be justified? Give some examples.

5. Patients who are poor or uninsured may be motivated to enter a clinical trial because of the monetary compensation it offers or because it is the only way for them to receive medical care. Does this amount to coercion? If so, how could it be prevented? If it is not coercive, is it ethically justifiable?

CASES

Nuremberg Tribunal (1945–47). A series of legal trials held over several years in Nuremberg, Germany. One of these, the Doctor's Trial, criminally charged twenty Nazi physicians and three medical administrators with subjecting unwilling victims to medical experimentation resulting in disfigurement, disability, or death. The Tribunal drew up the Nuremberg Code, consisting of ten basic principles involving moral, ethical, and legal requirements that all research on human subjects would have to meet. The most important of these are voluntary consent of human subjects to participate in research and the avoidance of unnecessary physical and mental suffering and injury.

Hyman v. Jewish Chronic Disease Hospital 42 Misc. 2d 427 NY (1963). Dr. Emanuel Mandel, Medical Director of the Jewish Chronic Disease Hospital in Brooklyn collaborated with Dr. Chester Southam of the Sloan-Kettering Institute for cancer research in studying the immunological effects of injecting cancer cells under the skin of debilitated elderly patients. A member of the Hospital's board of directors, William Hyman, took action that led the medical disciplinary board of New York State to bring disciplinary charges against Southam and Mandel. They were judged to have acted fraudulently and deceitfully in failing to obtain the informed consent of the experimental subjects.

Willowbrook (1954–71). The Willowbrook State School was an institution for mentally retarded children in Staten Island, New York. Some of the children were used as research subjects in order to develop an effective prophylactic agent against the strain of viral hepatitis prevalent in the institution. The research involved deliberately exposing the children to the virus. The main criticism was that it was unethical to expose children to infected material, particularly those who were mentally retarded, with or without parental consent, when there was no conceivable benefit to the child.

Tuskegee Syphilis Study (1932–72). The United States Public Health Service conducted a study involving six-hundred black men, mostly poor and uneducated, from Tuskegee, Alabama. Four-hundred of these men had been diagnosed with syphilis but were never told of their disease and never treated for it. Neither were they informed that they were research subjects nor that treatment for their condition could have been provided. The other two hundred served as controls. Subjects in both groups were told that they had "bad blood" and that they should have periodic medical examinations. (See the *Final Report of the Tuskegee Syphilis Study Ad Hoc Advisory Panel*. Washington, D. C.: U.S. Government Printing Office, 1973).

UCLA Schizophrenia Relapse Study (1982–93). A research study conducted at the Neuropsychiatric Institute of the University of California, Los Angeles. The study required schizophrenic patients who had recovered from their psychotic disorders to be withdrawn from medication, despite general acceptance that maintenance antipsychotic medication would benefit a substantial portion of chronic schizophrenics. The study aimed to produce a relapse in many patient-subjects to better predict relapse in schizophrenics in general. The consent form signed by the participants did not adequately disclose to them the risks that their participation entailed. In spite of this, the IRB approved the research protocol and the consent form.

SUGGESTED FURTHER READING

Angel, Marcia. "Investigators' Responsibilities for Human Subjects in Developing Countries." *N Engl J Med* 342: 967–969, 2000.

Beecher, Henry. "Ethics and Clinical Research." *N Engl J Med* 274: 1354–1360, 1966.

Brody, Baruch. *The Ethics of Biomedical Research: An International Perspective* New York: Oxford University Press, 1998.

Fried, Charles. *Medical Experimentation: Personal Integrity and Social Policy*. New York: American Elsevier, 1974.

Hellman, D.S., and Hellman, S. "Of Mice but not Men: Problems of the Randomized Clinical Trial." *N Engl J Med* 324: 1589–1592, 1991.

Johnson, N. et al. "At What Level of Collective Equipoise Does a Clinical Trial Become Ethical?" *J Medical Ethics* 17: 30–34, 1991.

Kahn, J.P., et al., eds. *Beyond Consent: Seeking Justice in Research*. New York: Oxford University Press, 1998.

Katz, Jay, et al. *Experimentation with Human Beings*. New York: Russell Sage, 1972.

Levine, Robert. *Ethics and Regulation of Clinical Research,* Second Edition. New Haven: Yale University Press, 1988.

Marquis, Don. "How to Resolve an Ethical Dilemma Concerning Randomized Clinical Trials." *N Engl J M* 341: 691–693, 1999.

Michels, Robert. "Are Research Ethics Bad for Our Mental Health?" *N Engl J Med* 340: 1427–1431, 1999.

Shalala, Donna. "Protecting Research Subjects—What Must Be Done." *N Engl J Med* 343: 808–810, 2000.

PART IV:

REPRODUCTIVE RIGHTS AND TECHNOLOGIES

In the case of *Roe v. Wade* in January of 1973, the U.S. Supreme Court ruled that state law could not restrict the right of a woman to abort a fetus during the first trimester of pregnancy. To support its ruling, the Court maintained that a fetus is not a person as interpreted under the 14th Amendment and, therefore, does not have the rights of persons generally guaranteed by the Constitution. The rights to an abortion elevated the autonomy of women to make decisions pertaining to their own bodies over any putative rights or claims of early-stage fetuses. Yet this ruling left the power to make laws regarding the safety of the abortion procedure relative to maternal health during the second trimester of pregnancy to the states. Moreover, in the third trimester, once the fetus was viable, or capable of existing outside the womb, state law could prohibit abortion except when it was necessary to preserve the life and health of the pregnant woman.

Reproductive ethics became much more complicated on July 25, 1978 with the birth of Louise Brown in England. Louise's mother had damage to her fallopian tubes and was unable to conceive through natural biological means. Ova were retrieved from Mrs. Brown through laparoscopy, fertilized with Mr. Brown's sperm in vitro, and the embryo was implanted in the uterus of Mrs. Brown, who became the first woman to carry an implanted embryo to term. This event was significant also because it marked the first time that a child was conceived without sexual coitus. It raised a new set of ethical questions. For example, do embryos have any moral status outside the womb? If they do not, then is it permissible to destroy them or use them for medical research? These questions, and the practice of in vitro fertilization (IVF) that generated them, broadened the ethical debate about human reproduction beyond the question of women's right to abortion.

Other advances in the science of reproductive technology complicated the ethical landscape even further. In 1985, the issue of surrogate gestation emerged with a high-profile case. William and Elizabeth Stern agreed to pay Mary Beth Whitehead $10,000 to bear a baby conceived through artificial insemination using Mr. Stern's sperm. After "Baby M" was delivered, Ms. Whitehead refused to surrender the child, claiming that she was its natural mother. The Sterns sued to enforce the surrogacy contract, which was upheld by the New Jersey Superior Court but then was ruled invalid by the state Supreme Court, which restored the surrogate Ms. Whitehead as the mother of the child. Among other things, this case showed that a child could have four mothers—genetic, gestational, lactational, and social—and two fathers—genetic and social.

The prospect of cloning human beings either through embryo splitting or nuclear transfer is important because it involves asexual human reproduction. While this idea had been raised and discussed earlier, the announcement in February of 1997 by Ian Wilmut and colleagues in Scotland that they had cloned a sheep through somatic cell nuclear transfer triggered a plethora of commentaries on the ethical implications of cloning humans. These included claims of genetic determinism and reductionism, whether cloned children would be instrumental means for the selfish ends of vainglorious parents, and more generally what cloning would mean for our understanding of ourselves as members of the human species.

The increased use of fertility drugs, such as Clomid and Pergonal, has led to an increased incidence of multiple gestations in pregnancy. One of the most notable cases in this regard has been that of the McCaughey septuplets who were born in Iowa in 1998. The main ethical question here is whether, given the risk of complications and harm to the fetuses as well as to the woman carrying them, it is permissible to selectively terminate some to reduce the risk to the others. Furthermore, there is the question of whether the use of fertility drugs should be permitted.

Amniocentesis and chorionic villus sampling during fetal gestation, or genetic testing of preimplantation embryos, can determine the sex, race, and perhaps even the sexual orientation of the child who would be born from an embryo or fetus. This raises questions about whether sex selection perpetuates sexism, racism, and homophobia, as well as how this concern weighs against the idea that parents' reproductive autonomy gives them the right to practice sex selection if they believe that it would be in the best interests of their child. All of the issues in Part IV have arisen from the dramatic advances in the science of reproductive technology over the last 25 years.

In the first selection, Mary Briody Mahowald explores the meaning of the right to have a baby. She discusses artificial insemination of sperm, the misleading notion of egg "donation," and surrogate gestation. Regarding the last issue, she distinguishes among four different types of mother and two different types of father to illustrate the complexity of the conflict between surrogate and real parenthood in determining the priority of parental rights to a child born from this type of assisted reproduction. Mahowald argues that if a surrogate intends to be the child's social parent, then, given the risk she undertakes in gestating and giving birth, she has a more compelling claim to the child than either of its genetic parents.

Lori Andrews continues the discussion of surrogacy by examining three arguments advanced by feminists in favor of banning the practice. These involve claims about potential harm to society, to surrogates themselves, and to children born through surrogacy. She skillfully dissects each of these arguments, exposing flaws in them that question their plausibility. Andrews claims that these arguments unwittingly work against women's reproductive autonomy and the efforts of feminists to uphold it. Surrogacy is constitutionally protected and should not be based on appeals to symbolism and tradition. There is nothing about surrogacy itself that threatens children. Moreover, to say that women are exploited by paid surrogacy agreements is demeaning to them and even sexist.

Susan Mattingly notes the shift in a physician's responsibility in obstetrics from a model in which the maternal-fetal dyad was one complex patient and the fetus was an integral part of the woman's body to a model in which the fetus is a distinct patient in its own right. She argues that the main professional conflict for physicians in the two-patient model is not between upholding the autonomy of the maternal patient and being nonmaleficent toward the fetal patient, but rather between discharging the duty of beneficence to the fetus and the duty of nonmaleficence to the maternal patient. To resolve this conflict, Mattingly proposes adapting the contextual approach of family practice medicine to obstetrics, where the maternal and fetal patients are not conceptually distinct but part of an integrated whole. Standards of family ethics would not always give priority to therapeutic intervention to benefit the fetus, but would consider such intervention in the light of the balance of benefits and harms of maternal and fetal patients understood as one unit.

Christine Overall's paper sheds interesting light on the question of the permissibility of selectively terminating some of the fetuses in a multiple pregnancy. She holds that ethical and policy questions about selective termination must be raised within the context of the technological manipulation of women's reproductive capacities. These questions, in turn, need to be addressed within a cultural context involving perceptions about female fertility and infertility. After distinguishing between abortion and selective termination, Overall distinguishes between the right to reproduce and the right not to reproduce and argues that the right to selectively terminate fetuses in a multiple pregnancy is an expression of the right not to reproduce. Understood in this way, selective termination is an expression of the more general reproductive autonomy of women.

The next two selections address different ethical aspects of the possibility of cloning human beings. John Harris argues that claims to the effect that cloning would undermine human dignity are vague and not well motivated. In particular, he maintains that appeals to the Kantian notion that clones would be used solely as means and not also as ends in themselves are unhelpful in assessing the ethics of human cloning. The mere possibility of abuse with any technique does not constitute a reason for banning it. Furthermore, Harris argues that the genetic identity entailed by cloning is not equivalent to personal identity, which, in addition to genetics, is a function of social and environmental factors. Harris concludes by suggesting that failure to permit cloning would violate people's procreative autonomy. In her second contribution, Lori Andrews similarly argues that cloning could fall under the more general idea of procreative freedom. This would entail the right to have access to cloning technology in order to have a child when all other forms of assisted reproductive technology have failed. Yet she holds that, even if such a right exists, cloning should be banned. She draws an analogy between incest and cloning to support this claim. Just as we ban incest because it involves the improper exercise of parental power over children, we can ban cloning for the same reason. Cloning would involve the exercise of parental power that would threaten a child's right to an open future.

In the last piece, Jonathan Berkowitz and Jack Snyder address the issue of selecting the sex and race of our children. They condemn these practices on the ground that they amount to calculating a child's worth in terms of the child's sex or race. In addition, these practices perpetuate social attitudes of sexism and racism. The authors suggest that there are limits to parents' procreative autonomy, despite any claims about sex selection being in the best interests of their children.

<hr/>

Fertility Enhancement and the Right to Have a Baby

Mary Briody Mahowald PhD

Discussions of reproductive issues are replete with references to rights: rights of women, men, children, fetuses or embryos, and rights of others in society. The "right to have a baby" is often invoked as grounds for providing women or couples with technical or social means of fertility enhancement or assisted reproduction. In this chapter, therefore, I begin with an examination of the concept of rights in order to set the context for addressing issues that arise with regard to artificial insemination, egg donor programs, and surrogate gestation.

RIGHTS AND RIGHTS LANGUAGE

Rights language is especially pervasive in American society because of its stress on individual liberty. Although deontological theories rely on rights more than other ethical theories do, utilitarian, contractarian, and even natural law theories may also be defended or explained in terms of rights. In addition, feminist arguments on reproductive issues are sometimes based on rights. Rights language, however, may not be congenial to a "feminine" model of moral reasoning. In an effort to develop a concept of equality compatible

Mary Briody Mahowald, *Women and Children in Health Care: An Unequal Majority*. New York: Oxford University Press, 1993.

with an ethic of care as well as justice, I avoided the term in developing guidelines that stress responsibilities rather than rights. Discussions of rights are so imbedded in our culture, however, that it seems impossible to address issues without that language. As Joan Callahan and Patricia Smith observe, it is not "rights" as such that present a problem, but a tendency to view the protection of rights as "the whole of the moral story." While insisting on the moral importance of rights, they propose that a "*preoccupation* with rights [be] abandoned in favor of a preoccupation with responsiveness to others, that urges the provision of care, preventing of harm, and maintaining relationships, including creating and maintaining the communities and social arrangements that make meaningful and morally appropriate relationships possible and natural for *all* persons."[1]

Such an interpretation is supported by explanations of rights as necessarily involving mutual or relation-based responsibilities. Stanley Benn, for example, defines a right as "a duty looked at from the standpoint of the other term in the same relationship."[2] Although the terms *duty, obligation,* and *responsibility* are often used interchangeably, I prefer the term responsibility because it is more suggestive (through its association with "response") of interpersonal relationships as grounds for moral judgments. Responsibilities arise not only because of impartially defined duties or obligations, but also because of ties formed by relationships or attachments among persons.

Rights may broadly be defined as justified or justifiable claims or entitlements. In applying the concept to concrete circumstances, the immediate questions that arise are: Claims or entitlements to what, for whom, and from whom? In the context of fertility enhancement, the first question is often answered as "the right to have a baby." Generally, the answer to the second question (a right for whom?) is a woman or couple who wish to have a child related to them genetically or gestationally. The answer to the third question (a right from whom?) may be anyone whose involvement is necessary in order to exer-

cise the right to have a baby—for example, a sexual partner, gamete donor, technician or clinician, or possibly an insurance company or government program that funds infertility treatment. At a more basic level, rights may be derived from the "law of nature," "consent of the governed," or from God.[3]

Unfortunately, when rights language is used in common parlance, and often when it is used in formal argument, different types of rights are not distinguished. Among the possible distinctions are human, natural, moral and legal, absolute or prima facie, and positive and negative rights. For each of these, there may be correlative responsibilities or duties.[4]

Human rights involve the basic needs or interests of all human beings.[5] They are thus associated with the principle of justice or a concept of equality: all human beings equally deserve to have their fundamental needs or interests fulfilled. In light of their applicability to all humans, human rights may also be construed as natural rights.[6] Within the context of natural law theory, both are identified with moral rights because what is natural to human beings is defined as moral. But moral rights generally include rights based on voluntary action as well as those based on human need or interest.

Moral rights are also broader than legal rights. Jeremy Bentham and John Austin view moral rights as based on public opinion rather than law or statue.[7] In contrast, legal rights assume the existence of a legal system whose rules govern their exercise, often restricting their application to certain groups. Although they often articulate moral or human rights, legal rights are formally stipulated by social conventions enacted through legislative or constitutional processes. Moral rights extend to informal as well as formal agreements or commitments among persons.

Whether or not the right to have a baby is a human or natural right depends on whether having a child is a basic need or interest of those who desire parenthood. Although social stigmas and personal disappointment sometimes accompany childlessness, becoming a parent is not necessary to survival, and therefore not a fundamental human need. Parenthood is in the *interest* of some individuals or couples, but whether this interest is so fundamental that it counts as a human or natural right remains questionable. Other interests, such as professional or economic success, clearly do not count as human or natural rights of individuals. Nonetheless, the right to have a baby is a claim that social convention both informally and formally supports, so long as its exercise does not impugn the rights of others. As a moral right, this right may appeal to obligations of beneficence or charity as its correlate.[8]

The distinction between absolute and prima facie duties has a parallel in discussions of rights. An absolute right is exceptionless in the demand it imposes on others. Although opposite sides of the abortion debate seem to regard their values in this way, it is difficult to see how either the right to life or the right to choose is truly absolute. A right to life does not obligate others to risk their lives in my behalf, and a right to choose is surely limited by the obligation of nonmaleficence. Yet either of these rights seems more compelling than a right to have a baby,[9] and a right to reproduce without another's assistance seems more compelling than a right to fertility enhancement or assisted reproduction. If these rights are not absolute, but may be overridden while recognizing their validity, they are prima facie rights.

The distinction between positive and negative rights, corresponding with a distinction between positive and negative duties, is particularly pertinent to issues of fertility enhancement. A negative right implies another's responsibility not to interfere with the expression of that right. A positive right implies the other's responsibility to support or facilitate its expression. If an individual's or couple's right to have a baby is a positive right, practitioners have an obligation to provide infertility treatment to those who require and desire it; if the right to have a baby is a negative right, such assistance is not obligatory. It thus seems clear that the right to have a baby is at most a prima facie negative right of individuals. Health professionals are not obligated to respond affirmatively to every individual or couple requesting reproductive assistance.

A RIGHT TO HAVE A BABY?

What does it mean, then, to assert one's right to have a baby? Ordinarily, when the claim is made by or on behalf of an infertile person or couple, it means the right to procreate by becoming a biological (genetic or gestational) parent. It may also mean the moral or legal right to become a social parent, through adoption or through one's committed relationship to a biological parent. Using Michael Bayles's terminology, we may therefore distinguish between the right to beget, the right to bear, and the right to rear a child. Presumably, the exercise of these rights is based on a desire on the part of a prospective parent. Bayles argues that the desire "to beget for its own sake" is irrational because fulfillment of the desire "will not contribute to one's life experiences."[10] The desire may become rational if begetting is seen as a means to fulfillment of other (rational) desires, such as the desire to rear a child. But the "right to have a baby" deserves analysis on another level, namely, critique of its key terms, *have* and *baby*.

To have has a different meaning when it applies to persons or subjects rather than to objects. To have an object means to own or possess it, and this implies a prima facie right to dispose of the object as one wishes. To own something is to treat it as property, which has no rights of its own. When we use the verb "have" in referring to persons (as in "I have a friend," or "I have a husband"), we refer to the relationship itself rather than to a person. We "have," for example, a relationship of friendship or marriage to a particular person. The "having" of such interpersonal relationships does not imply ownership.

Typically, it implies responsibility more than rights. As Antoine de Saint-Exupéry observed in *The Little Prince*, you become "responsible for what you have tamed,"[11] that is, for those with whom you have established ties. If having a baby means having a parental relationship with someone, it fulfills this view of responsibility toward another.

The right to *have* a baby may not be literally equivalent to the right *to* a son or daughter, but rather a right to "the having" or reproducing of one. In that context the claim to a biological tie with one's progeny is affirmed, and this may be expressed through gamete donation or surrogacy as well as through ordinary means of reproduction. One can then "have" a baby without a commitment to its nurturance. Obviously, this raises problems regarding the baby's rights. But what do we mean by the term *baby* in discussing the right to have one? The simplest and most direct answer is to say we mean a future baby or child, that is, a newborn. Because human gametes, embryos, and fetuses are not yet babies and may never be, the assertion of a right to have any of them is not equivalent to the right to have a baby. Moreover, if embryos and fetuses are not persons, the relationship signified by "having" is probably closer to a property relationship than an interpersonal relationship. Gametes are more like property than embryos or fetuses because they are formed entirely from within the "owner's" body, and are, in fact, a part of that body. If I may donate a kidney or blood because it is my property, I might also donate ova for the same reason. Legal restrictions on the selling of body parts do not imply that they are not owned by the person whose body contains them.

So long as they do not harm others, human beings have a right to do what they will with their own bodies. Nonetheless, American society has been loathe to treat human tissue or organs as mere property, that is, as subject to commerce. When the tissue involved is human ova or sperm, the term *donation* is used to characterize the exchange of money for tissue. As we will see subsequently, however, that characterization is misleading.

ARTIFICIAL INSEMINATION BY "DONORS"

Natural law theory opposes artificial insemination of women even when the semen donor is the woman's husband. In Roman Catholic teaching, this prohibition is based on the requisite of conformity with the natural law paradigm of sexual intercourse between married partners as crucial to the morality of reproduction.[12] Those who subscribe to a psychosomatic rather than physicalist view of human nature reject this interpretation of natural law ethics. Catholic theologian Lisa Soule Cahill, for example, argues in support of homologous but against heterologous reproductive technologies.[13] Homologous techniques are those that involve only the married couple as biological parents; heterologous methods involve third parties. "Artificial" insemination of a woman with her husband's sperm (AIH) is homologous; artificial insemination with another man's sperm (AID or TID) is heterologous.[14] Within the broader interpretation of natural law, the rationale for permitting artificial insemination of a woman with her husband's sperm is its fulfillment of the couple's commitment to have children within the context of the marital relationship as a whole, and not in the context of specific acts of sexual intercourse.

Cahill and others argue against artificial insemination with donor sperm on grounds that it violates the commitment to procreate only with one's spouse, which is essential to marriage.[15] In general, however, donor insemination presents more controversial issues with regard to its anonymity, and by the secrecy generally observed by couples who practice it. More recently, controversy has centered on the question of whether single women should be inseminated with donor sperm.[16] Each of these issues is assessable from an egalitarian perspective.

"Protection of donors" is the reason often given in support of their right to anonymity.[17]

Donor recruitment, it is thought, would be extremely difficult if donors' identities were known or knowable to the individuals in whose behalf their semen is utilized. Assurance of anonymity, however, along with the possible satisfactions of benefitting an infertile couple, or of passing on one's genetic endowment, has apparently not been considered an adequate incentive for semen donation in the United States. Financial remuneration undoubtedly provides persuasive incentive to those who might not otherwise "donate."[18]

Supposedly, semen donors have a right to anonymity as protection from possible legal, financial, and emotional claims on the part of future children to whom they are genetically related. Clinicians are generally so supportive of this prima facie right that they themselves remain unaware of donors' identities, keep incomplete records regarding them, and sometimes insist that the infertile husband's name be recorded on birth certificates of children born by donor insemination.[19]

The "protection of donors" rationale, with its utilitarian argument about maintaining a sufficient number of donors, ignores the interests of others who deserve protection when donor insemination is employed. Foremost among those whose interests may be compromised by secrecy are future offspring, who, on analogy with the rights of adopted children, have a right to know the facts regarding their origin and genetic parents.[20] The argument for the child's right to know is strongest when the information is medically relevant to her interests. As genetic knowledge escalates, so do the possibilities for genetic therapies. The relevant information can usually be provided without identifying the donor. In some cases, however, the information cannot be obtained without tracking down the donor, thus jeopardizing his anonymity.

In an age of AIDS (acquired immune deficiency syndrome), the argument regarding medically relevant information also applies to the woman who may be impregnated with donor semen, and to her husband. Both might be infected by viruses undetectable at the time of semen donation. Careful screening mechanisms have been set up at infertility clinics to eliminate that possibility and to test for other diseases also.[21]

Even if donor anonymity imposed no risk on the couple or their potential offspring, the question of whether it is truly supportive of the donor's own interests and of society's interests remains relevant. Anonymity is intended to assure the donor that he has no responsibility for the potential offspring or its parents. Minimally, however, he is responsible for honest and full disclosure of risk factors associated with his "donation." He is also responsible for facilitating the reproduction of another human being, whose existence is not always a moral desideratum. Donor insemination implies that genetic fatherhood is separable from social fatherhood, and anonymity suggests the appropriateness of maintaining that separation. It thus parallels the questionable view that procreation is not importantly related to sexual expression.[22] Society's interests may not be well served by reinforcing the separation between the two.

An egalitarian framework calls for balancing the rights and responsibilities of all of those affected by decisions regarding donor insemination: women, their partners, semen donors, potential children, and even the larger community. Possibly, laws could be introduced that would ensure some protection of donors' rights while also protecting others. But clearly the position that donor anonymity is an absolute requirement for donor insemination must be rejected. Interestingly, few have been as concerned about anonymity of ova donors as about that of semen donors. To treat men and women equally, however, the same standard of anonymity or confidentiality should apply to gamete donors of either sex.

Beyond the issue of identifying donors, couples prevalently tend to practice secrecy regarding donor insemination, and this distinguishes it from other methods of assisted reproduction. Judith Lasker and Susan Borg suggest that the main reason for this tendency is that donor insemination is used exclusively to solve the problem of male infertility, and "male infertility is a condition with greater stigma attached to it than female infertility."[23] While this observation may be correct with regard to couples, it obviously does not apply to situations where single women seek donor insemination. (I deal with this point shortly.) The secrecy practiced by those involved with donor insemination extends beyond donor anonymity to withholding information so as to mislead others regarding the fact of donor insemination. The others are relatives, friends, offspring, and sometimes even the couple themselves.[24] Some physicians continue to advocate not telling husbands of their infertility or that donor semen is going to be used, and most encourage couples to keep donor insemination a secret from everyone. Sometimes the semen of the infertile husband is mixed with that of the donor so as to provide the couple with some basis for believing that the child produced through the artificial insemination is genetically related to the husband.[25]

Parental reasons for secrecy regarding donor insemination are commonly framed in terms of the interests of the child, as well as those of the sperm donor and the legal father, usually the husband of the woman who is inseminated.[26] It is assumed that children might be teased by their peers if the latter know they were conceived through donor insemination. By itself this possibility is surely not an adequate reason for foregoing donor insemination, because children may be teased by peers for many inappropriate reasons (and may be complimented for inappropriate reasons also). Nonetheless, parents fear disapproval on the part of others, including family members and the children themselves, if conception by donor insemination is revealed.

Parents seldom offer the explanation of secrecy that may figure centrally in their own motivation—protection of the legal father from the embarrassment of infertility.[27] Although infertility is undoubtedly stressful for women, Lasker and Borg claim that men "are more likely than women

to want to keep donor insemination secret, and women are likely to cover up their husband's infertility by taking on the blame for reproductive problems."[28] The cover-up achievable with donor insemination is not achievable when other reproductive interventions or adoption is practiced, but it inevitably exacts a greater psychological toll. For some at least, there is the strain of "living the lie" that they are biological parents who have reproduced their offspring in the "normal" way. Despite such stresses, the cover-up is maintained to protect the man from what is apparently the greater harm of "a social stigma."[29]

Whether men in fact suffer more from the "stigma" of infertility remains an open question. Reasons offered in support of this point are the following: (1) unlike women, men tend to judge themselves by criteria of performance at work, in bed, and in producing offspring; (2) since the woman's ongoing role is crucial to produce offspring while the husband's is not, the traditional view of male dominance over their wives is thereby threatened; (3) donor insemination poses an additional threat to male dominance in society by barring the possibility of "patriarchal descent."[30] On examination, each of these reasons can be rejected as inegalitarian. Criteria of performance, after all, are no more (or less) legitimate for men than for women, and the reproductive performance exacted of women is surely a tougher requirement than that exacted of men. Male dominance, or for that matter female dominance, whether in families or society is clearly opposed to an egalitarian approach to these institutions. Sex differences thus provide justification for different but not unequal treatment. Should differences in marital status be treated similarly?

Possibly the issue of donor insemination for single women is the most controversial aspect of donor insemination. Consider, for example, the following case:

> A 35-year-old physician at a leading university hospital was not interested in marriage and had not dated for several years. Attempts to adopt a child had been unsuccessful. Although she was

aware that health problems of her own would be exacerbated by pregnancy, she requested donor insemination from her gynecologist. "More than anything else, I want to be a mother," she maintained, "and time is running out on my biological clock."

This case illustrates the fact that single women who request donor insemination tend to be well educated and economically independent.[31] They are often professional women, with ready access to the medical establishment. Given the circumstances of this case, it is surprising that the physician had not been able to arrange for a private adoption. However, the fact that she had tried to adopt a child suggests that she was not fixated on having a genetically related offspring.

If donor insemination is morally justified in cases such as the above, all of those affected by the decision should be treated fairly. Oddly enough, the one who might have been least fairly treated in this case was the patient herself, for whom pregnancy involved a special health risk. Nonetheless, her recognition and acceptance of the risk as necessary means to achievement of her goal made it possible for the physician to support her decision. If the medical risk the woman was ready to assume was so high that physician assistance would be tantamount to malpractice, it would have been wrong to perform the donor insemination.[32] Although the risk was not that severe, the physician still had a right to refuse the service because it was not medically necessary for the patient, or for reasons relevant to the possible offspring. If, for example, the physician considered it wrong to deliberately produce a child who would have only one social parent, he could deny the service on that basis. Many doctors and some institutions routinely deny reproductive technologies to unmarried individuals.[33] However, if their denial is based solely on *prejudice* against single parenthood, the refusal of treatment is morally unjustified.

The exercise of the right to deny medical services is based on the autonomy of the practitioner rather than his own reasons for the denial.

Obviously, autonomy and the reasons for its exercise are related, such that irrational or counterfactual reasons may render autonomy impossible or invalid. A parallel issue for refusal to provide donor insemination is that of abortion, which practitioners are neither legally nor morally bound to perform. Although some feminists disagree, so long as reproductive technologies or abortions are not necessary for women's health, physicians are not professionally obligated to provide them. The same standard applies to other medical treatments.

Whether or not infertility should be treated as a disease is a question that merits fuller consideration than I can give here.[34] The very fact that the question is raised suggests that conditions that are unquestionably diseases are more deserving of medical interventions. As medical technology introduces more and better means of satisfying people's desires to improve their lot in life, requests for interventions unrelated to health multiply, mainly from those who are affluent enough to pay for them.[35] It is ironic that infertility be considered a disease subject to treatment by medical personnel, while fertility or pregnancy is also a medicalized event. Both of the latter conditions, after all, are normal and healthy for most women, for part of their lives. As the stigma of single parenthood has lessened in society, requests for donor insemination by single women have increased.[36] To some the issue becomes especially troublesome if the women requesting donor insemination is an acknowledged lesbian. Among the questions raised for the endocrinologist who has elected to treat cases of infertility is the following: What right or competence do I have to refuse medical assistance to someone who wants to be a parent?

The endocrinologist who was involved in the case previously cited has a defensible but controversial practical response to this issue.[37] First of all, he acknowledges that he is responsible for making it possible for a woman to bear a child when she would not otherwise do so. He therefore agrees, albeit reluctantly, that he has some responsibility for the outcome, and should not provide assistance without considering the effect on the potential child. He is aware that children born to married couples are often raised for much of their lives by only one parent, and that one parent may be as effective as two. Reasoning that his own training has not equipped him to assess competence for parenthood, he notes that others in society are credited with such expertise, for example, adoption specialists. Accordingly, he asks persons who request donor insemination, in circumstances where society tends to question the appropriateness of parenthood, to consult such a specialist to obtain an evaluation of competence for parenthood. If the person refuses or the evaluation is negative, he declines to perform the procedure. If the evaluation is positive, he proceeds with donor insemination.

It may be objected that the logic of the endocrinologist's argument extends to requests for AIH as well as AID, and in general to married couples who seek access to reproductive technologies. The physician claims he has no right to deny infertility treatment to married couples because society generally supports their right to reproduce. However, so long as infertility is not a disease demanding treatment, he is not obligated to provide artificial insemination to anyone, married or single, homosexual or heterosexual. Women may inseminate themselves, do so with the assistance of nonmedical friends, or achieve pregnancy through casual sexual intercourse. Obviously, physicians have no control over such circumstances; they are responsible only for cases where their involvement makes a difference. The endocrinologist's practices fulfills that responsibility.

Suppose, however, the same endocrinologist were approached by a single man who wanted very much to have his own genetically related child. Suppose, further, that the man had a friend who was willing to be artificially inseminated with his sperm, to carry a resultant pregnancy to term, and to deliver a baby that she would then give to the man to nurture and raise. Would competence for parenthood be an adequate criterion for determining whether to proceed with the insemination? Would egalitarian considerations require a parallel policy for the endocrinologist? In addressing these questions, we need to examine whether in fact the two situations are parallel, whether egg donation or surrogate gestation by women for men who wish to be genetic fathers is comparable to sperm donation for women who wish to be biological mothers. Although the two types of donation by women often occur together, I treat them separately because the differences between them are morally relevant.

EGG "DONATION"

The process through which eggs are retrieved from women is clearly more difficult, costly, and riskier than the process through which sperm are obtained for artificial insemination. Sperm are provided through the nonclinical (and normally pleasurable) practice of masturbation, whereas eggs are obtained after drug induced hyperstimulation of the ovaries, followed by aspiration through the vagina.[38] The disparity in contribution of egg and sperm "donors" is acknowledged in the different "compensations" they receive: about $50 for sperm "donors," and $1500 or more for egg "donors."[39]

Both types of donation provide a means of overcoming infertility, or of avoiding transmission of a genetic defect. In egg donation, however, the recipient of the egg may also be the gestational mother. Unlike the infertile husband in donor insemination, the nongenetic (gestational) parent is biologically related to her offspring. In the ordinary process of reproduction, women contribute more, at greater risk and cost to themselves, for a much longer period than do men. Through egg donation and surrogate gestation, two aspects of biological motherhood are divided, but either aspect taken singly is still more demanding than biological (genetic) fatherhood. If equality of rights regarding offspring is based on the extent of contribution to their reproduction, the gestational mother has the most compelling claim, followed by the genetic mother, followed by the genetic father. As already indicated, however, having rights does not imply that they must be exercised. In fact, the exercise of rights relevant to reproduction may be freely forfeited, donated or sold, as occurs in donor insemination, egg donation, and surrogate gestation. Neither do the rights of gamete donors or gestational mothers alone suffice for determining the fate of embryos, fetuses, or infants when their fate is disputed by biological and social parents. I return to this point in the next section, but the concept of "donation" of gametes needs to be examined first.

A donation is a gift, and a gift is something of worth that is freely offered to another. Ordinarily, a gift is worth something to the giver also, or the process of obtaining the gift costs the giver something. It thus represents the giver. A gift is not equivalent to what is bought or sold, or exchanged for something of agreed value. When we discard items that are of no use to us, those who receive them are hardly receiving a gift. In fact, they may be giving us something by relieving us of objects we do not want. When human gametes are taken from would-be donors, the gametes themselves are of no intended "use" to the "donors" who are paid or compensated for inconvenience, pain, or risk that their "donation" entails. These aspects make the relationship one of exchange or commerce rather than gift. Accordingly, the term *donation* is misleading in that context.

In the context of ova donation, the term *compensation* is also misleading. Compensation is an attempt to reduce inequality between individuals or groups. The rationale for compensation of ovum donors thus involves recognition of the disparity between the recipient—who lacks ova, and the donor—who has ova and must undergo medical procedures in order to provide them for another. When (extra) ova are retrieved in conjunction with in vitro fertilization, there is no added risk for the donor. Ova may also be retrieved in conjunction with medical procedures such as tubal ligation, with little risk or inconvenience to the donor.

Compensation has not generally been provided in these cases, but it has been practiced when the donor would not otherwise undergo a medical procedure. At least one center in the United States has elicited egg donation through public announcement.[40] Allegedly, the announcement appealed to altruistic motives on the part of donors, that is, their desire to help an infertile couple. But provision of compensation while still calling the program egg donation presents a confusing message. The socioeconomic status of possible donors clearly influences whether participation in the program is undertaken. For example, a college student who had enrolled in an egg donor program made the following remark: "I would never go through this (drug-induced hyperstimulation and ova retrieval) if I weren't being paid $1000. After all, I'm a poor student."[41] Her comment illustrates the obvious point that compensation for some is enticement for others. Although society generally rejects the sale of human tissue or organs, the amount offered for ova retrieval apart from other medical procedures is clearly more than compensation. Thus "ova donation," as we know it, plainly amounts to "eggs for sale."

While the concept of commercial trafficking in human organs or tissue is worrisome to many, it is not without valid supportive arguments. Most of these appeal to the saliency of mutual informed consent or agreement between buyers and sellers, and consistency between this practice and other means of capitalizing on one's body in a capitalistic society. When the concept extends beyond sperm or ova to embryos and fetuses, however, commercialization becomes more troublesome still. At that point, the exchange has been labelled baby-selling. Whether the label is appropriate is considered in the next section.

SURROGATE GESTATION AND THE CASE OF BABY M

Ordinarily, a woman becomes a mother when her baby is born, that is, when her pregnancy is terminated through delivery (surgically or vaginally) of an infant. If we were to fix on a moment for the initiation of motherhood, it would be that moment at which the umbilical cord is cut so that the child is in fact separate (and not simply separable) from the mother. The man who impregnated the woman is generally regarded as becoming a father at the same moment. Both parents are regarded as parents even if the child is stillborn or later adopted. In the case of donor insemination, however, the fatherhood of the sperm donor is generally not acknowledged.

Women can and do become mothers in other ways as well. Such ways have long been available because social motherhood is separable from biological motherhood. Although there is a parallel distinction between social and biological fatherhood, a patriarchal pattern of the marital relationship has resulted in the tendency to attribute more importance to genetic than to social aspects of fatherhood. Men, in general, are defined by others and themselves in terms of their external roles in society rather than by the familial roles that predominate in perceptions of women.

More recently, biological motherhood has been separated into genetic and gestational components. Because women are capable of nursing children to whom they are neither genetically nor gestationally related, lactational motherhood provides an additional option that is rarely exercised apart from gestational motherhood. There are thus four possible forms of "surrogacy" for women: genetic, gestational, lactational, and social. Most women fulfill all four functions in their expression of motherhood.[42] When the functions are separated, the question of whose maternal rights and responsibilities have priority over others is inescapable. A second unavoidable question follows when conflicts regarding parental rights and responsibilities extend to genetic and social fathers. Before addressing these questions, however, we need to consider the different forms of surrogacy in more detail.

Literally, a *surrogate* is a substitute, that is, someone who stands in place of another. But whom does a surrogate mother stand in place of? If we define the paradigm case of "real" motherhood as one whose ovum is fertilized, who becomes pregnant, gives birth, nurses and raises her child, then a surrogate may fulfill any but not all of these roles. Yet I would not want to argue that "real" motherhood requires fulfillment of all of these functions. Many women do not nurse their children, and others assist in their nurturance, especially fathers. They are nonetheless "really" mothers of their offspring. Adoptive mothers are also "really" mothers, despite the fact that they are not biologically related to their children. They are not mothers in every sense in which they might be, but they are truly mothers. Similarly, genetic and social fathers are really fathers, although neither considered separately is a father in every possible sense.

What makes a woman a surrogate rather than a real mother? Or is the term surrogate inappropriate for multiple maternal roles? Comparable questions may be asked regarding sperm donation or genetic fatherhood and social fatherhood. Are sperm donors really fathers to their genetically related offspring, and are genetically unrelated social fathers real fathers?

On a very basic level, it must be admitted that all of these individuals are parents as well as surrogate parents. To the extent that any of us stands in place of parents toward others' children (for example, as teachers or health care providers), we serve as surrogates, and to the extent that others act parentally toward our children, they serve as surrogates. Thus the parentalism as a moral paradigm for interpersonal and social relations exemplifies a kind of generalized surrogacy. What we are trying to do when we distinguish between surrogate and real parenthood is to determine a priority of parental rights and responsibilities. In keeping with an egalitarian framework, the priority is determinable by considering differences among those who participate in parental arrangements. The differences involve two types of criteria, one subjective and the other objective. The subjective criterion is the intention of the participants; the objective criteria include the duration, cost, necessity, and effectiveness of their involvement in parenting.

If an egalitarian perspective entails respect for the choices of individuals, the intention to be a social parent is clearly relevant to its determination of whose parental tie has priority. Ironically, the intention not to be a parent while participating in the process of reproduction has generally characterized those considered surrogate mothers.[43] In contrast, the intention along with the desire to be a parent has characterized those who cannot participate in this process, who depute the surrogate to provide them with a child. In biblical times, the slave girl Agar was deputed by Sarah, the barren wife of Abraham, to bear them a child.[44] Similar "natural" arrangements are possible nowadays,[45] but artificial insemination rather than sexual intercourse is the usual means of achieving conception. According to Lori Andrews, one of the earliest cases of modern surrogacy involved insemination of a "surrogate" by one of the friends (a couple) for whom she had volunteered to bear a child. When the doctors they consulted were unwilling to perform donor insemination,

> the threesome finally handled the matter themselves. Debbie purchased a diabetic syringe at the drug store and filled it with her husband's sperm. Following the directions in a family medical guide, she successfully injected the sperm into her friend Sue, a twenty-four-year-old virgin, and their child was born nine months later.[46]

Because no money was exchanged, and because the surrogate was a friend of the infertile couple, the surrogate could be described as giving rather than selling the baby she bore to the infertile couple. Empirically, she was both the genetic and gestational mother, but her intent excluded her from being the social mother. Apparently, when she chose to be a surrogate she equated social motherhood with real motherhood. In contrast, some surrogates refer to the child they bear as solely the child of the men whose sperm are used for their insemination. Such men, however, also intend to be social fathers. Judge Harvey Sorkow affirmed this sentiment in the Baby M case by comparing the surrogate's position with that of a paid sperm donor who has no right to the offspring produced through his sperm.[47] Because the biological mother had agreed to accept payment for her surrogacy, the biological father alone had a right to Baby M. As Sorkow put it, "At birth the father does not purchase the child. It is his own biological genetically related child. He cannot purchase what is already his."[48]

Sorkow's decision was eventually overturned by the New Jersey Supreme Court, which acknowledged the full maternal rights of the woman who was both genetically and gestationally the child's mother.[49] Given the context in which this decision was made, intention was still crucial. Although the pregnancy had been initiated in fulfillment of a contract, the surrogate's intention had changed during the course of her pregnancy. By the time the baby was born, she regretted the commercial agreement and wanted to be the child's social mother.

Intention also seems to be crucial in cases where the surrogate is not genetically related to the child she gestates. The first reported case of this type occurred in Cleveland in 1985 when a woman requested in vitro fertilization of her egg with her husband's sperm, and embryo transfer of the resultant embryos to the uterus of a friend.[50] When this attempt failed, a paid surrogate was recruited, who eventually gave birth to a child who was genetically related to each of the partners who intended to raise the child. Before the baby was born, a court ruled that she should be considered the offspring of both genetic parents. Contradicting the traditional definition of mother as "a woman who has borne a child,"[51] the motherhood of the woman who gave birth was not acknowledged.

Like most surrogate arrangements, the preceding case did not result in conflict when the time came for the surrogate to give the baby to the infertile couple. In some cases, however, conflict arises because either of the contracting parties reneges on the original agreement. Usually it is the surrogate.[52] When she changes her mind and wants to be a social as well as biological mother, whose right to have the baby should prevail? From a deontological perspective, the contract between the surrogate and the infertile couple should be upheld no matter what consequences may ensue. From an egalitarian perspective, however, the objective differences among competing "parents" should be respected. Mary Beth Whitehead, who had conceived, gestated, given birth, and nursed her newborn might have remained a surrogate if she had completed the terms of her agreement with William and Elizabeth Stern to give them the child she bore in exchange for $10,000. Instead, Whitehead refused the money and took the child, claiming that her biological motherhood justified her doing so. The New Jersey Supreme Court supported her claim, describing the commercial surrogacy arrangement as babyselling.[53]

Gestation obviously involves a duration of commitment greater than that of gamete donation; it also involves risk and pain greater than that experienced through sperm donation. Accordingly, when weighing the parental right of Whitehead against that of William Stern, Whitehead's claim was more compelling so long as she also intended to be the child's social parent. This would be true even if Whitehead had not been both genetic and gestational mother. If the Sterns had *both* been the genetic parents, and Whitehead was only the gestational parent, Whitehead's maternal right would still be more compelling because the risk, duration, necessity and effectiveness of her parental role was clearly more substantial than either or both of the Sterns. I disagree, therefore, with a ruling by the California Court of Appeals, which held that the genetic relationship should take precedence over the gestational tie.[54] The justification for denying maternal rights to a gestator who is not ge-

netically related to the child she bears is dependent on the gestator's intention not to be a social mother, and on her decision not to exercise her right to have a baby to rear. She is then a biological parent who has chosen not to be a social mother.

The right to have a baby need not be exercised. When it is exercised, however, the expression of the right is not without moral limits. It would be wrong, for example, for a man to impregnate a woman against her wishes, or force her to maintain a pregnancy, solely because he wants to be a father. Similarly, a woman's right to have a baby does not impose an obligation on clinicians to provide technology necessary to facilitate that, for example, by prescribing infertility drugs or by performing in vitro fertilization. Neither does the right to have a baby imply the right to sell the baby.

In the Baby M Case, Judge Sorkow rejected the allegation of babyselling by claiming that Whitehead sold her services but not her child. Like men who sell their sperm so that an infertile couple might have a child, Whitehead agreed to accept money for providing an environment in which William Stern's child could develop. This rationale only makes sense if one negates or trivializes Whitehead's biological tie to her offspring. Surrogacy provides a conceptual framework for doing that. The very term surrogacy misleadingly suggests that a woman who conceives, gestates and gives birth to a child is not a mother.[55]

In general, a care model of moral reasoning stresses both social and biological ties between parents and their offspring. Because surrogacy sunders those relationships, it can only be supported by this model if its practice reinforces other basic ties, such as those between the surrogate and other family members. It is possible that the intention harbored by a surrogate who gives her child to an infertile couple epitomizes the nurturant responsibility of motherhood. Just as a woman who allows her child to be adopted may be acting heroically for the child's best interests, a surrogate may be acting similarly. Payment for the act suggests that it is based on self-interest rather than the child's interest, but this is not necessarily the case. It is possible that a woman who accepts $10,000 (or more) for undergoing pregnancy and childbirth in behalf of an infertile couple perceives herself as giving inestimably more to them than she is receiving. If human life is of inestimable value, the gift motif may still be valid in commercial surrogacy.

Nonetheless, most feminists are wary of the possibilities for exploitation of women that surrogacy, even more than egg donation programs, involves.[56] Socioeconomic differences between infertile persons who utilize reproductive "services" and those whose bodies provide such "services" were dramatically illustrated in the Baby M case.[57] Elizabeth Stern was a pediatrician, her husband a biochemist; Whitehead was an unemployed housewife, her husband a sanitation worker. The Sterns had postponed having children while pursuing their doctoral degrees; neither of the Whiteheads was educated beyond high school, they had married young and had children early, their financial status as well as their relationship had been "rocky" from time to time. Mary Beth Whitehead represented an opportunity for the Sterns to have a child genetically related to one of them. Apparently, that prospect was especially important to William Stern because he was an only child whose parents had experienced the holocaust. Although Elizabeth Stern was not infertile, the contract signed by Whitehead indicated that she was.[58] Elizabeth had a mild form of multiple sclerosis, and there had been concern that the disease could be exacerbated by pregnancy. The Sterns might also have been concerned that Elizabeth's age (40) increased the risk of genetic abnormality.

Exploitation occurs in an inegalitarian milieu, that is, one in which differences among individuals prompt evaluative judgments based on irrelevant criteria. Clearly, socioeconomic status is not an adequate guide for settling competing claims about the right to have a baby. Most feminists oppose surrogacy because of its implications regarding exploitation of women, but some liberal feminists support the practice as consistent with the principle of reproductive choice.[59] Those who oppose surrogacy sometimes compare it with prostitution: women's bodies are thus used in the interests of others.[60] The target of their critique is the set of social conditions that make surrogacy a genuine and unavoidable option for individual women. A free-market model may also use the analogy with prostitution, arguing in defense of surrogacy that reproductive choice entails women's right to do as they wish with their bodies and the products of their bodies. Unless infants have a moral status equivalent to that of more mature humans, the baby-selling that surrogacy may involve presents no problem for a free enterprise ethic. From an egalitarian perspective, however, it violates guideline 5, which requires that individuals not be "treated as other than who or what they are." If other human beings may not be bought or sold as commodities, then neither should newborn humans.

If competing rights to have the same baby are settled on the basis of objective differences among claimants, all of whom intend to be social parents, the woman who gestates and gives birth has the most compelling claim. Those who have no biological tie to the child have the least compelling claim. Although genetic mothers and fathers are equally related from a biological point of view, they differ regarding the prospect of child rearing. Even if a genetic mother does not nurse her child, she is more likely to be the crucial parental figure in the child's early development. This circumstance gives greater weight to her parental claim vis-à-vis the genetic father.

But competing rights of intentional social parents are not the only morally relevant factors in determining who should rear the baby. Clearly, the child has rights also, and these may override those of would-be parents, regardless of their biological tie to the child. Minimally the child has a prima facie right to receive the care necessary to survive and grow, but this does not imply that the child has a right to be placed in the parental situation that will provide the most advantages. Although the best interests of the child is the standard commonly invoked in settling custodial disputes between parents, that standard is vague and subject to biased interpretations.[61] By that standard, for example, financial advantages alone would have made the Sterns preferable parents for Baby M because they could buy her opportunities such as a large house, music lessons, and private school education. By that standard those of us who cannot do or be all that is best for our children might lose our custody of them to those who can provide greater material advantages.

To be invoked in an egalitarian framework, the principle of the child's best interests must not be regarded as an absolute criterion for settling questions of parental rights. So long as the Whiteheads had demonstrated adequate parenting skill, they might have been preferable parents for Baby M despite their lower income and educational level (as compared with the Sterns). As it was, however, two factors raised concerns about that adequacy: the possibility that Mary Beth Whitehead had become emotionally unstable,[62] and the fact that the child had already spent most of her infancy in the custody of the Sterns. It was not unreasonable, therefore, for the courts to give custody to the Sterns as a means of protecting the child from further instability. As a negative right, protection from possible harm is more compelling than the positive right to have one's best interests promoted. Had the child spent most of her infancy with the Whiteheads, and had that household provided a stable, although modest, environment, custody could reasonably have been awarded to the Whiteheads.

Summarily, the issue of surrogate motherhood, as the case of Baby M well illustrates, raises a plethora of thorny ethical questions about rights to have a baby. Here I have mainly considered the competing rights of parents, and I have suggested an egalitarian framework for those rights according to the intentions of, and objective differences among, the rights holders.

References and Notes

1. Joan C. Callahan and Patricia G. Smith, "Liberalism, Communitarianism, and Feminism," in *Liberalism and Community*, ed. Noel Reynolds, Cornelius Murphy, and Robert Moffat (Lewiston, New York: Edwin Mellen Press), forthcoming.

2. Stanley I. Benn, "Rights," in *Encyclopedia of Philosophy*, ed. Paul Edwards (New York: Macmillan Publishing Company, 1967), vol. 7, 196. Benn attributes this view to Wesley Hohfeld. That he endorses it himself is evident in the following statement from Stanley I. Benn and R. S. Peters, *The Principles of Political Thought* (New York: The Free Press, 1959), 102: "Rights and duty are different names for the same normative relation, according to the point of view from which it is regarded." He insists, nonetheless, that the correlation between rights and duties "is a logical, not a moral or legal relation."

3. Natural law theory supports the view that rights are based on the nature of human beings. This rationale may reflect the religious belief that nature is defined or ordered by God (Eternal Law). Social contract theorists such as Rousseau and Locke construe rights as derived from consent of the governed.

4. See Benn, *Encyclopedia*, 195–99; H. Tristram Engelhardt, *The Foundations of Bioethics* (New York: Oxford University Press, 1986), 94–97; Tom L. Beauchamp and James F. Childress, *Principles of Biomedical Ethics*, 3d ed. (New York: Oxford University Press, 1989), 56–60; and John Finnis, *Natural Law and Natural Rights* (Oxford: Clarendon Press, 1980). Beauchamp also distinguishes between fundamental and derivative rights. See his *Philosophical Ethics* (New York: McGraw-Hill Book Company, 1982), 194–95. Concerning the correlativity thesis, see Joel Feinberg, "The Nature and Value of Rights," *Journal of Value Inquiry* 4 (1970): 243–57. Feinberg rejects the correlativity thesis for some positive rights.

5. As Alan Gewirth states: "We may assume as true by definition, that human rights are rights that all persons have simply insofar as they are human" (in *Human Rights: Essays on Justification and Application* [Chicago: University of Chicago Press, 1983], 41). But human rights may also be possessed by humans who are not persons, or whose personhood is questionable.

6. See Abraham Irving Melden, *Rights and Persons* (Berkeley: University of California Press, 1977), 1.

7. Jeremy Bentham and John Austin in Benn, *Encyclopedia*, 197.

8. Some philosophers (e.g., libertarians) deny that there are any obligations of charity. Even if beneficence and charity are considered obligatory, however, their obligatoriness is less compelling than the obligation of nonmaleficence. As Hippocrates suggested, not harming is more important than doing good. See "Selections from the Hippocratic Corpus," in *Ethics in Medicine*, ed. Stanley Rieser, Arthur J. Dyck, and William Curran (Cambridge, Massachusetts: MIT Press, 1977), 7.

9. Although the two are often equated, the right to reproduce is not equivalent to the right to have a baby. For a woman, the right to reproduce includes the right to conceive, gestate, and give birth. The right to *have* a baby may be superseded by the child's right not to be harmed, even by a parent.

10. Michael Bayles, *Reproductive Ethics* (Englewood Cliffs, New Jersey: Prentice Hall, Inc., 1984), 13.

11. Antoine de Saint-Exupéry, *The Little Prince*, trans. Katherine Woods (New York: Harcourt, Brace and World, 1943), 71.

12. See Pope Pius XI, "Encyclical Letter on Christian Marriage" (Dec. 31, 1930), as cited in *Medical Ethics*, ed. Kevin D. O'Rourke and Philip Boyle (St. Louis: Catholic Health Association, 1989), 116.

13. Lisa Soule Cahill, "Women, Marriage, Parenthood: What Are Their 'Natures'?" *Logos* 9 (1988): 11–35.

14. AIH means "artificial insemination by husband"; AID means "artificial insemination by donor"; TID means "therapeutic insemination by donor." AID and TID are interchangeable terms. While not prevalently used, the acronym TID avoids the close association between AID and AIDS. My use of quotation marks in the first but not the second clause is intended to call attention to the difference between insemination from husband's sperm (artificial?) and from anonymous donor sperm.

15. Cahill, 22–26; and Benedict M. Ashley and Kevin D. O'Rourke, *Health Care Ethics: A Theological Analysis* (St. Louis: Catholic Health Association of the United States, 1982), 287–88.

16. Carson Strong and Jay S. Schinfield, "The Single Woman and Artificial Insemination by Donor," *Journal of Reproductive Medicine* 29 (1984): 293–99.

17. Kamran S. Moghissi, "The Technology of AID," in *New Approaches to Human Reproduction*, ed. Linda M. Whiteford and Marilyn L. Poland (Boulder, Colorado: Westview Press, 1989), 128. As Judith N. Lasker and Susan Borg suggest, however, protection of social fathers may be the main reason for secrecy regarding AID. See their "Secrecy and the New Reproductive Technologies," in Whiteford and Poland, 138–41.

18. According to Moghissi, remuneration currently ranges from $20 to $35 per ejaculate. See Moghissi, 122. But Lori Andrews says that the usual payment is $50 a "donation," as cited in Nadine Brozan, "Babies from Donated Eggs: Growing Use Stirs Questions," *New York Times* (Jan. 18, 1988), 9.

19. Moghissi, 128

20. George J. Annas, "Fathers Anonymous: Beyond the Best Interests of the Sperm Donor," in *Genetics and the Law II*, ed. Aubrey Milunsky and George J. Annas (New York: Plenum Press, 1980), 331–40.

21. Moghissi, 120–21.

22. Natural law theology probably provides the strongest support for an essential relation between procreation and sexuality, but the relation between the two can also be supported on utilitarian and deontological grounds, without arguing against contraception or Victorian mores.

23. Lasker and Borg, 133. AID is also used by couples who are carriers for debilitating genetic diseases. Observing secrecy about AID then obscures the fact that the male is carrier for the disease.

24. In 1884, when the first reported instance of successful AID occurred in Britain, the procedure was performed without revealing it to the couple. See Lasker and Borg, 134.

25. Ronald Munson calls this practice CAI (confused artificial insemination). See his *Intervention and Reflection*, 3d ed. (Belmont, California: Wadsworth Publishing Company, 1988), 415.

26. Lasker and Borg, 136–42.

27. Lasker and Borg, 138.

28. Lasker and Borg, 139.

29. Lasker and Borg, 140.

30. Lasker and Borg, 140–41.

31. Cheryl F. McCartney, "Decision by Single Women to Conceive by Artificial Insemination," *Journal of Psychosomatic Obstetrics and Gynecology* 4 (1985): 321;

Maureen McGuire and Nancy J. Alexander, "Artificial Insemination of Single Women," *Fertility and Sterility* 43 (Feb. 1985): 183; and Miriam B. Rosenthal, "Single Women Requesting Artificial Insemination by Donor" in *Psychiatric Aspects of Reproductive Technology*, ed. Nada L. Stotland (Chicago: American Psychiatric Press, Inc., 1990), 113–21.

32. The Hippocratic imperative, "to help, or at least to do no harm," would thus have been violated. See Reiser, Dyck, and Curran, 7.

33. Moghissi, 129. For example, Mount Sinai Hospital in Cleveland, Ohio, offered reproductive technologies to married couples only.

34. Leon Kass, *Toward a More Natural Science* (New York: Free Press, 1985), 159–64; and Christine Overall, *Ethics and Human Reproduction* (Boston: Allen and Unwin, 1987), 139–51.

35. Growth hormone therapy is a particularly apt example in this regard. I treat this further in Chapter 12.

36. Possible evidence of the increase of requests for artificial insemination by single women is the increase of articles on the topic, see note 31.

37. I wish to thank the reproductive endocrinologist involved in this case, Paul Schnatz, who is now at Providence Hospital in Southfield, Michigan, for sharing with me his rationale and practice regarding requests for artificial insemination from single women.

38. See John A. Robertson, "Ethical and Legal Issues in Human Egg Donation," *Fertility and Sterility* 52 (Sept. 1989): 358. Nonsurgical removal through the vagina is now the preferred means of ova retrieval from donors who are not undergoing medical procedures for themselves.

39. Brozan, 9; and Paula Monarez, "Halfway There," *Chicago Tribune* (Feb. 2, 1992), sect. 6, 4.

40. "Clinic in Ohio Starts Egg Donor Plan," *New York Times* (Sept. 15, 1987), 10.

41. The student took my course on "Moral Problems in Medicine" at Case Western Reserve University in 1987. After undergoing drug-induced hyperstimulation of her ovaries, this student underwent laparoscopic removal of her ova.

42. Although "wet nurses" have not socially been regarded as mothers, they fit the meaning of motherhood as one who fulfills an essential nurturant role.

43. See Phillip J. Parker, "Motivations of Surrogate Mothers: Initial Findings," *American Journal of Psychiatry* 140 (Jan. 1983): 117–18.

44. Genesis 16: 1–4. This early case of "surrogacy" had its problems. Once pregnant by Abraham, Agar despised Sarah, who in turn treated her so badly that she ran away from the household (16: 5–6).

45. One such "natural arrangement" is recounted by Juliette Zipper and Selina Sevenhuijsen in "Surrogacy: Feminist Notions of Motherhood Reconsidered," in *Reproductive Technologies*, ed. Michelle Stanworth (Minneapolis: University of Minnesota Press, 1987), 118.

46. Lori B. Andrews, *New Conceptions* (New York: St. Martin's Press, 1984), 202.

47. *In re Baby* M, New Jersey Superior court, No. FM-25314–86F (March 31, 1987).

48. "To Serve 'the Best Interests of a Child'," *New York Times* (April 1,1987), B2.

49. *In re matter of Baby* M, 1988 New Jersey Lexis 1, 79; New Jersey Supreme Court No. A-39, (February 1988).

50. Wulf Utian, Leon Sheeham, and James Goldfarb, "Successful Pregnancy after *In Vitro* Fertilization and Embryo Transfer from an Infertile Woman to a Surrogate," Letter, *New England Journal of Medicine* 313, no. 21 (Nov. 21, 1985): 1351–52.

51. *Webster's New World Dictionary*, 2d college ed. (New York: Simon and Schuster, 1982), 928.

52. Anna Johnson, for example, had agreed to be a gestational surrogate for Crispina Culvert, who with her husband had provided the gametes that produced a child. Although Johnson changed her mind and wanted to raise her son, a California court ruled that giving birth did not make her the child's mother. See *Anna J. vs. Mark C.*, 234 Cal. Ap. 3rd., 1557 (1991); and Susan Peterson and Susan Kelleher, "Genes Settle Legal Argument," *Chicago Tribune* (Oct. 10, 1991), sect. 1, 6.

53. *In re matter of Baby* M, February 1988. See Leonard Fleck, "Surrogate Motherhood: Is It Morally Equivalent to Selling Babies?" *Logos* 9 (1988): 135–45.

54. Peterson and Kelleher, 6.

55. LeRoy Walters reinforces this misleading interpretation by distinguishing between full and partial surrogacy. Full surrogacy occurs when the "surrogate" is both gestational and genetic mother. Partial surrogacy occurs when the "surrogate" is only the gestational mother. Moreover, despite the fact that neither adoptive fathers nor sperm donors are "surrogate

fathers," he treats the issue of surrogate motherhood under the heading "Surrogate Parenthood." See LeRoy Walters, "Genetics and Reproductive Technologies," in *Medical Ethics*, ed. Robert Veatch (Boston: Jones and Bartlett, Publishers, 1989), 210–12.

56. For example, Overall, 111–31. The following feminists joined a brief opposing surrogacy on behalf of Amici Curiae (*Foundation on Economic Trends*, In the Matter of Baby M, New Jersey Supreme Court, No. FM-25314-86E): Betty Friedan, Gloria Steinem, Gena Corea, Barbara Katz Rothman, Lois Gould, Michelle Harrison, Phyllis Chesler, and Letty Cottin Pogrebin.

57. Lisa H. Newton, "Surrogate Motherhood and the Limits of Rational Ethics," *Logos* 9 (1988): 113–14.

58. "The Baby M Contract: Is it Enforceable?" *New Jersey Law Journal* 119 (Feb. 26, 1987): 1.

59. Lori B. Andrews, "Feminism Revisited: Fallacies and Policies in the Surrogacy Debate," *Logos* 9 (1988): 81–96; also, Newton, 113–34.

60. Overall, 116–19.

61. Robert Hanley, "Baby M's 'Best Interests' May Decide Case without Firm Legal Precedent," *New York Times* (Feb. 2, 1987), 15. See my "Ethical Decisions in Neonatal Intensive Care," in *Human Values in Critical Care Medicine*, ed. Stuart J. Younger (New York: Praeger Press, 1986), 74–82. John J. Arras provides an excellent critique of this principle in his "Toward an Ethic of Ambiguity," *Hastings Center Report* 14, no. 2 (April 1984); 25–33.

62. As suggested, for example, in Whitehead's statement: "I'd rather see me and her [i.e., her baby] dead before you get her." George J. Annas, "Baby M: Babies (and Justice) for Sale," *Hastings Center Report* 17, no. 3 (June 1987): 13.

Surrogate Motherhood: The Challenge for Feminists

Lori B. Andrews JD

Surrogate motherhood presents an enormous challenge for feminists. During the course of the *Baby* M trial, the New Jersey chapter of the National Organization of Women met and could not reach consensus on the issue. "The feelings ranged the gamut," the head of the chapter, Linda Bowker, told the *New York Times*. "We did feel that it should not be made illegal, because we don't want to turn women into criminals. But other than that, what you may feel about the Baby M case may not be what you feel about another.

"We do believe that women ought to control their own bodies, and we don't want to play big brother or big sister and tell them what to do," Ms. Bowker continued. "But on the other

hand, we don't want to see the day when women are turned into breeding machines."[1]

Other feminist groups have likewise been split on the issue, but a vocal group of feminists came to the support of Mary Beth Whitehead with demonstrations[2] and an amicus brief[3]; they are now seeking laws that would ban surrogate motherhood altogether. However, the rationales that they and others are using to justify this governmental intrusion into reproductive choice may come back to haunt feminists in other areas of procreative policy and family law.

As science fiction has taught us, the types of technologies available shape the nature of a society. Equally important as the technologies—and having much farther-reaching implications—are the policies that a society devises and implements to deal with technology. In Margaret Atwood's *The Handmaid's Tale*, a book often cited as showing the dangers of the technology of surrogacy, it was actually policy changes—the criminalization of abortion and the banning of women from the paid labor force—that created the preconditions for a dehumanizing and harmful version of surrogacy.

THE FEMINIST LEGACY

In the past two decades, feminist policy arguments have refashioned legal policies on reproduction and the family. A cornerstone of this development has been the idea that women have a right to reproductive choice—to be able to contracept, abort, or get pregnant. They have the right to control their bodies during pregnancy, such as by refusing Cesarean sections. They have a right to create non-traditional family structures such as lesbian households or single-parent families facilitated by artificial insemination by donor. According to feminist arguments, these rights should not be overridden by possible symbolic harms or speculative risks to potential children.

Another hallmark of feminism has been that biology should not be destiny. The equal treatment of the sexes requires that decisions about men and women be made on other than biological grounds. Women police officers can be as good as men, despite their lesser strength on average. Women's larger role in bearing children does not mean they should have the larger responsibility in rearing children. And biological fathers, as well as nonbiological mothers or fathers, can be as good parents as biological mothers.

The legal doctrine upon which feminists have pinned much of their policy has been the constitutional protection of autonomy in decisions to bear and rear one's biological children.[4] Once this protection of the biologically related family was acknowledged, feminists and others

could argue for the protection of non-traditional, non-biological families on the grounds that they provide many of the same emotional, physical, and financial benefits that biological families do.[5]

In many ways, the very existence of surrogacy is a predictable outgrowth of the feminist movement. Feminist gains allowed women to pursue educational and career opportunities once reserved for men, such as Betsy Stern's position as a doctor and medical school professor. But this also meant that more women were postponing childbearing and suffering the natural decline in fertility that occurs with age. Women who exercised their right to contraception, such as by using the Dalkon Shield, sometimes found that their fertility was permanently compromised. Some women found that the chance for a child had slipped by them entirely and decided to turn to a surrogate mother.

Feminism also made it more likely for other women to feel comfortable being surrogates. Feminism taught that not all women relate to all pregnancies in the same way. A woman could choose not to be a rearing mother at all. She could choose to lead a child-free life by not getting pregnant. If she got pregnant, she could choose to abort. Reproduction was a condition of her body over which she, and no one else, should have control. For some women, those developments added up to the freedom to be a surrogate.

In the surrogacy context, feminist principles have provided the basis for a broadly held position that contracts and legislation should not restrict the surrogate's control over her body during pregnancy (such as by a requirement that the surrogate undergo amniocentesis or abort a fetus with a genetic defect). The argument against enforcing such contractual provisions resounds with the notion of gender equality, since it is in keeping with common law principles that protect the bodily integrity of both men and women, as well as with basic contract principles rejecting specific performance of personal-services provisions.[6] It is also in keeping with constitutional principles giving the pregnant woman, rather than the male progenitor, the right to make abortion decisions. In this area, feminist lobbying tactics have met with considerable success. Although early bills on surrogacy contained provisions that would have constrained surrogates' behavior during pregnancy, most bills regulating surrogacy that have been proposed in recent years specifically state that the surrogate shall have control over medical decisions during the pregnancy.[7] Even the trial court decision in the Baby M case, which enforced the surrogacy contract's termination of parental rights, voided the section that took from the surrogate the right to abort.[8]

Now a growing feminist contingent is moving beyond the issue of bodily control during pregnancy and is seeking to ban surrogacy altogether. But the rationales for such a ban are often the very rationales that feminists have fought against in the contexts of abortion, contraception, non-traditional families, and employment. The adoption of these rationales as the reason to regulate surrogacy could severely undercut the gains previously made in these other areas. These rationales fall into three general categories: the symbolic harm to society of allowing paid surrogacy, the potential risks to the woman of allowing paid surrogacy, and the potential risks to the potential child of allowing paid surrogacy.

THE SYMBOLIC HARM TO SOCIETY

For some feminists, the argument against surrogacy is a simple one: it demeans us all as a society to sell babies. And put that way, the argument is persuasive, at least on its face. But as a justification for policy, the argument is reminiscent of the argument that feminists roundly reject in the abortion context: that it demeans us as a society to kill babies.

Both arguments, equally heartfelt, need closer scrutiny if they are to serve as a basis for policy. In the abortion context, pro-choice people criticize the terms, saying we are not talking about "babies" when the abortion is done on an embryo or fetus still within the woman's womb.

In the surrogacy context, a similar assault can be made on the term "sale." The baby is not being transferred for money to a stranger who can then treat the child like a commodity, doing anything he or she wants with the child. The money is being paid to enable a man to procreate his biological child; this hardly seems to fit the characterization of a sale. Am I buying a child when I pay a physician to be my surrogate fallopian tubes through in vitro fertilization (when, without her aid, I would remain childless)? Am buying a child when I pay a physician to perform a needed Cesarean section, without which my child would never be born alive?

At most, in the surrogacy context, I am buying not a child but the preconception termination of the mother's parental rights. For decades, the preconception sale of a father's parental rights has been allowed with artificial insemination by donor. This practice, currently facilitated by statutes in at least thirty states, has received strong feminist support. In fact, when, on occasion, such sperm donors have later felt a bond to the child and wanted to be considered legal fathers, feminist groups have litigated to hold them to their pre-conception contract.[9]

Rather than focusing on the symbolic aspects of a sale, the policy discussion should instead analyze the advisability of pre-conception terminations for both women and men. For example, biological parenting may be so important to both the parent and the child that either parent should be able to assert these rights after birth (or even later in the child's life). This would provide sperm donors in artificial insemination with a chance to have a relationship with the child.

Symbolic arguments and pejorative language seem to make up the bulk of the policy arguments and media commentary against surrogacy. Surrogate motherhood had been described by its opponents not only as the buying and selling of children but as reproductive prostitution,[10] reproductive slavery,[11] the renting of a womb,[12] incubatory servitude,[13] the factory method of childbearing,[14] and cutting up women into genitalia.[15]

The women who are surrogates are labeled paid breeders,[16] biological entrepreneurs,[17] breeder women,[18] reproductive meat,[19] interchangeable parts in the birth machinery,[20] manufacturing plants,[21] human incubators,[22] incubators for men's sperm,[23] a commodity in the reproductive marketplace,[24] and prostitutes.[25] Their husbands are seen, alternatively, as pimps[26] or cuckolds.[27] The children conceived pursuant to a surrogacy agreement have been called chattel[28] or merchandise to be expected in perfect condition.[29]

Feminists opposing surrogacy have also relied heavily on a visual element in the debate over Baby M. They have been understandably upset at the vision of a baby being wrenched from its nursing mother or being slipped out a back window in a flight from governmental authorities. But relying on the visceral and visual, a long-standing tactic of the right-to-life groups, is not the way to make policy. Conceding the value of symbolic arguments for the procreative choice of surrogacy makes it hard to reject them for other procreative choices.

One of the greatest feminist contributions to policy debates on reproduction and the family has been the rejection of arguments relying on tradition and symbolism and an insistence on an understanding of the nature and effects of an actual practice in determining how it should be regulated. For example, the idea that it is necessary for children to grow up in two-parent, heterosexual families has been contested by empirical evidence that such traditional structures are not necessary for children to flourish,[30] This type of analysis should not be overlooked in favor of symbolism in discussions of surrogacy.

THE POTENTIAL HARM TO WOMEN

A second line of argument opposes surrogacy because of the potential psychological and physical risks that it presents for women. Many aspects of this argument, however, seem ill founded and potentially demeaning to women. They focus on protecting women against their own decisions be-cause those decisions might later cause them regret, be unduly influenced by others, or be forced by financial motivations.

Reproductive choices are tough choices, and any decision about reproduction—such as abortion, sterilization, sperm donation, or surrogacy—might later be regretted. The potential for later regrets, however, is usually not thought to be a valid reason to ban the right to choose the procedure in the first place.

With surrogacy, the potential for regret is thought by some to be enormously high. This is because it is argued (in biology-is-destiny terms) that it is unnatural for a mother to give up a child. It is assumed that because birth mothers in traditional adoption situations often regret relinquishing their children, surrogate mothers will feel the same way. But surrogate mothers are making their decisions about relinquishment under much different circumstances. The biological mother in the traditional adoption situation is already pregnant as part of a personal relationship of her own. In many, many instances, she would like to keep the child but cannot because the relationship is not supportive or she cannot afford to raise the child. She generally feels that the relinquishment was forced upon her (for example, by her parents, a counselor, or her lover).[31]

The biological mother in the surrogacy situation seeks out the opportunity to carry a child that would not exist were it not for the couple's desire to create a child as a part of their relationship. She makes her decision in advance of pregnancy for internal, not externally enforced reasons. While 75 percent of the biological mothers who give a child up for adoption later change their minds,[32] only around 1 percent of the surrogates have similar changes of heart.

Entering into a surrogacy arrangement does present potential psychological risks to women. But arguing for a ban on surrogacy seems to concede that the *government*, rather than the individual woman, should determine what risks a woman should be allowed to face. This conflicts with the general legal policy allowing competent individuals to engage in potentially risky behavior so long as they have given their voluntary, informed consent.

Perhaps recognizing the dangers of giving the government widespread powers to "protect" women, some feminists do acknowledge the validity of a general consent to assume risks. They argue, however, that the consent model is not appropriate to surrogacy since the surrogate's consent is neither informed nor voluntary.

It strikes me as odd to assume that the surrogate's consent is not informed. The surrogacy contracts contain lengthy riders detailing the myriad risks of pregnancy, so potential surrogates are much better informed on that topic than are most women who get pregnant in a more traditional fashion. In addition, with volumes of publicity given to the plight of Mary Beth Whitehead, all potential surrogates are now aware of the possibility that they may later regret their decisions. So, at that level, the decision is informed. Yet a strong element of the feminist argument against surrogacy is that women cannot give an informed consent until they have had the experience of giving birth. Robert Arenstein, an attorney for Mary Beth Whitehead, argued in congressional testimony that a "pre-birth or at-birth termination, is a termination without informed consent. I use the words informed consent to mean full understanding of the personal psychological consequences at the time of surrender of the child."[33] The feminist amicus brief in Baby M made a similar argument.[34]

The New Jersey Supreme Court picked up this characterization of informed consent, writing that "quite clearly any decision prior to the baby's birth is, in the most important sense, uninformed."[35] But such an approach is at odds with the legal doctrine of informed consent. Nowhere is it expected that one must have the experience first before one can make an informed judgment about whether to agree to the experience. Such a requirement would preclude people from ever giving informed consent to sterilizations, abortions, sex change operations, heart surgery, and so forth. The legal doctrine of informed consent presupposes that people will predict in advance of the experience whether a particular course will be beneficial to them.

A variation of the informed consent argument is that while most competent adults can make such predictions, hormonal changes during pregnancy may cause a woman to change her mind. Virtually a whole amicus brief in the Baby M appeal was devoted to arguing that a woman's hormonal changes during pregnancy make it impossible for her to predict in advance the consequences of her relinquishment.[36] Along those lines, adoption worker Elaine Rosenfeld argues that

> [t]he consent that the birth mother gives prior to conception is not the consent of . . . a woman who has gone through the chemical, biological, endocrinological changes that have taken place during pregnancy and birth, and no matter how well prepared or well intentioned she is in her decision prior to conception, it is impossible for her to predict how she will feel after she gives birth.[37]

In contrast, psychologist Joan Einwohner, who works with a surrogate mother program, points out that

> women are fully capable of entering into agreements in this area and of fulfilling the obligations of a contract. Women's hormonal changes have been utilized too frequently over the centuries to enable male dominated society to make decisions for them. The Victorian era allowed women no legal rights to enter into contracts. The Victorian era relegated them to the status of dependent children. Victorian ideas are given renewed life in the conviction of some people that women are so overwhelmed by their feelings at the time of birth that they must be protected from themselves.[38]

Surrogate Carol Pavek is similarly uncomfortable with hormonal arguments. She posits that if she is allowed the excuse of hormones to change her mind (thus harming the expectant couple and subjecting the child to the trauma of litigation), what's to stop men from using their hormones as an excuse for rape or other harms? In any case, feminists should be wary of a hormone-based argument, just as they have been wary of the hormone-related criminal defense of premenstrual syndrome.

The consent given by surrogates is also challenged as not being voluntary. Feminist Gena Corea, for example, in writing about another reproduction arrangement, in vitro fertilization, asks, "What is the real meaning of a woman's 'consent' . . . in a society in which men as a social group control not just the choices open to women but also women's *motivation* to choose?"[39]

Such an argument is a dangerous one for feminists to make. It would seem to be a step backward for women to argue that they are incapable of making decisions. That, after all, was the rationale for so many legal principles oppressing women for so long, such as the rationale behind the laws not allowing women to hold property. Clearly, any person's choices are motivated by a range of influences—economic, social, religious.

At a recent conference of law professors, it was suggested that surrogacy was wrong because women's boyfriends might talk them into being surrogates and because women might be surrogates for financial reasons. But women's boyfriends might talk them into having abortions or women might have abortions for financial reasons; nevertheless, feminists do not consider those to be adequate reasons to ban abortions. The fact that a woman's decision could be influenced by the individual men in her life or by male-dominated society does not by itself provide an adequate reason to ban surrogacy.

Various feminists have made the argument that the financial inducement to a surrogate vitiates the voluntariness of her consent. Many feminists have said that women are exploited by surrogacy.[40] They point out that in our society's social and economic conditions, some women—such as those on welfare or in dire financial need—will turn to surrogacy out of necessity rather than true choice. In my view, this is a harsh reality that must be guarded against by vigilant efforts to assure that women have equal access to the labor market and that there are sufficient social services so that poor women with children do not feel they must enter into a surrogacy arrangement in order to obtain money to provide care for their existing children.

However, the vast majority of women who have been surrogates do not allege that they have been tricked into surrogacy, nor have they done it because they needed to obtain a basic of life such as food or health care. Mary Beth Whitehead wanted to pay for her children's education. Kim Cotton wanted money to redecorate her house.[41] Another surrogate wanted money to buy a car. These do not seem to be cases of economic exploitation; there is no consensus, for example, that private education, interior decoration, and an automobile are basic needs, nor that society has an obligation to provide those items. Moreover, some surrogate mother programs specifically reject women who are below a certain income level to avoid the possibility of exploitation.

There is a sexist undertone to an argument that Mary Beth Whitehead was exploited by the paid surrogacy agreement into which she entered to get money for her children's education. If Mary Beth's husband, Rick, had taken a second job to pay for the children's education (or even to pay for their mortgage), he would not have been viewed as exploited. He would have been lauded as a responsible parent.

It undercuts the legitimacy of women's role in the workforce to assume that they are being exploited if they plan to use their money for serious purchases. It seems to harken back to a notion that women work (and should work) only for pin money (a stereotype that is the basis for justifying the firing of women in times of economic crisis). It is also disturbing that in most instances, when society suggests that a certain activity should be done for altruism, rather than money, it is generally a woman's activity.

Some people suggest that since there is a ban on payment for organs, there should be a ban on payment to a surrogate.[42] But the payment for organs is different from the payment to a surrogate, when viewed from either the side of the couple or the side of the surrogate. As the New Jersey Supreme Court has stated, surrogacy (unlike organ donation) implicates a fundamental constitutional right—the right to privacy in making procreative decisions.[43] The court erroneously assumed that the constitutional right did not extend to commercial applications. This is in conflict with the holdings of other right-to-privacy cases regarding reproductive decisions. In *Carey v. Population Services*, for example, it was acknowledged that constitutional protection of the use of contraceptives extended to their commercial availability.[44] The Court noted that "in practice, a prohibition against all sales, since more easily and less offensively enforced, might have an even more devastating effect on the freedom to choose contraception" than a ban on their use.[45]

Certainly, feminists would feel their right to an abortion was vitiated if a law were passed prohibiting payment to doctors performing abortions; such a law would erect a major barrier to access to the procedure. Similarly, a ban on payment to surrogates would inhibit the exercise of the right to produce a child with a surrogate. For such reasons, it could easily be argued that the couple's right to pay a surrogate is constitutionally protected (unlike the right to pay a kidney donor).

From the surrogate's standpoint, the situation is different as well. An organ is not meant to be removed from the body; it endangers the life of the donor to live without the organ. In contrast, babies are conceived to leave the body and the life of the surrogate is not endangered by living without the child.[46]

At various legislative hearings, women's groups have virtually begged that women be protected against themselves, against their own decisions. Adria Hillman testified against a New York surrogacy bill on behalf of the New York State Coalition on Women's Legislative Issues. One would think that a women's group would

criticize the bill as unduly intruding into women's decisions—it requires a double-check by a court on a contract made by a woman (the surrogate mother) to assure that she gave voluntary, informed consent and does not require oversight of contracts made by men. But the testimony was just the opposite. The bill was criticized as empowering the court to assess whether a surrogacy agreement protects the health and welfare of the potential child, without specifying that the judge should look into the agreement's potential effect on the natural mother.[47] What next? Will women have to go before a court when they are considering having an affair—to have a judge discern whether they will be psychologically harmed by, or later regret, the relationship?

Washington Post writer Jane Leavy has written:

> I have read volumes in defense of Mary Beth, her courage in taking on a lonely battle against the upper classes, the exploited wife of a sanitation man versus the wife of a biochemist, a woman with a 9th grade education versus a pediatrician. It all strikes me as a bit patronizing. Since when do we assume that a 29-year-old mother is incapable of making an adult decision and accepting the consequences of it?[48]

Surrogate mother Donna Regan similarly testified in New York that her will was not overborne in the surrogacy context: "No one came to ask me to be a surrogate mother. I went to them and asked them to allow me to be a surrogate mother.[49]

"I find it extremely insulting that there are people saying that, as a woman, I cannot make an informed choice about a pregnancy that I carry," she continued, pointing out that she, like everyone, "makes other difficult choices in her life."[50]

POTENTIAL HARM TO POTENTIAL CHILDREN

The third line of argument opposes surrogacy because of the potential harm it represents to potential children. Feminists have had a long-standing concern for the welfare of children. But much feminist policy in the area has been based on the idea that mothers (and family) are more appropriate decision-makers about the best interests of children than the government. Feminists have also fought against using traditions, stereotypes, and societal tolerance or intolerance as a driving force for determining what is in a child's best interest. In that respect, it is understandable that feminists rallied to the aid of Mary Beth Whitehead in order to expose and oppose the faulty grounds on which custody was being determined.[51]

However, the opposition to stereotypes being used to determine custody in a best-interests analysis is not a valid argument against surrogacy itself (which is premised not on stereotypes about the child's best interest being used to determine custody, but on a preconception agreement being used to determine custody). And when the larger issue of the advisability of surrogacy itself comes up, feminists risk falling into the trap of using arguments about potential harm to the child that have as faulty a basis as those they oppose in other areas of family law.

For example, one line of argument against surrogacy is that it is like adoption and adoption harms children. However, such an argument is not sufficiently borne out in fact. There is evidence that adopted children do as well as non-adopted children in terms of adjustment and achievement.[52] A family of two biological parents is not necessary to assure the child's well-being.

Surrogacy has also been analogized to baby-selling. Baby-selling is prohibited in our society, in part because children need a secure family life and should not have to worry that they will be sold and wrenched from their existing family. Surrogacy is distinguishable from baby-selling since the resulting child is never in a state of insecurity. From the moment of birth, he or she is under the care of the biological father and his wife, who cannot sell the child. There is thus no psychological stress to that child or to *any other existing child* that he or she may someday be sold.

Moreover, no matter how much money is paid through the surrogacy arrangement, the child, upon birth, cannot be treated like a commodity—a car or a television set. Laws against child abuse and neglect come into play.

Paying a biological mother to give her child up for traditional adoption is criticized since the child may go to an "undeserving" stranger, whose mere ability to pay does not signify sufficient merit for rearing a child. In paid surrogacy, by contrast, the child is turned over to the biological father. This biological bond has traditionally been considered to be a sufficient indicator of parental merit.

Another argument about potential harm to the resulting children is that parents will expect more of a surrogate child because of the $10,000 they have spent on her creation. But many couples spend more than that on infertility treatments without evidence that they expect more of the child. A Cesarean section costs twice as much as natural childbirth, yet the parents don't expect twice as much of the children. Certainly, the $10,000 is a modest amount compared to what parents will spend on their child over her lifespan.

Surrogacy has also been opposed because of its potential effect on the surrogate's other children. Traditionally, except in cases of clear abuse, parents have been held to be the best decision-makers about their children's best interests. Applying this to surrogacy, the surrogate (and not society) would be the best judge of whether on not her participation in a surrogacy program will harm her children. Not only are parents thought best able to judge their child's needs, but parents can profoundly influence the effects of surrogacy on the child. Children take their cues about things from the people around them. There is no reason to believe that the other children of the surrogate will necessarily feel threatened by their mother's contractual pregnancy. If the children are told from the beginning that this is the contracting couple's child—not a part of their own family—they will realize that they themselves are not in danger of being relinquished.

Surrogate Donna Regan told her child that "the reason we did this was because they [the contracting couple] wanted a child to love as much as we love him." Regan contrasted her case to the Whitehead case: "In the Mary Beth Whitehead case, the child did not see this as something her mother was doing for someone else, so, of course, the attitude that she got from that was that something was being taken away rather than something being given."[53]

It seems ironic for feminists to embrace the argument that certain activities might inherently lead their children to fear abandonment, and that consequently such activities should be banned. Feminists have fought hard to gain access for women to amniocentesis and late-stage abortions of fetuses with a genetic defect[54]— even in light of similarly anecdotal evidence that when the woman aborts, her *other* children will feel that, they too, might be "sent to heaven" by their mother.[55] Indeed, it could be argued that therapeutic abortion is more devastating to the remaining children than is surrogacy. After all, the brother or sister who is aborted was intended to be part of the family; moreover, he or she is dead, not just living with other people. I personally do not feel that the potential effect of either therapeutic abortion or surrogacy on the pregnant woman's other children is a sufficient reason to ban the procedures, particularly in light of the fact that parents can mediate how their children perceive and handle the experiences.

The reactions of outsiders to surrogacy may, however, be beyond the control of parents and may upset the children. But is this a sufficient reason to ban surrogacy? William Pierce seems to think so. He says that the children of surrogates "are being made fun of. Their lives are going to be ruined."[56] It would seem odd to let societal intolerance guide what relationships are permissible. Along those lines, a judge in a lesbian custody case replied to the argument that children could be harmed by stigma by stating:

It is just as reasonable to expect that they will emerge better equipped to search out their own standards of right and wrong, better able to perceive that the majority is not always correct in its moral judgments, and better able to understand the importance of conforming their beliefs to the requirements of reasons and tested knowledge, not the constraints of currently popular sentiment or prejudice.[57]

FEMINISM REVISITED

Feminists are taking great pride that they have mobilized public debate against surrogacy. But the precedent they are setting in their alliance with politicians like Henry Hyde and groups like the Catholic church is one whose policy is "protect women, even against their own decisions" and "protect children at all costs" (presumably, in latter applications even against the needs and desires of women). This is certainly the thrust of the New Jersey Supreme Court decision against surrogacy, which cites as support for its holding the notorious *In re A. C.* case. In that case a woman's decision to refuse a Cesarean section was overridden based on an unsubstantiated possibility of benefit to her future child.[58]

In fact, the tenor of the New Jersey Supreme Court decision is reminiscent of earlier decisions "protecting" women that have been roundly criticized by feminists. The U.S. Supreme Court in 1872 felt it was necessary to prevent Myra Bradwell and all other women from practicing law—in order to protect women and their children. And when courts upheld sexist employment laws that kept women out of employment that men were allowed to take, they used language that might have come right out of the New Jersey Supreme Court's decision in the Baby M case. A woman's

physical structure and a proper discharge of her maternal functions—having in view not merely her health, but the well-being of the race—justify legislation to protect her from the greed as well as the passion of man. The limitations which this statute place upon her contractual powers, upon her right to agree with her employer as to the time she shall labor, are not imposed solely for her benefit, but also largely for the benefit of all.[59]

The New Jersey Supreme Court rightly pointed out that not everything should be for sale in our society. But the examples given by the court, such as occupational safety and health laws prohibiting workers from voluntarily accepting money to work in an unsafe job, apply to both men and women. In addition, an unsafe job presents risks that we would not want people to undertake, whether or not they received pay. In contrast, a policy against paid surrogacy prevents women from taking risks (pregnancy and relinquishment) that they are allowed to take for free. It applies disparately—men are still allowed to relinquish their parental rights in advance of conception and to receive money for their role in providing the missing male factor for procreation.

Some feminists are comfortable with advocating disparate treatment on the grounds that gestation is such a unique experience that it has no male counterpart at law and so deserves a unique legal status.[60] The special nature of gestation, according to this argument, gives rise to special rights—such as the right for the surrogate to change her mind and assert her legal parenthood after the child is born.

The other side of the gestational coin, which has not been sufficiently addressed by these feminists, is that with special rights come special responsibilities. If gestation can be viewed as unique in surrogacy, then it can be viewed as unique in other areas. Pregnant women could be held to have responsibilities that other members of society do not have—such as the responsibility to have a Cesarean section against their wishes in order to protect the health of a child (since only pregnant women are in the unique position of being able to influence the health of the child).

Some feminists have criticized surrogacy as turning participating women, albeit with their consent, into reproductive vessels. I see the danger of the anti-surrogacy arguments as potentially turning *all* women into reproductive vessels, without their consent, by providing government oversight for women's decisions and creating a disparate legal category for gestation. Moreover, by breathing life into arguments that feminists have put to rest in other contexts, the current rationales opposing surrogacy could undermine a larger feminist agenda.

References and Notes

1. Iver Peterson, "Baby M Custody Trial Splits Ranks of Feminists over Issue of Exploitation." *New York Times*, Feb. 24, 1987 (quoting Linda Bowker).

2. Bob Port, "Feminists Come to the Aid of Whitehead's Case," *St. Petersburg Times*, Feb. 23, 1987, 1A.

3. Brief filed on behalf of Amici Curiae, the Foundation on Economic Trends et al., In the matter of Baby M, New Jersey Supreme Court, Docket No. FM-25314-86E (hereafter cited as "Brief"). (The feminists joining in the brief included Betty Friedan, Gloria Steinem, Gena Corea, Barbara Katz Rothman, Lois Gould, Michelle Harrison, Kathleen Lahey, Phyllis Chesler, and Letty Cottin Pogrebin.)

4. See, e.g., Roe v. Wade, 410 U.S. 113 (1973); Griswold v. Connecticut, 381 U.S. 479 (1965); Meyer v. Nebraska, 262 U.S. 390 (1923); Pierce v. Society of Sisters. 268 U.S. 510 (1928).

5. See, e.g., Karst, "The Freedom of Intimate Association." *Yale Law Journal*, 89 (1980): 624.

6. Prior to conception and during pregnancy, the surrogate mother contract is a personal service contract. However, after the child's birth, no further services on the part of the surrogate are needed. Thus, enforcing a provision providing for the father's custody of the child is not the enforcement of a personal services contract. It is like the enforcement of a court order on custody or the application of a paternity statute.

7. Lori Andrews, "The Aftermath of Baby M: Proposed State Laws on Surrogate Motherhood," *Hastings Center Report*, 17 (Oct./Nov. 1987): 31–40, at 37.

8. In re Baby M, 217 N.J. Super, 313, 525 A.2d 1128, 1159 (1987).

9. Jhordan C. v. Mary K., 179 Cal. App. 3d 386, 224 Cal. Rptr. 530 (1986).

10. *Surrogate Parenthood and New Reproductive Technologies, A Joint Public Hearing, before the N.Y. State Assembly, N.Y. State Senate, Judiciary Committees* (Oct. 16, 1986) (statement of Bob Arenstein at 103–4, 125); *In The Matter of a Hearing on Surrogate Parenting before the N.Y. Standing Committee on Child Care* (May 8, 1987) [statement of Adria Hillman at 174, statement of Mary Ann Dibari at 212 ("the prostitution of motherhood")].

11. *Surrogacy Arrangement Act of 1987: Hearing on H.R. 2433, before the Subcomm. on Transportation, Tourism, and Hazardous Materials,* 100th Cong., 1st sess (Oct. 15, 1987) (statement of Gena Corea at 3, 5); Robert Gould, N.Y. Testimony (May 8, 1987), supra note 10, at 233 (slavery).

12. Arthur Morrell, U.S. Testimony (Oct. 15, 1987), supra note 11, at 1.

13. William Pierce, U.S. Testimony (Oct. 15, 1987), supra note 11, at 2, citing Harvard Law Professor Lawrence Tribe.

14. Brief, supra note 3, at 19.

15. Port, supra note 2, at 7A, quoting Phyllis Chesler.

16. Gena Corea, U.S. Testimony (Oct. 15, 1987), supra note 11, at 3; Hillman, N.Y. Testimony (May 8, 1987), supra note 10, at 174.

17. Ellen Goodman, "Checking the Baby M Contract," *Boston Globe,* March 24, 1987, 15.

18. Gena Corea, U.S. Testimony (Oct. 15, 1987), supra note 11, at 5; Hillman, N. Y. Testimony (May 8, 1987) supra note 10, at 174.

19. Gena Corea, U.S. Testimony (Oct. 15, 1987), supra note 11, at 5.

20. Id.

21. Id.: 2.

22. Elizabeth Kane, U.S. Testimony (Oct. 15, 1987), supra note 11, at 1.

23. Kay Longcope, "Standing up for Mary Beth," *Boston Globe,* March 5, 1987, 81, 83 (quoting Janice Raymond).

24. Brief, supra note 3, at 14.

25. Robert Gould, N.Y. Testimony (May 8, 1987), supra note 10, at 232.

26. Judianne Densen-Gerber, N.Y. Testimony (May 8, 1987), supra note 10, at 253; Robert Gould, N.Y. Testimony (May 8, 1987), supra note 10, at 232.

27. Robert Gould, N.Y. Testimony (May 8, 1987), supra note 10, at 232.

28. Henry Hyde, U.S. Testimony (Oct. 15, 1987), supra note 11, at 1 ("Commercial surrogacy arrangements, by rendering children into chattel, are in my opinion, immoral."); DiBari, N.Y. Testimony (May 8, 1987), supra note 10, at 212.

29. John Ray, U.S. Testimony (Oct. 15, 1987), supra note 11, at 7.

30. See, e.g., Maureen McGuire and Nancy J. Alexander, "Artificial Insemination of Single Women," *Fertility and Sterility,* 43 (Feb, 1985): 182–84; Raschke and Raschke, "Family Conflict and Children's Self-Concept: A Comparison of Intact and Single Parent Families," *Journal of Marriage and the Family,* 41 (1979): 367; Weiss, "Growing up a Little Faster," *Journal of Social Issues,* 35 (1979): 97.

31. See, e.g., Rynearson, "Relinquishment and Its Maternal Complications: A Preliminary Study," *American Journal of Psychiatry,* 139 (1982): 338; Deykin, Campbell, Patti, "The Postadoption Experience of Surrendering Parents," *Amerian Journal of Orthopsychiatry,* 54 (1984): 271.

32. Betsy Aigen, N.Y. Testimony (May 8, 1987), supra note 10, at 18.

33. Robert Arenstein, U.S. Testimony (Oct. 15, 1987), supra note 11, at 9.

34. Brief, supra note 3, at 30–31.

35. In re Baby M, 109 N.J. 396; 537 A.2d 1227, 1248 (1988).

36. See Brief filed on behalf of Amicus Curiae the Gruter Institute, In the Matter of Baby M, New Jersey Supreme Court, Docket No. FM-25314-86E.

37. *Hearing in re Surrogate Parenting: Hearing on S.B. 1429, before Senators Goodhue, Dunne, Misters Balboni, Abramson, and Amgott* (April 10, 1987) (statement of Elaine Rosenfeld at 187). A similar argument made by Adria Hillman, N.Y. Testimony (May 8, 1987), supra note 10, at 175.

38. Joan Einwohner, N.Y. Testimony (April 10, 1987), supra note 37, at 110–11.

39. Gena Corea, *The Mother Machine* (New York: Harper & Row, 1985), 3.

40. Brief, supra note 3, at 10, 13; Judy Breidbart, N.Y. Testimony (May 8, 1987), supra note 10, at 168.

41. K. Cotton and D. Winn, *Baby Cotton: For Love and Money* (1985).

42. Karen Peters, N.Y. Testimony (May 8, 1987), supra note 10, at 121.

43. In re Baby M, 109 N.J. 396; 537 A.2d 1227, 1253 (1988).

44. Carey v. Population Services Int'l., 431 U.S. 678 (1977).

45. Carey v. Population Services, Int'l., 431 U.S. 678, 688 (1976) (citation omitted).

46. Besty Aigen, N.Y. Testimony (May 8, 1987), supra note 10, at 11–12.

47. Adria Hillman, N.Y. Testimony (May 8, 1987), supra note 10, at 177–78.

48. Jane Leavy, "It Doesn't Take Labor Pains to Make a Real Mom," *Washington Post*, April 4, 1987.

49. Donna Regan, N.Y. Testimony (May 8, 1987), supra note 10, at 157.

50. Id.

51. Michelle Harrison, "Social Construction of Mary Beth Whitehead," *Gender and Society*, 1 (Sept. 1987): 300–11.

52. Teasdale and Owens, "Influence of Paternal Social Class on Intelligence Level in Male Adoptees and Non-Adoptees," *British Journal of Educational Psychology*, 56 (1986): 3.

53. Donna Regan, N.Y. Testimony (May 8, 1987), supra note 10, at 156.

54. See, e.g., the briefs filed by feminist organizations in Thornburgh v. American College of Obstetricians, 476 U.S. 747 (1986).

55. See, e.g., J. Fletcher, *Coping with Genetic Disorders: A Guide for Counseling* (San Francisco: Harper & Row, 1982).

56. William Pierce, N.Y. Testimony (May 8, 1987), supra note 10, at 86. It should be pointed out that kids hassle other kids for a wide range of reasons. A child might equally be made fun of being the recipient of a kidney transplant or being the child of a garbage man.

57. M.P. v. S.P., 169 N.J. Super, 425, 438, 404 A.2d 1256, 1263 (Super. Ct. App. Div. 1979).

58. In re Baby M, 109 N.J. 396; 537 A.2d 1227, 1254 n. 13 (1988), citing In re A. C., 533 A.2d 611 (D.C. App. 1987).

59. Muller v. Oregon, 208 U.S. 412, 422 (1907).

60. See Brief, supra note 3, at 11.

The Maternal-Fetal Dyad
Exploring the Two-Patient Obstetric Model

Susan S. Mattingly PhD

For ages, medicine has had poor access to the fetus inside the mother's womb. But in relatively recent years, the human body has become transparent. The latest breakthroughs of technology have made it possible, from the very beginning of pregnancy, to consider the fetus as an individual who can be examined and sampled. His or her physician may now establish a diagnosis and prognosis and prescribe a treatment in the same way as in traditional medicine.

—Fernand Daffos[1]

Developments in obstetric medicine during the past ten to twenty years have transformed the clinical status of the fetus.[2] Traditionally physicians have been trained to assess fetal condition by indirect methods: palpating the fetus through the maternal abdominal wall and uterus, measuring hormonal milieu through maternal urine and serum, estimating statistical risks from parental medical histories. While the skillful use of these methods could produce highly reliable clues to

From *Hastings Center Report*, 22, 13–18, 1992.

fetal health and development, the fetus itself eluded direct examination. Throughout pregnancy the fetus could not be known, but only approached inferentially and probabilistically. Until recently suspected fetal anomalies have been treated indirectly too, by therapeutically managing the maternal environment. Unable to interact with the fetus in clear distinction from its host, physicians conceptualized the maternal-fetal dyad as one complex patient, the gravid female, of which the fetus was an integral part.

High-resolution ultrasonography and techniques for sampling fetal blood, urine, and other tissue have changed this conceptual scheme. These diagnostic tools penetrate the opaque environment and reveal the fetus to clinical observation in all its anatomical, physiological, and biochemical particularity. When anomalies are detected, *in utero* medical and surgical procedures are already beginning to offer alternatives to therapeutic delivery and neonatal treatment. The biological maternal-fetal relationship has not changed, of course, but the medical model of that relationship has shifted emphasis from unity to duality. Clinicians no longer look to the maternal host for diagnostic data and a therapeutic medium; they look through her to the fetal organism and regard it as a distinct patient in its own right.

What ethical implications flow from the fetus's transformation from inferred to observed entity? Unfortunately, legal developments have tended to preempt ethical exploration of the new two-patient obstetric model. Some physicians, assuming enhanced rights on the part of the fetal patient, have sought and obtained court orders to perform fetal therapies (notably cesarean deliveries) without maternal consent.[3] Although few in number, these cases raise the possibility of a new standard of clinical practice with far-reaching implications for civil and criminal liabilities to physicians and pregnant women. With legal stakes so high, it is not surprising that ethical inquiry has been displaced. Yet in the absence of independent and through ethical analysis one cannot judge whether these developments are compatible with fundamental values of medicine and medical care, and so one cannot know whether physicians have responsibilities, individually or collectively, to promote or resist them.

Well-grounded in law and ethics or not, cases of court-ordered fetal therapy have set the agenda for debate, focusing attention on the question, What should the physician do when a pregnant woman refuses medical or surgical treatment recommended for the well-being of the newly individuated fetal patient? The two-patient problem for the physician is seen to begin at the point of maternal refusal and is framed as a conflict between values of fetal benefit and maternal autonomy. The medical recommendation precipitating refusal is, presumably, unproblematic. But that presumption requires examination. Inherent in any conceptual shift is the potential for equivocation between the old paradigm and the new. If the physician's recommendation of fetal therapy incorporates one-patient thinking about the maternal-fetal relationship, questions about maternal refusal of that recommendation may be spurious, resting on a logically illicit hybrid of one-patient and two-patient conceptual schemes.

We need, I think, to gain a fresh perspective on this issue by stepping back from the legal debate and considering in a systematic way how ethical guidelines for prenatal medical care are altered by transition to the two-patient obstetric model. How do the familiar principles of beneficence, justice, and autonomy operate within the new model in contrast to the old? Fetal rights and fiduciary responsibilities of professionals, parents, and the state may all be affected by the fetus's newly acquired identity as a second individual patient, but to avoid blurring distinctions among these roles my focus will rest on ethical implications for physicians. After all, elevation of the fetus to patient status has occurred not because of any change in the fetus or in the maternal-fetal relationship but because of a change in physicians—in how they think about and relate to their patients during pregnancy—so it is in the physician-patient relationship that we should expect the ethical repercussions to begin.

FOR THE PATIENT'S OWN GOOD

The ethical principle guiding initial formulations of medical recommendations is beneficence. It directs physicians to recommend that course of therapy most likely to protect and promote patient health, based on estimates of medical benefits relative to burdens for the various treatment options. In making these complex comparisons, physicians are to ignore their own and third-party interests, responding compassionately to patient medical needs alone. For some purposes it is important to distinguish positive duties to offer benefits from negative duties not to inflict burdens. 'Beneficence' then refers more narrowly to the former duties, 'nonmaleficence' to the latter. Nonmaleficence requires that the risks, discomforts, and harms inherent in medical or surgical treatment be offset by proportionate therapeutic gains for the patient. Accordingly, treatment without therapeutic intent is categorically prohibited by the principle of nonmaleficence.

In cases where maternal and fetal burdens associated with fetal therapy are relatively small and prospective benefits to the fetus are substantial, the physician's duty of beneficence on the one-patient obstetric model is clearly to recommend treatment. This is true even if treatment offers *no* medical benefits, only burdens, to the woman in distinction from the fetus. When the maternal-fetal dyad is regarded as an organic whole, what matters is that *combined* maternal-fetal benefits outweigh *combined* maternal-fetal burdens. Distributions of benefits and burdens between fetal and maternal components of the one patient are not ethically relevant.

When fetus and pregnant woman are conceptualized as two individual patients, however, it is no longer appropriate to consider effects of treatment on the two combined. Physicians are to decide what is medically best for each patient considered separately. When fetal benefits out-weigh fetal burdens of intervention, beneficence dictates recommending therapy for the fetal patient. But when anomalous fetal conditions pose no threat to maternal health, caring for the fetal patient imposes some degree of discomfort, harm, or risk on the maternal patient with no offsetting therapeutic benefits to her.[4] Maternal medical burdens outweigh maternal medical benefits, such maleficence requires recommending *against* treatment for the maternal patient.

Here is an ethical two-patient problem for the physician that arises well before the point of maternal refusal: treatment medically indicated for one patient is contraindicated for the other, yet both must be treated (or not treated) alike. It is difficult to see a favorable ratio of fetal gains to maternal losses as a problem and not a solution, of course, for we are accustomed to maternal-fetal balancing on the one-patient model. Also, we know that in most cases pregnant women expect to assume reasonable risks to improve the chances of delivering a healthy baby. Willingness to do so is ideally implicit in the choice of pregnancy, and indeed the argument that the pregnant woman increases her responsibility for the fetus's well-being by choosing not to have an abortion is often cited to support the medical duty to provide fetal therapy.[5] Given persistent economic and social obstacles to abortion, not to mention its precarious legality, the degree to which abortion rights increase maternal responsibilities is, I think, dubious, but that is a side issue. The real question is how maternal duties affect professional duties and exactly which duties are affected. Since beneficence considerations are restricted to medical benefits and burdens, it seems clear that maternal morality must be a factor to be weighed against beneficence at a later stage of ethical analysis.

On the two-patient model of the maternal-fetal dyad, a single treatment recommendation for both patients cannot be justified in terms of the beneficence principle alone, for it includes no provision for balancing burdens to one patient against benefits to another. Indeed, tradeoffs *between* patients are expressly prohibited by the exclusion of third-party interests. Beneficence, applying as it does to patients one by one, is logically unequipped to produce a single recommendation for two linked patients with conflicting medical needs.

MEDIATING THE CONFLICT

Conflicts between duties of beneficence and nonmaleficence to multiple patients are rare in medicine but they do characteristically occur in two areas in addition to obstetrics: live-donor tissue transplantation and nontherapeutic research. In both fields physicians' unusual divided loyalties—to patients in need of medical help and to those put at medical risk to provide that help—have engendered considerable concern and an extensive ethical literature.[6] The resulting codes and practices resist any movement toward a utilitarian ethic whereby imperatives of medical rescue and medical progress would justify imposing relatively small harms and risks on donors and subjects. The rationale for rejecting an approach that trades off benefits against harms between patients hinges on the way medical moral authority is circumscribed. Professional ethical decisions are not generic judgments made from a neutral standpoint preferring always the lesser to the greater harm. They are choices made from the standpoint of the professional as moral agent, hence *causal responsibility* and *motivation* for harm are more significant variables than *quantity* of harm. If physicians do not intervene to help a patient in need of a kidney transplant, the patient suffers harm due to progress of the disease condition, and the physician's choice is at most a contributing factor; if physicians do intervene, the donor suffers harm directly and exclusively from medical intervention. The Hippocratic tradition is shaped by the presumption that moral liability for physician-caused harm to a patient is relieved only by therapeutic intent for that patient, whereas excusing conditions and motivations for failure to benefit a patient are many and varied.

Nonmaleficence constrains beneficence and not vice versa.

In transplantation and research ethics, nonmaleficence constraints have been cautiously qualified to permit physicians under narrowly specified conditions to treat some patients nontherapeutically in order to benefit others. First, the medical burdens inflicted must be smaller in relation to anticipated benefits than they are when they accrue to one and the same patient. Second, patients treated nontherapeutically must be volunteers. *Recommending* nontherapeutic treatment remains unethical, although *providing* it is permissible at the subject's or donor's request.

On the one-patient model for obstetric care, conflicts between maternal and fetal needs occur within, not between, patients; they are balanced and resolved by physicians under the principle of beneficence in determining the medically indicated course of therapy. On the two-patient model, however, competing maternal and fetal needs must be settled at a different level, by applying standards of justice. According to these standards, physicians are not at liberty to benefit one patient by inflicting medical harms on another, except under stringently qualified conditions. In most cases, pregnant women, continuing to identify fetal needs and interests with their own, will request treatment to promote fetal health, thereby lifting constraints of nonmaleficence and authorizing physicians to proceed with proportionate fetal therapy. For physicians to recommend fetal therapy as if it were medically indicated for both patients, however, would be misleading and unethical.

The question is whether, having removed fetal needs from the calculus of maternal medical interests and having divided one compound professional-patient obligation into two discrete fiduciary commitments, physicians may discount protective duties owed to the woman as an individual patient in her own right. Is this the stage at which professional duties are altered by maternal duties? In other areas of medicine, the injunction against intentional medical harm is not thought to be affected by patient morality or social role: neither moral debts to society nor obligations of family relationship authorize physicians to take a stronger-than-invitational approach in recruiting research subjects or tissue donors. Indeed, incarcerated felons and other institutionalized populations are virtually off-limits to medical researchers, since distinctions between *inviting, advising,* and *requiring* are difficult to maintain in coercive contexts. More to the point, in transplantation ethics, family pressures on the donor are considered a form of moral coercion, increasing rather than decreasing professional obligations to emphasize the optional nature of the transaction. When alternate volunteers or procedures are unavailable or unlikely to yield successful results, this restrained approach on the part of physicians may result in the loss of significant prospective benefits, including lives that might have been saved. That is the price of role-based limits on professional moral agency. But a professional ethics that allowed treatment recommendations to be based on moral diagnosis of patients and therapeutic intent for others would also exact a price: it would erode the fiduciary character of the physician-patient relationship, undermining the basis for patient trust.

By separating the maternal-fetal dyad conceptually into two individual patients, the new obstetric model bifurcates the process of formulating medical recommendations: physicians should recommend beneficial fetal therapy for the fetal patient, but recommending treatment for the maternal patient contrary to her best medical interests is prohibited by standards for the just resolution of conflicting duties to multiple patients. In two-patient obstetrics, physicians may at most invite and encourage the pregnant woman to submit voluntarily to burdensome treatment for the sake of proportionate fetal benefits. Usually the invitation will be readily accepted, so the distinction between inviting treatment and recommending it will have little

practical importance. It is of considerable theoretical importance, however, to the pregnant woman's autonomy.

HONORING THE PATIENT

On the one-patient obstetric model, recommended fetal therapy offers net medical benefits to the pregnant woman, the refusal of which, here as in other medical contexts, should trigger discussion to determine whether her needs and values are in fact incompatible with treatment. Although efforts to encourage consent are appropriate, paternalistic treatment of a competent dissenting patient is unlikely to be justified. In particular, her autonomy cannot be restricted on the grounds that she is causing harm to others, as the pregnant woman on the one-patient model causes harm only to herself.

Rejecting treatment on the two-patient obstetric model is more complicated. The physician's two treatment proposals—the recommendation of therapy for the fetus and the invitation to nontherapeutic maternal treatment as a means to fetal therapy—call for two distinct maternal replies, neither of which is a standard exercise of patient autonomy. First, the recommendation of therapy for the fetus requires a *maternal proxy decision* on behalf of the incompetent fetal patient. Maternal responsibility for fetal well-being is certainly relevant at this point, and physicians are morally authorized to challenge proxy decisions that are plainly contrary to the patient's best interests. Yet even if an alternate proxy (the father of the future child, for instance, or a court-appointed legal guardian) consents to therapy on behalf of the fetus, another ethical step remains. The physician's second proposal, the invitation to nontherapeutic maternal treatment, requires a *maternal patient decision.* This second step distinguishes fetal therapy from treatment of an infant or child. Treatment of an infant may impose substantial burdens of financial and personal care on parents, but physicians do not directly cause these harms through nontherapeutic practice of the medical art on parents *qua* patients. New technologies notwithstanding, diagnostic and therapeutic interventions on behalf of the fetus do entail medical invasion of the mother, and the proxy *for the fetus* has no ethical standing to consent to this invasion. What if the maternal patient declines treatment of herself?

When a proposed course of treatment is in a patient's medical best interests, refusal raises questions about the professional duty of respect for patient autonomy, because the harm caused by not treating her cannot be justified if the patient's refusal was not fully voluntary. When a patient *requests* treatment contrary to her medical best interests, the situation is the same: the request to donate a kidney, for instance, provokes questions about the duty of respect for patient autonomy because the harm caused by harvesting the kidney cannot be justified if the request was not fully voluntary.

In contrast to both of these cases, refusal of treatment contrary to a patient's medical best interests prompts no such questions about the duty to honor autonomy. When physicians disregard a patient's refusal of harmful treatment, the violation of patient autonomy is the least of their professional wrongs. Since ethical immunity against medical harm is independent of patient autonomy, it is uncompromised by limits on autonomy—incompetence, coercion, harm to others—that sometimes justify paternalism. *Harming* a patient without consent is not medical paternalism but medical maleficence.

A woman's failure to volunteer for fetal therapy may seriously violate her fiduciary responsibilities to the fetus, thus disqualifying her as proxy, but the physician's duties to her as patient remain intact. It is not the woman's moral obligation to consent that authorizes physicians to subject her to harm or risk without therapeutic intent; *consent itself* is necessary—consent that is to the highest degree competent, informed, uncoerced, and harmless to third parties. These ex-

acting standards rule out any attempt to substitute proxy or presumed consent for maternal dissent. As on the one-patient model, physicians would be remiss if they did not make every effort to elicit maternal consent to low-risk, high-gain fetal therapy by providing honest reassurance and encouragement, but in the principles and precedents of medical ethics as applied to the two-patient obstetric model we find no basis for overriding maternal refusals to volunteer for such procedures.

TWO-PATIENT ETHICS & THE MATERNAL-FETAL ECOSYSTEM

When the fetus is conceptualized in clinical obstetrics not as an integral part of the pregnant woman (her condition of pregnancy, as it were) but as a second individual patient, the physician's duties to promote fetal well-being are, *prima facie,* increased. Maternal harms no longer weigh against recommendations made for the sake of fetal benefit. Also, the pregnant woman no longer speaks inclusively as maternal-fetal patient; if her decisions are not sufficiently protective of fetal interests an alternate proxy may be sought. But this is only half of the story. The other half is that professional duties to the first patient—the maternal patient—are paradoxically increased as well. Detached conceptually from the fetus, the maternal patient suffers medical harms from fetal therapy that are no longer offset by fetal benefits. Her physician may not recommend fetal therapy for her, and the injunction against harming one patient involuntarily to help another is virtually absolute.

Drawing selectively and equivocally from both models—treating the fetus as an independent patient but continuing to regard the pregnant woman as a compound patient incorporating the fetus—has, I think, caused the physician's ethical dilemma to be misconstrued as a conflict between the duty to benefit the fetus and the duty to respect the woman's autonomy. If maternal refusal of fetal therapy were a standard exercise of patient autonomy, it would be subject to paternalistic review to guard against harms to others. But fetal therapy is beneficial to the pregnant woman only on the old model, where she *includes* the fetus, while fetal harm is harm to another only on the new model, where the fetus is independent and exclusive of the woman. In fact, maternal autonomy plays a peripheral role on the two-patient model: maternal autonomy *qua* proxy may be challenged, and maternal autonomy *qua* patient is redundant, a secondary defense against treatment that may not ethically be recommended for her in the first place. From the standpoint of professional ethics, the obstacle to fetal benefit is not maternal autonomy but maternal nonmaleficence. Newly strengthened duties to help the fetal patient are constrained by stronger duties to do no harm to the individualized maternal patient.

Despite the fetus's new clinical status as a second distinct patient, then, physicians' prerogatives to intervene on its behalf are no greater than before. Whether the maternal-fetal dyad is regarded as one patient or two is less relevant to providing ethical prenatal care than the fact of that dyad's biological unity. Literally, if not conceptually, the pregnant woman incorporates the fetus, so direct medical access to the fetal patient is as remote as ever. Ironically, when the fetus is construed as a second independent patient, physicians' prerogatives to act as fetal advocates are actually diminished. This consequence flows not from any assumed superiority of maternal rights over fetal rights but from differential professional duties to donors and recipients of medical benefits. Two-patient benefit-burden transactions require of physicians a deferential approach to those asked to assume medical risks for others and a readiness to shield reluctant or indecisive patients from involuntary harm. If the example of transplantation ethics is followed in obstetrics, physicians have acquired obligations to neutralize moral pressures on pregnant women arising from family relationships and ensure that any maternal sacrifices to benefit the fetus are strictly voluntary.

But surely our argument has carried us too far. If status as an independent patient affords the fetus relatively *less* protection than its previous state of dependency, instead of revising ethical standards of obstetric care to fit that counterintuitive conclusion one might simply retract the two-patient hypothesis. Perhaps developments in fetal medicine do not require reconceptualizing the obstetric patient after all. Alternatively, since the concept of the fetus as a second patient is already well entrenched in perinatal medical philosophy, one might challenge the orthodox view of the professional-patient relationship, which suppresses dependency relations among patients and posits them as strangers to one another.[7] Deeply ingrained in the Western Hippocratic tradition and in Eastern medical traditions as well, the assumption that physicians should treat patients as generic individuals without regard to social role or status reflects an ideal of egalitarian, compassionate, patient-centered medical care.[8] Can professional obligations be made sensitive to relationships of dependency between patients without detriment to that ideal and without simply making an *ad hoc* exception for the case at hand?

Efforts to reinterpret professional ethical principles to accommodate just such relationships are in fact under way in family practice medicine.[9] Family medicine rejects the reductionist model of illness, which focuses narrowly on proximate causes within the patient as a biological organism, espousing instead a biopsychosocial model of health and disease. It looks beyond organic conditions, even beyond the presenting patient, to family relationships and circumstances that affect and are affected by patient health. For diagnostic and therapeutic purposes, the patient is conceptualized in relation to the family ecosystem. This environmental medical model is not entirely compatible with an individualistic patient-centered professional ethics. Responsibilities of family practice physicians to their patients must be understood expansively to include the family context—guiding patients toward choices that are responsive to their family situations and helping family members fulfill obligations of care to one another.

Adapting the contextual approach of family practice medicine to obstetrics, we might think of the maternal-fetal dyad as an integrated, two-patient ecosystem whose individual components are not conceptually independent. Caring for one implicates the other and the family context. An environmental medical model would remove the specter of dueling specialists vying for medical control of a complicated pregnancy—the *reductio ad absurdum* of the two-patient thesis. It would counteract any tendency of physicians to discount the impact of fetal treatment on the pregnant woman, now effaced by her clinical transparency, and at the same time legitimize looking beyond the maternal patient to her protective biological and social role. Helping the pregnant woman fulfill her fiduciary duties to the fetus would again, as on the one-patient model, become a primary professional goal.

Once family roles and circumstances are drawn into the purview of patient care decisions, they may not be selectively considered only when they weigh in favor of treatment. Maternal fiduciary duties, for instance, typically extend beyond the fetus to other family members, and standards of family ethics do not always assign highest priority to fetal needs and claims. If the practice of fetal medicine were informed by an environmental maternal-fetal model, family demands would be acknowledged, not dismissed as irrelevant or even illicit conflicts of interest. By assuming obligations to address a wide range of health-related but nonmedical family problems, physicians may make it possible for the woman to accept therapy recommended for the fetus, but sometimes physicians must help patients and proxies make tragic choices forced by limited family circumstances, when resources cannot be stretched to meet the basic needs of all.[10] Also, family and medical values will sometimes diverge: increasing the chances for live delivery of a severely damaged fetus, for example, might be a medical value but a family disvalue. A context-sensitive perspective commits physicians to respect a family's well-considered value judgments unless basic family duties are violated.

Not surprisingly, ethical standards evolving in family practice medicine do not sanction doctors' enforcing a duty on the part of family members to sacrifice for each other, although reluctance to volunteer might be considered symptomatic of family dysfunction, to be treated through supportive intervention. In family practice, medical authority is exercised by negotiating medical goals and in collaborative decision-making. The physician's last resort in cases of severe and irremediable family problems—petitioning for the temporary or permanent removal to alternate caregivers of dependents at risk—is not available for the fetal dependent, of course, although planning for transfer of the neonate might be considered, but then the social meaning of the maternal-fetal relationship is changed. It reverts to the generic relationship of strangers, so the donor protections of two-person ethics apply: physicians should guard the woman from undue pressures to undergo medical harms for someone else's child.

Maternal-fetal conflicts are interesting out of proportion to their incidence in part because they raise in a compelling way questions about the integration of medical and family ethics, an important and underdeveloped topic. Conceptualizing the maternal-fetal dyad as two unrelated patients is bizarre whether the consequence is to tilt the ethical standard toward strongly weighted professional obligations to protect the maternal donor, as I have argued, or in the opposite direction. Yet the integration of family status into the patient role is not a simple or clearcut matter. Patients who voluntarily present assume *prima facie* duties to act in their own medical best interests, but neither medical ethics nor medical education addresses the task of helping patients combine these duties with the imperatives of their family roles. Family responsibilities are lumped together with patients' idiosyncratic preferences and masked by professional respect for individual patient autonomy. But while exclusion of family concerns from medical attention is often unsatisfactory, to select one familial duty that bolsters the case for medical intervention and graft it onto a medical model that otherwise suppresses family relationships clearly will not do.

To expand the medical gaze to encompass family status is to see patients as persons in social systems, and this in turn demands a broader view of professional care than is typical of modern scientific medicine. Family practice medicine is an exception, and a biopsychosocial perspective is implicit, as well, in the traditional medical and ethical values of obstetric care. Recent developments in obstetrics, however, particularly the emergence of a subspecialty in fetology, introduce a narrow focus that sees only the fetus as it survives the pathologies of pregnancy.

Constructing a model of the maternal-fetal dyad as a two-patient ecosystem would restore to medical relevance the relationship of dependence and protection characteristic of the dyad. The effect of such a model would be to join the professional-patient relationships to the two patients almost as closely as if they were a single compound commitment to one compound patient. Protections associated with dependence would be reinstated and the two-patient presumption against maternal medical sacrifice averted. Within a two-patient framework, it is possible, then, to approximate the one-patient standard of obstetric care, but there is no warrant for requiring or permitting physicians to move beyond it toward a stronger posture of fetal protection. One patient or two, independent or dependent, when the various possible models of the maternal-fetal dyad are consistently applied, they converge to reinforce the physician's customary ethical stance—working cooperatively with the pregnant woman for common, linked goals of infant, maternal, and family well-being.

References

1. Fernand Daffos, "Access to the Other Patient," *Seminars in Perinatology* 13, no. 4 (1989): 252.

2. F. A. Manning, "Reflections on Future Directions of Perinatal Medicine," *Seminars in Perinatology* 13, no. 4 (1989):342–51. In the introductory paragraphs I have relied heavily on Manning's excellent account of the way in which technical innovations in perinatal medicine have brought about subtle but far-reaching changes in underlying philosophy.

3. Veronika E. G. Kolder et al., "Court-Ordered Obstetrical Interventions," *NEJM* 316, no. 19 (1987): 1192–96.

4. Michael R. Harrison et al., "Management of the Fetus with a Correctable Congenital Defect," *JAMA* 246, no. 7 (1981): 774–77.

5. H. Tristram Engelhardt, Jr., "Current Controversies in Obstetrics: Wrongful Life and Forced Fetal Surgical Procedures," *American Journal of Obstetrics and Gynecology* 151 (1985): 313–18. Engelhardt's argument is cited, for example, by Frank A. Chervenak and Laurence B. McCullough, "Ethical Challenges in Perinatal Medicine: The Intrapartum Management of Pregnancy Complicated by Fetal Hydrocephalus with Macrocephaly," *Seminars in Perinatology* 11, no. 3 (1987): 232–39.

6. See, for instance, Gordon Wolstenholme and Maeve O'Connor, eds., *Law & Ethics of Transplantation* (formerly *Ethics in Medical Progress: With Special Reference to Transplantation*) (London: Churchill, 1966); Roberta G. Simmons et al., *Gift of Life: The Social & Psychological Impact of Organ Transplantation* (New York: John Wiley & Sons, 1977); Paul A. Freund, ed., *Experimentation with Human Subjects* (New York: George Braziller, 1970); Robert J. Levine, *Ethics and Regulation of Clinical Research* (Baltimore: Urban and Schwarzenberg, 1981).

7. Informal practice varies widely, but theoretical medical ethics assigns no relevance to family responsibilities in arriving at patient care decisions except to the extent that family members are acknowledged as proxy decisionmakers, and then, perversely, they are to ignore responsibilities they or the patient may have aside from their duty to represent the wishes and interests of the patient. For a different view, see John Hardwig, "What About the Family?" *Hastings Center Report* 20, no. 2 (1990): 5–10.

8. Albert Jonsen, "Do No Harm," in *Cross Cultural Perspectives in Medical Ethics: Readings*, ed. Robert M. Veatch (Boston: Jones and Bartlett, 1989), pp. 199–210.
9. See, for example, Ronald J. Christie and C. Barry Hoffmaster, *Ethical Issues in Family Medicine* (New York: Oxford University Press, 1986).

11. Physicians and parents have distinct fiduciary responsibilities for the fetal patient, reflecting differences of scope between the professional and parental ethical standpoints. I have developed this point more fully in "Fetal Needs, Physicians' Duties," *Midwest Medical Ethics* 7, no. 1 (1991): 8–11.

Selective Termination of Pregnancy and Women's Reproductive Autonomy

Christine Overall PhD

The development of techniques for selective termination of pregnancy has added further questions to debates about women's reproductive self-determination. The procedure is performed during the first or second trimester in some instances of multiple pregnancy, either to eliminate a fetus found through prenatal diagnosis to be handicapped or at risk of a disability, or simply to reduce the number of fetuses in the uterus. More than two hundred cases of selective termination are known to have been performed around the world.[1]

Physicians and ethicists have expressed reservations about selective termination, both with respect to its moral justification and to the formation of social policy governing access to and resource allocation for this procedure. Selective termination has been viewed as invoking a right to kill a fetus rather than to control one's body, as with abortion,[2] and some commentators have recommended restricting the procedure to pregnancies of three or more[3] and even stipulated a need for national guidelines for the procedure.[4]

Many discussions appear to assume that selective termination is primarily a matter of acting against some fetus(es) on behalf of others. For example, Diana Brahams describes the issue as follows:

> Is it ethical and legally appropriate to carry out a selective reduction of pregnancy—that is, to destroy one or more fetuses in order to give the remaining fetus or fetuses a better chance?[5]

However, this construction of the problem is radically incomplete, since it omits attention to the women—their bodies and their lives—who should be at the center of any discussion of selective termination. When Margaret Somerville, for example, expresses concern about "the right to kill a fetus who is competing with another for space," she neglects to mention that the "space" in question is the pregnant woman's uterus. In fact, selective termination vividly instantiates many of the central ethical and policy concerns that must be raised about the technological manipulation of women's reproductive capacities.

Evans and colleagues state that "the ethical issues [of selective termination] are the same in multiple pregnancies whether the cause is spontaneous conception or infertility treatment." Such a claim is typical of many discussions in contemporary bioethics, which abstract specific

From *Hastings Center Report* 20, 6–11, 1990.

moral and social problems from the cultural context that produced them. But the issue of selective termination of pregnancy demonstrates the necessity of examining the social and political environment in which issues in biomedical ethics arise.

Selective termination itself must be understood and evaluated with reference to its own particular context. The apparent need or demand for selective termination in fact is created and elaborated in response to prior technological interventions in women's reproductive processes, themselves the result of prevailing cultural interpretations of infertility.

Hence, it is essential to explore the significance of selective termination for women's reproductive autonomy. The issue acquires added urgency at this point in both Canada and the United States when access to and allocation of funding for abortion are the focus of renewed controversy. Although not precisely the same as abortion, selective termination is similar insofar as in both cases one or more fetuses are destroyed. They differ in that in abortion the pregnancy ends whereas in selective termination, ideally, the pregnancy continues with one or more fetuses still present. I will argue that, provided a permissive abortion policy is justified (that is, a policy that allows abortion until the end of the second trimester), a concern for women's reproductive autonomy precludes any general policy restricting access to selective termination of pregnancy, as well as clinical practices that discriminate on nonmedical grounds as to which women will be permitted to choose the procedure or how many fetuses they must retain.

A TECHNOLOGICAL FIX

In recent discussions of selective termination, women with multiple pregnancies are often represented as demanding the procedure—sometimes by threatening to abort the entire pregnancy if they are not allowed selective termination.[6]

The assumption that individual women "demand" selective termination of pregnancy places all moral responsibility for the procedure on the women themselves. However, neither the multiple pregnancies nor the "demands" for selective termination originated *ex nihilo*. An examination of their sources suggests both that moral responsibility for selective termination cannot rest solely on individual women and that the "demand" for selective termination is not just a straightforward exercise of reproductive freedom.

Deliberate societal and medical responses to the perceived problem of female infertility generate much of the demand for selective termination, which is but one result of a complex system of values and beliefs concerning fertility and infertility, maternity and children. Infertility is not merely a physical condition; it is both interpreted and evaluated within cultural contexts that help to specify the appropriate beliefs about and responses to the condition of being unable to reproduce. According to the prevailing ideology of pronatalism, women must reproduce, men must acquire offspring, and both parents should be biologically related to their offspring. A climate of acquisition and commodification encourages and reinforces the notion of child as possession. Infertility is seen as a problem for which the solution must be acquiring a child of one's own, biologically related to oneself, at almost any emotional, physical, or economic costs.[7]

The recent increase in numbers of multiple pregnancies comes largely from two steps taken in the treatment of infertility. The use of fertility drugs to prod women's bodies into ovulating and producing more than one ovum at a time results in an incidence of multiple gestation ranging from 16 to 39 percent.[8] Gamete intrafallopian transfer (GIFT) using several eggs, and in vitro fertilization (IVF) with subsequent implantation of several embryos in the woman's uterus to increase the likelihood that she will become pregnant may also result in multiple gestation. As Brahams notes, "Pregnancy rate increments are about 8 percent for each pre-embryo replaced in

IVF, giving expected pregnancy rates of 8, 16, 24, and 32 percent for 1, 2, 3, and 4 pre-embryos, respectively." A "try anything" mentality is fostered by the fact that prospective IVF patients are often not adequately informed about the very low clinical success rates ("failure rates" would be a more appropriate term) of the procedure.[9] A case reported by Evans and colleagues dramatically illustrates the potential effects of these treatments: One woman's reproductive history included three cesarean sections, a tubal ligation, a tuboplasty (after which she remained infertile), in vitro fertilization with subsequent implantation of four embryos, selective termination of two of the fetuses, revelation via ultrasound that one of the remaining twins had "severe oligohydramnios and no evidence of a bladder or kidneys," spontaneous miscarriage of the abnormal twin, and intrauterine death of the remaining fetus.

In a commentary critical of selective termination, Angela Holder quotes Oscar Wilde's dictum: "In this world, there are only two tragedies. One is not getting what one wants, and the other is getting it." But this begs the question of what is meant by saying that women "want" multiple pregnancy, or "want" selective termination of pregnancy.[10] What factors led these women to take infertility drugs and/or participate in an IVF program? How do they evaluate fertility, pregnancy, motherhood, children? How do they perceive themselves as women, as potential mothers, as infertile, and where do children fit into these visions? To what degree were they adequately informed of the likelihood that they would gestate more than one fetus? Were they provided with adequate support to enable them to clarify their own reasons and goals for seeking reproductive interventions, and to provide assistance throughout the emotionally and physically demanding aspects of the treatment? Barbara Katz Rothman's appraisal of women who abort fetuses with genetic defects has more general applicability:

> They are the victims of a social system that fails to take collective responsibility for the needs of its members, and leaves individual women to make impossible choices. We are spared collective responsibility, because we individualize the problem. We make it the woman's own. She "chooses," and so we owe her nothing.[11]

Uncritical use of the claim that certain women "demand" selective termination implies that they are just selfish, unable to extend their caring to more than one or two infants, particularly if one has a disability. But this interpretation appears unjustified. In general, participants in IVF programs are extremely eager for a child. They are encouraged to be self-sacrificing, to be acquiescent in the manipulations the medical system requires their bodies to undergo. As John C. Hobbins notes, these women "have often already volunteered for innovative treatments and may be desperate to try another." The little evidence so far available suggests that if anything these women are, by comparison to their male partners, somewhat passive in regard to the making of reproductive decisions.[12] There is no evidence to suggest that most are not willing to assume the challenges of multiple pregnancy.

An additional cause of multiple pregnancy is the conflicting attitudes toward the embryo and fetus manifested in infertility research and clinical practice. One report suggests that multiple pregnancies resulting from IVF are generated not only because clinicians are driven by the motive to succeed—and implantation of large numbers of embryos appears to offer that prospect—but also because of "intimidation of medical practitioners by critics and authorities who insist that all fertilized eggs or pre-embryos be immediately returned to the patient."[13] Such "intimidation" does not, of course, excuse clinicians who may sacrifice their patients' well-being. Nevertheless, conservative beliefs in the necessity and inevitability of procreation and the sacredness and "personhood" of the embryo may contribute to the production of multiple pregnancies.

Thus, the technological "solutions" to some forms of female infertility create an additional problem of female hyperfertility—to which a further technological "solution" of selective termination is then offered. Women's so-called "demand" for selective termination of pregnancy is not a primordial expression of individual need, but a socially constructed response to prior medical interventions.

The debate over access to selective pregnancy termination exemplifies a classic no-win situation for women, in which medical technology generates a solution to a problem itself generated by medical technology—yet women are regarded as immoral for seeking that solution. While women have been, in part, victimized through the use of reproductive interventions that fail to respect and facilitate their reproductive autonomy, they are nevertheless unjustifiably held responsible for their attempts to cope with the outcomes of these interventions in the forms made available to them. From this perspective, selective termination is not so much an extension of women's reproductive choice as it is the extension of control over women's reproductive capacity—through the use of fertility drugs, GIFT, and IVF as "solutions" to infertility that often result, when successful, in multiple gestations; through the provision of a technology, selective termination, to respond to multiple gestation that may create much of the same ambivalence for women as is generated by abortion; and finally through the imposition of limitations on women's access to the procedure.

In decisions about selective termination, women are not simply feckless, selfish, and irresponsible. Nor are they mere victims of their social conditioning and the machinations of the medical and scientific establishments. But they must make their choices in the face of extensive socialization for maternity, a limited range of options, and sometimes inadequate information about outcomes. When women "demand" selective termination of pregnancy they are attempting to take action in response to a situation not of their own making, in the only way that seems available to them. Hence my argument is not that women are merely helpless victims and therefore

must be permitted access to selective termination, but rather that it would be both socially irresponsible and unjust for a health care system that contributes to the generation of problematic multiple pregnancies to withhold access to a potential, if flawed, response to the situation.

SELECTIVE TERMINATION AND ABORTION

There is reason to believe that women's attitudes toward selective termination may be similar to their attitudes toward abortion. Although abortion is a solution to the problem of unwanted pregnancy, and the general availability of abortion accords women significant and essential reproductive freedom, it is often an occasion for ambivalence, and remains, as Caroline Whitbeck has pointed out, a "grim option" for most women.[14] Women who abort are, after all, undergoing a surgical invasion of their bodies, and some may also experience emotional distress. Moreover, for some women the death of the fetus is a source of grief, particularly when the pregnancy is wanted and the abortion is sought because of severe fetal disabilities.[15]

Comparable factors may contribute to women's reservations about selective termination of pregnancy. Those who resort to this procedure surely do not desire the invasion of their uterus, nor do they make it their aim to kill fetuses. In fact, unlike women who request abortions because their pregnancy is unwanted, most of those who seek selective termination are originally pregnant by choice. And as Evans and colleagues note, such pregnancies are "not only wanted but achieved at great psychological and economic cost after a lengthy struggle with infertility."

For such women a procedure that risks the loss of all fetuses as selective termination does, may be especially troubling. The procedure is still experimental, and its short- and long-term outcomes are largely unknown. Richard C. Berkowitz and colleagues suggest that "[a]lthough the risks associated with selective reduction are known, the dearth of experience with the procedure to date makes it impossible to assess their likelihood." Further, in their report on four cases of selective termination, Evans and coworkers state that:

> [A]ny attempt to reduce the number of fetuses [is] experimental and [can] result in miscarriage, and . . . infection, bleeding, and other unknown risks [are] possible. If successful, the attempt could theoretically damage the remaining fetuses.

Note that "success" in the latter case would be seriously limited, assuming that the pregnant woman's goal is to gestate and subsequently deliver one or more healthy infants. In fact, success in this more plausible sense is fairly low.[16] As a consequence, in their study of first trimester selective termination, Berkowitz *et al.* mention the "psychological difficulty of making the decision [to undergo selective termination]," a difficulty partly resulting from "emotional bonding" with the fetuses after repeated ultrasound examinations.

Thus, women undergoing selective termination, like those undergoing abortion, are choosing a grim option; they are ending the existence of one or more fetuses because the alternatives—aborting all the fetuses (and taking the risk that they will never again succeed in becoming pregnant), or attempting to maintain all the fetuses through pregnancy, delivery, and childrearing—are unacceptable, morally, medically, or practically.

THE CHALLENGES OF MULTIPLE GESTATION

Why don't women who seek selective termination simply continue their pregnancies? No matter how much it is taken for granted, the accomplishment of gestating and birthing even one child is an extraordinary event; perhaps even more praise should be given to the woman who births twins or triplets or quadruplets. Rather than setting policy limits on women who are not able or willing to gestate more than one or two

fetuses, we should recognize and understand the extraordinary challenges posed by multiple pregnancies.

There are good consequentialist reasons why a woman might choose to reduce the number of fetuses she carries. For the pregnant woman, continuation of a multiple pregnancy means, Evans notes, "almost certain preterm delivery, prefaced by early and lengthy hospitalization, higher risks of pregnancy-induced hypertension, polyhydramnions, severe anemia, preeclampsia, and postpartum blood transfusions."[17]

The so-called "minor discomforts" of pregnancy are increased in a multiple pregnancy, and women may suffer severe nausea and vomiting or become depressed or anxious. There is also an increased likelihood of cesarean delivery, entailing more pain and a longer recovery time after the birth.[18]

Infants born of multiple pregnancy risk "premature delivery, low infant birthweight, birth defects, and problems of infant immaturity, including physical and mental retardation."[19] Moreover, as Evans and colleagues note, there is a high likelihood that these infants "may . . . suffer a lengthy, costly process of dying in neonatal intensive care." Thus a woman carrying more than one fetus also faces the possibility of becoming a mother to infants who will be seriously physicaly impaired or will die.

It is also important to count the social costs of bearing several children simultaneously, where the responsibilities, burdens, and lost opportunities occasioned by childrearing fall primarily if not exclusively upon the woman rather than upon her male partner (if any) or more equitably upon the society as a whole—particularly when the infants are disabled. A recent article on Canada's first set of "test-tube quintuplets" reported that the babies' mother, Mae Collier, changes diapers fifty times a day, and goes through twelve litres of milk a day and 150 jars of baby food a week. Her husband works full time outside of the home and "spends much of his spare time building the family's new house."[20]

Moreover, while North American culture is strongly pronatalist, it is simultaneously anti-child. One of the most prevalent myths of the West is that North Americans love and spoil their children. A sensitive examination—perhaps from the perspective of a child or a loving parent—of the conditions in which many children grow up puts the lie to this myth.[21] Children are among the most vulnerable victims of poverty and malnutrition. Subjected to physical and sexual abuse, educated in schools that more often aim for custody and confinement than growth and learning, exploited as opportunities for the mass marketing of useless and sometimes dangerous foods and toys, children, the weakest members of our society, are often the least protected. Children are virtually the last social group in North America for whom discrimination and segregation are routinely countenanced. In many residential areas, businesses, restaurants, hotels, and other "public" places, children are not welcome, and except in preschools and nurseries, there is usually little or no accommodation to their physical needs and capacities.

A society that is simultaneously pronatalist but anti-child and only minimally supportive of mothering is unlikely to welcome quintuplets and other multiples—except for their novelty—any more than it welcomes single children. The issue, then, is not just how many fetuses a woman can be required to gestate, but also how many children she can be required to raise, and under what sort of societal conditions.

To this argument it is no adequate rejoinder to say that such women should continue their pregnancies and then surrender some but not all of the infants for adoption by eager childless and infertile couples. It is one thing for a woman to have the choice of making this decision after careful thought and with full support throughout the pregnancy and afterward when the infants have been given up. Such a choice may be hard enough. It would be another matter, however, to advocate a policy that would restrict selective termination in such a way that gestating all the fetuses and surrendering some becomes a woman's only option.

First, the presence of each additional fetus places further demands on the woman's physical and emotional resources; gestating triplets or quadruplets is not just the same as gestating twins. Second, to compel a woman to continue to gestate fetuses she does not want for the sake of others who do is to treat the woman as a mere breeder, a biological machine for the production of new human beings. Finally, it would be callous indeed to ignore the emotional turmoil and pain of the woman who must gestate and deliver a baby only to surrender it to others. In the case of a multiple gestation an added distress would arise because of the necessity of somehow choosing which infant(s) to keep and which to give up.

REPRODUCTIVE RIGHTS

Within the existing social context, therefore, access to selective termination must be understood as an essential component of women's reproductive rights. But it is important to distinguish between the right to reproduce and the right not to reproduce. Entitlement to access to selective termination, like entitlement to access to abortion, falls within the right not to reproduce.[22]

Entitlement to choose how many fetuses to gestate, and of what sort, is in this context a limited and negative one. If women are entitled to choose to end their pregnancies altogether, then they are also entitled to choose how many fetuses and of what sort they will carry. If it is unjustified to deny a woman access to an abortion of all fetuses in her uterus, then it is also unjustified to deny her access to the termination of some of those fetuses. Furthermore, if abortion is legally permitted in cases where the fetus is seriously handicapped, it is inconsistent to refuse to permit the termination of one handicapped fetus in a multiple pregnancy.

One way of understanding abortion as an exercise of the right not to reproduce is to see it as the premature emptying of the uterus, or the deliberate termination of the fetus's occupancy of the womb. If a woman has an entitlement to an abortion, that is to the emptying of her uterus of all of its occupants, then there is no ground to compel her to maintain all the occupants of her uterus if she chooses to retain only some of them. While the risks of multiple pregnancy for both the fetuses and the pregnant woman increase with the number of fetuses involved, it does not follow that restrictions on selective termination for pregnancies with smaller numbers of fetuses would be justified. Legal or medical policy cannot consistently say, "you may choose whether to be pregnant, that is, whether your uterus shall be occupied, but you may not choose how many shall occupy your uterus."

More generally, if abortion of a healthy singleton pregnancy is permitted for any reason, as a matter of the woman's choice, within the first five months or so of pregnancy, it is inconsistent to refuse to permit the termination of one or more healthy fetuses in a multiple pregnancy. To say otherwise is unjustifiably to accord the fetuses a right to occupancy of the woman's uterus. It is to say that two or more human entities, at an extremely immature stage in their development, have the right to use a human person's body. But no embryo or fetus has a right to the use of a pregnant woman's body—any more than any other human being, at whatever stage of development, has a right to use another's body.[23] The absence of that right is recognized through state-sanctioned access to abortion. Fetuses do not acquire a right, either collectively or individually, to use a woman's uterus simply because there are several of them present simultaneously. Even if a woman is willingly and happily pregnant she does not surrender her entitlement to bodily self-determination, and she does not, specifically, surrender her entitlement to determine how many human entities may occupy her uterus.

Although I defend a social policy that does not set limits on access to selective termination of pregnancy, there can be no denying that the procedure may raise serious moral problems. As some persons with disabilities have pointed out, there is a special moral significance to the termination of a fetus with a disability such as Down syndrome.[24] The use of prenatal diagnosis followed by abortion or selective termination may have eugenic overtones, when the presupposition is that we can ensure only high quality babies will be born, and that "defective" fetuses can be eliminated before birth.[25] The fetus is treated as a product for which "quality control" measures are appropriate. Moreover, as amniocentesis and chorionic villus sampling reveal the sex of offspring, there is also a possibility that selective termination of pregnancy could be used, as abortion already is, to eliminate fetuses of the "wrong" sex—in most cases, that is, those that are female.[26]

These possibilities are distressing and potentially dangerous to disabled persons and to women generally. The way to deal with these and other moral reservations about selective termination is not to prohibit the procedure or to limit access to it on such grounds as fetal disability or fetal sex choice. Instead, part of the answer is to change the conditions that promote large numbers of embryos and fetuses. For example, since as Evans and colleagues astutely note, "[m]any of the currently known instances of grand multiple pregnancies should have never happened," the administration of fertility drugs to induce ovulation can be carefully monitored, and for IVF and GIFT procedures, more use can be made of the natural ovulatory cycle and of cryopreservation of embryos.[27] The number of eggs implanted through GIFT and the number of embryos implanted after IVF can be limited—not by unilateral decision of the physician, but after careful consultation with the woman about the chances of multiple pregnancy and her attitudes toward it.[28] To that end, there is a need for further research on predicting the likelihood of multiple pregnancy.[29] And, given the experimental nature of selective termination, genuinely informed choice should be mandatory for prospective patients, who need to know both the short- and long-term risks and outcomes of the procedure. Acquiring this information will necessitate the "long-term follow-up of parents and children . . . to assess the psychological and physical effects of fetal reduction."[30] By these means the numbers of selective terminations can be reduced, and the women who seek selective termination can be both protected and empowered.

More generally, however, we should carefully reevaluate both the pronatalist ideology and the system of treatments of infertility that constitute the context in which selective termination of pregnancy comes to seem essential. There is also a need to improve social support for parenting, and to transform the conditions that make it difficult or impossible to be the mother of triplets, quadruplets, etc. or of a baby with a severe disability. Only through the provision of committed care for children and support for women's self-determination will genuine reproductive freedom and responsibility be attained.

References

1. Marie T. Mulcahy, Brian Roberman, and S.E. Reid, "Chorion Biopsy, Cytogenetic Diagnosis, and Selective Termination in a Twin Pregnancy at Risk of Haemophilia" (letter), *The Lancet*, 13 October 1984, 866; "Selective Fetal Reduction" (review article), *The Lancet*, 1 October 1988, 773; Dorothy Lipovenko, "Infertility Technology Forces People to Make Life and Death Choices," *The Globe and Mail*, 21 January 1989, A4.

2. "Multiple Pregnancies Create Moral Dilemma," *Kingston Whig Standard*, 21 January 1989, 3.

3. Mark I. Evans et al., "Selective First-Trimester Termination in Octuplet and Quadruplet Pregnancies: Clinical and Ethical Issues," *Obstetrics and Gynecology* 71:3, pt. 1 (1988), 289–296, at 293; Richard L. Berkowitz et al., "Selective Reduction of Multifetal Pregnancies in the First Trimester," *New England Journal of Medicine* 118:16 (1988), 1043. Berkowitz and colleagues regard even triplet pregnancies as constituting a "gray area" for physician and patient. However, it is not clear whether this hesitation is based on moral scruples in addition to the medical risks.

4. Lipovenko, "Infertility Technology."

5. Diana Brahams, "Assisted Reproduction and Selective Reduction of Pregnancy," *The Lancet*, 12 December 1987, 1409; cf. John C. Hobbins, "Selective Reduction—A Perinatal Necessity?," *New England Journal of Medicine* 318:16 (1988), 1063; Evans et al., "Selective First-Trimester Termination," 295.

6. One television interviewer who talked to me about this issue described women as "forcing" doctors to provide the procedure! See also "Multiple Pregnancies Create Moral Dilemma"; Angela R. Holder and Mary Sue Henifin, "Selective Termination of Pregnancy," *Hastings Center Report* 18:1 (1988), 21–22.

7. Christine Overall, *Ethics and Human Reproduction: A Feminist Analysis* (Boston: Allen & Unwin, 1987), 139–56.

8. Hobbins, "Selective Reduction," 1062.

9. Gena Corea and Susan Ince, "Report of a Survey of IVF Clinics in the U.S.," in *Made to Order: The Myth of Reproductive and Genetic Progress*, Patricia Spallone and Deborah Lynn Steinberg, eds. (Oxford: Pergamon Press, 1987), 133–45.

10. Compare the ambiguity of the claim "women want it" in connection with in vitro fertilization. See Christine Crowe, "Women Want It: In Vitro Fertilization and Women's Motivations for Participation" in Spallone and Steinberg, *Made to Order*, 84–93.

11. Barbara Katz Rothman, *The Tentative Pregnancy: Prenatal Diagnosis and the Future of Motherhood* (New York: Viking, 1986), 189.

12. Judith Lorber, "In Vitro Fertilization and Gender Politics," in *Embryos, Ethics, and Women's Rights*, Elaine Hoffman Baruch, Amadeo F. D'Adamo, Jr., and Joni Seager, eds. (New York: Haworth Press, 1988), 123–26.

13. "Selective Fetal Reduction," 774.

14. Caroline Whitbeck, "The Moral Implications of Regarding Women as People: New Perspectives on Pregnancy and Personhood," in *Abortion and the Status of the Fetus*, William B. Bondeson et al., eds. (Boston: Reidel, 1984), 251–52.

15. Rothman, *The Tentative Pregnancy*, 177–216. She describes abortion in the case of fetal defect as "the chosen tragedy" (180).

16. Evans et al. give a success rate of 50% (p. 289), while Berkowitz et al. give 66-2/3% (1043). Angela Holder quotes a success rate of 55% (21).

17. Cf. Berkowitz *et al.*, "Selective Reduction," 1045; and Alastair H. MacLennan, "Multiple Gestation: Clinical Characteristics and Management," in *Maternal-Fetal Medicine: Principles and Practice*, Robert K. Creasy and Robert Resnick, eds. (Philadelphia: W.B. Saunders, 2nd ed., 1989), 581–84.

18. Jose C. Scerbo, Powan Rattan, and Joan E. Drukker, "Twins and Other Multiple Gestations," in *High-Risk Pregnancy: A Team Approach*, Robert A. Knuppel and Joan E. Drukker, eds. (Philadelphia: W.B. Saunders, 1986) 347–48, 358; Martin L. Pernoll, Gerda I. Benda, and S. Gorham Babson, *Diagnosis and Management of the Fetus and Neonate at Risk: A Guide for Team Care* (St. Louis: C.V. Mosby, 5th ed., 1986), 192–93.

19. "Selective Fetal Reduction," 773.

20. Victoria Stevens, "Test-Tube Quints Celebrate First Birthday," *The Toronto Star*, 6 February 1989, A7.

21. See Letty Cottin Pogrebin, *Family Politics: Love and Power on an Intimate Frontier* (New York: McGraw-Hill, 1983), 42.

22. Overall, *Ethics and Human Reproduction*, 166–68.

23. Overall, *Ethics and Human Reproduction*, 76–79.

24. Adrienne Asch, "Reproductive Technology and Disability," in *Reproductive Laws for the 1990s*, Sherrill Cohen and Nadine Taub, eds. (Clifton, NJ: Humana Press, 1989), 69–117; Marsha Saxton, "Prenatal Screening and Discriminatory Attitudes About Disability," in *Embryos, Ethics, and Women's Rights*, 217–24.

25. Ruth Hubbard, "Eugenics: New Tools, Old Ideas," in *Embryos, Ethics, and Women's Rights*, 225–35.

26. Cf. Robyn Rowland, "Motherhood, Patriarchal Power, Alienation and the Issue of 'Choice' in Sex Preselection," in *Man-Made Women*, 74–87.

27. Hobbins, "Selective Reduction," 1063; "Selective Fetal Reduction," 773, 774.

28. Brahams, "Assisted Reproduction," 1409.

29. Ian Craft *et al.*, "Multiple Pregnancy, Selective Reduction, and Flexible Treatment" (letter), *The Lancet*, 5 November 1988, 1087.

30. "Selective Fetal Reduction," 775.

"Goodbye Dolly?" The Ethics of Human Cloning

John Harris DPhil

The recent announcement of a birth[1] in the press heralds an event probably unparalleled for two millennia and has highlighted the impact of the genetic revolution on our lives and personal choices. More importantly perhaps, it raises questions about the legitimacy of the sorts of control individuals and society purport to exercise over something, which while it must sound portentous, is nothing less than human destiny. This birth, that of "Dolly", the cloned sheep, is also illustrative of the responsibilities of science and scientists to the communities in which they live and which they serve, and of the public anxiety that sensational scientific achievements sometimes provokes.

The ethical implications of human clones have been much alluded to, but have seldom been examined with any rigour. Here I will examine the possible uses and abuses of human cloning and draw out the principal ethical dimensions, both of what might be done and its meaning, and of public and official responses.

There are two rather different techniques available for cloning individuals. One is by nuclear substitution, the technique used to create Dolly, and the other is by cell mass division or "embryo splitting". We'll start with cell mass division because this is the only technique for cloning that has, as yet, been used in humans.

From *J Medical Ethics*, 23:353–360, 1997.

CELL MASS DIVISION

Although the technique of cloning embryos by cell mass division has, for some time been used extensively in animal models, it was used as a way of multiplying human embryos for the first time in October 1993 when Jerry Hall and Robert Stillman[2] at George Washington Medical Center cloned human embryos by splitting early two- to eight-cell embryos into single embryo cells. Among other uses, cloning by cell mass division or embryo splitting could be used to provide a "twin" embryo for biopsy, permitting an embryo undamaged by invasive procedures to be available for implantation following the result of the biopsy on its twin, or to increase the number of embryos available for implantation in the treatment of infertility.[3] To what extent is such a practice unethical?

INDIVIDUALS, MULTIPLES AND GENETIC VARIATION

Cloning does not produce identical copies of the same individual person. It can only produce identical copies of the same genotype. Our experience of identical twins demonstrates that each is a separate individual with his or her own character, preferences and so on. Although there is some evidence of striking similarities with respect to these factors in twins, there is no question but that each twin is a distinct individual, as independent and as free as is anyone else. To clone Bill Clinton is not to create multiple Presidents of the United States. Artificial clones do not raise any difficulties not raised by the phenomenon of "natural" twins. We do not feel apprehensive when natural twins are born, why should we when twins are deliberately created?

If the objection to cloning is to the creation of identical individuals separated in time, (because the twin embryos might be implanted in different cycles, perhaps even years apart), it is a weak one at best. We should remember that such twins will be "identical" in the sense that they will each have the same genotype, but they will never (unlike some but by no means all natural monozygotic twins) be identical in the more familiar sense of looking identical at the same moment in time. If we think of expected similarities in character, tastes and so on, then the same is true. The further separated in time, the less likely they are to have similarities of *character* (the more different the environment, the more different environmental influence on individuality).

The significant ethical issue here is whether it would be morally defensible, by outlawing the creation of clones by cell mass division, to deny a woman the chance to have the child she desperately seeks. If this procedure would enable a woman to create a sufficient number of embryos to give her a reasonable chance of successfully implanting one or two of them, then the objections to it would have to be weighty indeed. If pre-implantation testing by cell biopsy might damage the embryo to be implanted, would it be defensible to prefer this to testing a clone, if technology permits such a clone to be created without damage, by separating a cell or two from the embryonic cell mass? If we assume each procedure to have been perfected and to be equally safe, we must ask what the ethical difference would be between taking a cell for cell biopsy and destroying it thereafter, and taking a cell to create a clone, and then destroying the clone? The answer can only be that destroying the cloned embryo would constitute a waste of human potential. But this same potential is wasted whenever an embryo is not implanted.

NUCLEAR SUBSTITUTION: THE BIRTH OF DOLLY

This technique involves (crudely described) deleting the nucleus of an egg cell and substituting the nucleus taken from the cell of another individual. This can be done using cells from an adult. The first viable offspring produced from fetal and adult mammalian cells was reported from an Edinburgh-based group in *Nature* on February

27, 1997.[4] The event caused an international sensation and was widely reported in the world press. President Clinton of the United States called for an investigation into the ethics of such procedures and announced a moratorium on public spending on human cloning; the British Nobel Prize winner, Joseph Rotblat, described it as science out of control, creating "a means of mass destruction",[5] and the German newspaper *Die Welt*, evoked the Third Reich, commenting: "The cloning of human beings would fit precisely into Adolph Hilter's world view".[6]

More sober commentators were similarly panicked into instant reaction. Dr Hiroshi Nakajima, Director General of the World Health Organisation said: "WHO considers the use of cloning for the replication of human individuals to be ethically unacceptable as it would violate some of the basic principles which govern medically assisted procreation. These include respect for the dignity of the human being and protection of the security of human genetic material".[7] The World Health Organisation followed up the line taken by Nakajima with a resolution of the Fiftieth World Health Assembly which saw fit to affirm "that the use of cloning for the replication of human individuals is ethically unacceptable and contrary to human integrity and morality".[8] Federico Mayor of UNESCO, equally quick off the mark, commented: "Human beings must not be cloned under any circumstances. Moreover, UNESCO's International Bioethics Committee (IBC), which has been reflecting on the ethics of scientific progress, has maintained that the human genome must be preserved as common heritage of humanity".[9]

The European parliament rushed through a resolution on cloning, the preamble of which asserted, (paragraph B):

> "[T]he cloning of human beings . . . , cannot under any circumstances be justified or tolerated by any society, because it is a serious violation of fundamental human rights and is contrary to the principle of equality of human beings as it permits a eugenic and racist selection of the human race,

it offends against human dignity and it requires experimentation on humans," And which went on to claim that, (clause 1) "each individual has a right to his or her own genetic identity and that human cloning is, and must continue to be, prohibited".[10]

These statements are, perhaps un-surprisingly, thin on argument and rationale; they appear to have been plucked from the air to justify an instant reaction. There are vague references to "human rights" or "basic principles" with little or no attempt to explain what these principles are, or to indicate how they might apply to cloning. The WHO statement, for example, refers to the basic principles which govern human reproduction and singles out "respect for the dignity of the human being" and "protection of the security of genetic material". How, we are entitled to ask, is the security of genetic material compromised? Is it less secure when inserted with precision by scientists, or when spread around with the characteristic negligence of the average human male?[11]

HUMAN DIGNITY

Appeals to human dignity, on the other hand, while universally attractive, are comprehensively vague and deserve separate attention. A first question to ask when the idea of human dignity is invoked is: whose dignity is attacked and how? Is it the duplication of a large part of the genome that is supposed to constitute the attack on human dignity? If so we might legitimately ask whether and how the dignity of a natural twin is threatened by the existence of her sister? The notion of human dignity is often also linked to Kantian ethics. A typical example, and one that attempts to provide some basis for objections to cloning based on human dignity, was Axel Kahn's invocation of this principle in his commentary on cloning in *Nature*.[12]

> "The creation of human clones solely for spare cell lines would, from a philosophical point of view, be in obvious contradiction to the principle expressed by Emmanuel Kant: that of human

dignity. This principle demands that an individual—and I would extend this to read human life—should never be thought of as a means, but always also as an end. Creating human life for the sole purpose of preparing therapeutic material would clearly not be for the dignity of the life created."

The Kantian principle, crudely invoked as it usually is without any qualification or gloss, is seldom helpful in medical or bio-science contexts. As formulated by Kahn, for example, it would outlaw blood transfusions. The beneficiary of blood donation, neither knowing of, nor usually caring about, the anonymous donor uses the blood (and its' donor) simply as a means to her own ends. It would also outlaw abortions to protect the life or health of the mother.

INSTRUMENTALIZATION

This idea of using individuals as a means to the purposes of others is sometimes termed "instrumentalization". Applying this idea coherently or consistently is not easy! If someone wants to have children in order to continue their genetic line do they act instrumentally? Where, as is standard practice in *in vitro* fertilisation (IVF), spare embryos are created, are these embryos created instrumentally? If not how do they differ from embryos created by embryo splitting for use in assisted reproduction?[13]

Kahn responded in the journal *Nature* to these objections.[14] He reminds us, rightly, that Kant's famous principle states: "respect for human dignity requires that an individual is *never* used . . . *exclusively* as a means" and suggests that I have ignored the crucial use of the term "exclusively". I did not of course, and I'm happy with Kahn's reformulation of the principle. It is not that Kant's principle does not have powerful intuitive force, but that it is so vague and so open to selective interpretation and its scope for application is consquently so limited, that its utility as one of the "fundamental principles of modern bioethical thought", as Kahn describes it, is virtually zero.

Kahn himself rightly points out that debates concerning the moral status of the human embryo are debates about whether embryos fall within the *scope* of Kant's or indeed any other moral principles concerning persons; so the principle itself is not illuminating in this context. Applied to the creation of individuals which are, or will become autonomous, it has limited application. True the Kantian principle rules out slavery, but so do a range of other principles based on autonomy and rights. If you are interested in the ethics of creating people then, so long as existence is in the created individual's own best interests, and the individual will have the capacity for autonomy like any other, then the motives for which the individual was created are either morally irrelevant or subordinate to other moral considerations. So that even where, for example, a child is engendered exclusively to provide "a son and heir" (as so often in so many cultures) it is unclear how or whether Kant' principle applies. Either other motives are also attributed to the parent to square parental purposes with Kant, or the child's eventual autonomy, and its clear and substantial interest in or benefit from existence, take precedence over the comparatively trivial issue of parental motives. Either way the "fundamental principle of modern bioethical thought" is unhelpful and debates about whether or not an individual has been used *exclusively* as a means are sterile and usually irresolvable.

We noted earlier the possibility of using embryo splitting to allow genetic and other screening by embryo biopsy. One embryo could be tested and then destroyed to ascertain the health and genetic status of the remaining clones. Again, an objection often voiced to this is that it would violate the Kantian principle, and that "one twin would be destroyed for the sake of another".

This is a bizarre and misleading objection both to using cell mass division to create clones for screening purposes, and to creating clones by nuclear substitution to generate spare cell lines. It is surely ethically dubious to object to one embryo being sacrificed for the sake of another, but not to object to it being sacrificed for nothing. In *in vitro* fertilisation, for example, it is, in the United Kingdom, currently regarded as good practice to store spare embryos for future use by the mother or for disposal at her direction, either to other women who require donor embryos, or for research, or simply to be destroyed. It cannot be morally worse to use an embryo to provide information about its sibling, than to use it for more abstract research or simply to destroy it. If it is permissible to use early embryos for research or to destroy them, their use in genetic and other health testing is surely also permissible. The same would surely go for their use in creating cell lines for therapeutic purposes.

IT IS BETTER TO DO GOOD

A moral principle, that has at least as much intuitive force as that recommended by Kant, is that it is better to do some good than to do no good. It cannot, from the ethical point of view, be better or more moral to waste human material that could be used for therapeutic purposes, than to use it to do good. And I cannot but think that if it is right to *use* embryos for research or therapy then it is also right to *produce* them for such purposes.[15] Kant's prohibition does after all refer principally to use. Of course some will think that the embryo is a full member of the moral community with all the rights and protections possessed by Kant himself. While this is a tenable position, it is not one held by any society which permits abortion, post-coital contraception, or research with human embryos.

The UNESCO approach to cloning is scarcely more coherent than that of WHO; how does cloning affect "the preservation of the human genome as common heritage of humanity"? Does this mean that the human genome must be "preserved intact", that is without variation, or does it mean simply that it must not be "reproduced a-sexually"? Cloning cannot be said to impact on the variability of the human genome, it merely repeats one infinitely small part of it, a

part that is repeated at a natural rate of about 3.5 per thousand births.[16]

GENETIC VARIABILITY

So many of the fears expressed about cloning, and indeed about genetic engineering more generally, invoke the idea of the effect on the gene pool or upon genetic variability or assert the sanctity of the human genome as a common resource or heritage. It is very difficult to understand what is allegedly at stake here. The issue of genetic variation need not detain us long. The numbers of twins produced by cloning will always be so small compared to the human gene pool in totality, that the effect on the variation of the human gene pool will be vanishingly small. We can say with confidence that the human genome and the human population were not threatened at the start of the present millennium in the year AD one, and yet the world population was then perhaps one per cent of what it is today. Natural species are usually said to be endangered when the population falls to about one thousand breeding individuals; by these standards fears for humankind and its genome may be said to have been somewhat exaggerated.[17]

The resolution of the European parliament goes into slightly more detail; having repeated the, now mandatory, waft in the direction of fundamental human rights and human dignity, it actually produces an argument. It suggests that cloning violates the principal of equality, "as it permits a eugenic and racist selection of the human race". Well, so does prenatal, and pre-implantation screening, not to mention egg donation, sperm donation, surrogacy, abortion and human preference in choice of sexual partner. The fact that a technique could be abused does not constitute an argument against the technique, unless there is no prospect of preventing the abuse or wrongful use. To ban cloning on the grounds that it might be used for racist purposes is trantamount to saying that sexual intercourse should be prohibited because it permits the possibility of rape.

GENETIC IDENTITY

The second principle appealed to by the European parliament states, that "each individual has a right to his or her own genetic identity". Leaving aside the inevitable contribution of mitochondrial DNA,[18] we have seen that, as in the case of natural identical twins, genetic identity is not an essential component of personal identity[19] nor is it necessary for "individuality". Moreover, unless genetic identity is required either for personal identity, or for individuality, it is not clear why there should be a right to such a thing. But if there is, what are we to do about the rights of identical twins?

Suppose there came into being a life-threatening (or even disabling) condition that affected pregnant women and that there was an effective treatment, the only side effect of which was that it caused the embryo to divide, resulting in twins. Would the existence of the supposed right conjured up by the European parliament mean that the therapy should be outlawed? Suppose that an effective vaccine for HIV was developed which had the effect of doubling the natural twinning rate; would this be a violation of fundamental human rights? Are we to foreclose the possible benefits to be derived from human cloning on so flimsy a basis? We should recall that the natural occurrence of monozygotic (identical) twins is one in 270 pregnancies. This means that in the United Kingdom, with a population of about 58 million, over 200 thousand such pregnancies have occurred. How are we to regard human rights violations on such a grand scale?

A RIGHT TO PARENTS

The apparently overwhelming imperative to identify some right that is violated by human cloning sometimes expresses itself in the assertion of "a right to have two parents" or as "the right to be the product of the mixture of the genes of two individuals". These are on the face of it highly artificial and problematic rights—where

have they sprung from, save from a desperate attempt to conjure some rights that have been violated by cloning? However, let's take them seriously for a moment and grant that they have some force. Are they necessarily violated by the nuclear transfer technique?

If the right to have two parents is understood to be the right to have two social parents, then it is of course only violated by cloning if the family identified as the one to rear the resulting child is a one-parent family. This is not of course necessarily any more likely a result of cloning, than of the use of any of the other new reproductive technologies (or indeed of sexual reproduction). Moreover if there is such a right, it is widely violated, creating countless "victims", and there is no significant evidence of any enduring harm from the violation of this supposed right. Indeed war widows throughout the world would find its assertion highly offensive.

If, on the other hand we interpret a right to two parents as the right to be the product of the mixture of the genes of two individuals, then the supposition that this right is violated when the nucleus of the cell of one individual is inserted into the de-nucleated egg of another, is false in the way this claim is usually understood. There is at least one sense in which a right expressed in this form might be violated by cloning, but not in any way which has force as an objection. Firstly it is false to think that the clone is the genetic child of the nucleus donor. It is not. The clone is the twin brother or sister of the nucleus donor and the genetic offspring of the nucleus donor's own parents. Thus this type of cloned individual is, and always must be, the genetic child of two separate genotypes, of two genetically different individuals, however often it is cloned or re-cloned.

TWO PARENTS GOOD, THREE PARENTS BETTER

However, the supposed right to be the product of two separate individuals is perhaps violated by cloning in a novel way. The de-nucleated egg contains mitochondrial DNA—genes from the female whose egg it is. The inevitable presence of the mitochondrial genome of the egg donor, means that the genetic inheritance of clones is in fact richer than that of other individuals, richer in the sense of being more variously derived.[20] This can be important if the nucleus donor is subject to mitochondrial diseases inherited from his or her mother and wants a child genetically related to her that will be free of these diseases. How this affects alleged rights to particular combinations of "parents" is more difficult to imagine, and perhaps underlines the confused nature of such claims.

WHAT GOOD IS CLONING?

One major reason for developing cloning in animals is said to be[4] to permit the study of genetic diseases and indeed genetic development more generally. Whether or not there would be major advantages in human cloning by nuclear substitution is not yet clear. Certainly it would enable some infertile people to have children genetically related to them, it offers the prospect, as we have noted, of preventing some diseases caused by mitochondrial DNA, and could help "carriers" of X-linked and autosomal recessive disorders to have their own genetic children without risk of passing on the disease. It is also possible that cloning could be used for the creation of "spare parts" by for example, growing stem cells for particular cell types from non-diseased parts of an adult.

Any attempt to use this technique in the United Kingdom, is widely thought to be illegal. Whether it would in fact be illegal might turn on whether it is plausible to regard such cloning as the product of "fertilisation". Apparently only fertilised embryos are covered by the *Human Fertilisation and Embryology Act 1990*.[21] The technique used in Edinburgh which involves deleting the nucleus of an unfertilised egg and then substituting a cell nucleus from an existing individual, by-passes what is normally considered to be

fertilisation completely and may therefore turn out not to be covered by existing legislation. On the other hand, if as seems logical, we consider "fertilisation" as the moment when all forty-six chromosomes are present and the zygote is formed the problem does not arise.

The unease caused by Dolly's birth may be due to the fact that it was just such a technique that informed the plot of the film "The Boys from Brazil" in which Hitler's genotype was cloned to produce a fuehrer for the future. The prospect of limitless numbers of clones of Hitler is rightly disturbing. However, the numbers of clones that could be produced of any one genotype will, for the foreseeable future, be limited not by the number of copies that could be made of one genotype (using serial nuclear transfer techniques 470 copies of a single nuclear gene in cattle have been reported),[22] but by the availability of host human mothers.[23] Mass production in any democracy could therefore scarcely be envisaged. Moreover, the futility of any such attempt is obvious. Hitler's genotype might conceivably produce a "gonadically challenged" individual of limited stature, but reliability in producing an evil and vicious megalomaniac is far more problematic, for reasons already noted in our consideration of cloning by cell mass division.

DOLLY COLLAPSES THE DIVIDE BETWEEN GERM AND SOMATIC CELLS

There are some interesting implications of cloning by nuclear substitution (which have been clear since frogs were cloned by this method in the 1950s) which have not apparently been noticed.[24] There is currently a world-wide moratorium on manipulation of the human germ line, while therapeutic somatic line interventions are, in principal, permitted.[13] However, inserting the mature nucleus of an adult cell into a denucleated egg turns the cells thus formed into germ line cells. This has three important effects. First, it effectively eradicates the firm divide between germ line and somatic line nuclei because each adult cell nucleus is in principle "translatable" into a germ line cell nucleus by transferring its nucleus and creating a clone. Secondly, it permits somatic line modifications to human cells to become germ line modifications. Suppose you permanently insert a normal copy of the adenosine deaminase gene into the bone marrow cells of an individual suffering from severe combined immuno-deficiency (which affects the so called "bubble boy" who has to live in a protective bubble of clean air) with obvious beneficial therapeutic effects. This is a somatic line modification. If you then cloned a permanently genetically modified bone marrow cell from this individual, the modified genome would be passed to the clone and become part of his or her genome, transmissible to her offspring indefinitely through the germ line. Thus a benefit that would have perished with the original recipient and not been passed on for the protection of her children, can be conferred on subsequent generations by cloning.[25] The third effect is that it shows the oft asserted moral divide between germ line and somatic line therapy to be even more ludicrous than was previously supposed.[15]

IMMORTALITY?

Of course some vainglorious individuals might wish to have offspring not simply with their genes but with a matching genotype. However, there is no way that they could make such an individual a duplicate of themselves. So many years later the environmental influences would be radically different, and since every choice, however insignificant, causes a life-path to branch with unpredictable consequences, the holy grail of duplication would be doomed to remain a fruitless quest. We can conclude that people who would clone themselves would probably be foolish and ill-advised, but would they be immoral and would their attempts harm society or their children significantly?

Whether we should legislate to prevent people reproducing, not 23 but all 46 chromosomes,

seems more problematic for reasons we have already examined, but we might have reason to be uncomfortable about the likely standards and effects of child-rearing by those who would clone themselves. Their attempts to mould their child in their own image would be likely to be more pronounced than the average. Whether they would likely be worse than so many people's attempts to duplicate race, religion and culture, which are widely accepted as respectable in the contemporary world, might well depend on the character and constitution of the genotype donor. Where identical twins occur naturally we might think of it as "horizontal twinning", where twins are created by nuclear substitution we have a sort of "vertical twinning". Although horizontal twins would be closer to one another in every way, we do not seem much disturbed by their natural occurrence. Why we should be disturbed either by artificial horizontal twinning or by vertical twinning (where differences between the twins would be greater) is entirely unclear.

Suppose a woman's only chance of having "her own" genetic child was by cloning herself; what are the strong arguments that should compel her to accept that it would be wrong to use nuclear substitution? We must assume that this cloning technique is safe, and that initial fears that individuals produced using nuclear substitution might age more rapidly have proved groundless.[26] We usually grant the so called "genetic imperative" as an important part of the right to found a family, of procreative autonomy.[27] The desire of people to have "their own" genetic children is widely accepted, and if we grant the legitimacy of genetic aspirations in so many cases, and the use of so many technologies to meet these aspirations,[28] we need appropriately serious and weighty reasons to deny them here.

It is perhaps salutary to remember that there is no necessary connection between phenomena, attitudes or actions that make us uneasy, or even those that disgust us, and those phenomena, attitudes, and actions that there are good reasons for judging unethical. Nor does it follow that those things we are confident *are* unethical must be prohibited by legislation or regulation.

We have looked at some of the objections to human cloning and found them less than plausible, we should now turn to one powerful argument that has recently been advanced in favour of a tolerant attitude to varieties of human reproduction.

PROCREATIVE AUTONOMY

We have examined the arguments for and against permitting the cloning of human individuals. At the heart of these questions is the issue of whether or not people have rights to control their reproductive destiny and, so far as they can do so without violating the rights of others or threatening society, to choose their own procreative path. We have seen that it has been claimed that cloning violates principles of human dignity. We will conclude by briefly examining an approach which suggests rather that failing to permit cloning might violate principles of dignity.

The American philosopher and legal theorist, Ronald Dworkin has outlined the arguments for a right to what he calls "procreative autonomy" and has defined this right as "a right to control their own role in procreation unless the state has a compelling reason for denying them that control".[20] Arguably, freedom to clone one's own genes might also be defended as a dimension of procreative autonomy because so many people and agencies have been attracted by the idea of the special nature of genes and have linked the procreative imperative to the genetic imperative.

> "The right of procreative autonomy follows from any competent interpretation of the due process clause and of the Supreme Court's past decisions applying it. . . . The First Amendment prohibits government from establishing any religion, and it guarantees all citizens free exercise of their own religion. The Fourteenth Amendment, which incorporates the First Amendment, imposes the same prohibition and same responsibility on states. These provisions also guarantee the right of procreative autonomy."[30]

The point is that the sorts of freedoms which freedom of religion guarantees, freedom to choose one's own way of life and live according to one's most deeply held beliefs are also at the heart of procreative choices. And Dworkin concludes:

> "that no one may be prevented from influencing the shared moral environment, through his own private choices, tastes, opinions, and example, just because these tastes or opinions disgust those who have the power to shurt him up or lock him up."[31]

Thus it may be that we should be prepared to accept both some degree of offence and some social disadvantages as a price we should be willing to pay in order to protect freedom of choice in matters of procreation and perhaps this applies to cloning as much as to more straightforward or usual procreative preferences.[32]

The nub of the argument is complex and abstract but it is worth stating at some length. I cannot improve upon Dworkin's formulation of it.

> "The right of procreative autonomy has an important place . . . in Western political culture more generally. The most important feature of that culture is a belief in individual human dignity: that people have the moral right—and the moral responsibility—to confront the most fundamental questions about the meaning and value of their own lives for themselves, answering to their own consciences and convictions. . . . The principle of procreative autonomy, in a broad sense, is embedded in any genuinely democratic culture."[33]

In so far as decisions to reproduce in particular ways or even using particular technologies constitute decisions concerning central issues of value, then arguably the freedom to make them is guaranteed by the constitution (written or not) of any democratic society, unless the state has a compelling reason for denying its citizens that control. To establish such a compelling reason the state (or indeed a federation or union of states, such as the European Union for example) would have to show that more was at stake than the fact that a majority found the ideas disturbing or even disgusting.

As yet, in the case of human cloning, such compelling reasons have not been produced. Suggestions have been made, but have not been sustained, that human dignity may be compromised by the techniques of cloning. Dworkin's arguments suggest that human dignity and indeed democratic constitutions may be compromised by attempts to limit procreative autonomy, at least where greater values cannot be shown to be thereby threatened.

In the absence of compelling arguments against human cloning, we can bid Dolly a cautious "hello". We surely have sufficient reasons to permit experiments on human embryos to proceed, provided, as with any such experiments, the embryos are destroyed at an early stage.[34] While we wait to see whether the technique will ever be established as safe, we should consider the best ways to regulate its uptake until we are in a position to know what will emerge both by way of benefits and in terms of burdens.

References and notes

1. The arguments concerning human dignity are developed in my Cloning and human dignity in *The Cambridge Quarterly of Healthcare Ethics* [in press]. The issues raised by cloning were discussed in a special issue of the *Kennedy Institute of Ethics Journal* 1994; **4,3** and in my *Wonderwoman and Superman: the ethics of human biotechnology*. Oxford University Press, Oxford 1992, especially ch 1.

2. Human embryo cloning reported. *Science* 1993; **262:** 652–3.

3. Where few eggs can be successfully recovered or where only one embryo has been successfully fertilised, this method can multiply the embryos available for implantation to increase the chances of successful infertility treatment.

4. Wilmut I *et al.* Viable offspring derived from fetal and adult mammalian cells. *Nature* 1997; **385:** 810–13.

5. Arlidge J. *The Guardian* 1997 Feb 26: 6.

6. Radford T. *The Guardian* 1997 Feb 28: 1.

7. WHO press release (WHO/20 1997 Mar 11).

8. WHO document (WHA50.37 1997 May 14). Despite the findings of a meeting of the Scientific and Eth-

ical Review Group (see **Acknowledgements**) which recommended that "the next step should be a thorough exploration and fuller discussion of the [issues]".

9. UNESCO press release No 97-29 1997 Feb 28.

10. The European parliament. Resolution on cloning. Motion dated March 11 1997. Passed March 13 1997.

11. Perhaps the sin of Onan was to compromise the security of his genetic material?

12. Kahn A. Clone mammals . . . clone man. *Nature* 1997; **386:** 119.

13. For use of the term and the idea of "instrumentalization" see: *Opinion of the group of advisers on the ethical implications of biotechnology to the European Commission No 9. 1997 28 May.* Rapporteur, Dr Anne McClaren.

14. Kahn A. Cloning, dignity and ethical revisionism. *Nature* 1997; **388:** 320. Harris J. Is cloning an attack on human dignity? *Nature* 1997; **387:** 754.

15. See my *Wonderwoman and Superman: the ethics of human biotechnology*. Oxford University press, Oxford 1992: ch 2.

16. It is unlikely that "artificial" cloning would ever approach such a rate on a global scale and we could, of course, use regulative mechanisms to prevent this without banning the process entirely. I take this figure of the rate of natural twinning from Moore KL and Persaud TVN. *The developing human* [5th ed]. Philadelphia: WB Saunders, 1993. The rate mentioned is 1 per 270 pregnancies.

17. Of course if *all* people were compulsorily sterilised and reproduced only by cloning, genetic variation would become fixed at current levels. This would halt the evolutionary process. How bad or good *this* would be could only be known if the course of future evolution and its effects could be accurately predicted.

18. Mitochondrial DNA individualises the genotype even of clones to some extent.

19. Although of course there would be implications for criminal justice since clones could not be differentiated by so called "genetic fingerprinting" techniques.

20. Unless of course the nucleus donor is also the egg donor.

21. Margaret Brazier alerted me to this possibility.

22. Apparently Alan Trounson's group in Melbourne Australia have recorded this result. *The Herald Sun* 1997 Mar 13.

23. What mad dictators might achieve is another matter; but such individuals are, almost by definition,

impervious to moral argument and can therefore, for present purposes, be ignored.

24. Except by Pedro Lowenstein, who pointed them out to me.

25. These possibilities were pointed out to me by Pedro Lowenstein who is currently working on the implications for human gene therapy.

26. Science and technology: *The Economist* 1997 Mar 1: 101-4.

27. *Universal Declaration of Human Rights* (article 16). *European Convention on Human Rights* (article 12). These are vague protections and do not mention any particular ways of founding families.

28. These include the use of reproductive technologies such as surrogacy and Intra Cytoplasmic Sperm Injection (ICSI).

29. Dworkin R. *Life's dominion*. London: Harper Collins, 1993: 148.

30. See reference 28: 160.

31. Dworkin R. *Freedom's law*. Oxford: Oxford University Press, 1996: 237-8.

32. Ronald Dworkin has produced an elegant account of the way the price we should be willing to pay for freedom might or might not be traded off against the costs. See his *Taking rights seriously*, London: Duckworth, 1977: ch 10. And his *A matter of principle*, Cambridge, Mass: Harvard University Press, 1985: ch 17.

33. See reference 27: 166-7.

34. The blanket objection to experimentation on humans suggested by the European parliament resolution would dramatically change current practice on the use of spare or experimental human embryos.

Mom, Dad, Clone: Implications for Reproductive Privacy

Lori B. Andrews JD

On 5 July 1996 a sheep named Dolly was born in Scotland, the result of the transfer of the nucleus of an adult mammary tissue cell to the enucleated egg cell of an unrelated sheep, and gestation in a third, surrogate mother sheep.[1] Although for the past ten years scientists have routinely cloned sheep and cows from embryo cells,[2] this was the first cloning experiment that apparently succeeded using the nucleus of an adult cell.[3]

Shortly after the report of the sheep cloning was published, President Clinton instituted a ban on federal funding for human cloning,[4] and asked the National Bioethics Advisory Commission (NBAC) to analyze the scientific, legal, and ethical status of human cloning and to make policy recommendations. In June 1997 NBAC recommended the passage of a federal statute that would, for a period of three to five years, ban the implantation of embryos created through human cloning, whether using private or public funding. President Clinton forwarded a bill to Congress prohibiting creating children through human cloning in the United States for at least five years.

If such a law were passed, it might be challenged as violating an individual's or a couple's right to create a biologically related child. This article explores whether such a right exists and whether, even if it does, a ban on creating children through cloning should nonetheless be upheld.

From *Cambridge Quarterly of Healthcare Ethics* 7:176–186, 1998.

THE RIGHT TO MAKE REPRODUCTIVE DECISIONS

The right to make decisions about whether to bear children is constitutionally protected under the constitutional right to privacy[5] and the constitutional right to liberty.[6] The U.S. Supreme Court in 1992 reaffirmed the "recognized protection accorded to liberty relating to intimate relationships, the family, and decisions about whether to bear and beget a child."[7] Early decisions protected married couples' right to privacy to make procreative decisions, but later decisions focussed on individuals' rights as well. The U.S. Supreme Court, in *Eisenstadt v. Baird*,[8] stated, "[i]f the right of privacy means anything, it is the right of the *individual*, married or single, to be free from unwarranted governmental intrusion into matters so fundamentally affecting a person as the decision whether to bear or beget a child."[9]

A federal district court has indicated that the right to make procreative decisions encompasses the right of an infertile couple to undergo medically assisted reproduction, including in vitro fertilization and the use of a donated embryo.[10] *Lifchez v. Hartigan*[11] held that a ban on research on conceptuses was unconstitutional because it impermissibly infringed upon a woman's fundamental right to privacy. Although the Illinois statute banning embryo and fetal research at issue in the case permitted in vitro fertilization, it did not allow embryo donation, embryo freezing, or experimental prenatal diagnostic procedures. The court stated:

> It takes no great leap of logic to see that within the cluster of constitutionally protected choices that includes the right to have access to contraceptives, there must be included within that cluster the right to submit to a medical procedure that may bring about, rather than prevent, pregnancy. Chorionic villi sampling is similarly protected. The cluster of constitutional choices that includes the right to abort a fetus within the first trimester must also include the right to submit to a procedure designed to give information about that fetus which can then lead to a decision to abort.[12]

Procreative freedom has been found to protect individuals' and couples' decisions to use contraception, abortion, and existing reproductive technology. Some commentators argue that the U.S. Constitution similarly protects the right to create a child through cloning.

There are a variety of scenarios in which such a right might be asserted. If both members of a couple are infertile, they may wish to clone one or the other of themselves.[13] If one member of the couple has a genetic disorder that the couple does not wish to pass on to a child, they could clone the unaffected member of the couple. In addition, if both husband and wife are carriers of a debilitating recessive genetic disease and are unwilling to run the 25% risk of bearing a child with the disorder, they may seek to clone one or the other of them.[14] This may be the only way in which the couple will be willing to have a child that will carry on their genetic line.

Even people who could reproduce coitally may desire to clone for a variety of reasons. People may want to clone themselves, deceased or living loved ones, or individuals with favored traits. A wealthy childless individual may wish to clone himself or herself to have an heir or to continue to control a family business. Parents who are unable to have another child may want to clone their dying child.[15] This is similar to the current situation in which a couple whose daughter died is making arrangements to have a cryopreserved in vitro embryo created with her egg and donor sperm implanted in a surrogate mother in an attempt to recreate their daughter.[16]

Additionally, an individual or couple might choose to clone a person with favored traits. Respected world figures and celebrities such as Mother Teresa, Michael Jordan, and Michelle Pfeiffer have been suggested as candidates for cloning. Less well-known individuals could also be cloned for specific traits. For example, people with a high pain threshold or resistance to radiation could be cloned.[17] People who can perform a particular job well, such as soldiers, might be cloned.[18] One biologist suggested cloning legless men for the low gravitational field and cramped quarters of a spaceship.[19]

Cloning also offers gay individuals a chance to procreate without using nuclear DNA from a member of the opposite sex. Clone Rights United Front, a group of gay activists based in New York, have been demonstrating against a proposed New York law that would ban nuclear transplantation research and human cloning. They oppose such a ban because they see human cloning as a significant means of legitimizing "same-sex reproduction."[20] Randolfe Wicker founded the Clone Rights United Front in order to pressure legislators not to ban human cloning research because he sees nuclear transplantation cloning as an inalienable reproductive right.[21] Wicker stated, "We're fighting for research, and we're defending people's reproductive rights. . . . I realize my clone would be my identical twin, and my identical twin has a right to be born."[22]

Ann Northrop, a columnist for the New York gay newspaper *LGNY*, says that nuclear transplantation is enticing to lesbians because it offers them a means of reproduction and has the potential of giving women complete control over reproduction.[23] "This is sort of the final nail in men's coffins," she says. "Men are going to have a very hard time justifying their existence on this planet, I think. Maybe women may not let men reproduce."[24]

The strongest claim for procreative freedom is that made by infertile individuals, for whom this is the only way to have a child with a genetic link to them. However, the number of people who will actually need cloning is quite limited. Many people can be helped by in vitro fertilization and its adjuncts; others are comfortable using a donated gamete. In all the other instances of creating a child through cloning, the individual is biologically able to have a child of his or her own, but is choosing not to because he or she prefers to have a child with certain traits. This made-to-order child-making is less compelling than the infertility scenario. Moreover, there is little legal basis to suggest that a person's procreative freedom includes a right to procreate using *someone else's* DNA, such as relatives, or a celebrity. Courts are

particularly unlikely to find that parents have a right to clone their young child. Procreative freedom is not a predatory right that would provide access to another individual's DNA.

The right of procreation is likely to be limited to situations in which an individual is creating a biologically related child. It could be argued that cloning oneself invokes that right to an even greater degree than normal reproduction. As lawyer Francis Pizzulli points out, "[i]n comparison with the parent who contributes half of the sexually reproduced child's genetic formula, the clonist is conferred with more than the requisite degree of biological parenthood, since he is the sole genetic parent."[25]

John Robertson argues that cloning is not qualitatively different from the practice of medically assisted reproduction and genetic selection that is currently occurring.[26] Consequently, he argues that "cloning . . . would appear to fall within the fundamental freedom of married couples, including infertile married couples to have biologically related offspring."[27] Similarly, June Coleman argues that the right to make reproductive decisions includes the right to decide in what manner to reproduce, including reproduction through, or made possible by, embryo cryopreservation and embryo twinning.[28] This argument could also be applied to nuclear transplantation by saying that a ban on cloning as a method of reproduction is tantamount to the state denying one's right to reproductive freedom.

In contrast, George Annas argues that cloning does not fall within the constitutional protection of reproductive decisions. "Cloning is replication, not reproduction, and represents a difference in kind, not in degree in the way humans continue the species."[29] He explains that "[t]his change in kind in the fundamental way in which humans can 'reproduce' represents such a challenge to human dignity and the potential devaluation of human life (even comparing the 'original' to the 'copy' in terms of which is to be more valued) that even the search for an analogy has come up empty handed."[30]

The process and resulting relationship created by cloning is profoundly different from that created through normal reproduction or even from that created through reproductive technologies such as in vitro fertilization, artificial insemination, or surrogate motherhood. In even the most high-tech reproductive technologies available, a mix of genes occurs to create an individual with a genotype that has never before existed on earth. In the case of twins, two such individuals are created. Their futures are open and the distinction between themselves and their parents is acknowledged. In the case of cloning, however, the genotype has already existed. Even though it is clear that the individual will develop into a person with different traits because of different social, environmental, and generational influences, there is evidence that the fact that he or she has a genotype that already existed will affect how the resulting clone is treated by himself, his family, and social institutions.

In that sense, cloning is sufficiently distinct from traditional reproduction or alternative reproduction to not be considered constitutionally protected. It is not a process of genetic mix, but of genetic duplication. It is not reproduction, but a sort of recycling, where a single individual's genome is made into someone else.

ASSUMING CONSTITUTIONAL PROTECTION

Let us assume, though, that courts were willing to make a large leap and find that the constitutional privacy and liberty protections of reproduction encompass cloning. If a constitutional right to clone was recognized, any legislation that would infringe unduly upon this fundamental right would be subject to a "strict standard" of judicial review.[31] Legislation prohibiting the ability to clone or prohibiting research would have to further a compelling interest in the least restrictive manner possible in order to survive this standard of review.[32]

The potential physical and psychological risks of cloning an entire individual are suffi-

ciently compelling to justify banning the procedure. There are many physical risks to the resulting child. Of 277 attempts, only one sheep lived. The high rate of laboratory deaths may suggest that cloning in fact damages the DNA of a cell. In addition, scientists urge that Dolly should be closely monitored for abnormal genetic anomalies that did not kill her as a fetus but may have long-term harmful effects.[33]

For example, all of the initial frog cloning experiments succeeded only to the point of the amphibian's tadpole stage.[34] In addition, some of the tadpoles were grossly malformed. Initial trials in human nuclear transplantation could also meet with disastrous results. Ian Wilmut and National Institutes of Health director Harold Varmus, testifying before Congress, specifically raised the concern that cloning technology is not scientifically ready to be applied to humans, even if it were permitted, because there are technical questions that can only be answered by continued animal research.[35] Dr. Wilmut is specifically concerned with the ethical issue that would be raised by any "defective births," which may be likely to occur if nuclear transplantation is attempted with humans.[36]

In addition, if all the genes in the adult DNA are not properly reactivated, there might be a problem at a later developmental stage in the resulting clone.[37] Some differentiated cells rearrange a subset of their genes. For example, immune cells rearrange some of their genes to make surface molecules.[38] That rearrangement could cause physical problems for the resulting clone.

Also, because scientists do not fully understand the cellular aging process, scientists do not know what 'age' or 'genetic clock' Dolly inherited.[39] On a cellular level, when the *Nature* article was published about her, was she a normal seven-month-old lamb, or was she six years old (the age of the mammary donor cell)?[40] Colin Stewart believes that Dolly's cells most likely are set to the genetic clock of the nucleus donor, and therefore are comparable to those of her six-year-old progenitor.[41] One commentator stated that if the hypotheses of a cellular, self-regulating genetic clock are correct, clones would be cellularly programmed to have much shorter life spans than the "original," which would seriously undermine many of the benefits that have been set forth in support of cloning—mostly agricultural justifications—and would psychologically lead people to view cloned animals and humans as short-lived, disposable copies.[42] This concern for premature aging has lead Dr. Sherman Elias, a geneticist and obstetrician at the Baylor College of Medicine, to call for further animal testing of nuclear transplantation as a safeguard to avoid subjecting human clones to premature aging and the potential harms associated with aged cells.[43]

The hidden mutations that may be passed on by using an adult cell raise concerns as well. Mutations are "a problem with every cell, and you don't even know where to check for them," notes Ralph Brinster of the University of Pennsylvania.[44] "If a brain cell is infected with a mutant skin gene, you would not know because it would not affect the way the cell develops because it is inactive. If you choose the wrong cell, then mutations would become apparent."[45]

WHEN PHYSICAL RISKS DECLINE

The proposed federal bill would put a five-year moratorium on creating a child through cloning. During that time period, though, the physical risks of cloning will probably diminish. Animal researchers around the world are rushing to try the Wilmut technique in a range of species. If cloning appeared to be physically safe and reached a certain level of efficiency, should it then be permissible in humans?

The NBAC recommendations left open the possibility of continuing the ban on human cloning based on psychological and social risks.[46] The notion of replicating existing humans seems to fundamentally conflict with our legal system, which emphatically protects individuality and uniqueness.[47] Banning procreation through nuclear transplantation is justifiable in light of the sanctity of the individual and personal privacy notions that

are found in different constitutional amendments, and protected by the Fourteenth Amendment.[48]

The clone has lost the ability to control disclosure of intimate personal information. A ban on cloning would "preserve the uniqueness of man's personality and thus safeguard the islands of privacy which surround individuality."[49] These privacy rights are implicated through a clone's right to "retain and control the disclosure of personal information—foreknowledge of the clonant's genetic predispositions."[50] Catherine Valerio Barrad argues that courts should recognize a privacy interest in one's DNA because science is increasingly able to decipher and gather personal information from one's genetic code.[51] The fear that potential employers and health insurers may use one's private genetic information discriminatorily is not only a problem for the original DNA possessor, but any clone "made" from that individual.[52] Even in cases in which the donor waives his privacy rights and releases genetic information about himself, the privacy rights of the clone are necessarily implicated due to the fact that the clone possesses the same nucleic genetic code.[53] This runs afoul of principles behind the Fifth Amendment's protection of a "person's ability to regulate the disclosure of information about himself."[54]

If a cloned person's genetic progenitor is a famous musician or athlete, parents may exert an improper amount of coercion to get the child to develop those talents. True, the same thing may happen—to a lesser degree—now, but the cloning scenario is more problematic. A parent might force a naturally conceived child to practice piano hours on end, but will probably eventually give up if the child seems disinterested or tone deaf. More fervent attempts to develop the child's musical ability will occur if the parents chose (or even paid for) nuclear material from a talented pianist. And pity the poor child who is the clone of a famous basketball player. If he breaks his kneecap at age ten, will his parents consider him worthless? Will he consider himself a failure?

In attempting to cull out from the resulting child the favored traits of the loved one or celebrity who has been cloned, the social parents will probably limit the environmental stimuli that the child is exposed to. The pianist's clone might not be allowed to play baseball or just hang out with other children. The clone of a dead child might not be exposed to food or experiences that the first child had rejected. The resulting clone may be viewed as being in a type of "genetic bondage"[55] with improper constraints on his or her freedom.

Some scientists argue that this possibility will not come to pass because everyone knows that a clone will be different from the original. The NBAC report puts it this way: "Thus the idea that one could make through somatic cell nuclear transfer a team of Michael Jordans, a physics department of Albert Einsteins, or an opera chorus of Pavarottis, is simply false."[56] But this overlooks the fact that we are in an era of genetic determinism, in which newspapers daily report the gene for this or that and top scientists tell us that we are a packet of genes unfolding.

James Watson, co-discoverer of deoxyribonucleic acid (DNA) and the first director of the Human Genome Project, has stated, "We used to think our fate was in the stars. Now we know, in large measure, our fate is in our genes."[57] Harvard zoologist Edward O. Wilson asserts that the human brain is not *tabula rasa* later filled in by experience but, "an exposed negative waiting to be slipped into developer fluid."[58] Genetics is alleged to be so important by some scientists that it caused psychiatrist David Reiss at George Washington University to declare that "the Cold War is over in the nature and nurture debate."[59]

Whether or not this is true, parents may raise the resulting clone as if it were true. After all, the only reason people want to clone is to assure that the child has a certain genetic makeup. Thus it seems absurd to think they will forget about that genetic makeup once the child comes into being. Elsewhere in our current social policies, though, we limit parents' genetic foreknowledge of their children because we believe it will improperly influence their rearing practices.

Cloning could undermine human dignity by threatening the replicant's sense of self and sense of autonomy. A vast body of developmental psychology research has signalled the need of children to have a sense of an independent self. This might be less likely to occur if they were the clones of a member of the couple raising them or of previous children who died.

The replicant individual may be made to feel that he is less of a free agent. Laurence Tribe argues that if one's genetic makeup is subject to prior determination, "one's ability to conceive of oneself as a free and rational being entitled to resist various social claims may gradually weaken and might finally disappear altogether."[60] Under such an analysis, it does not matter whether genetics actually determines a person's characteristics. Having a predetermined genetic makeup can be limiting if the person rearing the replicant and/or the replicant believes in genetic determinism.[61] In addition, there is much research on the impact of genetic information that demonstrates that a person's genetic foreknowledge about himself or herself (whether negative or positive) can threaten that individual's self-image, harm his or her relationships with family members, and cause social institutions to discriminate against him or her.[62]

Even though parents have a constitutional right to make childrearing decisions similar to their constitutional right to make childbearing decisions, parents do not have a right to receive genetic information about their children that is not of immediate medical benefit. The main concern is that a child about whom genetic information is known in advance will be limited in his or her horizons. A few years ago, a mother entered a Huntington disease testing facility with her two young children. "I'd like you to test my children for the HD gene," she said. "Because I only have enough money to send one to Harvard."[63] That request and similar requests to test young girls for the breast cancer gene or other young children for carrier status for recessive genetic disorders raise concerns about whether parents' genetic knowledge about their child will cause them to treat that child differently. A variety of studies have suggested that there may be risks to giving parents such information.

" 'Planning for the future,' perhaps the most frequently given reason for testing, may become 'restricting the future' (and also the present) by shifting family resources away from a child with a positive diagnosis," wrote Dorothy Wertz, Joanna Fanos, and Philip Reilly, in an article in the *Journal of the American Medical Association*.[64] Such a child "can grow up in a world of limited horizons and may be psychologically harmed even if treatment is subsequently found for the disorder."[65] A joint statement by the American Society of Human Genetics (ASHG) and the American College of Medical Genetics (ACMG) notes, "Presymptomatic diagnosis may preclude insurance coverage or may thwart long term goals such as advanced education or home ownership."[66]

The possibility that genetic testing of children can lead to a dangerous self-fulfilling prophecy led to the demise of one study involving testing children. Harvard researchers proposed to test children to see if they had the XYY chromosomal complement, which had been linked (by flimsy evidence) to criminality. They proposed to study the children for decades to see if those with that genetic makeup were more likely to engage in a crime than those without it. They intended to tell the mothers which children had XYY. Imagine the effect of that information—on the mother, and on the child. Each time the child took his little brother's toy, or lashed out in anger at a playmate, the mother might freeze in horror at the idea that her child's genetic predisposition was unfolding itself. She might intervene when other mothers would normally not, and thus distort the rearing of her child.

Because of the potential psychological and financial harm that genetic testing of children may cause, a growing number of commentators and advisory bodies have recommended that parents not be able to learn genetic information about their children. The Institute of Medicine Committee on Assessing Genetic Risks recommended that "in the clinical setting, children generally be tested only for disorders for which a curative or preventive treatment exists and should be instituted at that early stage. Childhood screening is not appropriate for carrier status, untreatable childhood diseases, and late-onset diseases that cannot be prevented or forestalled by early treatment."[67] The American Society of Human Genetics and American College of Medical Genetics made similar recommendations.

A cloned child will be a child who is likely to be exposed to limited experiences and limited opportunities. Even if he or she is cloned from a person who has favored traits, he may not get the benefit of that heritage. His environment might not provide him with the drive that made the original succeed. Or so many clones may be created from the favored original that their value and opportunities may be lessened. (If the entire NBA consisted of Michael Jordan clones, the game would be far less interesting and each individual less valuable.) In addition, even individuals with favored traits may have genes associated with diseases that could lead to insurance discrimination against the individuals cloned. If Jordan died young of an inheritable cardiac disorder, his clones would find their futures restricted. Banning cloning would be in keeping with philosopher Joel Feinberg's analysis that children have a right to an "open future."[68]

Some commentators argue that potential psychological and social harms from cloning are too speculative to provide the foundation for a government ban. Elsewhere, I have argued that speculative harms do not provide a sufficient reason to ban reproductive arrangements such as in vitro fertilization or surrogate motherhood.[69] But the risks of cloning go far beyond the potential psychological risks to the original whose expectations are not met in the cloning, or the risks to the child of having an unusual family arrangement if the original was not one of his or her rearing parents.

The risk here is of hubris, of abuse of power. Cloning represents the potential for "[a]buses of the power to control another person's destiny—both psychological and physical—of an unprecedented order."[70] Francis Pizzulli points out that legal discussions of whether the replicant is the property of the cloned individual, the same person as the cloned individual, or a resource for organs all show how easily the replicant's own autonomy can be swept aside.[71]

In that sense, maybe the best analogy to cloning is incest. Arguably, reproductive privacy and liberty are threatened as much by a ban on incest as by a ban on cloning. Arguably the harms are equally speculative. Yes, incest creates certain potential physical risks to the offspring, due to the potential for lethal recessive disorders to occur. But no one seriously thinks that this physical risk is the reason we ban incest. Arguably a father and daughter could avoid that risk by contracepting or agreeing to have prenatal diagnosis and abort affected fetuses. There might even be instances in which, because of their personalities, there is no psychological harm to either party.

Despite the fact that risks are speculative—and could be counterbalanced in many cases by other measures—we can ban incest because it is about improper parental power over children. We should ban the cloning of human beings through somatic cell nuclear transfer—even if physical safety is established—for that same reason.

References and Notes

1. Specter M, Kolata G. A new creation: the path to cloning—a special report. *New York Times* 1997; Mar 3:A1.

2. In 1993, embryologists at George Washington University split human embryos, making twins and triplets. See Sawyer K. Researchers clone human embryo cells; work is small step in aiding infertile. *Washington Post* 1993;Oct 25:A4. These embryos were not implanted into a woman for gestation. This procedure is distinguishable from cloning by nuclear transfer.

3. Begley S. Little lamb, who made thee? *Newsweek* 1997;Mar 10:53–7. See also Wilmut I, Schnieke AE, McWhir J, Kind AJ, Campbell KHS. Viable offspring derived from fetal and adult mammalian cells. *Nature* 1997;385:810–3.

4. Transcript of Clinton remarks on cloning. *U.S. Newswire* 1997;Mar 4.

5. E.g., Griswold v. Connecticut, 381 U.S. 379 (1965); Eisenstadt v. Baird, 405 U.S. 438 (1972).

6. Planned Parenthood v. Casey, 505 U.S. 833, 112 S.Ct. 2791 (1992).

7. Planned Parenthood v. Casey, 505 U.S. 833, 112 S.Ct. 2791, 2810 (1992).

8. Eisenstadt v. Baird, 405 U.S. 438 (1972).

9. Eisenstadt v. Baird, 405 U.S. 438, 453 (1972).

10. Lifchez v. Hartigan, 735 F.Supp. 1361 (N.D. Ill.), aff'd without opinion, *sub nom.*; Scholberg v. Lifchez, 914 F.2d 260 (7th Cir. 1990), cert. denied, 111 S.Ct. 787 (1991).

11. See note 10, Lifchez v. Hartigan 1991.

12. See note 10, Lifchez v. Hartigan 1991:1377 (citations omitted). The court also held that the statute was impermissibly vague because of its failure to define "experiment" or "therapeutic" (at 1376).

13. See Wray H, Sheler JL, Watson T. The world after cloning. *U.S. News & World Report* 1997;Mar 10:59.

14. Katz J. *Experimentation with Human Beings* 977 (1972).

15. Gaylin W. We have the awful knowledge to make exact copies of human beings. *New York Times* 1997;Mar 5:48.

16. Kolata G. Medicine's troubling bonus: surplus of human embryos. *New York Times* 1997;Mar 16:1. "Fox on Trends," Fox Television Broadcast, 19 March 1997.

17. Haldane JBS. Biological possibilities for the human species in the next thousand years. In Wolstenholme G, ed. *Man and His Future*. London: Churchill, 1963:337. Cited in Pizzulli FC. Asexual reproduction and genetic engineering: a constitutional assessment of the technology of cloning [Note]. *Southern California Law Review* 1974;47:490, n. 66.

18. Fletcher J. Ethical aspects of genetic controls. *New England Journal of Medicine* 1971;285:779.

19. See note 17, Pizzulli 1974:520.

20. Manning A. Pressing a 'right' to clone humans, some gays foresee reproduction option. *USA Today* 1997;Mar 6:D1.

21. See note 20, Manning 1997; see also Schilinger L. Postcard from New York. *The Independent* [London] 1997;Mar 16:2.

22. See note 21, Schilinger 1997.

23. See note 20, Manning 1997.

24. See note 21, Schilinger 1997.

25. See note 17, Pizzulli 1974:550. Charles Strom, director of genetics and the DNA laboratory at Illinois Masonic Medical Center, argues that the high rate of embryo death that has occurred in animal cloning should not dissuade people from considering cloning as a legitimate reproductive technique. Strom points out that all new reproductive technologies have been marred by high failure rates, and that it is just a matter of time before cloning could be as economically efficient as any other form of artificial reproduction. See Stolberg S. Sheep clone researcher calls for caution science. *Los Angeles Times* 1997;Mar 1:A18.

26. Robertson J. Statement to the National Bioethics Advisory Commission. 14 March 1997:83. This seems to be a reversal of Robertson's earlier position that cloning "may deviate too far from prevailing conception of what is valuable about reproduction to count as a protected reproductive experience. At some point attempts to control the entire genome of a new person pass beyond the central experiences of identity and meaning that make reproduction a valued experience." Robertson J. *Children of Choice: Freedom and the New Reproductive Technologies.* Princeton, New Jersey: Princeton University Press, 1994:169.

27. See note 26, Robertson 1994.

28. See Coleman J. Playing God or playing scientist: a constitutional analysis of laws banning embryological procedures. *Pacific Law Journal* 1996;27:1351.

29. Annas GJ. Human cloning. *ABA Journal* 1997;83:80–81.

30. Annas GJ. Testimony on scientific discoveries and cloning: challenges for public policy. Sub-committee on Public Health and Safety, Committee on Labor and Human Resources, United States Senate. 12 March 1977:4.

31. See, e.g., Griswold v. Connecticut, 381 U.S. 479 (1965); Eisenstadt v. Baird, 405 U.S. 438 (1972); Roe v. Wade, 410 U.S. 113 (1973); Planned Parenthood of Southern Pennsylvania v. Casey, 505 U.S. 833 (1992).

32. See note 10, Lifchez v. Hartigan.

33. See Nash JM. The age of cloning. *Time* 1997;Mar 10:62–65; see also Spotts PN, Marquand R. A lamb ignites a debate on the ethnics of cloning. *Christian Science Monitor* 1997;Feb. 26:3.

34. See The law and medicine. *The Economist* 1997;Mar 1:59; see also note 17, Pizzulli 1974:484.

35. See Recer P. Sheep cloner says cloning people would be inhumane. *Associated Press* 1997;Mar 12. Reported testimony of Dr. Ian Wilmut and of Dr. Harold Varmus before the Senate on 12 March 1997 regarding the banning of human cloning research.

36. See note 35, Recer 1997. Comments of Dr. Ian Wilmut, testifying that as of yet he does not know of "any reason why we would want to copy a person. I personally have still not heard of a potential use of this technique to produce a new person that I would find ethical or acceptable."

37. Tilghman S. Statement to National Bioethics Advisory Commission, 13 March 1997:173.

38. See note 37, Tilghman 1997:147.

39. See note 35, Recer 1997.

40. See note 35, Recer 1997; see also note 33, Nash 1997:62–65.

41. See note 35, Recer 1997; Laurence J, Hornsby M. Warning on human clones. *Times* [London] 1997;Feb 23. Whatever next? *The Economist* 1997;Mar 1:79 (discussing the problems associated with having mitochondria of egg interact with donor cell).

42. Hello Dolly. *The Economist* 1997;Mar 1:17, discussing the pros and cons of aging research that could result from nuclear transplantation cloning; cf. Monmaney T. Prospect of human cloning gives birth to volatile issues. *Los Angeles Times* 1997;Mar 2:A2.

43. See note 42, Monmaney 1997.

44. See note 33, Nash 1997.

45. See note 33, Nash 1997; see also note 37, Tilghman 1997:145.

46. National Bioethics Advisory Commission. *Cloning Human Beings: Report and Recommendations of the National Bioethics Advisory Commission.* Rockville, Maryland: National Bioethics Advisory Commission, 1997:9.

47. Mauro T. Sheep clone prompts U.S. panel review. *USA Today* 1997;Feb 25:A1.

48. See note 17, Pizzulli 1974:502.

49. See note 17, Pizzulli 1974:512.

50. See note 17, Pizzulli 1974. See also Amer MS, Breaking the mold: human embryo cloning and its implications for a right to individuality. *UCLA Law Review* 1996;4:1666.

51. Valerio Barrad CM. Genetic information and property theory [Comment]. *Northwestern University Law Review* 1993;87:1050.

52. See note 51, Valerio Barrad 1993.

53. See note 51, Valerio Barrad 1993.

54. See note 50, Amer 1996.

55. See note 17, Pizzulli 1974.

56. See note 46, National Bioethics Advisory Commission 1997:33.

57. Jaroff L. The gene hunt. *Time* 1989;Mar 20:63.

58. Wolfe T. Sorry, but your soul just died. *Forbes ASAP* 1996;Dec 2:212.

59. Mann CC. Behavioral genetics in transition. *Science* 1994;264:1686.

60. Tribe L. Technology assessment and the fourth discontinuity: the limits of instrumental rationality. *Southern California Law Review* 1973;46:648.

61. There is much evidence of the widespread belief in genetic determinism. See, e.g., Nelkin D, Lindee MS, *The DNA Mystique: The Gene as Cultural Icon.* New York: W.H. Freeman & Company, 1995.

62. For a review of the studies, see Andrews LB. Prenatal screening and the culture of motherhood. *Hastings Law Journal* 1996;47:967.

63. Wexler N. Clairvoyance and caution: repercussions from the Human Genome Project. In Kevles DJ, Hood L. *The Code of Codes: Scientific and Social Issues in the Human Genome Project.* Cambridge, Massachusetts: Harvard University Press, 1992:211–43, 233.

64. Wertz D, Fanos J, Reilly P. Genetic testing for children and adolescents: who decides? *JAMA* 1994; 274:878.

65. See note 64, Wertz et al. 1994. Similarly, the ASHG/ACMG Statement notes: "Expectations of others for education, social relationships and/or employment may be significantly altered when a child is found to carry a gene associated with a late-onset disease or susceptibility. Such individuals may not be encouraged to reach their full potential, or they may have difficulty obtaining education or employment if their risk for early death or disability is revealed." American Society of Human Genetics and American College of Medical Genetics. Points to consider: ethical, legal, and psychosocial implications of genetic testing in children and adolescents. *American Journal of Human Genetics* 1995;57:1233–41, 1236.

66. See note 65, ASGH/ACMG 1995.

67. Andrews LB, Fullarton JE, Holtzman NA, Motulsky AG, eds. *Assessing Genetic Risks: Implications for Health and Social Policy.* Washington, D.C.: National Academy of Sciences, 1994:276.

68. See note 46, National Bioethics Advisory Commission 1997:67.

69. Andrews LB. Surrogate motherhood: the challenge for feminists. *Law, Medicine & Health Care* 1988;72:16.

70. See note 17, Pizzulli 1974:497.

71. See note 17, Pizzulli 1974:492.

⑤

Racism and Sexism in Medically Assisted Conception

Jonathan M. Berkowitz MD, Jack W. Snyder MD

INTRODUCTION

In Italy, an infertile black female gave birth to a white infant following implantation with an egg harvested from a white woman. The parturient, whose husband is white, chose to have a 'white baby because she believed a white child had a better future than one of mixed race'.[1] In contrast, Dr Brinsden, director of the Bourne Hall

From *Bioethics* 12:25–44, 1998.

Clinic in Cambridge, stated that '[our] clinic had turned down a request from a Pakistani man requesting a 'blond, blue-eyed, fair-skinned daughter' because it would be easier to find her a husband.'[2] These cases illustrate an increasingly common dilemma faced by health care professionals who provide medically assisted conception, or MAC.[3] The problem arises from the question of whether or not the desire to manipulate race and sex reflects underlying cultural prejudice and hence, constitutes racism and sexism.

Parents have traditionally sought to influence their children; however, the ability to determine a child's sex[4] and race[5] prior to conception is a relatively recent development whose technology may soon allow determination of physical,[6] intellectual,[7] and psychological[8] characteristics. MAC is a generic term which includes many medical procedures: all of which involve non-coital reproduction in which medical technology is used to achieve pregnancy. Depending upon the pathogenesis of the infertility, sperm or ova can be procured from one or both partners, or wholly from donors. Sperm and ova, otherwise known as gametes, contain chromosomes. These chromosomes contain genetic instructions on melanin biosynthesis and distribution which, in turn, determines skin color. It is when gametes are obtained from donors that racial selection can occur. For instance, with in vitro fertilization (IVF) an egg is fertilized with sperm outside a woman's body and later implanted within her uterus. By careful selection of sperm and egg donors one can, prior to conception, influence a variety of physical characteristics including skin color, height, and eye color. Not all MAC procedures, however, can be used for pre-conceptive racial manipulation. For example, the use of exogenous hormones to enhance fertility cannot be used to manipulate race. With respect to sex selection, this usually involves various sperm separation techniques with sperm obtained from either a potential parent or donor.

This paper examines potential ethical consequences of preconceptive racial and sexual manipulation. First, it is suggested that the use of MAC to predetermine sex and race can be used as a vehicle through which racism and sexism are expressed. Second, it is maintained that facilitation of sexual and racial predetermination by governments and health workers represents *de facto* support of racism and sexism.

AN HISTORICAL PERSPECTIVE ON MALE DOMINATION

Sexism and racism, whose prevalence has been extensively documented,[9] influences the utilization of MAC. Most cultures, [10] including American culture,[11] express an almost universal preference for males as first born. That 'this has always been a man's world'[12] is reflected in a history written of men, for men[13] and, with respect to western history, by white men.[14] Even the Old Testament provides insight into the psyche of ancient man, abounding with proclamations of male domination.[15] This desire for male offspring and the devaluation of women is further expressed in the extreme by the continuing practices[16] of female infanticide[17] and 'bride burning'.[18] Even in contemporary America, a comparison of male versus female earnings[19] demonstrates that sexism is alive and well. With respect to race, in many countries, light skin color is often associated with greater social prestige. In America, despite significant advances against racism and sexism, it deserves emphasis that white males continue to wield disproportionate political and economic power.

DISABILITY: A RATIONALIZATION FOR GENETIC MANIPULATION

The perception that white maleness confers an advantage, drives the desire for white male offspring. This perception is frequently reinforced in our popular culture which often portrays successful individuals as white men.[20] The advertising industry has been particularly effective in exploiting this linkage of white-maleness and success. In this regard, any product of conception other than a white male may be viewed by potential parents as disabled. Thus, parents seeking optimum products of conception may invoke not only the ancient right to procreate,[21] but also a more contemporary right to 'enjoy the benefits of scientific progres and its applications'.[22]

To better appreciate the connection between a white, male-dominated society and the perception of non-white-maleness as disabling, it will help to define disability. Traditional approaches have narrowly linked disability to disease.[23] However, a broader, more colloquial definition describes disability (which is synonymous with handicap[24] as an

> inability to pursue an occupation because of physical or mental impairment.[25]

Handicap may be defined as

> a physical, mental, or emotional condition that interferes with an individual's normal functioning.[26]

Federal law[27] further broadens the definition of disability in at least three ways. First, one may be disabled by virtue of having

> a physical or mental impairment that substantially limits one or more major life activities.[28]

Second, one may be disabled due to a *record* of such impairment.[29] Finally, one may be disabled due to a *perception* by others of such impairment.[30]

Parents who *perceive* non-white maleness as disabling may be tempted to use MAC to stack the racial and sexual cards in their child's favor. In fact, numerous studies have documented increasing acceptance of sex selection.[31] Whereas some cultures have either excluded or frankly murdered unwanted offspring,[32] those that employ MAC will offer a precise method to express cultural prejudice. That is, the barbarism of infanticide will be replaced by the sterile and calculating selectivity of MAC.

SEXISM AND RACISM IN MEDICALLY ASSISTED CONCEPTION

The concept of perceived disability provides the philosophical framework upon which the desire for racial and sexual predetermination is based. In daily living however, pre-conceptive sexual and racial selection will most often be utilized by couples whose motivations are not so formally expressed but are potentially predicated on racism and sexism. While racism and sexism exist in most cultures, it deserves emphasis that basing individual worth upon race and sex is, with rare exceptions,[33] strongly discouraged and often illegal. Judgments on the value of a person are preferably based on more meaningful but nebulous variables such as personality and achievement. While we immediately perceive the sex and race of those around us, in our professional and daily lives we are encouraged, and often legally required, to be both color and sex blind. Pre-conceptive race and sex selection, however, forces individuals to think in terms of, and place value on, race and sex. While this may be intuitively disturbing, does pre-conceptive sexual and racial manipulation constitute racism or sexism? To answer these questions, it would be helpful to first define sexism. Sexism can be defined as

> belief in the superiority or supremacy of one sex over the other, . . . prejudice or discrimination against members of one sex, . . . the fostering of stereotyping of social roles for members of a given sex.[34]

There can be many reasons why parents may prefer a child of a certain sex. For instance, some couples may desire a daughter to avoid sex-linked disease. One could argue that this use of sex selection is sexist in that it assumes the 'supremacy of one sex over the other'; that is, being female is advantageous as one avoids sex-linked disease. This use of sex selection, however, is not sexist as it is not the sex of the child *per se* which is at issue. Rather, the decision to have a daughter is rooted in the desire to avoid the consequences of inevitable biological laws. There is an important difference between what we can control and what we can't control. Sexism is a consequence of assumed sex appropriate social roles, social roles which are of human invention and not genetically determined. For example, one would be hard pressed to call sexist the situation where only woman can bear children: an irrevocable result of natural law. It would, however, be sexist to assume that women are superior to men at child rearing as this assumes that women are better suited for a particular social task.

While many stereotypical social roles are historically rooted in the physical differences between the sexes, technology has made most of these dissimilarities inconsequential. Of course, there are physical/genetic differences between the sexes which remain significant as exemplified by sex-linked disease and pregnancy. Medicine has not eradicated many sex-linked maladies whose existence makes being either male or female have genuine inevitable consequences upon the welfare of the individual. While these MAC manipulations may ultimately become unnecessary as our ability to detect and treat heritable disease improves, MAC is presently one way to avoid devastating heritable illness. Though the use of science to avoid heritable disease may be controversial, pre-conceptive sex selection to avoid sex-linked disease is not sexist as decisions are based upon a desire to avoid predetermined genetic consequences; not upon the anticipated stereotypical social roles a child may ultimately perform.

When does sex selection represent sexism? Sexism in pre-conceptive sex selection occurs when parents choose the sex of a child in anticipation of the social roles that child will perform in the future. For example, a man may desire a son with whom he may pursue such 'masculine' activities as fishing or baseball. This preference implies that boys, when compared to girls, are more desirable or capable companions for these activities. Conversely, a woman may desire a daughter because she would like a shopping companion. Such assumptions are sexist in that they

presume one sex is superior to, or more appropriately suited for certain social tasks: presumptions which perpetuate and foster stereotypical social roles. Unlike the inability of men to become pregnant, there are no genetic barriers to girls fishing or boys shopping. In other words, pre-conceptive sex selection represents sexism when decisions about the sex of a child are based upon the anticipated social roles that that child will play, roles which often represent sex-based stereotypical social behavior.

The decision to have a child of a particular sex may not always be so well expressed as in the foregoing examples. Some parents may desire a boy or girl because, for ill-defined reasons, they feel better equipped to raise a child of a certain sex. It can be difficult to determine precisely why some parents prefer a child of a particular sex; however, when carefully examined, many of the motivations for preferring a certain sex are probably rooted in sexist preconceptions.

While individuals vary in their ability to articulate motivation, it is difficult to imagine that any decision, especially one involving the time, risk, and expense of pre-conceptive sex selection, would be made without anticipating gain. Furthermore, to perceive gain, one must predict the consequences of a decision. In gender selection, predicting gain necessitates assumptions to be made which are dependent upon the sex of the child. In other words, to choose a boy or girl, parents must have preconceived notions, however vague, about the ramifications of having a certain sexed child: notions which are fundamentally sexist as they are predicated upon anticipated gender based behavior.

Pre-conceptive sex selection is disturbing because it can be used as a vehicle for parents to express spoken or unspoken sexual prejudice. Furthermore, we can't always expect parents to be honest as to their reasons for preferring one sex. Parents who pursue pre-conceptive sex selection probably harbor strong feelings regarding their desire for a boy or girl. Given the substantial emotions, desires, and repercussions associated with sex selection, it is conceivable that some parents will not be completely honest when asked to explain their desire for a child of a particular sex. In other words, it is possible that some parents will say whatever is necessary so that they can have the freedom to choose the sex of their offspring.

Though it is unsettling that parents may use sex selection to perpetuate their own sexist assumptions, perhaps the most damaging and sexist aspects of pre-conceptive sex selection is that it forces one to think in terms of sex, to place a value upon sex, and to prefer one sex over another. With rare exception, it is difficult to imagine that anyone in making a decision intentionally chooses the least advantageous route. It is also doubtful that anyone would endure the expense and effort involved with pre-conceptive sex selection without a perceived potential for gain. Hence, parents will choose the sex of their child based upon the anticipated gain they will acquire by having a child of a particular sex. This forces parents to figure sex into the calculus of a child's worth, to place a value on sex. Furthermore, by making a choice, parents must essentially prefer one sex over another. This emphasis upon sex is in direct conflict with larger societal goals directed against sexism and which urge individuals to be sex-blind. Pre-conceptive sex selection represents sexism in its purest most blatant form as prior to conception, before any psychological or physical manifestations appear, before parents can possibly know anything about their child, a child's worth is based in large part upon its sex.

Similar arguments can be made about pre-conceptive race selection. Race selection is racist because it forces one to think in terms of race, to place a value upon race, and to prefer one race over another. This emphasis upon race is also in conflict with larger societal goals directed against racism which urge individuals to be race-blind. As with sex selection, pre-conceptive race selection represents racism in its purest form as prior to conception, a child's worth is based in part upon its race. Additionally, race selection may be

used as a vehicle to express parental racism. To demonstrate how racism may influence race selection, it would be helpful to define racism as,

> a belief that race determines human characteristics such as intelligence, physical ability, and the like, and hence that certain races may be genetically superior to or inferior to certain others in these qualities . . . [35]

While there are numerous studies concerning parental sex preferences,[36] race selection is relatively new and to our knowledge there have been no studies addressing why some parents desire to bear a child whose race differs from their own. For some, it may be inconceivable that an individual would consider another race preferable to his own; however, such beliefs are hardly novel. One may in fact wish they had been born a different race and make this desire a reality in their children through pre-conceptive race selection. It is fair to assume that the choice of race, like sex, will be based upon anticipated gain; that the child will benefit from its race. This perception of gain may be predicated upon the belief that genetically conferred intellectual or psychological differences exist between races, differences which are hoped to confer an advantage to the conceived child. This belief in genetically predetermined psychological or intellectual attributes exist is a premise which lies at the heart of racism.

It is conceivable that some parents who choose pre-conceptive race selection for behavioral diversity do not believe in the genetic predetermination of behavior. Rather, these parents may intend to raise their children in a manner 'appropriate' for that child's phenotype. This scenario is, however, also racist as these parents are assuming there are certain race appropriate behaviors and plan to impose their beliefs upon their children to achieve the desired effect. Both situations are essentially racist. To encourage behavior based on race is just as racist as is the belief that race specific behavior is inborn. Stereotypical racial behavior, if such behavior can be characterized, derives from cultural up-bringing, not genetic predisposition. To choose the race of a child in anticipation of race specific behavior is fundamentally racist.

Are there circumstances where race selection is not racist? One can argue that some families may simply desire racial diversity. Racial diversity can be characterized by either behavioral or phe-notypic expression of race. If parents desire racial diversity for phenotypic variance, then pre-conceptive race selection is not racist as parents anticipate gain from genetically determined phys-ical attributes. It is when parents desire racial di-versity because they expect their children to dis-play certain race specific behaviors that the use of preconceptive race selection becomes racist. In this situation parents anticipate behavioral di-versity based upon race; again, a fundamentally racist position.

There is another situation where pre-conceptive race selection is not racist but is a manifestation of racism. In the introductory ex-ample there is a black woman who desires a white child because 'a white child [has] a better future than one of mixed race'.[37] In this scenario, race selection is used to avoid racism and, as far as we can tell from the limited information, no racist assumptions are made. Nevertheless, this situa-tion is tragic as this woman allows herself to be-come a victim by permitting racism to influence a major life decision. One could argue that choos-ing race to avoid racism is similar to choosing sex to avoid sex-linked disease; that parents are re-sponding to pre-extant circumstances which are beyond their control. The difference, however, is that sex-linked disease is a consequence of natu-ral law which we presently have no choice but to accept. Racism is a man made construct which is wholly under human control: racism can be accepted or rejected.

Lastly, it must be emphasized that for health care professionals and governments to perform or permit pre-conceptive racial and sexual prede-termination represents de facto support of racism and sexism. Physicians are obligated to deliver health care objectively, without prejudice. Race and sex are not diseases necessitating treatment. Rather, sex and race selection reflect parental preferences which may be based on sexist and racist assumptions. To perform or allow these procedures implies that the delivery of health care can be based upon the sex and race of the individual. Furthermore, both governments and physicians symbolically represent authority whose participation in these fundamentally racist and sexist acts provides an aura of legitimacy to racism and sexism.

REASONABLE PHENOTYPIC APPROXIMATION

How can we prevent pre-conceptive racial and sexual selection from becoming a vehicle for racism and sexism? Preventing sexism is simple and can be achieved by insuring that the sex of the MAC conceived child is determined by the random association of sperm and egg. Preventing racism, however, is a bit more complicated. For millennia, children could only be the product of their fertile biological parents' genetic contribu-tions. Infertile couples simply produced no chil-dren of their own union. The advent of MAC, however, has enabled infertile couples to produce children which may or may not reflect the phe-notypic heritage of that couple. Current MAC techniques procure sperm or ova from either one or both partners, or from third parties.[38] The re-ality of obtaining ova or sperm from third parties has enabled racism to enter into the decision to have a child. Racism in MAC can be prevented by insisting that MAC conceived children only represent a Reasonable Phenotypic Approxima-tion (RPA) of their parents.

The concept of Reasonable Phenotypic Ap-proximation deserves further elaboration. By phe-notypic approximation, we are primarily referring to race with an emphasis on skin colour; how-ever, this term can also include the ethnic at-tributes of the infertile couple. While many vari-ables can be chosen to produce the best RPA;

those physical attributes which are readily perceptible to the casual observer and define an individual's racial heritage deserve increased fidelity. As previously indicated, RPA is primarily concerned with race which can be defined as,

> implying a distinct physical type with certain unchanging characteristics, as a particular color of skin or shape of skull.[39]

For the purposes of this discussion, race will be equated with skin color. Unfortunately, in many societies, skin color defines the social status of an individual. It is the perceived value of skin color, along with other physical attributes, which is at the heart of racism. Preselecting skin color entails the union of egg and sperm from individuals whose skin color is known. For instance, an infertile Hispanic female and an infertile Caucasian male desire a child. To produce the best racial RPA, sperm and ovum can be procured from a Caucasian male donor and a Hispanic female donor whose respective skin colors best approximates that of the infertile couple. This combination would produce a child whose skin color, while not perfectly matching the theoretical combined skin color of the infertile couple, approximates the color that would have resulted had the couple not been infertile.

Ethnicity represents a combination of genetic and cultural factors. Facial characteristics are heritable whereas more nebulous attributes such as mannerisms and food preferences are culturally determined. As with skin color, in some societies, certain ethnic groups hold higher social status. In contrast to skin color, which can usually be perceived immediately, ethnic origin is more subtle and may not be readily discerned by the casual observer. With respect to RPA, availability permitting, donors of similar ethnic background to the infertile couple can also be chosen. Careful ethnic selection of gamete donors moves further in the direction of best approximating the child which would have occurred had the couple not been infertile. However, since ethnicity is usually not an obvious physical characteristic,

more emphasis should be placed on choosing donors of similar skin color rather than on choosing donors of similar ethnic heritage.

Some couples prefer gamete donors of a particular religion. From a secular perspective, religious belief is not inborn but culturally determined. With the exception of religiously symbolic garments or markings, religious association is not physically perceptible. Hence, while parents may desire to match donors for religion, this is not absolutely necessary from a RPA perspective as one's religion is not physically manifest.

Sperm banks often tell prospective customers that their donors are medical students; thus, implying intelligence is a heritable trait. While certain aspects of intelligence may be heritable, the exact mechanisms of this remain obscure and controversial. Intelligence probably represents a complex interplay between environment and genetics. Like religion, however, intelligence usually cannot be determined by casual observation. Therefore, though parents may desire selection of gamete donors for intelligence, this prerequisite is not necessary for best achieving a RPA.

Some may object that by placing emphasis on skin color, by making race a 'meaningful classification', we are promoting racism. If we lived in a color blind society, perhaps we could avoid making such distinctions. Unfortunately, we do not live in a color blind world and as long as skin color and ethnic heritage confer privilege, we are forced to make these distinctions to prevent abuse. Not making such distinctions would deny there is a problem. To choose skin color implies that one skin color is preferable to another; an idea which is central to racism. The purposeful selection of gamete donors who best achieve a RPA is not racist as this selection provides the infertile couple a child whose skin color best resembles their own. That is, careful selection of donors by disinterested, objective health care professionals approximates what nature would have provided had the couple not been infertile. Sadly, as long as we live in a racist society race, and hence skin color, will remain a meaningful classification. RPA attempts to recapitulate nature without human bias.

LEGAL PROHIBITIONS OF RACISM AND SEXISM IN MAC

Is it possible to prohibit the racist and sexist use of racial and sexual predetermination? Although most cultures have recognized a general right, if not obligation,[40] to procreate, this right has been circumscribed. For example, some cultures encourage limiting the number of children born to each family.[41] Others prefer procreation within matrimony,[42] as 'it is the duty of every man to take a wife to himself, in order to fulfill the precept of propagation'.[43] Indeed, China has taken its family planning policies to extremes with programs of forced contraception, forced sterilization, and at times, forced abortions.[44] Similarly, the right to procreate via MAC has been limited[45] at various stages along the path of development from ovum/sperm, to conceptus (zygote), to embryo,[46] to fetus,[47] and finally, to newborn.[48] Usually, 'access is . . . limited to heterosexual married couples and to those heterosexual couples living in stable unions'.[49] Nevertheless, despite modest restrictions on access to MAC, and controversy as to the degree of sex selection acceptance by health professionals,[50] more than 70 clinics in the United States offer 'sex selection'.[51]

The American judiciary has clearly recognized a right to procreate.[52] Meanwhile, with medical advances, popular concepts of a right to health or health care have evolved.[53] These 'rights' have merged so that not only is there a right to procreate but also, there is a perception that parents have the right to use medical technology to ensure that their products of conception are as free from disease and defect as possible.[54]

As the legal and ethical controversies surrounding MAC have increased, so too has international legislation and regulation of reproductive technologies.[55] In the U.S., although some state statutes prohibit the use of MAC by unmarried women,[56] courts have been reluctant to decide who may use this technology. With the exception of legislation prohibiting abortion for sex selection,[57] most of the legal activity concerning MAC is reflected in court decisions involving legitimacy,[58] financial support,[59] parentage,[60] and visitation rights.[61] This relative legislative and judicial vacuum has left decisions on how to allocate MAC to medical professionals who lack consensus on its indications.[62] Consider, for example, a New York case involving the financial support of the child of a lesbian couple, one of whom was a transsexual and the other, a fertile biological female who bore the child via *in vitro* fertilization.[63] While many states and physicians would hesitate to permit the use of MAC under such circumstances, the fact that this case arose demonstrates the capricious nature of MAC utilization.

Does MAC Reflect a Fundamental Clash Between an Individual's Right to Privacy and Societal Prohibition of Discrimination?

The continued advances in MAC and trait-selection-technologies (TST's)[64] have created conflict between an individual's right to reproductive privacy and society's desire to eradicate racism and sexism. The right to procreate is rooted in constitutional decisions recognizing an individual's right to privacy. Indeed, some have argued that the use of MAC provides a vehicle to further the 'inclusive fitness' of individual reproductive efforts.[65] That is, MAC and other 'trait selection technologies' are private matters and should be afforded the same legal protections as other reproductive strategies (e.g., abortion and contraception).[66]

Although the use of MAC to manipulate race or sex may be viewed as an expression of personal privacy, such manipulations may reflect racism and sexism and be in conflict with larger societal goals. Both courts and legislators have been nearly unanimous in their decisions when choosing between individual privacy versus the best interests of society.[67] That is, when in conflict, society's interests generally supersede those of the individual. When pitted against society's commitment to eradicate racism and sexism, individual privacy can be secondary. 'There are manifold restraints to which every person is necessarily subject for the common good.'[68]

Despite the absence of specific legislation prohibiting MAC-based racism and sexism, The Americans With Disabilities Act of 1990, the Rehabilitation Act of 1973, and the Civil Rights Act of 1964 may provide a legal and intellectual foundation for future attempts to deter MAC racism and sexism. Although we are mindful of the challenges in enforcing anti-discrimination laws, and we are further concerned about potential negative consequences of any law that restricts procreative liberty, we nevertheless favor legislation that would control sex selection.

Of course, physicians who wish to minimize the potential for sexism may simply deny abortion services based on fetal sex. With the exception of sex-linked heritable illness, sex is certainly not a disease and no physician should be held derelict if she refuses to provide this information or service.

Some may argue that prohibiting sex selection infringes upon a woman's procreative liberty. Traditionally, reproductive autonomy has been defined as the freedom to determine when and if to become pregnant.[69] Major milestones in the advancement of procreative freedom include the legalization of contraception and abortion, thereby guaranteeing a woman's right to choose 'when' and 'if' to become pregnant. MAC has expanded the boundaries of reproductive autonomy in that not only can women choose if and when to become pregnant, but they can now, through MAC, choose how. The next logical step in the battle for procreative liberty is to control the 'what' of conception; that is, to pre-determine the end product of conception.

We recognize the necessity of reproductive autonomy and have no objection to women controlling the if, when, and how of procreation. We do however, abhor any action that, by its very nature, is sexist or racist. Anti-sex selection legislation would preserve the major goals of abortion, contraception, and MAC while, at the same time, prevent the sexism inherent in sex selection.

With respect to race, we reiterate the position that the child produced via MAC should be a RPA of his parents, no matter how racially diverse the parents may be. For this reason, legislation prohibiting the selection of a race which does not reasonably approximate the respective races of the mother and father is suggested.

CONCLUSIONS

The case of the infertile black woman in Italy establishes a disquieting precedent for parents who wish to design offspring to suit perceived needs— needs which often represent unspoken racial and sexual prejudice. When the health care community and government permit such manipulation, they lend de facto official sanction to racism and sexism.

At best, the predetermination of race and sex reflects cultural bias. At its worst, racial engineering is a harbinger of racial purity. For infertile couples, MAC offers the hope of parenthood and all the value attached to it.[70] However, with the exception of disabling disease, our procreative efforts should reflect the random luck of the genetic draw. To allow otherwise permits racism and sexism to flourish and enter our health care system. While the right to have children is protected, there are legitimate restrictions to which any responsible society is bound. Indeed, Pia Garavaglia, Italy's Health Minister has eloquently articulated this responsibility: 'Desires are not rights. A child is not a consumer good'.[71]

MAC has come a long way since it made international headlines in 1978 with the first 'test tube baby'.[72] Today, MAC is common and has made possible the predetermination of race and sex. Indeed, the future is likely to include the ability to manipulate the physical, emotional, and intellectual characteristics of our offspring. Imagine a world where we routinely produce children with IQs over 150. Imagine soldiers genetically engineered for aggression. This is not science fiction or fantasy. If history is a guide, we will elucidate the mechanisms behind our genetic inheritance.[73] Too often, vital issues such as nuclear weapon proliferation and MAC fall victim to the 'technological imperative'. That is, the technology is developed, market niches created, and precedents established in the absence of substantial debate over the consequences or outcomes. Put another way, appropriate technology assessment has not been undertaken in the case of MAC. Fortunately, it is not too late to prohibit the predetermination of race and sex. Unfortunately, the law has not kept pace with technology; thus, new legislation must be supported which limits the utilization of MAC.

Some believe that the combined wisdom of legislators, courts, and the medical community will never permit or facilitate attempts to 'enhance' our genetic endowment. However, we are not confident that there will be 'full public disclosure and extensive public discussion of each new or proposed procedure—just as should be done in every other area of medical technology'.[74] History does not necessarily support an abiding confidence in the 'wisdom' of the legal process or the medical profession. Consider, for example, federally supported experiments on the effects of radiation on live, unsuspecting human subjects begun in the 1940's and continuing into the 1970's.[75] Experiments on the sick, the weak,[76] the pregnant,[77] and infants.[78]

Consider also the professional and governmental *lassez faire* embodied by The Repository for Germinal Choice, a sperm bank established in 1979 to store and utilize the 'sperm [of] famous and exceptional people',[79] including Noble laureates. To our knowledge, no statute, regulation, court decision, or medical consensus document has in any way limited the activities of the Repository. William B. Shockley, a Repository donor and Winner of the 1956 Nobel Prize in physics, said of the bank, 'I am endorsing . . . [the] concept of increasing the people at the top of the population'.[80] Even to the uninitiated, it is obvious that the Repository represents a blatant attempt to manipulate intelligence.

Some may suggest we prohibit further research in genetic engineering, lest we open Pandora's Box. Not only would this prohibition be impossible to enforce, but it also goes against the grain of human nature. We will never suppress human curiosity, a quality which has made, for better or worse, that which we are today. Such suppression grates against the moral fabric of our existence and some may suggest it is tantamount to tyranny. Furthermore, by prohibiting these endeavors we compromise our never-ending efforts to modify, if not eradicate, medical disorders. Lastly, national security demands knowledge of the capacity of science as well as the ability to control its fruits. History shows us that there have been and will be those who do not share a sense of moral obligation, human rights, or international responsibility. We have witnessed the murder of millions, terrorism, and attempts at ethnic cleansing. It is foolish to assume our labors will not find a home in the arsenal of evil.

References and Notes

1. Willan, P. and Hawkes, N. 'White Baby Born To Black Mother', *The Times of London*, 1, 31 December 1993.

2. Ibid. 2.

3. Medically Assisted Conception is a generic term which includes many medical procedures and MAC involves non-coital reproduction in which medical technology is used to achieve pregnancy.

4. Beernick, F. J., Dmowski, W. P., Ericsson, R. J. 'Sex Preselection Through Albumin Separation of Sperm'. *Fertil. Steril.* 59, 1993, pp. 382–386.

5. The pre-selection of race is far simpler than that of sex as it entails the matching of egg and sperm from individuals whose race is known.

6. Ogata, T. and Matsuo, N. 'Sex Chromosome Aberrations and Stature: Deduction of the Principle Factors

Involved in the Determination of Adult Height'. *Hum. Genetics* 91, 1993, pp. 551–562.

7. Turner, G. and Partington, M.W., 'Genes for Intelligence on the X Chromosome'. *J. of Med. Gen.* 28, 1991, pp. 429–434.

8. Schuckit, M.A., 'A Clinical Model of Genetic Influences in Alcohol Dependence'. *J. Stud. Alcohol* 55, 1994, pp. 5–17.

9. See Ronald Sanders, *Lost Tribes and Promised Lands: The Origins of American Racism*, 1st ed., (Boston: Little, Brown, 1978). See also, Andrew Hacker, *Two Nations: Black And White, Separate, Hostile, Unequal*, 1st ed., (New York, Ballantine Books, 1993); Lee Sigelman, *Black Americans' View of Racial Inequality: The Dream Deferred* (Cambridge: Cambridge University Press, 1991); David T. Wellman, *Portraits of White Racism*, 2nd ed., (Cambridge: Cambridge University Press, 1993); Cynthia F. Epistein, *Deceptive Distinctions: Sex, Gender, and the Social Order*, (New Haven: Yale University Press, 1988); Walby, Sylvia *Theorizing Patriarchy*, (Cambridge: Oxford); Benokraitis, Nijole V. *Modern Sexism: Blatant, Subtle, and Covert Discrimination*, (Engelwood Cliffs: Prentice-Hall, 1986)

10. Holmes, Helen B. 'Sex Preselection: Eugenics for Everyone?' in James M. Humber and Robert F. Almeder (eds.) *Biomedical Ethics Review—1985*, Clifton, N. J.: Humana Press, 1985, pp. 38–71. See also, Jones, Owen D. Sex Selection: Regulating Technology Enabling the Predetermination of a Child's Gender. *Harvard Journal of Law and Technology* 6, 1992, pp. 11–12; WuDunn, Sheryl, China's Castaway Babies: Cruel Practice Lives On, *New York Times*, 26 February, 1991.

11. Jones O. D., Sex Selection: Regulating Technology Enabling the Predetermination of a Child's Gender. *Harvard Journal of Law and Technology* 6, 1992, pp. 12–14. See also, Pebley, A.R. and Westhoff, C.F. Women's Sex Preference in the United States: 1970–1975. *Demography* 19, 1982, pp. 177–189.

12. De Beauvoir, S. *The Second Sex*, New York: Knoff, First Modern Library Edition, 1968, p. 61.

13. Bradley, M.A. *The Iceman Inheritance: Prehistoric Sources of Western Man's Racism, Sexism, and Aggression*. New York: Kaydoe Publications, 1991.

14. Janssen-Jurreit, M. *Sexism: The Male Monopoly on History and Thought*, 1st ed. New York: Farrar Straus Giroux, 1992, p. 15.

15. Harris, K. *Sex, Ideology, and Religion: The Representation of Women in the Bible*. New York: Burning Bush Press, 1967, p. 30. See also, Larue, G. *Sex and the Bible*. Buffalo, NY: Prometheus Books, 1983, p. 15.

16. Kristof, Nicholas D. 'China's Crackdown on Births: A Stunning, and Harsh, Success'. *New York Times*, 25 April, 1. See also, Editorial Desk: China's Cruelty and Women's Rights. *New York Times*, 21 May 1993, A26; Kristof, Nicholas D. The Chosen Sex—A Special Report: Chinese Turn to Ultrasound, Scorning Baby Girls for Boys. *New York Times*, 21 July 1993, Al; Ferraro, Geraldine, Human Rights for Women. *New York Times*, 10 June 1993, A27; Gargan, Edward A. 'Bangalore Journal: For Many Brides in India, a Dowry Buys Death'. *New York Times*, 30 December 1993, A4; Thomson, Ann 'Why are Potential Women Being Killed?' *Midwifery*, 9, 181–82.

17. Miller, Barbara D. *The Endangered Sex: Neglect of Female Children in Rural North India* Ithaca, N.Y.: Cornell University Press, 1981. See also, Guttentag, Marcia *Too Many Woman?: The Sex Ratio Question* New Delhi, India: Sage Publications, 1983, 54. Fout, John C. ed., *Forbidden History: The State, Society, and the Regulation of Sexuality in Modern Europe: Essays from the Journal of the History of Sexuality* Chicago: University of Chicago Press, 1992, pp. 31–55.

18. Ghadially, R. and Kumar, P. *Bride Burning: The Psycho-Social Dynamics of Dowry Deaths*. In *Women in Indian Society*, edited by R. Ghadially. New Delhi: Sage Publications, 1988, pp. 167–177.

19. Goldin, C.D. *Understanding the Gender Gap: An Economic History of American Women*. New York: Oxford University Press, 1990, pp. 211–213. See also, Koziara, K.S. et al. *Working Women: Past, Present, Future*. Washington: Bureau of National Affairs, 1987, pp. 1–36.

20. Rudman W.J. and Hagiwara, A.F. 'Sexual Exploitation in Advertising Health and Wellness Products'. *Women and Health*, 18, 1992, pp. 77–89.

21. 'and God said unto them, Be fruiful, and multiply, and replenish the earth.' Genesis 1:28.

22. Article 15.1 (b) *The International Covenant on Economic, Social, and Cultural Rights*, 993 U.N.T.S. 3, 6 I.L.M. 360 (1967). This Covenant was adopted by the United Nations on 16 December 1966 (Annex to G.A. Res. 2000, 21 U.N. GAOR, 14th Sess., Supp. No 16, at 490, U.N. Doc. A/6316 (1976)).

23. Traditionally disability has been associated with disease which can be defined as ' . . . illness; sickness; an interruption, cessation, or disorder of body functions, systems, or organs . . . a morbid entity characterized usually by at least two of these criteria: recognized etiologic agent(s), identifiable group of signs and symptoms, or consistent anatomical alterations.' Hensl, W.R., ed. *Stedman's Medical Dictionary*, 25th ed. London: Williams & Wilkins, 1990, p. 444. This is a formal definition and in colloquial usage the concept of disease carries an assumed risk of mortality and morbidity which impacts upon 'normal' function. This effect upon function imparts a handicap or disability. *Webster's Ninth New Collegiate Dictionary* defines disease as 'a condition of the living animal . . . that impairs the performance of vital function.'

24. Chapman, Robert L. ed. *Roget's International Thesaurus*, 5th ed., New York: Harper Collins Publishers, 1992, p. 425. The terminology of disability has gradually evolved over the years. Those with disabilities were formerly considered handicapped, a term which has long since fallen from favor. Today there is a trend in referring to those who were once considered disabled as now being challenged. Eisenberg, Myron G. ed., *Key Words in Psychosocial Rehabilitation: A Guide to Contemporary Usage*, New York: Springer Publishing Company, 1994, pp. 40–42, 53–54. See also, World Health Organization, *International Classification of Impairments, Disabilities, and Handicaps*. Geneva: World Health Origination, 1980.

25. *Webster's Ninth New Collegiate Dictionary*, Springfield, MA: Merriam-Webster, 1990, p. 359.

26. Hensyl, W.R., ed *Stedman's Medical Dictionary*, 25th ed. London: Williams & Wilkins, 1990, p. 683.

27. Americans With Disabilities Act (ADA), 42 U.S.C.A. [189] [189] 12101 to 12213 West Supp. 1994.

28. Ibid.

29. Ibid.

30. Ibid.

31. Wertz, Dorothy C. and Fletcher, John C. 'Fatal Knowledge? Prenatal Diagnosis and Sex Selection'. *Hastings Center Report*, May/June, 1989, pp. 21–29. See also, Hartley, Shirley F. and Pietraczyk, Linda M. 'Preselecting the Sex of Offspring: Technologies, Attitudes, and Implications'. *Social Biology* 26, 1979, 232–46. Despite an increasing acceptance of sex selection technology by the public and health care professionals, there continue to be strong voices of caution. See, e.g., The Council of Ethical and Judicial Affairs, American Medical Association, Ethical Issues Related to Prenatal Genetic Testing. *Archives of Family Medicine* 3, 1994, 633–42.

32. Breiner, Sander J. *Slaughter of the Innocents: Child Abuse Through the Ages and Today*, New York: Plenum Press, 1990, pp. 49–50, 179–81, 191. See also, Kestenberg, Judith S. and Kestenberg, Milton *Child Killing and Child Rescuing*, New York: Human Sciences Press, 1989; Ullman, Jodic B. and Fidell, Linda S. *Gender Selection and Society*, Northridge, CA: California State University, 1989.

33. Such as in finding a significant other.

34. Wilson, K.G. *The Columbia Guide to Standard American English*, New York: Columbia University Press, 1993, p. 390.

35. Wilson, K.G. *The Columbia Guide to Standard American English*, New York: Columbia University Press, 1993, p. 358.

36. Pebley, A.R. and Westhoff, C.F. 'Women's Sex Preference in the United States: 1970–1975'. *Demography* 19, 1982, pp. 177–189.

37. Willan, P. and Hawkes, N. 'White Baby Born To Black Mother'. *The Times of London*, 1, Dec, 31, 1993.

38. Scibel, M.M. *Infertility: A Comprehensive Text*. Boston: Appleton & Lange, pp. 513–531. See also, Furrow, B.R., et al. *Health Law: Cases, Materials, and Problems*, 2nd ed. St Paul: West Publishing Co., 1991, p. 960.

39. Gove, P.B. Editor-in-Chief. *Webster's Third International Dictionary, Unabridged*. Springfield, MA: G. & C, Merriam Company, 1966, p. 1870.

40. Smith, J.E. *Humanea Vitae: A Generation Later*, Washington, DC: The Catholic University of America Press, 1991, pp. 42–54. See also, *infra*. 45.

41. Kaufman, J.A. *Billion and Counting: Family Planning Campaigns and Policies in the People's Republic of China*. San Francisco: San Francisco Press, 1983, p. 47. See also, Freedman, R. and Takeshita, J.Y. *Family Planning in Taiwan: An Experiment in Social Change*. Princeton: Princeton University Press, 1969, pp. 109–292.

42. See, e.g. Omran, A.R. *Family Planning in the Legacy of Islam*. New York: Routledge, 1992, pp. 13–26.

43. Rabbi Ganzfried, S. *Code of Jewish Law*, vol. 4. New York: Hebrew Publishing Company, 1963, p. 6.

44. Editorial Desk, China's Cruelty and Woman's Rights. *New York Times* 26, 21 May, 1993.

45. Physicians routinely screen applicants for MAC. A 1987 study by the Office of Technology Assessment found that physicians refused to perform MAC for many reasons, including child abuse, alcohol abuse, drug abuse, HIV seropositivity, and homosexuality.

46. *Davis v. Davis*, 50 U.S.L.W. 2205 app. granted, Sup. Ct. TN, 1990, (custody of fertilized ova).

47. *Roe v. Wade*, 401 U.S. 113, 165 (1973) (interests of fetus v. mother). See also, *In re A.C.* 533 A.2d 611 (D.C. 1990) (cesarean section ordered for woman with cancer); *Jefferson v. Griffin Spalding County Hospital Authority*, 247 Ga. 86, 274 S.E.2d 457 (1981) (cesarean section ordered for woman with placenta previa).

48. *In the Matter of Baby* M, 537 A.2d 1227 (N.J. 1988) (invalidating a surrogacy contract). See also, La. Rev. Stat. Ann. Section 722.851, (Louisiana law denying legal force to surrogacy contracts); Robertson, John A. 'Embryos, Families, and Procreative Liberty: The Legal Structure of the New Reproduction'. 59 *S. Cal. L. Rev.* 939, 1986.

49. Knoppers, B.M. and Lebris, S. 'Recent Advances in Medically Assisted Conception: Legal, Ethical, and Social Issues'. *Am. J. of Law and Med.* 42, 1991, 346–347.

50. Jones, Owen D. 'Sex Selection: Regulating Technology Enabling the Predetermination of a Child's Gender', 6 *Harvard Journal of Law and Technology*, 1, 1992, pp. 14–17, (indicating increasing acceptance). See also, Evans, Mark I. 'Attitudes on the Ethics of Abortion, Sex Selection, and Selective Pregnancy Termination Among Health Care Professionals, Ethicists, and Clergy Likely to Encounter Such Situations'. *American Journal of Obstetrics and Gynecology* 164 1991, pp. 1092–99, (concluding that 'sex selection was considered unethical by most respondents').

51. Blank, Robert H. *Regulating Reproduction*, New York: Columbia University Press, 1990, p. 46.

52. Procreational liberty rooted in constitutional protections of privacy, See, *Skinner v. Oklahoma*, 316 U.S. 535 (1942). See also, *Meyer v. Nebraska*, 262 U.S. 390, 399 (1923); *Stanley v. Illinois*, 405 U.S. 645, 651 (1972); John A. Robertson, Embryos, Families and Procreative Liberty: The Legal Structure of the New Reproduction, 59 *S. Cal. L. Rev.*, 942–1041, (1986);

Robertson, John A. 1983: Procreative Liberty and the Control of Conception, Pregnancy, and Childbirth, 60 *Va. L. Rev.* 405–464 (1983); Robertson, Procreative Liberty and the State's Burden of Proof in Regulating Noncoital Reproduction, 16 *L. Med. & Health Care* 18–26, 1988; Ikemoto, Lisa C. Providing Protection for Collaborative, Noncoital Reproduction: The Right of Intimate Association. 40 *Rutgers L. Rev.* 1273–1309, 1988. Comment, Prohibiting Payments to Surrogate Mothers: Love's Labor Lost and the Constitutional Right of Privacy, 20 *John. Marsh. L. Rev.* 715–741, 1987.

53. With the exception of lofty proclamations by various international agencies, few governments legally recognize a right to health care. The right to health and health care is, however, a popularly accepted belief. 'For years . . . the residents of Cold Spring [New York] have seen the hospital as evidence that they have a basic right to immediate and total health care.' See, Belkin, Lisa, Where Necessity Ends for Hospital Care. *New York Times*, 16 June 1993. B1. In his speech on national health care to Congress on 22 September 1993, President Clinton alluded to a potential federal right to health care when he spoke of 'giving every American health security, health care that can never be taken away, health care that is always there'. *Congressional Record*—House, Vol 139, No. 125, 22 September 1993, H6895–6900. See also, U.S. Congress, Senate, Special Committee on Aging. *Who Lives, Who Dies, Who Decides: The Ethics of Health Care Rationing: Hearing Before the Special Committee on Aging*, 102nd Cong., 1st sess., 19 June 1991; U.S. Congress, Senate, Committee on Labor and Human Resources. *Comprehensive Health Care Reform: The Need for Action: Hearing Before the Committee Labor and Human Resources*, 103rd Congress, 1st sess., 20 May 1993.

54. Article 15.1 (b). *The International Covenant on Economic, Social, and Cultural Rights*, 993 U.N.T.S. 3, 6 I.L.M. 360 (1967).

55. Knopper, B.M. and Le Bris, S. Ethical and Legal Concerns: Reproductive Technologies 1990–1993. *Curr. Opin. Obstet. Gynecol.* 5, 1993, pp. 630–635.

56. Curren, W.J., et al. Health Care Law, Forensic Science, and Public Policy. 4th ed. Boston: Little Brown and Company, 1990, p. 1073.

57. See 18 Pa. Stat. Ann. Section 3204(c) (Supp. 1993) and Ill. Ann. Stat. ch. 38 para. 81–26, §§ 6(8)

(Smith-Hurn Supp. 1990). See also, Lewin, Tamar, States Testing the Limits on Abortion. *New York Times*, 2 April 1990, A14.

58. *Gursky v. Gursky*, 39 Misc.2d 1083, 242 N.Y.S.2d 406 (Sup. Ct. 1963), child born through AID 'is not the legitimate 'issue' of the husband.' *Strnad v. Strnad*, 190 Misc. 786, 78 N.Y.S. 2d 390 (Sup. Ct. 1948), child born via AID is not illegitimate.

59. *Strnad v. Strnad*, 190 Misc. 786, 78 N.Y.S. 2d 390 (Sup. Ct. 1948). See also, *People v. Sorensen*, 68 Cal. 2d 280, 66 Cal. Rptr. 7, 437 P.2d 495 (Sup. Ct. 1968) (father is responsible for financial support of child conceived through artificial insemination).

60. *In the Matter of Baby M*, 537 A.2d 1227 (N.J. 1988). See also, *Strnad v. Strnad*, 190 Misc. 786, 78 N.Y.S.2d 390 (Sup. Ct. 1948).

61. C.M. v. C.C., 377 A.2d 821 (N.J. Super. 1977) one of the first cases concerning parenthood and visitation rights regarding a child produced by artificial insemination. See also Jordan C. v. Mary K., 224 Cal. Rptr. 530 (Cal. App. 1986); McIntyre v. Crouch, 780 P.2d 239 (Oreg. App. 1989); In re Baby Doc, 291 S.C. 389, 353 S.E.2d 877 (1987); R. v. F., 113 N.J. Super. 396 (Cty. Ct. 1971) (natural father has visitation rights for his illegitimate offspring).

62. Generally, indications for MAC are infertility, advanced age, and selected genetic disorders.

63. *Karin T. vs. Michael T.*, 484 N.Y.S. 2d 780 (Fam. Ct. 1985) (transsexual held responsible for child support).

64. Jones, O.D. 'Reproductive Autonomy and Evolutionary Biology: A Regulatory Framework for Trait-Selection Technologies'. *Am. J. of Law and Med.* 19, 1993, pp. 187–231.

65. Ibid.

66. Ibid.

67. Perhaps the most dramatic examples of societal interest superseding individual liberty are seen in cases involving mandatory immunizations; a situation where there is an actual invasion of a person's body. See, *Jacobson v. Massachusetts*, 197 U.S. 11 (1904) (Massachusetts statue requiring smallpox vaccine is not unconstitutional). See also, *Cude v. State*, 377 S.W.2d 816 (Ark. 1964) (children must be vaccinated despite parents' objections); *Prince v. Commonwealth*, 321 U.S. 158 (1943) (children must receive vaccinations despite parents' religious objections). Anti-

smoking legislation is another example where individual liberty is restricted for the common good. See, Center for Disease Control: Bureau of Health Education. *State Legislation on Smoking and Health*. (Atlanta: The Center for Disease Control, 1978). See also, Brody, Alvan *The Legal Rights of Nonsmokers*. New York: Avon Books, 1977, pp. 201–11. Environmental law is dedicated to protecting both the public and environment from the actions of the few. See, Findley, Roger W. and Farber, Daniel A. *Environmental Law: Cases and Materials*. 2nd ed. St. Paul: West Publishing Company, 1985. Anti-drunk driving laws are designed not only to protect the public against the irresponsible actions of drunk drivers but also intended to protect individuals from their own reckless behavior. Law Enforcement Study Center. *Alcohol, Alcoholism and Law Enforcement*. St Louis: Washington University Press, 1969.

68. *Jacobson v. Massachusetts*, 197 U.S. 11 (1904).

69. *Carey v. Population Services International*, 431 U.S. 678 (1977). See also, *Roe v. Wade*, 410 U.S. 113 (1973).

70. Aristotle, *Nicomachean Ethics*, 8: 12.

71. Associated Press. Debate Opens Over Pregnancy Ethics. *The Philadelphia Inquirer*. A2, 1 January, 1994.

72. Bonnicksen, A.L. *In Vitro Fertilization: Building Policy From Laboratories to Legislatures*. New York: Columbia University Press, 12–24.

73. Joseph Palca, 'James Watson to Head NIH Human Genome Project,' *Nature* 335 (1988) 193. See also, Smith, Lloyd M. 'Automated DNA Sequencing and the Analysis of the Human Genome, *Genome* 31, 1989, 929–37.

74. Warren, M.A. 'The Ethics of Sex Presclection'. In J. Humber and R.F. Almeder, eds. *Biomedical Ethics Review* Clifton, N.J.: Humana Press, 1985, p. 85.

75. Schncider, S. 'Secret Nuclear Research on People Comes to Light'. *New York Times*. A1, Dec, 17, 1993.

76. Ibid. B11.

77. Ibid.

78. Schneider, K. 'Energy Secretary Tells a Few More U.S. Nuclear Secrets'. *New York Times*. A10, June 28, 1994.

79. Broad, W.J. 'A Bank For Nobel Sperm'. *Science* 207:1326–1327, 1980.

80. Ibid, 1327.

QUESTIONS FOR DISCUSSION

1. Some argue that surrogacy is an expression of women's reproductive autonomy and that it is demeaning to women to say that it might be coercive or exploitative. Can you give any examples in which surrogacy could be coercive or exploitative? Explain.

2. Given the risks in a multiple pregnancy to the fetuses and the mother carrying them, and given that multiple pregnancy results from taking fertility drugs or producing multiple embryos through in vitro fertilization, are there justifiable grounds for banning these two practices altogether?

3. Is there an ethically significant difference between aborting a single fetus and selectively terminating one or more fetuses in a multiple pregnancy? How would the difference in reasons and intentions of the pregnant woman in either case be ethically significant?

4. Some argue that using cloning technology to produce children would involve parents' inappropriate exercise of power over their children. Explain how cloning would, or would not, threaten a child's right to an open future.

5. Given that the sex and sexual orientation of a fetus or embryo can be determined, many would argue that it would be morally reprehensible to select a male baby over a female, or to select a baby who likely will develop into a heterosexual rather than a homosexual person. But others might argue that, given discrimination and other social obstacles against women and homosexuals, parents would be acting in the best interests of their future child if they selected heterosexual males because they would have easier lives. How would you respond to this position?

CASES

Roe v. Wade. Supreme Court of the United States, 410 U.S. 113, 93 S. Ct. 705, 35L. Ed. 2d 147 (1973). The ruling in this case established a woman's right to choose whether or not to terminate a pregnancy, based on the concept of personal liberty embodied in the Due Process clause of the 14th Amendment to the Constitution. However, the right was not absolute and did not mean that a woman could terminate a pregnancy at any time. Rather it was limited to the first trimester of pregnancy before fetal viability, or the fetus' ability to live outside the womb.

Becker v. Schwartz. 46 N.Y. 2d 401, 411, 386 N.E. 807, 812, 413 N.Y.S 2d 895, 900 (1978). This case addressed the issue of wrongful life, or whether a child's physical condition is so bad that it would have been better for the child not to have been born. It was filed as a tort by a handicapped child against its parents on grounds of negligence but was rejected by the New York Supreme Court on the ground that the state should not become involved in deciding whether a person's life is or is not worthwhile.

Smith v. Cote. Supreme Court of New Hampshire. 128 N.H. 231, 513 A. 2d. 341 (1986). Linda Smith filed a wrongful birth claim against the obstetrician who was treating her during her pregnancy in 1979. She claimed that the defendant failed to exercise a duty of care to both Linda and Heather, her daughter who was born with multiple birth defects. The obstetrician breached his duty when he failed to discover Linda's exposure to rubella and failed to advise her of the possible effects of that exposure on her child's health. Had Linda been properly informed, she would have undergone an abortion and Heather would not have been born.

In the Matter of Baby M. 109 N.J. 396, 537 A. 2d. 1227 (1988). In this case, the New Jersey Superior Court ruled that once the terms of a surrogacy contract have been met by both parties, a surrogate mother has no parental rights and the natural biological (genetic) mother is entitled to retain her right to the child. But the New Jersey Supreme Court reversed the lower court's ruling that the surrogacy contract was valid. It held that a surrogacy contract that provides money for the surrogate and includes her irrevocable agreement to surrender the child at birth is invalid and unenforceable. While granting custody to the biological father, the court restored the surrogate as the mother of the child. William and Elizabeth Stern were the plaintiffs, and Mary Beth Whitehead was the defendant (surrogate).

Planned Parenthood of Southeastern Pennsylvania v. Casey. Supreme Court of the United States, 505 U.S. 833, 112 S.Ct. 2791, 120 L.Ed.2d 674 (1992). At issue here were five provisions of the Pennsylvania Abortion Control Act of 1982. These included different types of informed consent for adult and minor women to obtain abortions, as well as the requirement that a married woman seeking an abortion sign a statement indicating that she notified her husband of her intention. In its ruling on this case, the U.S. Supreme Court reaffirmed its three-part holding in *Roe v. Wade:* that a woman has a right to choose an abortion before fetal viability without undue interference from the state; that the state has the power to restrict abortions after fetal viability if the law contains exceptions for pregnancies that endanger a woman's life or health; and that the state has a legitimate interest from the outset of the pregnancy in protecting the health of the woman and the life of the fetus that may become a child.

Davis v. Davis. Supreme Court of Tennessee, 842 S.W. 2d 588 (1992). Mary Sue and Junior Lewis Davis divorced after producing seven embryos through in vitro fertilization; the embryos were then cryogenically preserved. Mary Sue originally asked for control of the frozen embryos, with the intention of having them transferred to her own uterus in a post-divorce effort to become pregnant. Junior Davis objected, saying that he preferred to leave the embryos in their frozen state until he decided whether or not he wanted to become a parent outside the bounds of marriage. The trial court awarded "custody" to Mary Sue Davis and directed that she be permitted to have the opportunity to bring the embryos to term as children through implantation. But the Court of Appeals reversed the decision, finding that Junior Davis had a constitutionally protected right not to beget a child when no pregnancy had taken place. Also, there was no compelling state interest to justify implanting embryos against the will of either genetic parent. Procreative autonomy consists of two equally significant rights—the right to procreate and the right to avoid procreation. On this ground, Junior Davis had the right to prevent implantation of the embryos.

SUGGESTED FURTHER READING

Cambridge Quarterly of Health Care Ethics. Special Issue on Human Cloning, Volume 7 (Spring 1998).

Glover, Jonathan, et al. *Ethics of New Reproductive Technologies: The Glover Report to the European Commission.* Dekalb, IL: Northern Illinois University Press, 1989.

Harris, John, and Holm, Soren, eds. *The Future of Human Reproduction: Ethics, Choice and Regulation.* Oxford: Clarendon Press, 1998.

Marquis, Don. "Why Abortion Is Immoral." *Journal of Philosophy* 86: 183–202, 1989

Robertson, John. "The Question of Human Cloning." *Hastings Center Report* 24: 6–14, 1994.

_____. *Children of Choice: Freedom and the New Reproductive Technologies.* Princeton: Princeton University Press, 1994.

Sherwin, Susan. *No Longer Patient.* Philadelphia: Temple University Press, 1992.

Stein, Edward. "Choosing the Sexual Orientation of Children." *Bioethics* 12: 1–24, 1998.

Steinbock, Bonnie. *Life Before Birth.* New York: Oxford University Press, 1992.

_____. "The McCaughey Septuplets: Medical Miracle or Gambling with Fertility Drugs?", in John Arras and Steinbock, eds., *Ethical Issues in Modern Medicine,* Fifth Edition, Mountain View, CA: Mayfield, pp. 375–384, 1999.

Thomson, Judith Jarvis. "A Defense of Abortion." *Philosophy & Public Affairs* 1: 47–66, 1971–1972.

Tong, Rosemarie. *Feminist Approaches to Bioethics,* Second Edition. Boulder, CO: Westview, 1999.

Warnock, Mary. *A Question of Life: The Warnock Report on Human Fertilization and Embryology.* Oxford: Blackwell, 1985.

Wolf, Susan. *Feminism and Bioethics: Beyond Reproduction.* New York: Oxford University Press, 1996.

PART V:
GENETICS

Since James Watson and Francis Crick announced the double helical structure of DNA in 1953, molecular biology in general and medical genetics in particular have advanced at a remarkable rate. In the 1960s, it became possible to test individuals and screen populations for certain genetic conditions. Phenylketonuria, a hereditary metabolic disorder involving the amino acid phenylalanine, which causes mental retardation in early childhood, was the first condition to be discovered through genetic testing. At approximately the same time, a blood test could reveal whether a person was a carrier of the defective gene that causes Tay-Sachs disease, a degenerative neurological disease that slowly kills infants. Screening programs were developed for certain populations within which particular diseases were prevalent. These included Tay-Sachs screening for Ashkenazi Jews, as well as screening for people of African ancestry who carried the genetic mutation causing sickle-cell anemia, a painful, debilitating, and often fatal disease. Direct genetic testing of individuals in families with dominantly inherited genetic disorders, such as Huntington's disease, and those with breast and ovarian cancer associated with the BRCA1 and BRCA2 genes, followed.

Ideally, genetic testing would lead to the development of therapies to treat genetically caused diseases. To date, however, few such interventions have been successful. With the notable exceptions of treatment of a few individuals for severe combined immune deficiency (SCID), familial hypercholesterolemia, and blood disorders, gene therapy has not

248

lived up to its promise. Gene therapy involves delivering a missing gene crucial for normal protein function in cells in the form of a vector consisting in a modified virus. This is a risky procedure, as vectors may act as misguided missiles that can kill normal-functioning cells, activate cancer-causing genes, or trigger an adverse immune response. Indeed, these risks have become palpably evident in the recently reported deaths of individuals treated with gene therapy for different conditions in both the United States and Canada. Presently, genetic testing is helpful only for prenatal diagnosis and selective abortion of embryos and fetuses affected with genetic abnormalities that would manifest in severe diseases in children who would be born with them.

Another obstacle to developing and successfully implementing gene therapy is that most genetically caused diseases result from the interaction between or among several different genes, as well as with environmental factors. Thus, in most cases, genetic testing only can tell us whether we are predisposed or susceptible to certain diseases, not that we will in fact have them. The multifactorial nature of most diseases casts suspicion on President Clinton's announcement in June, 2000 that, with the complete mapping and sequencing of the human genome, genetics would revolutionize medicine and lead to cures for many diseases. Nevertheless, the information yielded through genetic testing can be part of preventive measures, allowing individuals to modify their diet or lifestyle if they know that they are at risk of developing disease later in life. But there is a negative aspect to this as well. Knowing that one will have a disease that cannot be treated may be psychologically harmful. Specifically, in the case of a woman who knows that she has the BRCA1 or BRCA2 gene, she may have to choose between having a prophylactic mastectomy or constantly living under the shadow of a deadly disease. Moreover, genetic information may be abused by prospective employers and insurers if they know that some people are susceptible to developing certain diseases, even if they never will have them.

The intention to correct a mutation through gene therapy may take place in the somatic (body) or germ (sperm and egg) cells. Any harmful consequences of genetic intervention into somatic cells will remain with the affected individual. But the consequences of any errors in germ-line intervention would be much more serious because they would be passed on to offspring and future generations. Furthermore, many argue that there is no way to separate gene therapy and genetic enhancement neatly. Genetic intervention may aim to treat or prevent disease, to enhance genetic makeup, or to improve already normal physical and mental traits. This has generated worries about a possible return to the eugenics programs in Europe and the United States in the nineteenth and early twentieth centuries, with all of the morally repugnant practices that eugenics entails.

The Human Genome Project came into existence in 1989 with James Watson as its director. He recommended that a portion of the funding for human genome research be devoted to discussion of the ethical issues in this research and to develop public policy guidelines for it. The result was the Ethical, Legal, and Social Implications (ELSI) program. The papers in Part V address some of the ethical issues in genetics identified by or associated with the mandate of the ELSI program.

In the first paper, LeRoy Walters and Julie Gage Palmer raise and discuss seven ethical questions pertinent to somatic-cell gene therapy research in humans. The first four concern medical issues such as risk-benefit ratios in this research, whereas the last three concern procedural issues such as fairness in the selection of subjects, voluntary informed consent, and the protection of privacy and confidentiality. Many of these questions overlap with those raised in Part III regarding human subjects in medical research, because gene therapy still is very much an experimental procedure. The questions and principles that Walters and Palmer articulate and their discussion of them provide a helpful framework to guide gene therapy research in response to the question of when it is ethically justifiable.

Noting the degree of public misinformation about human genetics and the exaggerated claims that have been made with respect to the possible consequences of genetic alteration, Patricia Baird offers a clear and biologically well-informed analysis of three types of genetic alteration: genetic alteration of somatic cells to treat disease; genetic alteration of germ cells to prevent disease; and genetic alteration for improving human traits. She explains the differences between dominant and recessive genetic diseases, as well as why genetic diseases presently can be treated only by inserting an additional copy of a normal functioning gene, not by correcting the defective gene itself. She further points out that most genetic diseases are multifactorial, determined by the complex interaction between genetic predisposition and environmental influences. In addition, she explains why germ-cell intervention is not 'therapy' but instead a form of disease prevention. Because these three types of genetic intervention are different, each of them requires a different ethical response from us. Although the full ethical implications of these types of genetic interventions need to be thought through carefully, she concludes that the potential benefits of gene therapy make it ethical and not socially harmful to pursue.

Philip Kitcher acknowledges that prenatal genetic testing inevitably will lead us to pursue some form of eugenics. But he distinguishes between positive and negative eugenics. In the first, we select *for* certain traits in people according to perfectionist ideals. In the second, we select *against* traits that cause severe human disease and suffering. This would consist in testing embryos or fetuses and selectively aborting those found to have genetic abnormalities. It is the first type of eugenics that occasions ethical concern, suggesting the possibility of a return to the evil practices of Nazi Germany and sterilization programs in the United States. Kitcher proposes and defends a species of negative eugenics, or what he calls "laissez-faire eugenics." This would make prenatal testing available to all members of society who seek genetic counseling and would respect differences in phenotypic traits. Also, citizens would not be coerced into making reproductive decisions but would make them on the basis of their own values and goals.

The question of whether we can plausibly distinguish between genetic intervention to treat or prevent disease and intervention to enhance health is taken up by Eric Juengst. He argues that the distinction indeed can be drawn, but that it rests on two conditions. First, health and disease must be understood ontologically as objective entities involving dysfunction of biological systems. Second, genetic intervention should be limited to prevention of disease from pathogenic agents; it should not include changing our bodies to avoid or redress social inequalities. Genetic treatment of disease is ethically justifiable; genetic enhancement of normal healthy traits is not.

Using cases of Fragile X syndrome, cystic fibrosis, and deafness, Heather Draper and Ruth Chadwick illustrate how preimplantation genetic diagnosis (PIGD) may present dilemmas for parents who know from the testing that having a genetically related child entails a disease or disability that would not be in the best interests of that child. Yet their main focus is on how PIGD and the in vitro fertilization that makes it possible shift the question of responsibility from the mother or parents to the clinician. In particular, they address the question of whether it would be wrong for a clinician to implant a genetically abnormal embryo to satisfy parents' wishes. This shift in responsibility raises the further question of whether PIGD promotes greater reproductive autonomy and more choice for women and couples.

Maxwell Mehlman and Jeffrey Botkin discuss the issue of justice in access to genetic technology. If health is a primary good for all citizens, and if interventions such as genetic screening, testing, and gene therapy can promote health by reducing the severity of or preventing diseases, then all citizens should have access to this genetic technology. This idea is grounded in the moral and political principle of egalitarian distributive justice. Equal access to technology that will promote health by preventing disease will promote equal opportunity in pursuing projects and life plans for a reasonable level of lifetime well-being for all citizens. Mehlman and Botkin maintain that scarcity of health resources and current allocation policies could result in an unequal distribution of genetic technology, which could threaten social stability.

Human embryonic stem (ES) cell research holds considerable promise for treating degenerative diseases. But because human ES cells are derived from frozen human embryos scheduled to be discarded by fertility clinics, and because many argue that embryos have moral status, the research has significant ethical implications. The Geron Ethics Advisory Board considers these implications and spells out six conditions that must be met for the research to be ethical. They include: respect for early human embryonic tissue; informed consent from those donating such tissue for research; a prohibition on cloning and the creation of chimeras; compliance with accepted norms of human and animal research; respect for principles of global justice; and compliance with independent ethics advisory boards and institutional review boards.

ᏬᎻᏞᎾ

Ethical Issues

LeRoy Walters PhD, Julie Gage Palmer JD

AN INITIAL QUESTION: IS THIS KIND OF TREATMENT DIFFERENT?

In the ethical discussions that began in the late 1960s, commentators on human gene therapy sometimes seemed to assume that this technique was qualitatively different from other types of therapeutic interventions. However, as the ethical discussion of gene therapy has progressed,

From *The Ethics of Human Gene Therapy*, New York: Oxford University Press, 1997.

somatic cell gene therapy has increasingly been viewed as a natural and logical *extension* of current techniques for treating disease. Which of these views is correct?

On balance, the gene-therapy-as-extension view seems to be the more appropriate one. There are several reasons for adopting this view. First, because somatic cell gene therapy affects only nonreproductive cells, none of the genetic changes produced by somatic cell gene therapy will be passed on to the patient's children. Second, in some cases the products of the genetically modified somatic cells are similar to medications that patients can take as an alternative treatment. For example, there are enzyme therapies currently available for both ADA deficiency and Gaucher disease, but both enzyme therapies are very expensive and must be administered frequently. Third, some of the techniques currently used in somatic cell gene therapy closely resemble other widely used medical interventions—especially the transplantation of organs or tissues.

Several examples noted in the earlier part of this chapter illustrate how similar at least some somatic cell approaches are to transplantation. In the protocol for treating ADA deficiency, some of the patients' T cells were removed from their bodies and had the missing ADA gene added to them. The genetically modified cells were then returned to the patients' bodies, where they began to produce the missing enzyme, ADA. If the patients involved in this early gene therapy study had had healthy siblings whose cells closely matched their own, the alternative to gene therapy would have been a bone marrow transplant. In effect, the T cells of the healthy sibling (or more technically the stem cells that produce the T cells) would have replaced the patients' own ADA-deficient T cells.

The case is similar with cystic fibrosis (CF). Increasingly, lung transplants are being employed in the treatment of this disease. The cells in the transplanted lung will not have the genetic defect that causes CF and will therefore be able to function normally in the recipient. However, such transplants are expensive and highly invasive procedures, and there is a perpetual shortage of healthy organs for transplantation. Further, because transplanted organs never match the recipient's genotype exactly, except in the case of identical twins, the recipient will likely have to take drugs indefinitely to prevent his or her immune system from rejecting the transplant as foreign tissue. Somatic cell gene therapy seems to many observers to be a less invasive approach than the transplantation of a major organ. In addition, because it is the patient's own cells that are being genetically modified, there is a much lower probability that the cells will be rejected as foreign.

MAJOR ETHICAL QUESTIONS CONCERNING GENE-THERAPY RESEARCH

In the review of proposals to perform gene therapy research with human beings, seven questions are central:

1. What is the disease to be treated?
2. What alternative interventions are available for the treatment of this disease?
3. What is the anticipated or potential harm of the experimental gene therapy procedure?
4. What is the anticipated or potential benefit of the experimental gene therapy procedure?
5. What procedure will be followed to ensure fairness in the selection of patient–subjects?
6. What steps will be taken to ensure that patients, or their parents or guardians, give informed and voluntary consent to participating in the research?
7. How will the privacy of patients and the confidentiality of their medical information be protected?

Taken together, questions 1–4 constitute a kind of first hurdle, or initial threshold, that gene therapy research proposals must clear. If these questions are not satisfactorily answered, questions 5–7 will not even need to be asked.

However, if the first four questions are satisfactorily answered, and the risk–benefit ratio for the proposed research seems appropriate, questions 5–7 remain as a second hurdle—a set of important procedural safeguards for prospective subjects in the research.

What is the Disease to be Treated?

Question 1 asks both a simple and a more profound question. It asks simply for the name of a condition or a disorder that is regarded by reasonable people to be a malfunction in the human body. Thus, "cystic fibrosis" would be an acceptable answer to the first question, while "average height" would not. At a more profound level, question 1 asks whether the disease or condition put forward as an early candidate for somatic cell gene therapy is sufficiently serious or life-threatening to merit being treated with a highly experimental technique. As the list of disorders treated in the first 100 gene therapy studies indicates, the conditions proposed for possible treatment by means of gene therapy do gravely compromise the quality and duration of human life.

It must be acknowledged that two of the disorders included in the above list do not qualify as life-threatening: rheumatoid arthritis and peripheral artery disease. Rheumatoid arthritis is a chronic condition that often causes severe pain to the person who is suffering from it, but this disease alone generally does not cause a patient's death. Similarly, peripheral artery disease in, for example, the lower leg and ankle of a person with diabetes will not cause the patient's death. However, this condition can be limb-threatening. That is, a limb that does not receive a sufficient flow of oxygen may need to be amputated in order to prevent gangrene from developing in the limb. In the future, gene therapy protocols may also be submitted that seek to preserve sight by taking new approaches to the treatment of currently untreatable eye diseases.

Philosophers have argued at considerable length about the precise definitions of health and disease.[1] For our analysis we have adopted a rather standard definition of health, "species-typical functioning."[2] It seems clear that all of the conditions to be treated by the first 100 gene therapy protocols represent significant deviations from the physiological norm of species-typical functioning and therefore qualify as bona fide diseases. But are there reasonable limits to the notion of disease? How far would we will be willing to extend the concept? At the far extremes exemplified in discriminatory social programs both past and present, we would never want to see human characteristics like gender, ethnicity, or skin color regarded as diseases. However, serious mental illness would be included within the scope of our definition. We would not consider mild obesity or a crooked nose or larger-than-average ears to be significant deviations from species-typical functioning. However, serious obesity that threatened to shorten life might well qualify as a disease. In each case a condition will need to be evaluated in the light of species-typical functioning and a judgment will have to be made about the extent to which the condition compromises such functioning.[3]

What Alternative Interventions are Available for the Treatment of this Disease?

Question 2 asks about alternative therapies. If available modes of treatment provide relief from the most serious consequences of a disease without major side effects and at reasonable cost, the disease may not be a good candidate for early clinical trials of gene therapy in humans. For example, phenylketonuria (PKU) is a hereditary disorder that can be detected in newborns through a simple blood test. Dietary therapy suffices to prevent the brain damage that would otherwise occur in children afflicted with the disorder. Therefore, PKU is probably not a good early candidate for gene therapy. Similarly, the harmful effects of diabetes can be controlled quite well in most patients through the use of insulin produced by recombinant DNA techniques. Thus, diabetes may be a later rather than an earlier candidate for gene therapy research.

The determination that an alternative therapy is sufficiently effective is always a judgment call. In the review process for the first ADA deficiency study, it was noted that bone marrow transplantation was an effective treatment for children who had genetically matched siblings and that a synthetic form of ADA was available for use in ADA-deficient patients. The synthetic form of ADA was derived from the ADA produced by cattle and was linked, or conjugated, with the chemical PEG. The proponents of gene therapy for ADA deficiency pointed out that PEG-ADA could stimulate a hostile response by the human immune system because the synthetic compound was derived from cattle and thus might be perceived as foreign. The proponents also noted that, while most ADA-deficient patients benefited somewhat from treatment with PEG-ADA, they were still susceptible to many infections. Further, the high cost of PEG-ADA, about $250,000 per year, put this synthetic treatment out of the reach of most families. Thus, the reviewers of the initial ADA gene therapy protocol ultimately concluded that in families where children had no matched sibling donors, the alternative therapy of PEG-ADA was not wholly satisfactory. There was therefore space or justification for the development of gene therapy as a possibly superior approach to the treatment of this life-threatening pediatric disease.

As the field of gene therapy matures, the requirement that there be no effective alternative therapy may need to be relaxed. At some point there will need to be well-controlled studies that compare the gene therapy approach with alternative approaches to treatment of the same disease. However, given the novelty of gene therapy in 1990 and the uncertainty about its potential benefits and harms, it seems to us to have been appropriate to limit the earliest gene therapy trials to diseases and groups of patients for whom no alternative therapies were available.

What is the Anticipated or Potential Harm of the Experimental Gene-Therapy Procedure?

Question 3 concerns the anticipated or possible harm of somatic cell gene therapy. In responding to this question, researchers are asked to base their statements on the best available *data* from preclinical studies in vitro or in laboratory animal models like mice or monkeys. The use of domesticated (technically, replication-deficient) viruses as vectors in many somatic-cell gene-therapy studies raises one important safety question: How certain can researchers be that the domesticated viruses will not regain the genes that have been removed from them and thus regain the capacity to reproduce and cause an infection in the patient? A second kind of safety question arises from the "unguided-missile" quality of retroviral vectors. As noted earlier in this chapter, researchers cannot predict where a retroviral vector with its attached gene and marker will "land" within the nucleus of a target cell. It is possible that the vector will integrate into the middle of a gene that is essential to the functioning of the cell and will therefore kill the cell. A further concern is the theoretical possibility that a retroviral vector might integrate beside a quiescent oncogene (cancer-causing gene) and stimulate it into becoming active. If so, a previously healthy cell might begin to divide uncontrollably and even start a cancer in a particular site. Because of these concerns about risk and safety, researchers are asked to provide data about preclinical studies in animals that, insofar as possible, exactly duplicate the gene therapy studies that they propose to do in human subjects.

What is the Anticipated or Potential Benefit of the Experimental Gene Therapy Procedure?

The fourth question is in many ways the mirror image of the third. It asks researchers once again to provide data from preclinical studies, but in this case the data should indicate that there is a reasonable expectation of benefit to human patients from their participation in the gene therapy study. One step in the review process for the first approved human-gene therapy study in 1990 illustrates the importance of this point. Drs. Blaese and Anderson had provided impressive safety data to the RAC (the Recombinant DNA Advisory Committee—established in 1974 by NIH) based on their long-term studies in mice and monkeys. However, RAC members were not convinced that the genetic modification of ADA-deficient T cells would be beneficial to human patients. What if the T cells died off quickly, or what if they were overwhelmed by the patients' own ADA-deficient T cells? Fortunately there was a researcher in Milan, Italy, Dr. Claudio Bordignon, who was willing to speak to the RAC about his own research in mice that had an immune deficiency similar to the one that afflicts ADA-deficient human patients. In these animals Dr. Bordignon was able to show that *human* T cells that carry a functioning ADA gene survive longer than ADA-deficient T cells. This was the information that the RAC was seeking, and Dr. Bordignon's report helped to ensure the approval of the Blaese–Anderson proposal.

There has been considerable debate about the appropriate relationship between question 3 and question 4—or between anticipated harm and anticipated benefit of a gene therapy study. Some researchers have argued that if a gene therapy study is not likely to make patients worse off, it should be approved even if the probability of benefit is very low. This rationale may have been the basis for the controversial approval of a gene therapy protocol by former NIH director Bernadine Healy in December 1992. The proposal to treat a single cancer patient had not gone through regular view by the NIH RAC, and there was, in the opinion of most experts, little probability that it would benefit the terminally ill patient. Nonetheless, Dr. Healy approved the protocol on a "compassionate use" basis.[4] Since late 1992 the RAC has further discussed the requisite harm–benefit ratio in gene therapy studies. A majority

of the committee members seem to have adopted the following view: Even if a gene therapy protocol provides a satisfactory answer to question 3 (about harm), it must also offer at least a low probability of benefit to the patients who are invited to enter the protocol, *and* it must have an excellent scientific design, so that the information gathered from studying the early patients will be useful to later patients and to the entire field of gene therapy research. That is, there must also be a satisfactory answer to question 4.

If these first four questions are satisfactorily answered, researchers have cleared a first hurdle or crossed an important threshold. They have demonstrated that the ratio of probable benefit to probable harm in a proposed study is sufficiently positive to justify proceeding to research in human beings. The remaining three questions ask how the research will be done, or, in other words, outline procedural safeguards for the patients who will be invited to take part in the gene therapy studies.

What Procedure will be Followed to Ensure Fairness in the Selection of Patient–Subjects?

The first of the procedural questions, and the fifth question overall, asks how patients will be selected in a fair manner. With very rare disorders, like familial hypercholesterolemia and ADA deficiency, fairness in the selection process was relatively unproblematic. Virtually every patient with the condition who was not too ill to participate was considered a candidate for gene therapy and invited to enroll in the studies. However, when somatic cell gene therapy began to be used for more prevalent conditions like brain tumors, the selection process became much more difficult. For example, the first study of gene therapy for brain tumors was led by Edward Oldfield and Kenneth Culver at the National Institutes of Health. Their proposal was initially approved for the study of 20 patients. Within the first year of their study the offices of Drs. Oldfield and Culver received more than 1,000 inquiries by patients, their family members and friends, and even governors and legislators. It was therefore quite important that a fair procedure, like first-come first-served, be in place to use in selecting among the many candidates for treatment.

In the review of the first 100 gene therapy protocols two other questions of fairness in selecting subjects have also arisen. The first question is whether children should be included in the initial studies, assuming that some children do survive to adulthood with the disease. The first gene therapy study, for severe combined immune deficiency (SCID), involved children precisely because, until now, almost no children with this disorder live to complete their teenage years. However, some patients with familial hypercholesterolemia do live to be 30, as do an increasing number of cystic fibrosis (CF) patients. There are two opposing ethical perspectives on the involvement of children in the early stages of clinical trials. The classical position, formulated in the early 1970s in the United States, was that clinical trials should be completed in adults first, before children are exposed to the potential harms of such trials.[5] The revisionist position of the late 1980s and 1990s is that participants in clinical trials are carefully monitored and that they often are the first people in a society to have access to new and possibly effective treatments. Therefore no class of individuals, whether women or members of ethnic minorities or children, should be excluded from the potential benefits of timely participation in clinical trials.[6]

A second question is closely related to the alternative-therapy question discussed above. It concerns the stage of disease at which people with serious disease should receive gene therapy. Already in 1987, during the review of the "Preclinical Data Document," there had been vigorous debate about whether gene therapy should be regarded as last-ditch therapy. In the early studies of gene therapy, patients had generally not been helped by alternative therapies, or no alternative therapies were available. As the field has matured, and as researchers have gained more confidence in the safety of gene therapy (if not in its effectiveness), the question has increasingly been raised, "Why not employ gene therapy at earlier stages in the disease process where it might have a better chance to prevent the deterioration of the patient's condition?"

What Steps will be Taken to Ensure that Patients, or Their Parents or Guardians, Give Informed and Voluntary Consent to Participating in the Research?

The next procedural question, and the sixth question overall, concerns the voluntary and informed consent of patients or, in the case of minors, of their parents or guardians. It is always a challenge for researchers to convey to potential patient–subjects the important facts about their disease or condition, the major alternative treatments, and the precise procedures to be followed in the research. With a cutting-edge technology like human gene therapy this generic problem becomes even more difficult. For gene therapy studies, patients or their parents or guardians will frequently need a short course on how recombinant DNA research is conducted, how vectors are constructed, what cell types are targeted, how genes are inserted into cells, and how genes function in cells. In the case of specific gene therapy studies, additional modules may have to be added to the short course. For example, in the case of gene therapy for SCID, patients or their parents or guardians will need additional information on the human immune system and how specific kinds of cells, like T cells, function. While this educational responsibility may initially seem daunting, the question about voluntary, informed consent simply points to the importance of an extensive and ongoing dialogue between researchers and subjects, rather than the momentary act of signing a multiple-page consent form.

The response of researchers to question 6 has varied considerably. Some gene therapy proposals have included detailed information, including charts that outline the sequence and timing of proposed procedures, for patients. Other written consent forms have been woefully incomplete or have included ambiguous wording about who pays for procedures required by the research or about how the sponsoring institution deals with patients who are accidentally injured while they participate in research. Further, no external observers are present to monitor the quality of the consent *process* as patients are invited to take part in gene therapy studies. All that can be said with certainty is that the RAC has provided detailed guidance to researchers about the major points that RAC members think should be included in consent forms and that the consent forms themselves are reviewed in a public forum by peers who are not employees of the sponsoring institutions.

How will the Privacy of Patients and the Confidentiality of Their Medical Information be Protected?

The third procedural question, and the seventh question overall, concerns privacy and confidentiality. There is no single "correct" answer to this question. It merely asks researchers to think through in advance how they and the subjects participating in gene therapy studies will deal with inquiries from the press and the general public. A particular concern was that patients have sufficient privacy and rest following their treatment to allow them "space" to benefit from this experimental approach to treatment. Different researchers and families have adopted varying policies regarding privacy and confidentiality. In the case of the ADA-deficiency protocol, the first two young women treated remained relatively anonymous until the second anniversary (in September 1992) of the first child's initial treatment. Less than a year later, the two children were featured, named, and pictured in a *Time* magazine story.[7] In contrast, the parents of two newborns treated at birth (in a modification of the same protocol) by a different technique using stem cells from umbilical cord blood allowed

their names and pictures, and the names and pictures of their infants, to be disclosed almost immediately.[8] Similarly, the first patient in the study that aims to treat peripheral artery disease was interviewed by a reporter for the *New York Times* before he received his first gene transfer.[9]

This final question was included in the "Points to Consider" not to prescribe or proscribe any particular actions by patients or researchers but simply to encourage all parties involved in gene therapy studies to think through, in advance, a strategy for dealing with the press and the media. There had, in fact, been veritable media circuses when several earlier biomedical technologies had first been introduced. One thinks, for example, of the earliest heart transplant recipients, of Barney Clark and his artificial heart, of Baby Fae and her baboon heart, and of Louise Brown, the first "test tube baby." In general, the introduction of gene therapy has been, in our view, more respectful of patients and their families.

PUBLIC ATTITUDES AND EXPERT OPINION ABOUT SOMATIC CELL GENE THERAPY

The social context in which somatic-cell gene-therapy research occurs includes the response of both the general public and people who might be called "experts" to the concept as well as the practice of gene therapy. From the 1980s to the present we have a rather detailed record of both public attitudes in the United States and international expert opinion.

The Louis Harris polling organization has taken two snapshots of public attitudes toward gene therapy in the United States. The first survey, conducted by telephone between October 30th and November 17th, 1986, was commissioned by the Congressional Office of Technology Assessment (OTA).[10] In this initial survey, 1,273 telephone interviews were completed, and the sampling error was in the range of plus or minus 2–3%. The second survey, conducted by phone between April

17th and April 30th, 1992, was commissioned by the March of Dimes Birth Defects Foundation.[11] In this second survey a national cross section of 1,000 adults were interviewed, and the sampling error was plus or minus 3%.

Public knowledge of "genetic engineering" (1986) and "gene therapy" (1992) seems to be surprisingly meager. In answer to the 1986 question, "How much have you heard or read about genetic engineering?" in 1986, 24% of respondents said, "Almost nothing," and another 39% replied, "Relatively little."[12] Despite rather extensive news coverage of the initial gene therapy experiments in the intervening years, the 1992 survey discovered similar levels of professed ignorance. The 1992 question was, "How much have you heard or read about gene therapy?" Sixty percent of respondents said, "Almost nothing," and another 26% acknowledged that they had heard or read "Relatively little."[13]

Despite their lack of knowledge the telephone respondents in the two surveys proceeded to answer the remaining questions put to them by the interviewers. The respondents' general attitudes about the ethics of human gene therapy were elicited with rather different questions in 1986 and 1992. In the OTA survey of 1986 the question and response were as shown in Table 2.1.

In the 1992 survey, the corresponding question was much more positively phrased and included the assumption that the gene therapy procedure would be safe. Not surprisingly, the response was also much more positive (Table 2.2).

Another way of assessing public attitudes toward gene therapy is to ask whether people would be willing to make use of this new technique for themselves or one of their children. Tables 2.3 and 2.4 provide the responses to identical questions asked by the Louis Harris organization in 1986 and 1992 (1986 data in parentheses).

Two specific scenarios for somatic cell gene therapy were presented to the respondents in the 1986 and 1992 surveys. The word "genetic" was dropped from the first scenario in 1992, perhaps in part because multiple-gene-therapy proposals for treating cancers had been developed in the meantime. Otherwise the two scenarios were identical.

TABLE 2.1.   The Morality of Human Cell Manipulation

Some people believe that genetic alteration of human cells to treat disease is simply another form of medical treatment. Other people believe that changing the genetic makeup of human cells is morally wrong, regardless of the purpose. On balance, do you feel that changing the genetic makeup of human cells is morally wrong, or not?[14]

	Morally Wrong	Not Morally Wrong	Not Sure
Total (1,273)	42%	52%	6%

TABLE 2.2.   General Attitude About Gene Therapy

If it were safe, would you strongly approve, somewhat approve, somewhat disapprove, or strongly disapprove of gene therapy to treat or cure genetic diseases?[15]

Strongly Approve	Somewhat Approve	Somewhat Disapprove	Strongly Disapprove	Not Sure
47%	41%	4%	4%	4%

TABLE 2.3.   Willingness to Undergo Gene Therapy

If tests showed that you were likely to get a serious or fatal genetic disease late in life, how willing would you be to have those genes corrected before symptoms appear—very willing, somewhat willing, somewhat unwilling, very unwilling?[16]

Very Willing	Somewhat Willing	Somewhat Unwilling	Very Unwilling	Not Sure
30% (35)	49% (43)	10% (12)	9% (9)	2% (2)

1992 vs. (1986).

TABLE 2.4.   Willingness to Have a Child Undergo Gene Therapy

If you had a child with a usually fatal genetic disease, how willing would you be to have the child undergo therapy to have those genes corrected—very willing, somewhat willing, somewhat unwilling, very unwilling?[17]

Very Willing	Somewhat Willing	Somewhat Unwilling	Very Unwilling	Not Sure
52% (51)	36% (35)	5% (7)	4% (4)	3% (3)

1992 vs. (1986)

One final way to assess public attitudes toward somatic cell gene therapy is to inquire whether members of the public think that research in this arena should be continued or stopped. In the 1986 survey only a general question had been asked about whether "research into genetic engineering should be continued or should be stopped." Eighty-two percent of respondents replied, "Continued," while 13% said, "Stopped."[18] The 1992 survey asked more specifically whether "research into gene therapy should be continued or should be stopped." Eighty-nine percent of respondents favored continuation, while only 8% advocated the cessation of this line of research.[19]

What is the importance for ethical analysis of these ethical judgments by a random sample of the U.S. public? There is certainly no easy or automatic leap from the fact that a majority of the

TABLE 2.5.   Opinions about Specific Applications of Human Cell Manipulation

How do you feel about scientists changing the makeup of human cells to cure a usually fatal [genetic] disease? To reduce the risk of developing a fatal disease later in life? Would you strongly approve, somewhat approve, somewhat disapprove, or strongly disapprove?

	Strongly Approve	Somewhat Approve	Somewhat Disapprove	Strongly Disapprove	Not Sure
Cure a usually fatal [genetic] disease?	57% (48)	30% (35)	5% (7)	7% (7)	1% (2)
Reduce the risk of developing a fatal disease later in life?	41% (39)	37% (38)	11% (12)	8% (9)	3% (2)

1992 vs. (1986).

general public think that something is the case to its actually being the case—either in ethics or in science. In the realm of ethics, prejudice or bias sometimes interferes with making correct judgments. Think, for example, about traditional biases against members of various ethnic or racial groups, or about 19th-century majority views regarding voting rights for women. On the other hand, the moral judgments of the general public, as reflected in survey data, can be relevant in several ways. First, if people understand at least in a general way the questions they are answering, their judgments reflect a kind of common morality.[20] Thus, it seems clear from the survey data that a majority of the public is open to the use of genetic technology in the war against disease and has not been frightened into opposing genetic technology in principle by social critics like Jeremy Rifkin. Further, the more urgent the medical situation, the more likely respondents are to approve the use of gene therapy in the attempt to remedy the situation. The survey data also reveal a surprising willingness of the general public to consider gene therapy for themselves or their children—despite their admitted lack of knowledge on the topic. Finally, the poll data reflect strong support for research on gene therapy as one possible means for combating disease.

Second, data from polls like the two Harris surveys cited can serve as a salutary check on the rhetoric of politicians and public commentators. Any public figure who asserted, "The overwhelming majority of the American people oppose genetic engineering," could now be challenged to define what he or she meant by the term *genetic engineering*. If the answer were, "Any method of changing genes," the public figure could be asked about the specific techniques of gene addition currently being employed in somatic cell gene therapy. The results of the two Harris surveys could also be adduced, and the public figure could be asked whether he or she had any evidence from other public-opinion polls. In short, public opinion and its reflection in surveys can help to raise the level of public

discourse about important questions that are facing a society.

For international public opinion, similar surveys do not currently exist except for Japan and New Zealand.[21] However, beginning in 1980, numerous expert committees, commissions, and spokespeople for major religious groups have published policy positions on the ethics of human gene therapy. We have identified 28 policy statements on this topic from the years 1980 through 1993 (Table 2.6).

These 28 policy statements represent multiple professions, religious traditions, and cultures, including most advanced industrialized countries. Yet on somatic cell gene therapy a remarkable consensus emerges from the statements: All 28 agree that somatic cell gene therapy for the cure of serious disease is ethically acceptable in principle. There are few issues in all of biomedical ethics on which one would be able to discover such unanimous agreement!

Again in the case of the policy statements by experts there remains a nagging question. What is the importance for ethical analysis of the ethical judgments of experts from various fields? There is, of course, the possibility that various individuals and groups will read previous statements and merely follow, in lemming-like fashion, what their predecessors have said. In addition, the so-called experts may all be recruited from one academic field or area or from one social class and therefore may exhibit a systematic bias. However, on other issues in bioethics—like surrogate motherhood, for example—there are clear differences of opinion among experts in different countries and cultures.[22] Thus, a unanimous consensus of the 28 policy statements by representatives of multiple academic and professional fields suggests at least a measure of cross-cultural agreement on an important issue. To be sure, this consensus of the experts on the ethical acceptability of somatic cell gene therapy provides no guarantee that this practice is in fact ethically acceptable. However, ethical judgements do not allow for mathematical precision. In our judgment, we

TABLE 2.6.   Policy Statements on Human Gene Therapy: An International Chronology

1980   World Council of Churches, Conference on Faith, Science, and the Future, *Faith and Science in an Unjust World*

1982   Parliamentary Assembly, Council of Europe: Recommendation 934 (1982) on genetic engineering

World Council of Churches, Working Committee on Church and Society, *Manipulating Life*

United States, President's Commission for the Study of Ethical Problems in Medicine and Biomedical Research, *Splicing Life* report

1983   Pope John Paul II, Address on "The Ethics of Genetic Manipulation" to the 35th General Assembly of the World Medical Association in Venice

1984   Denmark, Indenrigsministeriet (Ministry of the Interior) *Fremskridtets Pris* (*The Price of Progress*)

Sweden, Gen-Ethikkommittén (Genetic Ethics Committee), *Genetisk Integritet* (*Genetic Integrity*)

U.S., Congress, Office of Technology Assessment, *Human Gene Therapy: Background Paper*

1985   U.S., National Institutes of Health, Human Gene Therapy Subcommittee (formerly, Working Group on Human Gene Therapy), "Points to Consider in the Design and Submission of Human Somatic-Cell Gene Therapy Protocols"

Federal Republic of Germany, Justice Minister and Minister for Research and Technology, Working Group (the Benda Commission), *In-Vitro Fertilisation, Genomanalyse und Gentherapie* (*In Vitro Fertilization, Genome-Analysis, and Gene Therapy*)

1986   National Council of Churches, Governing Board, policy statement on "Genetic Science for Human Benefit"

1987   German Federal Republic, Tenth Bundestag, Enquete-Kommission (Committee of Inquiry), *Chancen und Risiken der Gentechnologie* (*Opportunities and Risks of Genetic Technology*)

World Medical Association, "Statement on Genetic Counseling and Genetic Engineering" (39th World Medical Assembly, Madrid)

Canada, Medical Research Council, *Guidelines on Research Involving Human Subjects*

Australia, National Health and Medical Research Council, Medical Research Ethics Committee, *Ethical Aspects of Research on Human Gene Therapy*

1988   European Medical Research Councils, "Gene Therapy in Man"

American Medical Association, Council on Ethical and Judicial Affairs, "Opinion on Gene Therapy and Surrogate Mothers" [Report E: (I-88); title provided]

Switzerland, Commission d'Experts pour la Génétique Humaine et la Médecine de la Reproduction, *Rapport* (*The Amstad-Report*)

1989   Canada, Medical Research Council, *Discussion Paper: Research on Gene Therapy in Humans: Background and Guidelines*

European Commission, Working Party, *Ethics of New Reproductive Technologies* (*The Glover Report*)

World Council of Churches, Subunit on Church and Society, *Biotechnology: Its Challenge to the Churches and the World*

TABLE 2.6.   Continued

	Netherlands, Dutch Health Council, Committee, *Heredity: Science and Society: On the Possibilities and Limits of Genetic Testing and Gene Therapy*
1990	Council for International Organizations of Medical Sciences (CIOMS), "Genetics, Ethics and Human Values: Human Genome Mapping, Genetic Screening and Gene Therapy (The "Declaration of Inuyama")
	Canada, Medical Research Council, *Guidelines for Research on Somatic Cell Gene Therapy in Humans*
	France, Comité Consultatif National d'Ethique pour les Sciences de la Vie et de la Santé, *Avis sur la Thérapie Génique* (*Opinion on Gene Therapy*)
1991	Norway, Ministry of Health and Social Affairs, Ethics Committee, *Man and Biotechnology*
1992	United Kingdom, Committee on the Ethics of Human Gene Therapy [the Clothier committee], *Report*
1993	Canada, Royal Commission on New Reproductive Technologies, "Gene Therapy and Genetic Alteration," Chapter 29 in *Proceed with Care: Final Report*

are less likely to make a serious moral mistake if we are guided in our ethical analysis, at least in part, by the consensus view of the experts.[23]

OTHER MAJOR QUESTIONS ABOUT GENE THERAPY

In addition to the seven questions raised about gene therapy by the "Points to Consider," there are important questions about the current system for conducting and overseeing gene therapy, both in the United States and abroad. The following section of this chapter attempts to step back from the specifics of the first 100 U.S. gene therapy protocols to examine some of these broader issues.

Was Gene Therapy Attempted in Patients Too Soon?

This first question asks whether more laboratory research in cell cultures and in animal models should have preceded the first clinical studies with gene therapy. Some critics of current practice have noted that the available vectors for delivering genes to cells are relatively primitive. Other critics argue that basic research on how stem cells work and how they can be modified may facilitate new approaches to gene therapy. A

third line of criticism is that, while a few protocols submitted by researchers for review by the NIH RAC have represented excellent science, many of the protocols have been unoriginal and probably would not have been funded by NIH if the protocols had been reviewed according to the stringent standards of the usual NIH grant application process.

What can be said in response to these criticisms? First, the first somatic-cell gene-therapy studies in human beings were preceded by almost 20 years of public discussion and debate.[24] Even the initial protocol, approved in 1990, had been debated in near-final form from 1987 through early 1990. Thus, the introduction of gene therapy as a new biomedical technology has been more deliberate and more cautious than the first use of several other important techniques—for example, genetic screening for PKU in newborns, heart transplantation, and test tube (in vitro) fertilization. Second, even though the currently published evidence is sparse, there is at least a suggestion of clinical benefit in the initial gene therapy study for patients with SCID. At the same time, however, it must be acknowledged that the level of success in the first 60–70 gene therapy studies in the United States has been disappointing even to the technique's strongest advocates. In part because of this disappointment, the NIH director, Harold Varmus, recently asked an expert committee to review the NIH investment in gene therapy.[25]

Which Diseases are the Best Early Candidates for Gene Therapy?

We have seen in this chapter what the target diseases are in the first 100 U.S. gene therapy protocols. Are various types of cancers sufficiently important to merit having more than 60% of the protocols directed toward cancer? Is 22 of the first 100 studies the appropriate share for the thousands of genetic diseases? And do HIV infection and AIDS deserve more or less than 12% of the research effort?

The answers to these questions, like the answers to many resource allocation questions, stretch human knowledge and judgment to their limits. One approach to answering the questions is to ask: What is the burden of disease, in terms of premature death, suffering, lost work, and disability, caused by each disorder? The answer to this question provides at least one dimension of the answer to the larger question, although it should be noted that the comparison of death, permanent disability, pain and suffering, and temporary disability involves a series of value judgments.[26] However, the burden caused by a certain disease is only part of the picture. There must also be a genuine research opportunity. That is, enough progress in understanding and perhaps even in treating a disease must have been made to allow a next step to have a reasonable hope of succeeding. In the case of SCID, a very rare genetic disorder, one feature that made the disease a good early candidate for gene therapy studies was that it had been cured through bone marrow transplants from matched sibling donors. Thus, researchers had good leads in their quest to treat the disease in children who lacked such donors. Further, the gene for ADA had been isolated in the laboratory and was available for clinical use. One other safety feature for SCID was that the gene did not have to be carefully regulated. An overproduction of ADA by a turned-on gene would not, it seemed, harm the recipient patient. For these reasons SCID appeared to be an excellent early candidate for gene therapy, even though it is a rare disorder with a rather small national disease burden.

For the future the expert committee appointed by the NIH director may have some suggestions about an overall strategy for setting priorities among diseases, particularly if one or two diseases seem to have received inordinate attention thus far. On the other hand, centralized planning and long-term strategies may also have their pitfalls. There is much to be said for allowing considerable latitude to researchers in choosing the diseases that they consider to be plausible early candidates for gene therapy and in developing creative new approaches to the experimental treatment of those diseases. One of the most intriguing aspects of science is the factor of serendipity. One never knows in advance which scientists, which laboratory, which topic, and which approach will produce the next breakthrough, with unexpected benefits in a wide variety of seemingly unrelated fields.

To What Extent Should Commercial Considerations Drive the Selection of Target Diseases?

This question is closely related to the preceding question. It is not surprising that, with the increasing involvement of private industry in somatic cell gene therapy there has also been a increasing focus on diseases that are prevalent in the United States. The largest trials to date, in terms of the numbers of patients, are studies directed toward HIV infection and AIDS. As noted earlier, cancers of various types are the targets in almost two-thirds of the first 100 protocols. And among genetic diseases cystic fibrosis, the most prevalent genetic disorder among Caucasians, commands the most attention.

We should not be surprised that commercial firms would look, first and foremost, at larger rather than smaller markets. If gene therapy proves to be a successful strategy, these firms will one day provide the bridge from the laboratory to large numbers of patients. At the same time, however, there are the so-called *orphan diseases*, which strike people in numbers too small to provide a strong incentive for an investment in research. There are, again, no easy solutions to this general problem in the U.S. health care system. Public investment in research is no doubt one part of the solution: NIH researchers and researchers supported by federal funds have the option of targeting diseases that affect relatively few people. Success in treating rare diseases may, in turn, provide clues that will assist in the treatment of more prevalent diseases. However, by far the most important part of the solution to the problem of gene therapy for rare disorders will have to await major reform in the health care system.

How is National Oversight for Gene Therapy Working?

Virtually all U.S. gene therapy proposals go through a national public review process at the National Institutes of Health. Under a new consolidated review process with the Food and Drug Administration (FDA), only proposals that raise novel issues are reviewed publicly at quarterly RAC meetings. For the other proposals, basic information about the researchers, the title of the protocol, the target cell, the vectors, and the sponsors is made available in a public summary. All serious adverse events experienced by patients are also reported at each quarterly RAC meeting. In addition, at periodic intervals—annually in the future—a public report on virtually all U.S. gene therapy studies is compiled and presented at a public RAC meeting. This report allows any interested person to learn the most important facts, except for the effectiveness of treatment, about ongoing and already-closed clinical trials of gene therapy. For example, one can find out how many patients are enrolled in

each trial and how many adverse effects have occurred. If the results of a study have been published, the publication is cited.

One of the authors of this book has been much too closely involved with the public review process for gene therapy to be objective in judging it. However, several comments are in order. The level of public accountability that has existed for the early stages of gene therapy research is unprecedented in the history of clinical research. In fact, the NIH RAC has functioned as a kind of national research ethics committee (or institutional review board) for one new biomedical technology, gene therapy. Further, the RAC review process has provided a model for several other countries as they have established their own national review committees for gene therapy. In most cases the parallel committees in other nations do not meet in public, but their members often attend RAC meetings and sometimes report that RAC deliberations are helpful to them in evaluating protocols that come before them in their confidential review process.

Some U.S. commercial firms and some university researchers have found dual review to be burdensome and have campaigned to have the FDA provide the sole review for gene therapy studies. They argue that, even if the RAC was needed in the early 1990s for the earliest gene therapy studies, it has now outlived its usefulness. Our own view as authors is that the public review of selected protocols and the periodic reports on the current status of gene therapy are still important to the U.S. public, to the press and the media, and to members of the United States Congress. Public review and regular monitoring are essential to public accountability, in our view.

To What Extent are Researchers in Other Countries Involved in Gene Therapy Research?

We have focused primarily on gene therapy in the United States because more studies have been initiated here than in any other nation.

However, gene therapy research is proceeding in the United Kingdom, France, the Netherlands, Germany, Italy, Japan, and China—and in perhaps other nations as well. For the most part, the studies that have been made public parallel those that are being conducted in the United States. For example, SCID is the target disease in several countries. A study for which there is no parallel is the Chinese protocol that seeks to treat hemophilia B.[27]

How Useful will Somatic Cell Gene Therapy be in the Long Run?

The honest answer to this final question is, "It's too early to know the answer to this question with any degree of certainty."

Some critics of gene therapy have argued that the future does not look bright for this approach to treatment. They note that, using current techniques, gene therapy probably costs at least $100,000 per year per patient, with ongoing retreatment and monitoring being required for all patients. They also assert, quite rightly, that alternative treatments, like drug treatment for people with cystic fibrosis, are also improving and may ultimately make gene therapy unnecessary.

So long as gene therapy requires repeated treatments by very specialized laboratories that can introduce genes into target cells by means of engineered viral vectors, gene therapy will remain a relatively expensive approach to the treatment of disease. It will, under these conditions, be of very limited utility in the war on human disease. There are visionaries, however, who foresee at least the possibility that the gene therapy approach may become as routine and pervasive as current techniques like the use of immunizations or antibiotics. W. French Anderson, for example, dreams of a day when a "magic bullet" will be available that would "enable healing genes to enter the bloodstream and go directly to the cell that needs help."[28] In the words of Anderson, "I'd like to go to Africa with 10,000 vials and inject the gene to cure sickle-cell anemia."[29]

References and Notes

1. See, for example, Arthur L. Caplan, H. Tristram Engelhardt, Jr., and James J. McCartney, eds., *Concepts of Health and Disease: Interdisciplinary Perspectives* (Reading, MA: Addison-Wesley, 1981); and H. Tristram Engelhardt, Jr., and Kevin Wm. Wildes, "Health and Disease. IV. Philosophical Perspectives," in Warren T. Reich, ed.-in-chief, *Encyclopedia of Bioethics* (revised ed.; New York: Simon and Schuster Macmillan, 1995), Vol. II, pp. 1101–1106.

2. Norman Daniels, *Just Health Care* (Cambridge: Cambridge University Press, 1985), esp. pp. 26–32; Christopher Boorse, "Health as a Theoretical Concept," *Philosophy of Science* 44(4): 542–573; December 1977; and Christopher Boorse, "On the Distinction Between Disease and Illness," Philosophy and *Public Affairs* 5(1): 49–68; Fall 1975.

3. Two helpful discussions of the just allocation of human gene therapy are Norman Daniels, "The Genome Project, Individuals, and Just Health Care," in Timothy F. Murphy and Marc A. Lappé, eds., *Justice and the Human Genome Project* (Berkeley: University of California Press, 1994), pp. 110–132; and Leonard M. Fleck, "Just Genetics: A Problem Agenda," pp. 133–152.

4. For discussion of this case, see Larry Thompson, "Healy Approves an Unproven Treatment," *Science* 259 (5092): 172; 8 January 1993; and Larry Thompson, "Should Dying Patients Receive Untested Genetic Methods?," *Science* 259(5094): 452; 22 January 1993.

5. See, for example, Jay Katz, with Alexander Morgan Capron and Eleanor Swift Glass, *Experimentation with Human Beings: The Authority of the Investigator, Subject, Professions, and State in the Human Experimentation Process* (New York: Russell Sage Foundation, 1972).

6. See, for example, Anna C. Mastroianni, Ruth Faden, and Daniel Federman, eds., *Women and Health Research: Ethical and Legal Issues of Including Women in Clinical Studies* (2 vols.; Washington, DC: National Academy Press, 1994).

7. Larry Thompson, "The First Kids with New Genes," Time, June 7, 1993, pp. 50–53.

8. Leon Jaroff, "Brave New Babies," *Time*, May 31, 1993, pp. 56–57.

9. Gina Kolata, "Novel Bypass Method: A Dose of New Genes," *New York Times*, December 13, 1994, p. C1.

10. U.S., Congress, Office of Technology Assessment (OTA), *New Developments in Biotechnology—Background Paper: Public Perceptions of Biotechnology* (Washington, DC: U.S. Government Printing Office, May 1987).

11. March of Dimes (MOD) Birth Defects Foundation, "Genetic Testing and Gene Therapy Survey: Questionnaire and Responses" (White Plains, NY: March of Dimes Birth Defects Foundation, September 1992).

12. OTA, op. cit., p. 46, Table 28.

13. MOD, op. cit., p. 1, Question A1b.

14. OTA, op. cit., p. 71.

15. MOD, op. cit., p. 3. The heading for the table is the authors'.

16. OTA, p. 76, Table 58; MOD, p. 4. The heading is the authors'.

17. OTA, p. 77, Table 59; MOD, p. 4. The heading is the authors'.

18. OTA, p. 84, Table 63, Question (Q34).

19. MOD, Question A4, p. 2.

20. On common-morality theories, see Tom L. Beauchamp and James F. Childress, *Principles of Biomedical Ethics* (4th ed.; New York: Oxford University Press, 1994), pp. 100–111.

21. Darryl Macer, "Japanese Attitudes to Genetic Technology: National and International Comparisons," in Norio Fujiki and Darryl R.J. Macer, eds., *Human Genome Research and Society* (Christchurch, New Zealand: Eubios Ethics Institute, 1992), pp. 120–137.

22. See, for example, LeRoy Walters, "Ethics and New Reproductive Technologies: An International Review of Committee Statements," *Hastings Center Report* 17(3, Supplement): S3–S9; June 1987.

23. For a traditional defense of the role of wise people in guiding ethical judgments, see Thomas Aquinas, *Summa Theologiae*, I-II, question 95, 1 and 2.

24. For early discussion see Michael Hamilton, ed., *The New Genetics and the Future of Man* (Grand Rapids, MI: Eerdmans, 1972).

25. Eliot Marshall, "Gene Therapy's Growing Pains," *Science* 269(5227): 1050–1055; 25 August 1995. See also Gina Kolata, "In the Rush Toward Gene Therapy, Some See a High Risk of Failure," *New York Times*, July 25, 1995, p. C3.

26. For further discussion of this point, see Institute of Medicine, Division of Health Promotion and Disease Prevention, *New Vaccine Development: Establishing Priorities*, Volume I: *Diseases of Importance in the United States* (Washington, DC: National Academy Press, 1985), chapters 3 and 4.

27. For a summary of studies being conducted in countries other than the United States see a current issue of *Human Gene Therapy*. For a recent report on gene therapy research in the United Kingdom, see United Kingdom, Health Departments, Gene Therapy Advisory Committee, *First Annual Report: November 1993–December 1994* (London: Department of Health, January 1995).

28. Daniel Glick, "A Genetic Road Map," *Newsweek*, October 2, 1989, p. 46.

29. Ibid.

Altering Human Genes: Social, Ethical, and Legal Implications

Patricia A. Baird MD

It is important at the outset of any discussion on changing human DNA to take note of the current public context of discussion on this topic. It is worrisome that it is an area of great public mis-information. The possibility of altering the DNA of individuals elicits hype and exaggeration, both on the part of those who are for such use and on the part of those against. Mixtures of fact and

From *Perspectives in Biology and Medicine*, 37: 566–575, 1994.

fiction are used by opponents to portray the allegedly disastrous effects of using genetic knowledge to alter human DNA, with extrapolation to emotionally charged nightmare scenarios—usually making reference to Nazi Germany, to corporate conspiracy, or to agri-business. Proponents also extrapolate and exaggerate—with statements that many diseases will be wiped out, and with assumptions that human beings and their behaviour are simply the product of their genes—suggesting that having the full sequence of the human genome will reveal what makes us human.

For example, gene therapy is seen by some as miracle medicine; by others as tampering with nature and tempting fate. These simplistic and dichotomous views rise in part from the nature of media coverage of the topic. Given the time and space limitations imposed by media formats, reporters must portray fairly simple and clear messages. Given the real complexity of genetic technology and of the issues surrounding it, this is very unfortunate.

On the one hand, in an understandable desire to establish for media audiences the link between discovery and the ultimate application or treatment, the intervening developmental processes and difficulties of gene therapy are usually minimized. The length and uncertainty of the stage between initial discovery and clinically useful application are often compressed or ignored. This simplistic presentation of gene therapy as a simple, easy treatment also contributes to an over-simplified view of disease—the body analogous to a machine, the doctor analogous to a mechanic who fixes it. It means the genetic causes of disease are emphasized at the expense of the complex web of causation, involving social and cultural factors as well as physiological and immunological factors, that is relevant to the great majority of human ills. On the other hand, the coverage and reporting of the views of those who are opposed to genetic alteration and who raise concerns, also tends to be simplistic, without modulation, and without recognition of the complexities involved in this view as well.

This rhetoric on either side is not what is needed to come to principled judgments about what kinds of uses of genetic alteration are humane and beneficial. Responsible use should be founded neither on exaggerated claims of genetic success nor on exaggerated disaster scenarios. We need to take into account the reality that genetic knowledge can be misapplied or abused; we need to learn from the past; and we need to learn from open-minded social and ethical analyses of the implications of use for various groups and for society. At the same time, debate and analysis must be based on accurate information, on evidence, and on validated facts. It is essential that we work to develop a more informed and balanced public debate about the merits, limits, and dangers of altering genes in humans.

It is important in any discussion to define some terms, and this is particularly true in this field, since the way language has been used has led to lack of clarity of thinking on some of the issues raised. Using language inaccurately can frame the issues in a way that is misleading. Genetic alteration can be categorized into three uses:

1. Genetic alteration of somatic cells to treat disease (i.e., gene therapy)
2. Genetic alteration of germ cells (gonads) for prevention
3. Genetic alteration for "improvement"

The first of these three categories, human gene therapy, involves the insertion of genetic material into a human being with the intention of correcting a particular genetic disease. Specifically, a genetic defect resulting from an alteration in the DNA of a particular gene is corrected by inserting a normal DNA sequence for that gene into the individual's body cells. Gene therapy may be the only hope for some severely affected individuals who would otherwise die or be very severely disabled by genetic disease for which there is no currently known therapy. Since the altered genetic material is not inserted into the reproductive or germ cells, the alteration is not passed on to subsequent generations.

However, the term "gene therapy" has also been used to cover other uses of genetic alteration, and this is misleading. It is more accurate to refer to the other uses as "genetic alteration," because no treatment of an individual with a disorder is involved. Genetic alteration is possible that affects either the somatic cells or the germ cells (eggs and sperm). There are also purposes other than therapy for which DNA could be altered: one being prevention of disease, another being "improvement" of a person who is functioning within the normal range.

The issues raised by each of the three categories of use of genetic alteration are substantially different and the three categories should therefore be thought of differently, and discussed separately, which I now want to do.

I. GENE THERAPY

As context, it is important to note that existing or foreseeable gene therapy procedures do not apply to the great majority of severe human disorders. For example, chromosome disorders (such as Down's syndrome) are not amenable to this approach, as no techniques are available to insert or remove sufficient DNA to correct such large DNA segments. Similarly, most multifactorial disorders are beyond the reach of gene therapy. Multifactorial disorders are determined by a complex interaction between genetic predisposition and environmental influences, and the genetic components are not sufficiently understood to warrant serious contemplation of genetic intervention. Gene therapy is therefore primarily relevant to single gene disorders.

There are wide differences in the potential usefulness of gene therapy for various categories of genetic disease. With current knowledge it is feasible to insert a gene of normal DNA sequence somewhere in the chromosomes of an affected cell—that is, to insert a gene. Recessive disorders, where only one copy of the normal gene is usually sufficient to allow the person to function within the normal range, are therefore amenable

to treatment, because inserting one copy of the normal gene into someone with a double dose of the defective gene may be enough to restore health. Even so, there are still formidable obstacles in many recessive diseases: the affected tissue may not be accessible, the gene may need to be regulated very precisely, and damage may be irreversible by birth.

Dominant genetic disorders, on the other hand, are manifest even though the person has only a single copy of the defective gene. This is because they often alter the proteins which are the body's building blocks, making normal function impossible. Simply adding a normal gene in this case is not enough, because the aberrant dominant gene product interferes with the ability of the normal gene product to form normally functioning proteins. This means dominant disorders can only be corrected either by replacement of that dominant gene itself or of the aberrant nucleotides within the gene.

This is an important difference, because at present only gene insertion is feasible in human beings. It is possible to insert an additional, normal copy of the gene that is defective, but it is not yet possible to correct the mutation itself. Thus, only recessive disorders are amenable to gene therapy at present, and these are a relatively rare cause of serious human disease.

With regard to issues raised by the use of somatic cell gene therapy, there seems to be no reason to object in principle to somatic cell gene therapy, which can be seen as a natural extension of commonly used medical procedures. For example, people with hemophilia who are unable to produce normal amounts of a factor needed in blood clotting are given this missing gene product by injections. If the gene producing the blood-clotting factor could be inserted into someone with hemophilia, the effect would be the same as the injections, except the gene therapy could provide lifetime relief. The same permanent result would occur if the person with hemophilia received a tissue or organ transplant that would provide cells containing the normal gene. By itself then, the idea of somatic gene alteration does not seem to raise any new moral problems. Although somatic cell gene therapy is not inherently objectionable, its actual application raises several important issues, just as other therapies do, but these are not new or unique to gene therapy. They include issues such as assessment of risks, informed consent, confidentiality, and appropriate use of resources.

Risks

The method used to insert genetic material may expose the patient to an increased risk of cancer. At the current stage of the technology, it is not possible to control how or where the inserted DNA integrates into the host cell, so for those methods where it is integrated into the host genome, there is a risk that the integration of inserted genes could result in the inactivation or deactivation of genes that influence susceptibility to cancer or that promote the body's ability to suppress the development of tumors. Gene therapy could increase the chance that the person would subsequently develop cancer, although the probability is quite small. But a risk of cancer resulting from treatment is not unique to gene insertion; it also occurs in other life-saving treatments, such as anti-rejection medications used in kidney transplant patients.

Another risk is that the genetic material integrates successfully but the treatment is insufficient, so that the gene therapy procedure simply prolongs a severe disorder without actually curing the disease or even alleviating the suffering. Given these risks at this time, the use of somatic gene therapy is appropriate only for diseases that lead to severe debilitation or death, and that can't be treated successfully by any other means.

Informed Consent

As with all medical research, an individual's involvement in somatic cell gene therapy should be informed and voluntary. The person should be fully informed about the nature and risks of treatment and should make the decision about whether to participate completely free of any pressure. Sufficient information must therefore be provided about the proposed treatment and the patient's role in it, in a form that can be understood, to enable the patient to decide whether to participate. The patient should also know that it will remain unknown for many years whether adverse long-term effects occur. The level of disclosure should be such that even the remote possibility of adverse consequences should be made known.

Several problems arise with respect to informed consent for gene therapy. Often the individual for whom DNA treatment is proposed is a very young child and thus unable to give consent except via a proxy. In-depth counseling of the proxy—often the parents—should be provided to ensure full review of the state of knowledge concerning the risks of changing the DNA: what the known risks are, as well as what is unknown. The relative risks and benefits of alternative treatments and options should be fully discussed.

Confidentiality

Although confidentiality is an issue that is always important, it is of special relevance here because of the wide public interest in gene therapy research trials. The potential difficulty in maintaining anonymity should be disclosed as part of the process of informed consent, while at the same time any possible measures to protect confidentiality should be followed.

Appropriate Use of Resources

Another issue raised by somatic cell gene therapy is whether it is an appropriate use of resources: this kind of therapy is expensive, given the considerable expertise and laboratory support that are required. But there are also substantial costs associated with treating children born with a genetic disease. For example, children with immunodeficiency may have several bone marrow transplants, which are likely to be more expensive than gene therapy if the latter becomes part of clinical practice. It therefore seems appropriate to provide public funding for research into somatic cell gene therapy for serious disorders for which there are no alternative treatments, although this does not mean that other possible promising avenues of treatment should be neglected.

II. GERM-LINE GENETIC ALTERATION

The second category of genetic alteration involves the introduction of DNA into germ cells (that is, the gametes) of an individual so that the genetic change is passed on to subsequent generations, and future generations inherit the change. This has been suggested so as to prevent disease in future individuals.

Genetic alteration aimed specifically at the gonads to alter the gametes is not therapy: there are no existing affected individuals. It is incorrect, therefore, to refer to genetic alteration done in adults with the aim of altering the germ cells as "therapy"; rather, it is a preventive strategy. It is important not to describe or frame this as therapy, as there is much less willingness to undertake risk, both individually and societally, in order to prevent disease than in order to treat identified individuals with severe illnesses.

Germ-line genetic alteration has been discussed in terms of relevance to adults who either themselves have, or are carriers of, a genetic disorder. But if an adult manifests a genetic disease, then altering his or her germ cells won't treat that disease, which would continue to affect the body cells; it would mean simply that the DNA passed on to offspring would be altered. The difficulties associated with altering the gametes of adults are enormous, to the point where few proponents of germ-line alteration consider this a viable option.

Germ-line genetic alteration is much more complicated than somatic cell gene therapy. Germ-line therapy would require precise gene *replacement* in all the germ cells that are affected with the DNA anomaly. If a gene with the usual DNA sequence were simply inserted in addition, without taking out and replacing the mutant gene, then the genetic disease could still be passed on to future generations. At present genetic alteration in adults directed at affecting the germ-line is wholly speculative. As I will outline, it also seems both unnecessary and unwise.

As well as considering altering the gonads of adults, it is possible to consider genetic alteration aimed at curing disease in a zygote at an early stage of development. The developing human entity is theoretically accessible after in vitro fertilization (IVF), when preimplantation diagnosis can show that the zygote is affected with a genetic defect. If gene therapy of the zygote were to be done at this stage, before the process of cell differentiation and the development of body organs, then the genetic change would be part of the resulting cells; and if present in most or all cells, could thus affect the germ-line of the fetus that developed from that zygote.

Some have argued that this is a good thing, as it would not only treat that particular zygote but prevent the transmission of the gene to future generations. However, rather than taking the risk of altering genes that will be passed on to the next generation, there is the less risky option of simply not transferring affected zygotes. Couples who are at risk of passing on a genetic disorder have a very good chance that some of their zygotes will be normal, although the exact odds depends on the particular genetic disorder. The only scenario in which all zygotes will have the disease is when both members of the couple are affected by a recessive disorder and are not just carriers of it. In this case, it is virtually certain that all the zygotes they produce together will be affected by the disease. However, the likelihood that two similarly affected individuals would mate is rather small, given that the average birth incidence of an individual with a recessive disorder is one in many thousands. Moreover, even if they do, if they are both healthy and functional enough to achieve pregnancy, the disorder affecting them cannot be among the most devastating of genetic diseases. Indeed, such diseases are likely to be relatively mild, for example deafness, and certainly not devastating enough to warrant attempting manipulation of the DNA of the zygote. Further, couples in this situation could consider using donor gametes.

The same logic applies to the suggestion that germ-line genetic alteration could be applied to the adult who is a carrier of genetic disease to get rid of the risk in future generations. It isn't currently feasible to perform genetic alteration of sperm or eggs, but even if it were to become possible, in order to alter the carrier sperm, those sperm carrying the disease would have to be distinguished from those that do not; or else all the sperm would have to be altered.

A misguided argument has been made that even if other options are available to avoid or treat affected offspring, gene therapy on zygotes that also affects their germ-line is desirable, because it has the advantage of serving a preventive function by reducing the transmission of genetic disease to future generations. The argument goes that even if affected zygotes are not transferred, zygotes from couples who are carriers would still have a two out of three chance of being a carrier of the disease, and so still pass on the disorder to future generations. The argument continues that DNA alteration of such zygotes would eliminate this risk—that society should pursue the development of strategies for preventing or correcting such genes at the germ-line level as a way of ensuring that present and future couples can "exercise their rights to reproductive health."

The idea of eliminating the risk of transmitting genetic disease may sound attractive to some, but it is in fact based on quite erroneous information and a misunderstanding of human genetics. We are all carriers of various recessive disorders. We all carry genetic mutations that, if found in a double dose, would be deleterious or even fatal. To set as our aim the elimination of all risk of passing on genetic disease would involve genetic alteration of the gametes of virtually all adults. A risk of passing on genetic disease is in-

herent in the human condition. It makes no sense to try to alter this.

Moreover, even if it were feasible, it's not necessarily desirable from an evolutionary perspective. The fact that humans possess a certain amount of genetic mutation is what provides the reservoir for the species to adapt to changing environmental circumstances. The human genome has evolved over millions of years, in complex and subtle homeostasis with the environment. For example, we know that having carriers of certain genetic disorders has benefits in a population. The best known example is the gene for sickle-cell anemia, which provides greater resistance to malaria. But many other examples are suspected as well. We simply do not know enough to contemplate intentionally changing the human genome in the way required for a germ-line prevention program to have any appreciable effect.

It is important, however, not to exaggerate the possible impact of germ-line genetic alteration on the DNA of the human species as a whole. The behavior of humanity has always had consequences for the composition of the gene pool. Technological innovation and cultural change affect the human gene pool, which is enormous. There are over five and a half billion human beings, and to have any appreciable impact in a gene pool of that size would call for intervention on a great many people. Clearly cultural change and medical treatments of other kinds have a much greater effect on the gene pool by affecting the likelihood that people will become parents. However, germ-line genetic alteration is unique in that it involves intentional interference in human evolution, which imposes a greater responsibility to consider the impact of decisions regarding it on our species and on the interests of future generations.

III. Non-Therapeutic Genetic Alteration (Genetic Enhancement)

I turn now to my third category: genetic alteration intended to enhance particular desired qualities such as height or intelligence. This involves "the attempt to enhance or improve an already healthy genetic makeup by inserting a gene for improvement." Although this and the previous category are often discussed under the term "gene therapy," in my view it is not appropriate to refer to either of them as gene therapy; calling them this is misleading.

Genetic alteration to improve complex human traits, such as beauty, intelligence, vigor, or longevity, is far beyond our technical capabilities and will be so for the foreseeable future. These traits are a function of complex interactions between genetic and environmental factors. As a result, enhancement of any particular gene is not likely to have the desired effect. Genetic enhancement may be possible in principle for some simpler physical characteristics, such as height; however, the risks involved are totally disproportionate to any benefits that might be gained.

Moreover, the motivation for non-therapeutic gene alteration requires close examination. Some have argued that it is simply a way of helping individuals make the best of themselves. This is misleading and neglects the potential harms and social risks. A caring society values people for themselves and for their uniqueness. Genetic enhancement raises the prospect of a society in which individuals would be accepted only if they were "improved"; they would not be acceptable as themselves. This is a form of commodifying individuals. If it were permissible, it would be to treat people as things that can be changed, according to someone's notions of human perfection. This shows a lack of respect for human life and dignity and an intolerance for human diversity which is likely to lead to discrimination against, and devaluing of, certain categories of people.

Any use of genetic enhancement raises troubling and potentially discriminatory judgments about what sorts of enhancements would be allowed, and who would have access to them. In the case of gene therapy, the issue of who should receive the alteration is clear: those with a severe disease should be eligible for medical treatment. But in the case of genetic enhancement, the selection process by definition cannot be based on medical need. It must be based on other, as yet unspecified, criteria. Would it be a lottery or, more likely, the ability to pay?

As there is no therapeutic objective, the goal of such alteration would be to pursue non-medical objectives that might be economic, social, cultural, ethnic, or other. What are those objectives and whose objectives are they? There is also the danger that people might be pressured to undergo such a procedure and be subject to discrimination if they refused. Not only are the risks of inserting genetic material not yet well documented, but there are opportunity costs of using resources in this way. The non-therapeutic use of genetic alteration technology would draw away needed resources and skilled personnel from real medical problems. To allow DNA alteration in healthy individuals when there are so many other pressing calls on social attention and resources, would be irresponsible and unethical.

The desire to improve the longevity, talents, and vigor of ourselves and our children is not inherently objectionable. However, this can be best achieved by improving the social and environmental factors that shape our daily lives, such as improved education or a healthier environment, rather than through the risky and potentially discriminatory use of genetic enhancement by those with the money or the power to gain access to the technology.

CONCLUSION

Having discussed these three uses of genetic alteration—namely, somatic cell gene therapy, germ-cell genetic alteration, and alteration of DNA for enhancement purposes—it is clear that the issues they raise are different and that our response to them should also be different. The widespread and intense interest in all aspects of DNA technology that alter genetic makeup includes both ardent hopes for the development of cures for severe, often fatal genetic diseases, and equally intense concerns about potential abuses of science's increasing capacity for genetic manipulation. It is evident that the issues raised by each of the categories of DNA alteration I've discussed must be addressed, and their implications thought through.

There are both potential harms and potential benefits from using technology to alter the DNA of human beings. It is therefore essential in a field where patients and individuals do not have the knowledge to protect their own interests, that these vulnerable interests be protected through society's rules and regulation. Not only individuals have vulnerable interests that need protection; the wider community also embodies vulnerable interests. For example, we all have an interest in the nature of the community in which we live: that our society not be one in which people are treated as commodities, or one in which

technology is used in a way that offends human dignity. It is the role of governments and professional bodies to ensure that vulnerable interests, both of individuals and of society, are protected—in this field, as in others.

Policies must be put in place to set appropriate boundaries and to make sure activities are accountable and that the vulnerable interests of those involved and of society are protected. The implications for society of this evolving field warrant continued vigilance and public dialogue on whether and under what circumstances applications of scientific knowledge on altering DNA should be permitted to be applied. But for gene therapy, properly defined, provided that generally accepted safeguards relating to research trials with new therapies are in place, one must conclude that the potential benefits are such that gene therapy is ethical and it is not socially harmful to pursue it.

Inescapable Eugenics

Philip Kitcher PhD

For over two centuries, first British colonial officials and later the Indian government have struggled to stamp out the practice of female infanticide in rural villages of Northern India. Bound by the caste system, families view daughters as an economic burden and until recently have resorted to crude methods of freeing themselves from such expensive chattels. Baby girls have been killed at birth, usually through asphyxiation or drowning, and even those who are permitted to survive suffer abuse, neglect, and markedly higher mortality rates than their brothers. The arrival of more advanced medical techniques, including amniocentesis, has brought a more humane option. Preg-

nant women can discover the sex of the fetus and choose to terminate the pregnancy if they find they are carrying a female; in some regions of Northern India, dramatically skewed sex ratios at birth reveal that this has become a popular strategy.

It couldn't happen here, of course—or so you might suppose. Western societies are not governed by prejudices masquerading as religious doctrine, and though progress toward the acceptance of women as equals in the affluent world has been unsteady, imperfect, and incomplete, widespread prenatal testing would probably not issue in *dramatically* unbalanced sex ratios.

From *The Lives to Come: The Genetic Revolution and Human Possibilities*. New York: Simon & Schuster, 1996.

(Whether it would lead to a preponderance of two-child families, with elder brother and younger sister, is a further question.) But we should not congratulate ourselves too quickly, for we have preferences aplenty. Unlike Caesar, many people do not want to surround themselves with those who are fat. Even people who think it barbaric to persecute homosexuals are often disappointed to discover that a child is gay or lesbian, a fact reflected in the difficulty homosexuals frequently find in telling parents of their sexual orientation. And in many socioeconomic strata in meritocracies, where brains are taken to be key to at least modest levels of security and success, fathers and mothers hope fervently that their children will obtain an average score (or better) on the tests that are supposed to measure intelligence. Genes indicating low IQ or same-sex preference will be very hard to find—and may not exist—but researchers already claim to have found genetic causes of obesity. Although sex selection may be improbable in Western societies, ten years hence prospective parents sharing the attitudes now common may terminate pregnancies because tests disclose the presence of fetal genes indicating obesity, or perhaps genes that are suspected (quite possibly incorrectly) of causing homosexuality or low intelligence.

We have traveled roads like this before. The history of eugenics in Western societies offers a succession of prospects, some whimsical, most dismal, many tragic. Little harm was done by the eugenic exhibits at American state and county fairs, in which proud examples of prize human stock paraded before their neighbors, adorned with ribbons though presumably not decorated with rings through their noses or bells on their toes. Some of the work done at the former Eugenics Record Office at Cold Spring Harbor on Long Island, now transformed into one of the world's major centers in molecular genetics, bears a similar aura of dizziness. Convinced that the large number of naval officers in some families pointed to a hereditary yen for the sea, Charles Davenport, founding director of the Record Office, earnestly sought the allele for what he called "thalassophilia" (literally "love of the sea"), which he took to be a sex-linked recessive expressed only in males.

Most early-twentieth-century eugenic projects had far darker effects. Davenport's office also amassed studies to show the genetic inferiority and undesirability of the peoples from Eastern and Southern Europe. Congress responded by trumpeting the need for racial purity, and quickly transformed rhetoric into action. In 1924 a new Immigration Act greatly restricted the number of people who could enter the United States from the "undesirable" parts of Europe. Combining official immigration policy with the use of intelligence tests, tests whose cultural biases appear dumbfounding in retrospect, Henry Goddard, who pioneered the idea of screening for intelligence at Ellis Island, succeeded in returning to Europe thousands who would be destroyed by totalitarian regimes.

American obsessions with genetic purity were not simply directed at resisting corruption from without. It was also considered important to extirpate the putrescence of homegrown genetic infections spread by the shiftless and degenerate members of the population who often bred in far greater numbers than their respectable (middle-class, white, Protestant) counterparts. In the 1920s eugenicists publicly lamented the relatively low birthrates of graduates from elite universities. Determined to prevent America from being overrun with "the feebleminded," they campaigned for compulsory sterilization laws and won partial victories through legislation to "treat" the inmates of institutions in many states. Even during the 1940s and 1950s, sterilization was sometimes made a condition of discharge from mental hospitals and prisons.

By then, of course, knowledge of Nazi eugenic practices had caused changes in attitude, not only in those countries (such as Britain) in which eugenic pronouncements had not issued in social policy, but also in America. Beginning in 1933, Hitler had introduced compulsory sterilization on a far grander scale than anything enacted elsewhere, using it as the first instrument in the promotion of "race biology." Other tools followed, and by 1939 the Nazis were using more direct means to eliminate those they judged biologically inferior—people diagnosed as suffering from mental disorders, homosexuals, Gypsies, and Jews. Both the brutality of the methods and the patent attempt to portray social prejudice as objective biology appalled the world. "Eugenics" became a term tightly associated with Hitler's profoundly evil practices, a word with so powerful a stigma that it can instantly stop debate.

So when it is suggested that contemporary molecular biology will inevitably contribute to a revival of eugenics, the implications seem clear: We should have none of it. Genetic testing appears benign when it focuses on reducing the incidence of those rare but terrible diseases that afflict children with massive disruptions of development and early death. Some examples have figured in earlier chapters, but there are many others. Children born with Hurler syndrome show decelerated development toward the end of their first year. They typically deteriorate, growing abnormally and losing cognitive functions, and virtually all die before they are ten years old. Children with Sanfilippo syndrome may survive longer, but they are severely retarded, and their aggressive behavior is frequently difficult to manage. Unlike Hurler children, who are usually "placid and lovable," Sanfilippo patients may be wild and unreachable even when in the most tender and informed care. Many surely find the ability to predict these syndromes liberating, enabling prospective parents to prevent the inexorable decay of the Hurler child or the incomprehensible ferocity of children with Sanfilippo syndrome. Yet for at least some readers of the history of eugenics, these are the first steps on the road to a dreadful destination. In this view, once we begin thinking in terms of "innate defects," social pressures will expand the category of genetic deficiencies, and we shall end by cloaking injustice and prejudice in professions of biology, less monstrously than Hitler, or even than Davenport, but nonetheless harmfully enough.

Others harbor different fears. They are moved by fictional portrayals of individuals and societies who meddle with life and who try to shape people according to some distorted vision of the good. They see contemporary molecular biology as moving towards Baron Frankenstein's laboratory or the Central London Hatchery of *Brave New World*. Today we undertake timid ventures in prenatal testing and gene replacement; tomorrow we shall dispassionately design children and "decant" them into a ruthlessly planned world that has lost its humanity.

Because fine-grained genetic engineering is still remote and may be impossible, fear of Frankenstein is easier to dismiss than anxieties about repeating the errors of our eugenic past. At present, indeed for the foreseeable future, we cannot select *for* the human traits we deem desirable, shaping people according to our ideals, but we can select *against*, terminating those pregnancies in which fetuses bear unwanted alleles. Northern Indians already do it in a very particular way. Members of affluent societies will soon have the opportunity on a large scale. No doubt, initially, they will be moved by concern for the misery associated with the most devastating diseases—but where will they stop?

Eugenics was officially born in the writings of Charles Darwin's cousin, Francis Galton, who campaigned for applying knowledge of heredity to shape the characteristics of future generations. In retrospect, we can recognize the new theoretical science as a mixture of a study of heredity and some doctrines about the value of human lives. Galton's approach to studying inheritance, by looking for statistical features of the transmission of phenotypes, was original and was discarded by the growing number of his eugenic descendants who embraced Mendelian genetics. With characteristic Victorian confidence, however, Galton did not offer a critical discussion of the values underlying his judgments about proper and defective births. Assuming that his readers would agree about the characteristics that should be promoted, he set about the business of promoting them.

Separated from Galton by over a century, we can see how eugenic judgments have mixed science with the values of dominant groups and also how the prejudices have been so powerful as to distort scientific conclusions: Men with a mania for eradicating "feeblemindedness" convinced themselves that there must be genes to be found and duly "found" them. A fundamental objection to eugenics challenges the presupposition that there is *any* system of values that can properly be brought to bear on decisions about genetic worth. Galton's Olympian confidence that he could decide which lives would best be avoided easily provokes the reaction that we should abandon the pretense of being able to judge for others. People with severe disabilities who have attended workshops for human geneticists sometimes pose the question forcefully in words, sometimes even more vividly in their presence and determination: Who are you to decide if I should live?

Yet even as we admire those who have overcome extraordinary adversity to make rewarding lives for themselves, we should remember the dreadful clarity of some examples of genetic disease. Those who watch the inevitable decay of children born with Hurler syndrome or Canavan's disease, those who see the anguish of parents as they care for children whose genes prevent development beyond the abilities of an infant have no difficulty in deciding that similar sufferings should be avoided. In the spring of 1994, at a public discussion of the impact of the Human Genome Project in Washington, D.C., a man in late middle age protested the tendency to see only the problems of the Project, relating how his daughter had given birth to two children with neurofibromatosis. His tone, not his words, conveyed the grief of his family as well as his conviction that abstract fears of eugenic consequences should not block attempts to spare others similar agonies.

As a theoretical discipline, eugenics responds to our convictions that it is irresponsible not to do what can be done to prevent deep human suffering, yet it must face the challenge of showing that its claims about the values of lives are not the arrogant judgments of an elite group. Of course, if eugenics were *simply* a theoretical discipline, pursued by Galton's successors in their studies, there would be little fuss. Precisely because some are concerned about a revival of eugenic *practices*, while others fear that the label "eugenics" will be misapplied to humane and responsible attempts to eliminate pain and grief, questions about the eugenic implications of contemporary molecular biology have more than academic interest. Unless we look past the swastika and achieve a clearer picture of eugenics in action, these important questions will prove irresolvable.

Exactly when are people practicing eugenics? The Nazi doctors, the Americans worried about "racial degeneracy," would-be social reformers like Sidney Webb and George Bernard Shaw, and peasant families in Northern India, do not agree on very much, but all of them hope to modify the frequency with which various characteristics are present in future populations. Eugenic practice begins with an intention to affect the kinds of people who will be born.

Translating that intention into social action requires four types of important decision. First, eugenic engineers must select a group of people whose reproductive activities are to make the difference to future generations. Next, they have to determine whether these people will make their own reproductive decisions or whether they will be compelled to follow some centrally imposed policy. Third, they need to pick out certain characteristics whose frequency is to be increased or diminished. Finally, they must draw on some body of scientific information that is to be used in achieving their ends. Practical eugenics is not a single thing. Human history already shows a variety of social actions involving four quite separate components, each of which demands separate evaluation.

Introducing contemporary molecular biology into prenatal testing will lead us to engage in *some* form of eugenics, but that consequence, by itself, does not settle very much. For it is overwhelmingly obvious that some varieties are far worse than others. Greater evils seem to be introduced if we move in particular directions with respect to the four components: More discrimination in the first, more coercion in the second, focusing on traits bound up with social prejudices in the third, using inaccurate scientific information in the fourth. Unsurprisingly, Nazi eugenics was just as bad as we can imagine with respect to each component. The Nazis discriminated among particular populations for their reproductive efforts, selecting the "purest Aryans" for positive programs, using "special treatment" on groups of "undesirables." Starting with compulsory sterilization, they proceeded to the ultimate form of coercion in the gas chambers. The repeated comparison between Jews and vermin and the absurd—but monstrous—warnings about the threats to Nordic "racial health" display the extent to which prejudice pervaded their division of human characteristics. Minor, by comparison, is the fact that much of their genetics was mistaken.

Scientific inaccuracies infect other past eugenic practices in ways that appear more crucial. Henry Goddard's efforts to keep America pure led him to administer intelligence tests to newly arriving immigrants; even the staunchest contemporary advocate of IQ would have difficulty defending Goddard's assumption that his tests measured "innate hereditary tendencies." Those cast up at the foot of the Statue of Liberty found that their inability to produce facts about the recent history of baseball indicated their lack of native wit. Likewise, decisions to sterilize the inmates of state institutions often rested on abysmally poor evidence. Carrie Buck and her sister Doris were victims of the zeal to dam up the feebleminded flood, and it was Carrie's case that provoked one of the most chilling lines in the history of Supreme Court decisions. In 1927, finding in favor of the lower court decision in *Buck* v. *Bell*, Justice Oliver Wendell Holmes pronounced that "three generations of imbeciles are enough."

The three generations of imbeciles were three members of the Buck family. Carrie Buck's mother had been diagnosed as "feeble-minded," Carrie herself had been placed in the Virginia Colony for Epileptics and Feebleminded; on the basis of a Stanford-Binet intelligence test, she was assigned a mental age of nine. The third generation consisted of her illegitimate daughter, Vivian, seven months old at the time that the original decision for sterilization was made. Because a Red Cross worker thought that she had "a look" about her and a member of the Eugenics Record Office claimed, on the basis of a test for infants, that she had below-average intelligence, Vivian too was classified as feebleminded. Three generations of feeblemindedness demonstrated that the defect was hereditary.

At least the classifications of Carrie Buck and Vivian were quite erroneous. Vivian died while still a young child, but she had completed second grade and had impressed her teachers. In 1980, when she was in her seventies, Carrie Buck was rediscovered and was visited by doctors and scholars concerned with the history of sterilization laws. They found an ordinary woman who read the newspaper daily and who tackled crossword puzzles. The central figure in the tragic story was no "imbecile," not even according to the technical criterion which eugenic enthusiasts employed to grade the feebleminded (imbeciles were adults with a mental age between six and nine).

Failure to distinguish the components of eugenic practice blurs our vision of the injustices that have been done. What is the real moral of the case of Carrie Buck? Not simply that the judgment was mistaken, that Carrie and her sister Doris, both of whom were sterilized, did not carry genes for "feeblemindedness." Besides the scientific error, the practice of compulsory sterilization also destroyed something fundamental to people's lives. Even if Carrie, Doris, and Vivian had borne genes that set limits to their mental development, should they have been forced to give up all hopes of bearing children? Like the Nazis, albeit on a far smaller scale, American eugenicists carried out a coercive practice: They compelled some individuals to follow a social policy that was divorced from any aspirations that those who were treated may have had. Doris lived outside the asylum, married, and tried to have children. Only much later did she understand what had been done to her.

The brutal compulsion of the Nazi eugenics program prompted an important change in postwar efforts to apply genetic knowledge. Everyone is now to be her (or his) own eugenicist, taking advantage of the available genetic tests to make the reproductive decisions she (he) thinks correct. If genetic counseling, practiced either on the limited scale of recent decades or in the much more wide-ranging fashion that we can anticipate in the decades to come, is a form of eugenics, then it is surely *laissez-faire* eugenics. In principle, if not in actuality, prenatal testing is equally available to all members of the societies that invest resources in genetic counseling. Ideally, citizens are not coerced but make up their own minds, evaluating objective scientific information in light of their own values and goals. Moreover, the extensive successes of molecular genetics inspire confidence that our information about the facts of heredity is far more accurate than that applied by the early eugenicists. As for the traits that people attempt to promote or avoid, that is surely their own business, and within the limits of available knowledge, individuals may do as they see fit. Laissez-faire eugenics, the "eugenics" already in place and likely to become ever more prominent in years to come, is a very different form of eugenics from the endeavors of Davenport, Goddard, and Hitler's medical minions.

Identifying the gulf between laissez-faire eugenics and the horrors that underlie the stereotype makes room for discussing the important questions surrounding applications of molecular genetics but does not resolve them. Banning prenatal tests by tagging them with the ugly name "eugenics" should not substitute for careful thought about their proper scope and limits.

Everything depends on the *kind* of eugenics we practice.

We know that some genetic conditions cause their bearers to lead painful or truncated lives in all the environments that we know how to arrange for them. We know also how to identify, before a fetus is sentient, whether or not the fetus carries one of those conditions. Naively, we might try to avoid the smear of eugenics by insisting that nobody should use this information for selective abortions—we shall not interfere with the genetic composition of future populations. But once we have the option of intervening, this allegedly "noneugenic" decision shares important features with eugenic practices. Tacitly, it makes a value judgment to the effect that *unplanned* populations are preferable to *planned* populations. More overtly, it imposes a bar on decisions that individuals might have wished to make, depriving them of the chance to avoid great future suffering by terminating pregnancies in which fetuses are found to carry genes for Sanfilippo syndrome, neurofibromatosis, or any of a host of similarly devastating disorders. When we know how to shape future generations, the character of our descendants will reflect our decisions and the values that those decisions embody. For even if we compel one another to do nothing, that is to judge it preferable not to intervene in the procreation of human life, even to subordinate individual freedom to the goal of "letting what will be, be."

Molecular knowledge pitches us into some form of eugenic practice, and laissez-faire eugenics looks initially like an acceptable species. Yet its character deserves a closer look.

The most attractive feature of laissez-faire eugenics is its attempt to honor individual reproductive freedom. Does it succeed? Are the resources of prenatal testing in affluent societies equally open to all members of the population? Do they help people to make reproductive decisions that are genuinely their own? And is that really a proper goal? Since individual reproductive decisions have aggregate consequences for the composition of the population, should there not be restrictions to avoid potentially disastrous effects? Finally, because individual decisions may be morally misguided—as with those who would select on the basis of sex—will laissez-faire eugenics foster evil on a grand scale?

These serious questions emerge once we have appreciated the dimensions along which eugenic practices may be evaluated, for they correspond to three of the four components: discrimination, coercion, and division of traits. (Concern with the status of our molecular knowledge is less urgent when we concentrate on physiological characteristics, but will reappear later when we consider beliefs about the genetic basis of behavior.) Discrimination and coercion are prominent features of the history of eugenic excesses; only the gullible should believe that simple declarations that genetic testing will be open to all and free from social directives are enough to ensure that history will not repeat itself in these respects. Most obviously in the United States, but possibly in countries that already assure their citizens access to medical care, the costs of such medical technologies as prenatal tests and *in vitro* fertilization may prove an effective barrier to their broad availability: The poor may lack options that the affluent exercise. Predicting the likely consequences of these kinds of inequalities is not hard. If prenatal testing for genetic diseases is often used by members of more privileged strata of society and far more rarely by the underprivileged, then the genetic conditions the affluent are concerned to avoid will be far more common among the poor—they will become "lower-class" diseases, other people's problems. Interest in finding methods of treatment or for providing supportive environments for those born with the diseases may well wane.

The fault lines that run through our societies may threaten future prenatal decisions in other ways as well. Laissez-faire eugenics promises to enhance reproductive freedom. Prenatal testing is to provide unprecedented choices for prospective parents—and, indeed, it will sometimes spare mothers and fathers the anguish of watching young children degenerate and die. Yet the proclamation of reproductive freedom does not necessarily translate into increased autonomy in the clinic. Although the storm trooper's gun is the least subtle of a variety of ways in which social values may shape individual decisions, simply avoiding official decrees of "racial health" and announcing that prospective parents' decisions are to be their own does not ensure that people will act in ways that correspond to their most fundamental ideals.

There have already been women and couples for whom the bad genetic news has been doubly agonizing. Discovering that a fetus has an extra copy of chromosome 21—that it has Down syndrome—they know that the future person would have a more limited life. However, they also know that, with love, nurture, and support, people with Down syndrome can sometimes defy the gloomy predictions that used to lead some doctors to treat the extra chromosome as a marker for abortion. They are prepared to provide the love and nurture, but they cannot count on the support. For some, it is a matter of economics, of not being able to pay for special programs; for others, the problem stems from the attitudes prevalent in the segment of society they occupy, a tendency to view "mongol" children as defective and to write them off at birth. So, moved by concern for the future happiness of the child who would be born, they decide—reluctantly and against their own deep commitments—to terminate the pregnancy.

Individual choices are not made in a social vacuum, and unless changes in social attitudes keep pace with the proliferation of genetic tests, we can anticipate that many future prospective parents, acting to avoid misery for potential children, will have to bow to social attitudes they reject and resent. They will have to choose abortion even though they believe that a more caring or less prejudiced society might have enabled the child who would have been born to lead a happy and fulfilling life. Laissez-faire eugenics is in danger of retaining the most disturbing aspect of its historical predecessors—the tendency to try to transform the population in a particular direction, not to avoid suffering but to reflect a set of social values. In the actual world unequal wealth is likely to result in unequal access, and social attitudes will probably prove at least partially coercive. How are these problems to be solved?

Not by jettisoning the use of prenatal testing entirely. Parents who have seen their own children grieve over a child with neurofibromatosis or Hurler syndrome, who have watched marriages torn apart, bright lives quenched, rightly remind opponents of prenatal testing of the tragedies that the tests may prevent. Only the callous would refuse to allow some to benefit from the new resources of molecular genetics simply because those resources are not available to all. But even though unequal distribution might be tolerated temporarily, societies that introduce prenatal testing have a moral obligation to work toward making it available to all their citizens.

Similarly, if laissez-faire eugenics is to accord with the advertisement that it promotes individual reproductive freedom, our societies will have to combine attempts to bring into the world children whose lives are not sadly restricted with public commitment to assist those who are born to realize the highest possible degree of development. Disability activists already fear that the spread of prenatal tests will erode the tenuous systems of support that have made it possible for many people to go far beyond the limits once foreseen for them. If those systems decay, prospective parents will experience an ever more relentless pressure to eliminate those whom their society views as "defective." To make their decisions maximally free, they need to know not only how the genetic condition of the fetus would affect the life of the person who would be born, given the range of manageable environments, but also that their society is committed to helping them bring about an environment in which that life will flourish insofar as it can. Only if they are assured that all people have a serious chance of receiving respect and the support they need can

prospective parents decide on the basis of their own values.

Social change might make it possible for laissez-faire eugenics to live up to its billing, fastidiously promoting the reproductive freedom of all. But is that really desirable? Prenatal decisions do not affect only the parents; they have consequences, very directly, for the cluster of cells within the uterus and, more remotely, for other members of society who may have to contribute to support for the child who is born.

Those who believe that the cluster of cells already counts as a person view prenatal testing as a means of inspiring evil: Laissez-faire eugenics would hand out licenses to murder. Others do not oppose the taking of fetal lives in principle but doubt that prospective parents will make socially responsible decisions. One by one, the effects of terminating or continuing a pregnancy may be small; in the aggregate, they can make profound differences to the lives of our descendants.

If people proceed myopically, guided by their own dim lights, the consequences may prove disastrous. Seventy years ago unregulated breeding was widely assumed to lead to genetic catastrophe. Eugenicists everywhere suggested that *Homo sapiens* would be buried under a "load of mutations" and, more chauvinistically, Anglo-Saxons lamented "the passing of the great race." Today the concerns are expressed less stridently, more apologetically, and in terms of the *economic* impact on societies. Perhaps the commitment to fostering the full development of those born with genetic disabilities—a commitment which seems morally unassailable—would combine with shortsighted individual decisions to produce impossible obligations. Prospective parents, confident that their society will support a child with a genetic disorder, solemnly take on the responsibilities of providing love and care. As the product of their thoughtful, moral decisions, large social resources—resources that might have been used to promote the welfare of many other children—are consumed in compensating for the genetic misfortunes of their offspring.

In the presence of practical constraints, attractive ideals conflict. Reproductive freedom is important to us; providing support for all members of society, including people with expensive genetically imposed needs, is equally important. But our resources are finite. In a callous society, as we have seen, individual reproductive freedom is severely constrained. In a caring society individual reproductive freedom may lead to social disaster.

Not all chapters in the history of eugenics are unremittingly bleak, and the reflections of some earlier thinkers indicate a potential solution to our dilemma. British social reformers—George Bernard Shaw, Sidney and Beatrice Webb, and others who followed them—hardly correspond to the stereotypes of eugenic repression: They believed that eugenics, practiced freely, would be part of a systematic scheme of social reform. The society they envisaged would provide support for the full development of all its members and would use eugenic methods to ensure a population in which this commitment could be met. But they did not intend to dictate reproductive policy. How, then, were the reformers to guarantee that *right* choices would be made, that parents would procreate to achieve, collectively, a population of progeny who could be fully supported by the available resources? Their answer emphasized eugenic education. People would make the right decisions because they would understand the consequences of their decisions, both for their offspring and for society.

Today's enthusiasts for the use of molecular genetics in prenatal testing rarely call themselves "eugenicists," but their vision of future reproductive practice depicts a particular version of laissez-faire eugenics—*utopian eugenics*—which is remarkably similar to the ideas of Shaw and his friends. Utopian eugenics would use reliable genetic information in prenatal tests that would be available equally to all citizens. Although there would be widespread public discussion of values and of the social consequences of individual decisions, there would be no societally imposed restrictions on reproductive choices—citizens would be educated but not coerced. Finally, there would be universally shared respect for difference coupled with a public commitment to realizing the potential of all those who are born.

Who's afraid of utopian eugenics? Some critics surely fear that utopian eugenics deserves its name, that the conditions it requires cannot be sustained in any society. They might well concede that, in some attenuated sense, benign applications of molecular genetics are possible while maintaining that the results in practice will be far more disturbing. Has any society succeeded in giving its citizens reasonable access to medical resources, or in providing the basic support that all its children need to realize their potential? Can education be expected to succeed in promoting responsible reproductive decisions? Is it possible that an educational program would enhance reproductive freedom, rather than collapsing into a system of ideology that would reinforce widely held prejudices? If we are indeed committed to some form of eugenics, then utopian eugenics seems the most attractive option. But these questions will need to be answered if we are to forestall the worry that it will inevitably decay into something darker.

If prenatal tests are to be employed as a prelude to ending nascent human lives, then abortion must, at least sometimes, be morally defensible. Moreover, our descendants will have to arrive at a clearer conception of the ways in which genotypes influence human phenotypic traits: Repeating the determinist errors of earlier versions of eugenics would be truly tragic. We should also reflect on how the enterprise of choosing people changes our conceptions of human life and human freedom and of their value. If I am right in my diagnosis, human molecular genetics is already committed to that enterprise, and before we are carried onward by its momentum, there are important steps to take.

Most basic is the task of clarifying utopian eugenics, uncovering the considerations that should guide our reproductive choices. To envisage a practice in which reproductive decisions are both free and educated returns us to the problem with which this chapter began. The trouble is to identify the content of the education, to say what kinds of fetal characteristics would properly lead responsible people to terminate a pregnancy. In thinking about the proper form of eugenics, we have focused thus far on three important components: accurate information, open access, and freedom of choice. The issue of trait discrimination has figured only as an afterthought to the insistence on reproductive freedom: Laissez-faire eugenics allows people to make up their own minds about which traits to promote, which to avoid. Yet matters have proved to be not quite so simple. Utopian eugenics proposes that there should be some encouragement to draw the distinction in a particular way. Which way? The Northern Indians, we believe, do not have it right, whereas the doctors who helped reduce the frequency of Tay-Sachs recognize part of the truth. But exactly where between these polar cases is the line to be drawn?

There is an obvious answer. Abortion is appropriate when the fetus suffers from a genetic disease. Preventing disease has nothing to do with imposing social values, for whether or not something is a disease is a matter of objective fact.

Ultimately, this answer will prove inadequate, but understanding its difficulties will point us toward something better. Once we have left the garden of genetic innocence, some form of eugenics is inescapable, and our first task must be to discover where among the available options we can find the safest home.

Can Enhancement be Distinguished from Prevention in Genetic Medicine?

Eric T. Juengst Ph.D.

I. THE PROBLEM

In discussions of the ethics of human gene transfer, two distinctions have become standard rhetorical tools. The first distinction separates interventions that will only affect somatic cells from interventions aimed at modifying human germ-line cells. The second distinction contrasts the use of human gene transfer techniques to treat health problems with their use to enhance or improve normal human traits. Both distinctions are widely debated, but in practice they constitute the most influential moral matrix to date for evaluating new human gene transfer interventions. In this essay, I am interested in pursuing the debate over the second distinction. While the somatic/germ-line distinction is accused of lacking adequate ethical force, the conceptual line between those two classes of intervention is at least clear. The treatment/enhancement distinction, however, often seems in danger of evaporating entirely under its conceptual critiques, and to that extent seems to pose the larger risk to our efforts at assessing human gene transfer technology.

The treatment/enhancement distinction is usually used to argue that curative or therapeutic uses of genetic engineering fall within (and are protected by) the boundaries of medicine's traditional domain, while enhancement uses do not, and to that extent are more problematic as a

From *Journal of Medicine and Philosophy*, 22:125–142, 1997.

professional medical practice or a legitimate health care need.[1] There are several interesting rejoinders to this argument. Some argue that medicine has no essential domain of practice, so that a coherent distinction between medical and non-medical services can never be drawn in the first place. Others accept the distinction between treating and enhancing, but take on the traditional values of medicine, by arguing that privileging treatment over enhancement is itself wrong. Others argue that, in any case, for psychological and economic reasons, the line between treatment and enhancement will be impossible to hold in practice. The rejoinder I want to discuss, however, takes another tack. This response criticizes the distinction by showing how it dissolves in the case of using human gene transfer techniques to *prevent* disease when such interventions involve the enhancement of the body's health maintenance capacities. The argument is that to the extent that disease prevention is a proper goal of medicine, and the use of gene transfer techniques to strengthen or enhance human health maintenance capacities will help achieve that goal, then the treatment/enhancement distinction cannot confine or define the limits of the properly medical use of gene transfer techniques. This argument is bolstered by the fact that the technical prospects for such preventive-enhancement interventions already look good, given gene therapy protocols now underway to treat ill patients in just those ways. One gene therapist summarizes this current biomedical work by saying:

> Over the next few years, it appears that the greatest application will be in the treatment of cancer, where a number of genes that have been isolated have the potential to *empower* the immune system to eliminate cancer cells . . . . Human gene therapy cancer trials have also been initiated for insertion of the tumor necrosis factor (TNF) gene into T-lymphocytes in an effort *to enhance the ability* of T-lymphocytes to kill tumors. Another approach has been to insert the TNF gene into tumor cells in an effort *to induce a more vigorous immune response* against the tumor.

If human gene therapy protocols like these are acceptable as forms of preventive medicine, the critics ask, how can we claim that we should be "drawing the line" at enhancement?

Once accepted, this rejoinder to the treatment/enhancement distinction can be used to cut both ways in the normative discussion of human gene transfer. Critics of human gene transfer combine it with a slippery slope argument to warn against the whole enterprise of gene therapy. Defenders use it to put a foot in the door of the distinction, to keep open the possibility of some legitimate enhancement uses of human genetic engineering.

In this paper, I follow neither of these branches in the argument through to normative conclusions about the moral merits of gene therapy or genetic enhancement. Instead, I want to focus on their common rejoinder to the treatment/enhancement distinction, and address the problem they pose of distinguishing between enhancement and prevention in genetic medicine. I will argue that a line can be drawn between prevention and enhancement for gene therapy (and thus, perhaps, between properly medical and nonmedical uses of gene therapy), but only at a conceptual price that most commentators seem unaware of, even when they are already paying it.

The price of maintaining the prevention/enhancement distinction is that one must be willing to supplement the accounts of health and disease that currently dominate discussions of the boundaries of medical practice with an older, and somewhat old-fashioned way of looking at health problems. In short, in order to preserve a distinction between preventive and enhancement uses of genetic engineering, one must be willing to accept that some health problems (or "maladies," to borrow this useful generic term), in addition to being "reductions in the organizational readiness of an individual to perform functions within the efficiency range typical of members of its reference class (age, gender, species) in the absence of external sustaining causes," also need to be understood to be entities in their own right, reifiable as processes or parts in a biological system, with at least as much ontological objectivity and theoretical significance as the functions that they inhibit. On this view, legitimate preventive genetic health care needs, in addition to being limited to those that involve maintaining individuals within their personal (genetically constrained) subsets of the range of functional capabilities typical for members of their reference class, limited to efforts to defend people from attack by these more robust pathological entities. Or so I will try to argue.

First, though, I should point out a few more limits on my ambitions in this paper:

1. I am not concerned here with arguing whether distinguishing genetic prevention from genetic enhancement is the best way, in the final analysis, to settle the question of the moral limits of human genetic engineering. As I suggested above, there may be other considerations that undermine the whole line-drawing enterprise as well.

2. I will only point to, rather than pursue, the major implications of my thesis. If my thesis is correct, it looks as if it would raise considerations relevant to a number of larger issues. In short:

    a) My thesis seems to help resolve some "hard cases" for the currently dominant approach, suggesting that Daniels and company should pay its price and embrace it.

    b) It does improve the boundary defenses of medical practice, allowing health professionals to carry their commitment to prevention as well as cure into genetic medicine without opening the door to illegitimate enhancements. This suggests progress in the professional ethics of gene therapy, at least, if not in either "private" or social policy.

    c) On the other hand, it also increases the possibility of medical hegemony with respect to genetic engineering practices in our society, and preserves a traditional opening through which cultural values and prejudices can influence medical reasoning. This suggests that the slope remains slippery, and the story is not over yet.

    d) It also illuminates a theoretical weakness in the dominant model of health problems, and suggests that, far from being ready to dispense with the concept of disease, philosophers of medicine should pay more attention to the theoretical role that pathological entities play in the ways in which medicine frames its domain.

II. DRAWING A LINE BETWEEN PREVENTION AND ENHANCEMENT

A. The Treatment/Enhancement Distinction and "Normal Function" Theories of Health Needs

To understand the prevention/enhancement problem, it is useful to begin by looking back at the discussion of the treatment/enhancement distinction from whence it springs. Its most useful exposition comes through the writings of Norman Daniels and his co-authors, who attempt to use the distinction in the course of defining the limits of "legitimate health care needs" for health policy purposes. They argue that conceiving health problems and health care needs in terms of deviations from species-typical normal functioning and an individual's capability range—what Daniels has recently called the "Normal Function" model of health needs —is useful in helping to draw an objective distinction between curative treatments and enhancement uses of ordinary medical services like psychotherapy and prescriptions of human growth hormone. Others have used similar understandings of human malady to help explicate a distinction between "negative" (e.g., therapeutic) and "positive" (e.g., enhancing) human genetic engineering.

On these accounts, to be healthy is to function, under typical circumstances, with the typical efficiency of members of one's age, gender and species. Legitimate health care needs or "health problems" or "diseases" or "maladies" are all characterized by a fall from that level of functional readiness. All proper health care services, therefore, should be aimed at getting people back to "normal," e.g., restoring an individual's functional capability to the species-typical range for their reference class, and within that range to (the bottom of) the particular capability level which was the patient's genetic birthright. Interventions which take people to the top of their personal potential (like athletic training) or beyond their own birth range (like growth hormone), or to the top of the range of their reference class, or to the top of the species-typical range, or beyond(!), are all to be counted as enhancements and fall successively further beyond the domain or responsibility of medicine or health care.

The advantage of the Normal Function account is that it provides one relatively unified goal for health care, towards which the burdens and benefits of various interventions can be relatively objectively titrated, balanced, and integrated. By contrast, theories of "positive" health that would set the goals of medicine higher than the bottom of the individual's species typical capability range face the problem of having to compare different visions of human flourishing. As Boorse puts it, under these approaches:

> Not only is there no fixed goal of perfect health to advance towards, but there is also no unique direction of advance. This point reflects the familiar fact that realizing one potential is often inconsistent with realizing others. To enhance one function to the fullest, e.g., strength, may inhibit others e.g., speed. . . . Along any one functional dimension, comparative judgments of positive health can easily be made. What one cannot say is whether an advance along one dimension is healthier than an advance along another. . . . As it is, in negative health all therapeutic programs

converge towards one goal; in positive health they diverge further the greater the net improvement. . . . [Moreover] If the pursuit of positive health forces a choice between incompatible excellences, it requires an evaluative decision—by client, physician, or society—about what life goals are worthy of pursuit. . . . [thus] ideals of positive health are not discoverable, but only advocable. Their advocacy raises familiar ethical dilemmas about the good life for man, yet no medical procedure can possibly resolve them. . . . The trouble with calling physical or mental or moral excellence health is that it tends to unite under one term a value neutral notion—freedom from disease—with the most controversial of all prescriptions: the recipe for an ideal human being.

There are several implications here that are important for our purposes. First, the problem with "positive health" accounts of health care needs is not that they cannot draw a line between what they would count as restorative treatment and illegitimate enhancement: they can just as easily specify the top of the personal capability range, or the top of the species typical range for some function as their goal. The real problem with the positive health views is an epistemic one: positive health advocates cannot use the lines they would draw between treatment and enhancement, because they can never tell when they've crossed them. Daniels recognizes this when he complains that:

> Although the capability and welfare models capture basic moral insights, we believe that they cast too broad a net and pose severe problems for administration and cost. How are we to judge when the conditions for health insurance are met? If individuals invoke the capability model . . . do we simply take their assessment of need at face value? If not, how are we to investigate the claim? We have little idea of how to delve into questions like this.

Normal functionalists can use physiology to determine when they've achieved the species typical range and clinical histories to determine when they've brought a patient up to the baseline of his or her personal capability range. Thus Daniels stresses that, unlike positive health models of health care entitlements, the boundaries set for medicine by the Normal Function model are "the result of a highly public process open to scientific scrutiny, field testing and repetitive criticism over time." At the very least, death serves as clear indicator that one has left the range of normal function. But how does one know when one is at the top of a personal capability range, or the top of the species typical range? As far as we know, we've never seen the tops of the ranges. Performing better than one ever has before, or better than anyone ever has before, might just be a first step towards the true ceiling. In any case, we would not know the ceiling if we did see it, because there is nothing that sets a limit like death does at the other end of the range. To that extent, the positive health advocates cannot make a distinction with a difference between treatment and enhancement. This epistemic point about the need to be able to know when one has crossed a line is important to keep in mind in thinking about what separates genetic prevention from genetic enhancement, because in that context it applies equally forcefully to the Normal Function account as well.

B. Prevention and Normal Functioning

All the adherents to Normal Function accounts of health and health care needs include and endorse disease prevention as a legitimate health need and a proper goal for medical practice. Indeed, given the place of prevention and preventive efforts in the history and ideology of medicine, it would be a severe problem for their reconstruction of health care if it could not include preventive interventions within the sphere of legitimate medical practice. Unfortunately, without conceptual help, that is just what the Normal Function account cannot do in the case of preventive interventions that act by strengthening an organism's normal defenses against disease, like the gene transfer protocols mentioned above.

Daniels' recent work using the Normal Function account and the Treatment/Enhancement distinction to discuss questions about the bounds of legitimate medical practice is useful in explicating this limitation. Daniels summarizes his account by saying that:

> The central purpose of health care is to maintain, restore, or compensate for the restricted opportunity and loss of function caused by disease and disability. Successful health care restores people to the range of capabilities they would have had without the pathological condition, or prevents further deterioration.

If we rewrite this passage to focus on the preventive aspects of health care, we get:

> The central purpose of preventive health care is to maintain the range of opportunity and functional efficiency threatened by disease and disability. Successful preventive health care preserves for people the range of capabilities they have in the absence of pathological conditions, or prevents further deterioration.

Thus, for example, in genetic medicine, providing a low phenylalanine diet to individuals who lack the (species typical) capacity to metabolize phenylalanine will prevent the loss of normal mental capabilities that phenylketonuria otherwise typically will cause. Similarly, by artificially supplying individuals with hypcholesterolemia with the low-density lipo-protein receptors they lack, gene therapists can prevent further functional deterioration in the circulatory system from being caused by that genetic disease. Thus, both of these genetic interventions should count as legitimate medicine for the Normal Functionalists.

But what about preventive efforts that act by actually enhancing species-typical human health maintenance functions? Consider the case that LeRoy Walters and Julie Palmer make for including some genetic enhancements within the domain of legitimate medical needs. They start with the paradigm of a non-genetic preventive intervention: immunization against infectious disease:

In current medical practice, the best example of a widely-accepted health-related physical enhancement is *immunization against infectious disease*. With immunizations against diseases like polio or hepatitis B, what we are saying is in effect, "The immune system that we inherited from our parents may not be adequate to ward off certain viruses if we are exposed to them." Therefore, we will enhance the capabilities of our immune system by priming it to fight against these viruses.

From the current practice of immunizations against particular diseases, it would seem to be only a small step to try to enhance the general function of the immune system by genetic means. . . . In our view, the genetic enhancement of immune system function would be morally justifiable if this kind of enhancement assisted in preventing disease and did not cause offsetting harms to the people treated by the technique.

In fact, both normal immunization and the new "genetic immunizations" are hard cases for the Normal Function account. Susceptibility to infection by the polio virus is not a deviation from normal species typical functioning. Similarly, an individual's need for immunization does not require the loss of a functional efficiency or a disability. It simply reflects a human *inability*: the inability of the individual's immune system effectively to resist infection upon initial exposure to this virus. Yet in these cases, an intervention is performed that not only increases an individual's internal disease-resisting capability above their personal range of God-given abilities, but even enhances his or her capability beyond the functional range typical for the person's whole reference class within the species (e.g., the class of as yet unexposed children of either gender).[2]

The problem here for the Normal Functionalists is the same problem that Daniels identifies in efforts to call normal short stature a "handicap" in order to secure medical treatment. That is, medicine would be faced with "the need for a clear notion of handicap" and with "the challenge of trying to choose from amongst the many human differences which should count as legitimate

targets for medical amelioration." If the bare notion of a handicapping vulnerability were enough to secure preventive interventions, medicine would be faced with the need for some means of determining which human liabilities (aging?) it should attempt to prevent, and how one would know when one had succeeded in making an individual (or the species) impervious to them.

In other words, the Normal Function account is here faced with the same kind of limitation that "positive health accounts" faced in trying to distinguish legitimate treatment from improper enhancements: it can posit a line between prevention and treatment, but it cannot indicate, on its own, when that line is being crossed. This is why the "normal function" account seems blind to the difference between strengthening the body to resist disease and strengthening the body to gain other advantages.[3]

III. THE NEED FOR A MEDICAL ONTOLOGY

It is interesting that Daniels frames his criticism of the "handicapping" strategy as a set of "serious objections to dropping the reference to disease in drawing this version the treatment/enhancement distinction." In fact, references to disease and diseases play an even more important role in allowing medicine to distinguish between prevention and enhancement than Daniels seems to acknowledge.

In his discussions of boundary problems in medicine, Daniels distinguishes loss of function and opportunity from the diseases, disabilities and pathological conditions that cause them. He stresses that the Normal Function model "makes the health sector responsible for correcting only those conditions which—in DSM-IV terms—can be diagnosed as 'a symptom of a dysfunction,' that is as mental disorders." This is odd, because that distinction is not otherwise part of his general account of health care needs, which simply equates health problems with "deviations from the natural functional organization of a typical member of the species." Indeed, Daniels continues to cite and paraphrase this definition even as he casts diseases in these discussions as something distinct from the reductions in function they cause.[4] This makes his recurrent causal coupling of disease and function loss in these passages unusually (for Daniels) redundant.

Fortunately, this unusual redundancy itself is a clue, which points us back along Daniel's citation trail to the source of his definitions in Boorse's fuller account of health and its definition of disease as "internal states which depress a functional ability below species-typical levels."[5] The key point is that for Boorse, apparently, diseases do exist independently of the functional depression or deviance they can cause, as the "internal states" that cause them. That is still pretty mysterious, but such "internal states" do seem to be the suppressed causal concept in Daniels' short-hand summaries of Boorse's account that appear in his discussions of medicine's boundary problems under the labels "pathological conditions," "diseases," and "diagnosable disorders."

Moreover, Boorse says something important on this score in the process of setting up his own analysis. He says that:

> Diseases in the sense to be here analyzed—e.g., cystic fibrosis, bronchial asthma, trichinosis,—are universals, or types of unhealthy condition that occur in more than one person. Roughly corresponding to philosophical debates over universals, there have been recurrent controversies in the history of medicine about whether diseases or only ill patients are real. Sometimes the issue was whether diseases were independently existing external entities; at other times it was whether disease taxonomy is artificial or natural. Our legacy from these controversies is the term "disease entity", used to mean a natural unit of disease classification. Today, the strictest definition of a disease entity would be a constellation of signs, symptoms and pathology with specific etiology and prognosis . . . Our generic notion of disease looks wider than that of a disease entity. Fortunately, if our goal is to understand health as the absence of disease, we can abstract entirely from this problem of individuating diseases. Complete freedom from disease is the same

> however the field of disease is split up into units. . . . In this respect alone, we make no attempt to be faithful to the customary extension of "disease." The reader should bear this restriction in mind.

Daniels can also skirt the challenge of providing a fuller ontology of disease for his purposes, in defending the Normal Function model of medical needs for social policy purposes. ("Our endorsement of the normal function model does not rest on a view of disease or disability as ultimately real in a metaphysical sense.")

But if Boorse and Daniels can avoid the problem of disease ontology for their initial purposes, they cannot avoid it in attempting to distinguish prevention from enhancement. As their own language suggests, distinguishing effectively between prevention and enhancement depends less on the range of species-typical functioning than on the kind of challenge an intervention is designed to address: what distinguishes prevention from enhancement, in other words, is that medical prevention seeks to improve the body's defenses against *disease*.

Moreover, to do any work, "disease" in this context must mean more than deviation from species typical functioning. To be helpful in drawing a publicly defensible boundary for medical genetic engineering, it has to provide an independent epistemic ground for including an intervention within medicine's domain, above and beyond its ability to keep a person from succumbing to some species typical vulnerability and losing functional efficiency. In the next section, I argue that it is medicine's traditional concept of robust, objectively knowable disease entities—as "metaphysically real" as any natural biological process—that is what the Natural Function account needs in order to make the distinction necessary to defend the domain of medicine.

IV. TAKING DISEASES SERIOUSLY

What I've been calling the "Normal Function" account of health care needs and the account of health and disease it rests on are all descendants of an ancient tradition within Western medicine's

2000 year dialogue about its proper sphere. They reflect the perspective of what historians of medicine call the "physiological" school of thought about disease. "Physiologists" in pathology have always believed that only their patients were real, and diseases should be understood as relatively artificial descriptions of their patients' (malfunctioning) bodily processes. Different bodies, being constructed similarly and obeying the same natural laws, could be expected to go wrong in the same ways, and thereby appear to display the "same" disease, or even to 'communicate' it to other bodies. But the sophisticated physician would know those appearances to be illusions caused by the regularity with which biological systems operate: diseases need not be "metaphysically real" in themselves. The various incarnations of this perspective often led medical scholars to argue that, in principle, medicine could forego the concept of disease altogether, and reduce its explanation to the underlying laws of physiology, without compromising its ability to perform rationally and effectively (just as adherents of the Boorsian "normal function" account do today).

The other historical camp has traditionally been the "ontologists" of disease. Ontologists have always pointed out that, in terms of building a solid basis of reliable empirical knowledge for medical science, it makes more sense to take the observable constellations of complaints, physical signs, natural histories, pathogenetic processes and etiologies that constitute specific diseases as the primary data of medical science, since we are more confident about the reality of those systems than we are about the nature of the physiological laws they are supposed to reflect. Beyond that, the nature of that reality has been controversial for ontologists. Ontological thinking about disease has been pulled one direction and then another by theories of disease causation, because of its inclination to look for the specific pathognomic thread that ties particular constellations together as systems. Ontological reductionism usually takes the form of assuming that medical explanations can be reduced, ultimately,

to accounts of the behavior of these specific causes: germs, poisons, lesions, and genes.

I have argued elsewhere that causal explanation in medicine actually requires *both* ways thinking about health problems, and I think the effort to distinguish genetic prevention from enhancement is another piece of evidence for that thesis. Diseases are real in the same way as the "functionally organized systems" (e.g., the circulatory system) they inhibit and inhabit are real: as decompositions of more complex biological systems that can be discerned by multiple corroborating techniques, from multiple levels of biological organization and across multiple cases. In other words, they are susceptible to the same kind of robustness analysis that the natural sciences use to isolate natural entities from the flux of phenomena, even if they cannot exist independently of the patients who display them.

This epistemic robustness is what gives efforts to prevent diseases the intersubjective accessibility that grounds our confidence that such efforts are meeting legitimate medical needs. If proponents of a particular genetic enhancement intervention cannot describe an adequately robust story of the pathological process their improvement will defend against, the risk increases that they will not be able to tell when they have successfully forestalled or interrupted the process. If they cannot do that, as we have seen, they will not be able to avoid becoming embroiled in questions which "we have little idea of how to delve into" to the ultimate detriment of medicine and society.[6]

This also makes a good bit more sense out of our paraphrase of Daniels' description of the purpose of health care. Now it should read:

> The central purpose of preventive health care is to maintain the range of opportunity and functional efficiency threatened by a disease, e.g., a biological process that moves from discoverable causes (genes, germs, or environmental insults) through a robustly confirmable process of pathogenesis that yields characteristic signs and symptoms that, in turn, reduce function below species-typical norms.

V. The Consequences of Preventing Diseases

In conclusion, let me suggest three of the major implications of my analysis for further work. Most of these points have come out along the way, but all deserve better explication before their significance will be fully clear.

a) Reviving a robust concept of disease does seem to help resolve some "hard cases" for the currently dominant approach to medicine's boundary problems. It not only allows the "normal function" approach to explain why patients in equivalent levels of distress and facing equivalent hardships due to their short stature, gynecomastia, or depression may have different claims to medical care (because of the relative certainty of one's endpoints in cases of diagnosable disease), but it also helps the approach include paradigmatic preventive medical services like vaccination that would otherwise be serious anomalies for the model. Vaccinations against infection are now acceptable, because they are efforts to strengthen the body against specific diseases.

b) Incorporating a robust concept of disease thus does improve the boundary defenses of medical practice, allowing health professionals to carry their commitment to prevention as well as cure into genetic medicine without opening the door to illegitimate enhancements. This suggests progress in the professional ethics of gene therapy, at least, if not in either "private morality" or social policy.

c) On the other hand, giving the concept of disease a crucial role in delimiting medicine's domain does increase the possibility of medical hegemony with respect to genetic engineering practices in our society, and preserves a traditional opening through which cultural values and prejudices can influence medical reasoning. Thus, medicine regains the burden of inter-subjective proof in setting the limits of its own practice through the discovery and delineation of new disease entities. This makes it objective and regulatable, but it also makes it possible for medicine to spin stories of disease to suit various cultural or social values. For example, Kathy Davis, in her sociological study of cosmetic surgery, recounts the occasion in which she heard a well-known plastic surgeon rationalize performing a nose bob on a teenage Morrocan girl living in Holland by diagnosing her with an "inferiority complex due to racial characteristics."

d) Finally, this analysis, by illustrating one important theoretical role played by the robust concept of disease, suggests that, far from being ready to dispense with the concept of disease, as some have been suggesting, philosophers of medicine should pay even more attention to the theoretical role that pathological entities play in the ways in which medicine frames its domain.

When new issues return us to old problems, does it suggest that we have been traveling in a circle, or a spiral? I have argued that the best way to draw a distinction for policy purposes between preventive and enhancement uses of medicine's emerging gene transfer techniques is to embrace the very old notion of a "disease entity" and to test proposed interventions against the robustness of the diseases they would forestall. Where the human problems anticipated by an intervention cannot be tied together into a diagnosable disease entity, with its recognizable constellation of subjective symptoms, physical signs and causes, it should not be adopted as a proper part of medical practice. If this helps, it may be that we are ready for next turn in the helix: Is anything wrong with genetic self-improvement pursued *without* the help of a doctor?

Notes

1. The treatment/enhancement distinction is almost always used, and discussed, in the context of germ-line gene transfer, where it is used to demarcate the limits of permissible practice. Where the distinction is raised in the context of somatic cell interventions, it is much more likely to be raised as a question of resource allocation and legitimate medical needs.

2. But perhaps this is just a problem of specifying the right reference class? One might say that in this case the age of the individuals is irrelevant: unexposed humans of any age are equally susceptible to infection. Further, one might argue that the unexposed do fall below the resistance typical for the whole species, because immunity to polio is a trait of all those who survive their first exposure, whether by virtue of superior capabilities, luck or vaccine. By definition, at any one time the immune class will be the vast majority of living members of the species, and will represent the statistical norm. Against this norm, the non-immunized suffer, if not a dysfunction, a distinct handicap, which they might claim help in overcoming.

One way to analyze this argument would be to pursue a discussion of the relative roles of statistical and teleological conceptions of "normality" in biomedical thinking. Without even pursuing that, however, we can note that the immunized gain their immunity much more efficiently than those who must survive infection by the disease, and indeed than would be normal for the species as a whole if left to its own natural devices. Even though vaccination preserves species-typical functioning, it results in a net gain for the immunized: an enhancement of their ability to respond effectively to infection over that provided by the human immune system's "natural functional organization."

3. For some other interesting challenges that the body's natural defense mechanisms raise for the "normal function" account of health, see Nordenfelt, 1987, pp. 23–35.

4. Elsewhere Daniels makes this definitional link explicitly in the text: "We have obligations to provide services whenever someone desires that a medical need be met. Generally this is taken to mean that the service involves the treatment of a disease or disability when disease and disability are seen as departures from species typical normal functional organization or functioning."

5. Or more formally, "A disease is a type of internal state which is either an impairment of normal functional ability, i.e., a reduction of one or more functional abilities below typical efficiency, or a limitation on functional ability caused by environmental agents."

6. Interestingly, support for this view of the role of "disease entities" in defining the scope of "prevention" in genetic medicine can be found in the way in which the field of preventive medicine already describes its own domain:

> Prevention is said to have three components: primary, secondary and tertiary. Primary prevention means preventing the occurrence of disease or injury, for example, by immunization against infectious diseases and by the use of safety equipment to protect workers in hazardous occupations. Secondary prevention means early detection and intervention, preferably before the condition is clinically apparent, and has the aim of reversing, halting or at least retarding the progress of a condition. Secondary prevention is epitomized in screening programs in which people with early, often preclinical manifestations of disease are identified and offered a regimen to prevent its progression. Tertiary prevention means minimizing the effects of disease and disability by surveillance and maintenance aimed at preventing complications and premature deterioration.

Each of the three traditional components or forms of prevention corresponds to one of the major explanatory levels in a robust disease entity. Primary prevention addresses the etiologic level, by preventing exposure to or infection by the causes of disease. Secondary prevention attempts to interrupt a disease process by interfering with the cascade of broken parts and dysfunctional processes that constitute the pathogenesis of the disease. Tertiary prevention is aimed primarily at preventing the known signs and symptoms of a mature disease process. The field is deployed against the organizing principle of the ontological disease entity because it is what provides the clues to intervention and the criteria for success. This, after all, is what being "medically defined" or "diagnosable" means!

ᏩᎲᎲᎲᎾ

Beware! Preimplantation Genetic Diagnosis may Solve Some Old Problems but It Also Raises New Ones

Heather Draper BA, MA, PhD, Ruth Chadwick BPhil, MA, DPhil, LLB, FRSA

PREIMPLANTATION GENETIC TESTING

Preimplantation genetic diagnosis (PIGD) is the result of combining our increasing knowledge about the human genome with techniques employed in assisted conception. It is currently employed when a couple have had one affected child and/or one or more termination of pregnancy (TOP) following conventional antenatal testing. Superovulation, egg collection and in vitro fertilisation (IVF) are followed by the genetic testing of each of the resulting embryos. Non-affected embryos are then implanted using the same protocols covering IVF for infertility. Preimplantation genetic diagnosis enables couples to found their family with greater confidence that they will neither give birth to an(other) affected child nor subject themselves to a series of terminations of pregnancy.

ADVANTAGES OF PREIMPLANTATION DIAGNOSIS

The most obvious advantage of PIGD is that it enables couples to have an unaffected child without also having to have a series of terminations of pregnancy. These terminations can be particularly stressful for a woman (and her partner) because each aborted fetus is potentially a wanted child. Moreover, the knowledge that each pregnancy is conditional upon a clear test result also constrains the usual joy with which news of a new pregnancy is greeted by those "trying for a baby". The potential of PIGD to reduce the physical and psychological wear and tear on the woman and her partner is one advantage. Another is that the failure to implant an embryo is viewed by many as

morally preferable to the killing of a more fully developed fetus. This view is attractive to those who believe that the embryo gradually acquires greater moral status as it develops both physically and towards viability—hence the various cut-off points in its development which have been used to demark appropriate behaviour (the primitive streak for embryo research or the increased ability to exist independently which seems to mark the cut-off point for termination of pregnancy etc).[1] Preimplantation genetic diagnosis is also attractive to those who wish to draw a distinction between actively destroying life (termination of pregnancy) and a failure to save life (the decision not to implant an embryo). Indeed, we speak of "allowing embryos to perish" rather than "embryo killing".

There remains, however, a sizeable contingent for whom PIGD does not resolve any ethical problems because for them, morally significant human life begins at conception. Obviously those holding this view may be as opposed to PIGD as they are to IVF, unless they are prepared to endorse "embryo euthanasia". According to this view, the human embryo has a moral status akin to that of the fetus, infant or fully developed human. This position need not be incompatible with the view that what makes life worth living is its quality. Thus, it could both be held that the embryo has moral significance and that it is in the best interests of the embryo that it is not implanted, provided that its life is not worth living. Such a view might also justify termination of a pregnancy (feticide) or non-voluntary euthanasia (of both small infants and incompetent adults).

Another perceived advantage of preimplantation diagnosis is that it gives greater choice to

From *Journal of Medical Ethics*, 25: 114–120, 1999.

couples because it gives them the scope to make a decision about which of the embryos to implant, whereas TOP simply presents the choice of whether or not to terminate a pregnancy. This choice is, as we will show, somewhat of a mixed blessing. On the positive side it enables couples to maximise the advantages for their future child but within the limits of what nature provides (ie the number of embryos they have to choose between). So, whilst not actually manipulating the genes of their offspring, they are able to choose not to implant, for instance, not just those embryos which will be directly affected by some genetic disorder, but also any embryo which carries recessive genes for some disorder. Thus, parents are able to protect their future children not just from the direct burdens of genetic disorder, but also the worries which they have themselves experienced to ensure that their own children will not suffer. In time couples may even be able to select according to other genetic traits just as they can now select the sex of their future progeny.

Of course, even as these perceived advantages are listed, old problems begin to emerge. It is one thing to accept, as some people do, that no injustice is done to the embryo if it is not implanted. It is quite another to endorse the policies and justifications which motivate the decision not to implant. For instance, what counts as a life not worth living? Is sex selection permissible? What makes a particular genetic formation a disorder rather than a difference? Is it permissible to maximise advantage as well as to minimise disadvantage? Should we be eradicating difference or intolerance to difference? These larger questions cut across the debate even if we are prepared to accept that no one of moral significance is affected by our decision not to implant any one of the embryos in question. We do not intend to dwell on these old problems, but intend instead to explore some of the new problems which PIGD has introduced, concerning whether it is always wrong to implant an affected embryo; and the extent to which PIGD involves a transfer of power away from women. There is also a third problem,

concerning the greater potential for eugenic implications in PIGD because of the possibility that embryos might be selected on the basis of carrier status for recessive conditions, but this will not be discussed here for reasons of space.

First New Problem: Is It Always Wrong to Implant an Affected Embryo?

It would be easy to assume that the purpose of PIGD is to ensure that only unaffected children are born, and that since the rationale for desiring this end is to avoid the life of suffering which affected children are perceived to have, in the absence of available and effective treatment for the condition in question, it must be wrong to deliberately or knowingly implant an affected embryo. It is one thing, it could be argued, for couples to refuse to undertake PIGD, but quite another for them to request that an affected embryo be implanted. The assumption that it is wrong knowingly to implant an affected embryo seems to be a shift away from the rhetoric of choice which dominates when the context is counselling concerning termination of pregnancy. Yet if it is so obviously wrong to implant an affected embryo, why is it not equally obviously wrong to continue to term under similar circumstances? One answer is that embryos have less moral worth than fetuses. Another is that termination is wrapped up with the autonomy of women whereas the ex-utero embryo is the responsibility of the clinician. We will return to this point later. The assumption that it is obviously wrong to implant affected embryos also ignores at least two other issues in the wider debate about reproductive technologies. The first is the extent to which parents can expect—where possible—to be genetically related to their offspring. The second is the extent to which we are prepared to entertain debate about what makes a life worth living, what constitutes a disadvantaged life, and under what circumstances, if any, an individual could be said to be harmed by being brought into existence.

Let's put this into the context of some examples.

1. Simon and Claire are both in their mid-40s. They have been referred for PIGD because ten years ago they had a child with Fragile X who died six months ago. Since the birth of this child, Claire has had two TOPs following positive antenatal tests for Fragile X. Following the death of their first child, they are more than ever determined to extend their family, but acknowledge that time is running out for them. Claire is superovulated but even so only five gametes are collected. Only two of these become fertilised when mixed with Simon's sperm. Both embryos are affected by Fragile X. Simon and Claire decide that they are getting too old to wait any longer for a child and ask the clinician to implant the embryos. As an alternative, he offers them a place on his IVF waiting list, arguing that they should try IVF with donor gametes. They refuse because they want a child which is genetically related to both of them. He offers further PIGD, they refuse again, concerned that next time they may not even manage to produce a single embryo and that there is no guarantee that even if they do, it will be unaffected by Fragile X. They prefer instead to take the chance that this second child—if a pregnancy is established—will be less badly affected than was their first.

2. Judith and Paul are carriers for cystic fibrosis. They have both had experience of living with sufferers and want to avoid having an affected child. Following PIGD they are informed that they have six viable embryos, but one is affected with Down's syndrome. They ask for four of the embryos to be frozen for later use and for two of them to be implanted. They are not in the least concerned about Down's syndrome, saying that they believe that it is possible to have Down's and

still have a good quality of life. They want the affected embryo to be implanted/frozen without discrimination and at random.

3. Philip and Linda are both deaf. Linda is infertile and the couple have been accepted for IVF. Once on the programme they were offered PIGD by a well-meaning clinician who assumed that they would not want any of their children to be deaf. He is shocked when they steadfastly insist that out of their nine embryos the one with congenital deafness be implanted first—along with any one of the other unaffected embryos. The remaining embryos should be frozen for later use. They justify their decision by arguing that their quality of life is better than that of the hearing. As far as they are concerned, giving preference to the affected embryo is giving preference to the one which will have the best quality of life. They are very concerned that any hearing child they have will be an "outsider"—part neither of the deaf nor of the hearing community at least for the first five or so years of his/her life.

Case Number 1: Simon and Claire

This case challenges us to determine whether it is permissible for a couple to put the desire for a child which is genetically related to them above the interests of the child, once born; and also, whether it is acceptable to offset the risk that they will not manage to have another successful attempt against the risk that the child may have a very disadvantaged life. To address these issues, we have to look at reproductive freedoms and parental responsibility.

There has been systematic and unresolved discussion over what makes an individual a parent, even more debate about what makes a woman a mother. This discussion has been provoked by what is perceived as the division of motherhood into, for instance, the social, the bearer and the genetic. Although most people agree that it is not a necessary criterion of parenting that one has a genetic relationship with a child, it is usually considered a sufficient qualification. The strength of this assumption has been revealed in a variety of contexts: the "father" distressed because a woman is going to abort "his" child; the reluctance of some to donate genetic material or frozen embryos; mothers who only reluctantly handed over children for adoption; men who discover that unbeknown to them, they have a child in the world whom they have never met. Likewise, as many of those experiencing the discomfort and expense of infertility treatment attest, the desire to have a genetically related child is an enormously strong one. From this perspective, it is not difficult to have sympathy with what Simon and Claire are proposing to do.

Their claim does, however, highlight the weakness of considering the conceptual issue of parenting in isolation from the responsibilities which flow from parenting. Simon and Claire are asserting a right to be parents of a particular kind—genetic parents. Whether such a right exists and if so what its content might be is contested.[2] Yet if such a right exists, it stands to protect the goods which flow from parenting.[3] These goods are arguably of two kinds—the fundamental and the incidental. Incidental goods include goods which one obtains as a known side effect of having children; for instance, securing council housing, producing a football team, or having company and security in one's old age. Fundamental goods, on the other hand, are the moral goods of parenting, the goods which parenting represent and which, without parenting, might never be achieved. These goods include the care and nurture of a child, the sense of affection and community found in loving families and the moral good of being responsible for the wellbeing of another. It is these kinds of goods which the concept of a right to parent seems to protect.

The question which Simon and Claire's case raises is whether being genetically related to the child is an incidental or fundamental good of parenting. Or, put another way, does the right to found a family include the right to be genetically related to one's child? On balance, the answer to

this question is no. Being genetically related to one's child seems more appropriately located as an incidental good of parenting because it lacks sufficient weight to count as a fundamental good. This way of looking at the dilemma faced by Simon and Claire yields a quite different result from that which concentrates solely on future persons. In conclusion then, it would seem that Simon and Claire cannot insist upon having either of the embryos implanted on the grounds that they have a right to a child genetically related to them.

Cases 2 and 3 Judith and Paul, Philip and Linda

In some respects both of these cases raise the same issue—that there is no definitive view either about what makes a life worth living, or about what constitutes quality of life. These are not new issues. The new dimension in PIGD is the possibility of actively choosing to have an affected child; in Judith and Paul's case because they do not see Down's as a condition incompatible with quality of life; and in Philip and Linda's case, because they think that being deaf is positively life-enhancing.

Of course, making an assessment of an individual's quality of life is a moral decision because other morally important decisions will be based upon the answer reached. In this respect, one has to look at the context in which the decision is being made to gain a full appreciation of the morality of the decision itself. So, for instance, if a quality-of-life decision is being used to allocate scarce resources, we want to locate this decision in the context of debate about justice. The context for our two couples is that they are claiming the parental authority to make decisions about the welfare of their children. The context in which their decision has to be discussed is that of whether they are making a responsible or irresponsible *parental* judgment. The moral basis for respecting the judgment of parents is the presumption that parents have the best interests of their children at heart, that they of all people can be trusted to do what is best for their children.

This is the basis upon which parental judgments command moral authority. Sometimes parents do not seem to exercise good judgment when it comes to protecting their children's best interests. When this happens, we may consider them to be bad or even unfit parents, or sometimes no kind of parent at all! These kinds of judgments reinforce the view expressed above that it is almost impossible to look at what being a parent means without also considering parental responsibility. In this sense, not only might it be argued that the term parent is actually a moral term (as opposed to a term related to bearing, genetics or social roles), but also that it is perhaps inappropriate to separate our understanding of good parents from our understanding of what it means to be a parent.[3] Whilst attractive, this leaves us in danger of denying that parents can make mistakes without losing, as it were, the right to parent. We have, therefore, to accept that parents can make *misguided* judgments as well as *bad* judgments. Also, because there is an acceptably wide understanding of what constitutes a child's best interests, different parents may arrive at different decisions for their children without being either misguided or irresponsible in their judgment.

Now we need to apply these observations to the decisions made by Judith and Paul, Linda and Philip. We will then be in a better position to determine whether it is wrong for them to want to have affected embryos implanted.

Judith and Paul

To assess the strength of Judith and Paul's claim, we may actually need to know more about their views about the status of the embryo. If they are making an embryo euthanasia decision (ie attempting to make a decision about the future quality of life for what they consider to be an existing child) and if they believe that Down's is compatible with a quality of life worth having, then we will have to accept that they are making a responsible parental judgment—whether or not it is the one which we would be prepared to make for our own child.

But what if they are making a more political statement—perhaps one about the wrongness of a policy of testing for Down's? This is a much more difficult issue to resolve because the couple are much more vulnerable to the criticism of harming the future child, particularly if they believe that the embryo itself has no moral status. Judith and Paul cast as proponents of embryo euthanasia are balancing the harm of ceasing to exist against the harm of existing with Down's. Judith and Paul cast as a couple who believe that the embryo does not have moral worth (because it does not yet have a life at all) seem rather to be choosing to create a person with Down's. We need to be aware that there are different points coming together here. First there is the issue unique to PIGD—that of the active choice to implant a particular embryo. Second is the old dilemma of the extent to which parents can allow their own political views to affect the decisions they take about reproduction, rather than being motivated by considerations of the interests of their future children.

It might be argued that since Down's syndrome is not deemed to be incompatible with a life worth living, Judith and Paul do not wrong a child by bringing it into existence with Down's. But however much value is attached to the lives of those who have Down's, it nevertheless remains the case that is it not good to have the disabilities which those who have Down's have to suffer. It is one thing to say that those who have Down's are valuable and quite another to say that the choice between choosing to implant an affected or an unaffected embryo has no moral significance. Whether a condition is so severe as to make life not worth living is one question. Whether it is permissible to implant an embryo with a condition that will result in disability, but a disability that is not so severe that it makes life not worth living, is another. If the answer is not clear then there is a case for leaving it to parental choice. There remains an issue, however, about the sorts of considerations that are relevant to that choice.

What if, however, they argue that for them the moral significance in having the affected embryo implanted lies precisely in making a political statement about the value of those with Down's, a symbol of their belief that a life with Down's is nevertheless a valuable life? We cannot do justice to the wider issue here, so we will simply describe it rather than discussing it at length. In its broadest sense this question asks us to decide which takes precedence, our obligations as citizens or our obligations as parents.

The extent to which we can impose the effects of our political beliefs on our children is raised in many different contexts. The conscientious objector in an oppressive regime knows that her objections place not just herself but her children at risk of physical harm and death. Those who believe in public education for children have to decide whether or not to send their children to private schools when their children have special needs or happen to live in the catchment areas of substandard state schools. We might be happy to conclude that making these decisions is one of those areas where, once again, the boundary for responsible parental decision making is quite a wide one. Nevertheless, we also conclude that once parents cite their moral authority as parents as the reason to allow them to make such decisions for their children, the interests of the children do have to figure to a significant degree in the calculations, whatever the final decision which is reached.

Linda and Philip

Linda and Philip also want to implant an affected embryo, but in their case what they believe themselves to be doing is maximising the advantages for their future child. This decision is a difficult one to challenge. By offering a choice between possible future persons, PIGD provides not only the opportunity to avoid avoidable harms, but also the possibility of maximising advantage or enhancing quality of life.

Why are Linda and Philip able to argue that deafness is life-enhancing? One answer is that they are themselves deaf and are therefore in a good position to judge, whereas we who can hear are not. Equally, however, it could be argued that

Linda and Philip because of their deafness are not in a position to appreciate what they are missing. In one sense this argument is intractable; it is impossible to claim that one form of life is better than another unless one has experienced both and even then one's preference could be said to be subjective. One could, of course, refuse to give their claim any credibility at all by arguing that it is harming a child to engineer that she is born without the capacity to enjoy all of her senses or do all that it is possible for humans to do.[4] This is surely the kind of judgment to which we appeal when we observe that whatever value attaches to the life of the person with Down's, nevertheless having Down's is a disadvantage. But Linda and Philip's claim is more difficult to dismiss than this. Few if any of us claim that the pressure of intellectual capacity is so great that we wish we'd been born without it. We might claim that the pressures of responsibilities we have as a result are so great that we'd like to give them up in favour of a more simple life, but in considering the possibilities for this more simple life, irreversible brain damage rarely, if ever, features. Many of us have, however, found noise to be obtrusive. Too much uninvited noise is itself a recognised medical condition (tinnitus) but too much intellectual capacity is not. Some of us regularly resort to ear-plugs in order to sleep or work in environments we cannot control. Thus whilst we do not literally deafen ourselves, we certainly are prepared to trade hearing for peace and quiet.

The argument, however, may be less in terms of the quality of sound-related experience or its lack, but as indicated above, in terms of a sense of belonging to a community, a language and a culture. It is this that marks out deafness from other conditions. Linda and Philip are not simply making a political claim that people like them should not be discriminated against through programmes to screen out deaf future persons, although there are arguments for the view that screening for deafness harms the deaf community. They are motivated by the genuine belief that they are acting in their child's best interests.

Perhaps the best that can be argued against them is that they should allow their child to decide for herself whether she thinks that their quality of life is better than hers. This choice is removed from her if she is born irreversibly deaf. But even this solution does not address the point which they make about being an outsider.

This case highlights one of the disadvantages of giving parental decision making moral authority, namely that it can act as a trump card in those areas where there is no right answer, but where the decision which parents want to make, to choose a state in which a child is born with a hearing system which does not work, is one that most rational bystanders would not take. On the other hand, as has been suggested above, in cases where it is not the case that the child would be so disadvantaged that its life would not be worth living, it may be argued that parental choice is the best option, particularly where motivated by the child's best interests. It is precisely this that may be undermined by PIGD, however, and this is where we turn to our second problem.

SECOND NEW PROBLEM: DOES PIGD SHIFT REPRODUCTIVE POWER FROM WOMEN TO PHYSICIANS?

To date, quality-of-life decisions have largely rested with women because it was impossible to make decisions over the life or death of fetuses without effecting these decisions on women's bodies. Once pregnant, a woman is free to decide whether or not to seek antenatal screening, and irrespective of this decision she is free (within legal boundaries) to determine whether or not the child is a wanted one, irrespective of any advice given to the contrary by her clinician.[5] Although women cannot be compelled to participate in PIGD, once they have parted with their gametes and once the resulting embryos are tested, it is possible for them to lose control over what happens next. Clinicians participating in IVF have a clear statutory obligation (and some would argue that this reflects an absolute moral obligation) to

consider the interests of the future child. Just as the clinician cannot compel a woman to give up her gametes, or have a TOP, or be implanted, she cannot compel him to implant embryos against his wishes. Does this mean that in all the cases we discussed above, we were wrong to assume that the decisions were the parents to make at all? The clinician, it seems, has the final say in whether or not to implant.[6]

Or does he? There are several points to be made here. The first concerns the extent to which the clinician needs to rely solely on his own judgment. He can of course take account of the arguments of the parents—or indeed, his own ethics committee. However, the net effect of this could be to split hairs, since although he takes account of the parents' views he still has the final power to decide whether or not to be bound by their decision. Also, the 1990 Human Fertilisation and Embryology Act was formulated on an assumption that the clinician would arrive at this judgment *before* deciding whether or not to treat. When disagreements arise in PIGD, treatment (if this is the correct term) is already well underway. Any dispute concerns whether or not to implant *existing* embryos. In deciding not to implant on the basis of disagreement about the interests of the future child, the clinician not only retains his considerable power over reproductive freedom, he also gains power over what could be described as the property of the couple—the embryo—which is the product of their own gametes, which arguably are their property.

But, is it fair to assume that if gametes are property embryos are also property? If we consider that the embryo has an independent moral status, the claim about ownership diminishes because we readily accept that humans cannot be owned in any sense. If, however, we are working on the assumption that the embryo has no independent moral status it does seem reasonable to suppose that it can be owned and therefore belongs to the couple jointly (let's leave aside totally the issue of what to do if they disagree among themselves). This puts the clinician in an impossible position.

He cannot implant because he does not think that it is in the interests of the child to do so, equally he cannot simply freeze the embryo since the purpose of this would be to afford the couple the chance of successfully finding a clinician who will agree to implant and this may result in a child whose interests he believes are best served by not coming into existence. Both freezing and implanting are using his skills to bring about a child. Of course, there is a precedent for suggesting that he should freeze and refer, namely the practice of clinicians who have a conscientious objection to abortion but who are expected to offer to refer patients to someone who will perform an abortion for them. The moral inconsistency of this position is obvious and needs no further explanation.

It seems to us highly probable that this tension is likely to cause problems in the future. The couple will, not unreasonably, assume that the decision in the case of PIGD will be theirs to make —because in antenatal screening it is. Likewise, the clinician cannot be blamed for assuming that he has the final word since in infertility treatment he does. Moreover, it seems likely that any "contract" which the couple make with their clinician as part of their consent prior to PIGD will be impossible to enforce—particularly in a case like that of Simon and Claire, where the embryos in question became endowed with the additional status of being the ONLY chance for them to have a genetically related child. It remains to be seen,

then, whether PIGD should be marketed as affording greater autonomy and reproductive freedom to couples when, as things stand, they are effectively putting the decision in the hands of the treating clinician.

References and Notes

1. For instance in the amendment to the Abortion Act 1967 found in the Human Fertilisation and Embryology Act 1990.

2. See for example, Chadwick RF, ed. *Ethics, reproduction and genetic control* [2nd ed]. London: Routledge, 1992.

3. For the complete development of this argument see Draper H. Assisted conception techniques, parent selection and the interests of children to adequate parents. *Bioetica* 1997;5:391–9.

4. For a discussion of this issue see Chadwick R, Levitt M.A. The end of deafness? Deaf people, deaf genes and deaf ethics. *Deaf Worlds* 1997; 13:2–9.

5. Granted, conditions such as extent of knowledge, subtle coercion, tests made available and other circumstances may erode autonomy.

6. Steinberg DL. *Bodies in glass: genetics, eugenics, embryo ethics.* Manchester: Manchester University Press, 1997. As Deborah Lynn Steinberg has argued, while preimplantation diagnosis may be debated in the gender-neutral language of genetic risks, it "obscures social inequalities between practitioners and female patients and between patients and their male partners, while implicitly reinforcing and relying on these power imbalances".

Genetic Technologies and the Challenge to Equality

Maxwell Mehlman JD and Jeffrey Botkin MD, MPH

As it stands now, many future genetic technologies will be accessible only to those people who have insurance coverage or who can afford to purchase such technologies with private funds.

This will deny access to persons who lack health insurance—currently estimated to be around forty million individuals—unless they have sufficient personal wealth. Even those persons who

From *Access to the Genome*, Washington, D.C.: Georgetown University Press, 1998.

possessed health insurance might be unable to obtain access to expensive genetic technologies that were not part of the insurers' benefits packages, either because the technologies were experimental or because they were too costly. One particular set of genetic technologies—genetic enhancements—are likely to be excluded entirely from coverage and will only be available to those persons who can purchase them with private funds.

Some people, particularly some economists, will defend this method of allocating genetic services. Allocating resources on the basis of willingness to pay is consistent with the belief that, all other things being equal, the best way to identify and measure the strength of an individual's demand for goods and services is to rely on the individual's own choices. This enables the market to price goods and services efficiently and to avoid wasting production capacity by producing goods and services for which people are not willing to pay. Allocating resources on the basis of a person's willingness to pay arguably also maximizes the individual's decision-making autonomy. No one else—not the government or a private insurance plan—is in a position to interfere with the individual's wants.

These attractions account for the popularity of proposals to replace government health insurance programs with medical savings accounts. These would allow people to put earnings in interest-bearing accounts without paying taxes on them and to withdraw funds to purchase desired medical care. Money in the account that was not spent could be used for other purposes or become part of a person's estate upon death.

But willingness to pay runs into a fundamental problem. It might be a satisfactory and perhaps even superior way of allocating access to genetic technologies so long as individuals are able to afford the technologies they desire. Part of what economists who advocate willingness-to-pay approaches mean when they assume that "all other things are equal" is that everyone has roughly the same amount of wealth. As we know,

however, from personal experience, this clearly is not the case. Not only are some people wealthier than others, but some have health insurance while others do not, and some insurance plans cover services that others exclude.

Another assumption that economists make is that everyone has the same basic needs for the desired goods, for example, the same risk factors that cause them to need genetic technologies. But this assumption also is false. People differ in their inherited characteristics and life-time experiences so that some need different types and amounts of health care than others. A willingness-to-pay approach could still result in an efficient allocation of genetic services if those people who had a greater need for these services also were more likely to possess the wealth to pay for them. But this, too, is not the case. As Richard Epstein, a distinguished law professor who is a proponent of free market economics, points out, ability to pay does not correlate well with medical need.[1] Sick people are not wealthier than healthy people. If anything, the opposite is true; poor people tend to suffer more illness than those with greater financial resources, due to the lack of access to timely care and to the poorer quality of their nutrition and living environments. Under a pure willingness-to-pay approach, then, some people with a need for genetic technologies would have access to them while others with the same need would not. From an economist's standpoint, this result would be inefficient.

Economic efficiency is not the only reason to be concerned about a system that would make many important genetic technologies accessible only to those who could pay for them. Arguably, nothing is as essential to a good life as good health. If we think of some desired goods as "wants" and others as "needs," good health is as close as anything to being a "need." To the extent that health care is necessary for the good life, it is a "primary" good, along with such necessities as food and shelter. Even if we thought that people ought to obtain access to most goods on the basis of what they chose and what they could pay, we might believe that we had a collective responsibility to ensure that everyone had at least a minimum set of primary goods, including access to health care.

If health care in general is a primary good, so are many genetic technologies, and people who cannot obtain genetic services will be denied critical health benefits. Without access to genetic testing, they will lack much of the ability to forestall or reduce the severity of genetic disorders. People lacking access to effective gene therapies will be forced to rely on less effective conventional therapies that, in many cases, somewhat ameliorate the symptoms of their ailments rather than curing them. The more the Human Genome Project leads to the discovery of genetic tests and successful therapies for genetic disorders, the more the health of those without access to these services will decline in comparison to those with access.

Genetic testing and therapy are not the only types of genetic services that might be considered primary goods, however. Genetic manipulation may be able to alter significantly a person's physical appearance—such as his or her height or attractiveness. Genetically engineered human growth hormone may make it possible to increase height, although it is unclear whether this will occur without troublesome side effects.[2] Once the right genetic precursors are located by the Human Genome Project, the same techniques that permit us to correct genetic errors should enable us to alter other physical attributes such as strength, stamina, and visual and aural acuity.

Ultimately, the most significant result of the Human Genome Project may be the ability to enhance a person's mental abilities. We are only beginning to understand the extent to which mental characteristics are the product of a person's genetic endowment. Research in this area is mired in controversy, with critics concerned that it could lead to everything from cuts in social welfare programs and increased discrimination against certain genetically defined races and ethnic groups to Nazi-like eugenics

programs in which governments try to breed a better citizenry.[3] Even so, it may only be a matter of time before we are able to improve a person's memory, concentration, or IQ through genetic manipulation.

While lack of access to gene testing and gene therapy would deprive people of primary health care services, lack of access to genetic enhancements could deny them the ability to satisfy primary social needs. Many people would consider the resulting society to be intolerably unjust. One of the leading experts on justice and health care, Norman Daniels, maintains that individuals must have a fairly equal opportunity to obtain those health care services that will provide a "normal range of opportunity."[4] Daniels' notion of a normal opportunity range refers to those opportunities he considers necessary for an individual to formulate and carry out a life plan. Health care is important in this scheme because a certain level of healthy physical and mental functioning is necessary for an individual's prospects to fall within an acceptable range of opportunity. If physical health conditions and mental abilities achievable with genetic technologies come to be regarded as necessary to enable individuals to carry out a life plan with a normal range of opportunity, then it would be unjust to deny individuals that chance.

Many individuals would not obtain access to a number of important genetic technologies under the present system. Access would be unequal, and would depend primarily on whether an individual had insurance that covered the genetic services in question, or could pay for them with private funds.

Philosophers and political theorists have struggled for centuries to construct models of society that justify certain types of inequality. One way of analyzing whether our prediction of unequal access to genetic technologies would be acceptable from an ethical standpoint is to see if it can be justified under any of these theories.

A leading theory of inequality is utilitarianism, developed originally by Jeremy Bentham and

John Stuart Mill in the nineteenth century. The principle of utility is well-known. It holds that we should act (or arrange our institutions) so that the results of the act bring about the greatest good for the largest number of people. The "good" may be a general good, such as happiness, or a specific good, such as health care.

Utilitarians speak of maximizing either aggregate utility or average utility. Distributing a good to maximize aggregate utility refers to adding together the utility for each individual affected.[5] If we conceived of utility in terms of units, for example, one would simply add together the units that all persons affected would receive by a particular distribution. For example, if there were five individuals, A through E, and A received three units, B received five units, C seven, D four, and E six, the total utility gained, or aggregate utility, would be twenty-five units.

Distributing a good to maximize average utility refers to the aggregate utility divided by the number of persons who receive it.[6] Thus, the average utility in the example above is five (twenty-five units divided by five persons affected).

The principle of utility might be applied to the allocation of health care resources by assessing the consequences of alternative distribution systems and determining which system would provide the greatest number of units of good (either in the aggregate or on average). One way of evaluating the consequences is through the use of cost-benefit analysis. The benefits and costs of alternative distributions could be calculated to determine the distribution with the greatest amount of net benefit or the best ratio of costs to benefits. A system that delivered five units of benefit at three units of cost would be preferred over a system that delivered five units of benefit at four units of cost.

Preventive health services often fare well under a utilitarian scheme because their cost is low and the benefit is generally deemed to be high, in part because often they prevent serious illnesses and their benefit endures for a long time. Utilitarians, therefore, might call for widespread access to genetic testing and gene therapy that detect and prevent serious genetic illnesses.

"Rescue medicine" is another story. The cost of providing gene therapy to save *one person* with a catastrophic illness may be the same as providing genetic testing and preventive therapy for *many individuals*. The total units of utility produced in both cases might be the same. A genetic test that would lead to preventive treatment might add ten years of life to five individuals, while a life-saving gene therapy might save the life of a child with a life expectancy of fifty years. In each case, the same amount of utility, measured in terms of additional years of life, would result, and a utilitarian would have trouble deciding whether to provide access to one or the other. The fact that the benefit was enjoyed by one individual in the first case and by five individuals in the second would be irrelevant. Some would say that utilitarianism produces unjust results on this account.

Another problem with utilitarianism concerns how to determine just what the distributive result would be. In terms of health care, just as there are many different ways of measuring costs and benefits, so there are many different ways of distributing access to health care that would be consistent with utilitarian principles. Yet each of these approaches would yield a different result.[7] To maximize the number of years of life that would be saved by a genetic therapy, we might limit access for the elderly. If benefit to society were the primary objective, we might limit access for criminals and give preferences to philanthropists and medical researchers.

In terms of genetic technologies, utilitarian theories would support a wide range of distributive systems, depending on how utility, costs, and benefits were calculated. Utilitarians might sanction a broad pattern of distribution in which many people, or at least a majority, obtained some access to some services. They might opt instead for a highly restricted system in which access to genetic technologies was concentrated in those individuals with the poorest genetic endowments.

Or, utilitarians might support giving access only to those who already possessed good health and superior traits, on the theory that the resulting super-persons would provide the most benefit to society, thereby indirectly maximizing everyone's utilities.

There simply is no ready means of determining which genetic technologies would be available to which persons under a utilitarian approach. The only point that is obvious is that the interests of individuals can be subordinated to the interests of others in order to maximize the sum of utility. Utilitarianism, therefore, could sanction a broad range of inequality in terms of access to genetic technologies.

A number of other theories of justice insist that individuals have rights that cannot be sacrificed in order to create more utility for others. The most well-known and influential of these rights-based theorists is John Rawls. In his landmark work, *A Theory of Justice*,[8] Rawls asks us to imagine that we are in a position to choose principles to govern societal institutions without knowing the kind of society in which we would live or the position in society into which we would be born. Under these circumstances, argues Rawls, we would choose two principles.

One is the principle of greatest equal liberty. According to this principle, "each person is to have an equal right to the most extensive basic liberty compatible with a similar liberty for others."[9] In other words, we must maximize liberty, but we may do so only to the extent that it is possible to ensure the same liberty for everyone.

The second principle Rawls calls the "difference" principle. It holds that people should have equal opportunity to participate in important societal institutions and that the only differences in wealth or social status that would be acceptable would be those that would make everyone better off. In other words, one individual or group may have an unequal advantage only if all others realize some betterment from the unequal distribution of the wealth or benefit.

Although Rawls himself has not written about the implications of his theory of justice for health care, others have tried to derive working policies using his principles of justice.[10] Each attempt has encountered difficulties in taking what is a very abstract theory of distributive justice and trying to fashion particular rules to govern hard choices in actual situations. Much of the problem stems from what others see as one of Rawls' strengths: the flexibility of his principles. By being flexible, his principles allow for any particular society to set up institutions in a number of different ways, depending on the culture, the scarcity of resources, the peculiarities of the underlying distribution of wealth in that society, and so on. Yet this seems to permit a wide range of choices for specific policies. For example, Rawls' second principle, encompassing both equality of opportunity and the difference principle, has been invoked to support both the most minimal rights to health care and the most extensive access that society can afford. In terms of genetic technologies, Rawls might be comfortable with a considerable degree of unequal access, so long as he could be persuaded that this was the approach in which everyone had the greatest liberty and in which everyone derived at least some benefit from the inequality of access.

Another theory, libertarianism, rejects the notion that society can compel individuals to relinquish their wealth or power for the benefit of others. According to Robert Nozick, a leading libertarian philosopher,[11] people are entitled to the holdings they acquire justly. Answering the question of whether a holding was justly acquired requires looking to the past. Does the person have a natural talent or ability? A libertarian would say that income or wealth acquired as a result of a natural talent is justly held and deserved in that sense. If the wealth is justly held, it may be voluntarily exchanged for other goods.[12] Thus, if a person has perfect pitch and becomes a famous and wealthy opera singer, the holdings she has as a result are justly held and she may exchange them for other goods and services, e.g., health care. According to this view, requiring the opera singer to give up some of her wealth so that others might also receive health care is unjust. Rather, a libertarian would rely on people making charitable gifts for this purpose.

Philosopher Paul Menzel has argued that the libertarian view can be used to design an ethically sound model for unequal access to health care in a democratic society.[13] Menzel looks at individuals' willingness to pay to avoid risks of future harm (pain, suffering, disability, or early death from illness). A good example is health insurance pools in which groups of persons choose a plan to protect themselves against future risk of illness. The key to Menzel's approach is that he holds individuals to their past preferences. A person who purchased a cheap insurance policy would be deemed to give consent to forgo services not included in the plan, including services needed to treat a serious or life-threatening illness. It may seem unfortunate both that the particular illness has struck the individual and that its treatment is not covered by the plan that the individual purchased in the past, but, according to Menzel, it would not be unfair to withhold the treatment the individual now needs and wants.

At the same time, if the individual has the resources to purchase the services, the libertarian would argue that she must be allowed to do so. A person who needed an autologous bone marrow transplant for breast cancer that was not covered by her insurance plan should be able to purchase those services in the free market.

The libertarian viewpoint thus is clear about how it would allocate access to genetic technologies. Those who could afford to purchase them would receive them, and except for those who received services through charity, the rest of the population would not. The result would be a much greater degree of inequality than would result under our current system, where government programs, such as Medicare and Medicaid, and the tax deductibility of insurance premiums, subsidize health care.

A major objection to libertarian theory generally, and to Menzel's version of it in particular, is that it rests on the assumptions that individual holdings have been justly acquired and that we can distinguish those that have been so acquired from those that have not. Can we reasonably say that anyone's wealth is the result of an unbroken chain of just acquisition and transfers? If not, then perhaps some redistribution is warranted to rectify past injustices.

Unlike utilitarian and rights theories, the libertarian view also does not take into account the overall benefit of its citizens' good health to a society.[14] A healthy citizenry contributes to the general level of production and flourishing of a society; an unhealthy citizenry impedes progress. Therefore, there might be value even in a libertarian society in funding public institutions that promote good health.

One particular set of theories, called communitarianism, goes even further and emphasizes that the common good, or the good of society, takes precedence over the good of the individual. Daniel Callahan has written extensively on this topic as it relates to health care.[15] He claims that the individual only benefits when the community in which he or she lives is good (however good is defined). The primary effort should be to assure societal welfare; individuals then receive the benefit of living in a just society. Similarly, the provision of health care services should be geared toward improving or maintaining the overall health of a society, rather than ensuring that each individual's needs or wants are met. Citizens should be guaranteed a decent baseline of health care,[16] but everyone should not get whatever they need or want. Where curative treatment is not provided, an individual must receive supportive care. According to Callahan, caring is the foundation of respect for human dignity and worth and must always be provided in a just society.[17]

In regard to distributing genetic technologies, a communitarian approach would be willing to constrain individual access to the extent necessary to achieve communitarian objectives.

Thus, if it were felt that certain technologies, such as germ cell engineering, were a serious threat to the safety or stability of society, communitarians would support restrictions on the personal freedom to acquire them. On the other hand, if allowing some individuals to obtain access to certain genetic technologies, even though others could not, were believed to provide sufficient benefit to the community, there would be no communitarian objection.

Identifying and achieving communitarian objectives, however, would be difficult, and perhaps highly controversial. Would it be appropriate to require certain persons to relinquish access to life-saving gene therapy in order that the community might devote the resources to others? What about the elderly? Could we say that they "owed it" to the community to decline expensive genetic treatments so that younger people might live, or so that genetically healthier babies might be born?

Daniel Callahan has advocated just such a position. The best method of allocating access to medical technologies, in his opinion, is according to age. To cope with the scarcity of medical resources, he originally proposed that scarce medical resources be concentrated on the population below a certain age cut-off.[18] Although he never specified the precise age limit, it seemed to be around eighty years old. People over the age limit would be given access only to comfort care, not to what Callahan considered to be heroic, life-saving treatments, such as dialysis or major organ transplantation.

Callahan's proposal for age-based rationing triggered a storm of protest. Advocates for older Americans objected to singling out age as the chief characteristic that determined whether a patient would be given access to particular treatments.[19] Others criticized Callahan's approach as really a wealth-based rationing scheme in disguise, since the only elderly patients who would be denied medical services by his scheme would be those who could not afford to purchase them with their own funds.

Callahan attempted to counter this by suggesting that the government should prevent technologies for the extremely elderly from being developed in the first place, but he ran into insurmountable problems in defining which technologies the government should restrict, since virtually all technologies used in elderly patients also are employed in the treatment of younger persons whom Callahan thought were entitled to those treatments.[20]

Callahan has since switched his approach to one that does not emphasize prioritization based on age so much as on an assessment of the costs and benefits of medical technologies.[21] Moreover, he is less focused on mandatory government limits on access than on convincing people to limit voluntarily their consumption of expensive health care services, especially when these services merely prolong rather than improve the quality of life. But it is still clear that his goal is to persuade individuals to sacrifice their personal interests for the greater good of the community.

In the end, it is evident that all of these theories would tolerate a significant amount of unequal access to genetic technologies. Utilitarians and rights-based theorists such as Rawls would accept inequality on the grounds that it maximized total utility or benefitted the least well-off along with others, although Rawls might have trouble with a distribution method that limited liberty. Libertarians would sanction a free market system, or one in which individuals were held to their earlier decisions about how much to spend on health care; in either case, inequality would be rampant. Since communitarians would sacrifice the welfare of the individual for the welfare of the community, they would support an unequal system if they thought it necessary in order to promote community goals, such as containing health care spending. If we are worried about unequal access to genetic technologies, in short, we need to look beyond these theories for the reasons for our concerns.

Let us suppose, therefore, that we proceeded to allocate access to genetic technologies according to the principles that govern the current system. The result would be that many technologies would be available only to those with insurance or to those who could pay. Moreover, one whole set of technologies—genetic enhancements—would not be covered by insurance at all and would be accessible only to those individuals with the personal wealth to purchase them. What would such a society be like?

In this "postgenorevolutionary" society, those who could afford to would have their children by *in vitro* fertilization, which, as now, would not be covered by insurance. They would employ the techniques to select only superior embryos for implantation, or would manipulate the genetic characteristics of the embryos to make them free of inherited diseases. Most people would be relegated to whatever gene therapies government or private insurers chose to cover. Even these technologies would be beyond the reach of persons who could not afford to pay the corresponding deductibles and copayments. Insurers would most likely cover only relatively inexpensive therapies that were highly effective.

The one type of genetic technology that would be most likely to be widely available, even for those persons who were not insured, would be genetic screening services. Insurers and government programs would provide generous coverage of these services in the hopes that people would avail themselves of the most common techniques of gene therapy: birth control and abortion. In the face of the growing availability of genetic tests for inherited diseases, the government would come under increasing pressure not only to reject pro-life opposition to abortion, but to cover abortion generously under government health insurance programs and to provide inducements, such as tax advantages, to persons who would agree to be screened and then decline to give birth to genetically diseased children.

Genetic enhancements, meanwhile, would be available only to a narrow, wealthy segment of society. This "genobility," already privileged by its wealth, would experience an unprecedented burst of positive evolution. The privileged status of its members would become more and more unassailable, particularly if genetic enhancements were installed through germ cell manipulation and, therefore, were passed on from one generation to the next.

Widespread genetic screening, coupled with birth control and abortion, whether voluntary or under pressure, would enable people to avoid passing on genetic disorders to their offspring. But there would be little opportunity for the average person to ascend the genetic ladder. There might be some intermarriage between the genetic aristocracy and the genetic underclass, reminiscent of the "poor boy (or girl) marries rich girl (or boy)" scenario, but this is not likely to be very common. Studies show that, by and large, Americans tend to marry people very much like themselves—that is, from their own social class.[22] Occasionally an Horatio Alger story would enable a member of the genetic underclass to accumulate enough wealth to purchase the genetic means to become part of the aristocracy, but this is likely to occur even less frequently than it does now, as genetically engineered advantages enable the "genobility" to monopolize the most lucrative jobs and investment opportunities.

In short, providing access to genetic technologies according to current coverage policies would create a widening gulf between the genetically privileged and the genetic underclass. One group would be virtually free of inherited disorders, would receive powerful genetic therapies for acquired diseases, and would be engineered with superior physical and mental abilities. The other group would continue to suffer from genetic illnesses and would have to content itself with less effective, conventional medical treatments. Its members would be able to improve their mental and physical traits only through comparatively laborious traditional methods of self-improvement.

The division of society into a genetic aristocracy and a genetic underclass would have momentous consequences not only for individuals, but for democratic society as well. It would undermine the fundamental precept upon which such a society rests: the maxim of social equality. As the Declaration of Independence states: "We hold these truths to be self-evident: that all men are created equal; that they are endowed by their creator with certain inalienable rights; that among these rights are life, liberty, and the pursuit of happiness." These are more than just lofty, idealistic sentiments. They are the glue that holds our society together.

Social inequality is inherently destabilizing. As one sociologist has observed:

> Inequality in the distribution of rewards is always a potential source of political and social instability. Because upper, relatively advantaged strata are generally fewer in number than disadvantaged lower strata, the former are faced with crucial problems of social control over the latter. One way of approaching this issue is to ask not why the disprivileged often rebel against the privileged but why they do not rebel more often than they do.[23]

Obviously, people are not endowed with the same genetic traits. The Human Genome Project will have taught us this at least: that some people are healthier, prettier, craftier, stronger, or more intelligent than others, due in large part to their genetic makeup. But these differences do not make it impossible to ground society on a foundation of social equality. Western democratic societies accommodate these differences by means of a widespread belief in equality of opportunity. What matters is not that people are the same, or even that they believe that they are equal. What matters is that people believe that they have just as good an opportunity to succeed as the next person:

> Whereas most Americans are willing to tolerate sizeable inequalities in the distribution of resources, they typically insist that individuals from all backgrounds should have an equal opportunity to secure these resources.[24]

The belief in equality of opportunity performs the key function of enabling our society to remain relatively stable politically despite significant actual inequalities. As a noted political theorist, John Shaar, observes: "No policy formula is better designed to fortify the dominant institutions, values, and ends of the American social order than the formula of equality of opportunity, for it offers *everyone* a fair and equal chance to find a place within that order."[25] The lower classes accept the existing order because a sufficient number of them believe that there is equality of opportunity. In essence, equality of opportunity means that it is possible for a person, through talent and effort, to move up the social ladder.

The importance of upward mobility was recognized as far back as the ancient Greeks. In *The Republic*, for example, Plato conceptualized that society was divided into groups of "gold," "silver," and "bronze" individuals. Individuals were born into these conditions, he acknowledged, but they had to be allowed to move up or down, depending upon their abilities. Thus, bronze children of gold parents and gold children of bronze parents deserved to be given their rightful places in the hierarchy of leadership.[26]

Upward mobility provides the main evidence that equality of opportunity, in fact, exists. A belief in upward mobility also motivates members of the lower classes to produce and achieve in the hopes that they will move up on the social scale. More importantly, upward mobility is a primary stabilizing mechanism in unequal Western democratic societies:

> There is a long-standing and widespread idea that circulation of individuals and families among the different levels of an otherwise divided society acts as a kind of safety valve to keep the pressures of discontent low. Hopes among the unprivileged may then, it is assumed, be centered on personal achievement rather than on collective resistance, rebellion or revolution.[27]

Marxist scholars, for example, attribute the lack of revolutionary fervor among lower classes in

Western societies to their belief in upward mobility:

> Capitalism is taken to lose a good part of its sting in so far as wage-earning dependency is not a fixed and inherited condition. Class barriers are seen as dissolving, the more individuals can move across the face of the social structure; as the possibility of movement helps to generate personal aspirations among workers that either they, or at least their children, may be able to reach the security of supervisory, managerial or professional positions.[28]

As one famous sociologist remarked almost seventy years ago about the impact of upward mobility on the lower classes: "Instead of becoming leaders of a revolution, they are turned into protectors of social order."[29]

Upward mobility not only soothes the restlessness that inequality creates among the lower classes, but syphons off those individuals who are most accomplished and, therefore, most likely to be the instigators of unrest, reassigning them to higher status positions: "Mobility provides an escape route for large numbers of the most able and ambitious members of the underclass, thereby easing some of the tensions generated by inequality."[30] Even if individuals come to realize that they are destined to remain at a fixed social level or, even worse, to move down, equality of opportunity can continue to tranquilize them by holding out the possibility that the pattern will be reversed in their children.[31]

A genetically stratified society such as we envision would challenge the concept of social equality in three fundamental ways. By enabling a genetic aristocracy to achieve greater genetic health and talent than those who do not have access to genetic technologies, genetic stratification would substantially increase actual inequality. By allowing the members of this aristocracy to manipulate their genetic endowment and possibly even to pass genetic advantages on to succeeding generations, it would undermine the belief in equality of opportunity. Finally, stratification would freeze up the crucial safety valve of

upward social mobility. The genobility would monopolize desirable occupations and fill higher status social roles. Members of the lower classes no longer would be able to count on traditional methods of advancement, such as education and intermarriage, to improve their status.

If the reduction in upward mobility were substantial enough, the lower classes, who could not afford to better themselves genetically, would remain locked into their genetic class. With genetic superiority predisposing individuals to social and economic success, and this success in turn permitting families to preserve their genetic advantages, membership in the upper classes would be genetically preordained by virtue of the genetic opportunities given to offspring by their parents. Membership in different genetic classes would become a matter of inheritance.

Inherited, largely fixed social status is no stranger to the human condition. In feudal Europe, individuals were born into their classes and, with rare exceptions in which peasants were able to obtain education in religious institutions or became apprenticed and eventually squired to knights, they stayed there. In slave-owning societies, people were born into bondage, although they could be freed at the pleasure of their masters. Perhaps the most immutable type of social strata is represented by caste systems, such as those of traditional India.

Static social strata may be compatible with some forms of human society, but they are not compatible with that type of society known as Western democracy. The demise of feudalism, slavery, and the caste system is generally believed to have been indispensable to the rise and survival of democratic systems.

Genetic social stratification, then, clearly threatens democracy, but it is not clear how seriously. Perhaps society will adapt to the social artifacts of the genetic revolution and the result, while markedly different from present arrangements, will be relatively stable. The planetary motto of Aldous Huxley's *Brave New World,* in which scientists produced large numbers of standardized individuals, was "Community, Identity,

Stability." As one of Huxley's characters observed: "You really know where you are."

In one vision of our future, for example, the genetic underclass might cede power to their genetic superiors in return for enjoying the material benefits made possible by genetic advances. The underclass would accept the division between social strata, and be content with being upwardly mobile only within the confines of their own class. The genobility, in turn, would rule according to enlightened principles of noblesse oblige, being careful to permit sufficient benefits to trickle down so that political and social equilibrium was maintained. A democracy of sorts might even persist, with the underclass electing representatives who either belonged to the upper class or who were committed to preserving its privileges. Such a system might not look very different from our own, given the extent to which we increasingly elect representatives who are considerably more privileged than their constituents.

Such a system seems highly unstable, however. For one thing, the members of the upper class would need great self-control to avoid overreaching. At a minimum, they would need to maintain effective means of monitoring and regulating the behavior of their peers to prevent antisocial excesses of greed. Even so, the media—assuming it remained free—could be counted upon to glamorize the lifestyles of the genetically rich and famous in graphic contrast to the more mundane existences of the underclass. The fact that genetically superior persons owed their advantages to accidents of birth or to their starting positions of wealth would reduce the admiration that the underclass might feel for them, while leaving unchanged, or perhaps increasing, underclass admiration for those who had gained their privileged status through hard work or the development of great skill.

Such a system would be vulnerable to demagogues who came to power by promising to redistribute genetic endowments more evenly. Assuming that the principle of one-person/one-vote persisted, a numerically inferior genetic upper class could be out-voted by the underclass. Congress could become dominated by elected officials pledged to employ the full force of government to rectify genetic imbalances.

The genobility would respond with reprisals in an effort to preserve its privileged status. These could range from threats to withhold the fruits of genetic medicine from nonprivileged segments of society to overt interference with the democratic process. At the least, the genetic upper class is liable to have amassed sufficient wealth and influence to enable it to control the media, which would permit it to affect the outcome of elections in a manner quite out of proportion to its numbers. Efforts by the underclass to preserve its majoritarian hegemony may prove no more successful than have current efforts to reform campaign financing in order to dilute the power of special interests.

The end result might be an era of social chaos as the system swung in ever-widening arcs between rule by underclass demagogues and domination by the genetic aristocracy. This could degenerate into mob rule and anarchy. To rid itself of its status as the class of the genetically disadvantaged, the mob might even destroy the scientific foundations of the genetic revolution, perhaps by physically dismantling research centers and erasing mapping and sequencing data.

From our current vantage point, the exact nature of postgenorevolutionary society is obscure. Alternatively, postgenorevolutionary society could devolve into totalitarian rule by a genetic autocracy. The genetic upper class would employ whatever repressive techniques were needed in order to obtain power and keep the underclass in check. Given the advances in genetic science that would have made genetic class distinctions so marked, techniques might even be developed to manipulate the underclass genetically to make it more docile.

What is clear is that the genetic technologies of the future come with a curse. They promise great advances in our ability to forecast and forestall disease and to improve the capabilities of the human species. But, judging from the increasing scarcity of resources and the dislocations that are likely to result from distributing genetic technologies according to current allocation principles, genetic technologies represent a serious and fundamental threat to our social and political system. Rather than blessing us with unprecedented social progress, the genetic revolution may plunge us into a new Dark Age.

But perhaps we are going too far. This bleak future arguably is only one of a number of possible alternatives. Many people may dismiss our warning that the development of genetic technologies could provoke the decline of democratic civilization. This is nothing more, they may say, than the equivalent of Chicken Little alarming the barnyard due to a genetic acorn.

The introduction of these technologies will be so distant and so gradual, some may chide, that society will have a chance to adjust to them naturally without cataclysm. Given enough time, the means of coping with these advances will evolve within our democratic institutions, just as these institutions have adjusted to other profound technological changes, such as the advent of electronic media, nuclear weapons, and the computer. The postgenetic social and political system may look different, we may be told, but it will retain the tell-tale characteristics that make a relatively stable, free society possible.

The problem with this viewpoint is that it ignores the degree to which genetic advances, if distributed along current lines, will alter the fundamental assumptions that underlie democratic society. There has never been a challenge to the principle of equal opportunity as powerful as the threat posed by these technologies, with the possible, hardly democratic, exception of slavery.

Another more rosy view of the future rejects the assumption that access to genetic technologies will be confined only to those who can afford to pay for them. For one thing, genetic technologies may not be as costly as we predict. Genetic technologies may become so inexpensive, both in an absolute sense and in comparison with the costs of providing conventional medical care, that

we will be able to generate enough savings to provide genetic services to everyone. But the fact remains that, when they are first introduced, genetic technologies, like most new medical services, are likely to be very expensive. Moreover, even if the price of a genetic technology decreases over time, the total cost is likely to increase as the usefulness of the technology spreads to broader numbers of patients.

A related viewpoint is that we may save so much money by preventing certain genetic disorders that we will have the resources to provide genetic technologies to everyone. This argument is a familiar one in terms of reducing health care spending. If we immunized enough people, or detected enough cancers early enough that they can still be treated, or stopped enough people from smoking, we are told, we would be able to redirect our health care expenditures so that we can provide such expensive services as hospitalization, surgery, and life-saving drugs to everyone who needs them.[32] Similarly, if we prevented people from dying from fatal or life-threatening genetic disorders, such as cystic fibrosis or inherited forms of cancer, we would save enough money so that we could provide genetic technologies to everyone.

The problem is that, surprising as it may sound, it simply is not clear that preventing illness saves money. No doubt it may reduce the costs of acute care in the short run, but in the long run, the people who would have died from acute ailments would go on to live longer and to contract the expensive, chronic illnesses of old age. For example, an article on the costs of cigarette smoking in the *Journal of the American Medical Association* found that, while every pack of cigarettes smoked increased health care costs by thirty-eight cents, it saved $1.82 in pension costs.[33] An earlier British study found that a 40 percent reduction in smoking would save that country sixteen million pounds in the first ten years, but would cost a net thirteen million pounds after thirty years due to the additional costs of social security payments.[34] Similarly, physicians studying prenatal care programs for low-income women have found no conclusive evidence that these programs save money.[35] This is not to say that we should not prevent disease when we can, but only that there may be better arguments for doing so than reducing long-term health care costs.

The final objection to a doomsday scenario is that, even if genetic technologies were tremendously expensive, and regardless of how much money we were already spending on health care, the government would do whatever was necessary to make genetic technologies available to everyone. This was essentially society's solution to the shortage of kidney dialysis machines in the late 1960s.[36] Congress included patients suffering from end-stage kidney disease within the Medicare program even if they were under the age of sixty-five or not otherwise eligible and mandated that dialysis was a covered service under Medicare. While a number of health policy analysts criticize this program because of its cost and because dialysis is not a cure and does not permit patients to enjoy a completely normal lifestyle,[37] others commend the program for saving lives and reflecting a societal commitment to the ill.

This same approach of including genetic technologies under Medicare, and extending eligibility to persons regardless of their age, could be employed in regard to genetic services. Or, in the event Congress enacted a national health care reform program that guaranteed universal coverage, it could include genetic services within the congressionally mandated basic benefits package.[38] If everyone received access to important genetic benefits, the adverse social effects of genetic stratification might be avoided. The only technologies that might be excluded from coverage due to cost would be those that were expected to yield only trivial benefits.

What technologies might be regarded as trivial? They might include genetic tests to detect disorders that could not be treated, or to identify extremely low probabilities that persons being tested would suffer from inherited disorders in the future, or that predicted the susceptibility to relatively minor ailments. Trivial genetic therapies might be those that treated or prevented minor disorders, or disorders in patients with no hope of long-term survival, or with severely compromised qualities of life, such as patients in persistent vegetative states or anencephalic newborns. In terms of genetic enhancements, perhaps those that altered relatively insignificant aspects of physical appearance, such as eye or hair color, might be denied.

However, this assumes that we could define which benefits were trivial. What might be trivial to one person might be important or even critical to another, or at least significant enough that, in order to get it, the individual would be willing to trade off something that others would regard as more desirable. At least, this is the basic assumption behind the well-entrenched ethical and legal doctrine of informed consent, which requires that a physician allow a patient to decide which medical interventions he or she will accept, based on the patient's own assessment of the relative importance of different sets of risks and benefits.[39] To avoid making blanket prioritization decisions that potentially could waste resources by providing certain genetic technologies to people who did not value them highly, we instead might have to establish limits on the amount that individuals could spend on genetic technologies—a sort of voucher system—and then permit them to make their own selections.

The notion that important genetic technologies can be provided to everyone is unrealistic, however. It is naive to expect that the price of genetic technologies will drop to such an extent, or that the societal savings from their use will be so great, or that voters will be willing to commit sufficient funds, that we will be able to provide everyone with everything that they deem important. The contrasting precedent of the end-stage renal disease program discussed earlier may turn out to be an historical anomaly. After all, that program sprung from a fortuitous combination of technological break-throughs, media attention, clever lobbying in Congress, and the unique cultural context of the sixties.[40] It is unlikely that similar circumstances would coincide in the case of future genetic technologies.

Moreover, there simply is no precedent for providing people with widespread access to genetic enhancements. The closest nonmedical analogy might be public education, where there seems to be a societal commitment to providing at least a basic level of education to everyone regardless of ability to pay. But even here, families that can afford the expense can send their children to superior private schools; the right to education does not entail the right to an equal education.

Perhaps, in order to refute the genetic doomsday scenario, one need not assume that everyone will have access to the genetic technologies that they desire. The division in society between the genetic have's and have not's may be far less clear-cut than has been suggested. Instead of a two-tiered society comprised of a genetic upper class and an underclass, a complex arrangement is likely to develop in which a large genetic middle class acts as a buffer and stabilizer between the upper and lower classes.

One way this might occur would be if sufficient genetic benefits were distributed to the middle class to persuade it to support a system that denied many genetic technologies to the underclass. A prime vehicle for making some genetic technologies available to the middle class but not to the underclass would be through employment benefits, in much the same way that the middle class now obtains health insurance. However, employers are likely to provide access to genetic technologies only in ways that benefit the firm. For example, they are likely to focus on providing access to technologies that increase employee productivity. Employers also would favor approaches that tended to increase employee loyalty. For example, they would be unlikely to provide younger employees with access to germ cell manipulations, which would automatically confer genetic benefits on subsequent generations, even if the employees left the company. Rational employers would prefer genetic interventions that required periodic renewal, such as the early aerosol gene therapy for cystic fibrosis that had to be repeated periodically to maintain its therapeutic efficacy. This way, the employer could hold the threat of losing the genetic benefit over the employee's head. Employees would end up being indentured to their firms in a genetic counterpart to the job-lock created by the threat of losing health insurance or coverage for preexisting conditions. It is unlikely that unions would be any more successful in regulating these employer practices than they are now at preventing the loss of health insurance if an employee leaves the company.

Even if a genetic middle class arose between the upper and lower classes, it is unclear that such a society would be able to forestall the socially destructive consequences of selective access to genetic technologies. We have assumed that the middle class would be co-opted by the genetic upper class. But it also potentially might ally with the underclass to force the upper class to disgorge more of its genetic privileges. The result could be a genetic tug-of-war that constantly threatened to degenerate into class warfare. Perpetuating such a system would take a deft hand at the controls of the mechanisms for allocating access to genetic technologies. The upper class might find it simpler to forestall an alliance between the middle and lower classes by resorting to undemocratic political means. Or the middle class might simply decide to supplant the upper class and attempt to gain genetic ascendancy for itself.

The point is that it cannot be assumed that society somehow *automatically* will figure out how to allocate access to genetic technologies in such a way that the socially disruptive scenarios we have envisioned will be avoided, much less that the net effect of the development of genetic technologies will be socially beneficial. Instead, we need to investigate whether there are any steps that might be taken to minimize the chances that the Human Genome Project will be socially disruptive. Rather than leaving the genetic future to the unplanned interaction of social forces, we need to use the political process to increase the chances that our genetic future will be democratic and harmonious.

References and Notes

1. See Richard A. Epstein, *Why Is Health Care Special?*, 40 U. Kan L. Rev. 307 (1993).

2. Sally Lehrman, "Doctors Challenge Child Growth Hormone Tests," *The Phoenix Gazette*, 31 May 1993, p. 10B; Shari Roan, "Growth Drug Debate: What Is Too Short?" *Los Angeles Times*, 2 February 1993, p. 1E.

3. William Saffire, "Of I.Q. and Genes," *New York Times*, 20 October 1994, p. 27A; Ralph Heimer, "Smart Genes?" *New York Times*, 25 December 1994, p. 8; Myron A. Hofer, "Behind the Curve," *New York Times*, 26 December 1994, p. 39.

4. Norman Daniels, *Just Health Care* (Cambridge: Cambridge University Press, 1985).

5. Allen Buchanan, "The Right to a Decent Minimum of Health Care," in *Securing Access to Health Care*, ed. President's Commission for the Study of Ethical Problems in Medicine and Biomedical and Behavioral Research (Washington, D.C.: U.S. Government Printing Office, 1983), 207–238.

6. Ibid., 216.

7. See, for example, Gerald R. Winslow, *Triage and Justice* (Berkeley: University of California Press, 1982), 63–86.

8. John Rawls, *A Theory of Justice* (Cambridge: Harvard University Press, 1971).

9. Ibid., 60.

10. See, for example, Thomas C. Shevory, *Applying Rawls to Medical Cases: An Investigation into the Usages of Analytical Philosophy*, 11 J. Health Pol., Pol'y & L. 749 (1986).

11. Larry R. Churchill, *Rationing Health Care in America: Perceptions and Principles of Justice* (Notre Dame, Indiana: University of Notre Dame Press, 1987), 49.

12. Robert Nozick, *Anarchy, State, and Utopia* (New York: Basic Books, 1974).

13. Paul T. Menzel, *Strong Medicine: The Ethical Rationing of Health Care* (New York: Oxford University Press, 1990).

14. Charles J. Dougherty, *American Health Care: Realities, Rights, & Reforms* (New York: Oxford University Press, 1988), 86.

15. Daniel Callahan, *What Kind of Life: The Limits of Medical Progress* (New York: Simon and Schuster, 1990); Daniel Callahan, *Settings Limits: Medical Goals in an Aging Society* (New York: Simon and Schuster, 1987).

16. Callahan, *What Kind of Life*, 255.

17. Ibid., 143–49.

18. Callahan, *Setting Limits*.

19. Robert H. Binstock and Stephen G. Post, *Too Old For Health Care? Controversies in Need, Law, Economics & Ethics* (Baltimore, Maryland: Johns Hopkins University Press, 1991); William J. Bricknell, "Set No Limits: A Rebuttal to Daniel Callahan's Proposal to Limit Health Care for the Elderly," *Journal of the American Medical Association* 269 (1993): 2148.

20. Maxwell J. Mehlman, *Age-Based Rationing and Technological Development*, 33 St. Louis U. L. Rev. 671 (1989).

21. Callahan, *What Kind of Life*.

22. Jane E. Brody, "Making It Work When Opposites Attract," *New York Times*, 23 November 1994, p. 7C.

23. Frank Parkin, *Class Inequality and Political Order: Social Stratification in Capitalist and Communist Societies* (New York: Praeger, 1971), 48.

24. David B. Grusky and Azumi Ann Takata, "Social Stratification," in *Encyclopedia of Sociology*, ed. Edgar F. Borgatta and Marie L. Borgatta (New York: Macmillan, 1992).

25. John H. Schaar, *Legitimacy in the Modern State* (New Brunswick, New Jersey: Transaction Books, 1981), 195 (emphasis added).

26. Plato, *The Republic*, trans. and ed. H.D.P. Lee (Harmondsworth, England: Penguin, 1955).

27. Ibid., 285.

28. Ibid., 280.

29. Pitirim A. Sorokin, *Social Mobility* (New York: Harper, 1927), 533.

30. Parkin, *Class Inequality*, 50.

31. Ibid., 57.

32. Joseph A. Califano, Jr., *Radical Surgery: What's Next for America's Health Care* (New York: Times Books, 1995); Willard Gaylin, "Faulty Diagnosis," *New York Times*, 12 June 1994, p. 4A.

33. Willard G. Manning, et al., "The Taxes of Sin: Do Smokers and Drinkers Pay Their Way?" *Journal of the American Medical Association* 261 (1989): 1604.

34. Howard Leichter, "Public Policy and the British Experience," *Hastings Center Report*, (October 1982): 32.

35. Frederick A. Connell and Jane Huntington, "For Every Dollar Spent—The Cost-Savings Argument for Prenatal Care," *New England Journal of Medicine* 331 (1994): 1303–1307.

36. See Chapter Five.

37. See Callahan, *Setting Limits*.

38. See discussion of coverage of genetic services under national health reform in Chapter Five.

39. Maxwell J. Mehlman, *The Patient-Physician Relationship in an Era of Scarce Resources: Is There a Duty to Treat?* 25 Conn. L. Rev. 349 (1993).

40. For a description of the interplay of these factors, see Richard Rettig, *The Policy Debate on Patient Care Financing for Victims of End-Stage Renal Disease*, 40 Law & Contemp. Probs. 201, 202 (1976).

Research with Human Embryonic Stem Cells: Ethical Considerations

GERON ETHICS ADVISORY BOARD:

*Karen Lebacqz (chair), Michael M. Mendiola,
Ted Peters, Ernlé W. D. Young, Laurie Zoloth-Dorfman*

On 5 November 1998 Geron Corporation announced that scientists working in collaboration with Geron had succeeded in establishing cell culture lines of human embryonic stem (hES) cells. Because these cells are considered pluripotent (capable of being the precursors to a variety of human cell types) and immortal (sustainable in culture and reproducing themselves indefinitely), they represent a major breakthrough in scientific research, with potential for significant advances in tissue transplantation, pharmaceutical testing, and embryology.

Prior to the November announcement, the Geron Ethics Advisory Board developed "A Statement on Human Embryonic Stem Cells"[1] as a set of guidelines for hES research. This essay provides an expansion and elaboration of the particular warrants and moral reasoning for that statement.

The EAB did not offer a *carte blanche* approval of research on hES cells undertaken by Geron or any other entity. The board unanimously affirmed that such research can be undertaken ethically, contingent upon meeting a range of qualifying conditions. The initial work of the board has been to specify such conditions; its continued work will consist of assessing Geron's developing research in light of them. Hence here we also include some preliminary reflections on ethical issues in human embryonic germ cell (hEG) research.

Moreover, the EAB perceived the need for and urged continued public discussion of the complex ethical issues emerging from such research. Thus the statement and this companion essay should be seen not only as an initial clarification of the EAB's own position, but also as an effort to contribute to and invite that

From *Hastings Center Report* 29: 31–36, 1999.

public discourse. We enumerate some specific questions for further reflection at the end of this essay.

1. "THE BLASTOCYST MUST BE TREATED WITH THE RESPECT APPROPRIATE TO EARLY HUMAN EMBRYONIC TISSUE."

The creation of hES cells involves isolation of cells from the blastocyst.[2] The blastocyst consists of an outer cellular layer, which would develop as the placenta, and an inner cell mass, which would develop as the body of the fetus. The outer layer is dissolved and the resulting mass of cells is used for research. Thus a central ethical issue is the moral status of the blastocyst.

To raise the matter of "moral status" is to ask, Does a given entity possess the requisite qualities or characteristics that entitle it to moral consideration and concern? "Moral status" thus functions as a threshold idea: entities with moral status should be treated in a manner differently from entities without that status. The EAB affirms that the blastocyst has moral status and hence should be treated with respect.[3]

What sort of moral status does the blastocyst have? This question has riveted political, religious, and ethical attention, and profound and substantial disagreement is based not only on contending biological interpretations but also on deeply held philosophical and theological considerations. Some have argued for conception as the relevant consideration, others for the development of the "primitive streak" (the precursor to the spinal cord of an individual fetus) as a defining moment, and some for utilizing implantation as the crucial threshold for moral status.[4]

Reviewing the complex literature on this topic, Ted Peters, following Daniel Callahan, distinguishes three basic schools of thought.[5] The *genetic school* locates the beginning of human personhood, and thus claims of moral status and dignity, at the genetic beginning—that is, at conception, at the point where one's individual genome is set. Here, a criterion for moral status

(human genetic heritage) is linked to a particular point in human life (conception). The *developmental school*, while granting that human life begins at conception, holds equally that human *personhood*—and hence full moral status—is a later development. Here, moral status is understood developmentally: as the conceptus develops from blastocyst to fetus and beyond so too does moral status grow (although proponents differ on when exactly the threshold of moral status is reached). The *social consequences school* shares with the developmental school the belief that human personhood is a process and an achievement over time. Advocates deny, however, that personhood is achieved at any particular moment. Rather, "personhood" is a matter of definition rather than biological fact, based on socially constructed norms.

In its work, the National Institutes of Health Human Embryo Research Panel focused less on the time when moral status might be acquired and more on the *criteria* for its determination. The panel noted two broad approaches in the debates: one proposes a single criterion a constitutive of moral personhood, while a second, "pluralistic," approach emphasizes a number of different, interacting criteria. As the panel noted

> Among the qualities considered under a pluralistic approach are those mentioned in single-criterion on views: genetic uniqueness, potentiality for development, sentience, brain activity, and degree of cognitive development. Other qualities often mentioned are human form, capacity for survival outside the mother's womb, and degree of relational presence (whether to the mother herself or to others). Although none of these qualities is by itself sufficient to establish personhood, their developing presence in an entity increases its moral status until, at some point, full and equal protectability is required.[6]

The panel proposed the pluralistic approach as the more adequate of the two, with moral status (and hence protectability) understood developmentally, culminating at birth in full and equal personhood.[7]

Drawing upon this wealth of philosophical and theological reflection and situating ourselves relative to it, the EAB affirmed our understanding of moral status as developmental and consonant with the pluralistic approach. This developmental view is in accord with Jewish tradition,[8] with the views of many Roman Catholics[9] (although not the Vatican), and with the majority of Protestant traditions as well as with legal traditions that provide different protections at different stages of fetal development.

We hold that a fundamental principle of respect for human life applies at all stages of human development. The developmental view that we affirm does not mean that the principle of respect can be ignored; it means that the principle requires different considerations and entails different obligations at different developmental stages. For example, Lisa Sowle Cahill argues that "Few doubt that there exists from conception some form of 'human life' in the literal sense; the crucial question is whether from conception or at any subsequent time during pregnancy that life deserves the same respect and protection due an infant."[10] Once there is evidence of capacity for sensation, for example, respect requires minimization of pain. In this very early embryonic tissue there is no capacity for sensation; thus minimization of pain does not apply. Rather, early embryonic tissue is respected by ensuring that it is used with care only in research that incorporates substantive values such as reduction of human suffering.[11] We believe that the purposes of the hES research—its potential to contribute to fundamental knowledge of human development and to medical and pharmaceutical interventions to alleviate suffering—provide such substantive values.

A second source of cells is human embryonic germ (hEG) cells derived from gamete ridge tissue removed from early fetal tissue following elective abortion. These cells have been cultured using similar but not identical methods as are used for the hES cells, and may have both properties of pluripotency and immortality. However, this research raises ethical questions distinct from those in the use of the early blastocyst. The tissue is taken (much as cadaver organs might be taken) from an aborted fetus within the first eight weeks after conception. At stake in this debate is whether licit use can be made of tissue collected after abortion in a society in which the act of abortion is seen by some as murderous and by others (and by law) as acceptable.

The EAB cannot resolve the contentious abortion debate. We are developing guidelines for hEG research. Preliminary reflections suggest at least the following concerns: First, all agree that the demise of the fetus is not caused by the research procedures. Second, the moral obligation to save life may be a sufficiently strong warrant to justify certain uses of the tissue of the dead and hence to support such research. Third, the tissue of the dead must be used with respect. Respect for tissue taken from a dead fetus would take into account the need for closure, grief, and ritual that families might have in these cases. Respect would include the confidential and dignified handling of the tissue when collected and used. Finally, issues of informed consent would apply with the same stringency required in the case of hES research.

2. "WOMEN/COUPLES DONATING BLASTOCYSTS PRODUCED IN THE PROCESS OF IN VITRO FERTILIZATION MUST GIVE FULL AND INFORMED CONSENT FOR THE USE OF THE BLASTOCYSTS IN RESEARCH AND IN THE DEVELOPMENT OF CELL LINES FROM THAT TISSUE."

Human embryonic stem cells are derived from embryos produced for clinical purposes and then donated for research purposes. Hence of crucial ethical significance is the character and quality of the consent given by women and couples to such donation. As with the issue of moral status, the ethical and legal literature on consent and refusal is voluminous.[12] What is needed for valid consent to donate embryonic tissue for research purposes?

Tom Beauchamp and James Childress argue that the core meaning of informed consent is an *autonomous authorization* of a medical intervention or involvement in research. An informed consent occurs "if and only if a patient or subject, with substantial understanding and in substantial absence of control by others, intentionally authorizes a professional to do something."[13] Thus informed consent or refusal is not simply a matter of what the professional should disclose to the patient, but is a matter of ensuring that the conditions necessary for autonomous authorization are met—i.e., that consent is intentional, with substantial understanding, and without controlling influences. Authority for participation in research, expressed in an informed consent, resides with and is to be exercised by the subject.

Consent to utilize embryos for *clinical* purposes of IVF does not therefore suffice as consent for their use in research and cell-line development. Explicit consent must be elicited for such use. We concur with Arthur Caplan that "when research is the goal, whether for profit or not, those whose materials are to be used have a right to know and consent to such use."[14] Other commentators agree that fairness and respect for persons dictate that explicit information be provided to patients regarding the use of their tissues and cells, especially when those may be used for commercial purposes.[15] For these reasons, the EAB determined that women/couples donating embryos for this research should understand clearly the nature of the research and also should understand whether there are commercial implications and if so, whether they hold any proprietary rights in the tissue lines developed from embryonic cells.[16]

Moreover, we believe that the context of embryo donation within the process of IVF renders the need for careful consent even more important. The IVF process is often physically painful, emotionally burdensome, and financially costly. These factors may make IVF patients particularly vulnerable.[17] Such possible vulnerability demands careful and consistent efforts on the part of researchers not to exercise a controlling or coercive influence over these patients. A recent study of patients who consented to participate in therapeutic research found that "Physicians' recommendation were . . . powerful factors influencing patients' decisions to become research subjects."[18] Authors of the study recommended that research ethics "be enriched with a sensitivity to the profound trust participants place in researchers and the research enterprise." The context of a study regarding participation in therapeutic research is clearly different from the context of IVF embryo donation for hES cell research. In the latter context, the consent is "twice removed": women/couples are not consenting to therapeutic research, nor does the research involve their own bodies or persons. Nevertheless, even in the IVF context some measure of trust in the researchers may be involved and this possibility raises a warning regarding the ways in which trust can be manipulated to researchers' advantage, thus possibly leading to undue influence over subjects. Moreover, while this research does not involve their own bodies, it does involve entities that they may well consider as potential progeny, a factor that must be considered in this research.

Informed consent also requires "substantial understanding." Hence the EAB requires certain informational elements in the context of embryo donation for hES cell research. First, as the derived hES cells are of significant market potential, donors should understand those potential market implications. Second, they should be advised as to whether there are any proprietary rights in the tissue. The achievement of substantial understanding requires a process that builds trust over time, an admittedly difficult requirement yet one that will be critical in all stages of this research for it to be carried out ethically.[19] Adequate time for eliciting and answering donor questions is necessary, as is ensuring that donors are genuinely free to refuse as well as to consent.

In the course of our deliberations, we reviewed an exemplary form used in soliciting consent for embryo donation for research.[20] This form states explicitly: "cells that may be derived from embryos donated for this research could have clinical and commercial value in the event that the study is successful." It further specifies:

> This research will not benefit your clinical care, and you will not benefit financially from it. The physicians/clinicians involved in your care will not benefit financially from this study. The investigators conducting this study could benefit financially from clinical or commercial values that may result from it. The cells derived in this study may be shared with Geron Corporation, located in Menlo Park, CA, as part of the study. Geron Corporation may benefit financially from the development and clinical use of the cells derived in this study.

Such explicit statements embody well the kinds of financial disclosure that a consent form should contain.

3. "The hES Research will not Involve Any Cloning for Purposes of Human Reproduction, Any Transfer to a Uterus, or Any Creation of Human Chimeras or Human-Animal Hybrids."

Corporate representatives have stated clearly to the EAB that human reproduction was not a goal, purpose, or intent of Geron's research on hES (and hEG) cells. Any effort to produce a living being out of this research would raise a host of ethical issues, in particular the risk of harms to potential offspring,[21] to parenting women and couples, and to the human community itself through genetic manipulation and transmission. Because Geron is not engaged in these activities, and has made clear its intention not to do so, the EAB did not take them up for extended assessment in its deliberations. Should Geron consider initiating any such activities, the EAB will undertake the necessary ethical analysis.

4. "Acquisition and Development of the Feeder Layer Necessary for the Growth of hES Cells in Vitro Must not Violate Accepted Norms for Human or Animal Research."

To keep hES cells in an undifferentiated state, they are cultured and maintained on layers of nutrients called "feeder layers." Currently, irradiated mouse embryonic fibroblast feeder layers are utilized, but it is possible that other tissues would be used in the future. The acquisition and development of the feeder layers must be in accord with norms for research appropriate to the source from which the feeder layers are drawn.[22]

Geron's use of mouse embryonic cells would seem to fall well within a judgment of ethical use of animal tissue. The research holds great potential therapeutic value. In addition, mouse embryos fall below the threshold of sentience (the ability to experience pain) or of other capacities of organic animal being and activity. Nevertheless, we mandate continued attention to animal welfare.

5. "All Such Research Must be Done in a Context of Concern for Global Justice."

One of the primary justifications of hES research is beneficence based: its therapeutic potential to alleviate human suffering and to promote the health and well-being of human populations. However, to justify a practice on the basis of its benefits makes moral sense only if people in need actually have access to those benefits. Hence the justification gains credibility only when it is wedded to a commitment to justice, rooted in "a recognition of our sociality and mutual vulnerability to disease and death."[23] *The EAB considers concerns about social justice in public health to be of overriding importance.* Thus in the EAB's judgment, it is morally paramount that research development include attention to the global distribution of and access to these therapeutic interventions.

Two features of Geron's research render this commitment to just access particularly challenging. First, the research is undertaken in the private sector—in the context of market forces, patenting of products, interests of shareholders and investors, and a consideration of profit. These varied interests may compete with—but should not override—a concern for equitable access.[24] Second, the research is highly technological and expensive, as well as under the proprietary rights of a U.S. company. How to ensure adequate access for insured, underinsured, and noninsured patients in the United States, let alone on a global basis, will be an ethically and financially challenging task. The EAB will continue to work with Geron on these matters.

6. "ALL SUCH RESEARCH SHOULD BE APPROVED BY AN INDEPENDENT ETHICS ADVISORY BOARD IN ADDITION TO AN INSTITUTIONAL REVIEW BOARD."

At its own initiative, Geron established the EAB. Given the kinds of ethical issues already emerging from hES research and those yet to come, the EAB reaffirmed the necessity of an independent board for ethical analysis and consultation. In addition, the research undertaken should receive IRB review and approval in order to protect subjects involved.

ISSUES REQUIRING FURTHER DELIBERATION

As indicated above, the EAB wishes to generate public discourse on a wide range of issues related to emerging research arenas. Among those are some that surfaced during our discussions but are not reviewed in this essay:

1. Who should exercise control over the disposition of fetal or embryo tissue? In our discussion of consent, we refer to both "women" and "couples." The appropriate locus of consent/refusal may be disputed.

2. What is the proper relationship of ethicists to proprietary companies? Who should constitute an ethics board, and who should serve on it? Under what conditions (e.g., remuneration, stock options, etc.)?[25]

3. As noted above, how can difficult issues of global justice and fair distribution be handled in research involving private enterprise?

4. What is the role of consensus in a society that is both pluralistic and often deeply divided over appropriate norms? How can we develop appropriate language for public debate and decisionmaking while remaining respectful of differences and accountable to substantive moral disagreements?[26]

References and Notes

1. The statement was drafted in September 1998 by Karen Lebacqz, revised by the EAB, and was finalized on 20 October 1998.

2. The blastocyst is approximately 140 cells, fourteen days post-conception.

3. Michael M. Mendiola, "Some Background Thoughts on the Concept of 'Moral Status' Relative to the Early Embryo." Background paper for the EAB.

4. Jacques Cohen and Robert Lee Hotz, "Toward Policies Regarding Assisted Reproductive Technologies," in *Setting Allocation Priorities: Genetic and Reproductive Technologies*, ed. Robert H. Blank and Andrea Bonnicksen (New York: Columbia University Press, 1992), pp. 228–29.

5. Ted Peters, *For the Love of Children* (Louisville, KY: Westminster/John Knox Press, 1996), pp. 96–100.

6. National Institutes of Health, *Report of the Human Embryo Research Panel* (Bethesda, Md.: National Institutes of Health, 1994), p. 49. Mary Anne Warren offers a critique similar in structure, arguing for a "multi-criterial" view of moral status, instead of "uni-criterial" approaches. Mary Anne Warren, *Moral Status: Obligations to Persons and Other Living Things* (Oxford: Clarendon Press, 1997).

7. National Institutes of Health, *Report of the Human Embryo Research Panel*, pp. 49–51. Cohen and Holtz echo this position: "New life does not appear suddenly; it is created gradually, with each new phase differing

from that which preceded it." Cohen and Holtz, "Toward Policies Regarding Assisted Reproductive Technologies," p. 230.

8. Laurie Zoloth-Dorfman, "The Ethics of the Eighth Day: Jewish Bioethics and Genetic Medicine," Background paper for the EAB.

9. See, for example, Thomas A. Shannon and Allan B. Wolter, "Reflections on the Moral Status of the Pre-Embryo," *Theological Studies* 51 (1990): 603–626.

10. Lisa Sowle Cahill, "Abortion," in *The Westminster Dictionary of Christian Ethics*, ed. James F. Childress and John Macquarrie (Philadelphia: The Westminster Press, 1986), p. 3.

11. Ernlé W. D. Young, "The Moral Status of Human Embryonic Tissue." Background paper for the EAB. The EAB holds that "substantive" values are those supported by prima facie moral duties such as nonmaleficence.

12. See Ruth R. Faden and Tom L. Beauchamp, *A History and Theory of Informed Consent* (New York: Oxford University Press, 1986), for a good overview of the historical development and philosophical treatment of informed consent in the clinical and research contexts.

13. Tom L. Beauchamp and James F. Childress, *Principles of Biomedical Ethics*, 4th ed. (New York: Oxford University Press, 1994), p. 143.

14. Arthur L. Caplan, "Blood, Sweat, Tears and Profits: The Ethics of the Sale and Use of Patient Derived Materials in Biomedicine," *Clinical Research* 33, no. 4 (1985): 448–51, at 451.

15. See, for example, George J. Annas, "Outrageous Fortune: Selling Other People's Cells," *Hastings Center Report* 20, no. 6 (1990): 36–39; also George J. Annas, "Whose Waste Is It Anyway? The Case of John Moore," *Hastings Center Report* 18, no. 5 (1988): 37–39.

16. The most celebrated legal case dealing with the issue of use of tissue without consent is that of Moore v. Regents of the University of California (51 Cal 3rd 120, 1990). For an extended discussion, see E. Richard Gold, *Body Parts: Property Rights and the Ownership of Human Biological Materials* (Washington, D.C.: Georgetown University Press, 1996).

17. Judith Lorber has argued that IVF may also involve a coercive element for women when undertaken to treat male infertility. Such women may have to strike a "patriarchal bargain" to maintain a relationship and have a child within the constraints of monogamy, the nuclear family, and the valorization of biological parenthood. Judith Lorber, "Choice, Gift, or Patriarchal Bargain? Women's Consent to In Vitro Fertilization in Male Fertility," in *Feminist Perspectives in Medical Ethics*, ed. Helen Bequaert Holmes and Laura M. Purdy (Bloomington: Indiana University press, 1992), pp. 169–80.

18. Nancy E. Kass, Jeremy Sugarman, Ruth Faden, Monica Schoch-Spana, "Trust: The Fragile Foundation of Contemporary Biomedical Research," *Hastings Center Report* 26, no. 5 (1996): 25–34, at 26.

19. Mark G. Kuczewski, "Reconceiving the Family: The Process of Consent in Medical Decisionmaking," *Hastings Center Report* 26, no. 2 (1996): 30–37, at 32.

20. The form was developed by Roger Pedersen, Ph.D., of the Department of Obstetrics, Gynecology and Reproductive Sciences, University of California, San Francisco, and is used with permission.

21. It is for this reason that the NIH Human Embryo Research Panel distinguished between research on embryos intended for and not intended for transfer. Research on the former must include consideration of potential harms to the future child—a concern not raised by the latter. (National Institutes of Health, *Report of the Human Embryo Research Panel*, pp. 51–52.) It should also be noted that hES cells are derived cells and are not the cellular equivalent of an intact embryo. Even if transferred, hES cells would not form an embryo because they lack other cells necessary for implantation and embryogenesis.

22. The current usage of mouse embryo cells raises ethical concerns about the use of animals in hES research. A number of criteria have been proposed to weigh ethical versus unethical uses of animals in biomedical research. However, as Strachan Donnelley notes, no single, unambiguous standard or guideline exists for assessing each and every use of animals in science. Ethical attention must be directed to the specific purposes, types, and contexts of animal use. See Strachan Donnelley and Kathleen Nolan, eds., "Animals, Science, and Ethics" [Special Supplement], *Hastings Center Report* 20, no. 3 (1990), pp. S11–S12.

23. Larry R. Churchill, *Rationing Health Care in America: Perceptions and Principles of Justice* (Notre Dame: University of Notre Dame Press, 1987), p. 135.

24. Zoloth-Dorfman, "The Ethics of the Eighth Day."

25. Members of the EAB receive a very modest honorarium for the time spent in scheduled meetings with

Geron staff and officers. We are not compensated for time spent in research, writing, or other conversations with Geron, nor does any of us hold any stock in the corporation.

26. See, for example, Alta Charo, "The Hunting of the Snark: The Moral Status of Embryos, RighttoLifers, and Third World Women," *Stanford Law and Policy Review* 6, no. 2 (1995): 11–38.

✺

QUESTIONS FOR DISCUSSION

1. Gene therapy is a very expensive procedure and thus far has resulted in only a few successful interventions and several deaths. Are the potential benefits of gene therapy significant enough to outweigh the costs and risks and justify continued research and development of it? Explain.
2. Can negative eugenics, understood as selecting *against* genetic traits that cause disease and disability, be justified? If it can, then how would you respond to the claim that there is a slippery slope from negative to positive eugenics, or selecting *for* genetic traits in accord with perfectionist ideals?
3. Would it be unfair to make access to genetic technology for medical treatment contingent on ability to pay? If so, then on what grounds would it be unfair? Does fairness require that everyone have access to genetic enhancement technology?
4. What are some of the ethical arguments for and against preimplantation genetic diagnosis of embryos?
5. Human embryonic stem cell research may lead to treatment of many degenerative diseases and may even cure them. Discuss the ethical significance of the fact that these cells are derived from discarded human embryos.

CASES

Zeitzoff v. Katz, Supreme Court of Israel (1986). Prior to her marriage, a woman consulted with a genetic counselor about the chances of having the gene causing Hunter's disease and how it might affect her future offspring. Hunter's is traceable to a mutation on the X chromosome, which is passed on by women to 50% of male offspring. The genetic counselor concluded that no such risk existed, and on the basis of his advice, the woman became pregnant and bore a son. But the son had the disease, which severely handicapped his physical and mental development. If the woman had known this, she would not have had any male children. The child brought a personal injury suit for wrongful life against the genetic counselor on grounds of negligence in genetic testing and counseling.

Mayfield v. Dalton, U.S. District Court of Hawaii 901 F. Supp., 300 (1995). Beginning with operation Desert Storm in 1991, the United States Military has used DNA analysis to help with the identification of soldiers' remains. Because of problems with obtaining reliable DNA samples during the Gulf War, the Department of Defense began a program to collect and store reference specimens of DNA from members of active duty and reserve armed forces. The reference samples would then be available for use in identifying remains in future conflicts. Two members of the U.S. Marine Corps stationed in Hawaii were ordered to provide specimens of DNA for the repository. They refused, holding that the collection, storage, and use of DNA samples violated their rights to freedom of expression, privacy, and due process under the First, Fifth, and Ninth Amendments of the U.S. Constitution. They were charged with violation of an order from a Supreme Commanding Officer. But the charges were dismissed on the ground that the regulations were not punitive and that no disciplinary action could be taken for refusal to provide the samples.

Pate v. Threlkel, Supreme Court of Florida, 661 So. 2d 278 (1995). This case addressed the issue of whether health care providers were under a duty to warn a patient of the importance of testing her children for a genetically transmissible carcinoma. It was ruled that in any circumstance in which a physician has a duty to warn of a genetically transmissible disease, the duty is satisfied by warning the patient. It does not extend to warning the patient's offspring as well.

Safer v. Pack, Superior Court of New Jersey, Appellate Division, 291 N.J. Super. 619, 677 A. 2d. 1188 (1996). In February 1990, Donna Safer, 36, began to experience lower abdominal pain, caused by a cancerous blockage of the colon and multiple polyps. She underwent a total abdominal colectomy, and a primary tumor in the colon was found to have extended throughout the entire bowel. She then underwent chemotherapy. In 1991, Ms. Safer obtained the medical records of her deceased father, Robert Batkin, from which she learned that he also suffered from multiple polyposis. She contended that the disease was hereditary, could lead to metastatic colorectal cancer, and that her father's doctor, Dr. Pack, had a duty to warn her. She filed a suit against him for failing to do so. The trial court dismissed the suit, holding that a physician had no legal duty to warn a child of a patient of a genetic risk.

Jesse Gelsinger (Reported January 26, 2000, *New York Times*). This case involved the death of an 18-year-old male, Jesse Gelsinger, in a gene therapy experiment conducted at the University of Pennsylvania. He suffered from the genetic disorder ornithine transcarbamylase (OTC) deficiency, where the liver cannot process ammonia, a toxic breakdown product of food. Jesse suffered from a mild form of the disease, which could be controlled through diet and drugs. A gene-altered virus meant to correct the enzyme deficiency triggered an adverse immune response that spiraled out of control. There were numerous deficiencies in the way the clinical trial in which Jesse was entered was carried out. Specifically, neither Jesse nor his father was informed of the risks of the intervention. Nor were they told that despite 300 clinical trials, gene therapy had never cured anyone of any disorder. In September, 2000, Jesse's family filed a lawsuit against the research team and the ethicist who offered advice on the experiment on grounds of negligence.

SUGGESTED FURTHER READING

Anderson, W. French. "Human Gene Therapy: Why Draw a Line?" *Journal of Medicine and Philosophy* 14:681–693, 1989.

Berger, E., and Gert, B. "Genetic Disorders and the Ethical Status of Germ-Line Gene Therapy," *Journal of Medicine and Philosophy* 16:667–685, 1991.

Brock, D., Buchanan, A., Daniels, N., and Wikler, D. *From Chance to Choice: Genetics and Justice*. New York: Cambridge University Press, 2000.

Buchanan, Allen. "Choosing Who Will Be Disabled: Genetic Intervention and the Morality of Inclusion." *Social Philosophy & Policy* 13:18–46, 1996.

Davis, Dena. "Genetic Dilemmas and the Child's Right to an Open Future." *Hastings Center Report* 25:7–15, 1997.

Hood, L., and Kevles, D., eds. *The Code of Codes: Scientific and Social Issues in the Human Genome Project*. Cambridge, MA: Harvard University Press, 1992.

Kevles, Daniel. *In the Name of Eugenics: Genetics and the Uses of Human Heredity*. Berkeley: University of California Press, 1986.

Marteau, T., and Richards, M., eds. *The Troubled Helix: Social and Psychological Implications of the New Human Genetics*. Cambridge: Cambridge University Press, 1996.

Nelkin, D., and Lindee, M.S. *The DNA Mystique: The Gene as a Cultural Icon*. New York: Freeman, 1995.

Parens, Eric, ed. *Enhancing Human Traits*. Washington, D.C.: Georgetown University Press, 1998.

Rothstein, Mark. *Genetic Secrets*. New Haven, CT: Yale University Press, 1997.

Shapira, Amos. "Wrongful Life Lawsuits for Faulty Genetic Counseling: Should the Impaired Newborn Be Entitled to Sue?" *Journal of Medical Ethics* 24:369–375, 1998.

Suzuki, D., and Knudsen, P. *Genethics: The Clash Between the New Genetics and Human Values*. Cambridge, MA: Harvard University Press, 1990.

PART VI:

DEATH AND DYING

Until the second half of the twentieth century, death was a relatively straightforward phenomenon. People were declared dead when they ceased breathing and their heart stopped
beating. Dying was not a prolonged process because most people died from diseases that
could not be cured or controlled by the few available medical interventions. But with
the development of mechanical life support, especially in the form of the artificial respirator, the last stage of dying patients' lives could be prolonged indefinitely. Respiration
and heart rate now can be mechanically maintained even when one's higher-brain functions have permanently and irreversibly ceased. And yet most of us believe that when
these brain functions have ceased, a person ceases to exist. The technology that has made
artificial respiration, hydration, and nutrition possible apparently has given medicine the
mandate to not only cure and treat disease but also to prolong life as long as possible.

The question of the ethical justification for extending a patient's life indefinitely has
to be treated on a par with such questions as when it is permissible to withhold or withdraw treatment from terminally ill patients. This question is complex because it turns on
the more fundamental question of whether these patients can give informed consent to
continuation or discontinuation of treatment. It also may involve substitute decision-
making by family members or others acting on behalf of incompetent patients who cannot give consent on their own. The issue of end-of-life decision-making also raises the
question of what the duties of physicians are to the patients for whom they care and

whether what patients want them to do accords with accepted standards of care and their professional integrity as physicians.

In some cases, a dying patient may have intractable pain that is not responsive to any pain medication or may have lost control over so many bodily functions that they have lost their dignity as well. The patient may not just ask that treatment be withdrawn or withheld, but that the physician assist in bringing about death. Or if a patient is physically unable to carry out the intention to die he or she may ask the physician to directly inject a lethal dose of morphine or some other drug or perform some other act that would directly kill him or her. These cases of physician-assisted suicide (PAS) and euthanasia may generate an ethical dilemma for physicians involved in end-of-life care. On the one hand, they have a duty not to harm and to benefit their patients, and causing them to die seems to contradict this duty blatantly. On the other hand, it would seem that in some instances a physician acts mercifully and, thus, benefits a patient by killing that patient if it is the only way to relieve pain and suffering. Prolonging such a life would be harming the patient, and therefore, killing or helping the patient to die benefits him or her.

What does it mean to say that a physician has a duty to benefit and not harm a patient at the end of the patient's life? Do patients have a right to die? And if so, does this entail a corresponding obligation on the part of the physician to do whatever the patient wishes, even if the physician conscientiously objects to both directly causing and assisting in a patient's death? Would better pain management and palliative care obviate the need for such measures? Are there cases in which continuing medical treatment would be futile, and that despite a patient's or family's wishes to continue treatment, a physician would have a right to unilaterally stop it? These particular questions need to be framed by the more general questions of what the goals of medicine are regarding the last stage of life, and both types of questions are addressed by the articles in Part VI.

In the first selection, Timothy Quill offers a poignant and eloquent account of his assisting a patient to die by prescribing a dose of barbiturates sufficient for her to commit suicide. He had known her for some time and, thus, understood her values and fears. When she refused chemotherapy for acute myelomonocytic leukemia and her condition deteriorated, she feared having to make the choice between pain and sedation. Quill comes across as a compassionate physician for whom caring for his patient means enabling her to die with as much control and dignity as possible. As Quill points out, by prescribing the barbiturates he only indirectly assisted her in bringing about her death on her own terms. In this regard, he was only an advocate of patient self-determination in controlling the time and manner of her death.

Edmund Pellegrino repudiates the position advocated by Quill, arguing that any form of physician assistance in bringing about a patient's death conflicts with the duty to heal. PAS is an abrogation of a physician's responsibility of caring for a patient. Pellegrino emphasizes the physician's beneficence over the patient's self-determination and argues that beneficence entails a patient's right to a good death, but not death by killing. He further argues that euthanasia could lead to an erosion of the trust essential to the healing relationship and questions the claim that killing patients could benefit them. PAS is a distortion of patient autonomy, trust, and healing. Indeed, Pellegrino goes so far as to say that Quill's action is no different from, and even may be more dangerous than, Jack Kevorkian's use of his "suicide machine."

Dan Brock argues that PAS and euthanasia may be permissible in some cases. He maintains that it is misleading to differentiate between these two practices on the basis of who performs the act that causes the patient's death. If the intention in both cases is to cause death, and thus both involve killing, then there is no intrinsic moral difference between PAS and euthanasia. The same holds for killing and allowing to die. Again, if the act or omission is the cause that brings about the patient's death, and if the intention behind the doing or allowing is the same, then there is no substantial moral difference between the two. If one is permissible, then the other should be as well. Significantly, for Brock, what makes intentionally killing a patient wrong and impermissible is that it violates the patient's right not to be killed. The focus should not be on the physician's intention but rather on the patient's consent and thus her autonomy. PAS and euthanasia may be permissible when a patient has waived her right not to be killed. Brock then addresses the objection that these practices would put us on a slippery slope to nonvoluntary active euthanasia, maintaining that the slide could be preempted by appropriate safeguards implemented and enforced at the policy level.

Complementing Brock's ideas in many respects, Margaret Battin grounds her argument for PAS in two principles: self-determination and mercy. The latter incorporates both nonmaleficence and beneficence. More specifically, the principle of mercy says that one ought both to refrain from causing pain or suffering and act to relieve it. Together, these two principles provide justification for the right to PAS in some cases of terminal illness. If a patient has a right to assistance in ending her life, then this entails a corresponding obligation of the physician to assist the patient. This does not imply that physicians are required to honor any patient request during the dying process. Yet as a patient's condition deteriorates, the physician has a greater obligation to provide care for the patient, and at some point in the patient's decline the principles of self-determination and mercy may obligate or at least permit the physician to assist in bringing about the patient's death. However, this can be justified only after a careful assessment of the patient's values and determining that there are no alternatives for relieving the patient's pain and suffering.

Unlike the right of a competent patient to refuse treatment, which is a negative right based on liberty, the right of a patient to die is a positive right based on welfare. Leon Kass raises the question of whether there are any positive rights and answers in the negative. And insofar as the right to die is a positive right, it follows that there is no right to die and no obligation on the part of physicians to help patients die. Kass notes the irony in the idea of a right whose exercise eliminates those who have this putative right. The 'right to die' is a confused and meaningless concept. Kass's main point is that the positive liberty right of one to be aided cannot serve as the basis of a right to have another assist one in suicide. For the obligation to assist would restrict the other person's more fundamental right to autonomy. Although Kass defends the idea of allowing to die, he opposes the practice of deliberate killing in both PAS and euthanasia. The concept of autonomy means that if there is no right to eliminate another person, then there is no right to have others do it to ourselves. Hence there is no defensible right to die.

The last two articles address the concept of futility, one of the more controversial concepts in medical decision-making at the end of life. The basic idea behind futility is that once it has been determined that a given treatment is of no benefit to a patient, a physician can withdraw or discontinue treatment unilaterally, even over the objections of a competent patient or the patient's family. Yet, as Stuart Youngner points out, the meaning of 'futility' is unclear because it allows for different definitions and interpretations. Youngner maintains that all interpretations of futility, with the exception of physiological futility, involve value judgments. And when futility takes on qualitative connotations, there often are conflicts between what the physician believes is beneficial to the patient and what the patient or the patient's family believes is beneficial. This can result in conflict about whether to continue or discontinue treatment. If physicians unilaterally invoke futility to justify stopping treatment, then they run the risk of a shift backward to paternalism and a failure to adequately respect patient and family values. Instead, Youngner recommends that what physicians should do in these situations is to encourage and initiate honest communication about the issues at hand, with the aim of reaching a decision to which all parties can reasonably agree would be in the patient's best interests.

Rosamond Rhodes frames the question of futility with the broader concept of the goals of medicine. When a patient or patient's family demand aggressive life-extending treatment that a physician believes is of no medical benefit to the patient, appeal to the goals of medicine might lead to a resolution of at least some of these conflicts. Rhodes says that these goals are determined partly by science and partly by society, and they include healing, preserving life, preserving function, and alleviating suffering. Generally, when requests for treatment are consonant with the goals of medicine, the physician is required to respect and accede to the patient's or family's request. But when their requests fall outside the boundary set by these goals, the physician is permitted, if not required, to withhold or discontinue treatment. This model can serve as a guide by which physicians can discharge their fiduciary responsibility of caring for patients and uphold their professional and personal integrity at the same time, as well as a way of adjudicating conflicts involving claims of medical futility.

☙

Death and Dignity: A Case of Individualized Decision Making

Timothy E. Quill MD

Diane was feeling tired and had a rash. A common scenario, though there was something subliminally worrisome that prompted me to check her blood count. Her hematocrit was 22, and the white-cell count was 4.3 with some metamyelocytes and unusual white cells. I wanted it to be

From *New England Journal of Medicine*, 324: 691–694, 1991.

viral, trying to deny what was staring me in the face. Perhaps in a repeated count it would disappear. I called Diane and told her it might be more serious than I had initially thought—that the test needed to be repeated and that if she felt worse, we might have to move quickly. When she pressed for the possibilities, I reluctantly opened the door to leukemia. Hearing the word seemed to make it exist. "Oh, shit!" she said. "Don't tell me that." Oh, shit! I thought, I wish I didn't have to.

Diane was no ordinary person (although no one I have ever come to know has been really ordinary). She was raised in an alcoholic family and had felt alone for much of her life. She had vaginal cancer as a young woman. Through much of her adult life, she had struggled with depression and her own alcoholism. I had come to know, respect, and admire her over the previous eight years as she confronted these problems and gradually overcame them. She was an incredibly clear, at times brutally honest, thinker and communicator. As she took control of her life, she developed a strong sense of independence and confidence. In the previous 3½ years, her hard work had paid off. She was completely abstinent from alcohol, she had established much deeper connections with her husband, college-age son, and several friends, and her business and her artistic work were blossoming. She felt she was really living fully for the first time.

Not surprisingly, the repeated blood count was abnormal, and detailed examination of the peripheral-blood smear showed myelocytes. I advised her to come into the hospital, explaining that we needed to do a bone marrow biopsy and make some decisions relatively rapidly. She came to the hospital knowing what we would find. She was terrified, angry, and sad. Although we knew the odds, we both clung to the thread of possibility that it might be something else.

The bone marrow confirmed the worst: acute myelomonocytic leukemia. In the face of this tragedy, we looked for signs of hope. This is an area of medicine in which technological intervention has been successful, with cures 25 per-

cent of the time—long-term cures. As I probed the costs of thes cures, I heard about induction chemotherapy (three weeks in the hospital, prolonged neutropenia, probable infectious complications, and hair loss: 75 percent of patients respond, 25 percent do not). For the survivors, this is followed by consolidation chemotherapy (with similar side effects; another 25 percent die, for a net survival of 50 percent). Those still alive, to have a reasonable chance of long-term survival, then need bone marrow transplantation (hospitalization for two months and whole-body irradiation, with complete killing of the bone marrow, infectious complications, and the possibility for graft-versus-host disease—with a survival of approximately 50 percent, or 25 percent of the original group). Though hematologists may argue over the exact percentages, they don't argue about the outcome of no treatment—certain death in days, weeks, or at most a few months.

Believing that delay was dangerous, our oncologist broke the news to Diane and began making plans to insert a Hickman catheter and begin induction chemotherapy that afternoon. When I saw her shortly thereafter, she was enraged at his presumption that she would want treatment, and devastated by the finality of the diagnosis. All she wanted to do was go home and be with her family. She had no further questions about treatment and in fact had decided that she wanted none. Together we lamented her tragedy and the unfairness of life. Before she left, I felt the need to be sure that she and her husband understood that there was some risk in delay, that the problem was not going to go away, and that we needed to keep considering the options over the next several days. We agreed to meet in two days.

She returned in two days with her husband and son. They had talked extensively about the problem and the options. She remained very clear about her wish not to undergo chemotherapy and to live whatever time she had left outside the hospital. As we explored her thinking further, it became clear that she was convinced she would die during the period of treatment and would suffer unspeakably in the process (from hospitalization, from lack of control over the body, from the side effects of chemotherapy, and from pain and anguish.) Although I could offer support and my best effort to minimize her suffering if she chose treatment, there was no way I could say any of this would not occur. In fact, the last four patients with acute leukemia at our hospital had died very painful deaths in the hospital during various stages of treatment (a fact I did *not* share with her). Her family wished she would choose treatment but sadly accepted her decision. She articulated very clearly that it was she who would be experiencing all the side effects of treatment and that odds of 25 percent were not good enough for her to undergo so toxic a course of therapy, given her expectations of chemotherapy and hospitalization and the absence of a closely matched bone marrow donor. I had her repeat her understanding of the treatment, the odds, and what to expect if there were no treatment. I clarified a few misunderstandings, but she had a remarkable grasp of the options and implications.

I have been a longtime advocate of active, informed patient choice of treatment or nontreatment, and of a patient's right to die with as much control and dignity as possible. Yet there was something about her giving up a 25 percent chance of long-term survival in favor of almost certain death that disturbed me. I had seen Diane fight and use her considerable inner resources to overcome alcoholism and depression, and I half expected her to change her mind over the next week. Since the window of time in which effective treatment can be initiated is rather narrow, we met several times that week. We obtained a second hematology consultation and talked at length about the meaning and implications of treatment and nontreatment. She talked to a psychologist she had seen in the past. I gradually understood the decision from her perspective and became convinced that it was the right decision for her. We arranged for home hospice care (although at that time Diane felt reasonably well, was active, and looked healthy), left the door

open for her to change her mind, and tried to anticipate how to keep her comfortable in the time she had left.

Just as I was adjusting to her decision, she opened up another area that would stretch me profoundly. It was extraordinarily important to Diane to maintain control of herself and her own dignity during the time remaining to her. When this was no longer possible, she clearly wanted to die. As a former director of a hospice program, I know how to use pain medicines to keep patients comfortable and lessen suffering. I explained the philosophy of comfort care, which I strongly believe in. Although Diane understood and appreciated this, she had known of people lingering in what was called relative comfort, and she wanted no part of it. When the time came, she wanted to take her life in the least painful way possible. Knowing of her desire for independence and her decision to stay in control, I thought this request made perfect sense. I acknowledged and explored this wish but also thought that it was out of the realm of currently accepted medical practice and that it was more than I could offer or promise. In our discussion, it became clear that preoccupation with her fear of a lingering death would interfere with Diane's getting the most out of the time she had left until she found a safe way to ensure her death. I feared the effects of a violent death on her family, the consequences of an ineffective suicide that would leave her lingering in precisely the state she dreaded so much, and the possibility that a family member would be forced to assist her, with all the legal and personal repercussions that would follow. She discussed this at length with her family. They believed that they should respect her choice. With this in mind, I told Diane that information was available from the Hemlock Society that might be helpful to her.

A week later she phoned me with a request for barbiturates for sleep. Since I knew that this was an essential ingredient in a Hemlock Society suicide, I asked her to come to the office to talk things over. She was more than willing to protect me by participating in a superficial conversation about her insomnia, but it was important to me to know how she planned to use the drugs and to be sure that she was not in despair or overwhelmed in a way that might color her judgment. In our discussion, it was apparent that she was having trouble sleeping, but it was also evident that the security of having enough barbiturates available to commit suicide when and if the time came would leave her secure enough to live fully and concentrate on the present. It was clear that she was not despondent and that in fact she was making deep, personal connections with her family and close friends. I made sure that she knew how to use the barbiturates for sleep, and also that she knew the amount needed to commit suicide. We agreed to meet regularly, and she promised to meet with me before taking her life, to ensure that all other avenues had been exhausted. I wrote the prescription with an uneasy feeling about the boundaries I was exploring—spiritual, legal, professional, and personal. Yet I also felt strongly that I was setting her free to get the most out of the time she had left, and to maintain dignity and control on her own terms until her death.

The next several months were very intense and important for Diane. Her son stayed home from college, and they were able to be with one another and say much that had not been said earlier. Her husband did his work at home so that he and Diane could spend more time together. She spent time with her closest friends. I had her come into the hospital for a conference with our residents, at which she illustrated in a most profound and personal way the importance of informed decision making, the right to refuse treatment, and the extraordinarily personal effects of illness and interaction with the medical system. There were emotional and physical hardships as well. She had periods of intense sadness and anger. Several times she became very weak, but she received transfusions as an outpatient and responded with marked improvement of symptoms. She had two serious infections that responded surprisingly well to empirical courses of oral antibiotics. After three tumultuous months, there

were two weeks of relative calm and well-being, and fantasies of a miracle began to surface.

Unfortunately, we had no miracle. Bone pain, weakness, fatigue, and fevers began to dominate her life. Although the hospice workers, family members, and I tried our best to minimize the suffering and promote comfort, it was clear that the end was approaching. Diane's immediate future held what she feared the most—increasing discomfort, dependence, and hard choices between pain and sedation. She called up her closest friends and asked them to come over to say goodbye, telling them that she would be leaving soon. As we had agreed, she let me know as well. When we met, it was clear that she knew what she was doing, that she was sad and frightened to be leaving, but that she would be even more terrified to stay and suffer. In our tearful goodbye, she promised a reunion in the future at her favorite spot on the edge of Lake Geneva, with dragons swimming in the sunset.

Two days later her husband called to say that Diane had died. She had said her final goodbyes to her husband and son that morning, and asked them to leave her alone for an hour. After an hour, which must have seemed like an eternity, they found her on the couch, lying very still and covered by her favorite shawl. There was no sign of struggle. She seemed to be at peace. They called me for advice about how to proceed. When I arrived at their house, Diane indeed seemed peaceful. Her husband and son were quiet. We talked about what a remarkable person she had been. They seemed to have no doubts about the course she had chosen or about their cooperation, although the unfairness of her illness and the finality of her death were overwhelming to us all.

I called the medical examiner to inform him that a hospice patient had died. When asked about the cause of death, I said, "acute leukemia." He said that was fine and that we should call a funeral director. Although acute leukemia was the truth, it was not the whole story. Yet any mention of suicide would have given rise to a police investigation and probably brought the arrival of an ambulance crew for resuscitation. Diane would have become a "coroner's case," and the decision to perform an autopsy would have been made at the discretion of the medical examiner. The family or I could have been subject to criminal prosecution, and I to professional review, for our roles in support of Diane's choices. Although I truly believe that the family and I gave her the best care possible, allowing her to define her limits and directions as much as possible, I am not sure the law, society, or the medical profession would agree. So I said "acute leukemia" to protect all of us, to protect Diane from an invasion into her past and her body, and to continue to shield society from the knowledge of the degree of suffering that people often undergo in the process of dying. Suffering can be lessened to some extent, but in no way eliminated or made benign, by the careful intervention of a competent, caring physician, given current social constraints.

Diane taught me about the range of help I can provide if I know people well and if I allow them to say what they really want. She taught me about life, death, and honesty and about taking charge and facing tragedy squarely when it strikes. She taught me that I can take small risks for people that I really know and care about. Although I did not assist in her suicide directly, I helped indirectly to make it possible, successful, and relatively painless. Although I know we have measures to help control pain and lessen suffering, to think that people do not suffer in the process of dying is an illusion. Prolonged dying can occasionally be peaceful, but more often the role of the physician and family is limited to lessening but not eliminating severe suffering.

I wonder how many families and physicians secretly help patients over the edge into death in the face of such severe suffering. I wonder how many severely ill or dying patients secretly take their lives, dying alone in despair. I wonder whether the image of Diane's final aloneness will persist in the minds of her family, or if they will remember more the intense meaningful months they had together before she died. I wonder whether Diane struggled in that last hour, and whether the Hemlock Society's way of death by suicide is the most benign. I wonder why Diane, who gave so much to so many of us, had to be alone for the last hour of her life. I wonder whether I will see Diane again, on the shore of Lake Geneva at sunset, with dragons swimming on the horizon.

Distortion of the Healing Relationship

Edmund D. Pellegrino MD

DISTORTIONS OF BENEFICENCE

The strongest arguments in favor of euthanasia and assisted suicide are based in appeals to two basic principles of contemporary medical ethics—beneficence and respect for autonomy. Protagonists of intentional death argue when the patient is suffering intolerably, is ready to meet death, and able to give consent, that it is compassionate, merciful, and beneficent to kill the

From T. L. Beauchamp and R.M. Veatch (eds.), *Ethical Issues in Death and Dying*, Second Edition. Upper Saddle River, NJ; Prentice-Hall, 1996; 161–165.

patient or assist him or her in killing oneself. Not to do so would be to act maleficently, to violate the dignity and autonomy of the suffering person, and to inflict harm on another human—in effect, to abandon a person in a time of greatest need. Since the doctor has the requisite knowledge to make death easy and painless, it is not only cruel but immoral not to accede to the patient's request.[1,2,3] Some would carry the argument further into the realm of justice. They would make euthanasia a moral obligation. Not to "assist" an incompetent patient is to act discriminatorily, for it deprives the comatose, the retarded, and infants the "benefit" of an early death. When the patient's intention cannot be expressed, the obligation, in justice, is to provide involuntary or nonvoluntary access to the same benefit of death accessible to the competent patient.[4] The Dutch Pediatric Society is already moving in this direction in the case of badly handicapped infants.[5]

It will not do to argue that one is not intending to kill but only to relieve suffering. This is a misuse of the principle of double effect. In this regard, it is interesting that the Remmelink Report shows that only 10 of the 187 cases of patients studied who asked for active euthanasia in Holland did so for relief of pain alone, while 46% mentioned pain in combination with loss of dignity, unworthy dying, dependence, or surfeit with life.[6]

At this juncture, those who see euthanasia as beneficent may reply that, in fact, physicians do not manage pain optimally, that they are not educated to do so, and that they ignore contemporary methods of analgesia. It is concluded that we cannot realistically expect or trust physicians to control pain and this justifies killing the patient out of compassion. In this way, we make the victim of medical ineptitude a victim twice over. In fact, legitimating euthanasia in any form would relieve physicians of the time, effort, and care required to control *both* pain and suffering. The moral mandate is not to extinguish the life of the patient because doctors are inept at pain control

but to better educate physicians in modern methods of analgesia.

A familiar argument used in many contexts today is that what is illegal or morally forbidden but desired by many should be "regularized" to keep it within respectable bounds. Examples of this kind of thinking include legalization of drug use, prostitution, commercialization of organ procurement, and so on. This argument misses the fact that the more decorous and regulated injection of a lethal dose of morphine or potassium chloride to bring about death in a hospital or one's own bedroom by one's family practitioner is not morally different from Kevorkian's crude methodology. The intention is the same—to kill or to help the patient kill oneself. Efficiency in the killing does not eradicate the unethical nature of the act.

Arguments based on euthanasia as a way to preserve the patient's dignity in dying are grounded in a misconception about dignity.[7] Patients do not lose their dignity as humans simply because they are suffering, in pain, perhaps disfigured by illness, incontinent, or comatose. A patient's dignity resides in his humanity. It cannot be lost, even through the ravages of disease. When proponents of euthanasia speak of loss of dignity, they are speaking more for their own reactions to seeing, living with, or treating terminally ill patients. When patients speak of their fear of a loss of "dignity," for the most part, they are speaking of the way they appear to, or are regarded by, others—by physicians, nurses, other patients, and even their families. This type of "dignity" is the fabrication of the observer, not a quality of the person observed.[8]

For the patient, this is not death with "dignity"; it is more like death as a remedy for the shame they feel, or are made to feel. Shame is a potent cause of suffering. It is far more human to treat that cause by treating the patient with true dignity. Acceding to the patient's request to die is not helping to restore his dignity. It is a confirmation of the loss of worth he has suffered in the eyes of those who behold him as an object of pity.

DISTORTION OF AUTONOMY

Protagonists of euthanasia and assisted suicide argue that assisting the patient to die is a beneficent act since it respects the principle of autonomy. On this view, those who refuse to comply with the autonomous request of a competent patient are in violation of respect for persons.[9] Such absolutization of autonomy has two serious moral limitations that make any form of euthanasia or assisted suicide a maleficent rather than a beneficent act. For one thing, the mere assertion of a request cannot, of itself, bind another person within, or outside the physician-patient relationship. When a demand becomes a command, it can violate another person's autonomy. Even more problematic is whether a person desperate enough to ask to be killed or assisted in killing herself can act autonomously. In the end, the person who opts for euthanasia uses her autonomy to give up her autonomy. She chooses to eradicate the basis on which autonomy is possible— consciousness and rationality.

At the other extreme, when death is imminent, the empirical questions of autonomy are equally problematic. The person who is fatally ill is a person, often in pain, anxious, and rejected by those who are healthy, afflicted with a sense of guilt and unworthiness, perceiving himself as a social, economic, and emotional burden to others. Can a person in this state satisfy the criteria for autonomous choice?[10] How well could these patients safeguard their autonomy if euthanasia were legalized? Chronically ill and dying patients are extremely sensitive to even the most subtle suggestions of unworthiness by their medical attendants, family, and friends. Any sign—verbal or nonverbal—that reinforces guilt or shame will be picked up as a subtle suggestion to take the "noble" way out.

The degree to which pain, guilt, and unworthiness may compromise autonomy is evident in the fact that when these are removed or ameliorated, patients do not ask to be killed.[11] Even if euthanasia were legalized, a first obligation under both principles of beneficence and autonomy would be to diagnose, ameliorate, or remove those causes of the patient's despondency and suffering that lead to a request for euthanasia in the first place.

DISTORTION OF TRUST

Trust plays an inescapable role in whatever model of physician-patient relationship one chooses.[12] The patient trusts the physician to do what is in the patient's best interests as it is indicated by the diagnosis, prognosis, and therapeutic possibilities. When patients know that euthanasia is a legitimate choice and that some physicians may see killing as healing, they know they are vulnerable to violations of trust.

A much more common danger at present is the possibility that the physician's values and acceptance of euthanasia may unconsciously shape how vigorously she treats the patient or presents the possibility of assisted suicide. How is the patient to know when his doctor is persuading or even subtly coercing him to choose death? The doctor's motives may be unconsciously to advance her own beliefs that euthanasia is a social good to relieve herself of the frustrating difficulties of caring for the patient, of her distress with the quality of life the patient is forced to lead, or promote her desire to conserve society's resources, etc. How will a patient ever be sure of the true motive for his doctor's recommendation? When is the doctor depreciating the value of available methods of pain relief or comprehensive palliative care because he believes the really "good" death is a planned death?

The power of physicians to shape their patient's choices is well-known to every experienced clinician. Physicians can get a patient to agree to almost any decision they want by the way they present the alternatives. All judgments may be influenced by the physician's attitude on euthanasia or her emotional and physical frustrations in treating a difficult patient. How realistic is patient autonomy in such circumstances? How effective can the criteria proposed to prevent abuses of legalized euthanasia really be?

ASSISTED SUICIDE: IS THERE A MORAL DIFFERENCE BETWEEN QUILL AND KEVORKIAN?

What I have attempted to show is the way in which intentional killing, if accepted into the body of medical ethics, would distort the ethics and purposes of the healing relationship in at least three of its dimensions—beneficence, protection of autonomy, and fidelity to trust. One may justifiably ask: Is the ethical situation different if the physician intends only to advise the patient on how to attain the goal of a "good" death by assisting the patient to kill oneself? Is not the causal and intentional relationship of the physician to the death of the patient essentially different?

I do not believe a convincing case can be made for a moral difference between the two. This is a classical instance of a distinction without a difference in kind. The intentional end sought in either case is the death of the patient: in active euthanasia, the physician is the immediate cause; in assisted suicide, the physician is the necessary cooperating cause, a moral accomplice without whom the patient could not kill oneself. In assisted suicide, the doctor fully shares the patient's intention to end his or her life. The doctor provides the lethal medication, advises on the proper dose, on how it should be taken to be most effective, and on what to do if the dose is regurgitated. The physician's cooperation is necessary if the act is to be carried out at all. The physician shares equal responsibility with the patient just as she or he would in active euthanasia.

This moral complicity is obvious in the cases reported by Dr. Timothy Quill and Dr. Jack Kevorkian. In both cases, the physician provided the means fully knowing the patient would use them and encouraging the patients to do so when they felt the time was right. Kevorkian's "death machine" was operated by the patient but designed and provided by Kevorkian. Quill's patient took the sedatives he prescribed. To be sure, Quill's account of his assistance in the death of a young woman with leukemia elicits more sympathy because of the length and intensity of his professional relationship with her. Kevorkian's cases, in contrast, are remarkable for the brevity of the relationships, the absence of any serious attempt to provide palliative medical or psychiatric assistance, and the brusqueness with which the decisions are made and carried out. Kevorkian is the technician of death; Quill, its artist.

Quill's *modus operandi* is gentler and more deliberate, but this does not change the nature of the action in any essential way. Indeed, in some ways, Quill's approach is more dangerous to patient beneficence and autonomy because it compromises the patient more subtly and is conducted under the intention of "treatment." But when does the intention to treat become synonymous with the intent to assist in, or actively accelerate, death? Kevorkian's patients at least approach him with the intention already in their minds to commit suicide and to gain access to his machine. He is, after all, a pathologist, and his patients do not start out thinking he might be able to treat their illnesses. Quill's patients presumably come to him as a physician primarily, not as a minister of death. This may well change now that Quill has attained so much notoriety through his public zeal for assisted suicide.

References and Notes

1. J.H. Van Den Berg. *Medical Power and Medical Ethics.* New York: W. W. Norton, 1978.

2. T.E. Quill. "Doctor, I Want to Die, Will You Help Me?" *Journal of the American Medical Association* 270(7): (1993):870–873.

3. C.K. Cassell and D.E. Meier. "Morals and Moralism in the Debate Over Euthanasia and Assisted Suicide." *New England Journal of Medicine* 323 (1990):750–752.

4. J. Lachs, "Active Euthanasia." *Journal of Clinical Ethics* 1(2) (1993):113–115.

5. E. Van Leeuwen and G.K. Kimsma. "Acting or Letting Go: Medical Decision Making in Neonatology in the Netherlands." *Cambridge Quarterly of Health Care Ethics* 2(3) (1993):265–269.

6. Commission on the Study of Medical Practice Concerning Euthanasia. "Medical Decisions Concerning the End of Life" (The Hague: Staatsuitgeverij, 1991). See also P.J. van der Maas, J.J.M. van Delden, et al. "Euthanasia and Other Medical Decisions Concerning the End of Life." *Lancet* 338 (1991):669–674.

7. T. Quill. *Death and Dignity: Making Choices and Taking Charge.* New York: W. W. Norton, 1992.

8. D.P. Sulmasy. "Death and Human Dignity." *Linacre Quarterly* 61(4) (1994):27–36.

9. J. Kevorkian. "The Goodness of a Planned Death: An Interview with Jack Kevorkian." *Free Inquiry* (Fall 1991):14–18.

10. Y. Conwell and E. Caine. "Rational Suicide and the Right to Die," *New England Journal of Medicine* 325 (Oct. 10, 1991):100–103.

11. N. Coyle. "The Last Weeks of Life." *American Journal of Nursing* (1990):75–78.

12. E.D. Pellegrino. "Trust and Distrust in Professional Ethics." In E.D. Pellegrino, et al. (eds.) *Ethics, Trust and the Professions.* Washington, DC: Georgetown University Press, 1991, pp. 69–92.

Voluntary Active Euthanasia

Dan Brock PhD

Since the case of Karen Quinlan first seized public attention fifteen years ago, no issue in biomedical ethics has been more prominent than the debate about foregoing life-sustaining treatment. Controversy continues regarding some aspects of that debate, such as forgoing life-sustaining nutrition and hydration, and relevant law varies some from state to state. Nevertheless, I believe it is possible to identify an emerging consensus that competent patients, or the surrogates of incompetent patients, should be permitted to weigh the benefits and burdens of alternative treatments, including the alternative of no treatment, according to the patient's values, and either to refuse any treatment or to select from among available alternative treatments. This consensus is reflected in bioethics scholarship, in reports of prestigious bodies such as the President's Commission for the Study of Ethical Problems in Medicine, The Hastings Center, and the American Medical Association, in a large body of judicial decisions in courts around the country, and finally in the beliefs and practices of health care professionals who care for dying patients.[1]

More recently, significant public and professional attention has shifted from life-sustaining treatment to euthanasia—more specifically, voluntary active euthanasia—and to physician-assisted suicide. Several factors have contributed to the increased interest in euthanasia. In the Netherlands, it has been openly practiced by physicians for several years with the acceptance of the country's highest court.[2] In 1988 there was an unsuccessful attempt to get the question of whether it should be made legally permissible on the ballot in California. In November 1991 voters in the state of Washington defeated a widely publicized referendum proposal to legalize both voluntary active euthanasia and physician-assisted suicide. Finally, some cases of this kind,

From *Hastings Center Report* 22: 10–22, 1992.

such as "It's Over, Debbie," described in the *Journal of the American Medical Association*, the "suicide machine" of Dr. Jack Kevorkian, and the cancer patient "Diane" of Dr. Timothy Quill, have captured wide public and professional attention.[3] Unfortunately, the first two of these cases were sufficiently problematic that even most supporters of euthanasia or assisted suicide did not defend the physicians' actions in them. As a result, the subsequent debate they spawned has often shed more heat than light. My aim is to increase the light, and perhaps as well to reduce the heat, on this important subject by formulating and evaluating the central ethical arguments for and against voluntary active euthanasia and physician-assisted suicide. My evaluation of the arguments leads me, with reservations to be noted, to support permitting both practices. My primary aim, however, is not to argue for euthanasia, but to identify confusions in some common arguments, and problematic assumptions and claims that need more defense or data in others. The issues are considerably more complex than either supporters or opponents often make out; my hope is to advance the debate by focusing attention on what I believe the real issues under discussion should be.

In the recent bioethics literature some have endorsed physician-assisted suicide but not euthanasia.[4] Are they sufficiently different that the moral arguments for one often do not apply to the other? A paradigm case of physician-assisted suicide is a patient's ending his or her life with a lethal dose of a medication requested of and provided by a physician for that purpose. A paradigm case of voluntary active euthanasia is a physician's administering the lethal dose, often because the patient is unable to do so. The only difference that need exist between the two is the person who actually administers the lethal dose—the physician or the patient. In each, the physician plays an active and necessary causal role.

In physician-assisted suicide the patient acts last (for example, Janet Adkins herself pushed the button after Dr. Kevorkian hooked her up to his suicide machine), whereas in euthanasia the physician acts last by performing the physical equivalent of pushing the button. In both cases, however, the choice rests fully with the patient. In both the patient acts last in the sense of retaining the right to change his or her mind until the point at which the lethal process becomes irreversible. How could there be a substantial moral difference between the two based only on this small difference in the part played by the physician in the causal process resulting in death? Of course, it might be held that the moral difference is clear and important—in euthanasia the physician kills the patient whereas in physician-assisted suicide the patient kills him- or herself. But this is misleading at best. In assisted suicide the physician and patient together kill the patient. To see this, suppose a physician supplied a lethal dose to a patient with the knowledge and intent that the patient will wrongfully administer it to another. We would have no difficulty in morality or the law recognizing this as a case of joint action to kill for which both are responsible.

If there is no significant, intrinsic moral difference between the two, it is also difficult to see why public or legal policy should permit one but not the other; worries about abuse or about giving anyone dominion over the lives of others apply equally to either. As a result, I will take the arguments evaluated below to apply to both and will focus on euthanasia.

My concern here will be with *voluntary* euthanasia only—that is, with the case in which a clearly competent patient makes a fully voluntary and persistent request for aid in dying. Involuntary euthanasia, in which a competent patient explicitly refuses or opposes receiving euthanasia, and non-voluntary euthanasia, in which a patient is incompetent and unable to express his or her wishes about euthanasia, will be considered here only as potential unwanted side effects of permitting voluntary euthanasia. I emphasize as well that I am concerned with *active* euthanasia, not withholding or withdrawing life-sustaining treatment, which some commentators characterize as "passive euthanasia." Finally, I will be concerned with euthanasia where the motive of those who perform it is to respect the wishes of the patient and to provide the patient with a "good death," though one important issue is whether a change in legal policy could restrict the performance of euthanasia to only those cases.

A last introductory point is that I will be examining only secular arguments about euthanasia, though of course many people's attitudes to it are inextricable from their religious views. The policy issue is only whether euthanasia should be permissible, and no one who has religious objections to it should be required to take any part in it, though of course this would not fully satisfy some opponents.

THE CENTRAL ETHICAL ARGUMENT FOR VOLUNTARY ACTIVE EUTHANASIA

The central ethical argument for euthanasia is familiar. It is that the very same two fundamental ethical values supporting the consensus on patients' rights to decide about life-sustaining treatment also support the ethical permissibility of euthanasia. These values are individual self-determination or autonomy and individual well-being. By self-determination as it bears on euthanasia, I mean people's interest in making important decisions about their lives for themselves according to their own values or conceptions of a good life, and in being left free to act on those decisions. Self-determination is valuable because it permits people to form and live in accordance with their own conception of a good life, at least within the bounds of justice and consistent with others doing so as well. In exercising self-determination people take responsibility for their lives and for the kinds of persons they become. A central aspect of human dignity lies in people's capacity to direct their lives in this way. The value of exercising self-determination presupposes some minimum of decisionmaking capacities or competence, which thus limits

the scope of euthanasia supported by self-determination; it cannot justifiably be administered, for example, in cases of serious dementia or treatable clinical depression.

Does the value of individual self-determination extend to the time and manner of one's death? Most people are very concerned about the nature of the last stage of their lives. This reflects not just a fear of experiencing substantial suffering when dying, but also a desire to retain dignity and control during this last period of life. Death is today increasingly preceded by a long period of significant physical and mental decline, due in part to the technological interventions of modern medicine. Many people adjust to these disabilities and find meaning and value in new activities and ways. Others find the impairments and burdens in the last stage of their lives at some point sufficiently great to make life no longer worth living. For many patients near death, maintaining the quality of one's life, avoiding great suffering, maintaining one's dignity, and insuring that others remember us as we wish them to become of paramount importance and outweigh merely extending one's life. But there is no single, objectively correct answer for everyone as to when, if at all, one's life becomes all things considered a burden and unwanted. If self-determination is a fundamental value, then the great variability among people on this question makes it especially important that individuals control the manner, circumstances, and timing of their dying and death.

The other main value that supports euthanasia is individual well-being. It might seem that individual well-being conflicts with a person's self-determination when the person requests euthanasia. Life itself is commonly taken to be a central good for persons, often valued for its own sake, as well as necessary for pursuit of all other goods within a life. But when a competent patient decides to forgo all further life-sustaining treatment then the patient, either explicitly or implicitly, commonly decides that the best life possible for him or her with treatment is of sufficiently poor quality that it is worse than no further life at all. Life is no longer considered a benefit by the patient, but has now become a burden. The same judgment underlies a request for euthanasia: continued life is seen by the patient as no longer a benefit, but now a burden. Especially in the often severely compromised and debilitated states of many critically ill or dying patients, there is no objective standard, but only the competent patient's judgment of whether continued life is no longer a benefit.

Of course, sometimes there are conditions, such as clinical depression, that call into question whether the patient has made a competent choice, either to forgo life-sustaining treatment or to seek euthanasia, and then the patient's choice need not be evidence that continued life is no longer a benefit for him or her. Just as with decisions about treatment, a determination of incompetence can warrant not honoring the patient's choice; in the case of treatment, we then transfer decisional authority to a surrogate, though in the case of voluntary active euthanasia a determination that the patient is incompetent means that choice is not possible.

The value or right of self-determination does not entitle patients to compel physicians to act contrary to their own moral or professional values. Physicians are moral and professional agents whose own self-determination or integrity should be respected as well. If performing euthanasia became legally permissible, but conflicted with a particular physician's reasonable understanding of his or her moral or professional responsibilities, the care of a patient who requested euthanasia should be transferred to another.

Most opponents do not deny that there are some cases in which the values of patient self-determination and well-being support euthanasia. Instead, they commonly offer two kinds of arguments against it that on their view outweigh or override this support. The first kind of argument is that in any individual case where considerations of the patient's self-determination and well-being do support euthanasia, it is nevertheless always ethically wrong or impermissible. The second kind of argument grants that in some individual cases euthanasia may *not* be ethically wrong, but maintains nonetheless that public and legal policy should never permit it. The first kind of argument focuses on features of any individual case of euthanasia, while the second kind focuses on social or legal policy. In the next section I consider the first kind of argument.

EUTHANASIA IS THE DELIBERATE KILLING OF AN INNOCENT PERSON

The claim that any individual instance of euthanasia is a case of deliberate killing of an innocent person is, with only minor qualifications, correct. Unlike forgoing life-sustaining treatment, commonly understood as allowing to die, euthanasia is clearly killing, defined as depriving of life or causing the death of a living being. While providing morphine for pain relief at doses where the risk of respiratory depression and an earlier death may be a foreseen but unintended side effect of treating the patient's pain, in a case of euthanasia the patient's death is deliberate or intended even if in both the physician's ultimate end may be respecting the patient's wishes. If the deliberate killing of an innocent person is wrong, euthanasia would be nearly always impermissible.

In the context of medicine, the ethical prohibition against deliberately killing the innocent derives some of its plausibility from the belief that nothing in the currently accepted practice of medicine is deliberate killing. Thus, in commenting on the "It's Over, Debbie" case, four prominent physicians and bioethicists could entitle their paper "Doctors Must Not Kill."[5] The belief that doctors do not in fact kill requires the corollary belief that forgoing life-sustaining treatment, whether by not starting or by stopping treatment, is allowing to die, not killing. Common though this view is, I shall argue that it is confused and mistaken.

Why is the common view mistaken? Consider the case of a patient terminally ill with ALS disease. She is completely respirator dependent with no hope of ever being weaned. She is unquestionably competent but finds her condition intolerable and persistently requests to be removed from the respirator and allowed to die. Most people and physicians would agree that the patient's physician should respect the patient's wishes and remove her from the respirator, though this will certainly cause the patient's death. The common understanding is that the physician thereby allows the patient to die. But is that correct?

Suppose the patient has a greedy and hostile son who mistakenly believes that his mother will never decide to stop her life-sustaining treatment and that even if she did her physician would not remove her from the respirator. Afraid that his inheritance will be dissipated by a long and expensive hospitalization, he enters his mother's room while she is sedated, extubates her, and she dies. Shortly thereafter the medical staff discovers what he has done and confronts the son. He replies, "I didn't kill her, I merely allowed her to die. It was her ALS disease that caused her death." I think this would rightly be dismissed as transparent sophistry—the son went into his mother's room and deliberately killed her. But, of course, the son performed just the same physical actions, did just the same thing, that the physician would have done. If that is so, then doesn't the physician also kill the patient when he extubates her?

I underline immediately that there are important ethical differences between what the physician and the greedy son do. First, the physician acts with the patient's consent whereas the son does not. Second, the physician acts with a good motive—to respect the patient's wishes and self-determination—whereas the son acts with a bad motive—to protect his own inheritance. Third, the physician acts in a social role through which he is legally authorized to carry out the patient's wishes regarding treatment whereas the son has no such authorization. These and perhaps other ethically important differences show that

what the physician did was morally justified whereas what the son did was morally wrong. What they do *not* show, however, is that the son killed while the physician allowed to die. One can either kill or allow to die with or without consent, with a good or bad motive, within or outside of a social role that authorizes one to do so.

The difference between killing and allowing to die that I have been implicitly appealing to here is roughly that between acts and omissions resulting in death.[6] Both the physician and the greedy son act in a manner intended to cause death, do cause death, and so both kill. One reason this conclusion is resisted is that on a different understanding of the distinction between killing and allowing to die, what the physician does is allow to die. In this account, the mother's ALS is a lethal disease whose normal progression is being held back or blocked by the life-sustaining respirator treatment. Removing this artificial intervention is then viewed as standing aside and allowing the patient to die of her underlying disease. I have argued elsewhere that this alternative account is deeply problematic, in part because it commits us to accepting that what the greedy son does is to allow to die, not kill.[7] Here, I want to note two other reasons why the conclusion that stopping life support is killing is resisted.

The first reason is that killing is often understood, especially within medicine, as unjustified causing of death; in medicine it is thought to be done only accidentally or negligently. It is also increasingly widely accepted that a physician is ethically justified in stopping life support in a case like that of the ALS patient. But if these two beliefs are correct, then what the physician does cannot be killing, and so must be allowing to die. Killing patients is not, to put it flippantly, understood to be part of physicians' job description. What is mistaken in this line of reasoning is the assumption that all killings are *unjustified* causings of death. Instead, some killings are ethically justified, including many instances of stopping life support.

Another reason for resisting the conclusion that stopping life support is often killing is that it is psychologically uncomfortable. Suppose the physician had stopped the ALS patient's respirator and had made the son's claim, "I didn't kill her, I merely allowed her to die. It was her ALS disease that caused her death." The clue to the psychological role here is how naturally the "merely" modifies "allowed her to die." The characterization as allowing to die is meant to shift felt responsibility away from the agent—the physician—and to the lethal disease process. Other language common in death and dying contexts plays a similar role; "letting nature take its course" or "stopping prolonging the dying process" both seem to shift responsibility from the physician who stops life support to the fatal disease process. However psychologically helpful these conceptualizations may be in making the difficult responsibility of a physician's role in the patient's death bearable, they nevertheless are confusions. Both physicians and family members can instead be helped to understand that it is the patient's decision and consent to stopping treatment that limits their responsibility for the patient's death and that shifts that responsibility to the patient.

Many who accept the difference between killing and allowing to die as the distinction between acts and omissions resulting in death have gone on to argue that killing is not in itself morally different from allowing to die.[8] In this account, very roughly, one kills when one performs an action that causes the death of a person (we are in a boat, you cannot swim, I push you overboard, and you drown), and one allows to die when one has the ability and opportunity to prevent the death of another, knows this, and omits doing so, with the result that the person dies (we are in a boat, you cannot swim, you fall overboard, I don't throw you an available life ring, and you drown). Those who see no moral difference between killing and allowing to die typically employ the strategy of comparing cases that differ in these and no other potentially morally im-

portant respects. This will allow people to consider whether the mere difference that one is a case of killing and the other of allowing to die matters morally, or whether instead it is other features that make most cases of killing worse than most instances of allowing to die. Here is such a pair of cases:

Case 1. A very gravely ill patient is brought to a hospital emergency room and sent up to the ICU. The patient begins to develop respiratory failure that is likely to require intubation very soon. At that point the patient's family members and long-standing physician arrive at the ICU and inform the ICU staff that there had been extensive discussion about future care with the patient when he was unquestionably competent. Given his grave and terminal illness, as well as his state of debilitation, the patient had firmly rejected being placed on a respirator under any circumstances, and the family and physician produce the patient's advance directive to that effect. The ICU staff do not intubate the patient, who dies of respiratory failure.

Case 2. The same as Case 1 except that the family and physician are slightly delayed in traffic and arrive shortly after the patient has been intubated and placed on the respirator. The ICU staff extubate the patient, who dies of respiratory failure.

In Case 1 the patient is allowed to die, in Case 2 he is killed, but it is hard to see why what is done in Case 2 is significantly different morally than what is done in Case 1. It must be other factors that make most killings worse than most allowings to die, and if so, euthanasia cannot be wrong simply because it is killing instead of allowing to die.

Suppose both my arguments are mistaken. Suppose that killing is worse than allowing to die and that withdrawing life support is not killing, although euthanasia is. Euthanasia still need not for that reason be morally wrong. To see this, we need to determine the basic principle for the moral evaluation of killing persons. What is it that makes paradigm cases of wrongful killing wrongful? One very plausible answer is that killing denies the victim something that he or she values greatly—continued life or a future. Moreover, since continued life is necessary for pursuing any of a person's plans and purposes, killing brings the frustration of all of these plans and desires as well. In a nutshell, wrongful killing deprives a person of a valued future, and of all the person wanted and planned to do in that future.

A natural expression of this account of the wrongness of killing is that people have a moral right not to be killed.[9] But in this account of the wrongness of killing, the right not to be killed, like other rights, should be waivable when the person makes a competent decision that continued life is no longer wanted or a good, but is instead worse than no further life at all. In this view, euthanasia is properly understood as a case of a person having waived his or her right not to be killed.

This rights view of the wrongness of killing is not, of course, universally shared. Many people's moral views about killing have their origins in religious views that human life comes from God and cannot be justifiably destroyed or taken away, either by the person whose life it is or by another. But in a pluralistic society like our own with a strong commitment to freedom of religion, public policy should not be grounded in religious beliefs which many in that society reject. I turn now to the general evaluation of public policy on euthanasia.

WOULD THE BAD CONSEQUENCES OF EUTHANASIA OUTWEIGH THE GOOD?

The argument against euthanasia at the policy level is stronger than at the level of individual cases, though even here I believe the case is ultimately unpersuasive, or at best indecisive. The policy level is the place where the main issues lie, however, and where moral considerations that might override arguments in favor of euthanasia will be found, if they are found anywhere. It is important to note two kinds of disagreement about the consequences for public policy of per-

mitting euthanasia. First, there is empirical or factual disagreement about what the consequences would be. This disagreement is greatly exacerbated by the lack of firm data on the issue. Second, since on any reasonable assessment there would be both good and bad consequences, there are moral disagreements about the relative importance of different effects. In addition to these two sources of disagreement, there is also no single, well-specified policy proposal for legalizing euthanasia on which policy assessments can focus. But without such specification, and especially without explicit procedures for protecting against well-intentioned misuse and ill-intentioned abuse, the consequences for policy are largely speculative. Despite these difficulties, a preliminary account of the main likely good and bad consequences is possible. This should help clarify where better data or more moral analysis and argument are needed, as well as where policy safeguards must be developed.

Potential Good Consequences of Permitting Euthanasia

What are the likely good consequences? First, if euthanasia were permitted it would be possible to respect the self-determination of competent patients who want it, but now cannot get it because of its illegality. We simply do not know how many such patients and people there are. In the Netherlands, with a population of about 14.5 million (in 1987), estimates in a recent study were that about 1,900 cases of voluntary active euthanasia or physician-assisted suicide occur annually. No straightforward extrapolation to the United States is possible for many reasons, among them, that we do not know how many people here who want euthanasia now get it, despite its illegality. Even with better data on the number of persons who want euthanasia but cannot get it, significant moral disagreement would remain about how much weight should be given to any instance of failure to respect a person's self-determination in this way.

One important factor substantially affecting the number of persons who would seek euthanasia is the extent to which an alternative is available. The widespread acceptance in the law, social policy, and medical practice of the right of a competent patient to forgo life-sustaining treatment suggests that the number of competent persons in the United States who would want euthanasia if it were permitted is probably relatively small.

A second good consequence of making euthanasia legally permissible benefits a much larger group. Polls have shown that a majority of the American public believes that people should have a right to obtain euthanasia if they want it.[10] No doubt the vast majority of those who support this right to euthanasia will never in fact come to want euthanasia for themselves. Nevertheless, making it legally permissible would reassure many people that if they ever do want euthanasia they would be able to obtain it. This reassurance would supplement the broader control over the process of dying given by the right to decide about life-sustaining treatment. Having fire insurance on one's house benefits all who have it, not just those whose houses actually burn down, by reassuring them that in the unlikely event of their house burning down, they will receive the money needed to rebuild it. Likewise, the legalization of euthanasia can be thought of as a kind of insurance policy against being forced to endure a protracted dying process that one has come to find burdensome and unwanted, especially when there is no life-sustaining treatment to forgo. The strong concern about losing control of their care expressed by many people who face serious illness likely to end in death suggests that they give substantial importance to the legalization of euthanasia as a means of maintaining this control.

A third good consequence of the legalization of euthanasia concerns patients whose dying is filled with severe and unrelievable pain of suffering. When there is a life-sustaining treatment that, if forgone, will lead relatively quickly to death, then doing so can bring an end to these patients' suffering without recourse to euthanasia. For patients receiving no such treatment, however, euthanasia may be the only release from their otherwise prolonged suffering and agony. This argument from mercy has always been the strongest argument for euthanasia in those cases to which it applies.[11]

The importance of relieving pain and suffering is less controversial than is the frequency with which patients are forced to undergo untreatable agony that only euthanasia could relieve. If we focus first on suffering caused by physical pain, it is crucial to distinguish pain that *could* be adequately relieved with modern methods of pain control, though it in fact is not, from pain that is relievable only by death.[12] For a variety of reasons, including some physicians' fear of hastening the patient's death, as well as the lack of a publicly accessible means for assessing the amount of the patient's pain, many patients suffer pain that could be, but is not, relieved.

Specialists in pain control, as for example the pain of terminally ill cancer patients, argue that there are very few patients whose pain could not be adequately controlled, though sometimes at the cost of so sedating them that they are effectively unable to interact with other people or their environment. Thus, the argument from mercy in cases of physical pain can probably be met in a large majority of cases by providing adequate measures of pain relief. This should be a high priority, whatever our legal policy on euthanasia— the relief of pain and suffering has long been, quite properly, one of the central goals of medicine. Those cases in which pain could be effectively relieved, but in fact is not, should only count significantly in favor of legalizing euthanasia if all reasonable efforts to change pain management techniques have been tried and have failed.

Dying patients often undergo substantial psychological suffering that is not fully or even principally the result of physical pain.[13] The knowledge about how to relieve this suffering is much more limited than in the case of relieving pain, and efforts to do so are probably more often unsuccessful. If the argument from mercy is extended to patients experiencing great and unrelievable psychological suffering, the numbers of patients to which it applies are much greater.

One last good consequence of legalizing euthanasia is that once death has been accepted, it is often more humane to end life quickly and peacefully, when that is what the patient wants. Such a death will often be seen as better than a more prolonged one. People who suffer a sudden and unexpected death, for example by dying quickly or in their sleep from a heart attack or stroke, are often considered lucky to have died in this way. We care about how we die in part because we care about how others remember us, and we hope they will remember us as we were in "good times" with them and not as we might be when disease has robbed us of our dignity as human beings. As with much in the treatment and care of the dying, people's concerns differ in this respect, but for at least some people, euthanasia will be a more humane death than what they have often experienced with other loved ones and might otherwise expect for themselves.

Some opponents of euthanasia challenge how much importance should be given to any of these good consequences of permitting it, or even whether some would be good consequences at all. But more frequently, opponents cite a number of bad consequences that permitting euthanasia would or could produce, and it is to their assessment that I now turn.

Potential Bad Consequences of Permitting Euthanasia

Some of the arguments against permitting euthanasia are aimed specifically against physicians, while others are aimed against anyone being permitted to perform it. I shall first consider one argument of the former sort. Permitting physicians to perform euthanasia, it is said, would be incompatible with their fundamental moral and professional commitment as healers to care for patients and to protect life. Moreover, if eu-

thanasia by physicians became common, patients would come to fear that a medication was intended not to treat or care, but instead to kill, and would thus lose trust in their physicians. This position was forcefully stated in a paper by Willard Gaylin and his colleagues:

> The very soul of medicine is on trial. . . . This issue touches medicine at its moral center; if this moral center collapses, if physicians become killers or are even licensed to kill, the profession—and, therewith, each physician—will never again be worthy of trust and respect as healer and comforter and protector of life in all its frailty.

These authors go on to make clear that, while they oppose permitting anyone to perform euthanasia, their special concern is with physicians doing so:

> We call on fellow physicians to say that they will not deliberately kill. We must also say to each of our fellow physicians that we will not tolerate killing of patients and that we shall take disciplinary action against doctors who kill. And we must say to the broader community that if it insists on tolerating or legalizing active euthanasia, it will have to find nonphysicians to do its killing.[14]

If permitting physicians to kill would undermine the very "moral center" of medicine, then almost certainly physicians should not be permitted to perform euthanasia. But how persuasive is this claim? Patients should not fear, as a consequence of permitting *voluntary* active euthanasia, that their physicians will substitute a lethal injection for what patients want and believe is part of their care. If active euthanasia is restricted to cases in which it is truly voluntary, then no patient should fear getting it unless she or he has voluntarily requested it. (The fear that we might in time also come to accept nonvoluntary, or even involuntary, active euthanasia is a slippery slope worry I address below.) Patients' trust of their physicians could be increased, not eroded, by knowledge that physicians will provide aid in dying when patients seek it.

Might Gaylin and his colleagues nevertheless be correct in their claim that the moral center of medicine would collapse if physicians were to become killers? This question raises what at the deepest level should be the guiding aims of medicine, a question that obviously cannot be fully explored here. But I do want to say enough to indicate the direction that I believe an appropriate response to this challenge should take. In spelling out above what I called the positive argument for voluntary active euthanasia, I suggested that two principal values—respecting patients' self-determination and promoting their well-being—underlie the consensus that competent patients, or the surrogates of incompetent patients, are entitled to refuse any life-sustaining treatment and to choose from among available alternative treatments. It is the commitment to these two values in guiding physicians' actions as healers, comforters, and protectors of their patients' lives that should be at the "moral center" of medicine, and these two values support physicians' administering euthanasia when their patients make competent requests for it.

What should not be at that moral center is a commitment to preserving patients' lives as such, without regard to whether those patients want their lives preserved or judge their preservation a benefit to them. Vitalism has been rejected by most physicians, and despite some statements that suggest it, is almost certainly not what Gaylin and colleagues intended. One of them, Leon Kass, has elaborated elsewhere the view that medicine is a moral profession whose proper aim is "the naturally given end of health," understood as the wholeness and well-working of the human being; "for the physician, at least, human life in living bodies commands respect and reverence—*by its very nature.*" Kass continues, "the deepest ethical principle restraining the physician's power is not the autonomy or freedom of the patient; neither is it his own compassion or good intention. Rather, it is the dignity and mysterious power of human life itself."[15] I believe Kass is in the end mistaken about the proper account of the aims of medicine and the limits on physicians' power, but this difficult issue will certainly be one of the central themes in the continuing debate about euthanasia.

A second bad consequence that some foresee is that permitting euthanasia would weaken society's commitment to provide optimal care for dying patients. We live at a time in which the control of health care costs has become, and is likely to continue to be, the dominant focus of health care policy. If euthanasia is seen as a cheaper alternative to adequate care and treatment, then we might become less scrupulous about providing sometimes costly support and other services to dying patients. Particularly if our society comes to embrace deeper and more explicit rationing of health care, frail, elderly, and dying patients will need to be strong and effective advocates for their own health care and other needs, although they are hardly in a position to do this. We should do nothing to weaken their ability to obtain adequate care and services.

This second worry is difficult to assess because there is little firm evidence about the likelihood of the feared erosion in the care of dying patients. There are at least two reasons, however, for skepticism about this argument. The first is that the same worry could have been directed at recognizing patients' or surrogates' rights to forego life-sustaining treatment, yet there is no persuasive evidence that recognizing the right to refuse treatment has caused a serious erosion in the quality of care of dying patients. The second reason for skepticism about this worry is that only a very small proportion of deaths would occur from euthanasia if it were permitted. In the Netherlands, where euthanasia under specified circumstances is permitted by the courts, though not authorized by statute, the best estimate of the proportion of overall deaths that result from it is about 2 percent.[16] Thus, the vast majority of critically ill and dying patients will not request it, and so will still have to be cared for by physicians, families, and others. Permitting euthanasia should not diminish people's commitment and concern to maintain and improve the care of these patients.

A third possible bad consequence of permitting euthanasia (or even a public discourse in which strong support for euthanasia is evident) is to threaten the progress made in securing the rights of patients or their surrogates to decide about and to refuse life-sustaining treatment.[17] This progress has been made against the backdrop of a clear and firm legal prohibition of euthanasia, which has provided a relatively bright line limiting the dominion of others over patients' lives. It has therefore been an important reassurance to concerns about how the authority to take steps ending life might be misused, abused, or wrongly extended.

Many supporters of the right of patients or their surrogates to refuse treatment strongly oppose euthanasia, and if forced to choose might well withdraw their support of the right to refuse treatment rather than accept euthanasia. Public policy in the last fifteen years has generally let life-sustaining treatment decisions be made in health care settings between physicians and patients or their surrogates, and without the involvement of the courts. However, if euthanasia is made legally permissible greater involvement of the courts is likely, which could in turn extend to a greater court involvement in life-sustaining treatment decisions. Most agree, however, that increased involvement of the courts in these decisions would be undesirable, as it would make sound decision-making more cumbersome and difficult without sufficient compensating benefits.

As with the second potential bad consequence of permitting euthanasia, this third consideration too is speculative and difficult to assess. The feared erosion of patients' or surrogates' rights to decide about life-sustaining treatment, together with greater court involvement in those decisions, are both possible. However, I believe there is reason to discount this general worry. The legal rights of competent patients and, to a lesser degree, surrogates of incompetent patients to decide about treatment are very firmly embedded in a long line of informed consent and life-sustaining treatment cases, and are not likely to be eroded by a debate over, or even acceptance of, euthanasia. It will not be accepted without safeguards that reassure the public about abuse, and if that debate shows the need for similar safeguards for some life-sustaining treatment decisions they should be adopted there as well. In neither case are the only possible safeguards greater court involvement, as the recent growth of institutional ethics committees shows.

The fourth potential bad consequence of permitting euthanasia has been developed by David Velleman and turns on the subtle point that making a new option or choice available to people can sometimes make them worse off, even if once they have the choice they go on to choose what is best for them.[18] Ordinarily, people's continued existence is viewed by them as given, a fixed condition with which they must cope. Making euthanasia available to people as an option denies them the alternative of staying alive by default. If people are offered the option of euthanasia, their continued existence is now a choice for which they can be held responsible and which they can be asked by others to justify. We care, and are right to care, about being able to justify ourselves to others. To the extent that our society is unsympathetic to justifying a severely dependent or impaired existence, a heavy psychological burden of proof may be placed on patients who think their terminal illness or chronic infirmity is not a sufficient reason for dying. Even if they otherwise view their life as worth living, the opinion of others around them that it is not can threaten their reason for living and make euthanasia a rational choice. Thus the existence of the option becomes a subtle pressure to request it.

This argument correctly identifies the reason why offering some patients the option of euthanasia would not benefit them. Velleman takes it not as a reason for opposing all euthanasia, but for restricting it to circumstances where there are "unmistakable and overpowering reasons for persons to want the option of euthanasia," and for denying the option in all other cases. But there are at least three reasons why such restriction may not be warranted. First, polls and other evidence support that most Americans believe euthanasia should be permitted (though the recent defeat of the referendum to permit it in the state of Washington raises some doubt about this support). Thus, many more people seem to want the choice than would be made worse off by getting it. Second, if giving people the option of ending their life really makes them worse off, then we should not only prohibit euthanasia, but also take back from people the right they now have to decide about life-sustaining treatment. The feared harmful effect should already have occurred from securing people's right to refuse life-sustaining treatment, yet there is no evidence of any such widespread harm or any broad public desire to rescind that right. Third, since there is a wide range of conditions in which reasonable people can and do disagree about whether they would want continued life, it is not possible to restrict the permissibility of euthanasia as narrowly as Velleman suggests without thereby denying it to most persons who would want it; to permit it only in cases in which virtually everyone would want it would be to deny it to most who would want it.

A fifth potential bad consequence of making euthanasia legally permissible is that it might weaken the general legal prohibition of homicide. This prohibition is so fundamental to civilized society, it is argued, that we should do nothing that erodes it. If most cases of stopping life support are killing, as I have already argued, then the court cases permitting such killing have already in effect weakened this prohibition. However, neither the courts nor most people have seen these cases as killing and so as challenging the prohibition of homicide. The courts have usually grounded patients' or their surrogates' rights to refuse life-sustaining treatment in rights to privacy, liberty, self-determination, or bodily integrity, not in exceptions to homicide laws.

Legal permission for physicians or others to perform euthanasia could not be grounded in patients' rights to decide about medical treatment. Permitting euthanasia would require qualifying, at least in effect, the legal prohibition against homicide, a prohibition that in general does not allow the consent of the victim to justify or excuse the act. Nevertheless, the very same fundamental basis of the right to decide about life-sustaining treatment—respecting a person's self-determination—does support euthanasia as well. Individual self-determination has long been a well-entrenched and fundamental value in the law, and so extending it to euthanasia would not require appeal to novel legal values or principles. That suicide or attempted suicide is no longer a criminal offense in virtually all states indicates an acceptance of individual self-determination in the taking of one's own life analogous to that required for voluntary active euthanasia. The legal prohibition (in most states) of assisting in suicide and the refusal in the law to accept the consent of the victim as a possible justification of homicide are both arguably a result of difficulties in the legal process of establishing the consent of the victim after the fact. If procedures can be designed that clearly establish the voluntariness of the person's request for euthanasia, it would under those procedures represent a carefully circumscribed qualification on the legal prohibition of homicide. Nevertheless, some remaining worries about this weakening can be captured in the final potential bad consequence, to which I will now turn.

This final potential bad consequence is the central concern of many opponents of euthanasia and, I believe, is the most serious objection to a legal policy permitting it. According to this "slippery slope" worry, although active euthanasia may be morally permissible in cases in which it is unequivocally voluntary and the patient finds his or her condition unbearable, a legal policy permitting euthanasia would inevitably lead to active euthanasia being performed in many other cases in which it would be morally wrong. To prevent those other wrongful cases of euthanasia we should not permit even morally justified performance of it.

Slippery slope arguments of this form are problematic and difficult to evaluate.[19] From one perspective, they are the last refuge of conservative defenders of the status quo. When all the opponent's objections to the wrongness of euthanasia itself have been met, the opponent then shifts ground and acknowledges both that it is not in itself wrong and that a legal policy which resulted only in its being performed would not be bad. Nevertheless, the opponent maintains, it should still not be permitted because doing so would result in its being performed in other cases in which it is not voluntary and would be wrong. In this argument's most extreme form, permitting euthanasia is the first and fateful step down the slippery slope to Nazism. Once on the slope we will be unable to get off.

Now it cannot be denied that it is *possible* that permitting euthanasia could have these fateful consequences, but that cannot be enough to warrant prohibiting it if it is otherwise justified. A similar *possible* slippery slope worry could have been raised to securing competent patients' rights to decide about life support, but recent history shows such a worry would have been unfounded. It must be relevant how likely it is that we will end with horrendous consequences and an unjustified practice of euthanasia. How *likely* and *widespread* would the abuses and unwarranted extensions of permitting it be? By abuses, I mean the performance of euthanasia that fails to satisfy the conditions required for voluntary active euthanasia, for example, if the patient has been subtly pressured to accept it. By unwarranted extensions of policy, I mean later changes in legal policy to permit not just voluntary euthanasia, but also euthanasia in cases in which, for example, it need not be fully voluntary. Opponents of voluntary euthanasia on slippery slope grounds have not provided the data or evidence necessary to turn their speculative concerns into well-grounded likelihoods.

It is at least clear, however, that both the character and likelihood of abuses of a legal policy permitting euthanasia depend in significant part on the procedures put in place to protect against them. I will not try to detail fully what such procedures might be, but will just give some examples of what they might include:

1. The patient should be provided with all relevant information about his or her medical condition, current prognosis, available alternative treatments, and the prognosis of each.
2. Procedures should ensure that the patient's request for euthanasia is stable or enduring (a brief waiting period could be required) and fully voluntary (an advocate for the patient might be appointed to ensure this).
3. All reasonable alternatives must have been explored for improving the patient's quality of life and relieving any pain or suffering.
4. A psychiatric evaluation should ensure that the patient's request is not the result of a treatable psychological impairment such as depression.[20]

These examples of procedural safeguards are all designed to ensure that the patient's choice is fully informed, voluntary, and competent, and so a true exercise of self-determination. Other proposals for euthanasia would restrict its permissibility further—for example, to the terminally ill—a restriction that cannot be supported by self-determination. Such additional restrictions might, however, be justified by concern for limiting potential harms from abuse. At the same time, it is important not to impose procedural or substantive safeguards so restrictive as to make euthanasia impermissible or practically infeasible in a wide range of justified cases.

These examples of procedural safeguards make clear that it is possible to substantially reduce, though not to eliminate, the potential for abuse of a policy permitting voluntary active euthanasia. Any legalization of the practice should be accompanied by a well-considered set of procedural safeguards together with an ongoing evaluation of its use. Introducing euthanasia into only a few states could be a form of carefully limited and controlled social experiment that would give us evidence about the benefits and harms of the practice. Even then firm and uncontroversial data may remain elusive, as the continuing controversy over what has taken place in the Netherlands in recent years indicates.[21]

The Slip into Nonvoluntary Active Euthanasia

While I believe slippery slope worries can largely be limited by making necessary distinctions both in principle and in practice, one slippery slope concern is legitimate. There is reason to expect that legalization of voluntary active euthanasia might soon be followed by strong pressure to legalize some nonvoluntary euthanasia of incompetent patients unable to express their own wishes. Respecting a person's self-determination and recognizing that continued life is not always of value to a person can support not only voluntary active euthanasia, but some nonvoluntary euthanasia as well. These are the same values that ground competent patients' right to refuse life-sustaining treatment. Recent history here is instructive. In the medical ethics literature, in the courts since Quinlan, and in norms of medical practice, that right has been extended to incompetent patients and exercised by a surrogate who is to decide as the patient would have decided in the circumstances if competent.[22] It has been held unreasonable to continue life-sustaining treatment that the patient would not have wanted just because the patient now lacks the capacity to tell us that. Life-sustaining treatment for incompetent patients is today frequently foregone on the basis of a surrogate's decision, or less frequently on the basis of an advance directive executed by the patient while still competent. The very same logic that has extended the right to refuse life-sustaining treatment from a competent patient to the surrogate of an incompetent patient (acting with or without a formal advance directive from the patient) may well extend the scope of ac-

tive euthanasia. The argument will be, Why continue to force unwanted life on patients just because they have now lost the capacity to request euthanasia from us?

A related phenomenon may reinforce this slippery slope concern. In the Netherlands, what the courts have sanctioned has been clearly restricted to voluntary euthanasia. In itself, this serves as some evidence that permitting it need *not* lead to permitting the nonvoluntary variety. There is some indication, however, that for many Dutch physicians euthanasia is no longer viewed as a special action, set apart from their usual practice and restricted only to competent persons.[23] Instead, it is seen as one end of a spectrum of caring for dying patients. When viewed in this way it will be difficult to deny euthanasia to a patient for whom it is seen as the best or most appropriate form of care simply because that patient is now incompetent and cannot request it.

Even if voluntary active euthanasia should slip into nonvoluntary active euthanasia, with surrogates acting for incompetent patients, the ethical evaluation is more complex than many opponents of euthanasia allow. Just as in the case of surrogates' decisions to forego life-sustaining treatment for incompetent patients, so also surrogates' decisions to request euthanasia for incompetent persons would often accurately reflect what the incompetent person would have wanted and would deny the person nothing that he or she would have considered worth having. Making nonvoluntary active euthanasia legally permissible, however, would greatly enlarge the number of patients on whom it might be performed and substantially enlarge the potential for misuse and abuse. As noted above, frail and debilitated elderly people, often demented or otherwise incompetent and thereby unable to defend and assert their own interests, may be especially vulnerable to unwanted euthanasia.

For some people, this risk is more than sufficient reason to oppose the legalization of voluntary euthanasia. But while we should in general be cautious about inferring much from the experience in the Netherlands to what our own experience in the United States might be, there may be one important lesson that we can learn from them. One commentator has noted that in the Netherlands families of incompetent patients have less authority than do families in the United States to act as surrogates for incompetent patients in making decisions to forego life-sustaining treatment.[24] From the Dutch perspective, it may be we in the United States who are *already* on the slippery slope in having given surrogates broad authority to forego life-sustaining treatment for incompetent persons. In this view, the more important moral divide, and the more important with regard to potential for abuse, is not between foregoing life-sustaining treatment and euthanasia, but instead between voluntary and nonvoluntary performance of either. If this is correct, then the more important issue is ensuring the appropriate principles and procedural safeguards for the exercise of decisionmaking authority by surrogates for incompetent persons in *all* decisions at the end of life. This may be the correct response to slippery slope worries about euthanasia.

I have cited both good and bad consequences that have been thought likely from a policy change permitting voluntary active euthanasia, and have tried to evaluate their like-lihood and relative importance. Nevertheless, as I noted earlier, reasonable disagreement remains both about the consequences of permitting euthanasia and about which of these consequences are more important. The depth and strength of public and professional debate about whether, all things considered, permitting euthanasia would be desirable or undesirable reflects these disagreements. While my own view is that the balance of considerations supports permitting the practice, my principal purpose here has been to clarify the main issues.

THE ROLE OF PHYSICIANS

If euthanasia is made legally permissible, should physicians take part in it? Should only physicians be permitted to perform it, as is the case in the Netherlands? In discussing whether euthanasia is incompatible with medicine's commitment to curing, caring for, and comforting patients, I argued that it is not at odds with a proper understanding of the aims of medicine, and so need not undermine patients' trust in their physicians. If that argument is correct, then physicians probably should not be prohibited, either by law or by professional norms, from taking part in a legally permissible practice of euthanasia (nor, of course, should they be compelled to do so if their personal or professional scruples forbid it). Most physicians in the Netherlands appear not to understand euthanasia to be incompatible with their professional commitments.

Sometimes patients who would be able to end their lives on their own nevertheless seek the assistance of physicians. Physician involvement in such cases may have important benefits to patients and others beyond simply assuring the use of effective means. Historically, in the United States suicide has carried a strong negative stigma that many today believe unwarranted. Seeking a physician's assistance, or what can almost seem a physician's blessing, may be a way of trying to remove that stigma and show others that the decision of suicide was made with due seriousness and was justified under the circumstances. The physician's involvement provides a kind of social approval, or more accurately helps counter what would otherwise be unwarranted social disapproval.

There are also at least two reasons for restricting the practice of euthanasia to physicians only. First, physicians would inevitably be involved in some of the important procedural safeguards necessary to a defensible practice, such as seeing to it that the patient is well-informed about his or her condition, prognosis, and possible treatments, and ensuring that all reasonable means have been taken to improve the quality of the patient's life. Second, and probably more important, one necessary protection against abuse of the practice is to limit the persons given authority to perform it, so that they can be held accountable for their exercise of that authority. Physicians, whose training and professional norms give some assurance that they would perform euthanasia responsibly, are an appropriate group of persons to whom the practice may be restricted.

References and Notes

1. President's Commission for the Study of Ethical Problems in Medicine and Biomedical and Behavioral Research, *Deciding to Forego Life-Sustaining Treatment* (Washington, D.C.: U.S. Government Printing Office, 1983); The Hastings Center, *Guidelines on the Termination of Life-Sustaining Treatment and Care of the Dying* (Bloomington: Indiana University Press, 1987); *Current Opinions of the Council on Ethical and Judicial Affairs of the American Medical Association — 1989: Withholding or Withdrawing Life-Prolonging Treatment* (Chicago: American Medical Association, 1989); George Annas and Leonard Glantz, "The Right of Elderly Patients to Refuse Life-Sustaining Treatment," *Millbank Memorial Quarterly* 64, suppl. 2 (1986): 95–162; Robert F. Weir, *Abating Treatment with Critically Ill Patients* (New York: Oxford University Press, 1989); Sidney J. Wanzer et al., "The Physician's Responsibility toward Hopelessly Ill Patients," *NEJM* 310 (1984): 955–59.

2. M.A.M. de Wachter, "Active Euthanasia in the Netherlands," *JAMA* 262, no. 23 (1989): 3315–19.

3. Anonymous, "It's Over, Debbie," *JAMA* 259 (1988): 272; Timothy E. Quill, "Death and Dignity," *NEJM* 322 (1990): 1881–83.

4. Wanzer et al., "The Physician's Responsibility toward Hopelessly Ill Patients: A Second Look," *NEJM* 320 (1989): 844–49.

5. Willard Gaylin, Leon R. Kass, Edmund D. Pellegrino, and Mark Siegler, "Doctors Must Not Kill," *JAMA* 259 (1988): 2139–40.

6. Bonnie Steinbock, ed., *Killing and Allowing to Die* (Englewood Cliffs, N.J.: Prentice Hall, 1980).

7. See Chapter 7 of this volume, "Forgoing Life-Sustaining Food and Water: Is it Killing?"

8. James Rachels, "Active and Passive Euthanasia," *NEJM* 292 (1975): 78–80; Michael Tooley, *Abortion and Infanticide* (Oxford: Oxford University Press, 1983). In Chapter 5 of this volume, "Taking Human Life," I argue in more detail that killing in itself is not morally different from allowing to die and defend the strategy of argument employed in this and the succeeding two paragraphs in the text.

9. See Chapter 4 of this volume, "Moral Rights and Permissible Killing."

10. P. Painton and E. Taylor, "Love or Let Die," *Time*, 19 March 1990, pp. 62–71; *Boston Globe*/Harvard University Poll, *Boston Globe*, 3 November 1991.

11. James Rachels, *The End of Life* (Oxford: Oxford University Press, 1986).

12. Marcia Angell, "The Quality of Mercy," *NEJM* 306 (1982): 98–99; M. Donovan, P. Dillon, and L. Mcguire, "Incidence and Characteristics of Pain in a Sample of Medical-Surgical Inpatients," *Pain* 30 (1987): 69–78.

13. Eric Cassell, *The Nature of Suffering and the Goals of Medicine* (New York: Oxford University Press, 1991).

14. Gaylin et al., "Doctors Must Not Kill."

15. Leon R. Kass, "Neither for Love Nor Money: Why Doctors Must Not Kill," *The Public Interest* 94 (1989): 25–46; cf. also his *Toward a More Natural Science: Biology and Human Affairs* (New York: The Free Press, 1985), chs. 6–9.

16. Paul J. Van der Maas et al., "Euthanasia and Other Medical Decisions Concerning the End of Life," *Lancet* 338 (1991): 669–74.

17. Susan M. Wolf, "Holding the Line on Euthanasia," Special Supplement, *Hastings Center Report* 19, no. 1 (1989): 13–15.

18. My formulation of this argument derives from David Velleman's statement of it in his commentary on an earlier version of this paper delivered at the American Philosophical Association Central Division meetings; a similar point was made to me by Elisha Milgram in discussion on another occasion. For more general development of the point see Thomas Schelling, *The Strategy of Conflict* (Cambridge, Mass.: Harvard University Press, 1960); and Gerald Dworkin, "Is More Choice Better Than Less?" in *The Theory and Practice of Autonomy* (Cambridge: Cambridge University Press, 1988).

19. Frederick Schauer, "Slippery Slopes," *Harvard Law Review* 99 (1985): 361–83; Wibren van der Burg, "The Slippery Slope Argument," *Ethics* 102 (October 1991): 42–65.

20. There is evidence that physicians commonly fail to diagnose depression. See Robert I. Misbin, "Physicians Aid in Dying," *NEJM* 325 (1991): 1304–7.

21. Richard Fenigsen, "A Case against Dutch Euthanasia," Special Supplement, *Hastings Center Report* 19, no. 1 (1989): 22–30.

22. Allen E. Buchanan and Dan W. Brock, *Deciding for Others: The Ethics of Surrogate Decisionmaking* (Cambridge: Cambridge University Press, 1989).

23. Van der Maas et al., "Euthanasia and Other Medical Decisions."

24. Margaret P. Battin, "Seven Caveats Concerning the Discussion of Euthanasia in Holland," *American Philosophical Association Newsletter on Philosophy and Medicine* 89, no. 2 (1990).

Is a Physician Ever Obligated to Help a Patient Die?

Margaret P. Battin PhD

Physician-assisted suicide will probably soon become legal on a state-by-state basis, culturally tolerated, and openly practiced. But while this change will resolve some moral issues, it will raise others. One particular question which, I suspect, covertly fuels many physicians' anxieties about legalization of physician-as-sisted suicide is this: Is a physician ever *obligated* to help a patient die? If physician-assisted suicide were to become legal or legally tolerated, would the patient have a right to assistance, a right held against the physician for performance of this duty?

It may seem obvious that physicians can never be obligated to do something they regard as morally wrong—especially not something that may seem to them to be as profoundly morally wrong as contributing to the self-killing of their patient. Whatever the law says, for some physicians, conscience still may not permit it. All proposals for the legalization of physician-assisted suicide that have been proposed to date take this stance: that the physician may elect to help, but is not obligated to do so. In voter initiatives in Washington, California, and Oregon, in state legislative initiatives, in model statutes such as that of the Boston Working Group,[1] and so on, all proposals have opt-out provisions, or "conscience clauses," that permit the physician to refuse to participate in a suicide. Oregon's Measure 16, which passed at the polls in November 1994 and withstood a repeal measure in 1997, is representative. It says: "No health care provider shall be under any duty, whether by contract, by statute or by any other legal requirement to participate in the provision to a qualified patient of medication to end his or her life in a humane and dignified manner."[2]

But the basis of opt-out clauses—the ubiquitous assumption that a physician's scruples provide adequate justification, legally and morally, for excusing him or her from assisting in suicide—is rarely challenged. Furthermore, there is little challenge to the informal understanding that if the practice of assisting suicides were to remain extralegal but still become widely accepted, physicians could nevertheless choose to opt out, based on their conscience or any other personal consideration. It is just this assumption that I wish to examine here. It is my view that even the physician with the most profound moral scruples against physician-assisted suicide can, in certain circumstances, incur an obligation to provide this assistance. But when this turns out to be the case, it is almost always the product of that physician's own doing, and thus could have been avoided.

From Linda L. Emanuel. (ed.), *Regulating How We Die; The Ethical, Medical and Legal Issues Surrounding Physician-Assisted Suicide*, Cambridge, MA: Harvard University Press, 1998.

I hasten to add that I support the legal recognition of opt-out provisions in legislation concerning physician-assisted suicide. But that does not mean that a physician has no *moral* obligation to help, even if there is no legal one. Opt-out clauses, whether explicitly stated in legal documents or informally embedded in culturally understood social expectations, cannot always provide moral protection, even if they do shield a physician from legal action or social blame.

This paper has two principal parts: a long background section that examines the argument over physician-assisted suicide and shows how a positive right to assistance is generated from two basic moral principles, and a more sharply focused applications section that examines how a patient's right to assistance in suicide can impose an obligation on the physician to assist, even if the physician has scruples against doing so.

To address the question of physician obligation, we must first review the principal arguments for and against physician-assisted suicide in terminal illness, since these arguments establish whether the dying patient has rights to assistance in suicide. These rights would at a minimum include the "negative" right not to be interfered with or prevented from committing suicide if the means are available from a willing physician, and they might also include the "positive" right to require a physician to provide such help if requested.[3] If there are such rights, do they impose obligations upon physicians, even when as physicians they do not want to participate and even when the law provides opt-out clauses protecting them from any legal obligation to do so?

THE CASE FOR PHYSICIAN-ASSISTED SUICIDE

The moral argument in favor of permitting physician assistance in suicide is grounded in the conjunction of two principles: self-determination (or, as bioethicists put it, autonomy) and mercy (or the avoidance of suffering). The moral right of self-determination is the right to live one's life as one

sees fit, subject only to the constraint that this not involve harm to others. Because living one's life as one chooses must also include living the very end of one's life as one chooses, the matter of how to die is as fully protected by the principle of self-determination as any other part of one's life. Choosing how to die is part of choosing how to live.

The second component of the moral argument in favor of physician assistance in suicide is grounded in the joint obligations to avoid doing harm and to do good (the principles of nonmaleficence and beneficence, as bioethicists often put them). In medical-ethics discussions, some writers call this the principle of patient interests or patient welfare, but in the specific context of end-of-life questions, I like to call this the principle of mercy—the principle that one ought both to refrain from causing pain or suffering and act to relieve it.[4] The principle of mercy, or avoidance of suffering, underwrites the right of a dying person to an easy death, to whatever extent possible, and clearly supports physician-assisted suicide in many cases. Suicide assisted by a humane physician spares the patient the pain and suffering that may be part of the dying process, and grants the patient a "mercifully" easy death.

The principle of mercy is relevant in two general classes of cases, one comparatively unproblematic, the other far more disputed. In the first case, the dying patient is currently enduring pain or other intolerable physical symptoms (such as continuous breathlessness, nausea, vomiting) or is suffering from emotional and psychological anguish. In the second case, the patient with a terminal illness anticipates and seeks to avoid pain and suffering, knowing that they are highly likely to occur in the future course of the disease. Narrow constructions of the principle of mercy are typically interpreted to support just the patient's right to avoid current pain and suffering; the requirement that the patient be undergoing "intolerable suffering" is often read in this way. Broader constructions support preemptive strategies intended to avoid anticipated pain and suffering before they begin.

Of course, with modern pain-management techniques—especially those pioneered by the hospice movement for treating pain before it develops, on a regular schedule, rather than as needed after the patient already experiences it—most pain in terminal illness can be avoided. Other symptoms caused either by the disease itself or by the treatments employed to arrest it (including diarrhea, itching, restlessness, confusion, hallucinations, and many others) can also be controlled at least to some extent with adequate management. And suffering—that constellation of emotional and psychological factors often described as anguish, despair, hopelessness, fear, and dread—can be greatly relieved by sensitive counseling and plain old-fashioning caring.

But not all pain, symptoms, and suffering are amenable to treatment or actually receive treatment. The 1995 SUPPORT study, for example, showed that about half of patients dying in five major teaching hospitals experienced moderate to severe pain at least 50 percent of the time during their last two or three days of life.[5] Many other studies both in the United States and worldwide document inadequate treatment of pain from cancer and other causes. Sometimes this failure is due to fears of creating addiction to narcotics, sometimes to ignorance of contemporary escalating or "ladder" methods of pain management, and sometimes to lack of adequate drugs, facilities, personnel, and other resources. Whether or not nearly all pain *could* be controlled, the reality is that much pain in dying patients is not effectively treated.

It is always possible to relieve pain, other symptoms, and suffering by producing partial or complete unconsciousness through sedation. But some patients do not want this sort of relief, even if it could be effectively managed over time. They regard as repugnant programs that stress the heavy use of analgesics, especially opiates, because this treatment does not accord with their conceptions of death with dignity, or with the sort of easy passage they wish for themselves and for the family members who will be close observers of it. They do not want a medicalized, drugged dying process; they do not want "terminal sedation." They want a death they can meet consciously, in the company of their family, at a time and place and in a manner of their own choosing.

It is these two basic moral principles, self-determination and mercy, in which the right to suicide in terminal illness is grounded. Like rights of self-determination generally, the right to suicide in terminal illness is initially the negative right (sometimes called a liberty right) not to be interfered with; patients retain the right to control what is done to them in the sense of preventing what they do not want. That is what liberty, in the negative-right sense of the term, is. In the circumstances of terminal illness, however, self-determination may become a positive right as well—a right to require someone to help, a right to request or demand what one actively wants. This transformation can occur because endstage terminally ill patients, dying of degenerative processes in a long, debilitating illness, may not be able to exercise their right to influence the circumstances of their death without assistance from another person. They are often institutionalized in a hospital or other facility or bedridden at home, with constant surveillance ("care"), perhaps in pain or with other disturbing symptoms. And while some terminally ill patients do find alternative means of committing suicide—shooting themselves or jumping from buildings—for most of them this is completely unrealistic or utterly repugnant. The right to control one's own dying as far as possible in order to avoid suffering or pain is the right to seek an *easy* death. It is not merely the "right to die"; it is the right to try to die without suffering and with what is often called dignity, in a way, perhaps, that underscores the importance of the very end of life. But this is a right nullified without the assistance of someone who can provide both technical and emotional support.

The most plausible party for providing such assistance is the physician. It is the physician who has access to drugs, who has specialized knowledge of appropriate dosages, and who knows how to prevent side effects such as nausea and vomiting.[6] Equally important, the physician can be a source of emotional support for both patient and family. Seen in this light, the right to assistance in suicide is plausibly construed as the dying patient's right to help from his or her own physician, at least where there is a personal physician who knows the patient well, who has been directly, extensively, and intimately connected with and responsible for that person's care, who may know the family, and who understands, better than any other physician or other party able to provide assistance in suicide, that person's hopes, fears, and wishes about how to die.

The realistic physician also knows how the sort of death the patient seeks is likely to contrast with the expected course of events if assistance is not provided. Not only is the right to suicide in order to achieve an easier, more acceptable death not much of a right if one cannot exercise it by oneself, but it is only fully supported where such help is provided by the most effective person in this role, the patient's own physician, or, if there is no such arrangement, the physician currently responsible for providing the patient's terminal care.

It is important to recognize that in serving as the basis for the rights of dying patients, self-determination and mercy do not function as independent principles, each sufficient in itself. A mere request for physician-assisted suicide by a perfectly healthy person does not justify a physician's assistance. Similarly, the mere fact of pain or suffering in a terminal patient does not license a physician to end that person's life, if the person does not seek physician-assisted suicide.[7] Fears that legalization would license assisted suicide for a healthy person without pain or suffering, or involuntary or nonvoluntary mercy-killing, are often expressed by those who oppose it, but this is to misunderstand what the bases of a patient's right would be under any of the current proposals. *Both* principles, self-determination and mercy,

must be applicable for the patient to have any substantial claim on the physician's help.

In practice, these two principles do not always function in independent ways. The principle of self-determination may play a large role in what constitutes acceptable and unacceptable forms of pain relief to the patient. The principle of mercy likewise plays a role in what the patient conceives of as an easy death, taking into consideration both his or her own comfort and the comfort of family members or others who will be observers of the death or directly affected by it.

A person's background views about the significance of the final parts of one's life—the last months, weeks, days, hours—may also influence how patients exercise their rights. In a contemporary secular view, perhaps borrowed from medieval theology but often (though not always) cleansed of its religious underpinnings, these last moments are given special weight in a way that makes the physician's role particularly important. In medieval Christian theology, the final moments of life were the last chance for repentance, perhaps made in the religious ritual of extreme unction but in any case held within the conscience of the dying person. Repentance and complete acceptance of God in the last moments of life were held to the crucial, in that they might pave the way for salvation. A lot rode on these last moments.

The modern secularized version of this scene recognizes, at a minimum, that the very last part of one's life can be of paramount emotional, reflective, and social significance; it can be viewed as the conclusion, the resolution, the culmination of a life now completely lived. That is the reason some people choose to end their lives directly, so that they can finish their lives as themselves, able to think, communicate, and (for some) to pray, rather than be overtaken by pain or sedated into oblivion.

Thus we begin to see the basic structure of the argument about physician-assisted suicide. The side favoring physician-assisted suicide argues from the conjunction of the moral principles of self-determination and mercy to establish the right to direct assistance in dying—a right which in turn generates obligations on the part of the physician. At a minimum, the physician is obligated to refrain from attempting to prevent the suicide, whether by threat, force, or involuntary hospitalization. And insofar as the patient's right becomes a positive claim to assistance, the physician, as the party most knowledgeable in medical matters, must provide help in doing what the patient seeks. And because the patient's trust and comfort with a familiar caregiver is also crucial in seeking an easy death, the obligation to assist is particularly strong for the patient's own physician.

To be sure, relabeling might take some of the sting out of this obligation. Were the physician's role redescribed as "attending" in a "patient-directed" or "self-enacted" death, rather than "assisting" a "suicide," it might not seem so controversial or so difficult for physicians with scruples against "suicide" to comply with.[8] That is why the practice is often called "aid-in-dying" or other less freighted names, and why legislative measures, including Oregon's Measure 16, can insist that what is authorized "shall not constitute a suicide."

But relabeling is not the point. The point is that if the patient has a right to physician-assisted suicide, aid-in-dying, or whatever the act is called, the two underlying moral principles clearly show that at least in some circumstances, the patient's personal physician has a corresponding obligation to provide the assistance the patient seeks—despite whatever opt-out legal clauses or social expectations may be available.

THE CASE AGAINST PHYSICIAN-ASSISTED SUICIDE

If the patient has the right to seek an easy, merciful death, including death by means of physician-assisted suicide, the corresponding obligation on the part of the physician to provide assistance can be overridden only by other relevant considerations of equal or greater weight. The two basic arguments most frequently used to oppose physician-assisted suicide are the slippery-slope argument, which points to the likelihood of abuse, and the principled argument, which points to the intrinsic wrongness of killing.

The slippery-slope argument, backbone of the literature opposed to physician-assisted suicide, claims that legal and societal recognition of physician-assisted suicide will lead by gradual degrees to outright abuse: from a few sympathetic cases of suffering, we will move to the coercion of dying patients by malevolent family members who harbor long resentments or fragile ones who cannot bear the stress, to the callousness of cost-cutting insurers and health-maintenance organizations, and the greed, arrogance, or impatience of physicians who for a variety of reasons do not take adequate care of their dying patients. Finally we will reach the point where patients with disabilities or chronic illnesses or other conditions requiring extraordinary care are forced into "choosing" suicide when that would otherwise not have been their choice.

Focusing on physicians, the slippery-slope argument points to inadequate training in terminal care, fatalism about patients who are dying, overwork and severe time pressures in clinical settings, endemic racism, prejudice against the elderly, the disabled, those who have mental illnesses, and those who do not speak English, frustration with patients who are not improving, and many other factors which, it claims, will lead physicians to nudge, push, or force their patients in this direction. In its extreme forms, the slippery-slope argument predicts that we will end with medical holocaust: widespread involuntary killing, disguised only by the fact that its victims are not herded into concentration camps but remain dispersed in various hospitals, nursing homes, long-term care facilities, and bedrooms of their own homes. Patients will be killed against their will, it is argued, once we open these flood-gates.

Slippery-slope claims have been the focus of most objection to legalization of physician-assisted suicide. But claims of this type are notoriously difficult to defend, since they require both adequate evidence of causal factors that will lead to the feared future circumstance and reasons for thinking there are no adequate ways to prevent the predicted slide. But while cost pressures within a currently chaotic medical care system may provide reason for expecting manipulative pressures on terminally ill patients to choose suicide (in addition to or in spite of equally manipulative pressures to extend treatment), there are many resources for erecting barriers to abuse—waiting times, documentation of requests, prohibition of fees, mandatory counseling, and the analysis of records after the fact to identify deviant patterns of physician practice.[9] Certainly, we must be continuously alert to the risks of abuse. But this risk, like most risks in slippery-slope arguments, is not predictable with sufficient probability to warrant the undercutting of terminally ill patients' basic rights to a physician's assistance—especially their own physician's assistance—in suicide if they choose.

The second moral claim of the opposition to physician-assisted suicide, that killing is intrinsically wrong, is often presented with religious defenses. This argument is not so much concerned with future abuse but with the very fact of killing that physician-assisted suicide involves right now. Killing, it is argued, has been repudiated by religious codes from ancient times to the present; killing violates the sanctity of life; killing destroys the Creator's work. That killing is wrong, it is asserted, is a basic moral principle, regardless of whether it is set in a religious context or not and regardless of whether one kills another or kills oneself. While the argument concerning the wrongness of killing is more often used against active euthanasia, it is also employed against physician-assisted suicide.

Most religious and ethical systems recognize some forms of killing as justified: killing in war, killing in self-defense, killing in capital punish-

ment, and so on. In discussions of physician-assisted suicide and euthanasia, the claim that killing is intrinsically wrong is often transmuted into the claim that *doctors* should not kill. Though it might be permissible for soldiers in combat, jailers acting at the orders of the justice system, and innocent persons defending themselves from aggressors to kill in specific circumstances, it is never permissible for doctors, acting *as doctors*, to kill. It is simply outside the physician's role, a basic violation of it, in fact. Healing, the doctor's professional task, precludes killing.

But does the physician's role really preclude direct involvement in a patient's death? Clearly the physician's role centers on healing, but when healing is no longer possible and the patient is dying (after all, everyone must die eventually), what is the physician's role in this circumstance? Historical precedent will not resolve the issue: while physicians in some time periods have at least officially rejected assistance in a patient's suicide, physicians have at other times accepted it. For instance, the mainstream Greek physicians of ancient times regarded it as part of their role to provide patients whom they could not treat with a lethal drug, either at the patient's or the family's request; hemlock was developed for this purpose.[10] At the same time, the Hippocratic school of medicine held that the physician ought not to do this; this view is the one incorporated in the Hippocratic Oath. Indeed, there has been dispute about this issue throughout Western medical history.

But the issue here is not just whether doctors throughout the ages do or do not agree about their roles in caring for a dying patient and whether that may include direct killing. Such a determination would hardly answer an issue about *rights*. It is possible that physicians throughout the ages have rejected any involvement in ending life; it is also possible—and there is much evidence to suggest this—that they have been quietly willing to do so in sympathetic circumstances. One thinks, for instance, of Freud's physician, who promised and delivered a lethal drug at Freud's request after Freud had endured many years of oral cancer. But that possibility is changing as physician roles vis-à-vis the dying become a matter of broad public concern.

In the late twentieth century in the developed world, most people face death from diseases with characteristically prolonged downhill courses (cancer, cardiovascular conditions, organ failure at various sites, neurological diseases, and so on), and these often involve extended pain, limitation of function, and suffering. Physician-aided death has always been an issue, but not a frequent one, since previously there were not many cases in which dying took this extended, more difficult form; now, at the end of this century, it is becoming an issue of massive scope.

It is also important to observe cultural differences in notions about the proper duties of physicians. Doctors in the Netherlands, where physician-assisted suicide and euthanasia are broadly accepted and legally tolerated, take direct aid-in-dying to be among the duties of the conscientious doctor. While many physicians report that performing euthanasia is personally difficult, they say they believe it to be part of the physician's role, and expect one another not to desert their patients at the end. As the Remmelink Commission, which examined the practice of euthanasia and physician-assisted suicide in that country, reported, under certain circumstances, "a large majority of physicians in the Netherlands see euthanasia as an accepted element of medical practice."[11]

Nor is the religious conception of "innocence" of much help in explicating the principle of the wrongness of killing. Especially within Catholic teaching, this principle holds that it is wrong to kill the innocent, not that it is wrong to kill altogether. But not only is it difficult to separate the innocent from the guilty in any nontheological sense that could be used in public policy (aside from singling out convicts, enemy soldiers, and assailants of nonaggressive people), it

would also mean, applied in the context of assisted suicide in terminal illness, that it was just the guilty, not the innocent, who could hope to have their pleas for assistance in suicide answered. But this, of course, seems backwards: if anyone is to be forced to suffer when they choose not to do so, it should not be the innocent but the guilty.

Are these arguments—the slippery-slope argument concerning abuse and the argument from the wrongness of killing—sufficient to undercut the patient's rights of self-determination and mercy that jointly support a moral right to physician assistance in suicide? It is crucial that the arguments favoring physician-assisted suicide and the arguments opposing it are of different structures. The arguments in favor of assisted suicide appeal to the conjunction of two fundamental moral principles: self-determination and mercy. These two basic moral principles are acknowledged by all parties, including physicians, patients, and observers (both opponents and proponents of physician-assisted suicide), as just that: basic moral principles. Even physicians who oppose physician-assisted suicide accept the principle of self-determination—it is, after all, what underlies the opt-out conscience-clause provisions in legislation concerning physician-assisted suicide.

The same principle is also recognized by the patient seeking help as the basis of his or her own right of self-determination. Physicians and patients alike also recognize obligations of mercy: relieving pain and suffering is a central part of the physician's task, as well as what the patient seeks from the physician.

Furthermore, opponents of physician-assisted suicide also appeal to both these principles: autonomy or self-determination is the basis of the right not to be killed against one's will (feared as the consequence of the slide down the slippery slope) and mercy is the basis of the patient's right to avoid the fear and emotional pain that the prospect of being killed against one's will would involve. All sides, then, recognize these two fundamental moral principles, though they may differ about their relevance in the issue of physician-assisted suicide.

The arguments *against* physician-assisted suicide, however, have a different structure; they are not based on fundamental moral principles. The principle "do not kill" cannot be directly defended without qualification, it is widely assumed, since it would also prohibit killing in war, self-defense, and capital punishment. Even the more limited principle of not killing the innocent, though defensible elsewhere, backfires in terminal-illness contexts. The more focused application "doctors should not kill" is not usually treated as an argument in principle, since it would run afoul of historical and contemporary cross-cultural variation, but as a form of slippery-slope argument. Why shouldn't doctors kill? The answers characteristically point to the bad consequences that would ensue if doctors were to kill or assist in the suicide of even those patients who asked for this help. Patients, it is said, would no longer be able to trust their doctors. Doctors would overstep the bounds of legally permitted assistance in suicide, moving on to killing that is in no way sanctioned by law. Perhaps the law, too, might expand its scope, permitting doctors to kill patients, especially patients with disabilities, where there were no acceptable moral grounds for doing so. Furthermore, the integrity of the medical profession would be threatened.

But when the question is pursued in this way, a principle-based argument is thus transmuted into a consequentialist one that points to the harms killing might cause. Unless it is held that *all* killing causes harm sufficient so that it cannot be permitted (a view almost never consistently advanced by opponents in the current public discussions of physician-assisted suicide), it is difficult to show why, if their dying patients earnestly request it in preference to irremediable suffering, physicians in particular should not kill, without appealing to a consequentialist argument. But this is not an argument in principle; it is an argument about possible future practice.

Given this difference in the structure of the arguments for and against physician-assisted suicide, we may conclude that the burden of proof runs in favor of recognizing dying patients' rights to physician-assisted suicide if they are suffering intolerably or if they anticipate intolerable suffering. Only principle-based claims of equal or greater weight, or predictive proof that widespread bad consequences and medical holocaust would really ensue, can override this right. Moreover, claims about possible harms cannot be merely conjectural, speculative guesses about what could happen but must provide clear, incontrovertible evidence of genuine threats that can be avoided in no other way. Slippery-slope arguments against rights succeed only if they can provide good evidence that the projected future harm is really great and truly inevitable.

Claims about abuse in Holland are often used to try to make this point, but many of those given broadest circulation in the United States involve substantial distortion of the facts. Despite claims about the notorious "1,000 cases" in which suffering patients were euthanized without a current explicit request, there is no evidence of abuse that would be sufficient to prove that allowing physician-assisted suicide and euthanasia leads to medical holocaust.[12] Indeed, many observers think protections for patients in the Netherlands are improving as legal regulation and social recognition of a formerly underground practice increases. There is no sound evidence of a pattern of generalized abuse.

The overall structure of the argument invites (though does not require) proponents of the physician-assisted suicide to show that widespread, serious abuse will not result, and this, I think, they are able to do. Certainly the possibility of abuse should always be taken seriously, by proponents and opponents alike, regardless of the structure of the argument. Even with the weight of principle on their side, proponents have been working to show that it is possible to devise adequate barriers against abuse. No compelling case has been made by opponents that legalizing or otherwise accepting physician-assisted suicide will cause overridingly great harms, sufficient to override the patient's basic rights of autonomy and mercy in the first place, and much of their argument has involved the kind of diffuse threat often employed in slippery slope argumentation but without real corroboration. But if the opposition cannot reasonably establish that substantial harms would ensue, it has not produced a case strong enough for overriding a right.

The error many interpreters of the physician-assisted suicide debate have made, sizing up the arguments concerning self-determination and mercy on one side and the arguments concerning the wrongness of killing and the possibility of abuse on the other, is to treat these as equal, not just in content but in structure. But they are not equal in structure; the self-determination and mercy side is logically stronger, being grounded in basic moral principles, while the argument from the wrongness of killing (which is focused in practice, as we have seen, on the wrongness of *doctors'* killing and is argued primarily on slippery-slope grounds, or grounds of projected consequences) and the slippery-slope argument itself function as challenges to it. This structure of rights grounded in basic moral principles and correlative obligations (articulated by proponents) and reasons for overridings (articulated by opponents) captures all the elements of both sides of the argument.

THE PHYSICIAN'S OBLIGATION

This elaborate analysis, based on the structure of the arguments for and against physician-assisted suicide, may seem entirely irrelevant to the practicing physician. What bothers the physician is the claim that patients have a *right*—a right "against" the physician—for performance of an "obligation" to help patients kill themselves. Actual clinical situations in the real world are often not simple, and the relevance of ideals such as self-determination and mercy are far from clear. Even among physicians who recognize a moral

obligation to assist dying patients with suicide, putting that policy into practice in actual situations is often problematic.

For example, a patient may seek help in suicide because of anticipated pain and suffering that lies in the future but has not yet occurred. Honoring this request is likely to be a problem where statutes define eligibility for physician-assisted suicide in terms of time to projected death. Oregon's Measure 16 and most other U.S. proposals make eligibility for assistance a function of expected outcome (death within six months), but they do not specify what degree of medical deterioration must already have occurred. What if the physician cannot be certain that death will occur in six months? Or what about a suffering patient who articulated a wish for suicide in the past but has since become incompetent? This is the problem with more than half of the notorious 1,000 Dutch cases, where wishes for euthanasia had been expressed but there was no current explicit request. What should physicians do about conscious, competent patients who earnestly wish assistance in suicide and are enduring irremediable pain or suffering but cannot administer the means of death to themselves—for instance, patients who are unable to take oral drugs, or who are too disabled to use other means of administration such as self-injections or suppositories? Here, if the physician feels a moral obligation to provide assistance, it must be by physician-administered euthanasia, not physician-assisted suicide.

Of particular relevance is the situation some Dutch physicians report in assisting patients with suicide. Though the suicide may begin with the patient's self-administration of a lethal oral solution, suppository, or pills, if the effect is not complete or if vomiting occurs (as sometimes happens with oral drugs not preceded by an antiemetic), or if the effect cannot be complete because the volume required for one-time administration would be too large (as with patients who have difficulty swallowing), the physician must be prepared to perform euthanasia at the end.

Other situations also make things far less clear, as is the case with patients who are chronically but not terminally ill, or who suffer from paralysis, or who have some but not overwhelming pain, or whose suffering is exclusively anticipatory, at some distant and undetermined point in the future, and so on. Each of these mixed, difficult cases presents a different challenge.

The obligations of physicians in these situations are best expressed in terms of a double axis of continuums: the stronger the patient's current wish for a physician-assisted death (this is the self-determination axis) and the greater the patient's experience of unrelievable pain and suffering in the process of dying (this is the mercy axis), the stronger the dual basis of the patient's right, and hence the stronger the physician's correlative obligation to provide the patient with assistance in dying. At the other end of this double axis of continuums, where the patient does not want to commit suicide and is not suffering from a terminal illness, the physician has an obligation *not* to assist the patient's death. Intermediate points yield a range of somewhat weaker to somewhat stronger claims on the physician. In many of these, a physician may choose to respond to a patient's request for assistance but is not morally required to do so. Only toward that end of the continuum, where earnest request and a real need for mercy coincide, where the patient seeks an easier death but cannot accomplish this with ease or dignity acting alone, does the possibility of obligation to the dying patient arise. Thus, obligation to assist a patient in suicide may be a comparatively rare thing, but it nevertheless can arise. It is this obligation which, I think, physicians' scruples are too easily assumed to defeat.

What about the physician who objects? Even where physician-assisted suicide has been fully legalized and no legal penalty or other harm to the physician, family members, or others is anticipated, and where there are no issues about borderline cases like those above, a physician may still have scruples against participating in this practice. The opt-out clauses that are part of all current public initiatives and legislative proposals permit the physician to decline to participate. But in order to evaluate the moral weight of these opt-outs and determine whether they outweigh a patient's rights, we must know something about the reasons for them.

Consider the sorts of explanations various physicians might provide for declining to meet a patient's request for assistance in suicide. Some explanations involve doubts about the psychological and medical appropriateness of ending life in the specific case, such as "The patient is ambivalent" or "The patient's pain could still be alleviated." These reasons, in effect, challenge the criteria of eligibility by asserting that self-determination and mercy do not in this case fully apply. Other reasons could involve points of self-interest or self-protection, such as "It's too time-consuming," "I'll lose respect around the hospital," or "I don't want to dirty my hands." Reasons of self-interest may include both reasons of trivial concern, like "It takes too much paperwork," and concerns about more substantial personal risks, as in "I don't want to subject myself or my family to social ostracism or legal risk."

But some of the reasons a physician might offer, if being truthful, for not wishing to participate are rooted in more basic moral scruples: the beliefs that it is contrary to the physician's religion, that it is sinful, that it is a violation of the law, and that it is profoundly morally wrong. These are not trivial or merely self-interested excuses but serious, earnest reservations. It is important not to minimize the force of some physicians' objections or the range of behaviors such objections might proscribe. Kevin Wildes, a Jesuit, points out that because suicide is held in the Roman Catholic tradition to be inherently evil, so is assisting in a suicide.[13] But Wildes also argues that for a physician to refer a patient to another, more compliant physician would likewise be complicity in evil, and hence evil itself. A conscientious believer not only would make use of an opt-out clause but would refuse to have anything to do with the suicide at all, not even providing advice, confirming a terminal diagnosis, or transferring a patient's records to another physician (as most opt-out clauses, including that of Measure 16, would require), for this too would be tantamount to complicity in evil itself.

It may seem self-evident that scruples of this intensity should be honored without reservation, perhaps especially where they have a religious basis. Clearly, it would do substantial psychological, emotional, and spiritual harm to physicians to force them to violate their own consciences, and under most circumstances this would be unnecessary: after all, patients may be easily able to find other physicians willing and prepared to provide the aid they seek. In such cases, the patient's rights of self-determination and mercy would still be satisfied, though by some other physician, and real harm to the physician with scruples would be avoided.

While genuine scruples on the part of the physician should be honored whenever possible, there are circumstances where the patient's right overrides these scruples. The patient may have a particularly strong relationship with the original physician, and may find it impossible to achieve such a relationship with another. Or there may be no other physician available with equal technical skill in terminal care or similar specialization in the patient's particular disease. Or there may be no other physician available at all. Or there may be no other physician available who is willing to assist in a suicide, a circumstance particularly likely in a practice area or facility where physicians tend to share the same values and views. If all physicians were to decline to participate, this would render the patient's right to assistance nil.

While in many situations it will be comparatively easy for a patient to find a physician willing to assist in suicide, especially if full legalization has occurred, there still may be circumstances in which a particular physician is the only one who could reasonably be called upon to provide assistance. Because in these circumstances the patient cannot find an alternative, the case for expecting this physician to cooperate, despite his or her scruples, is far stronger.

This may seem to be a rare circumstance, but it is closely related to another, far more common situation in which the physician does not tell the patient about his scruples until quite late in the downhill course of the disease. By this time the patient is often seriously incapacitated and in substantial need of ongoing medical care. As the patient deteriorates, it becomes increasingly difficult for the patient to transfer to the care of another physician—with whom, in any case, there would be no longstanding relationship or pattern of mutual understanding. By not informing the patient of his or her scruples in a timely way, the physician has in effect made himself or herself the only one available to this patient.

Nor can it be supposed that it is the patient's responsibility rather than the physician's to bring the matter up early on (though the prudent patient will certainly do so). The patient cannot be expected to understand the probable course of the disease, the likelihood of pain or other symptoms that are inherently untreatable, possible limitations of the physician's capacity to relieve pain and suffering (whether because of a lack of skill, a lack of information, or institutional priorities), or other factors in the medical course that lies ahead. The effect of delay is compounded if the physician—perhaps seeking to avoid "dirty hands" or any complicity in "evil"—refuses to consult, refer, confirm a diagnosis, transfer records, or cooperate in any way.

In short, because it has become too late for the patient to switch to another doctor to receive that aid to which the patient has a right, it has likewise become too late for the doctor to announce any principled reservations he or she may have. Although the individual physician with serious reservations may not have an obligation to assist in the suicide of a patient where it is easy for the patient to transfer, in this case it is the physician's own behavior that has led to a situation in which that physician has become the patient's only choice.

Furthermore, the patient may have come to rely on expectations that the physician will help. Consciously or unconsciously, physicians often foster a patient's trust in their capacity to negotiate a peaceful, dignified death. Especially if physician-assisted suicide is legal, patients may come to expect that their physician will provide assistance in suicide if asked to do so. Furthermore, the physician may even believe there is some medical reason to encourage this expectation, since evidence suggests that when patients believe they can count on the physician to provide aid-in-dying on request at a later date, this expectation allows them to extend their lives longer.[14] The patient who believes that help will be available whenever it is finally needed will often hang on until the very last minute.

Of course, the obligation may be different when the patient's terminal condition is of sudden onset or could not be foreseen: for instance, in unexpected, massive stroke, in accidental trauma, and in various other conditions. But the majority of cases are not like this. In the contemporary world, at least in developed countries, most dying involves a downhill, deteriorative trajectory, the general outlines of which the experienced physician can readily foresee. This includes virtually all cases of cancer, much cardiovascular disease, most neurological conditions, most organ disease or failure, virtually all AIDS, and so on. It may be particularly true when the patient is hospitalized or institutionalized in a nursing home or other health care facility (as is the case for the vast majority of deaths occurring in the United States) or otherwise under close surveillance. The physician *can* foresee what is coming and how the patient is likely to die; by remaining in a position of care for the patient, the physician incurs a growing obligation, as the patient's capacity for self-determination diminishes and the need for mercy grows, to assist in easing the patient's death in the way that the patient desires.

To put this in another way, the physician's obligation to help arises primarily within a relationship that develops during the course of providing care for a dying patient. As time goes on and the patient's condition declines, the patient's rights grow stronger both on grounds of self-determination and of mercy, and thus the physician's obligation grows correspondingly more difficult to evade.

Nor is it adequate to argue that the patient's death can always be softened by either of the two principal means of negotiating death that are already legal and already widely employed: first, the withholding or withdrawing of treatment without which the patient will die, such as respiratory support or artificial nutrition or hydration, and second, the over-ample use of pain-relieving drugs, especially morphine, which, although ostensibly used with the intention of relieving pain, also decrease respiration and thus hasten death. These two strategies, now ubiquitous in U.S. medical practice, are not adequate means of satisfying the physician's obligation to the dying patient who seeks assistance in suicide, since the physician's obligation is rooted not just in the principle of mercy, which these means of negotiating death might provide, but also in the principle of autonomy or self-determination. Of course, if these strategies are satisfactory to the patient, then the physician's obligation to assist the patient in dying can be met in this way. But to repeat, some patients find these strategies distasteful or repugnant and, as an expression of their basic right of self-determination, seek means of dying they perceive as more dignified and more humane, more in keeping with their own basic values. They reject a form of dying they perceive as drawn-out, overmedicalized, drugged, undignified, and cruel, and they are not willing to settle for this, even to salve the physician's conscience—especially if they believe the physician's conscience or religious commitment is being used to trump their own rights.

Many physicians try to avoid such situations with promises like "I won't let you suffer," seeking to reduce the patient's fears and to give the patient the courage to continue. But the physician's obligation is *strengthened*, not relieved, by such tactics. If the physician proves unable to treat the patient's pain or suffering adequately, this simple, consoling phrase actually reinforces the obligation the physician now incurs. It is mercy that is promised in that little phrase, and it is the need for mercy that is part of the basis of the patient's right to assistance in dying.

"I won't let you suffer" may covertly promise something else as well—a period of dying that is not only pain-free but lived in a conscious, alert, still-autonomous way. This promise is certainly not explicit; but to at least some patients, "not suffering" does not suggest the absence of conscious experience, as in terminal sedation, but rather the enjoyment of conscious experience in which suffering does not occur. To some, at least, "I won't let you suffer" will seem to mean "I'll see that you can remain alert, still capable of emotion, communication, and other things that may be important to you, like final goodbyes or prayer, in a way that is not distorted by suffering."

The development of increasingly stronger rights on the part of the patient as the patient's condition declines and correspondingly stronger obligations on the part of the physician caring for the patient during that decline is exacerbated by medicine's tendency to delay decision-making as long as possible, waiting until a crisis or change of status to raise most questions about withholding or withdrawing treatment, using opiates for pain management, or addressing other elements of terminal care.[15] This may reinforce patients' tendencies to evade and delay discussion of issues they find it painful to think about, especially if denial is part of their defense against bad news. But it is not only hesitation, fear of raising painful issues, or perhaps even cowardice on the part of both the patient and the physician that favors postponing discussion of these issues. Longstanding institutional practice contributes as well. Despite legal requirements like that imposed by the Patient Self-Determination Act, which requires hospitals and other institutions to ask patients if they have advance directives, and despite

other recent changes, the institutional ethos of medicine tends to put decision-making about end-of-life situations off as long as possible, until virtually the last minute at which an effective decision can be made. Not only do these patterns of delayed decision-making tend to displace responsibility away from the patient onto the physician, family members, and others, as the patient becomes increasingly incapacitated and less and less capable of genuine participation in them, but these patterns also tend to put physicians into an increasing moral bind and make them still more vulnerable targets for moral blame—though blame of a different sort, and even harder to see for a physician who objects in principle.

If decision-making is postponed long enough, the patient who would perhaps have requested the physician's assistance in suicide may become incompetent, delirious, or comatose. As these final stages of deterioration occur, self-determination and mercy—the principles that formed the basis of the patient's original right to aid—cease to be relevant in any direct way. The incompetent or delirious patient is no longer capable of current, self-directing autonomous choice and cannot effectively request assistance in suicide, and may not be able to carry it out even if assistance were provided; and if unconscious, the patient is no longer capable of experiencing suffering or feeling pain. Since neither autonomy nor mercy is relevant any longer, the patient's original right to assistance in suicide may seem to evaporate, and with it the physician's obligation to assist. Thus, it may seem, if the physician with scruples delays long enough, he or she is home free.

But I think not. There is a new basis for moral blame here, and blame of a stronger sort. The physician no longer merely fails to meet the obligation a patient's right to assistance generates, but now is blameworthy for suppression of that right as well. If the singular importance of this right is rooted in the secularized medieval view that the last moments of life can be of particular significance, it is not a trivial right that is being suppressed, and the physician's blameworthiness in doing so is greater than it would be for suppressing other rights, such as rights to information about a prognosis, or informed consent to procedures, or access to certain treatment. If the kinds of rights suppressed in caring for a patient near death are far more substantial than those that might be violated during other periods of caring for a patient who is temporarily ill but will recover, then a physician does particularly grave moral wrong in delaying, prevaricating, and eluding the patient's claim.

CONCLUSIONS

That physicians may come to have obligations to provide direct assistance in the matter of dying does not mean that they are required to honor any patient request. It is still up to the physician to assess as carefully as possible (preferably in consultation with others, especially those with expertise in diagnosing depression or other psychologically confounding states) whether the request is stable, unambivalent, uncoerced, fully informed, and reflects the patient's most basic values—in short, whether it is a rational request, rationally made. It is also up to the physician (again, preferably in consultation with others, especially experts in the treatment of pain) to ascertain that there are no alternative ways acceptable to the patient of relieving the current pain and suffering or that which is about to occur.

But where the patient's request really does originate in autonomy and in the claim to mercy, it does mean that the physician is obligated not to entrap the patient into compliance with the physician's values rather than the patient's own values, which is what happens when choices are ignored or decision-making is delayed. This will be the particular temptation (though it would not be phrased in this way) of those physicians who have the strongest reservations and scruples against killing or assistance in suicide. After all, these are the physicians who are most likely to want to avoid the issue, to delay any discussion of dying, to promise not to let the patient suffer at the end so as to avoid having the patient raise the question of suicide assistance in the first place, and to delay assistance until the patient's own deterioration renders the issue moot. Perhaps these physicians will signal, albeit unconsciously, that physician-assisted suicide is not a topic open to discussion. But in doing so, especially if physician-assisted suicide is legal or broadly accepted in the culture, they become the physicians most likely to have generated for themselves a strong moral obligation, one they will most bitterly resent. Paradoxically, it is physicians with the firmest moral scruples who may be the most likely to find themselves in this profoundly unwanted situation.

This conclusion is not a palatable one, especially for physicians who have the strongest moral reservations but who are not alert to the moral consequences of their own behavior. Physicians who entrap patients into compliance with their own values paradoxically also entrap themselves into having moral obligations they do not want. Even if the law protects these physicians from being forced to honor them, the moral obligations they have brought upon themselves will remain. Opt-out clauses may provide legal protection, but they do not guarantee moral protection too. Of course, a patient's right to assistance from a particular physician may be overridden where both the psychic damage to the physician's conscience would be genuinely grave and the disruption to the patient of transferring to another physician comparatively small, but it is not always the case that both these conditions are met. There may be little moral sympathy for physicians whose own behavior creates the dilemma they seek to avoid.

This conclusion applies not only to physician-assisted suicide but to any mode of life-ending assistance to which a patient has a right but to which a physician has scrupled objections, be it withholding or withdrawing of treatment, the overuse of opiates, the cessation of nutrition and hydration, the induction of terminal sedation, and so on. The irony is that in most situations it is fairly easy for physicians to protect themselves from such obligations. All it requires is announcing in advance—*well* in advance—what scruples one has and whether these would preclude one's willingness to assist, so that the patient can seek care somewhere else and not become dependent on aid from this physician. Ideally, such a discussion might occur at the beginning of a continuing relationship between a physician and patient, long before any evidence of terminal illness might arise, so that both physician and patient would be aware of differences in individual values that might some day be relevant in the matter of terminal care. After all, if the vast majority of people in the developed world die of diseases with characteristically long downhill courses, there is a substantial chance for any individual patient that the issue will eventually arise. Of course, in the comparatively transitory climate of contemporary medicine, the possibility of such conversations between patients and their personal physicians so far in advance may be wishful thinking; but there is no reason they could not occur far, far earlier than such conversations ordinarily do.

Physicians must also be careful not to lean too heavily on assertions of scruple by the institutions in which they practice. Catholic hospitals, Hospice, and the VA system, for example, have all articulated opposition to physician-assisted suicide, as have other organizations. Although institutional announcement of scruples in effect involves institutional refusal to honor patients' particularly important rights, the patient cannot assume that the physician's scruples track those of the institution or are significant to the physician to the same depth or degree. It may be easier for institutions than for physicians to announce scruples about physician-assisted suicide; for an institution, announcing scruples requires merely issuing a position statement or policy directive—and making sure the patient is informed of this. Physicians, by contrast, have to talk

clearly, directly, even intimately with their patients—their *own* patients—who are dying. Prior, clear announcement of their own personal scruples will perhaps be less difficult for doctors in a future in which physician-assisted suicide is legal, but only if the current climate of medical decision-making also changes.

But physicians' own behavior is not the only culprit in engendering moral obligations they do not want. Public attitudes and practices contribute to this as well, paradoxically reinforcing obligation-producing behavior on the part of physicians. Believing that physicians' objections to assisted suicide excuses them across the board, the public has not demanded full, compelling evidence for any claim that would have the effect of overriding a patient's principle-based rights. Society leads physicians to assume that trivial, self-interested objections will trump patients' rights as easily as profoundly held scruples (though the Boston Working Group's model statute would not do so), and society does not notice the way in which the legal structures now being developed to protect genuine, profoundly held scruples invite this. Society does not require physicians with either trivially or profoundly held scruples to own up to them in advance, and to put them forward for the patient's inspection. And society lets physicians and institutions delay decision-making so long that the patient's rights, and the physician's corresponding obligations, are effectively eclipsed. We think that we have solved the moral problem in this way. We haven't. On the contrary, we have only made it worse.

References and Notes

1. The Boston Working Group's model statue provides: "No individual who is conscientiously opposed to providing a patient with medical means of suicide may be required to do so or to assist a responsible physician in doing so." Charles H. Baron, Clyde Bergstresser, Dan W. Brock, Garrick F. Cole, Nancy S. Dorfman, Judith A. Johnson, Lowell E. Schnipper, James Vorenberg, Sidney H. Wanzer, "A model state act to

authorize and regulate physician-assisted suicide," *Harvard Journal on Legislation* 33, no. 1 (1996): 1–34.

2. Oregon Death with Dignity Act, Section 4.04. The Act does require, however, that if a health care provider is unable or unwilling to carry out a patient's request under the Act, and the patient transfers his or her care to a new health care provider, that the prior health care provider shall transfer, upon request, a copy of the patient's relevant medical records to the new health care provider (Section 4.04). To be sure, a health care provider would be legally obligated to transfer the patient's records at the patient's request in any case.

3. Many of these arguments can also be made for and against physician performance of active euthanasia, though since that is no longer the focus of most legislative proposals in the U.S., I won't discuss it further here.

4. For example, Dan Brock uses the term mercy in his *Life and Death* (Cambridge: Cambridge University Press, 1993). I've discussed at some length the relationship between the principles of nonmaleficence and beneficence, now canonical in the bioethics literature, and what I like to call the principle of mercy. The former are comparatively narrow principles, requiring not doing harm and doing good, respectively. The latter, the principle of mercy, is a broader principle that amalgamates both in the context of suffering. Thus the principle of mercy requires not just refraining from causing pain or suffering, which the principle of nonmaleficence would require, but also acting to relieve pain or suffering, as the principle of beneficence would require.

To call this principle the principle of mercy, then, is to use shorthand for much more cumbersome terms, but it is also to invoke traditional conceptions of the physician's role in the matter of pain and suffering. See my account "Euthanasia: the fundamental issues," originally appearing in *Health Care Ethics*, ed. D. Van DeVeer and T. Regan (Philadelphia: Temple University Press, 1987), reprinted in Margaret P. Battin, *The Least Worst Death* (New York: Oxford University Press, 1994).

5. The SUPPORT Principal Investigators, "A controlled trial to improve care for seriously ill hospitalized patients," *JAMA* 274, no. 20 (1995): 1591–1598. Objections to the methodology of this study include the fact that these reports were taken from family members or other survivors, not the patients themselves.

6. When the practices of euthanasia and physician-assisted suicide first came to light in the Netherlands, it became clear that some physicians did not know the appropriate drugs or dosages to use; some attempted to use wholly inappropriate drugs, such as insulin or morphine. In response, anesthesiologist Dr. Pieter Admiraal published the appropriate information in a booklet sent to all Dutch physicians; this information has been revised and updated repeatedly. See Gerrit K. Kimsma, "Euthanasia and euthanising drugs in the Netherlands," *Journal of Pharmaceutical Care in Pain and Symptom Control* 3, nos. 3/4 (1995) and 4, nos. 1/2 (1996), also published as *Drug Use in Assisted Suicide and Euthanasia*, ed. Margaret P. Battin and Arthur G. Lipman (Binghamton, NY: Haworth Press, 1996).

For information on methods of physician assistance in suicide used by Compassion in Dying, Seattle, see Thomas A. Preston and Ralph Mero, "Observations concerning terminally ill patients who choose suicide," in the same volume. Derek Humphrey's *Final Exit: The Practicalities of Self-Deliverance and Assisted Suicide for the Dying* (Eugene, OR: The Hemlock Society, 1991), has also provided drug information to the general public.

7. Some authors argue for the legitimacy of directly caused death on grounds of mercy in the absence of patient request when the patient is no longer competent and cannot make a request or express any wishes but is suffering severely. No contemporary writer with whom I'm familiar argues for directly caused death where that is contrary to the patient's wishes.

8. The term "patient-directed" is from Totie Oberman, personal communication, American Association of Suicidology, May 1995. The term "self-enacted" is from Stephen Jamison.

9. Actual cost savings from physician-assisted suicide may be far smaller than generally believed. See E. J. Emanuel and M. P. Battin, "The economics of euthanasia: what are the potential cost savings from legalizing physician-assisted suicide?" (*New England Journal of Medicine*, forthcoming), where we estimate that the cost savings from patients who would choose physician-assisted suicide or euthanasis, were these legal, would be less than 1 percent of the total U.S. health-care budget. For a more detailed discussion of safeguards against abuse, see Battin, "Voluntary euthanasia and the risks of abuse," in Battin, *Least Worst Death*, pp. 163–181.

10. Ludwig Edelstein, "The Hippocratic Oath: text, translation, and interpretation," in *Supplements to the Bulletin of the History of Medicine* no. 1 (1943), and in *Ancient Medicine: Selected Papers of Ludwig Edelstein*, ed. Owsei Temkin and C. Lillian Temkin (Baltimore: Johns Hopkins University Press, 1967). Also see Danielle Gourevitch, "Suicide among the sick in classical antiquity," *Bulletin of the History of Medicine* 43 (1969): 501–518; Darrel W. Amundsen, "The physician's obligation to prolong life: a medical duty without classical roots," *Hastings Center Report* 8, no. 4 (1978): 23–30; Margaret Pabst Battin, *Ethical Issues in Suicide* (Englewood Cliffs, NJ: Prentice-Hall, 1995); and Ezekiel Emanuel, "The history of euthanasia debates in the United States and Britain," *Annals of Internal Medicine* 121, no. 10 (1994): 793–802.

11. Paul J. van der Maas, Johannes J. M. van Delden, Loes Pijnenborg, and Caspar W. N. Looman, "Euthanasia and other medical decisions concerning the end of life," *The Lancet* 338 (1991): 609–674. The first Remmelink report is available in full in English as a special issue of *Health Policy* 22, nos. 1 and 2 (1992); the follow-up report is available in condensed form in Paul J. van der Maas et al., "Euthanasia, physician-assisted suicide, and other medical practices involving the end of life in the Netherlands, 1990–1995," *New England Journal of Medicine* 335 (1996): 1699–1705.

12. See Loes Pijnenborg, Paul J. van der Maas, Johannes J. M. van Delden, and Caspar W. N. Looman, "Life-terminating acts without explicit request of patient," *The Lancet* 341 (1993): 1196–1199. This more detailed examination of the approximately 1,000 cases of euthanasia without explicit request uncovered in the original Remmelink Commission report shows that in about 59 percent of them the physician did have some information about the patient's wish, though short of a full, current request; in nearly all of the other 41 percent of cases, the patient had become no longer capable of discussion, was suffering unbearably, there was no chance of improvement, and palliative possibilities were exhausted. While the Dutch do not seek to defend every case that occurs, it is clearly not the case, as outside observers often insinuate, that in the Netherlands patients are routinely killed against their will.

13. Kevin W. Wildes, S.J., "Conscience, referral, and physician assisted suicide," in *Journal of Medicine and Philosophy* 18, no. 3 (1993): 323–328, a special issue entitled "Legal Euthanasia: Ethical Issues in an Era of Legalized Aid in Dying," ed. Margaret P. Battin and Thomas J. Bole, III.

14. Thomas A. Preston and Ralph Mero, "Observations concerning terminally ill patients who choose suicide," *Journal of Pharmaceutical Care in Pain and Symptom Control* 3 (1995): 3–4; also in *Drug Use in Assisted Suicide and Euthanasia*, ed. Battin and Lipman.

15. See Margaret Battin, "The eclipse of altruism: the moral costs of deciding for others," in Battin, *The Least Worst Death*, pp. 40–57.

Is There a Right to Die?

Leon R. Kass MD, PhD

It has been fashionable for some time now and in many aspects of American public life for people to demand what they want or need as a matter of rights. During the past few decades we have heard claims of a right to health or health care, a right to education or employment, a right to privacy (embracing also a right to abort or to enjoy pornography, or to commit suicide or sodomy), a right to clean air, a right to dance naked, a right to be born, and a right not to have been born. Most recently we have been presented with the ultimate new rights claim, a "right to die."

From *Hastings Center Report* 23: 34–43, 1993.

This claim has surfaced in the context of changed circumstances and burgeoning concerns regarding the end of life. Thanks in part to the power of medicine to preserve and prolong life, many of us are fated to end our once-flourishing lives in years of debility, dependence, and disgrace. Thanks to the respirator and other powerful technologies that can, all by themselves, hold comatose and other severely debilitated patients on this side of the line between life and death, many who would be dead are alive only because of sustained mechanical intervention. Of the 2.2 million annual deaths in the United States, 80 percent occur in health care facilities; in roughly 1.5 million of these cases, death is preceded by some explicit decision about stopping or not starting medical treatment. Thus, death in America is not only medically managed, but its timing is also increasingly subject to deliberate choice. It is from this background that the claims of a right to die emerge.

I do not think that the language and approach of rights are well suited either to sound personal decision-making or to sensible public policy in this very difficult and troubling matter. In most of the heartrending end-of-life situations, it is hard enough for practical wisdom to try to figure out what is morally right and humanly good, without having to contend with intransigent and absolute demands of a legal or moral right to die. And, on both philosophical and legal grounds, I am inclined to believe that there can be no such thing as a *right* to die—that the notion is groundless and perhaps even logically incoherent. Even its proponents usually put "right to die" in quotation marks, acknowledging that it is at best a misnomer.

Nevertheless, we cannot simply dismiss this claim, for it raises important and interesting practical and philosophical questions. Practically, a right to die is increasingly asserted and gaining popular strength; increasingly, we see it in print without the quotation marks. The former Euthanasia Society of America, shedding the Nazi-tainted and easily criticized "E" word, changed its name to the more politically correct Society for the Right to Die before becoming Choice In Dying. End-of-life cases coming before the courts, nearly always making their arguments in terms of rights, have gained support for some sort of "right to die." The one case to be decided by a conservative Supreme Court, the *Cruzan* case, has advanced the cause, as I will show.

The voter initiatives to legalize physician-assisted suicide and euthanasia in Washington and California were narrowly defeated, in part because they were badly drafted laws; yet the proponents of such practices seem to be winning the larger social battle over principle. According to several public opinion polls, most Americans now believe that "if life is miserable, one has the right to get out, actively and with help if necessary." Though the burden of philosophical proof for establishing new rights (especially one as bizarre as a "right to die") should always fall on the proponents, the social burden of proof has shifted to those who would oppose the voluntary choice of death through assisted suicide. Thus it has become politically necessary—and at the same time exceedingly difficult—to make principled arguments about why doctors must not kill, about why euthanasia is not the proper human response to human finitude, and about why there is no right to die, natural or constitutional. This is not a merely academic matter: our society's willingness and ability to protect vulnerable life hang in the balance.

An examination of "right to die" is even more interesting philosophically. It reveals the dangers and the limits of the liberal—that is, rights-based—political philosophy and jurisprudence to which we Americans are wedded. As the ultimate new right, grounded neither in nature nor in reason, it demonstrates the nihilistic implication of a new ("postliberal") doctrine of rights, rooted in the self-creating will. And as liberal society's response to the bittersweet victories of the medical project to conquer death, it reveals in pure form the tragic meaning of the entire modern project, both scientific and political.

The claim of a right to die is made only in Western liberal societies—not surprisingly, for only in Western liberal societies do human beings look first to the rights of individuals. Also, only here do we find the high-tech medicine capable of keeping people from dying when they might wish. Yet the claim of a right to die is also a profoundly strange claim, especially in a liberal society founded on the primacy of the right to life. We Americans hold as a self-evident truth that governments exist to secure inalienable rights, first of all, to self-preservation; now we are being encouraged to use government to secure a putative right of self-destruction. A "right to die" is surely strange and unprecedented, and hardly innocent. Accordingly, we need to consider carefully what it could possibly mean, why it is being asserted, and whether it really exists—that is, whether it can be given a principled grounding or defense.

A *RIGHT* TO DIE

Though the major ambiguity concerns the substance of the right—namely, to die—we begin by reminding ourselves of what it means, in general, to say that someone has a right to something. I depart for now from the original notion of *natural* rights, and indeed abstract altogether from the question of the source of rights. I focus instead on our contemporary usage, for it is only in contemporary usage that this current claim of a right to die can be understood.

A right, whether legal or moral, is not identical to a need or a desire or an interest or a capacity. I may have both a need and a desire for, and also an interest in, the possessions of another, and the capacity or power to take them by force or stealth—yet I can hardly be said to have a right to them. A right, to begin with, is a species of liberty. Thomas Hobbes, the first teacher of rights, held a right to be a *blameless* liberty. Not everything we are free to do, morally or legally, do we have a right to do: I may be at liberty to wear offensive perfumes or to sass my parents or

to engage in unnatural sex, but it does not follow that I have a right to do so. Even the decriminalization of a once-forbidden act does not yet establish a legal right, not even if I can give reasons for doing it. Thus, the freedom to take my life—"I have inclination, means, reasons, opportunity, and you cannot stop me, and it is not against the law"—does not suffice to establish the *right* to take my life. A true right would be at least a blameless or permitted liberty, at best a praiseworthy or even rightful liberty, to do or not to do, without anyone else's interference or opposition.

Historically, the likelihood of outside interference and opposition was in fact the necessary condition for the assertion of rights. Rights were and are, to begin with, *political* creatures, the first principles of liberal politics. The rhetoric of claiming rights, which are in principle always absolute and unconditional, performs an important function of defense, but only because the sphere of life in which they are asserted is limited. Rights are asserted to protect, by deeming them blameless or rightful, certain liberties that others are denying or threatening to curtail. Rights are claimed to defend the safety and dignity of the individual against the dominion of tyrant, king, or prelate, and against those high-minded moralizers and zealous meddlers who seek to save man's soul or to preserve his honor at the cost of his life and liberty.

To these more classical, negative rights against interference with our liberties, modern thought has sought to add certain so-called welfare rights—rights that entitle us to certain opportunities or goods to which, it is argued, we have a rightful claim on others, usually government, to provide. The rhetoric of welfare rights extends the power of absolute and unqualified claims beyond the goals of defense against tyranny and beyond the limited sphere of endangered liberties; for these reasons their legitimacy as rights is often questioned. Yet even these ever-expanding lists of rights are not unlimited. I cannot be said to have a right to be loved by those whom I hope will love me, or a right to become wise. There are many good things that I may rightfully possess and enjoy, but to which I have no claim if they are lacking. Most generally, then, having a right means having a *justified* claim against others that they act in a fitting manner: either that they refrain from interfering or that they deliver what is justly owed. It goes without saying that the mere assertion of a claim or demand, or the stipulation of a right, is insufficient to establish it; making a claim and actually having a rightful claim to make are not identical. In considering an alleged right to die, we must be careful to look for a *justifiable* liberty or claim, and not merely a desire, interest, power, or demand.

Rights seem to entail obligations: one person's right, whether to noninterference or to some entitled good or service, necessarily implies another person's obligation. It will be important later to consider what obligations on others might be entailed by enshrining a right to die.

A RIGHT *TO DIE*

Taken literally, a right to die would denote merely a right to the inevitable; the certainty of death for all that lives is the touchstone of fated inevitability. Why claim a right to what is not only unavoidable, but is even, generally speaking, an evil? Is death in danger of losing its inevitability? Are we in danger of bodily immortality? Has death, for us, become a good to be claimed rather than an evil to be shunned or conquered?

Not exactly and not yet, though these questions posed by the literal reading of "right to die" are surely germane. They hint at our growing disenchantment with the biomedical project, which seeks, in principle, to prolong life indefinitely. It is the already available means to sustain life for prolonged periods—not indefinitely, but far longer than is in many cases reasonable or desirable—that has made death so untimely late as to seem less than inevitable, that has made death, when it finally does occur, appear to be a blessing.

For we now have medical "treatments" (that is, interventions) that do not treat (that is, cure or ameliorate) specific diseases, but do nothing more than keep people alive by sustaining vital functions. The most notorious such device is the respirator. Others include simple yet still artificial devices for supplying food and water and the kidney dialysis machine for removing wastes. And, in the future, we shall have the artificial heart. These devices, backed by aggressive institutional policies favoring their use, are capable of keeping people alive, even when comatose, often for decades. The "right to die," in today's discourse, often refers to—and certainly is meant to embrace—a right to refuse such life-sustaining medical treatment.

But the "right to die" usually embraces also something more. The ambiguity of the term blurs over the difference in content and intention between the already well-established common-law right to refuse surgery or other unwanted medical treatments and hospitalization and the newly alleged "right to die." The former permits the refusal of therapy, even a respirator, even if it means accepting an increased risk of death. The latter permits the refusal of therapy, such as renal dialysis or the feeding tube, *so that* death *will* occur. The former seems more concerned with choosing how to live while dying; the latter seems mainly concerned with a choice *for death*. In this sense the claimed "right to die" is not a misnomer.

Still less is it a misnomer when we consider that some people who are claiming it demand not merely the discontinuance of treatment but positive assistance in bringing about their deaths. Here the right to die embraces the (welfare!) right to a lethal injection or an overdose of pills administered by oneself, by one's physician, or by someone else. This "right to die" would better be called a right to assisted suicide or a right to be mercifully killed—in short, a right *to become dead*, by assistance if necessary.

This, of course, looks a lot like a claim to a right to commit suicide, which need not have any connection to the problems of dying or medical technology. Some people in fact argue that the "right to die" through euthanasia or medically assisted suicide grows not from a right to refuse medical treatment but rather from this putative right to commit suicide (suicide is now decriminalized in most states). There does seem to be a world of moral difference between submitting to death (when the time has come) and killing yourself (in or out of season), or between permitting to die and causing death. But the boundary becomes fuzzy with the alleged right to refuse food and water, artificially delivered. Though few proponents of a right to die want the taint of a general defense of suicide (which though decriminalized remains in bad odor), they in fact presuppose its permissibility and go well beyond it. They claim not only a right to attempt suicide but a right to succeed, and this means, in practice, a *right to the deadly assistance of others*. It is thus certainly proper to understand the "right to die" in its most radical sense, namely, as a right to become or to be made dead, by whatever means.

This way of putting the matter will not sit well with those who see the right to die less as a matter of life and death, more as a matter of autonomy or dignity. For them the right to die means the right to continue, despite disability, to exercise control over one's own destiny. It means, in one formulation, not the right to become dead, but the right to choose the manner, the timing, and the circumstances of one's death, or the right to choose what one regards as the most humane or dignified way to finish out one's life. Here the right to die means either the right to self-command or the right to death with dignity—claims that would oblige others, at a minimum, to stop interfering, but also, quite commonly, to "assist self-command" or to "provide dignity" by participating in bringing one's life to an end, according to plan. In the end, these proper and high-minded demands for autonomy and dignity turn out in most cases to embrace also a right to become dead, with assistance if necessary.

This analysis of current usage shows why one might be properly confused about the meaning of the term "right to die." In public discourse today, it merges all the aforementioned meanings: right to refuse treatment even if, or so that, death may occur; right to be killed or to become dead; right to control one's own dying; right to die with dignity; right to assistance in death. Some of this confusion inheres in the term; some of it is deliberately fostered by proponents of all these "rights," who hope thereby to gain assent to the more extreme claims by merging them with the more modest ones. Partly for this reason, however, we do well to regard the "right to die" at its most radical—and I will do so in this essay—as a right to become dead, by active means and if necessary with the assistance of others. In this way we take seriously and do justice to the novelty and boldness of the claim, a claim that intends to go beyond both the existing common-law right to refuse unwanted medical treatment and the so-called right to commit suicide all by oneself. (The first right is indisputable, the second, while debatable, will not be contested in this essay. What concerns us here is those aspects of the "right to die" that go beyond a right to attempt suicide and a right to refuse treatment.)

Having sought to clarify the meaning of "right to die," we face next the even greater confusion about who it is that allegedly has such a right. Is it only those who are "certifiably" terminally ill and irreversibly dying, with or without medical treatment? Also those who are incurably ill and severely incapacitated, although definitely not dying? Everyone, mentally competent or not? Does a senile person have a "right to die" if he is incapable of claiming it for himself? Do I need to be able to claim *and act* on such a right in order to have it, or can proxies be designated to exercise my right to die on my behalf? If the right to die is essentially an expression of my autonomy, how can anyone else exercise it for me?

Equally puzzling is the question, Against whom or what is a right to die being asserted? Is it a liberty right mainly against those officious meddlers who keep me from dying—against those doctors, nurses, hospitals, right-to-life groups, and district attorneys who interfere either with my ability to die (by machinery and hospitalization) or with my ability to gain help in ending my life (by criminal sanctions against assisting suicide)? If it is a right to become dead, is it not also a welfare right claimed against those who do not yet assist—a right demanding also the provision of the poison that I have permission to take? (Compare the liberty right to seek an abortion with the welfare right to obtain one.) Or is it, at bottom, a demand asserted also *against nature*, which has dealt me a bad hand by keeping me alive, beyond my wishes and beneath my dignity, and alas without terminal illness, too senile or enfeebled to make matters right?

The most radical formulations, whether in the form of "a right to become dead" or "a right to control my destiny" or "a right to dignity," are, I am convinced, the complaint of human pride against what our tyrannical tendencies lead us to experience as "cosmic injustice, directed against me." Here the ill-fated demand a right not to be ill-fated; those who want to die, but cannot, claim a right to die, which becomes, as Harvey Mansfield has put it, a tort claim against nature. It thus becomes the business of the well-fated to correct nature's mistreatment of the ill-fated *by making them dead*. Thus would the same act that was only yesterday declared a crime against humanity become a mandated act, not only of compassionate charity but of compensatory justice!

WHY ASSERT A RIGHT TO DIE?

Before proceeding to the more challenging question of the existence and ground of a "right to die," it would be useful briefly to consider why such a right is being asserted, and by whom. Some of the reasons have already been noted in passing:

- fear of prolongation of dying due to medical intervention; hence, a right to refuse treatment or hospitalization, even if death occurs as a result;

- fear of living too long, without fatal illness to carry one off; hence, a right to assisted suicide;
- fear of the degradations of senility and dependence; hence, a right to death with dignity;
- fear of loss of control; hence, a right to choose the time and manner of one's death.

Equally important for many people is the fear of becoming a burden to others—financial, psychic, social. Few parents, however eager or willing they might be to stay alive, are pleased by the prospect that they might thereby destroy their children's and grandchildren's opportunities for happiness. Indeed, my own greatest weakening on the subject of euthanasia is precisely this: I would confess a strong temptation to remove myself from life to spare my children the anguish of years of attending my demented self and the horrible likelihood that they will come, hatefully to themselves, to resent my continued existence. Such reasons in favor of death might even lead me to think I had a *duty* to die—they do not, however, establish for me any right to become dead.[1]

But the advocates of a "right to die" are not always so generous. On the contrary, much dishonesty and mischief are afoot. Many people have seen the advantage of using the language of individual rights, implying voluntary action, to shift the national attitudes regarding life and death, to prepare the way for the practice of terminating "useless" lives.[2]

Many who argue for a right to die mean for people not merely to have it but to exercise it with dispatch, so as to decrease the mounting socioeconomic costs of caring for the irreversibly ill and dying. In fact, most of the people now agitating for a "right to die" are themselves neither ill nor dying. Children looking at parents who are not dying fast enough, hospital administrators and health economists concerned about cost-cutting and waste, doctors disgusted with caring for incurables, people with eugenic or aesthetic interests who are repelled by the prospect of a society in which the young and vigorous expend enormous energy to keep alive the virtually dead—all these want to change our hard-won ethic in favor of life.

But they are either too ashamed or too shrewd to state their true intentions. Much better to trumpet a right to die, and encourage people to exercise it. These advocates understand all too well that the present American climate requires one to talk of rights if one wishes to have one's way in such moral matters. Consider the analogous use of arguments for abortion rights by organizations which hope thereby to get women—especially the poor, the unmarried, and the nonwhite—to exercise their "right to choose," to do their supposed duty toward limiting population growth and the size of the underclass.

This is not to say that all reasons for promoting a "right to die" are suspect. Nor do I mean to suggest that it would never be right or good for someone to elect to die. But it might be dangerous folly to circumvent the grave need for prudence in these matters by substituting the confused yet absolutized principle of a "right to die," especially given the mixed motives and dangerous purposes of some of its proponents.

Truth to tell, public discourse about moral matters in the United States is much impoverished by our eagerness to transform questions of the right and the good into questions about individual rights. Partly, this is a legacy of modern liberalism, the political philosophy on which the genius of the American republic mainly rests. But it is augmented by American self-assertion and individualism, increasingly so in an age when family and other mediating institutions are in decline and the naked individual is left face to face with the bureaucratic state.

But the language of rights gained a tremendous boost from the moral absolutism of the 1960s, with the discovery that the nonnegotiable and absolutized character of all rights claims provides the most durable battering ram against the status quo. Never mind that it fuels resentments and breeds hatreds, that it ignores the consequences to society, or that it short-circuits a political process that is more amenable to working out a balanced view of the common good. Never

mind all that: go to court and demand your rights. And the courts have been all too willing to oblige, finding or inventing new rights in the process.

These sociocultural changes, having nothing to do with death and dying, surely are part of the reason we are now confronted with vociferous claims of a right to die. These changes are also part of the reason why, despite its notorious difficulties, a right to die is the leading moral concept advanced to address these most complicated and delicate human matters at the end of life. Yet the reasons for the assertion, even if suspect, do not settle the question of truth, to which, at long last, we finally turn. Let us examine whether philosophically or legally we can truly speak of a right to die.

Is There a Right to Die?

Philosophically speaking, it makes sense to take our bearings from those great thinkers of modernity who are the originators and most thoughtful exponents of our rights-based thinking. They above all are likely to have understood the purpose, character, grounds, and limits for the assertion of rights. If a newly asserted right, such as the right to die, cannot be established on the natural or rational ground for rights offered by these thinkers, the burden of proof must fall on the proponents of novel rights, to provide a new yet equally solid ground in support of their novel claims.

If we start at the beginning, with the great philosophical teachers of natural rights, the very notion of a right to die would be nonsensical. As we learn from Hobbes and from John Locke, all the rights of man, given by nature, presuppose our self-interested attachment to our own lives. All natural rights trace home to the primary right to life, or better, the right to self-preservation—itself rooted in the powerful, self-loving impulses and passions that seek our own continuance, and asserted first against deadly, oppressive polities or against those who might insist that morality requires me to turn the other cheek when my life is threatened. Mansfield summarizes the classical position elegantly:

> Rights are given to men by nature, but they are needed because men are also subject to nature's improvidence. Since life is in danger, men's equal rights would be to life, to the liberty that protects life, and to the pursuit of the happiness with which life, or a tenuous life, is occupied.
>
> In practice, the pursuit of happiness will be the pursuit of property, for even though property is less valuable than life or liberty, it serves as guard for them. Quite apart from the pleasures of being rich, having secure property shows that one has liberty secure from invasion either by the government or by others; and secure liberty is the best sign of a secure life.[3]

Because death, my extinction, is the evil whose avoidance is the condition of the possibility of my having any and all of my goods, my right to secure my life against death—that is, my rightful liberty to self-preservative conduct—is the bedrock of all other rights and of all politically relevant morality. Even Hans Jonas, writing to defend "the right to die," acknowledges that it stands alone, and concedes that "every other right ever argued, claimed, granted, or denied can be viewed as an extension of this primary right [to life], since every particular right concerns the exercise of some faculty of life, the access to some necessity of life, the satisfaction of some aspiration of life."[4] It is obvious that one cannot found on this rock any right to die or right to become dead. Life loves to live, and it needs all the help it can get.

This is not to say that these early modern thinkers were unaware that men might tire of life or might come to find existence burdensome. But the decline in the will to live did not for them drive out or nullify the right to life, much less lead to a trumping new right, a right to die. For the right to life is a matter of nature, not will. Locke addresses and rejects a natural right to suicide, in his discussion of the state of nature:

> But though this be a state of liberty, yet it is not a state of license; though man in that state has an uncontrollable liberty to dispose of his person or possessions, yet he has not liberty to destroy himself, or so much as any creature in his possession, but where some nobler use than its bare preservation calls for it. The state of nature has a law of nature to govern it, which obliges everyone; and reason, which is that law, teaches all mankind who will but consult it, that, being all equal and independent, no one ought to harm another in his life, health, liberty, or possessions.[5]

Admittedly, the argument here turns explicitly theological—we are said to be our wise Maker's property. But the argument against a man's willful "quitting of his station" seems, for Locke, to be a corollary of the natural inclination and right of self-preservation.

Some try to argue, wrongly in my view, that Locke's teaching on property rests on a principle of self-ownership, which can then be used to justify self-destruction: since I own my body and my life, I may do with them as I please. As this argument has much currency, it is worth examining in greater detail. Locke does indeed say something that seems at first glance to suggest self-ownership:

> Though the earth and all inferior creatures be common to all men, *yet every man has a property in his own person;* this nobody has a right to but himself. The labor of his body and the work of his hands we may say are properly his.[6]

But the context defines and constricts the claim. Unlike the property rights in the fruits of his labor, the property a man has in his own person is inalienable: a man cannot transfer title to himself by selling himself into slavery. The "property in his own person" is less a metaphysical statement declaring self-ownership, more a political statement denying ownership by another. This right removes each and every human being from the commons available to all human beings for appropriation and use. My body and my life are my property *only in the limited sense* that they are *not yours.* They are different from my alienable property—my house, my car, my shoes. My body and my life, while mine to use, are not mine to dispose of. In the deepest sense, my body is nobody's body, not even mine.[7]

Even if one continues, against reason, to hold to strict self-ownership and self-disposability, there is a further argument, one that is decisive. Self-ownership might enable one at most to justify *attempting* suicide; it cannot justify a right to succeed or, more important, a right to the assistance of others. The designated potential assistant-in-death has neither a natural duty nor a natural right to become an actual assistant-in-death, and the liberal state, instituted above all to protect life, can never countenance such a right to kill, even on request. A right to become dead or to be made dead cannot be sustained on classical liberal grounds.

Later thinkers in the liberal tradition, including those who prized freedom above preservation, also make no room for a "right to die." Jean-Jacques Rousseau's complaints about the ills of civil society centered especially and most powerfully on the threats to life and limb from a social order whose main purpose should have been to protect them.[8] And Immanuel Kant, for whom rights are founded not in nature but in reason, holds that the self-willed act of self-destruction is simply self-contradictory.

> It seems absurd that a man can injure himself (*volenti non fit injuria* [Injury cannot happen to one who is willing]). The Stoic therefore considered it a prerogative of his personality as a wise man to walk out of his life with an undisturbed mind whenever he liked (as out of a smoke-filled room), not because he was afflicted by actual or anticipated ills, but simply because he could make use of nothing more in this life. And yet this very courage, this strength of mind—of not fearing death and of knowing of something which man can prize more highly than his life—ought to have been an ever so much greater motive for him not to destroy himself, a being having such authoritative superiority over the strongest sensible incentives; consequently, it ought to have been a motive for him not to deprive himself of life.

Man cannot deprive himself of his personhood so long as one speaks of duties, thus so long as he lives. That man ought to have the authorization to withdraw himself from all obligation, i.e., to be free to act as if no authorization at all were required for this withdrawal, involves a contradiction. To destroy the subject of morality in his own person is tantamount to obliterating from the world, as far as he can, the very existence of morality itself; but morality is, nevertheless, an end in itself. Accordingly, to dispose of oneself as a mere means to some end of one's own liking is to degrade the humanity in one's person (*homo noumenon*), which, after all, was entrusted to man (*homo phænomenon*) to preserve.[9]

It is a heavy irony that it should be autonomy, the moral notion that the world owes mainly to Kant, that is now invoked as the justifying ground of a right to die. For Kant, autonomy, which literally means self-legislation, requires acting in accordance with one's true self—that is, with one's rational will determined by a universalizable, that is, rational, maxim. Being autonomous means not being a slave to instinct, impulse, or whim, but rather doing as one ought, as a rational being. But autonomy has now come to mean "doing as you please," compatible no less with self-indulgence than with self-control. Here-with one sees clearly the triumph of the Nietzschean self, who finds reason just as enslaving as blind instinct and who finds his true "self" rather in unconditioned acts of pure creative will.

Yet even in its willful modern meaning, "autonomy" cannot ground a right to die. First, one cannot establish on this basis a right to have *someone else's* assistance in committing suicide—a right, by the way, that would impose an obligation on someone else and thereby restrict *his* autonomy. Second, even if my choice for death were "reasonable" and my chosen assistant freely willing, my autonomy cannot ground *his right* to kill me, and, hence, it cannot ground my right to become dead. Third, a liberty right to an assisted death (that is, a right against interference) can at most approve assisted suicide or euthanasia for the mentally competent and alert—a restriction that would prohibit effecting the deaths of the mentally incompetent or comatose patients who have not left explicit instructions regarding their treatment. It is, by the way, a long philosophical question whether all such instructions must be obeyed, for the person who gave them long ago may no longer be "the same person" when they become relevant. Can my fifty-three-year-old self truly prescribe today the best interests for my seventy-five-year-old and senile self?

In contrast to arguments presented in recent court cases, it is self-contradictory to assert that a proxy not chosen by the patient can exercise the patient's rights of autonomy. Can a citizen have a right to vote that would be irrevocably exercised "on his behalf," and in the name of his autonomy, by the government?[10] Finally, if autonomy and dignity lie in the free exercise of will and choice, it is at least paradoxical to say that our autonomy licenses an act that puts our autonomy permanently out of business.

It is precisely this paradox that appeals to the Nietzschean creative self, the bearer of so many of this century's "new rights." As Mansfield brilliantly shows, the creative ones are not bound by normality or good sense:

> Creative beings are open-ended. They are open-ended in fact and not merely in their formal potentialities. Such beings do not have interests; for who can say what is in the interest of a being that is becoming something unknown? Thus the society of new rights is characterized by a loss of predictability and normality: no one knows what to expect, even from his closest companions.[11]

The most authentic self-creative self revels in the unpredictable, the extreme, the perverse. He does not even flinch before self-contradiction; indeed, he can display the triumph of his will most especially in self-negation. And though it may revolt us, who are we to deny him this form of self-

expression? Supremely tolerant of the rights of others to their own eccentricities, we avert our glance and turn the other moral cheek. Here at last is the only possible philosophical ground for a right to die: arbitrary will, backed by moral relativism. Which is to say, no ground at all.

IS THERE A LEGAL RIGHT TO DIE?

Such foreign philosophic doctrines, prominent among the elite, are slowly working their relativistic way through the broader culture. But in America, rights are still largely defined by law. Turning, then, from political and moral philosophy to American law, we should be surprised to discover any constitutional basis for a legal right to die, given that the framers understood rights and the role of government more or less as did Locke. Perusal of the original Constitution of 1787 or of the Bill of Rights finds absolutely nothing on which even the most creative of jurists could try to hang such a right.

But the notorious due process clause of the Fourteenth Amendment, under the ruling but still oxymoronic "substantive due process" interpretation, has provided such a possible peg, as it has for so many other new rights, notwithstanding the fact that the majority of states at the time the Fourteenth Amendment was ratified had laws that prohibited assisting suicide. The one "right-to-die" case to reach the Supreme Court, *Cruzan by Cruzan v. Director, Missouri Department of Health* (decided by a five-to-four vote in June 1990) explored the Fourteenth Amendment in connection with such a right.[12] This case may well have prepared the way for finding constitutional protection, at least for a right-to-refuse-lifesustaining-treatment-in-order-that-death-may-occur.

The parents of Nancy Cruzan, a comatose young woman living for seven years in a persistent vegetative state, petitioned to remove the gastrostomy feeding and hydration tube in order that Nancy be allowed to die. The trial court found for the parents but the Missouri supreme court reversed; when the Cruzans appealed, the United States Supreme Court took the case to consider "whether Cruzan has a right under the United States Constitution which would require the hospital to withdraw life-sustaining treatment from her under the circumstances."

At first glance, the Court's decision in *Cruzan* disappointed proponents of a right to die, because it upheld the decision of the Missouri supreme court: it held that Missouri's interest in safeguarding life allowed it to demand clear and convincing evidence that the incompetent person truly wished to withdraw from treatment, evidence that in Nancy Cruzan's case was lacking. Nevertheless, the reasoning of the majority decision was widely interpreted as conceding such a right to die for a competent person—a misinterpretation, to be sure, but not without some ground.

Chief Justice William Rehnquist, writing for the majority, scrupulously avoided any mention of a "right to die," and he wisely eschewed taking up the question under the so-called right of privacy. Instead, following precedent in Fourteenth Amendment jurisprudence and relying on the doctrine that informed consent is required for medical invasion of the body, he reasoned that "the principle that a competent person has a constitutionally protected *liberty interest* in refusing unwanted medical treatment may be inferred from our previous decisions." (A "liberty interest" is a technical term denoting a liberty less firmly protected by the due process clause than a "fundamental right"; generally speaking, restrictions on the latter may be justified only by a compelling state interest but restraints on the former may be upheld if they do not unduly burden its exercise.) But on the crucial question of whether the protected liberty interest to refuse medical treatment embraces also refusing *life-sustaining* food and water, Rehnquist waffled skillfully:

> Petitioners insist that under the general holdings of our cases, the forced administration of life-sustaining medical treatment, and even of artifi-

cially-delivered food and water essential to life, would implicate a competent person's liberty interest. Although we think the logic of the cases discussed above would embrace such a liberty interest, the dramatic consequences involved in refusal of such treatment [namely, death] would inform the inquiry whether the deprivation of that interest is constitutionally permissible. *But for purposes of this case, we assume that the United States Constitution would grant a competent person a constitutionally protected right to refuse lifesaving hydration and nutrition.* (p. 2852) (Emphasis added)

Because the decision in *Cruzan* concerned an incompetent person incapable of exercising "a hypothetical right to refuse treatment or any other right," the right that Rehnquist was willing to assume had no bearing on the decision. But the chief justice could have put the matter differently. He might have said, "Whether or not a competent person has such a right, Nancy Cruzan, being incompetent, does not." True, he drew back from accepting in his own name the petitioner's claim, indicating instead that an inquiry would still be needed to determine whether a state may constitutionally deprive a competent person of his "liberty interest" to elect death by refusing artificial hydration and nutrition. But he was willing to stipulate for the purposes of this case—(one suspects that he really means for the purpose of getting a majority on his side in this case)—a constitutionally protected right-to-refuse-treatment-so-that-death-will-occur. This stipulation, missing the qualification "for the purposes of this case," was heralded in many newspapers and magazines around the country as establishing a constitutional right to die for competent persons.

Justice Sandra Day O'Connor, apparently the swing vote in the case, wrote a concurring opinion solely to indicate why the stipulated right was a right indeed. It is clear from her opinion that, if the case had in fact involved a competent patient, a right-to-elect-death-by-refusing-food-and-water would have been judicially established, for she would have sided with the four-member minority who were ready to grant it even to incompetents:

> I agree that a [constitutionally] protected liberty interest in refusing unwanted medical treatment may be inferred from our prior decisions . . . and that the refusal of artificially delivered food and water is encompassed within that liberty interest. I write separately to clarify why I believe this to be so. (p. 2856)

What Chief Justice Rehnquist treats as hypothetical, Justice O'Connor treats as actual, and she presents her argument for its establishment. In the end she even speaks about the need to safeguard similar liberty interests for incompetents, giving shockingly little attention to the duty of the state to protect the life of incompetent people against those who would exercise on their behalf their putative right to die.[13]

Only Justice Antonin Scalia, writing a separate concurring opinion, seems to have gotten it right, insisting that the Constitution has absolutely nothing to say in this matter. He argues, first, that the liberty protected by the Fourteenth Amendment could not and does not include a "right to suicide," and second, that arguments attempting to separate the withdrawal of the feeding tube from Nancy Cruzan from ordinary suicide all fail. He reasons (to me convincingly) that a right to refuse treatment here means necessarily a right to put an end to her life.

> What I have said above is not meant to suggest that I would think it desirable, if we were sure that Nancy Cruzan wanted to die, to keep her alive by the means at issue here. I only assert that the Constitution has nothing to say about the subject. To raise up a constitutional right here we would have to create out of nothing (for it exists neither in text nor tradition) some constitutional principle whereby, although the State may insist that an individual come in out of the cold and eat food, it may not insist that he take medicine; and although it may pump his stomach empty of poison he has ingested, it may not fill his stomach with food he has failed to ingest. (p. 2863)

Yet paradoxically, Justice Scalia's powerful argument, which identifies the refusal of food and water as suicide, may come back to haunt us, especially when conjoined with Justice O'Connor's insistence that such right of refusal is already constitutionally protected. For should Justice O'Connor's view prevail, Justice Scalia's powerful intellect will have provided the reasons for regarding the newly protected right as indeed a right to die. The elements are all in place for inventing a constitutional right to suicide and, in the case of competents, for assistance with suicide, that is, a right to die. Justice Scalia's worry is not misplaced:

> I am concerned, from the tenor of today's opinions, that we are poised to confuse that enterprise [legislating with regard to end-of-life decisions] as successfully as we have confused the enterprise of legislating concerning abortion. (p. 2859)

Almost no one seems to have noticed a painful irony in this proceeding.[14] The Fourteenth Amendment prohibits the states from depriving persons not only of liberty but also of life and property, without due process of law. A so-called vitalist state, like Missouri, has at least for now been vindicated in its efforts to protect an incompetent person's life against those who assert the superiority of his "liberty interest" to elect death by starvation. But no thought seems to have been given to the conduct of the so-called nonvitalist states, like New Jersey, that go the other way and give the benefit of incompetency to death—all in the name of liberty. In abandoning those vulnerable persons whom others insist have lives no longer worth living, these states come much closer to violating the strict letter of the Fourteenth Amendment's insistence that the state not take life than does Missouri in allegedly thwarting Cruzan's liberty to elect death.

THE TRAGIC MEANING OF "RIGHT TO DIE"

The claim of a "right to die," asserted especially against physicians bent on prolonging life, clearly exposes certain deep difficulties in the foundations of modern society. Modern liberal, technological society rests especially upon two philosophical pillars raised first in the seventeenth century, at the beginning of the modern era: the preeminence of the human individual, embodied in the doctrine of natural rights as espoused first by Hobbes and Locke; and the idea of mastery of nature, attained through a radically new science of nature as proposed by Francis Bacon and René Descartes.

Both ideas were responses to the perceived partial inhospitality of nature to human need. Both encouraged man's opposition to nature, the first through the flight from the state of nature into civil society for the purpose of safeguarding the precarious rights to life and liberty; the second through the subduing of nature for the purpose of making life longer, healthier, and more commodious. One might even say that it is especially an opposition to death that grounds these twin responses. Politically, the fear of violent death at the hands of warring men requires law and legitimate authority to secure natural rights, especially life. Technologically, the fear of death as such at the hands of unfriendly nature inspires a bolder approach, namely, a scientific medicine to wage war against disease and even against death itself, ultimately with a promise of bodily immortality.

Drunk on its political and scientific successes, modern thought and practice have abandoned the modest and moderate beginnings of political modernity. In civil society the natural rights of self-preservation, secured through active but moderate self-assertion, have given way to the nonnatural rights of self-creation and self-expression; the new rights have no connection to nature or to reason, but appear as the rights of the untrammeled will. The "self" that here asserts itself is not a natural self, with the predictable interests given it by a universal human nature with its bodily needs, but a uniquely individuated and self-made self. Its authentic selfhood is demonstrated by its ability to say no to the needs of the body, the rules of society, and the dictates of reason. For such a self, self-negation through suicide and the right to die can be the ultimate form of self-assertion.

In medical science, the unlimited battle against death has found nature unwilling to roll over and play dead. The successes of medicine so far are partial at best and the victory incomplete, to say the least. The welcome triumphs against disease have been purchased at the price of the medicalized dehumanization of the end of life: to put it starkly, once we lick cancer and stroke, we can all live long enough to get Alzheimer's disease. And if the insurance holds out, we can die in the intensive care unit, suitably intubated. Fear of the very medical power we engaged to do battle against death now leads us to demand that it give us poison.

Finally, both the triumph of individualism and our reliance on technology (not only in medicine) and on government to satisfy our new wants-demanded-as-rights have weakened our more natural human associations—especially the family, on which we all need to rely when our pretense to autonomy and mastery is eventually exposed by unavoidable decline. Old age and death have been taken out of the bosom of family life and turned over to state-supported nursing homes and hospitals. Not the clergyman but the doctor (in truth, the nurse) presides over the end of life, in sterile surroundings that make no concessions to our finitude. Both the autonomous will and the will's partner in pride, the death-denying doctor, ignore the unavoidable limits on will and technique that nature insists on. Failure to recognize these limits now threatens the entire venture, for rebellion against the project through a "right to die" will only radicalize its difficulties. Vulnerable life will no longer be protected by the state, medicine will become a death-dealing profession, and isolated individuals will be technically dispatched to avoid the troubles of finding human ways to keep company with them in their time of ultimate need.

That the right to die should today be asserted to win release from a hyperpowerful medical futility is thus more than tragic irony: it is also very dangerous. Three dangers especially stand out.

First, the right to die, especially as it comes to embrace a right to "aid-in-dying," or assisted suicide, or euthanasia, will translate into an obligation on the part of others to kill or help kill. Even if we refuse to impose such a duty but merely allow those to practice it who are freely willing, our society would be drastically altered. For unless the state accepts the job of euthanizer, which God forbid that it should, it would thus surrender its monopoly on the legal use of lethal force, a monopoly it holds and needs if it is to protect innocent life, its first responsibility.

Second, there can be no way to confine the practice to those who knowingly and freely request death. The vast majority of persons who are candidates for assisted death are, and will increasingly be, incapable of choosing and effecting such a course of action for themselves. No one with an expensive or troublesome infirmity will be safe from the pressure to have his right to die exercised.

Third, the medical's profession's devotion to healing and refusal to kill—its ethical center—will be permanently destroyed, and with it, patient trust and physicianly self-restraint. Here is yet another case where acceding to a putative personal right would wreak havoc on the common good.

Nothing I have said should be taken to mean that I believe life should be extended under all circumstances and at all costs. Far from it. I continue, with fear and trembling, to defend the practice of allowing to die while opposing the practice of deliberately killing—despite the blurring of this morally bright line implicit in the artificial food and water cases, and despite the slide toward the retailing of death that continues on the sled of a right to refuse treatment. I welcome efforts to give patients as much choice as possible in how they are to live out the end of their lives. I continue to applaud those courageous patients and family members and those conscientious physicians who try prudently to discern, in each case, just what form of treatment or nontreatment is truly good for the patient, even if it embraces an increased likelihood of death. But I continue to insist that we cannot serve the patient's good by deliberately eliminating the patient. And if we have no right to do this to another, we have no right to have others do this to ourselves. There is, when all is said and done, no defensible right to die.

A CODA: ABOUT RIGHTS

The rhetoric of rights still performs today the noble, time-honored function of protecting individual life and liberty, a function now perhaps even more necessary than the originators of such rhetoric could have imagined, given the tyrannical possibilities of the modern bureaucratic and technologically competent state. But with the claim of a "right to die," as with so many of the novel rights being asserted in recent years, we face an extension of this rhetoric into areas where it no longer relates to that protective function, and beyond the limited area of life in which rights claims are clearly appropriate and indeed crucial. As a result, we face a number of serious and potentially dangerous distortions in our thought and in our practice. We distort our understanding of rights and weaken their respectability in their proper sphere by allowing them to be invented—without ground in nature or in reason—in response to moral questions that lie outside the limited domain of rights. We distort our understanding of moral deliberation and the moral life by reducing all complicated questions of right and good to questions of individual rights. We subvert the primacy and necessity of prudence by pretending that the assertion of rights will produce the best—and most moral—results. In trying to batter our way through the human condition with the bludgeon of personal rights, we allow ourselves to be deceived about the most fundamental matters: about death and dying, about our unavoidable finitude, and about the sustaining interdependencies of our lives.

Let us, by all means, continue to deliberate about whether and when and why it might make sense for someone to give up on his life, or even actively to choose death. But let us call a halt to all this dangerous thoughtlessness about rights. Let us refuse to talk any longer about a "right to die."

References and Notes

1. For my "generosity" to succeed, I would, of course, have to commit suicide without assistance and without anyone's discovering it—i.e., well before I were demented. I would not want my children to believe that I suspected them of being incapable of loving me through my inevitable decline. There is another still more powerful reason for resisting this temptation: is it not unreasonably paternalistic of me to try to order the world so as to free my children from the usual intergenerational experiences, ties, obligations, and burdens? What principle of family life am I enacting and endorsing with my "altruistic suicide"?

2. Here is a recent example from a professor of sociology who objected to my condemnation of Derek Humphry's *Final Exit*:

> Is Mr. Kass absolutely opposed to suicide? Would he have dissuaded Hitler? Would he disapprove of suicide by Pol Pot? . . . If we would welcome suicide by certain figures on limited occasions, should we prolong the lives of people who lived useless, degrading or dehumanized lives; who inflicted these indignities upon others; or who led vital lives but were reduced to uselessness and degradation by incurable disease? (*Commentary*, May 1992, p. 12).

3. Harvey C. Mansfield, Jr., "The Old Rights and the New: Responsibility vs. Self-Expression," in *Old Rights and New*, ed. Robert A. Licht (Washington: American Enterprise Institute, 1993), in press.

4. Hans Jonas, "The Right to Die," *Hastings Center Report* 8, no. 4 (1978): 31–36, at 31.

5. John Locke, *Second Treatise on Civil Government*, ch. 2, "Of the State of Nature," para. 6.

6. Locke, *Second Treatise*, ch. 5, "Of Property," para. 27. Emphasis added.

7. Later, in discussing the extent of legislative power, Locke denies to the legislative, though it be the supreme power in every commonwealth, arbitrary power over the individual and, in particular, power to destroy his life. "For nobody can transfer to another more power than he has in himself; and nobody has an absolute arbitrary power over himself, or over any other to destroy his own life, or take away the life or property of another." *Second Treatise*, ch. 9, "Of the Extent of the Legislative Power," para. 135. Because the state's power derives from the people's power, the person's lack of arbitrary power over himself is the ground for restricting the state's power to kill him.

8. See, for example, Rousseau, *Discourse on the Origin and Foundations of Inequality among Men*, note 9, especially paragraphs four and five.

9. Immanuel Kant, *The Metaphysical Principles of Virtue*, trans. James Ellington (Indianapolis: Bobbs-Merrill, 1964), pp. 83–84. My purpose in citing Kant here is not to defend Kantian morality—and I am not myself a Kantian—but simply to show that the thinker who thought most deeply about rights in relation to *reason* and *autonomy* would have found the idea of a "right to die" utterly indefensible on these grounds.

10. The attempt to ground a right to die in the so-called right to privacy fails for the same reasons. A right to make independent judgments regarding one's body in one's private sphere, free of governmental inference, cannot be the basis of the right of someone else, appointed by or protected by government, to put an end to one's bodily life.

11. Mansfield, "The Old Rights and the New." This permanent instability of "the self" defeats the main benefit of a rightsbased politics, which knows how to respect individual rights precisely because they are understood to be rooted in a common human nature, with reliable common interests, both natural and rational. The self-determining self, because it is variable, also turns out to be an embarrassment for attempts to respect prior acts of self-determination, as in the case of living wills. For if the "self" is truly constantly being re-created, there is no reason to honor today "its" prescriptions of yesterday; for the two selves are not the same.

12. 110 S. Ct. 2841 (1990).

13. Justice William Brennan, in his dissenting opinion, denies that the state has even a legitimate interest in—much less a duty toward—someone's life that could ever outweigh the person's choice to avoid medical treatment. And in the presence of a patient who can no longer choose for herself, the state has an interest *only* in trying to determine as accurately as

possible "how she would exercise her rights under these circumstances. . . . [U]ntil Nancy's wishes have been determined, the only [!] state interest that may be asserted is an interest in safeguarding the accuracy of that determination." (This is, by the way, a seemingly impossible task, given the view of the self that is implicit in Justice Brennan's reasoning.) Not the security of life but the self-assertion of the self-determining will is, for Justice Brennan, the primary interest of the state. We

see here how Nietzschean thinking threatens to replace classical American liberalism, even in constitutional interpretation.

14. A notable exception is Yale Kamisar, professor of law at the University of Michigan Law School. In my view, Kamisar is our finest legal commentator on this subject. See his "When Is There a Constitutional 'Right to Die'? When Is There *No* Constitutional 'Right to Live'?" *Georgia Law Review* 25 (1991): 1203–42.

Who Defines Futility?

Stuart J. Youngner MD

For the past two decades, our society has struggled to identify the proper circumstances under which life-sustaining medical treatment should be limited. In fact, we seem to have reached a consensus on some aspects of the problem. It is generally agreed that a competent patient has the right to refuse life-sustaining treatment; when the patient is not competent, family members may limit treatment to serve the patient's best interests.

The report by Murphy[1] in this issue of THE JOURNAL examines a more controversial question that is currently at the forefront of the treatment-limitation debate—ie, under what circumstances can life-sustaining interventions be limited *without* the informed consent of the patient or family?

Murphy notes correctly that cardiopulmonary resuscitation (CPR) is "rarely effective and in many cases futile" in the setting of a long-term-care facility, where many elderly patients are chronically ill or severely demented. He proposes a policy that "enables health care providers to make ethically sound, *unilateral* [emphasis mine] decisions regarding CPR. . . ." Physicians should

only discuss the resuscitation decision with patients and families if resuscitation offers "some level of benefit" or the patient's prognosis is "at all equivocal."

Murphy argues that such a policy would avoid "futile" therapy that "can be harmful" because it prevents "a timely death." By acting unilaterally, physicians would avoid causing unnecessary suffering for the patient as well as an unfair "burden of guilt" for the family. Moreover, he argues, families' treatment decisions may be based on factors (eg, guilt over not visiting the patient or fear of death) that have little to do with what the patient desired. (He believes, I assume, that health professionals are less likely than family members to have interests or values that potentially conflict with those of the patient.) Finally, he raises the question of whether society should provide the "substantial resources" that aggressive treatment of long-term–care patients would require.

Murphy justifies these claims with two ethical arguments. First, physicians' scientific knowledge and clinical experience enable them to recognize when a life-sustaining treatment is "futile." At this point, they should "reconsider the emphasis on

From *Journal of the American Medical Association,* 260: 2094–2095, 1988 autonomy" and exercise a strong paternalism that promotes patient (and family) well-being by limiting such treatment unilaterally and without even informing the patient and/or family. The second argument involves the broader social issue of the proper allocation of our nation's resources. In other words, does society have an interest in limiting "futile" interventions to divert limited resources to more productive use within, or even outside, the health care system? While these justifications have initial appeal, closer scrutiny reveals an alarming vagueness and confounding of issues.

The word "futile" has a categorical ring that masks a more subtle complexity. To delineate its meaning in specific situations, we must first examine the potential goals of the medical intervention in question.[2] For example, we can understand futility in purely *physiological* terms. Will a given vasopressor actually raise or maintain the patient's blood pressure? Will careful attention to fluid management be successful in maintaining electrolyte balance? Or, in the case of resuscitation, will CPR reestablish spontaneous heartbeat? We can also understand futility in terms of *postponing death*. We might, with diligent attention, be able to keep the serum sodium level within normal limits in a patient whose condition is rapidly deteriorating, but still fail to postpone death by even a few minutes. According to one standard, our efforts were futile; according to another, they were quite effective. *Length of life* represents another standard for judging futility. If our attention to fluid and electrolyte balance manages to postpone the patient's death for 24 hours, were our efforts futile? Many of the studies to which Murphy refers measure futility of CPR by whether or not the resuscitated patients lived to leave the hospital. Using this standard, CPR was futile if the patient lived a week, but died before discharge. And what about the *quality of life*? An intervention that kept a patient alive for six months might well be judged futile because it did not achieve an important goal of the patient—eg, being able to walk and take care of his or her own personal hygiene. Finally, we might think of futility in terms of *probability*. A given intervention could be judged futile if the chance of achieving one or more of the goals just examined is not entirely absent, but is highly unlikely. But how low must the probability of success be before an intervention is judged futile? One percent? Five percent? Should statisticians define futility? When is an outside chance a chance worth taking?

Physicians are in the best position to know the empirical facts about the many aspects of futility. I would argue, however, that all, except for physiological futility and an absolute inability to postpone death, also involve value judgments. Physicians may be best suited to frame the choices by describing prognosis and quality of life—as well as the odds for achieving them. Physicians should not offer treatments that are physiologically futile or certain not to prolong life, and they could ethically refuse patient and family requests for such treatments. Beyond that, they run the risk of "giving opinions disguised as data."[3]

Living for five more days might give some patients the opportunity to say good-byes, to wait for the arrival of a loved one from another city, or to live to see the birth of a grandchild. For one patient, a life with extreme disability and pain might be quite tolerable; for another, it might be totally unacceptable. Risk takers might see a 3% chance as worth taking, while others might give more weight to the 97% chance of failure.

Nonetheless, the aggressive intervention of CPR in the event of cardiac arrest seems intuitively contraindicated in the long-term–care population described by Murphy. Murphy became understandably concerned when he discovered that only 10% of multiply impaired, very elderly patients had do-not-resuscitate orders. His solution (as opposed to his proposed policy) was eminently reasonable and extremely effective. He stopped avoiding discussion or using misleading euphemisms, such as, "Would you want us to do everything possible to save your life if your heart stopped beating?" Patients and families predictably answered this question by saying, "Why of course, doctor." He started talking turkey. He provided patients and family members with accurate descriptions of their medical conditions, poor prognoses, and the grisly realities of dying in a critical care unit. He presented the options as objectively as he could. The results were gratifying: 23 of 24 patients opposed resuscitation. None refused to discuss the tough issues because they felt uncomfortable. When patients were incompetent, all but one relative indicated that the patient would not have opted for resuscitation.

Why then does Murphy propose excluding patients and families from the decision-making process, and the even more radical step of not informing them of the do-not-resuscitate decision made unilaterally by the physician? Such a policy seems unnecessary; by communicating frankly with patients and families, he achieved the desired outcome. Why take the next step? Murphy seems to lapse back into an outdated (but perhaps yearned for) notion of paternalism. After giving ample evidence to the contrary, he worries that families will feel too guilty or will fail to "fully understand the implications of resuscitation despite detailed explanations." He goes on to say that making do-not-resuscitate decisions unilaterally and not informing patients and families will enable us to save time "better spent discussing other therapies and plans . . . that may have potential benefit." Acceptance of this position would also provide a justification for having physicians make unilateral and secret decisions about other "useless" therapies.

This latter reasoning becomes even more alarming when Murphy shifts from a paternalistic concern about what is best for the patient and family to a worry about how society should use its resources. He is not the first to be concerned about the massive resources consumed by the elderly in their final months, weeks, and even days of life—a problem that has been likened to a medical "avalanche."[4] As more and more elderly patients with chronic illnesses and severe de-

mentia fill beds in long-term–care facilities in the decades ahead, the problem may become monumental.

While everyone seems to agree that the avalanche is coming, there is little consensus in our society about a national policy to handle the situation. Responsible persons, such as philosophers Daniel Callahan and Norman Daniels, as well as former Colorado Governor Lamm, have suggested that care to the elderly be limited; their ideas have met with loud and often harsh criticism. Public opinion polls and surveys reveal the ambivalence of the American public about these issues."[5-9] On one hand, they want more access to high-technology interventions, believe that we spend too little on health care, and generally are unwilling to limit health care to the elderly. On the other hand, Americans are not enthusiastic about paying more taxes to achieve these goals.

These are issues that must be decided at the public policy level. Americans may well choose explicitly to ration medical resources by denying them to those persons with the least chance of deriving benefit; other countries have chosen this course implicitly, by tradition. While rationing is always a painful process, the potential success of treatment may be a more ethically acceptable criterion than others, such as social worth or ability to pay.[10,11]

Until we reach a public consensus about how to deal with these very difficult issues, individual clinicians and institutions should continue to separate concerns about patient welfare from broader social and economic policy issues.[12] As professionals, we are there to serve our patients. As citizens, we can vote or lobby for policies that limit individual choice in the interests of a broader social good.

Murphy's proposal is a regressive step. Under the guise of medical expertise and concern for proper resource allocation, it encourages physicians to substitute their own value judgments for those of their patients. He urges physicians to cut off communication with patients and families about the futility of resuscitation, an intervention imbued with complex and powerful symbolism.[13]

His actions were much more appealing. By engaging in honest communication, he was able to use his clinical knowledge and judgment to help families and patients make wise choices about painful but inescapable issues. Physicians would do well to follow Dr Murphy's example—not his proposal.

References

1. Murphy DJ: Do-not-resuscitate orders: Time for reappraisal in long-term–care institutions. JAMA 1988;260:2098–2101.

2. Tomlinson T, Brody H: Ethics and communication in do-not-resuscitate orders. N Engl J Med 1988; 318:43–46.

3. McQuillen MP: Ethics of life support and resuscitation. N Engl J Med 1988;318:1756.

4. Callahan D: Setting Limits: Medical Goals in an Aging Society. New York, Simon & Schuster Inc Publishers, 1987.

5. Evans RW: Health care technology and the inevitability of resource allocation and rationing decisions. Part I. JAMA 1983;249:2047–2052.

6. Evans RW: Health care technology and the inevitability of resource allocation and rationing decisions. Part II. JAMA 1983;249:2208–2219.

7. Callahan D: Allocating health resources. Hastings Cent Rep 1988;18:14–20.

8. Blendon RJ, Altman DE: Public attitudes about health-care costs: A lesson in national schizophrenia. N Engl J Med 1984;311:613–616.

9. Blendon RJ: The public's view of the future of health care. JAMA 1988;259:3587–3593.

10. Rescher N: The allocation of exotic medical lifesaving therapy. Ethics 1969;79:173–186.

11. Childress J: Who shall live when not all can live? Soundings 1970;53:339–355.

12. Angell M: Cost containment and the physician. JAMA 1985;254:1203–1207.

13. Nolan K: In death's shadow: The meanings of withholding resuscitation. Hastings Cent Rep 1987;17:9–14.

Futility and the Goals of Medicine

Rosamond Rhodes PhD

CASE

Mrs. Briggs is 73 years old. She is at the end of a long course of multiple myeloma. Chemotherapy has failed. Because of her disease she has suffered multiple fractures. The disease has metastasized to her peritoneum. She had been admitted to the hospital with nausea and vomiting, and diagnosed with obstructed bowel, which was surgically diverted with a colostomy. Post-operatively she did not do well. Gastro-intestinal (GI) bleeding continued. Her mental function deteriorated and then she lapsed into a coma.

Mrs. Briggs is in the intensive care unit (ICU), where she is being maintained with ventilator support, intravenous feeding and hydration, and antibiotics. In addition, since she is bleeding and her own bone marrow is no longer functioning, she daily receives one or two units of packed cells and some fresh frozen plasma. There is no expectation that Mrs. Briggs's condition will improve because none of her problems are reversible.

From *Journal of Clinical Ethics*, 9:194–205, 1998.

Mrs. Briggs's husband and son have been attentive throughout her hospitalization. They are religious people who pray at her bedside for a miracle. They emphatically assert that they want "everything done" to keep Mrs. Briggs alive until her heart stops. Since they consider someone whose heart stops to be dead, they have signed a do-not-resuscitate (DNR) order.

The physicians on the team describe the treatment as "futile." They would like to discontinue all treatment, or at least to stop the transfusions and have Mrs. Briggs transferred out of the ICU.[1]

ANALYSIS

This case raises a cascade of questions: Is the treatment futile? Does labelling treatment "futile" justify discontinuing it? Is the physician always required to comply with the wishes of the patient or surrogate? What would justify a physician's refusal? Can a physician invoke conscience or integrity as the grounds for refusing to comply with a patient's request? Is the physician free to obey personal morality, or is the doctor bound by professional responsibility?

At this point what should be clear is that an ethical resolution of this case will require working through a complex nest of moral concepts. Refusing treatment on the grounds that it is futile is troubling precisely because it seems to involve either overriding a patient's autonomy or complying with an unconscionable demand. In arguing for my own position on this kind of futility case, I will first sketch the general problem of saying "no" to patients or their surrogates, and explain the concept of autonomy that is the usual ground for respecting a patient's choice. Then I will discuss professional obligation, and try to make a case for thinking about futility in terms of the goals of medicine. Finally, I will refer to the goals of medicine in sketching a moral position for the case of Mrs. Briggs. In general, I will be arguing that physicians are required to accede to patient's wishes only if those wishes are consonant with the goals of medicine.

Saying "No" to Patients

Should treatment be provided for someone who is dying from a fatal illness that, at this point, has no cure? Once the inevitability of the outcome is recognized, some physicians could accept moving from aggressive treatment to a plan of palliative care. Physicians might be especially inclined to take that route when the patient and family signal their acceptance of it. Such a shift has also become well-accepted by many non-physicians in our society to the extent that a 1995 op ed piece in the *New York Times* described the practice.[2] The *Times* piece asserted that some physicians might be willing to order a morphine drip to ease a patient's suffering, even when it could be expected to hasten death. And, more recently, the June 1997 U.S. Supreme Court decisions in *Vacco v. Quill* and *Washington v. Glucksberg* proclaimed out society's adjustment to non-aggressive medical treatment and aggressive pain management.[3] In its decision on these cases, which questioned the constitutionality of prohibitions on physician-assisted suicide, the Court explicitly endorsed palliative care and even terminal sedation.

But if the patient and family instead demand more vigorous efforts, more treatment, more tests, a respirator, dialysis, an ICU bed, and resuscitation, some physicians are inclined to call such treatment "futile," and to design policies to protect themselves from having to comply with these directions. Such scenarios raise a challenging question for bioethics: Does respect for patients' autonomy require physicians to follow such orders from patients? And, if not, how can physicians' refusals be justified? This is a troubling issue that bioethics has not been particularly helpful in answering. If we can find an acceptable answer to the problem of when a physician is justified in saying no to a patient, we might be able to resolve at least some cases involving demands for futile treatment.

Respect for the autonomy of persons has been accepted as a cornerstone principle of bioethics. Autonomy, along with beneficence and justice, are acknowledged in the literature as the moral principles with the greatest bearing on medical practice.[4] The principle of autonomy is the basis for requiring truth-telling in physician/patient communications, informed consent in medical research, and confidentiality in handling personal information. Respect for autonomy requires that we allow people to make their own choices and to live by their own lights. And respect for autonomy prohibits physicians from imposing their personal judgment on patients so that patients can act on choices that reflect their own values.

While respect for patients' autonomy has become well entrenched in medical education and medical practice, the parameters of physicians' autonomy have hardly been discussed.[5] But physicians are obviously autonomous beings with values and goals of their own that may be different from those of their patients. When a patient's choice conflicts with a physician's, respect for autonomy dictates that physicians must respect their patients' decisions to *refuse* recommended treatments or tests. The Jehovah's Witness who refuses a blood transfusion would be an example. On the other hand, when a patient's choice conflicts with a physician's, and the patient *demands* treatments or tests that the physician would *not* choose to give, it is not clear whether physicians are required to comply or whether they are morally permitted to refuse. Examples of what I have in mind include a physician's choice not to prescribe antibiotics for a viral sore throat or more morphine for the patient with end-stage lung cancer when it appears that an additional amount will shorten the patient's life; or a physician's decision not to perform surgery when a patient has a DNR order in place, or not to intubate a dying patient. Does respect for autonomy allow physicians to act on their autonomous choices, or must the patient's choice always rule in the physician/patient relationship? Certainly physicians in these situations might have very different reasons for refusing to go along with their patients' choices. In what follows I will argue that those doctors' reasons have

different moral status, and that only reasons of a certain sort are legitimate.

Autonomy

So that we can better appreciate what is required, let us briefly examine the concept of autonomy. Because the centrality of autonomy in bioethics derives primarily from Kantian kinds of moral theory, I will explain the concept from that perspective. It is autonomy that distinguishes moral beings from other creatures. Autonomous beings must be able to do three things: conceive of moral principles or rules, choose actions in accordance with those principles, and constrain their actions to conform with their principles. These capacities enable people to take responsibility for their actions; beings who are incapable of any one of these capacities cannot be held responsible. These abilities are, therefore, the grounds both for moral treatment and moral accountability. The choices of beings who can be moral must be treated as if they do flow from moral principles. In other words, it is the ability to be moral that entitles people to moral treatment, that is, to respect.

While it is clear that everyone is not fully autonomous and that people sometimes act without considering moral rules, respect for autonomy requires that we presume that others are autonomous and that we allow them to make their own choices. In the words of Candace Cummins Gauthier, "We recognize that as a free and rational being the other has the capacity to choose his own goals and projects on the basis of moral principles known by reason and, thus, to act on a personal conception of what is right. Only when we respect and do not interfere with others' goals, projects, and actions, chosen on their own conception of what is right, are we respecting their autonomy as rational agents."[6] This means that we must tolerate the decisions other people make about their own lives even when it seems that they are not doing what is best.

In medical practice, respect for autonomy gives the patient what have been called negative rights, primarily the right to be left alone. Thus, competent patients or their designated surrogates have the right to refuse any recommended diagnostic procedure or therapy. Autonomous patients can check out of the hospital or choose to be treated by a different physician. However, according to this analysis, respect for autonomy does not give patients the right to dictate to their physician which treatments they will be given.

PROFESSIONAL OBLIGATION

Even though physicians are obliged to respect patients' autonomy, that duty may not always square with the full range of professional medical obligations. A brief account of their professional responsibility will bring this problem into focus and contribute to a framework for under-standing the issue of futility.

In descriptions of the professions, the professional is often cast as the agent of the client. In law, the attorney is described as the "mouth-piece" who speaks on behalf of the client and who only utters what he is authorized to say. Similarly, in an article in the *Journal of the American Medical Association* on alternative models of the physician-patient relationship, Ezekiel and Linda Emanuel draw on an earlier account by Robert Veatch,[7] and describe the informative or consumer model in which the patient dictates what is to be done and "the physician execute[s] the selected interventions."[8] According to this model, patients can legitimately regard their physicians as their agents and ask their physicians to do things on their behalf. The physician is the instrument of the patient's will. Whether or not this is the most appropriate way to conceptualize the physician-patient relationship (and the Emanuels argue that it is not), the model helps to frame the question at issue: Can physicians justifiably refuse to comply with their patients' requests? And, if so, which requests, and why?

Furthermore, asking this question in light of a discussion of autonomy illuminates a problem with the model that the Emanuels overlooked. They recognized that when physicians are merely

agents, there is no place left in the relationship for caring. But the problem is deeper, and the displacement of caring is only a symptom of the flaw in this conceptualization. To see physicians as simply instruments of their patients would absolve them from responsibility for what they do. A cog is not held accountable for the motion of the machine, and a physician who is merely a tool is not responsible for what occurs. But physicians are autonomous beings, and they are responsible for what they do. And as autonomous beings, they should try to do what they think is right.

This last turn in the argument leaves us with patient-clients who seem to have the right to dictate instructions to their physicians and with physicians who have a moral obligation to follow their own lights. When patient and physician agree on what should be done, there is no problem. When they disagree, we still do not know whose choices should rule.

In his article, "Doing What the Patient Orders," Jeffrey Blustein tries to resolve conflicts between patients' choices and physicians' objections by an appeal to integrity or conscience.[9] People with integrity act according to the principles they embrace, and they do not violate the dictates of their own conscience. According to Blustein, the physician who feels that doing what the patient orders will violate his integrity should simply refer the patient to another doctor who has less conscience or who has different principles.

While this kind of appeal to conscience may captivate physicians who feel entitled to refuse to do whatever they do not want to do, the analysis does not stand up to the test of consistency. Although it is hard to imagine that any physician would feel free of pangs of conscience while allowing a Jehovah's Witness to die from the need for blood, it is widely accepted that physicians must accede to the competent patient's choice of refusing blood. And it is not hard to imagine that a physician could feel guilty about initiating tortuous treatment or resuscitative efforts for a patient who will soon die anyway, but, nevertheless, most physicians will provide the treatment when the patient demands it. These examples illustrate that physicians can feel obligated to act in opposition to their own consciences. In both cases the physicians are actually allowing respect for their patients' choices to override their personal moral judgments about what should be done.

In other cases, physicians' integrity properly overrides patients' choices: most physicians will refuse to prescribe antibiotics for a viral sore throat, and most will refuse to initiate ineffectual chemotherapy in spite of their patients' demands. How can physicians who value autonomy justify those occasions when they must oppose it? Integrity does not tell us whether reluctant physicians should follow patients' orders or their own consciences, and so appealing to integrity cannot be the foundation for a distinction.

We need a way of thinking about the issue of when the physician must comply with a patient's demands, a way that will distinguish between responsibilities and dictate which obligation must be followed. To frame the question in another way, if medicine were to regulate itself, when should the profession require physicians to follow their patients' orders and when should physicians be required to refuse?[10]

A Distinguishing Principle—the Goals of Medicine

I would like to suggest a way of making the distinction that comes from medicine itself. Most broadly, medicine is committed to using the knowledge of science and employing it for patients' good. But as Aristotle pointed out, the word "good" is ambiguous.[11] Different kinds of things appear good to different people, and the same person calls different things good at different times. In fact, whatever anyone wants or values at any time can be called "good." Medicine is not committed to promoting anything that may be a good to a patient; medicine is only committed to promoting goods in relation to another *qua* patient. In other words, medicine has a commitment to achieving appropriate goals. The specific

parameters of the goals of medicine are determined in part by the developments of science and in part by society. So, while the goals of medicine are evolving, at any time there are some clearly identifiable activities that are consistent with the goals. The goals of medicine certainly include: healing, preserving life, preserving function, alleviating suffering.[12] No particular individual is allowed to determine the goals of medicine. And, while the goals may evolve, and while borderline cases and transitional commitments are likely to be controversial, they are not subject to personal choice.

Professions are marked by mastery of skills and a body of knowledge, and, beyond that, by a fiduciary relationship requiring the professional to employ those professional competencies for the benefit of clients/patients. The goals of medicine are not an arbitrary list of goods, but an enumeration of the unique goods that can be achieved by using medical knowledge. Listing them helps us appreciate the scope of duties that individuals take on when they become physicians. It helps us see what it means to act for a patient's good.

The over-arching duty to pursue a patient's good also provides another way of appreciating the place of respect for patients' autonomy. Because the physician's duty is focused on promoting the good of the patient, and since that good is largely subjective, the patient's perspective (that is, a patient's hierarchy of goods, respect for a patient's autonomy) must be factored into the content of the physician's obligation. Furthermore, because the vast majority of patients see the achievement of the goals of medicine as good, at least most of the time, we have an additional reason to see their achievement as the content of medical obligation.

The goals of medicine provide boundaries for patients' choices. Generally, physicians are only obligated to comply with patients' requests that are related to health. When patients ask for treatments that are consistent with medical science and the goals of medicine, their choices must be respected. When patients ask their physicians to comply with requests that are at odds with science or the goals of medicine, their physicians must refuse to cooperate. Patients who want antibiotics or chemotherapy when they will do no good and are likely to cause harm must be refused, because the goals of medicine require the physician to do no harm. However, a patient who wants a double mastectomy because she does not want to worry about her cancer returning, either in the breast that originally had the disease or in the breast that appears to be disease-free, should have her choice respected, even when her physician believes that a lumpectomy would be preferable because it is less disfiguring and, in this case, offers as good a prognosis as the more radical surgery. Here the patient's goals of life preservation and freedom from suffering—including worry about the cancer's return—are consistent with the goals of medicine. The physician's goal of wanting to avoid harm is also consistent with the goals of medicine. Valuing the patient's autonomy gives preference to the patient's priorities when goals conflict, and requires the physician to accede to the patient's request because her choice is consonant with the goals of medicine.

This is not to suggest that discussion, exploration, and negotiation have no place in medical practice. They are valuable in aiding physician and patient to appreciate each other's concerns and understandings. They are essential to forging a cooperative, caring, and trusting relationship that provides an environment that allows medicine to be practiced.[13] The point is rather that there are limitations on what physicians should do, and bounds beyond which they must not negotiate. Those constraints come from the goals that are the commitments of medicine. Viewing them as freely assumed special obligations gives us a *prima facie* reason for believing that they override the background duties of personal morality.[14]

Committing oneself to the achievement of the goals of medicine both limits the obligations of healthcare providers and constrains their liberty by providing boundaries for conscientious objection by physicians. The physician in the case of the woman who wanted a double mastectomy would have her conscience most at ease by performing the more limited surgery. Personally, she may see great value in preserving the aesthetics of the body and preserving sexual identity. But by choosing to be a physician, she commits herself to acting according to the goals of medicine in her professional life. So, when she acts as a physician, her personal morality must yield to the inherent standards of the goals of medicine. Since her patient's orders are consistent with the goals of medicine, she has no grounds for refusing to comply.

As another example, if this physician was deeply committed to the work ethic, wholeheartedly opposed to "government support of sloth," and voted for every candidate who promised to attack "the public dole," she would still be obliged to sacrifice her personal morality and to follow the demanding professional standards for respectful, compassionate medical care in treating the ill patient who appeared to be abusing alcohol and the welfare system. A physician of integrity organizes her commitment to morality by putting her professional values first, at least in her professional life.[15]

Bioethicist Samuel Gorovitz has written, "at the level of clinical practice, medicine should be value-free in the sense that the personal values of the physician should not distort the making of medical decisions."[16] I am suggesting that we see the situation in just the opposite way. Medicine is not value-free, but value-laden and, therefore, medical practice must be guided by those values. The goals of medicine must guide medical practice, and when they clash with the dictates of the ethics of either the physician or the patient the personal must yield.

With this much of the decision-making scheme sketched out, I would like to return to the issue of futility and our case in order to test the usefulness of the concept—that is, to see whether considering the goals of medicine can be effective in providing answers and whether the answers are intuitively acceptable.

Futility

The *Oxford English Dictionary* defines "futile" as "1. Incapable of producing any results; useless, ineffectual, vain. 2. Lacking in purpose."[17] It also tells us that the word comes from the Latin *futilis* and the French, *fundere*, to pour out. Unfortunately, this term that seems straightforward in the dictionary becomes much more ambiguous when applied in today's hospital setting. Starting with the two relevant and hardly distinct senses of the lexicon, we develop four senses of futility in modern medicine.

1. A remedy is futile when it is "useless, ineffectual, vain." The use of coffee enemas to treat cancer is futile in this sense.
2. Using an antibiotic for a viral infection or using a kind of chemotherapy that has been shown not to work against cancer to be treated are also called "futile." Although these treatments produce no *desired* results, they may produce some untoward effects.
3. New York State's Do-Not-Resuscitate Law defines "medical futility" in a closely related yet distinct sense. According to this law, the term applies only to a resuscitative procedure which is "medically futile," and hence, need not be undertaken, when "it is not expected to be successful or would have to be repeated again in a short time," usually understood to be within 24 hours.[18]

These first three senses of futility are relatively uncontroversial. Within medicine there may be dispute about whether or not some particular therapy meets the criteria of being futile, but there is little debate about whether the criteria should be used to rule out taking an action. The arguments arise over the fourth sense of futility.

4. A treatment is called "futile" when it is "lacking in purpose." But, as previously mentioned, medicine has a variety of purposes.

There is the goal of restoring health and curing disease, the goal of preserving life, the goal of restoring, improving, or maintaining function, the goal of alleviating pain. The issue of futility arises in cases where the patient or surrogate takes the simple prolonging of life to be a legitimate goal for medical care, while the healthcare team does not since all other medical goals are unattainable. "Futility," in this sense, is lacking a purpose that has value to me or us.[19]

Although we sometimes have common goals, we frequently have different purposes, even with respect to medical care. Groups have distinctive goals, and individuals can have idiosyncratic goals. Respect for autonomy requires us to allow others to act according to their own purposes. And beyond that, the goals of medicine commit physicians to act on their patients' behalf in ways that further the goals of medicine. Steven Miles has pointed out that no individual patient should be allowed to dictate the goals of medicine.[20] But neither should an individual physician or a particular group of healthcare providers. If, as I have maintained, the goals of medicine are determined in part by science and in part by society,[21] the issue turns on whether simply preserving life is a goal of medicine. This issue must be distinguished from the related question of whether extending biological life *should be* a goal of medicine, which is the subject of ongoing and extended public and professional debate.[22] But the present question is whether or not, in our society today, it is reasonable to expect medicine to act toward this goal.

Certainly 50 years ago, before cardiopulmonary resuscitation, before ventilators, before dialysis, before continuous veno-venous hemofiltration, this was not an issue. It was understood that good physicians were supposed to try to keep their patients alive. Those who lived functioned cognitively and physically, or they did not survive very long. But now, with and because of new knowledge and treatment modalities, physicians recognize that there can be a significant gap between restoring function or cognitive status and merely maintaining life without restoring function or cognitive status, and patients who cannot be restored may live for a very long time. Many physicians see providing treatment merely to sustain life as "futile," and appeal to personal integrity as a justification for refusing to treat. But the argument above suggests that only an appeal to the goals of medicine would justify such a refusal. So, in light of the gap between treatment that can be expected to accomplish some other goal of medicine, and treatment that will merely sustain life, does the latter still belong within the goals of the profession?

Although I am personally uncomfortable with an affirmative answer and committed to advocating for a change, and although science has moved to a new plateau that would accommodate omitting the mere preservation of life from the goals of medicine, today's society has not been acclimated to the change. Philosophically, the distinction that scientific medicine would like to make turns on a concept of persons as "beings with moral status," who can be distinguished from "mere humans." This distinction between personhood and human life is at the heart of the abortion debate, which still has our country embroiled in contention. Furthermore, drawing lines between "persons" and "mere humans" is associated with dangerous moves toward genocide and genetic cleansing. And we want to hold fast to the emotional force and moral power that comes from identifying with distant others as fellow human beings: the starving in Somalia, the liberated in Eastern Europe, the oppressed in Haiti. From that perspective, medicine can hardly count on consensus.

Furthermore, when not focusing on cases like the one I used to start this discussion, most people in our society, including nurses and physicians, would still list "preserve life" as one of the legitimate goals of medicine. Actually, the idea that medicine is committed to saving patients' lives is expressed repeatedly in the extensive literature on the goals of clinical practice.[23] It is also held to be implicit in the licensure promise that physi-

cians make to the state.[24] Given this broadly shared social understanding, it does not yet seem legitimate to claim that the goals of medicine have been revised to exclude treatment that would merely preserve life without accomplishing any other of the accepted goals. And further still, numerous court decisions from our recent past (for example, *Wanglie*, *Baby K*), which can be taken to express the social content of the goals of medicine, uphold the position that the preservation of life falls within the goals of medicine.[25] And then New York and New Jersey have state laws that permit families to refuse brain death as a standard for declaration of death. When people have the legal right to demand medical treatment for a loved one who is dead by the reigning clinical standard, it is easy to appreciate the gulf that may exist between social and clinical conceptions.

For the public, the goals of medicine have *not* shifted to accommodate a change in treatments that may be seen as "required" treatments.[26] On the other hand, the intuition that continuing a treatment is "futile" and immoral is commonly shared by medical professionals. The pronounced chasm between these views invites our speculation. Here some anecdotal data may be useful. In discussions of cases like Mrs. Briggs's, when the house staff is frustrated with the family and adamant about wanting to discontinue treatment, I typically ask if they would be willing to continue for another few days until "the granddaughter from far away" could arrive and see her before she dies. The house staff has always been most willing to accommodate this hypothetical delay.

I suggest that the professional commitments of medicine account for both the reluctance to treat the patient who can merely be kept alive and the change of perspective in light of "waiting for the granddaughter." Throughout its history, medicine has been committed to acting for the good of patients and doing no harm. Most medical and surgical treatments, and most of what is routinely done to patients in the critical-care setting, would count as harm but for the greater good that they promise. From the medical perspective, when the promise of greater good can no longer be maintained, all that is left is the harm. What physicians and nurses see is someone suffering for nothing, and suffering for nothing looks like torture, even when the medically enlightened know that the patient is beyond the cognitive possibility of suffering. The hypothetical granddaughter's hypothetical visit provides a way of seeing something worth while coming of the suffering so that it is no longer for nothing.[27]

CONCLUSION

If this last analysis is correct, it shows that medical professionals generally accept an obligation to rely upon their professional commitments to guide their professional behavior. In turn, this result suggests that pointing to the goals of medicine is, in principle, the model for adjudicating the case of Mrs. Briggs and similar problematic cases of medical futility. Treatment that will merely preserve her life must be provided when it is requested by the family. While it certainly looks as if the treatment is futile, as if blood is being poured on sand or down the drain, because it does maintain life it does realize one of medicine's current goals.

At some time in the future, the power of medical economics and moral argument may lead to a change in the goals of medicine. Meanwhile, as physicians remain committed to acting according to the current professional standard of practice, those who want a change must lead an educational charge against the status quo. A way from the bedside, physicians and nurses need to inform the public about the changes wrought by medical science. They should share their concerns about cases like Mrs. Briggs's and articulate the powerful arguments for a reconstruction of the goals of medicine to reflect the view that merely prolonging life is not worthwhile.

Policy Recommendations

Some institutions (for example, John's Hopkins Hospital in Baltimore and the Veterans Affairs Medical Center in Seattle, Washington)[28] have promulgated policies to refuse treatment that would merely preserve life. In that they are intended to deny patients treatments that are still consistent with the goals of medicine, these policies are problematic.

But there is an alternative policy route that may be more fitting for this dilemma. While the larger institution has the commitment to try to meet medicine's goals, that obligation only extends so far as the available resources can be stretched. When patients' needs exceed the bounds of the available resources, justice dictates that we carefully consider how medical attention, equipment, finances, and energy should be distributed. The reality of scarcity prompts us to employ some conception of distributive justice in order to allocate limited medical resources among the many who need them. Triage according to likelihood of benefit is the guiding vision that has been most commonly invoked in transplantation. The fact that there are not enough transplant organs to meet the needs of all those who could benefit from having one allows the team to adopt a policy of not listing some who might benefit from a transplant. Arguments in the transplant literature have been persuasive in moving the transplant community to adopt the view that those who would derive the least benefit from a new organ should be denied.[29] Even though more beds can be created in a way that more transplant organs cannot be, presently beds in ICUs are scarce and, in some states (for example, New York), the number is actually limited by state regulation. Frequently patients who could have benefitted from critical care are turned away because there is no room in the unit. This scarcity justifies an institutional policy to designate that ICU care will be denied to patients who are least likely to benefit from it.[30]

A policy would have to be written that sincerely attempted to fulfill the goals of medicine within the constraint of the resources of the institution. Then, aiming at a just distribution of what was available, the policy should clearly state medical criteria for the exclusion of some patients (for example, that critical care was reserved for patients who had medical problems that were potentially reversible or could at least be restored to mental competency). The policy would have to apply to all patients and consistently be used as a criterion for admission to or discharge from the unit.[31] The institution would also have to commit itself to trying to provide the care required by the goals of medicine, to the extent possible, for all of the patients who did not meet the standard for receiving critical care. This could include provisions for patients to have ventilator support continued outside of the ICU. It might also be reasonable for a policy to include an appeal procedure.[32]

Addressing futility from the perspective of the goals of medicine and using the triage model to limit care has several advantages over other views, which have discussed the issue from the perspective of cost containment or the best interest of the patient. Focusing on cost containment puts other social goods ahead of the good of the patient, an inimicable stand for a doctor. And discussing futility from the point of view of a patient's best interest is irrelevant when the patient is beyond the capacity to experience. The position I have advocated has the significant advantages of maintaining medicine's historical commitments to its traditional goals and to the doctor's fiduciary relationship to the patient.[33]

References and Notes

1. A version of this case was presented at SICU Ethics Rounds by Dr. Mayur Patel on 8 February 1995 at Mount Sinai Hospital, New York.

2. G. Kolata, "Withholding Care From Patients: Boston Case Asks, Who Decides?" *New York Times*, 3 April 1995, A1.

3. *Vacco v. Quill*, U.S. SupCt, No. 95–1858, 6/26/97; *Washington v. Glucksburg*, U.S. SupC:. No. 96–100, 6/22/97.

4. T.L. Beauchamp and J.F. Childress, *Principles of Biomedical Ethics*, 4th ed. (New York: Oxford University Press, 1994).

5. A few articles have discussed this issue, for example: M. Siegler, "Physicians' Refusals of Patient Demands: An Application of Medical Discernment," in *Search Of Equity: Health Needs and the Health Care System*, ed. R. Bayer, A.L. Caplan, and N. Daniels (New York: Plenum, 1983); A.S. Brett and L.B. McCullough, "When Patients Request Specific Interventions: Defining the Limits of the Physician's Obligation," *New England Journal of Medicine* 315 (1986): 1347–51; S. Leiken, "When Parents Demand Treatment," *Pediatric Annals* 4 (1989): 266–68.

6. C.C. Gauthier, "Philosophical Foundations of Respect for Autonomy," *Kennedy Institute of Ethics Journal* 3, no. 1 (1993): 21–37.

7. R. Veatch, "Models for Ethical Medicine in a Revolutionary Age," *Hastings Center Report* 2, no. 3 (June 1972): 5–7.

8. E.J. Emanuel and L.L. Emanuel, "Four Models of the Physician-Patient Relationship," *Journal of the American Medical Association* 267 (1992): 2221–26.

9. J. Blustein, "Doing What the Patient Orders: Maintaining Integrity in the Doctor-Patient Relationship," *Bioethics* 7, no. 4 (1993): 289–314.

10. This point was made by Daniel A. Moros in conversation.

11. Aristotle, *Nicomachean Ethics*, 1.1.

12. The goals of medicine have been discussed by a number of authors who offer variations on the list of goals, for example: A.R. Jonsen, M. Siegler, and W.J. Winslade, *Clinical Ethics*, 2d ed. (New York: MacMillan, 1986); A.E. Buchanan and W. Brock, *Deciding for Others: The Ethics of Surrogate Decision Making* (Cambridge: Cambridge University Press, 1989); R.M. Veatch, "Why Physicians Cannot Determine if Care Is Futile," *Journal of the American Geriatrics Society* 42, no. 8 (1994): 871–74; K. Kipnis, "Clinical Goals and the Concept of Medical Futility," *American Philosophical Association Newsletter on Philosophy and Medicine* (Fall 1995): 66–70.

It is beyond the scope of the present discussion to offer an argument in defense of any particular version of the list of goals. In this article it will be sufficient to recognize that the goals of medicine include preserving life.

I also recognize the controversy surrounding the "goals of medicine." Some bioethicists (e.g., R.M. Veatch, 4 April 1995, on the bioethics network) deny that there are goals. Without argument, this article will assume the majority position that there are goals that mark the profession and that these goals are normative.

13. R. Rhodes, "Love Thy Patient: Justice, Caring and the Doctor-Patient Relationship," *Cambridge Quarterly of Health Care Ethics* 4, no. 3 (1995): 434–47.

14. This is a complex and controversial position. A full discussion is beyond the scope of this article. In brief, however, the reason for the priority of special obligations is that special obligations are duties that individuals get only by taking them on. Awareness of the implications of special undertakings suggests that whoever commits to them grants them overriding status. That people sometimes or frequently act from moral blindness or with limited imagination does not refute the point about how they should behave. Furthermore, acknowledging the *prima facie* standing of special obligations does not imply that conflicts of duties should always turn in their favor. Also, ordinary morality provides constraints on the kinds of special obligations that can count as moral commitments (e.g., a hit-man's promise would not count).

For a discussion of this last claim, see C.M. Korsgaard, *The Sources of Normativity* (Cambridge, Cambridge University Press, 1996), or T. Hobbes, *Leviathan*.

15. Since the "goals of medicine" approach presumes that there are several legitimate goals for the profession, in particular cases conflict between the goals is certainly possible. For example, such conflict is at the core of controversies about abortion and physician-assisted suicide. Does preserving life or alleviating suffering take precedence? Are the rankings rigid or variable? Without here addressing the problem, I want to acknowledge that giving a *prima facie* ranking preference to professional commitments over personal commitments does not resolve all conflicts. It only addresses conflicts of a certain sort.

16. S. Gorovitz, *Doctor's Dilemmas: Moral Conflict and Medical Care* (New York: Oxford University Press, 1982), chapter 6.

17. *The Shorter Oxford English Dictionary*, 3d ed. (London: Oxford at the Clarendon Press, 1965), 765.

18. New York State Task Force on Life and the Law, *Do Not Resuscitate Order: The Proposed Legislation and Report of the New York State Task Force on Life and the Law*, 2d ed. (New York: Task Force, 1988).

19. R.M. Veatch makes a similar distinction in "Why Physicians Cannot Determine If Care Is Futile," see note 12 above.

"Futility" is also sometimes used to describe treatment in which the burdens are greater than the benefits. Although a comparison of benefits to burdens may provide an excellent reason for deciding not to initiate or continue a treatment, I take this to be a misappropriation of the term "futility."

20. S. Miles, "Medical Futility: The End of Medical Professionalism," *Seton Hall Law Review* 25, no. 3 (1995): 873–82.

21. In John Rawls's book, *Political Liberalism* (New York: Columbia University Press, 1993), he discusses the "overlapping consensus" as the normative model of just and fair social agreement. I am invoking this Rawlsian sense for socially accepted medical norms. Overlapping consensus is significantly different from majority positions which only reflect a "*modus vivendi*." Overlapping consensus expresses a sincere effort to achieve an unbiased and informed agreement. The conclusion of this article alludes to how a new overlapping consensus might be achieved about medical treatment for people whose lives could merely be prolonged.

22. E.g., S. Wear and G. Logue, "The Problem of Medically Futile Treatment: Falling Back on a Preventive Ethics Approach," *The Journal of Clinical Ethics* 6, no. 2 (Summer 1995): 138–48; D.B. Waisel and R.D. Truog, "The Cardiopulmonary Resuscitation-Not Indicated Order: Futility Revisited," *Annals of Internal Medicine* 122 (1995): 304–08; L. Schneiderman, K. Faber-Langendoen, and N.S. Jecker, "Beyond Futility to an Ethic of Care," *American Journal of Medicine* 96 (1994): 110–14; Veatch, "Why Physicians Cannot Determine," see note 11 above; J. Savulescu, "Rational Desires and the Limitation of Life-Sustaining Treatment," *Bioethics* 8, no. 3 (1994): 191–222; J.J. Paris et al., "Sounding Board: Beyond Autonomy—Physicians' Refusal to use Life-Prolonging Extracorporeal Membrane Oxygenation," *New England Journal of Medicine* 329 (1993): 354–57; N.S. Jecker and L.J. Schneiderman, "Medical Futility: The Duty Not to Treat," *Cambridge Quarterly of Healthcare Ethics* 2 (1993): 151–59; L.J. Schneiderman and N.S. Jecker, "Futility in Practice," *Archives of Internal Medicine* 153 (1993): 437–41; L.K. Stell, "Stopping Treatment on Grounds of Futility: A Role for Institutional Policy," *Saint Louis University Public Law Review* 11 (1992): 481–97; R.D. Truog, A.S. Brett, and J. Frader, "The Problem with Futility," *New England*

Journal of Medicine 326 (1992): 1560–64; R.M. Veatch and C.M. Spicer, "Medically Futile Care: The Role of the Physician in Setting Limits," American Journal of Law and Medicine 18 (1992): 15–36; N.S. Jecker and R.A. Pearlman, "Medical Futility: Who Decides?" Archives of Internal Medicine 152 (1992): 1140–44; S.H. Miles, "Informed Demand for 'Non-Beneficial' Medical Treatment," New England Journal of Medicine 325 (1991): 512–15; T. Tomlinson and H. Brody, "Futility and the Ethics of Resuscitation," Journal of the American Medical Association 264 (1990) 1276–80; S.M. Wolf, " 'Near Death'—In the Moment of Decision," New England Journal of Medicine 322 (1990): 208–10; E.D. Pellegrino, "Ethics in AIDS Treatment Decisions," Origins 19 (1990): 539–44; D.W. Brock and S.A. Wartman, "When Competent Patients Make Irrational Choices," New England Journal of Medicine 322 (1990): 1595–99; J.J. Paris, R.K. Crone and F. Reardon, "Occasional Notes: Physicians' Refusal of Requested Treatment—The Case of Baby L," New England Journal of Medicine 322 (1990): 1012–14. S.J. Younger, "Who Defines Futility? Journal of the American Medical Association 260 (1988): 2094–95.

23. Jonsen, Siegler, and Winslade, Clinical Ethics, see note 11 above; Buchanan and Brock, Deciding for Others, see note 12 above; Veatch, "Why Physicians Cannot Determine," see note 12 above.

24. Veatch, "Why Physicians Cannot Determine," see note 12 above; Veatch and Spicer, "Medically Futile Care," see note 22 above.

25. In re Wanglie, no PX-91–283 (4th Judicial Dist. Minnesota, Hennepin County, July 1991); In Re Baby K, 16 F.3d 590 (4th Cir. Feb. 10, 1994), cert. denied, 115 S.Ct.91 (1994). Recent legal decisions on cases of "futile" treatment are discussed at length in the bioethics literature, e.g., Paris, Crone, and Reardon, "Occasional Notes," see note 22 above; J.J. Paris and F.E. Reardon, "Physician Refusal of Requests for Futile or Ineffective Interventions," Cambridge Quarterly of Healthcare Ethics 2 (1992): 126–34; Paris et al., "Sounding Board," see note 20 above.

26. Court cases (e.g., Quinlan, Cruzan, Brophy, Glucksburg, Quill) have shown a shift in our society's position on allowing families to forgo treatment and allowing patients to request physician-assisted suicide. These changes do not, however, alter our view of the treatment that patients and families may demand. In Re Quinlan, 70 N.J. 10, 355 A.2d 647 (1976), cert. denied, 429 U.S.922 (1976); Brophy v. New England Sinai Hospital, 389 Mass., 417, 497 N.E.2d 626 (1986); Cruzan v. Director, Mo. Dep't of Health, 497 U.S.110 S Ct.2841 (1990); Washington v. Glucksberg, US SupCt, No. 96–110, 6/26/97; Vacco v. Quill, US SupCt, No. 95–1858, 6/26/97.

27. The analysis offered in this paragraph is mere speculation about behavior. Individuals may have very different views about the meaning of life. This article is not meant to engage the range of those alternative positions.

28. D.B. Waisel and R.D. Truog, "The Cardiopulmonary Resuscitation-Not-Indicated Order: Futility Revisited," Annals of Internal Medicine 122, no. 4 (1995): 304–08.

29. R. Rhodes, C. Miller, and M. Schwartz, "Transplant Recipient Selection: Peacetime vs. Wartime Triage," Cambridge Quarterly of Healthcare Ethics 4 (1992): 327–31.

30. The intermittent scarcity of ICU beds is discussed in the literature, for example: P.N. Lanken, P.B. Terry, and M.L. Osborne, "Ethics of Allocating Intensive Care Unit Resources," New Horizon 5, no. 1 (1997): 38–50; M.S. Johannes, "A New Dimension of the PACU: The Dilemma of the ICU Overflow Patient," Journal of Post-Anesthesia Nursing 9, no. 5 (1994): 297–300; D. Teres, "Civilian Triage in the Intensive Care Unit: The Ritual of the Last Bed," Critical Care Medicine 21, no. 4 (1993): 598–606.

31. It seems more practically and psychologically feasible to create ICU admission/discharge policy based on futility assessment (FA) than to invoke futility (relative futility, FR) only when a bed was needed by a patient with a better prognosis. FA as a limit on admission would allow the ICU team to commit itself to each of its patients, a commitment that would end only when the team's efforts could no longer be expected to achieve their limited goals (i.e., restored health or mental capacity). The alternative FR would leave them with merely tentative commitments to patients who could be "bumped" as soon as a more promising patient came along, and then re-admitted as soon as there was an available bed or a shift in the patient's standing, relative to the others in the unit.

Unfortunately, luck would be a factor in the implementation of both futility standards. If FA were adopted, the beds could all be filled with patients who had poor, but not futile, prognoses when a new patient with a better likelihood of success arrived at the hospital. If FR were adopted, a patient like Mrs. Briggs might be bounced out of the unit one day and, if she survived, treated vigorously in the unit the next.

It is hard to imagine that a team could maintain the requisite emotional stance toward a patient like Mrs. Briggs under a policy like FR. It is also hard to imagine that they could make objective relative judgments about their patients, as required by FR, in the face of the emotional and political pressures from family members and physicians that could surely be anticipated.

32. Appeals of denial of critical care or discharge from an ICU could be referred to the hospital ethics committee. Such steps are usually unnecessary in transplantation, where the patient typically applies for treatment. Since surrogates, rather than patients, are typically the ones asking for futile treatment, an appeal procedure could help meet their psychological need to advocate for their loved one to the utmost.

33. R.M. Veatch discussed the fiduciary duties of the physician in a Bioethics Network entry "Re: Baby K," 3/17/95.

QUESTIONS FOR DISCUSSION

1. It has been argued that physician-assisted suicide (PAS) enables patients to control the time and manner of their death, which in turn upholds their dignity and autonomy. Explain how this position can be reconciled with the physician's duty to do no harm to and benefit patients.

2. Some have maintained that there is no ethically significant difference between acts and omissions that lead to a patient's death, but rather between acts and omissions that are intended to cause death and those that are not. On this view, if the physician's intention is the same, is there any ethical difference between discontinuing mechanical life support and giving terminal sedation?

3. If a patient has a right to assistance in bringing about his or her own death, then presumably a physician has a corresponding obligation to assist the patient to realize this end. But some would argue that this is beyond the pale of physicians' professional obligation and therefore they can justifiably refuse to assist. Does this effectively mean that there is no right to PAS?

4. Many requests for PAS are caused by intractable pain and suffering. Would adequate pain management and palliative care obviate the need for PAS? Why are such measures not already in place in medical practice?

5. When a patient's condition has deteriorated beyond a certain point, a physician may invoke physiological futility to justify discontinuation of treatment. But patients and their families may believe that continued treatment is not qualitatively futile because living longer has value for them. How can such conflicts be resolved? If it would be more helpful to eliminate the concept of futility, then what alternative concept should guide patients, families, and physicians in reaching agreement in end-of-life decision–making?

CASES:

In Re Quinlan. 355 A. 2d 647 N.J. (1976) In April 1975 21-year-old Karen Ann Quinlan was brought comatose to hospital emergency because of cardiac arrest induced by ingestion of barbiturates, Valium, and alcohol. She was put on a respirator to assist her breathing, but her neurological condition deteriorated and she fell into a persistent vegetative state (PVS). Her father petitioned to have the mechanical ventilator withdrawn. Karen's attending physician, the state's attorney, and the trial court refused, claiming that the duty to preserve life and the right of her physician to administer medical treatment according to his best judgment were sufficient to override her constitutional privacy right to refuse further life-sustaining treatment. But the New Jersey Supreme Court ruled in favor of Mr. Quinlan and ordered discontinuation of the respirator. Karen then unexpectedly began to breathe spontaneously. She was moved to a nursing home where she lived in a PVS for ten years, dying in 1985 at the age of 31.

Bouvia v. Superior Court. 179 Cal. App. 3d 1127, 225 Cal. Rptr. 297 (1986). Elizabeth Bouvia was a quadriplegic affected from birth with severe cerebral palsy and suffered from constant pain. While she was in a public hospital receiving artificial nutrition, she competently requested that her nasogastric feeding tube be removed so that she could starve to death. The hospital refused, citing a duty to continue necessary life-sustaining treatment. The California Court of Appeals overruled the hospital and ordered that the tube be removed, holding that competent patients are entitled to forego any treatments, including those that sustain life. Later, Elizabeth changed her mind and decided to continue living until nature took its course. The appellate court suggested not only that there was a right of privacy to refuse treatment, but also that courts and physicians should make it possible for physicians to assist patients in ending their lives in dignity and comfort.

Cruzan v. Director, Missouri Department of Health. 497 U.S. 261, 110 S.Ct. 2841, 111 L.Ed. 2d 224 (1990). In 1983, Nancy Cruzan lost control of her car and sustained injuries resulting in a coma. It then progressed into an unconscious state in which she was unable to ingest nutrition orally. Surgeons implanted a gastrostomy feeding and hydration tube in Nancy with the consent of her then husband. Her parents sought a court order directing the withdrawal of the tube. But the Supreme Court of Missouri overruled it, holding that there was no clear and convincing evidence of Nancy's desire to have life-sustaining treatment withdrawn under such circumstances. In 1990, the U.S. Supreme Court upheld the right of the State of Missouri to require strict standards of evidence regarding the patient's preferences. At the same time, however, it affirmed the fundamental principle of a patient's right (or "liberty interest") to forego life-sustaining treatment and ordered the discontinuation of the artificial feeding and hydration.

In Re: The Conservatorship of Helga M. Wanglie. State of Minnesota District Court (1991). Helga Wanglie, 87-year-old, was in a PVS being maintained on a respirator. Her physicians maintained that further artificial respiration was futile because it could not restore her to consciousness. But Mrs. Wanglie's husband pointed out that, while she still was competent, his wife never had indicated her preference about life-sustaining treatment. He maintained that her doctors should not play "God," and that life support should be continued. The hospital sought a court order to have a conservator appointed who might consent to the removal of the respirator. The judicial ruling denied the hospital's request and instead upheld Mr. Wanglie's request that treatment continue. Helga Wanglie died three days after the court ruling despite continued aggressive treatment. This case focused debate on the idea of medical futility.

Washington v. Glucksberg. 117 U.S. S. Ct. 2258 (1997). This case raised the question of whether the State of Washington's prohibition against causing or aiding a suicide offended the 14th Amendment of the U.S. Constitution. The U.S. Supreme Court reversed the decision of the Ninth Court of Appeals, which had decided in 1996 that state prohibitions on physicians assisting competent terminally ill patients to commit suicide were unconstitutional. Specifically, the Ninth Circuit had ruled that Washington's laws deprived dying patients of a fundamental aspect of self-determination, the right to determine the time and manner of one's death. The U.S. Supreme Court rejected the Ninth Circuit's recognition of a fundamental right, citing a long U.S. history of state prohibition against suicide. States have legitimate interests in prohibiting any medical practice that assists patients in hastening their death because states have legitimate interests in preserving citizens' lives, preventing citizens from taking their own lives, protecting vulnerable groups against euthanasia, and maintaining trust in the medical profession's commitment not to take patients' lives.

Vacco v. Quill. 117 U.S. S. Ct. 2258 (1997). This was treated as a companion case to *Washington v. Glucksberg* because it addressed the same issue, and both cases were decided by the U.S. Supreme Court on the same day, June 26, 1997. In this case, the Court examined the question of whether New York State's prohibition against assisting suicide violated the Equal Protection clause of the 14th Amendment. In holding that it did not, the Court found that the New York law applied equally to everyone in that all citizens have the right to refuse medical life support; but no citizen has a right to a physician's assistance in dying.

SUGGESTED FURTHER READING

Battin, Margaret et al., eds. *Physician-Assisted Suicide: Expanding the Debate.* London: Routledge, 1998.

Brody, Howard. "Assisted Death: A Compassionate Response to Medical Failure." *New England Journal of Medicine* 327:1384–1388, 1992.

Burt, Robert. "The Supreme Court Speaks: Not Assisted Suicide but a Constitutional Right to Palliative Care." *New England Journal of Medicine* 337:1234–1236, 1997.

Dworkin, Gerald et al. *Euthanasia and Physician-Assisted Suicide: For and Against.* New York: Cambridge University Press, 1998.

Dworkin, Ronald et al. "Assisted Suicide: The Philosophers' Brief." *New York Review of Books* 44:41–47, 1997.

Gaylin, Willard et al. "Doctors Must not Kill." *Journal of the American Medical Association* 259:2139–2140, 1988.

Helft, Paul et al. "The Rise and Fall of the Futility Movement." *New England Journal of Medicine* 343:293–296, 2000.

Lantos, John et al. "The Illusion of Futility in Clinical Practice." *American Journal of Medicine* 87:81–84, 1989.

President's Commission for the Study of Ethical Problems in Medicine and Biomedical and Behavioral Research: *Deciding to Forego Life-Sustaining Treatment.* Washington, D.C.: U.S. Govt. Printing Office, 1983.

Quill, Timothy et al. "Care of the Hopelessly Ill: Proposed Clinical Criteria for Physician-Assisted Suicide." *New England Journal of Medicine* 327:1380–1384, 1992.

———"The Rule of Double Effect: A Critique of its Role in End-of-Life Decision Making." *New England Journal of Medicine* 337:1768–1771, 1997.

Randall, F. and Downie, R. S. *Palliative Care Ethics,* Second Edition. Oxford: Oxford University Press, 1998.

Veatch, Robert. *Death, Dying, and the Biological Revolution,* Second Edition. New Haven: Yale University Press, 1989

PART VII:

ALLOCATION OF SCARCE
MEDICAL RESOURCES

Maintaining an adequate level of health care for all people is a costly enterprise. Indeed, at 14% of Gross Domestic Product (GDP), health care expenditures in the United States are far ahead of those of other countries in the Organization for Economic Cooperation and Development (OECD). Although health care arguably is the most important social good, education, housing, and environmental protection are also important. No liberal democratic society can afford to spend too much on health care, not only because of the way it affects these other social goods, but also because it adds to the national debt and thus is unfair to future generations, saddling them with higher taxes and perhaps even affecting their own access to adequate health care.

Rationing is necessary to control health care costs. It consists in limiting services and procedures within predetermined levels. Unfortunately, rationing means that some people will be denied care that they need. Because not all the needs of all people can be met, we have to find ways of rationing care that will meet people's medical needs as best we can. This requires that medical resources be allocated efficiently, maximizing health benefits while keeping costs down. At the same time, we must ensure that resources are distributed fairly by giving equal weight to people's claims on these resources. This entails ensuring that all people have access to a decent minimum of care, which could include a basic package of immunizations, prenatal care, antibiotics, insulin for diabetes, emergency care, and continuity of care with an overseeing primary care physician. This is necessary for people to have equal opportunity to formulate life plans and to undertake and complete the projects that contribute to a decent minimum level of well-being. To be viable, any health care system must combine the economic principle of efficiency with the ethical principle of fairness as complementary goals.

Of the four ethical principles that serve as the foundation of biomedical ethics, justice is the most important on the matter of allocating scarce medical resources. There are different conceptions of justice, but for the issue at hand the egalitarian theory of justice associated with Rawls is the most plausible. Recall from Part I the two principles of justice by Rawls, the second of which, the difference principle, says that inequalities are justified only if they benefit the least advantaged members of society. This embodies a "prioritarian" interpretation of egalitarian (as distinct from utilitarian or libertarian) justice. The point is not that equality as such has value, but rather that in any distribution policy priority should be given to the needs of the worse off. Moreover, a smaller benefit to the worse off matters more morally than a larger benefit to the better off. Extending this principle to the domain of health care, the worse off are those with worse health status, or sick people. Fairness is one aspect of a theory of justice. On the egalitarian theory adopted here, a fair allocation of a scarce resource will be one that meets people's claims in proportion to their strength, where the strength of these claims is a function of the degree of need. Since sick people have greater needs and, therefore, stronger claims than healthy people, a fair allocation will be one that meets the claims of sick people first.

But we must distinguish between those who are acutely sick and in urgent need of care, on the one hand, and those who are chronically sick over a longer period of time and have more basic medical needs, on the other. Each of these groups is worse off than those who are healthy but have different needs that require different applications of the difference principle and the idea of fairness. In the case of the acutely sick, we should give all who have urgent medical needs an equal chance to receive immediate medical care. In the case of the chronically sick, we should ensure that they have equal access to a basic package of health benefits that will enable them to have the same opportunity for achievement and well-being enjoyed by those who are healthier. Many of those worse off in the more general chronic sense of sickness are the poor and uninsured, which at last count totaled 44 million Americans. The papers in Part VII address the issues of fairness and efficiency in the distribution of scarce resources in both acute and chronic senses of medical need.

In the first selection, Daniel Callahan discusses the claims of the elderly on medical resources within a framework of intergenerational justice. More specifically, how do claims to receive life-extending medical care by those who have lived for, say, 75 or more years affect the welfare of working-age Americans and children? Motivating this question is a communitarian political philosophy, which aims at a shared consensus about how health care should contribute to the good of society. Callahan is not arguing for a reduction in health care expenditures to the elderly but instead for a revised understanding of aging that will benefit the lives of the elderly as much as those of the young. He claims that our social obligation to the elderly is only to help them to live out a natural life span of 75–80 years, and that generally the government is only obligated to provide health care to them to achieve that goal. Beyond that point, health care should not aim at extending life but rather at relieving suffering. An appropriate understanding of the meaning of aging must be coupled with an understanding of the obligations the elderly have to the young and to future generations. By the same token, there is an obligation for the young to ensure that the elderly live out a life span with dignity and security. Life-extending technology and the increase in chronic illness have generated painful moral choices about how to care for the elderly. These choices should be informed by a communitarian conception of the place of aging and death within life.

Norman Daniels and Robert Veatch further discuss age as a factor in allocating health care. Daniels begins with Rawls' idea of fair equality of opportunity and extends it to the distribution of health care over the course of people's lives, arguing that a just distribution of health care will be one that guarantees fair equality of opportunity. He defends what he calls the "prudential lifespan account." This says that distribution of health resources between different age groups should be seen as a problem of prudential reasoning for a single individual about how to distribute resources over the different stages of his or her life, taking into account the likelihood of disease at these different stages. If we reason in this way, then rationing on the basis of age need not be unjust when compared with allocating resources to meet needs at specific times.

Veatch considers both Callahan's and Daniels' accounts of age-based rationing in developing and defending his own position. He argues that people who have had more opportunities for life experience are better off than those who have had less, suggesting that younger people are worse off than older people because they have not had an equal amount of opportunities. In this respect, it would not be unfair to give general priority to younger over older individuals in allocating scarce health resources. Significantly, Veatch's argument is not motivated by consequentialist considerations of welfare or health outcomes. Rather, it is motivated by non-consequentialist, deontological considerations of fairness. By shifting the justification for such a policy from consequentialism to egalitarian justice, Veatch effectively disarms the criticism that the position he defends would be ageist and hence unjust.

The concept of quality adjusted life-years (QALYs) was introduced by health economists in the 1980s as a means of testing the cost-effectiveness of medical procedures. Roughly, a QALY is a measure of the additional life-years adjusted for quality that any given procedure would yield. A QALY takes a year of healthy life expectancy to be worth 1 and a year of unhealthy life expectancy to be less than 1. John Harris examines this concept and argues that QALYs are untenable on several counts. First, by focusing on quantitative and qualitative aspects of life-years, QALYs ignore the value that lives have for people. Furthermore, QALYs are ageist because they emphasize life expectancy to be gained from treatment, and younger people have more life expectancy to gain from any given treatment than do older people. QALYs also can be sexist and racist to the extent that they discriminate against certain vulnerable groups who are identified by race, gender, and color. The upshot is that QALYs violate the principle of equal access to health care for all people.

Shifting to more specific rationing problems, Robert Truog takes up the issue of rationing care in the hospital intensive care unit (ICU), stating at the outset that all intensive care therapies are fundamentally scarce. He argues that a patient's autonomy and right to care are not absolute but *prima facie* and must be weighed against the benefit that he or she is likely to receive from treatment. He develops a model whereby patients and their families are made to prospectively understand the "rules" of allocation in the ICU. Borrowing from the traditional concept of triage in a battlefield setting, Truog maintains that patients should be prioritized according to their likelihood of benefiting from ICU therapy. The best use of ICU resources is that which maximizes health benefits. However, when treatment is withdrawn from a patient because it is not in *that* patient's best interest, the interests of any other patient do not arise.

The next selection addresses the issue of prioritization of candidates for transplantation of scarce organs such as livers. The Council on Ethical and Judicial Affairs of the American Medical Association lists five ethically acceptable conditions in the selection of candidates for organ transplantation: (1) the likelihood of benefit to the patient with a transplant; (2) the impact of treatment in improving the patient's quality of life; (3) the duration of benefit with a transplant; (4) the urgency of the patient's condition, and (5) the amount of resources required for successful treatment. These criteria serve more general goals of medical treatment, which include number of lives saved, number of life-years saved, and improvement in quality of life. The Council argues that differences in the magnitude of change in functional status among patients are ethically relevant only when they are substantial. It rejects social worth, patient contribution to diseases, and past use of resources as factors worthy of consideration on the ground that they are not ethically relevant criteria for setting priorities in organ transplantation. The Council then goes on to consider different strategies for implementing the five criteria, pointing out that no single approach can be applied to every case.

In the final piece, Charles Dougherty brings matters full circle by offering a general discussion of the need for a policy of cost-containment in health care. He defines health care rationing as denying or limiting access to needed and potentially beneficial health care and formulates eight criteria for an ethically acceptable system of rationing: (1) it must ensure a basic level of care for everyone; (2) it must preserve care and trust at both clinical and policy levels; (3) it must protect vulnerable groups; (4) it must serve the common good by contributing to the overall health of communities; (5) it must be necessary; (6) it must result from an open public process of debate about the goals and methods of rationing; (7) it must exclude all forms of discrimination; and (8) the same rationing standard must apply to all citizens. Dougherty concludes by stating that medical rationing is probably the only way to achieve the twin goals of expanded access and cost containment.

Allocating Resources to the Elderly

Daniel Callahan PhD

The political decision to shift the primary burden of health care and social security for the elderly from their children and families to government was one of great and still-unfolding consequence. While it by no means relieved children and families of most traditional obligations toward their elderly parents and relatives, the intent was to shift their weight from the economic to the affectional sphere. As it has turned out, however, the domestic burdens within that sphere can be heavy and at times overwhelming, and exacerbated by greater longevity and changing family patterns. Outside help has been sought. Nor have all financial pressures on families by any means been relieved, especially when long-term institutional care of elderly relatives is required; a need for still greater financial relief for families has emerged. As the number and proportion of the elderly have grown, the economic pressure upon government continues to increase at a rapid pace.

What is the extent of the government's obligation? Or, to put the matter more precisely, what is the extent of our common obligation as a society—using the instruments of government—to provide health care for the elderly? If we must acknowledge that the families of the elderly cannot meet all their legitimate needs, that there are limits to familial obligation, does that mean that the duties of government are thus unlimited? The only prudent answer to that question is no. Government cannot be expected to bear, without restraint, the growing social and economic costs of health care for the elderly. It must draw lines, because technological advances almost guarantee escalating and unlimited costs which cannot be met, and because in any case it has a responsibility to other age groups and other social needs, not just to the welfare of the elderly.

My purpose is to develop a rationale for limiting health resources to the elderly, first at the level of public policy and then at the level of clinical practice and the bedside. Our common social obligation to the elderly is only to help them live out a natural life span; that is, the government is obliged to provide deliberately life-extending health care only to the age which is necessary to achieve that goal. Despite its widespread, almost universal rejection, I believe an age-based standard for the termination of life-extending treatment would be legitimate. Although economic pressures have put the question of health care for the elderly before the public eye, and constitute a serious issue, it is also part of my purpose to argue that, no less importantly, the meaning and significance of life for the elderly themselves is best founded on a sense of limits to health care. Even if we had unlimited resources, we would still be wise to establish boundaries. Our affluence and refusal to accept limits have led and allowed us to evade some deeper truths about the living of a good life and the place of aging and death in that life.

My underlying intention is to affirm the inestimable value of individual human life, of the old as much as the young, and the value of old age as part of our individual and collective life. I must then meet a severe challenge: to propose a way of limiting resources to the elderly, and a spirit behind that way, which are compatible with that affirmation. What does that affirmation mean in practice, and not merely in rhetoric? It means that individual human life is respected for its own sake, not for its social or economic benefits, and that individuals may not be deprived of life to serve the welfare, alleged or real, of others—individuals are not to be used to achieve the

From *Setting Limits: Medical Goals in an Aging Society*. New York: Simon and Schuster, 1987.

ends of others. To affirm the value of the aged is to continue according them every civil benefit and right acknowledged for other age groups unless it can be shown that their good is better achieved by some variation; to respect their past contributions when young and their present contributions now that they are old; and never, under any circumstances, to use their age as the occasion to demean or devalue them. That is the test my approach to allocation must meet.

The greatest social benefit now enjoyed by the American elderly comes from a social security system that provides a minimal level of financial maintenance and heavily subsidized health care. What those who designed the health portion of the system—beginning with Medicare in 1965—did not reckon with was that its high and ever-escalating costs could in the long run threaten its viability. Federal expenditures for Medicare, for example, have been projected to rise from $74 billion in 1985 to $120 billion in 1989—a 60-percent increase in only four years. The threat that escalating figures of that kind portend—an eventual need to scale down benefits and to reconceive health care for the elderly—seems a cruel blow to the gains that have so recently been achieved. It is a basic assault upon the dream of a modernizing, aging society: that old age and good health are biologically compatible and financially affordable.

Initially, the economic issues of health care for the elderly seem to present an array of issues that are difficult but not unfamiliar. Among them are cost effectiveness in the delivery of care, the fair allocation of resources, effective and affordable methods of insurance, and the establishment of priorities for research. Is there, then, any reason to think that the economic problems of health care for the old are unique? Similarities can surely be noted in the case, say, of caring for severely handicapped newborns or for other groups of patients wherein the interventions are exotic, the costs high, and the ultimate results often problematic. Yet the difficulties of caring for the elderly display three unique features. The first

is the increasingly endemic nature of their illnesses, which are less curable than they are controllable. The price of an extended life span for the elderly is an increase in chronic illness. The second feature follows from the first: the sheer number and proportion of the elderly as a pool of ill or impaired people. The third is the growing necessity to make painful moral choices in the care of the elderly dying as a class, particularly among those who end their days incompetent and grossly incapacitated, more dead than alive.

Health care for the elderly encompasses, then, some features shared with other age groups and some that are unique. How should we, therefore, think about the allocation of health resources to the elderly? I want to approach that question from the moral perspectives I have laid out in earlier chapters. The main points to be included within such an approach are that the allocation of resources to the elderly should be based upon (1) suitable goals for medicine, by which I mean achievement of a natural life span and, beyond that, only the relief of suffering; (2) an appropriate understanding of the meaning and ends of aging, particularly in terms of the search for personal meaning coupled with service to the young and coming generations; (3) a commitment by the young to assist the elderly to achieve their end in dignity and security, but in a way compatible with the other familial and social obligations of the young and without placing excessive or unreasonable demands upon them; and (4) the achievement of a death by the elderly that is human. To these points I would add two additional ideals not previously developed: (5) a deployment of economic and other resources oriented to the good of society and its different age groups, not simply to the health and welfare of elderly individuals; and (6) the goal of minimizing as far as possible economic and social anxieties about growing old and being old. This last point requires making credible the belief that in one's old age one will be treated with dignity and respect, be assured of minimally adequate welfare and health care, and be supported by society in one's effort to find meaning and significance in aging and death.

FACTS, PROJECTIONS, SIGNIFICANCE

I have been working with the assumption that there is a growing problem of allocating health care to the elderly. There is enormous resistance to that idea. Is it true? As with any other definition of what is or is not a "problem," everything will depend on how we interpret the available evidence. Carroll L. Estes, for one, has suggested that the whole debate about the future viability of Social Security is a manufactured "crisis," one designed to delegitimate the elderly as a deserving group. Reality, he argues, is being defined to make old age and an aging society a problem; thus can the elderly be "blamed for their predicament and for the economy" and domestic spending reduced as a consequence.[1] That is not a wholly farfetched idea and might be applied to Medicare as well as Social Security. Yet what are the available facts and projections about the health-care needs of the elderly? How reliable, in particular, are the projections for future needs? What is the significance of those projections, and in what sense do they indicate a problem?

The basic facts of the present situation can be briefly summarized. In 1980, the 11 percent of our population over age 65 consumed some 29 percent of the total American health-care expenditures of $219.4 billion. By 1984, the percentage had increased to 31 percent and total expenditures to $387 billion. Medicare expenditures reached $59 billion in 1984, while Medicaid and other government health expenditures on the elderly came to an additional $15 billion. Taken together, these government programs covered approximately 67 percent of the health outlay of the elderly (compared with 31 percent for those under 65).[2] Some 30.1 percent of the elderly classified their health as fair or poor in 1981, with some 45.7 percent of that number reporting some limitation of activity due to poor health.[3] In 1984, personal health-care expenditures for those 65 and older came to a total of $4,202 per capita (in comparison with $1,785 in 1977).

Projections for the future are less certain, but some typical figures are as follows. Between 1965 and 1980, there was an increase in the life expectancy of those who reached age 65 from 14.6 to 16.4 years, with a projected increase by the year 2000 to 19.1 years. Between 1980 and 2040, a 41-percent general population increase is expected, but a 160-percent increase in those 65 or over. An increase of 27 percent in hospital days is expected for the general population by 2000, but a 42-percent increase for those 65 and over and a 91.2 percent increase for those 75 and over. The number of those 85 or older will go from 2.2 million in 1980 to 3.4 million in 1990 and 5.1 million in 2000; and those 65 and older from 25.5 million in 1980 to 31.7 million in 1990 and 35.0 million in 2000.[4] Whereas in 1985 the elderly population of 11 percent consumed 29 percent of health-care expenditures, the expected 21-percent elderly population will consume 45 percent of such expenditures in 2040. The distinguished statistician Dorothy Rice, on summarizing the evidence, has written that "the number of very old people is increasing rapidly; the average period of diminished vigor will probably rise; chronic diseases will probably occupy a larger proportion of our life span, and the needs for medical care in later life are likely to increase substantially."[5] Karen Davis, formerly director of the federal Health Care Financing Administration (HCFA), has stated that "Future demographic and economic trends will strain the ability of public programs to maintain the current level of assistance, and will further magnify the gaps. Even with the uncertainties of technological change, biomedical research, and health-related behavior of the population in future years, it seems safe to predict that the gap between expanding health-care needs and limited economic resources will widen."[6]

Need we accept the judgements of Rice and Davis, or of others who believe (as I do) that the projections point to a grave problem? There are some who think the whole debate that is emerging over the costs of health care for the old, and particularly the possible strains it might create between the generations, is misplaced. There are also a few who think that one reform in particular, a control of useless and expensive care in the case of the dying elderly, would provide major economic relief. These reservations are serious and deserve reflection. I want to look at four general lines of criticism of the belief that there is a "problem" as well as to examine the view that the elimination of excessive spending on the elderly dying would be the single most efficacious way of reducing the health-care costs of the elderly.

The Heterogeneity of the Old and Long-Term Projections

Two objections to any supposed need for rationing are frequently joined. The first is that it is a mistake to allow future projections based on extrapolations from present data to dominate our thought, as if projections could give us an accurate picture of the future, or as if the future were immutable, not subject to policy manipulation. The second is that it is no less a mistake to think we can make illuminating projections about the aged as a group. They are too diverse to make that a meaningful exercise. It also contributes to a stereo-typing of the old and a consequent failure to attend to the specific needs of specific individuals and subgroups among the aged.[7]

All projections into the future are, to be sure, uncertain, especially in the case of societies that change as rapidly as the United States. Yet as a general rule, there is no other way to plan for the future than to make extrapolations from present trends. That they may turn out to be wrong, or may be subject to great variation, is no good reason to evade the responsibility of making them in the first place. In the case of the aging, moreover, the palpable vastness of the demographic changes now taking place, their undeniably great implications for social and personal planning, and

the harmful possible consequences of not having some kind of strategy (however tentative) for dealing with them would seem flagrantly irresponsible and irrational. While past projections about health-care needs and costs concerning the elderly have been wrong, they were almost always *underestimates* of mortality and morbidity trends and of health-care costs.[8] Two trends in particular were underestimated: that of life expectancy beyond the age of 65, and that of the number and proportion of those over 85. The health-care costs of the later have become particularly pronounced. There is, more generally, little room to doubt that the number and proportion of the elderly are growing rapidly at present, that the number of young people in the demographic pipeline ensures a continuing growth of the elderly in the future, and that the old have greater health needs than the young. That is a trend which cannot be ignored; and there is no reason whatever to believe it will be reversed. Even if the inflationary costs of health-care delivery generally can be controlled, the combination of steady-state general costs combined with a growing pool of aged would guarantee a substantial increase in costs of care for the elderly. In the meantime, of course, health-care costs continue to outstrip the pace of inflation, so far impervious to cost-containment remedies.

The objection that the old are too heterogeneous a group to allow for any meaningful generalizations raises more serious problems. It incorporates both a technical issue (the validity of statistical or other generalizations) and a value-laden policy issue (the moral and social implications of categorizing people on the basis of their age and not merely their needs). Regarding the technical issue, while it is true that the aged are a remarkably heterogeneous group—and generalizations or predictions about any given elderly individual difficult to make—that does not mean group generalizations of some soundness cannot reliably be made. Many groups of people are heterogeneous, displaying a wide range of personal traits along a broad spectrum. But both because our language requires the use of general terms if we are to communicate at all, and because moral and policy considerations force some degree of generalization, there is no escaping the use of broad terms regardless of individual variation.

We know, for instance, that people over the age of 65 have greater health-care needs as a group than those under 65, that they are more in danger of death, that they are less suitable for physical-contact sports, that they tend to look different from those under the age of 10 (in ways that can be well characterized). That there are border-line disputes about just which age should be called "old" (whether 65, or 75, or 80) hardly proves that the word "old" is a meaningless category. It is simply a category encompassing great diversity and open to dispute. Many general and socially necessary terms (as an instance, "adolescence") have the same characteristics; that just means some care is required in using them, not that they should be dismissed altogether.

There would be little concern over these linguistic matters but for their political and moral implications. A concern about stereotyping typically underlies the wariness toward generalizations about the old: that they will be thought of as homogeneous, and in harmful ways. Some of that wariness has, of late, also been urged on advocacy groups for the aging. They have been accused, in the name of publicizing the problems of their constituents, of exacerbating a public image of the old as uniformly weak, frail, and poor. A newer stereotype of the elderly as affluent and pampered is no less rejected.[9] The worry about stereotyping is certainly legitimate. Yet many true generalizations about the elderly that are not offensive stereotypes can be made, particularly about their health status *as an age group* in comparison with other age groups. No general statement, however true in general, will be exactly true about any given individual. That does not invalidate their general truth. To say that the aged have greater health-care needs than other age groups is true. To say that death comes to all the old is also true.

Generalizations are also politically necessary. Since many of those most concerned about the stereotyping of the old are those who have worked hard on their behalf, their own cause would be threatened by a successful effort to eliminate all group generalizations. There are also related hazards in making too many distinctions about the aged and overstressing their heterogeneity. An excessively large number of subcategories of the aged, one way of coping with the diversity problem, could create bureaucratic and public confusion and could lead to competition among the aged themselves. The need for some coordinated political strategies on their behalf makes it therefore all the more important that the heterogeneity be of a recognizable general group: the elderly. Otherwise the sheer diversity of the needs and demands may confuse both government and the public.[10] The question is: For what purposes are we grouping and generalizing, and are they valid? An effort to focus exclusively on the needs of the elderly as individuals, rather than as members of a distinct group, is not a viable policy direction. It would threaten solid and helpful traditions that enhance respect for the elderly, would ignore perfectly valid generalizations about the elderly, and would force the pretense that age is a trivial or irrelevant human characteristic.

Is Rationing Necessary?

In April of 1983, Roger Evans published a two-part article in the *Journal of the American Medical Association* with the title "Health Care Technology and the Inevitability of Resource Allocation and Rationing Decisions."[11] That article was by no means the first to stress the eventual need for rationing decisions, but by its emphasis on the "inevitability" of that development, it expressed a major (though hardly undisputed) trend in policy thought. The factors that produce the inevitability are an aging population, an increase in the prevalence of chronic disease, and the emergence of an array of expensive medical technologies to cope with those developments. "In short," he concluded, "the demand for health care will doubtless outstrip available resources."[12] In a much-discussed 1984 book, *The Painful Prescription: Rationing Hospital Care*, Henry J. Aaron and William B. Schwartz compared the British and American health-care systems to see what Americans might learn from the British about rationing, which they took to be inevitable also in the United States.[13] That the elderly are more subject to rationing in Great Britain than children or younger adults was one not-unexpected finding.

While it is difficult to gauge just what the present balance of opinion is among those in the health-care field on the need and justification for rationing of health care in general, two lines of objection have emerged. One of these is that even though the United States now spends close to 11 percent of its GNP on health care, there is nothing magical about that figure or any need to assume it should stay there or be lower. Why, it has been asked, could not the percentage go to 12 percent or 14 percent or 15 percent? That is theoretically possible, but it fails to take into account the important reality of political acceptability. That the United States already devotes a larger portion of its GNP to health care, 10.8 percent in 1986, than other developed countries with excellent health-care systems is itself a good reason for politicians and health planners to believe that more money would not in itself guarantee any greatly improved level of health care.[14] On what basis other than that might they persuade the public to tolerate a higher proportion of expenditures on health? While public-opinion polls often indicate a willingness on the part of the public to spend more money on health care, the apparent political perception is that there is little tolerance for greatly increased expenditures.

Another objection is that any talk of rationing is premature. The gerontologist Robert Binstock has said that future economic strains should not be blamed upon the elderly, but instead "lie in our unwillingness to confront and control the causes of runaway health care costs."[15] Others agree. Marcia Angell, Deputy Editor of *The New England Journal of Medicine*, has argued not only that more health care is not necessarily better care, but also that much present care is wasteful and unnecessary. This includes needless laboratory and diagnostic tests, "big-ticket" operations and procedures, and aggressive care of terminally ill patients.[16] Two other analysts contend that "evidence that rationing effective services in the United States may be unnecessary comes from three areas: the wide variation in per-person rates of use of all forms of medical care, the unproved effectiveness of many procedures used to diagnose and treat illness, and the unquestioned assumption among both medical practitioners and the public that doing more or at least doing something is preferable to doing nothing."[17] Another commentator, also stressing the inefficiencies and waste of the present system, has gone even further and contended that "invoking the language of rationing . . . has been at best, poorly thought through and, at worst, unethical."[18]

There can be little doubt that the present system is wasteful. The prospective-payment system based on diagnosis-related groups (DRGs) initiated in 1983 to control the costs of hospitalization under Medicare has shown that patients can be moved out of hospitals more quickly, and the proliferation of outpatient surgical and other medical procedures shows still other ways of reducing hospital costs. Research has demonstrated a striking variation from one community to another in the number of surgical procedures performed, a variation pointing to a lack of criteria for and control of necessary care.[19]

Nonetheless, despite some cost reductions here and there, there is so far no significant evidence that any striking savings of the kind envisioned by Binstock or Angell can, or at least will, in fact be made. Despite efforts dating back to the late 1970s to control or reduce health-care costs, they continue to rise in an uninterrupted fashion. Despite occasional claims that costs are beginning to come under control—*no one* has claimed that they are in fact already under control—the evidence is solid that health-care expenditures rose more rapidly after 1980 than earlier, and that relative to the overall consumer price index, more rapidly after 1980 than in the late 1970s. That trend continued with no abatement at all right through 1986.[20] Despite the politically inspired, and not implausible, belief that competition among providers would reduce costs, it seems instead to have raised them.

To look to theoretically possible efficiencies as a way out of our problems in caring for the aged thus seems to be wishful thinking with little historical or present basis. Even if *some* savings can be made, which surely is possible, new technologies are constantly being introduced that drive the costs higher, and technologies originally introduced to help the young are extended to care of the aged. Heart transplants, for instance, have now been extended to patients in their 60s, and a liver transplant was successfully carried out on a 76-year-old patient in 1986. As late as 1980, such patients would have been considered too old. Medicare was extended in 1987 to include heart and other organ transplants.[21] With an aging population, there will be an ever-larger pool of candidates to use those technologies—hardly a recipe for cost reduction. The evidence, on balance, suggests the need both to "cut the fat" (as the most common expression has it) and to ration as well. To depend on the former's doing a sufficient job in time would seem an act of unjustified faith; while to depend on the latter without strenuous efforts at the former would seem harsh and unfair. No one has been known to suggest that we could spend less money in the future on health care, either in real dollars or as a percentage of GNP; it has been suggested only that we might not have to see continued high growth rates. Moreover, while we might imagine a great change in the direction of stabilized or reduced costs, or simply muddling through with higher costs, that still leaves open the question I have been pressing: even if we can find the money, and

avoid rationing, are large expenditures on health care for the elderly a wise way of allocating resources? That question is rarely if ever addressed in discussions of ways to avoid rationing or by those intent on denying its need.

Guns or Canes?

An important variant on the objections to the need for rationing of health care is what has been called the "guns versus canes" argument.[22] It has a number of versions. If we can afford to spend more than $300 billion on national defense each year (much of it notoriously wasteful), another $25 billion on tobacco products, and $500,000 for a Super Bowl commercial, why should we entertain at all any serious discussion of cutting back or holding down expenditures on the sick and the elderly?[23] A heavy focus on the costs of care for the aged may simply serve to divert attention from other costs that are far less acceptable. Another version—in response to data supposedly showing that the elderly are benefiting more from government programs than the young—holds that even if this is true, it would be foolish for advocates of the aged to reduce their demands as a way of benefiting children. There is no guarantee whatsoever in our political system that any savings on the old would actually be transferred to children. Why risk a sacrifice of the needs of the aged in a circumstance of that kind?

These are potent arguments. The lack of any coordinated health, welfare, and social planning means that each group has powerful incentives to pursue its own interests, even if it is known that other valid interests exist. They each have little reason to believe their interests would otherwise be fully acknowledged or that any sacrifice on their part would be met by similar action on the part of other interest groups. We lack a system designed to be a just way of allocating scarce resources, either within the health-care system itself or between health and other social needs. There thus seems to be no good reason for any one group to forgo its demands and needs in favor of other groups, at least if the motive is to help the other groups.[24]

There are some problems with that approach. It serves all too readily to encourage some diversionary thinking of its own, turning attention away from a full and candid evaluation of the real needs of the elderly and the costs of meeting them. The fact that worse economic villains can be found, or more foolish expenditures in other realms discovered, provides no justification for avoiding that self-examination. More fundamentally, one of the prices of living in a democracy is that people are allowed to have other needs and interests than those of health and health-care delivery. A goodly number of Americans, patently enough, want to spend large amounts of money on national defense, and cosmetics, and wasteful advertising. One can complain about that, and label the present policies as stupid, narrow, and self-interested or self-indulgent. I am prepared to do so. One should also work politically to correct the situation and not be willing to settle for the status quo. I am ready to join that cause. But it is in the nature of our political system to tolerate such harms until peaceably and democratically changed.

Even within that democratic context, however, if one group pursues its needs with single-minded zeal and achieves excessive success, that increases the likelihood that other groups will not get what they need. In theory there is no zero-sum game in a country as affluent (at the moment) as ours, but the political reality includes a limit to the tolerance of taxpayers. They will not pay equally well or generously for everything. A practical consequence of the large amounts of funds now going to the elderly (together with the strong political support they enjoy) is to make it highly likely that new funds will not be appropriated for the young or for other social needs; it is the economic status quo (which includes high defense spending) that will have priority. We then end with a painful paradox. A reduction of spending on the elderly in no way guarantees that the money saved would be spent wisely or well.

But an escalation of spending on the elderly almost ensures that money will not be adequately available for other needs, including those of children. The fate of Medicaid, ironically, perfectly illustrates this truism. Whereas it was originally designed to provide general health care for the poor, its originally incidental inclusion of long-term care of the elderly has meant that as the latter's costs have risen, funds for the other poor have proportionately declined (to only 40 percent), driven down by the costs of long-term care.

The "Common Stake" in Care for the Old

While the subject of allocation of resources among the generations will receive further discussion in my last chapter, it is pertinent to touch on it in this context. The argument has been made, in effect, that there is no real problem of allocation of resources to the elderly for two important reasons. The first is that because everyone either is already old or will become old, a social policy of expenditures on the elderly benefits all generations in the long run; that is our "common stake."[25] Second, health-care benefits for the aged have some immediate value for younger generations. They help relieve the young of burdens of care for the elderly they would otherwise have to bear. Research on those diseases which particularly affect the elderly has the side benefit of frequently producing health knowledge of pertinence to the young and their diseases. It also promises the young relief, when they are old, from diseases which they would otherwise be forced to anticipate. They are reassured about their own future to a greater extent.

That is a plausible viewpoint. Called, in one of its variants, the "life course perspective," it "clarifies the reciprocity of giving and receiving that exists between individuals and generations over time."[26] Yet it also obscures some important considerations. It is a view that could be taken to imply that any amount of health care for the present old would be beneficial to society because it would benefit everyone else as well. If this is an implication, it does not follow. We must first and independently decide, in the context of comparison with other social needs, just how high a priority health care for the aged should have in relation to other social goods. Would too high a priority, with no fixed limits, be a sensible way to allocate health-care benefits in comparison with such other benefits as education, housing, or economic development? In the absence of such a determination, moreover, we could inadvertently do harm by gradually increasing health-care allocations to the present generation of aged (and those who will join them over the next decade or so), thus overpoweringly burdening with indebtedness the younger generations, guaranteeing that they could not, when old, have comparable benefits. We might, that is, establish a precedent of care and a financial debt for that care which could not be managed in the future.

If the aged proportion of the population promised to remain stationary over the next few generations, and if there were no great chance of any increase in the average life expectancy of the old or in the burden of chronic illness among them, and if the introduction of further life-extending technologies were unlikely—then, in that case, a "life course perspective" could be put immediately to work. But it cannot now rationally be used without the prior exercise of freshly deciding what we want old age to be, which kind and proportion of resources we ought to devote to old age, and what the long-range implications of our choices for both old and young may be. Precisely because the future of aging, medically and socially, is so open-ended, so subject to some conscious ethical and policy decisions, it would be a mistake to simply leap into the middle of an indeterminate "life course perspective." We have to fashion that idea anew, taking into account as a necessary first step some basic judgment about how much and what kind of health care would be right for the elderly in the future. A "life course perspective" does not obviate the need to determine appropriate health care for the elderly, but

logically requires it (together with a similar determination for other age groups) as a first step.

Costs of the Dying Elderly

The suggestion has been made by a distinguished medical economist that control of the costs of the elderly dying would be a major step toward eliminating the excessively heavy health-care costs of that age group. "At present," Victor Fuchs has written, "the United States spends about 1 percent of the gross national product on health care for elderly persons who are in their last year of life. . . . One of the biggest challenges facing policy makers for the rest of this century will be how to strike an appropriate balance between care of the [elderly] dying and health services for the rest of the population."[27] It is understandable that the gross figure—1 percent of the GNP—attracts attention. There are few physicians and increasingly few lay people who cannot find in their own experience of the elderly some cases of seemingly outrageous and futile expenditures to keep an elderly person alive. Bills running into the tens of thousands of dollars are common, and those in six figures hardly rare any longer. That kind of personal experience has solid empirical support. Studies of Medicare expenditures have shown that some 25 to 35 percent of Medicare expenditures in any given year go to the 5 to 6 percent of those enrollees who will die within that year, and that the high medical expenses of those who die are a major reason that health-care expenditures of the old rise with increasing age.[28] In addition to Medicare studies, a number of other analyses of the care of the critically ill indicate that the costs of caring for those who die are often much higher than for those who survive, and that the elderly are of course a high proportion of those who die.[29]

There is less here than meets the eye. Two issues need to be discentangled. The first is empirical. What exactly do the financial data show, and do they suggest that substantial savings would be possible if expensive care were withheld from the elderly dying? The second is ethical. Even if large amounts of money are spent on the elderly dying, is it an unreasonable and unjust amount?

The available data, while they support the charge of high expenditures, reveal a complex problem. The pertinent studies, for example, are all retrospective in nature; that is, they show only after the fact that someone died that large amounts of money were spent prior to the death. They do not tell us whether the initial prognosis was that of a terminal illness, whether care was taken not to waste money, and whether less expensive options for equally humane care were available. The point about prognosis is the most important. Can physicians ordinarily (save at the last moment) *know* that an elderly person is dying and that further sophisticated medical care will do the patient no significant good? Apparently not. As one of the more important studies concludes: "Among nonsurvivors, the highest charges were due to caring for patients who were perceived at the time of admission as having the greatest chance of recovery. Among survivors, the highest charges were incurred by those thought to have the least chance of recovery. Patients with unexpected outcomes . . . incurred the greatest costs . . . For the clinician, the problem may seem hopelessly complex. Simple cost-saving solutions, such as withholding resources from the hopelessly ill or earlier transfer of those requiring only anticipatory care, are difficult to apply to an individual patient because prognosis is always uncertain."[30]

A no less important finding is that the high expenses at the end of life are not largely the result of aggressive, intensive high-technology medical care. A Health Care Financing Administration (HCFA) study showed that only 3 percent of all Medicare reimbursements (some 24,000 decedents) went to those who incurred charges greater than $20,000 in the last year of life. Even the use of a lower threshold figure—of charges greater than $15,000—showed only 6 percent (56,000 decedents) incurring such costs.[31] Thus the economist Anne Scitovsky was

justified in concluding that "the bulk of Medicare reimbursements for all elderly patients who die is accounted for by patients other than those who received intensive medical care in their last year of life."[32]

The combination of data of that kind and the clinical difficulty of an accurate prognosis that a patient is actually terminal means that optimism about the possibility of large-scale savings is misplaced. The constant innovation in critical-care medicine, most of it expensive, could well nullify other economies in any case. An additional important implication suggests itself: there is little basis to the moral conclusion that the money being spent on the elderly dying is unjust or unreasonable, even if quantitatively disproportionate to the spending on other age groups. That the aged are, as a group, going to be more expensive to care for than other medically needy groups is inevitable, inherent in the aging process. The expenditures could be judged unreasonable or unfair only if there were evidence that money was spent more inefficiently on the aged dying than on other patients—and no such evidence exists; or that, in the face of a known prognosis of certain or highly likely death, resources were nonetheless expended as if that were not known—and there is no basis to support that kind of general accusation. It then becomes rash to conclude that the spending is unjust. Since more money will proportionately and inescapably be spent on the old than on the young, and more of the old proportionately are likely to die despite such care, it is hard to see what is prima facie unreasonable and wasteful about that situation.

Does that mean there is *no* economic or moral problem? Not necessarily. I want only to conclude that the charge of wasted, useless expenditure on care of the dying elderly cannot be supported. There is, actually, an even more disturbing outcome of the studies to be discerned, well articulated by Anne Scitovsky: " . . . if further studies bear out the tentative conclusion that the high medical costs at the end of life are due not so much to intensive treatment of clearly terminal patients but to ordinary medical care of very sick patients, this raises much more complex and difficult issues than have been discussed in the literature to date. . . . A consensus has gradually developed about the ethics of forgoing treatment for such patients for whom care is, in some real way, futile. But no such consensus exists for patients who, although very sick, might still be helped by various diagnostic or therapeutic procedures and whose days might be prolonged. Thus, if we ask whether the costs of care for this group are excessive, we face new ethical problems of major proportions."[33] She bases this conclusion on evidence that the sickest elderly patients are actually treated less aggressively than younger elderly patients, and that the largest costs turn out to be those of providing long-term home and nursing care for the very frail and debilitated (and often demented) elderly, costs that can well exceed their acute-care hospital and physician costs.[34] Perhaps better solutions can routinely be found to the problem of those clearly identified as terminal (different hospital routines, expanded hospice options, for example). Even so, we will still be left with that other but much larger group of elderly, those who are patently, though slowly, declining but not yet imminently dying.

SETTING LIMITS

I have considered five responses pertinent to the contention that there is a need to ration health care for the elderly; while each of them has a certain plausibility, none is wholly convincing: It is possible and necessary to generalize about the elderly. It is possible that benefits to the aged will not automatically benefit other age groups. It is not premature to take the idea of rationing seriously. It is not a mistake to consider limitations on health care for the elderly even if there continue to be other social expenditures that we individually think wasteful. And it is more wishful thinking than anything else to believe that more efficient care of the elderly dying could save vast amounts of money. All those objections reflect a laudable desire to avoid any future policies that would require limiting benefits to the aging and that would use age as a standard for that limitation. They also betray a wish that economic realities would be happily coincidental with a commitment to the unrestricted good of the elderly. That may no longer be possible. A carefully drawn, widely discussed allocation policy is likely to be one safer in the long run for the elderly than the kind of ad hoc rationing (such as increased cost-sharing under Medicare) now present and increasing.

How might we devise a plan to limit health care for the aged that is fair, humane, and sensitive to the special requirements and dignity of the aged? Neither in moral theory nor in the various recent traditions of the welfare state is there any single and consistent basis for health care for the elderly. The ideas of veteranship, of earned merit, of need, of respect for a age as such, and various pragmatic motives have all played a part in different societies and in our own as well. The earlier presumption of a basic obligation on the part of families to take care of their elderly, rooted in filial obligation, has gradually given way to the acceptance of a state obligation for basic welfare and medical needs. While the need and dependency of the elderly would appear to be the strongest basis of the obligation, it has never been clear just how medical "need" is to be understood or the extent of the claim that can be drawn from it. Minimal requirements for food, clothing, shelter, and income for the aged can be calculated with some degree of accuracy and, if inflation is taken into account, can remain reasonably stable and predictable. Medical "needs," by contrast, admit of no such stable calculations. Forecasts about life expectancy and about health needs have, as noted, consistently been mistaken underestimates in the past. Constant technological innovation and refinement means not only that new ways are always being found to extend life or improve therapy, but also that "need" itself becomes redefined in the process. New horizons for research are created, new desires for cures encouraged, and new hopes for relief of disability engendered. Together they induce and shape changing and, ordinarily, escalating perceptions of need. Medical need is not a fixed concept but a function of technological possibility and regnant social expectations.

If this is true of medical care in general, it seems all the more true of health care for the aged: it is a new medical frontier, and the possibilities for improvement are open, beckoning, and flexible. Medical need on that frontier in principle knows no boundaries; death and illness will always be waiting no matter how far we go. The young can already for the most part be given an adequate level of health care to ensure their likely survival to old age (even if there also remain struggles about what their needs are). For the aged, however, the forestalling of bodily deterioration and an eventually inevitable death provide the motivation for a constant, never-ending struggle. That struggle will turn on the meaning of medical need, an always malleable concept, and will move on from there to a struggle about the claims of the elderly relative to other age groups and other social needs. That these struggles are carried on in a society wary about the propriety of even trying to achieve a consensus on appropriate individual needs does not help matters.

For all of its difficulties, nonetheless, only some acceptable and reasonably stable notion of need is likely to provide a foundation for resources allocation. The use of merit, or wealth, or social worth as a standard for distributing life-saving benefits through governmental mechanisms would seem both unfair at best and morally outrageous at worst. We must try, then, to establish a consensus on the health needs of different age groups, especially the elderly, and establish priorities to meet them. At the same time, those standards of need must have the capacity to resist the redefining, escalating power of technological change; otherwise they will lack all solidity. The nexus between need and technological possibility has to be broken, not only that some

stability can be brought to a definition of adequate health care, but also that the dominance of technology as a determinant of values can be overcome.

Need will not be a manageable idea, however, unless we forthrightly recognize that it is only in part an empirical concept. It can make use of physical indicators, but it will also be a reflection of our values, what we think people require for an acceptable life. In the case of the aged, I have proposed that our ideal of old age should be achieving a life span that enables each of us to accomplish the ordinary scope of possibilities that life affords, recognizing that this may encompass a range of time rather than pointing to a precise age. On the basis of that ideal, the aged would need only those resources which would allow them a solid chance to live that long and, once they had passed that stage, to finish out their years free of pain and avoidable suffering. I will, therefore, define need in the old as primarily to achieve a natural life span and thereafter to have their suffering relieved.

The needs of the aged, as so defined, would therefore be based on a general and socially established ideal of old age and not exclusively, as at present, on individual desires—even the widespread desire to live a longer life. That standard would make possible an allocation of resources to the aged which rested upon criteria that were at once age-based (aiming to achieve a natural life span) and need-based (sensitive to the differing health needs of individuals in achieving that goal). A fair basis for limits to health care for the aged would be established, making a clear use of age as a standard, but also recognizing the heterogeneity of the needs of the old within those limits.

Norman Daniels has helpfully formulated a key principle for my purposes: the concept of a "normal opportunity range" for the allocation of resources to different individuals and age groups. The foundation of his idea is that "meeting health-care needs is of special importance because it promotes fair equality of opportunity. It helps guarantee individuals a fair chance to enjoy the normal opportunity range for their society." A "fair chance," however, is one that recognizes different needs and different opportunities for each stage of life; it is an "age-relative opportunity range."[35] Even though fairness in this conception is based upon age distinctions, it is not unfairly discriminatory: it aims to provide people with that level of medical care necessary to allow them to pursue the opportunities ordinarily available to those of their age. Everyone needs to walk, for example, but some require an artificial hip to do so. It also recognizes that different ages entail different needs and opportunities. A principle of limitation is also implicit: "Only where differences in talents and skills are the results of disease and disability, not merely normal variation, is some effort required to correct for the effects of the 'natural lottery.' "[36]

Yet there are two emendations to this approach that would help it better serve my purposes. For one thing, moral and normative possibilities of what *ought* to count as "normal opportunity range" are left unaddressed. For another, the concept should be extended to encompass what I will call a normal "life-span opportunity range"—what opportunities is it reasonable for people to hope for over their lifetimes?—and we will need to know what *ought* to count as "normal" within that range also. For those purposes we will have to resist the implications of the modernizing view of old age, which would deliberately make it an unending frontier, constantly to be pushed back, subject to no fixed standards of "normal" at all. Otherwise the combination of that ideology and technological progress could make Daniels' idea of a normal opportunity range for the elderly as an age group and my concept of a life-span opportunity range for individuals intractable and useless as a standard for fair allocation among the generations. The aged, always at the edge of death, would inevitably have medical needs—if defined as the avoidance of decline and death—greater than other age groups. No other claims could ever trump theirs.

Those considerations underscore the urgency of devising an ideal of old age that offers serious resistance to an unlimited claim on resources in the name of medical need, and yet also aims to help everyone achieve a minimally adequate standard. For that purpose we require an understanding of a "normal opportunity range" that is not determined by the state-of-the-art of medicine and consequently by fluctuating values of what counts as a need. "Need" will have no fixed reference point at all apart from a technology-free (or nearly so) definition. Where Daniels uses the term "normal" in a statistical sense, it should instead be given a normative meaning; that is, what counts as morally and socially adequate and generally acceptable. That is the aim of my standard of a natural life span, one that I believe is morally defensible for policy purposes. Such a life can be achieved within a certain, roughly specifiable, number of years and can be relatively impervious to technological advances. The minimal purpose is to try to bring everyone up to this standard, leaving any decision to extend life beyond that point as a separate social choice (though one I think we should reject, available resources or not). Daniels recognizes that his strategy has the implication that it "would dictate giving greater emphasis to enhancing individual chances of reaching a normal lifespan than to extending the normal lifespan."[37] But I think that that implication, to me highly desirable, really follows only if taken in conjunction with some theory of what *ought* to count as a "normal opportunity range" and not simply what happens to so count at any given historical and technological moment. The notion of a natural life span fills that gap.

With those general points as background, I offer these principles:

1. Government has a duty, based on our collective social obligations, to help people live out a natural life span, but not actively to help extend life medically beyond that point. By life-extending treatment, I will

mean any medical intervention, technology, procedure, or medication whose ordinary effect is to forestall the moment of death, whether or not the treatment affects the underlying life-threatening disease or biological process.[38]

2. Government is obliged to develop, employ, and pay for only that kind and degree of life-extending technology necessary for medicine to achieve and serve the end of a natural life span; the question is not whether a technology is available that can save a life, but whether there is an obligation to use the technology.

3. Beyond the point of a natural life span, government should provide only the means necessary for the relief of suffering, not life-extending technology.

These principles both establish an upper age limit on life-extending care and yet recognize that great diversity can mark the needs of individuals to attain that limit or, beyond it, to attain relief of suffering.

AGE OR NEED?

The use of age as a principle for the allocation of resources can be perfectly valid.[39] I believe it is a necessary and legitimate basis for providing health care to the elderly. It is a necessary basis because there is not likely to be any better or less arbitrary criterion for the limiting of resources in the face of the open-ended possibilities of medical advancement in therapy for the aged.[40] Medical "need" can no longer work as an allocation principle; it is too elastic a concept. Age is a legitimate basis because it is a meaningful and universal category. It can be understood at the level of common sense, can be made relatively clear for policy purposes, and can ultimately be of value to the aged themselves if combined with an ideal of old age that focuses on its quality rather than its indefinite extension.

This may be a most distasteful proposal for many of those trying to combat ageist stereotypes and to protect the deepest interests of the elderly. The main currents of gerontology (with the tacit support of medical tradition) have moved in the opposite direction, toward stressing individual needs and the heterogeneity of the elderly. That emphasis has already led to a serious exploration of the possibility of shifting some old-age entitlement programs from an age to a need basis, and it has also been suggested that a national health-insurance program which provided care for everyone on the basis of individual need rather than age (as with the present Medicare program) would better serve the aged in the long run.[41] Thus while age classifications have some recognizably powerful political assets, a consensus seems to be emerging—clearly contrary to what I propose—that need is a preferable direction for the future. "Perhaps," as the Neugartens have written, "the most constructive ways of adapting to an aging society will emerge by focusing, not on age at all, but on more relevant dimensions of human needs, human competencies, and human diversity."[42] While that is an understandable impulse, I think it cannot for long remain possible or desirable in the case of allocating health care to the aged.

The common objections against age as a basis for allocating resources are varied. If joined, as it often is, with the prevalent use of cost–benefit analysis, an age standard is said to guarantee that the elderly will be slighted; their care cannot be readily justified in terms of their economic productivity.[43] The same can be said more generally of efforts to measure the social utility of health care for the old in comparison with other social needs; the elderly will ordinarily lose in comparisons of that kind. By fastening on a general biological trait, age as a standard threatens a respect for the value and inherent diversity of individual lives. There is the hazard of the bureaucratization of the aged, indifferent to their differences.[44] Since age, like sex and race, is a category for which individuals are not responsible, it is unfair to use it as a measure of what they deserve in the way of benefits.[45] The use of an age standard for limiting care could have the negative symbolic significance of social abandonment.[46] Finally, its use will run counter to established principles of medical tradition and ethics, which focus on individual need, and will instead, in an "Age of Bureaucratic Parsimony. . . . be based upon institutional and societal efficiency, or expediency, and upon cost concerns—all emerging rapidly as major elements in decision making."[47]

References and Notes

1. Carroll L. Estes, "Social Security: The Social Construction of a Crisis," *Milbank Memorial Fund Quarterly* 61:3 (Summer 1983), pp. 445–61.

2. *A Profile of Older Americans: 1985*, American Association of Retired Persons (AARP), Washington, DC; Dorothy P. Rice, "The Medical Care System: Past Trends and Future Projections," *New York Medical Quarterly* 6 (1986), pp. 39–70.

3. See Daniel R. Waldo and Helen C. Lazenby, "Demographic Characteristics and Health Care Use and Expenditures by the Aged in the United States: 1977–1984," *Health Care Financing Review* 6 (Fall 1984), pp. 1–29.

4. Rice, "Past Trends and Future Projections," p. 61.

5. *Ibid.*, p. 46.

6. Karen Davis, "Aging and the Health-Care System: Economic and Structural Issues," *Daedalus* 115 (Winter 1986), pp. 234–35. Dr. Davis does, however, in another place say that "Extended life expectancy and improved health of the elderly will bring with it a cost—one that is clearly affordable to a growing and prosperous society": in Karen Davis and Diane Rowland, *Medicare Policy* (Baltimore: Johns Hopkins Press, 1983), p. 33. She does not explain why an "increase from about $83 billion in 1981 to almost $200 billion in 2000, in constant 1980 dollars" (*ibid.*) is "clearly affordable," much less whether it would be wise.

7. Robert H. Binstock, "The Aged as a Scapegoat," *Gerontologist* 23 (1983), pp. 136–43: "The Oldest Old: A Fresh Perspective or Compassionate Ageism Revisited?" *Milbank Memorial Fund Quarterly* 63:1 (Spring 1985), pp. 420–51; Bernice L. Neugarten and Dail A. Neugarten, "Age in the Aging Society," *Daedalus* 115 (Winter 1986), pp. 31–49.

8. Samuel H. Preston, "Children and the Elderly: Divergent Paths for America's Dependents," *Demography* 21 (November 1984), p. 435.

9. *Cf.* Binstock, "Scapegoat."

10. Thomas Halper, "The Double-Edged Sword: Paternalism as a Policy in the Problems of Aging," *Milbank Memorial Fund Quarterly* 58:3 (1980), p. 486; Fernando Torres-Gil and Jon Pynoos, "Long-Term Care Policy and Interest Group Struggles," *Gerontologist* 26:5 (1986), pp. 488–95.

11. Roger W. Evans, "Health Care Technology and the Inevitability of Resource Allocation and Rationing Decisions," *Journal of the American Medical Association* 249 (April 1983), pp. 2047–53, 2208–19.

12. *Ibid.*, p. 2052.

13. Henry J. Aaron and William B. Schwartz, *The Painful Prescription: Rationing Hospital Care.* (Washington, DC: The Brookings Institution, 1984).

14. The comparative figures are: United Kingdom, 6.2 percent; Canada, 8.5 percent; Denmark, 6.6 percent; France, 9.3 percent; Japan, 6.7 percent; Netherlands, 8.8 percent; Sweden, 9.6 percent. John K. Iglehart, "Canada's Health Care System," *New England Journal of Medicine* 315:3 (July 1986), p. 205.

15. Binstock, "Scapegoat," p. 139; see also Noralou P. Roos *et al.*, "Aging and the Demand for Health Services: Which Aged and Whose Demand?" *Gerontologist* 24:1 (1984), pp. 31–36.

16. Marcia Angell, "Cost Containment and the Physician," *Journal of the American Medical Association* 254 (September 1985), p. 1204. Erdman B. Palmore has argued that a trend toward better health among the elderly should reduce their health-care costs: "Trends in the Health of the Aged," *Gerontologist* 26:3 (1986), pp. 298–302. That seems to me optimistic and not supported by other trends.

17. Robert H. Brook and Kathleen N. Lohr, "Will We Need to Ration Effective Health Care?" in press, *Issues in Science and Technology* (National Academy of Sciences).

18. Arthur L. Caplan, "A New Dilemma: Quality, Ethics and Expansive Medical Technologies," *New York Medical Quarterly* 6 (1986), p. 23.

19. John Wennberg and Alan Gittlesohn, "Variations in Medical Care Among Small Areas," *Scientific American* 246:4 (April 1982), pp. 120–34.

20. Uwe E. Reinhardt, "Battle Over Medical Costs Isn't Over," *Wall Street Journal*, October 22, 1986, p. 16. See also William B. Schwartz, "The Inevitable Failure of Current Cost-Containment Strategies," *Journal of the American Medical Association* 257 (January 1987), pp. 220–24.

21. P.L. 99–509, Sixth Omnibus Reconciliation Act (SOBRA), Conference Report, October 18, 1986.

22. B. Torrey, "Guns Versus Canes: The Fiscal Implications of an Aging Population," *American Economic Review* 72 (1982), p. 309ff.

23. Angell, "Cost Containment," p. 1207.

24. Cf. Norman Daniels, "Why Saying No to Patients in the United States Is So Hard: Cost Containment, Justice, and Provider Autonomy," *New England Journal of Medicine* 314 (May 1986), pp. 1380–83.

25. This argument is developed at length in Eric R. Kingson, Barbara A. Hirshorn, and John M. Cornman, *Ties That Bind: The Interdependence of Generations* (Washington, DC: Seven Locks Press, 1986).

26. *Ibid.*, p. 26.

27. Victor R. Fuchs, "Though Much Is Taken: Reflections on Aging, Health, and Medical Care," *Milbank Memorial Fund Quarterly* 62:1 (Spring 1984), pp. 464–65.

28. J. Lubitz and R. Prihoda, "Uses and Costs of Medicare Services in the Last Two Years of Life," *Health Care Financing Review* 5 (Spring 1984), pp. 117–31.

29. See Ronald Bayer, Daniel Callahan, *et al.*, "The Care of the Terminally Ill: Morality and Economics," *New England Journal of Medicine* 309 (December 1983), pp. 1490–94.

30. A. S. Detsky *et al.*, "Prognosis, Survival, and the Expenditure of Hospital Resources for Patients in an Intensive-Care Unit," *New England Journal of Medicine* 305 (1981), p. 668.

31. Lubitz and Prihoda, "Costs of Medicare Services," p. 122.

32. Anne A. Scitovsky, "'The High Cost of Dying': What Do the Data Show?" *Milbank Memorial Fund Quarterly* 62:4 (Fall 1984), pp. 606–7.

33. *Ibid.*

34. Anne A. Scitovsky and Alexander M. Capron, "Medical Care at the End of Life: The Interaction of Economics and Ethics," *Annual Review of Public Health* 7 (1986), p. 71; and Anne A. Scitovsky, "Medical Care

Expenditures in the Last Twelve Months of Life" (unpublished paper, March 1986).

35. Norman Daniels, *Just Health Care.* (Cambridge: Cambridge University Press, 1985), pp. 104–5.

36. Norman Daniels, "Family Responsibility Initiatives and Justice Between Age Groups," *Law, Medicine and Health Care* (September 1985), p. 156; cf. Phillip G. Clark, "The Social Allocation of Health Care Resources: Ethical Dilemmas in Age-Group Competition," *Gerontologist* 25 (April 1985), pp. 119–25; and B. J. Diggs, "The Ethics of Providing for the Economic Well-Being of the Aged," in Bernice L. Neugarten and Robert J. Havighurst, ed., *Social Policy, Social Ethics, and the Aging Society* (Washington, D.C.: GPO, 038-000-0029-6).

37. Daniels, *Just Health Care*, p. 106.

38. This general definition is drawn from *Guidelines on the Termination of Life-Sustaining Treatment and the Case of Dying*, Susan Wolf, Daniel Callahan, Bruce Jennings, Cynthia B. Cohen, eds. (Briarcliff Manor, N. Y.: The Hastings Center, 1987), Introduction.

39. One of the first articles to explore the idea of an age basis for allocation was Harry R. Moody's "Is It Right to Allocate Health Care Resources on Grounds of Age?" In Elsie L. Bandman and Bertram Bandman, *Bioethics and Human Rights* (Boston: Little, Brown, 1978), pp. 197–201.

40. For a good general discussion of age as an allocation principle, see Leslie Pickering Francis, "Poverty, Age Discrimination, and Health Care," in George R. Lucas, Jr., ed., *Poverty, Justice, and the Law* (Lanham, MD: University Press of America, 1986), pp. 117–29.

41. Bernice L. Neugarten, ed., *Age or Need?: Public Policies for Older People.* (Beverly Hills: Sage Publications, 1982); see Douglas W. Nelson, "Alternative Images of Old Age as the Bases for Policy," in *Age or Need*, ed. Neugarten.

42. Neugarten and Neugarten, "Age in the Aging Society," p. 47.

43. Jerome L. Avorn, "Benefit and Cost Analysis in Geriatric Care: Turning Age Discrimination into Health Policy," *New England Journal of Medicine* 310 (May 1984), pp. 1294–1301.

44. Carole Haber has written well on this problem in *Beyond Sixty-Five: The Dilemma of Old Age in America's Past* (New York: Cambridge University Press, 1983), especially pp. 125–29.

45. "Life-Sustaining Technologies and the Elderly: Ethical Issues," Chapter 4 of U.S. Congress, Office of Technology Assessment, Biological Applications Program, *Life-Sustaining Technologies and the Elderly* (Washington, D.C.: OTA, July 1987).

46. James F. Childress, "Ensuring Care, Respect, and Fairness for the Elderly," *Hastings Center Report* 14 (October 1984), p. 29.

47. Mark Siegler, "Should Age be a Criterion in Health Care?" *Hastings Center Report* 14 (October 1984), p. 25.

A Lifespan Approach to Health Care

Norman Daniels PhD

Some general theories of justice, most notably Rawls', provide foundations for a principle protecting fair equality of opportunity. If such a principle is indeed a requirement of an acceptable general theory of justice, then I believe we have a natural way to extend such general theories to govern the distribution of health care. We should include health care institutions among those basic institutions of a society that are governed by the fair equality of opportunity principle. If this approach to a theory of just health care is correct, it means that there are social obligations to provide health care services that protect and restore normal functioning. In short, the principle of justice that should govern the design of health care institutions is a principle that calls for guaranteeing fair equality of opportunity.

This principle of justice has implications for both access and resource allocation. It implies that there should be no financial, geographical, or discriminatory barriers to a level of care that promotes normal functioning. It also implies that resources be allocated in ways that are effective in promoting normal functioning. That is, since we can use the effect on normal opportunity range as a crude way of ranking the moral importance of health care services, we can guide hard public policy choices about which services are more important to provide. Thus, the principle does not imply that every technology that might have a positive impact on normal functioning for some individuals should be introduced: we must weigh new technologies against alternatives to judge the overall impact of introducing them on fair equality of opportunity—this gives a slightly new sense to the term "opportunity cost." The point is that social obligations to provide just health care must be met within the conditions of moderate scarcity that we face. This is not an approach that gives individuals a basic right to have all their health care needs met. There are social obligations to provide individuals only with those services that are part of the design of a system that, on the whole, protects equal opportunity.

We must refine this account so that it applies more directly to the problem of allocating health care over the lifespan—among different age groups. I draw on three basic observations. First, there is the banal fact we have all noticed: we age. By contrast, we do not change sex or race. This contrast has important implications for the

From *Aging and Ethics*. N. Jecker, ed. Clifton, N.J.: The Humana Press, 1991. pp. 235–238.

problem of equality. If I treat blacks and whites or men and women differently, than I produce an inequality, and such inequalities raise questions about justice. If I treat the old and the young differently, I may or may not produce an inequality. If I treat them differently just occasionally and arbitrarily, then I will treat different persons unequally, but if I treat as a matter of policy the old one way and the young another, and I do so over their whole lives, then I treat all persons the same way. No inequality is produced. Thus, the fact that we all notice, that we age, means age is different from race or sex when we think about distributive justice.

Second, as we age, we pass through institutions that redistribute wealth and income in a way that performs a "savings" function. The observation is trivial with regard to income support institutions, such as the Social Security system. It is not often noticed that our health care system does the same thing. When we reach age 65, we consume health care resources at about 3.5 times the rate (in dollars) that we do prior to age 65. However, we pay, as working people, a combined health care insurance premium—through private premiums, through employee contributions, and through Social Security taxes—that covers not just our actuarially fair costs, but the costs of the elderly and of children as well. If this system continues as we age, others will pay "inflated premiums" that will cover our higher costs when we are elderly. In effect, the system allows us to defer the use of resources from one stage of our lives to a later one. It "saves" health care for our old age—when we need more of it.

Third, our health care system is not prudently designed, given that it plays this role as a savings institution. It lavishes life-extending resources on us as we are dying, but it withholds other kinds of services, such as personal care and social support services, which may be crucial to our well-being when our lives are not under immediate threat. The system could be far more pru-

dently designed. It could pay better attention to matching services to needs at different stages of our lives and, thus, be more effective in its savings function.

Earlier, I claimed that the just design of our health care institutions should rest on a principle protecting fair equality of opportunity. Imagine that each of us has a lifetime allocation of health care services, which we can claim only if the appropriate needs arise, as a result of appealing to such a principle. Our task now is to allocate that fair share over the lifespan—and to do so prudently. In this exercise, we will find out what is just or fair between age groups by discovering what it is prudent to do between stages of life, over the whole lifespan. One way to make sure we do not bias this allocation, favoring one stage of life and, thus, one age group over another is to pretend that we do not know how old we are. We must allocate these resources imagining that we must live our whole lives with the result of our choices. One way we would refine our earlier principle of justice is to conclude that we should protect our fair shares of the normal opportunity range at each stage of life. Since we must live through each stage, we will not treat any one stage as less important than another.

Notice what this rather abstract perspective—I call it the Prudential Lifespan Account—accomplishes: it tells us that we should not think of age groups as competing with each other, but as sharing a whole life. We want to make that life go as well as possible, and we must therefore make the appropriate decisions about what needs it is most important to meet at each stage of life. If we do this prudently, we will learn how it is fair to treat each age group. Instead of focusing on competition, we have a unifying perspective or vision. I am suggesting that, as individuals and as a society, we must think through the decisions we must make about our health care system from this perspective.

How Age Should Matter: Justice as the Basis for Limiting Care to the Elderly

Robert M. Veatch PhD

THE ROLE OF AGE IN AGE-BASED ALLOCATION

It is not as easy as one might think to figure out exactly what the role of age is in apparently age-based allocation policies. It could be that age is used as a crude predictor of the benefit from treatment. A policy committed to using resources where they will do the most good might include the view that in cases where older people will not do as well with an intervention, age should be used as an indirect, approximating measure of where resources will do the most good. Even if the medical benefit measured in terms of cure rates or incidence of side effects is the same for older patients, the benefit measured in years will predictably not be as great. The elderly will not benefit as long, if the treatment is a success. Allocators might argue that it would be impractical to assess outcomes on a case-by-case basis and choose, instead, to use chronological age as a predictor of benefit.

This raises the ethical issue of the use of sociological measures as predictors of outcome. In the United States, in many situations, it is considered unethical (as well as illegal) in allocating goods to use sociological categories to predict expected outcome. . . . We cannot use sex, race, or other sociological measures as a basis for excluding individual members of their groups even if we can show that the group as a whole will use the resource less efficiently. We need evidence for the individual.

Then can we insist that age be used only when we can show that age is a predictor of a poor outcome in the case of the individual elderly person? If so, that would be almost impossible to show.

CONSEQUENTIALIST ARGUMENT PERTAINING TO THE USE OF AGE

Consequentialist Arguments for Age-Based Allocation

The arguments that appear most readily are grounded in appeals to the consequences of allocating on the basis of age. These appeals necessarily look at the benefits and social costs of using age as a criterion in allocation. The argument begins with the conclusion we have just reached: Resources are inevitably scarce. Those committed to one or another version of utilitarian, normative ethical theory hold that in such cases the ethical imperative is to do the greatest good for the greatest number; we need to maximize the net good in aggregate. For health care the ethical imperative is the use of health planning and cost-benefit analyses to make sure we use our health-care dollars to do the most good possible. As we have seen, it is impossibly inefficient to measure the benefits for each individual patient. The process itself would have great disutilities. The prudent, efficient thing to do would be to opt for the allocation formula that will do the greatest good overall. If age is a reasonably good predictor of good, then it morally must be used according to utilitarian theory. The welfare of individuals may have to be sacrificed in certain cases in order to produce the greatest aggregate benefit. A true consequentialist would

From *Facing Limits: Ethics and Health Care for the Elderly.* Gerald R. Winslow and James W. Walters, eds. Boulder, CO: Westview Press, 1993, pp. 211–229.

not be dissuaded from this conclusion by concern that such a policy might be unfair to certain elderly persons.

Many American health planners find this persuasive. They assume that if we must ration—and we must—then the rationing must be on the basis of maximizing the common or aggregate good. There are reasons, however, why these utilitarian reasons for using age as a basis for allocating health resources should be resisted.

Consequentialist Arguments Against Using Age

Some critics of the use of age buy the principle, but reject the moral calculation. They accept that the goal is to serve the aggregate good, but then reject the claim that using age as a criterion will maximize the aggregate good. Their arguments are as follows:

First, some elderly can be very productive citizens. . . . That consequentialist argument against the use of age, however, overlooks the fact that statistically the elderly are not as productive as the young. . . . Statistically, it seems clear that more good will be done if the younger patients get the resources. Even the process of figuring out who is physiologically young could have severe disutilities both in terms of cost and in terms of inevitable conflicts.

Second, critics of the use of age might argue that the psychological burden of anticipating reaching old age without life-sustaining medical care would be a serious disutility of using age as a criterion.

But one must also take into account the psychological burdens that would result from knowing that younger people might not get the benefits of needed medical care if resources are going to the elderly.

Third, utilitarian critics of the use of age as a criterion might appeal to the psychological and economic burdens on families whose elderly members were excluded from health care that could offer at least marginal benefits. Once again, however, these would be offset by the psychological and economic burdens on families whose younger members would be deprived of care if resources went to the elderly.

On balance, the consequentialist case for using age as a criterion in allocating resources seems to be convincing, provided the utilitarian principle of maximizing aggregate net outcome is morally legitimate in the first place. To the surprise of many, however, it may turn out that even if we move to nonconsequentialist (or deontological) ethical theory, age may be a legitimate basis for allocating health resources.

NONCONSEQUENTIALIST CONSIDERATIONS

Some ethical systems hold that morality is not just a matter of producing good and avoiding evil consequences. This characteristic is shared by the ethics of Kant, the Jewish ethics of the Ten Commandments, and by much Protestant thought. It is central to secular, liberal political philosophy that places the rights of the individual over against the aggregate welfare at least in some cases. In the Ten Commandments, for instance, the command is "Thou shalt not." There is no clause added "except when it would produce good consequences."

One nonconsequentialist principle is the principle of justice. It is social and allocational but, as an independent ethical principle, does not focus on the aggregate amount of consequences produced. It is the nature of morally interesting allocational problems that the pattern that produces the greatest aggregate good is not the same as the one that distributes the good most justly. The criterion for what is a just or equitable pattern of distribution is itself a controversy among those who are committed to justice as a patterned principle. One particularly appealing formulation recognizes distributions as just when they provide opportunities for net welfare that are equal among people. The policy implication is that resources should be allocated in such a way as to give people an opportunity for equality of well being.[1]

Often the conflict between utility and justice is an uninteresting one since distributing resources to those who are worst off will do the most good. That is what economists refer to as decreasing marginal utility. However, often in health care the worst off—the ones who have the strongest claims of justice—are the sickest and, as such, they are just the ones whom it is most difficult to benefit. They are chronically ill with incurable, perhaps hopeless conditions. Here spending resources on the worst off will do the least good rather than the most good. Thus in health care the conflict between utility and justice is often a real one. This is particularly true with the elderly. Thus it will be critical to see whether the principle of justice militates against using age as a criterion for allocating health resources.

Justice-Based Arguments Against the Use of Age

It seems at first like justice weighs in against the use of age as an allocation criterion. A number of commentators who are committed to justice as an allocational principle have criticized the use of age as a criterion.[2] The logic is that justice requires that resources be used to provide opportunities to have needs met. Elderly people are often precisely the ones who are most needy medically. Therefore, they deserve priority. They at least deserve to be treated identically to those younger people who are medically in equal need.

This appears to set a battle between consequentialists and nonconsequentialists, with consequentialists arguing for the use of an age-based allocation criterion to promote efficient use of resources and nonconsequentialists wringing their hands, screaming it is unfair and unjust.

Justice-Based Arguments for the Use of Age

There is, of course, one other possibility. One might mount a justice-based argument in favor of the use of age as a criterion. That is precisely what

I believe is called for and shall attempt to do in the remainder of this essay.

It should be noted that there have been other efforts along these lines recently. Philosophers Daniel Callahan and Norman Daniels have both made important attempts to argue for limits on health care for the elderly that have not been grounded exclusively in considerations of utility. I am now convinced that, while they are on the right track, their approaches fail. I shall briefly summarize what I consider to be the problems with their approaches before presenting my own version of a justice-based defense of the use of age as a criterion for allocating health resources.

Daniel Callahan's Setting of Limits[3]

His claim is that there is a natural end to the life-span. Medical resources should be used to get people up to that natural completion and then only to use resources for the elderly to provide comfort and inexpensive treatments of acute illness.

The result is that medical care needed to complete the major phases of the life cycle generates a higher moral claim than care to sustain life after the life cycle is completed. According to Callahan, "The old should step aside in an active way."[4]

To be fair, Callahan has sometimes been terribly misunderstood. He was not suggesting that we be cruel.[5] Rather his position was that all of us ought to have a realistic conception of what counts as a full life. There comes a time when life is complete. While Callahan does not directly make his argument in terms of justice, it seems to be an appeal to fairness considerations rather than aggregate utility.

The problem with Callahan's approach is that it rests on a controversial stance regarding the value of life after what he takes to be the end of the natural life-span. Moreover, it rests on an even more controversial claim about life having a natural span. His use of age as a criterion for limiting certain life-sustaining resources for the elderly rests on a conviction that life after some purported natural end point is not very valuable in any case. For him, it is, thus, all too easy to argue that it deserves low priority.

There is a more practical problem as well. The notion that life after its natural end point calls for a lower priority in health resource allocation seems to call for a precipitous cessation of claims for a certain group of life-sustaining services at some age—the age at which the life cycle has been completed. As one is "over the hill," there is a precipitous fall "over the cliff." Yet, even if we are willing to accept the notion of a natural life-span, many of us would be acutely uncomfortable with the idea that there is some identifiable end point at which, for public policy purposes, some health-care resources would no longer be funded.

Yet, we would need some easily administered, if arbitrary, age cut-off. We could not tell insurance companies and hospital administrators to cut people off whenever it appears they have completed their life span without giving them some specific age. Callahan, at one point early in the discussion, suggested that a life span of 75 years was as good as any.[6] In *Setting Limits*, he was slightly more conservative, identifying the range of the late 70s to early 80s.

Whether we pick 75 or 85, administrators and clinicians would have to have some specific, cut-off age. It is the precipitous cut-off that seems both necessary and implausible in a theory grounded in the notion of completing a life-span. Consider, for example, two patients medically similar in need of some high-tech, life-extending technology such as a transplant. If one were 74 and the other 76 (or 84 and 86), the former would get the full treatment (because he has not yet completed his life-span) while the latter would get no life-extending interventions. I doubt that such a cut-off would be tolerable, yet it seems appropriate based on a theory that differentiates people into two groups, one which has completed the life-span and one that has not.

There is one final problem with Callahan's theory. He readily acknowledges the continuing need for relief of suffering, basic nursing care for cleanliness and dignity, and so forth. What the "life-span completion" theory cannot explain is why we should spend resources on these when others will never reach their full life-span. If these lives are over, why do they have claims for even these services? Would not those whose life span is not over have claims for these resources as well?

Here Callahan's instincts are stronger than his theory. It is intuitively obvious that we should continue to provide comfort care. I do not think Callahan's theory can explain why.

Norman Daniels' Prudential Life-Span Account

The account of Norman Daniels attempts to rectify some of these problems.[7]

There are problems, however, with Daniels' account as well. It is not obvious that it is only a matter of prudence how the resources get allocated to different stages of one's life-cycle. Even if it is prudent for people to save for their old age, it may not be just or fair.

The problem is especially acute when one takes into account the fact that not all people will reach old age. Daniels implies at one point that a prudent allocation would be one in which an equal portion of each age-specific need was met.[8] That seems reasonable, provided we are dealing with a group who will live through all stages of the life-cycle. The Rawls-Daniels scheme is based on a model in which rational, self-interested heads of households (blinded as to their specific interests and needs) are viewed as the ones making the allocation choices. That model, however, has built into it the implication that all will at least reach adulthood. They therefore have a very high probability of reaching old age, and it would be rational to include a prudent amount (if only a prudent amount) for their period of old age.

In the real world, however, some are treated more harshly by the natural lottery. They are born with congenital and genetic problems such that they will suffer from critical, fatal, or permanently handicapping conditions. If a majority of rational adults would spend equally on conditions of infancy, middle age, and old age, it does not follow that it is fair to those who will never reach adulthood. The real ethical issue is what is fair or just. In the same way that I would say to Callahan that completion of the life-span is not the relevant criterion, so I would say to Daniels that prudence is not. The real question is whether justice either permits or requires limits on care to the elderly.

A JUSTICE-BASED LIMIT ON CARE TO THE ELDERLY

I think there is another nonconsequentialist argument that supports limits on some care to the elderly, one based more directly on appeals to justice. I agree with Daniels, and with the work of Ronald Dworkin that precedes Daniels,[9] that an ethical health insurance is one that is based on intrapersonal allocational decisions made by those behind a veil of ignorance about their own personal desires, needs, and interests. I would, however, see them further constrained to choose what is fair rather than simply what seems prudent.[10] In particular, I would see them as obliged by the principle of fairness to deal with the just claims of those who have critical or fatal conditions in infancy. It is not just a matter of being prudent. It is not a matter of efficiently serving the common good. Rather, it is a question of which allocation is fair. Justice requires identifying the worst-off individuals and allocating resources so as to give those persons an opportunity to be as well off as others. I shall argue for certain kinds of health care that give priority to the young.

Age in Deciding Who Is Worse Off

Consider two dialysis patients, medically similar, both of whom have a five-year life expectancy if dialyzed and both of whom will die soon if not dialyzed. One is age 40; the other age 60. Can we identify one of them as worse off or do we say that they are equally poorly off? In a hypotheti-

cal situation in which there was only one dialysis machine, can we identify who should get it?

If we add the further assumption that we can expect the two to lead equally useful lives during their remaining five years, it should be clear that a utilitarian should be indifferent. For the non-consequentialist considering egalitarian justice, the problem is more complex.

The Slice-of-Time and Over-a-Lifetime Perspectives

We should consider two different ways of calculating who is worse off. The first, call it the slice-of-time perspective, asks who is worse off at a given moment, say, when the two patients are near death. The second, call it the over-a-lifetime perspective, views well-being cumulated over the lifetimes of the individuals involved. From the slice-of-time perspective these two patients seem equally poorly off. They are both about to die if they do not get the machine and will live for five years with it. From the over-a-lifetime perspective, however, they seem to be in significantly different positions. The 60-year-old has had twenty more years of life. From the slice-of-time perspective they are equal. On a per–lifetime basis, the 40-year-old has had much less opportunity for well-being. He would seem to have a much greater claim of egalitarian justice.

Justifying Acute Care and Basic Care Needed for Dignity and Pain Relief

This brings us back to the problem faced by Callahan of why the elderly have a claim for basic medical care, for treatment of acute illness and relief of suffering, and for nursing care for cleanliness and dignity. It seems that the relevant consideration has nothing to do with whether a lifespan is deemed to have been completed. Rather, it seems related to whether it is legitimate to cumulate one's well-being.

I see the problem as related to contemporary debates over the theory of personal identity. A person is one who has continuity of personal identity over a period of time. That continuity of identity requires continuity of awareness of oneself such that one can say, "I am the same person who existed at some previous time."

For some conditions, well-being (or lack thereof) is easily seen as cumulating over time. It makes good sense for people to say that, since they have lived a long time, they have had many opportunities for well-being. In fact, the longer one has lived, the more such opportunities one has had.

By contrast some needs present themselves anew at each moment in time. They cannot be cumulated over a lifetime. There is noncontinuity of personal identity that prohibits the summing up of acute, severe pain over a lifetime. We cannot plausibly say that because one's first eighty years have been relatively pain-free, the acute, severe pain one experiences at age eighty-one gets low priority morally. Acute pain forces radical discontinuity with one's previous life. Life in acute pain is detached from experiences accumulated over the years. Past life experiences seem irrelevant in deciding whether one in acute pain is among the worst off. A similar conclusion seems right regarding significant assaults on personal dignity such as those that come from absence of basic nursing care.

The slice-of-time perspective is appropriate in these cases because people in acute, severe pain or in a state in which they experience significant assault on dignity are entities separate from their life-histories. They are comparable to the child trapped in a well who cries out for assistance. Deciding whether it is ethical to respond is independent of any cool calculation of utility *or* of who is worst off over a lifetime. For those conditions that separate oneself from one's personal identity over a lifetime, the slice-of-time perspective is the correct one in deciding who is worst off. For those conditions such as chronic threat to continued existence, which still leave one recognizing personal identity over a lifetime, the cumulative time perspective is the correct one. That seems to me to explain how we should differentiate kinds of care for the elderly much

better than either the "natural lifespan" view of Callahan or the "prudential lifespan" account of Daniels. My conclusion is that for these conditions that permit accumulating over-a-lifetime, age is one relevant factor in deciding who is worse off and therefore a *prima facie*, justice-based reason for allocating scarce resources.

References and Notes

1. See Robert M. Veatch, *The Foundations of Justice: Why the Retarded and the Rest of Us Have Claims to Equality.* New York: Oxford University Press, 1986, for my development of the case for this interpretation.

2. Jerry Avorn. "Benefit and Cost Analysis in Geriatric Care: Turning Age Discrimination into Health Policy," *New England Journal of Medicine* 310 (May 17, 1984): 1294–1300; Nancy S. Jecker, "Disenfranchising the Elderly from Life-Extending Medical Care," *Public Affairs Quarterly* 2 (July 1988):51–68; John F. Kilner, "Age Criteria in Medicine: Are the Medical Justifications Ethical?" *Archives of Internal Medicine* 149 (Oct., 1989):2343–2346; Eric Munoz, Fred Rosner, Don Chalfin, et al., "Age, Resource Consumption, and Outcome of Medical Patients at an Academic Medical Center," *Archives of Internal Medicine* 149 (Sept. 1989):1946–1950; Margaret P. Battin, "Age Rationing and the Just Distribution of Health Care: Is There a Duty to Die?" *Ethics* 97 (January 1987):317–340; Larry R. Churchill, "Should We Ration Health Care by Age?" *Journal of the American Geriatrics Society* 36 (July, 1988):644–647.

3. Daniel Callahan. *Setting Limits: Medical Goals in an Aging Society.* New York: Simon & Schuster, 1987.

4. Ibid., p. 43.

5. In his sequel, Daniel Callahan, *What Kind of Life: The Limits of Medical Progress.* New York: Simon and Schuster, 1990, Callahan is much more bold about appealing to "the common good" as a criterion for health resource allocation.

6. Daniel Callahan, "Natural Death and Public Policy," *Life Span: Values and Life-Extending Technologies*, edited by Robert M. Veatch. San Francisco: Harper and Row, Publishers, 1979, p. 174.

7. See Norman Daniels, *Am I My Parents' Keeper?: An Essay on Justice Between the Young and the Old.* New York: Oxford University Press, 1988.

8. Ibid., pp. 58–59.

9. See Ronald Dworkin, "What is Equality? Part I: Equality of Welfare," *Philosophy and Public Affairs* 10 (Summer 1981):185–246; and "What Is Equality? Part 2: Equality of Resources," *Philosophy and Public Affairs* 10 (Fall 1981):283–345.

10. It should be clear that this commits me to a different version of the hypothetical contract than that supported by Rawls and Daniels. I view contractors as discovering a preexisting moral structure, not simply choosing what is prudent.

QALYfying the Value of Life

John Harris DPhil

Against a background of permanently scarce resources it is clearly crucial that such health care resources as are available be not used wastefully. This point is often made in terms of 'efficiency' and it is argued, not implausibly, that to talk of efficiency implies that we are able to distinguish between efficient and inefficient use of health care resources, and hence that we are in some sense able to measure the results of treatment. To do so of course we need a standard of measurement. Traditionally, in life-endangering conditions, that standard has been easy to find. Successful treatment removes the danger to life, or at least postpones it, and so the survival rates of treatment have been regarded as a good indicator of success.[1] However, equally clearly, it is also of crucial importance to those treated that the help offered them not only removes the threat to life, but leaves them able to enjoy the remission granted. In short, gives them reasonable quality, as well as extended quantity of life.

A new measure of quality of life which combines length of survival with an attempt to measure the quality of that survival has recently[2] been suggested and is becoming influential. The need for such a measure has been thus described by one of its chief architects: 'We need a simple, versatile, measure of success which incorporates both life expectancy and quality of life, and which reflects the values and ethics of the community served. The "Quality Adjusted Life Year" (QALY) measure fulfils such a role'.[3] This is a large claim and an important one, if it can be sustained its consequences for health care will be profound indeed.

There are, however, substantial theoretical problems in the development of such a measure, and more important by far, grave dangers of its misuse. I shall argue that the dangers of misuse, which partly derive from inadequacies in the theory which generates them, make this measure itself a life-threatening device. In showing why this is so I shall attempt to say something positive about just what is involved in making scrupulous choices between people in situations of scarce resources, and I will end by saying something about the entitlement to claim in particular circumstances, that resources are indeed scarce.

We must first turn to the task of examining the QALY and the possible consequences of its use in resource allocation. A task incidentally which, because it aims at the identification and eradication of a life-threatening condition, itself (surprisingly perhaps for a philosophical paper) counts also as a piece of medical research,[4] which if successful will prove genuinely therapeutic.

From *Journal of Medical Ethics*, 13:117–122, 1987.

THE QALY

What are QALYS?

It is important to be as clear as possible as to just what a QALY is and what it might be used for. I cannot do better than let Alan Williams, the architect of QALYs referred to above, tell you in his own words:

> 'The essence of a QALY is that it takes a year of healthy life expectancy to be worth one, but regards a year of unhealthy life expectancy as worth less than 1. Its precise value is lower the worse the quality of life of the unhealthy person (which is what the "quality adjusted" bit is all about). If being dead is worth zero, it is, in principle, possible for a QALY to be negative, ie for the quality of someone's life to be judged worse than being dead.
>
> The general idea is that a beneficial health care activity is one that generates a positive amount of QALYs, and that an efficient health care activity is one where the cost per QALY is as low as it can be. A high priority health care activity is one where the cost-per-QALY is low, and a low priority activity is one where cost-per-QALY is high'.[5]

The plausibility of the QALY derives from the idea that 'given the choice, a person would prefer a shorter healthier life to a longer period of survival in a state of severe discomfort and disability'.[6] The idea that any rational person would endorse this preference provides the moral and political force behind the QALY. Its acceptability as a measurement of health then depends upon its doing all the theoretical tasks assigned to it, and on its being what people want, or would want, for themselves.

How Will QALYs Be Used?

There are two ways in which QALYs might be used. One is unexceptionable and useful, and fully in line with the assumptions which give QALYs their plausibility. The other is none of these.

QALYs might be used to determine which of rival therapies to give to a particular patient or which procedure to use to treat a particular condition. Clearly the one generating the most QALYs will be the better bet, both for the patient and for a society with scarce resources. However, QALYs might also be used to determine not what treatment to give *these* patients, but which group of patients to treat, or which conditions to give priority in the allocation of health care resources. It is clear that it is this latter use which Williams has in mind, for he specifically cites as one of the rewards of the development of QALYs, their use in 'priority setting in the health care system in general'. It is this use which is likely to be of greatest interest,[7] to all those concerned with efficiency in the health service. And it is for this reason that it is likely to be both the most influential and to have the most far-reaching effects. It is this use which is I believe positively dangerous and morally indefensible. Why?

What's Wrong with QALYs?

It is crucial to realise that the whole plausibility of QALYs depends upon our accepting that they simply involve the generalisation of the 'truth'[8] that 'given the choice a person would prefer a shorter healthier life to a longer period of survival in a state of severe discomfort'. On this view giving priority to treatments which produce more QALYs or for which the cost-per-QALY is low, is both efficient and is also what the community as a whole, and those at risk in particular, actually want. But whereas it follows from the fact that given the choice a person would prefer a shorter healthier life to a longer one of severe discomfort, that the best treatment *for that person* is the one yielding the most QALYs, it does not follow that treatments yielding more QALYs are preferable to treatments yielding fewer where *different people* are to receive the treatments. That is to say, while it follows from the fact (if it is a fact) that I and everyone else would prefer to have, say one year of healthy life rather than three years of severe discomfort, that we value healthy existence more than uncomfortable existence for ourselves, it does not follow that where the choice is between three years of discomfort for *me* or immediate death on the one hand, and one year of health for *you*, or immediate death on the other, that I am somehow committed to the judgement that you ought to be saved rather than me.

Suppose that Andrew, Brian, Charles, Dorothy, Elizabeth, Fiona and George all have zero life-expectancy without treatment, but with medical care, all but George will get one year complete remission and George will get seven years' remission. The costs of treating each of the six are equal but George's operation costs five times as much as the cost of the other operations. It does not follow that even if each person, if asked, would prefer seven years' remission to one for themselves, that they are all committed to the view that George should be treated rather than that they should. Nor does it follow that this is a preference that society should endorse. But it is the preference that QALYs dictate.

Such a policy does not value life or lives at all, for it is individuals who are alive, and individuals who lose their lives. And when they do the loss is principally their loss. The value of someone's life is, primarily and overwhelmingly, its value to him or her; the wrong done when an individual's life is cut short is a wrong to that individual. The victim of a murder or a fatal accident is the person who loses his life. A disaster is the greater the more victims there are, the more lives that are lost. A society which values the lives of its citizens is one which tries to ensure that as few of them die prematurely (that is when their lives could continue) as possible. Giving value to life-years or QALYs, has the effect in this case of sacrificing six lives for one. If each of the seven *wants* to go on living for as long as he or she can, if each values the prospective term of remission available, then to choose between them on the basis of life-years (quality adjusted or not), is in this case to give no value to the lives of six people.

The Ethics of QALYs

Although we might be right to claim that people are not committed to QALYs as a measurement

of health simply in virtue of their acceptance of the idea that each would prefer to have more QALYs rather than fewer for themselves, are there good moral reasons why QALYs should none the less be accepted?

The idea, which is at the root of both democratic theory and of most conceptions of justice, that each person is as morally important as any other and hence, that the life and interests of each is to be given equal weight, while apparently referred to and employed by Williams plays no part at all in the theory of QALYs. That which is to be given equal weight is not persons and their interests and preferences, but quality-adjusted life-years. And giving priority to the manufacture of QALYs can mean them all going to a few at the expense of the interests and wishes of the many. It will also mean that all available resources will tend to be deployed to assist those who will thereby gain the maximum QALYs—the young.

The Fallacy of Valuing Time

There is a general problem for any position which holds that time-spans are of equal value no matter who gets them, and it stems from the practice of valuing life-units (life-years) rather than people's lives.

If what matters most is the number of life-years the world contains, then the best thing we can do is devote our resources to increasing the population. Birth control, abortion and sex education come out very badly on the QALY scale of priorities.

In the face of a problem like this, the QALY advocate must insist that what he wants is to select the therapy that generates the most QALYs for those people who already exist, and not simply to create the maximum number of QALYs. But if it is people and not units of life-span that matter, if the QALY is advocated because it is seen as a moral and efficient way to fulfil our obligation to provide care for our fellows, then it does matter who gets the QALYs—because it matters how people are treated. And this is where the ageism of QALYs and their other discriminatory features become important.

QALYs are Ageist

Maximising QALYs involves an implicit and comprehensive ageist bias. For saving the lives of younger people is, other things being equal, always likely to be productive of more QALYs than saving older people. Thus on the QALY arithmetic we always have a reason to prefer, for example, neonatal or paediatric care to all 'later' branches of medicine. This is because any calculation of the life-years generated for a particular patient by a particular therapy, must be based on the life expectancy of that patient. The older a patient is when treated, the fewer the life-years that can be achieved by the therapy.

It is true that QALYs dictate that we prefer people, not simply who have *more life expectancy*, but rather people who have *more life expectancy to be gained from treatment*. But wherever treatment saves a life, and this will be frequently, for quite simple treatments, like a timely antibiotic, can be life-saving, it will, other things being equal, be the case that younger people have more life expectancy to gain from the treatment than do older people.

Ageism and Aid

Another problem with such a view is that it seems to imply, for example, that when looking at societies from the outside, those with a lower average age have somehow a greater claim on our aid. This might have important consequences in looking at questions concerning aid policy on a global scale. Of course it is true that a society's having a low average age might be a good indicator of its need for help, in that it would imply that people were dying prematurely. However, we can imagine a society suffering a disaster which killed off many of its young people (war perhaps) and which was consequently left with a high average age but was equally deserving of aid despite the fact that such aid would inevitably benefit the old. If QALYs were applied to the decision as to whether to provide aid to this society or another much less populous and perhaps with less pressing problems, but with a more normal age distri-bution, the 'older' society might well be judged 'not worth' helping.

QALYs can be Racist and Sexist

If a 'high priority health care activity is one where the cost-per-QALY is low, and a low priority activity is one where cost-per-QALY is high' then people who just happen to have conditions which are relatively cheap to treat are always going to be given priority over those who happen to have conditions which are relatively expensive to treat. This will inevitably involve not only a systematic pattern of disadvantage to particular groups of patients, or to people afflicted with particular diseases or conditions, but perhaps also a systematic preference for the survival of some kinds of patients at the expense of others. We usually think that justice requires that we do not allow certain sections of the community or certain types of individual to become the victims of systematic disadvantage and that there are good moral reasons for doing justice, not just when it costs us nothing or when it is convenient or efficient, but also and particularly, when there is a price to be paid. We'll return shortly to this crucial issue of justice, but it is important to be clear about the possible social consequences of adopting QALYs.

Adoption of QALYs as the rationale for the distribution of health care resources may, for the above reasons, involve the creation of a systematic pattern of preference for certain racial groups or for a particular gender or, what is the same thing, a certain pattern of discrimination against such groups. Suppose that medical statistics reveal that say women, or Asian males, do better than others after a particular operation or course of treatment, or, that a particular condition that has a very poor prognosis in terms of QALYs afflicts only Jews, or gay men. Such statistics abound and the adoption of QALYs may well dictate very severe and systematic discrimination against groups identified primarily by race, gender or colour, in the allocation of health resources, where it turns out that such groups are vulnerable to conditions that are not QALY-efficient.[9]

Of course it is just a fact of life and far from sinister that different races and genders are subject to different conditions, but the problem is that QALYs may tend to reinforce and perpetuate these 'structural' disadvantages.

Double Jeopardy

Relatedly, suppose a particular terminal condition was treatable, and would, with treatment, give indefinite remission but with a very poor quality of life. Suppose for example that if an accident victim were treated, he would survive, but with paraplegia. This might always cash out at fewer QALYs than a condition which with treatment would give a patient perfect remission for about five years after which the patient would die. Suppose that both candidates wanted to go on living as long as they could and so both wanted, equally fervently, to be given the treatment that would save their lives. Is it clear that the candidate with most QALYs on offer should always and inevitably be the one to have priority? To judge so would be to count the paraplegic's desire to live the life that was available to him as of less value than his rival's—what price equal weight to the preferences of each individual?

This feature of QALYs involves a sort of double jeopardy. QALYs dictate that because an individual is unfortunate, because she has once become a victim of disaster, we are required to visit upon her a second and perhaps graver misfortune. The first disaster leaves her with a poor quality of life and QALYs then require that in virtue of this she be ruled out as a candidate for life-saving treatment, or at best, that she be given little or no chance of benefiting from what little amelioration her condition admits of. Her first disaster leaves her with a poor quality of life and when she presents herself for help, along come QALYs and finish her off!

Life-Saving and Life-Enhancing

A distinction, consideration of which is long overdue, is that between treatments which are life-saving (or death-postponing) and those which are simply life-enhancing, in the sense that they improve the quality of life without improving life-expectancy. Most people think, and for good as well as for prudential reasons, that life-saving has priority over life-enhancement and that we should first allocate resources to those areas where they are immediately needed to save life and only when this has been done should the remainder be allocated to alleviating non-fatal conditions. Of course there are exceptions even here and some conditions, while not life-threatening, are so painful that to leave someone in a state of suffering while we attend even to the saving of life, would constitute unjustifiable cruelty. But these situations are rare and for the vast majority of cases we judge that life-saving should have priority.

It is important to notice that QALYs make no such distinction between types of treatment. Defenders of QALYs often cite with pride the example of hip-replacement operations which are more QALY-efficient than say kidney dialysis.[10] While the difficulty of choosing between treating very different groups of patients, some of whom need treatment simply to stay alive, while others need it to relieve pain and distress, is clearly very acute, and while it may be that life-saving should not *always* have priority over life-enhancement, the dangers of adopting QALYs which regard only one dimension of the rival claims, and a dubious one at that, as morally relevant, should be clear enough.

There is surely something fishy about QALYs. They can hardly from 'an appropriate basis for health service policy'. Can we give an account of just where they are deficient from the point of view of morality? We can, and indeed we have already started to do so. In addition to their other problems, QALYs and their use for priority setting in health care or for choosing not which treatment to give these patients, but for selecting which patients or conditions to treat, involve profound injustice, and if implemented would constitute a denial of the most basic civil rights. Why is this?

MORAL CONSTRAINTS

One general constraint that is widely accepted and that I think most people would judge should govern life and death decisions, is the idea that many people believe expresses the values animating the health service as a whole. These are the belief that the life and health of each person matters, and matters as much as that of any other and that each person is entitled to be treated with equal concern and respect both in the way health resources are distributed and in the way they are treated generally by health care professionals, however much their personal circumstances may differ from that of others.

This popular belief about the values which animate the health service depends on a more abstract view about the source and structure of such values and it is worth saying just a bit about this now.

The Value of Life

One such value is the value of life itself. Our own continued existence as individuals is the *sine qua non* of almost everything. So long as we want to go on living, practically everything we value or want depends upon our continued existence. This is one reason why we generally give priority to life-saving over life-enhancing.

To think that *life is valuable*, that in most circumstances, the worst thing that can happen to an individual is that she lose her life when this need not happen, and that the worst thing we can do is make decisions, a consequence of which, is that others die prematurely, we must think that *each life is valuable*. Each life counts for one and that is why more count for more. For this reason we should give priority to saving as many lives as we can, not as many life-years.[11]

One important point must be emphasised at this stage. We talk of 'life-saving' but of course this must always be understood as 'death-postponing'. Normally we want to have our death postponed for as long as possible but where what's possible is the gaining of only very short periods of remission, hours or days, these may not be worth having. Even those who are moribund in this sense can usually recognise this fact, particularly if they are aware that the cost of postponing their death for a few hours or days at the most will mean suffering or death for others. However, even brief remission can be valuable in enabling the individual to put her affairs in order, make farewells and so on, and this can be important. It is for the individual to decide whether the remission that she can be granted is worth having. This is a delicate point that needs more discussion than I can give it here. However, inasmuch as QALYs do not help us to understand the features of a short and painful remission that might none the less make that period of vital importance to the individual, perhaps in terms of making something worthwhile out of her life as a whole, the difficulties of these sorts of circumstances, while real enough, do not undermine the case against QALYs.[12]

Treating People as Equals

If each life counts for one, then the life of each has the same value as that of any. This is why accepting the value of life generates a principle of equality. This principle does not of course entail that we treat each person equally in the sense of treating each person *the same*. This would be absurd and self-defeating. What it does involve is the idea that we treat each person with the same concern and respect. An illustration provided by Ronald Dworkin, whose work on equality informs this entire discussion, best illustrates this point: 'If I have two children, and one is dying from a disease that is making the other uncomfortable, I do not show equal concern if I flip a coin to decide which should have the remaining dose of a drug'.[13]

It is not surprising then that the pattern of protections for individuals that we think of in terms of civil rights[14] centres on the physical protection of the individual and of her most fundamental interests. One of the prime functions of the State is to protect the lives and fundamental interests of its citizens and to treat each citizen as the equal of any other. This is why the State has a basic obligation, *inter alia*, to treat all citizens as equals in the distribution of benefits and opportunities which affect their civil rights. The State must, in short, treat each citizen with equal concern and respect. The civil rights generated by this principle will of course include rights to the allocation of such things as legal protections and educational and health care resources. And this requirement that the State uphold the civil rights of citizens and deal justly between them, means that it must not choose between individuals, or permit choices to be made between individuals, that abridge their civil rights or in ways that attack their right to treatment as equals.

Whatever else this means, it certainly means that a society, through its public institutions, is not entitled to discriminate between individuals in ways that mean life or death for them on grounds which count the lives or fundamental interests of some as worth less than those of others. If for example some people were given life-saving treatment in preference to others because they had a better quality of life than those others, or more dependants and friends, or because they were considered more useful, this would amount to regarding such people as more valuable than others on that account. Indeed it would be tantamount, literally, to sacrificing the lives of others so that they might continue to live.[15]

Because my own life would be better and even of more value to me if I were healthier, fitter, had more money, more friends, more lovers, more children, more life expectancy, more everything I want, it does not follow that others are entitled to decide that because I lack some or all of these things I am less entitled to health care resources, or less worthy to receive those resources, than are others, or that those resources would somehow be wasted on me.

Civil Rights

I have spoken in terms of civil rights advisedly. If we think of the parallel with our attitude to the system of criminal justice the reasons will be obvious. We think that the liberty of the subject is of fundamental importance and that no one should be wrongfully detained. This is why there are no financial constraints on society's obligation to attempt to ensure equality before the law. An individual is entitled to fair trial no matter what the financial costs to society (and they can be substantial). We don't adopt rubrics for the allocation of justice which dictate that only those for whom justice can be cheaply provided will receive it. And the reason is that something of fundamental importance is at stake—the liberty of the individual.

In health care something of arguably greater importance is often at stake—the very life of the individual. Indeed, since the abolition of capital punishment, the importance of seeing that individuals' civil rights are respected in health care is pre-eminent.

Discrimination

The only way to deal between individuals in a way which treats them as equals when resources are scarce, is to allocate those resources in a way which exhibits no preference. To discriminate between people on the grounds of quality of life, or QALY, or life-expectancy, is as unwarranted as it would be to discriminate on the grounds of race or gender.

So, the problem of choosing how to allocate scarce resources is simple. And by that of course I mean 'theoretically simple', not that the decisions will be easy to make or that it will be anything but agonisingly difficult actually to determine, however justly, who should live and who should die. Life-saving resources should simply be allocated in ways which do not violate the individual's entitlement to be treated as the equal of any other individual in the society: and that means the individual's entitlement to have his interests and desires weighed at the same value as those of anyone else. The QALY and the other bases of preference we have considered are irrelevant.

If health professionals are forced by the scarcity of resources, to choose, they should avoid unjust discrimination. But how are they to do this?

JUST DISTRIBUTION

If there were a satisfactory principle or theory of just distribution now would be the time to recommend its use.[14] Unfortunately there is not a satisfactory principle available. The task is to allocate resources between competing claimants in a way that does not violate the individual's entitlement to be treated as the equal of any other individual—and that means her entitlement to have her fundamental interests and desires weighed at the same value as those of anyone else. The QALY and other quality-of-life criteria are, as we have seen, both dangerous and irrelevant as are considerations based on life-expectancy or on 'life-years' generated by the proposed treatment. If health professionals are forced by the scarcity of resources to choose, not *whether* to treat but *who* to treat, they must avoid any method that amounts to unjust discrimination.

I do not pretend that the task of achieving this will be an easy one, nor that I have any satisfactory solution. I do have views on how to approach a solution, but the development of those ideas is a task for another occasion.[12] I will be content for the moment if I have shown that QALYs are not the answer and that efforts to find one will have to take a different direction.

Defensive Medicine

While it is true that resources will always be limited it is far from clear that resources for health care are justifiably as limited as they are sometimes made to appear. People within health care are too often forced to consider simply the question of the best way of allocating the *health care budget,* and consequently are forced to compete with each other for resources. Where lives are at

stake however, the issue is a moral issue which faces the whole community, and in such circumstances, is one which calls for a fundamental reappraisal of priorities. The question should therefore be posed in terms, not of the health care budget alone, but of the *national budget.*[16] If this is done it will be clearer that it is simply not true that the resources necessary to save the lives of citizens are not available. Since the citizens in question are in real and present danger of death, the issue of the allocation of resources to life-saving is naturally one of, among other things, national defence. Clearly then health professionals who require additional resources simply to save the lives of citizens, have a prior and priority claim on the defence budget.

QALYs encourage the idea that the task for health economics is to find more efficient ways of doing the wrong thing—in this case sacrificing the lives of patients who could be saved. All people concerned with health care should have as their priority defensive medicine: defending their patients against unjust and lethal policies, and guarding themselves against devices that tend to disguise the immorality of what they are asked to do.

Priority in Life-Saving

It is implausible to suppose that we cannot deploy vastly greater resources than we do at present to save the lives of all those in immediate mortal danger. It should be only in exceptional circumstances—unforeseen and massive disasters for example—that we cannot achieve this. However, in such circumstances our first duty is to try to save the maximum number of lives possible. This is because, since each person's life is valuable, and since we are committed to treating each person with the same concern and respect that we show to any, we must preserve the lives of as many individuals as we can. To fail to do so would be to value at zero the lives and fundamental interests of those extra people we could, but do not, save. Where we cannot save all, we should select those who are not to be saved in a way that shows no unjust preference.

We should be very clear that the obligation to save as many lives as possible is *not the obligation to save as many lives as we can cheaply or economically save*. Among the sorts of disasters that force us to choose between lives, is not the disaster of overspending a limited health care budget!

There are multifarious examples of what I have in mind here and just a couple must suffice to illustrate the point. Suppose, as is often the case, providing health care in one region of a country[17] is more expensive than doing so in another, or where saving the lives of people with particular conditions, is radically more expensive than other life-saving procedures, and a given health care budget won't run to the saving of all. Then any formula employed to choose priorities should do just that. Instead of attempting to measure the value of people's lives and select which are worth saving, any rubric for resource allocation should *examine the national budget afresh* to see whether there are any headings of expenditure that are more important to the community than rescuing citizens in mortal danger. For only if all other claims on funding are plausibly more important than that, is it true that resources for life-saving are limited.

Conclusion

The principle of equal access to health care is sustained by the very same reasons that sustain both the principle of equality before the law and the civil rights required to defend the freedom of the individual. These are rightly considered so important that no limit is set on the cost of sustaining them. Equal access to health care is of equal importance and should be accorded the same priority for analogous reasons. Indeed, since the abolition of capital punishment, due process of law is arguably of less vital importance than is access to health care. We have seen that QALYs involve denying that the life and health of each citizen is as important as that of any. If, for example, we applied the QALY principle to the administration of criminal justice we might find that those with little life expectancy would have less to gain from securing their freedom and therefore should not be defended at all, or perhaps given a jury trial only if not in competition for such things with younger or fitter fellow citizens.

A recent BBC television programme calculated[18] that if a health authority had £200,000 to spend it would get 10 QALYs from dialysis of kidney patients, 266 QALYs from hip-replacement operations or 1197 QALYs from anti-smoking propaganda. While this information is undoubtedly useful and while advice to stop smoking is an important part of health care, we should be wary of a formula which seems to dictate that such a health authority would use its resources most efficiently if it abandoned hip replacements and dialysis in favour of advice to stop smoking.

References and Notes

1. See the excellent discussion of the recent history of this line of thought in the Office of Health Economics publication *The measurement of health* London, 1985.

2. Williams A. Economics of coronary artery bypass grafting. *British medical journal* 1985; 291; and his contribution to the article, Centre eight—in search of efficiency. *Health and social service journal* 1985. These are by no means the first such attempts. See reference (1).

3. Williams A. The value of QALYs. *Health and social service journal* 1985.

4. I mention this in case anyone should think that it is only medical scientists who do medical research.

5. See reference (3): 3.

6. See reference (1): 16.

7. See reference (3): 5, and reference (3).

8. I'll assume this can be described as 'true' for the sake of argument.

9. I am indebted to Dr S G Potts for pointing out to me some of these statistics and for other helpful comments.

10. For examples see reference (1) and reference (2).

11. See Parfit D. Innumerate ethics. *Philosophy and public affairs* 1978; 7, 4. Parfit's arguments provide a detailed defence of the principle that each is to count for one.

12. I consider these problems in more detail in my: eQALYty. In: Byrne P, ed. *King's College studies*. London: King's Fund Press, 1987/8. Forthcoming.

13. Dworkin R. *Taking rights seriously*. London: Duckworth. 1977: 227.

14. I do not of course mean to imply that there are such things as rights, merely that our use of the language of rights captures the special importance we attach to certain freedoms and protections. The term 'civil rights' is used here as a 'term of art' referring to those freedoms and protections that are customarily classed as 'civil rights'.

15. For an interesting attempt to fill this gap see Dworkin R. What is equality? *Philosophy and public affairs* 1981; 4 and 5.

16. And of course the international budget; see my *The value of life*. London: Routledge & Kegan Paul 1985: chapter 3.

17. See Townsend P, Davidson N, eds. *Inequalities in health: the Black Report*. Harmondsworth, Penguin: 1982.

18. BBC 1. *The heart of the matter* 1986, Oct.

Triage in the ICU

Robert D. Truog MD

The United States has a seemingly limitless need for intensive care resources. More than 15 percent of our acute hospital beds are devoted to critical care, as compared with only 1 percent in Great Britain.[1] While some new technologies such as transluminal angioplasty have decreased the need for critical care beds, most are demanding ever more intense levels of care for longer periods of time. These dramatic changes in the demographics of hospital care have created new dilemmas for physicians and other caregivers.

Extracorporeal membrane oxygenation (ECMO) provides a case in point. ECMO is a form of cardiopulmonary bypass used primarily to support newborns with life-threatening respiratory failure. It is a truly "scarce" resource, available in few centers and requiring the presence of highly trained personnel around the clock. Patients can be supported with this technology for more than a month if necessary; but data from the National ECMO Registry indicates that over 99 percent of newborns who will survive ECMO therapy can be weaned off support in less than two weeks.[2] Nevertheless, some parents (and caregivers) believe that as long as there is "one chance in a million," their child should remain on ECMO. Continuation of this therapy despite a very poor prognosis is potentially wasteful of this expensive resource. More importantly, however, this practice can (and does) adversely affect the health and survival of other ill newborns. Infants who require ECMO frequently die if they cannot gain access to the therapy within several hours, and many are too ill to survive an extended transport to an alternate ECMO center. Should we withdraw ECMO from a newborn with a poor prognosis in favor of another newborn with a good prognosis if the child more likely to benefit needs the therapy to survive and cannot be safely transferred to another facility? This question is a concrete example of the kind of dilemmas

From *Hastings Center Report* 22 13–17, 1992.

increasingly encountered in many areas of critical care medicine.

The generally accepted answer to the question is straightforward. It is commonly considered ethically unacceptable to remove one patient from life-sustaining therapy to make room for another. Just as respect for a patient's autonomy requires consent before *initiating* therapy, so must we obtain consent before *withdrawing* it. In addition, the fiduciary relationship between physician and patient is commonly held to require physicians to be exclusively committed to the particular interests of their patients. "In caring for an individual patient, the doctor must act solely as that patient's advocate, against the apparent interests of society as a whole, if necessary."[3]

These considerations, however, are not absolute. The principle of respect for autonomy is only *prima facie*, and must be balanced against competing claims of justice. The mere fact that one patient needed ECMO sooner than another may not be a sufficient moral reason for giving it to that patient. "First come, first served" has been advocated as a method for allocating scarce resources between patients with similar needs, but it is less useful when the claims are not equal. Even if we assume that all patients have an *a priori* equal right to a scarce resource, a patient with a poor prognosis who has already consumed an appreciable part of that resource has less right to the continued use of it than someone with a better prognosis who has had no use of it at all. Simply because a patient is already receiving a benefit does not give that patient an ironclad right to further use of that benefit, nor does it imply that the caregivers have made a morally binding commitment to giving that benefit exclusively to him.

The fiduciary relationship between physicians and patients likewise does not commit physicians to tunnel vision in allocating scarce resources. Physicians routinely allocate resources among the patients under their care and between their patients and the rest of society.

The surgeon who cancels her afternoon clinic because she is tied up with a complicated case in the operating room has allocated her limited time among her patients. The physician who agrees to put off a CT scan on his patient until tomorrow because other patients need the procedure more urgently is distributing a scarce resource between his patient and others in the community. Even when the therapy is life-sustaining, a physician's decision to shift the resource from one patient to another may be seen as a necessary exception to the general principle of exclusive commitment, as when a psychiatrist violates confidentiality to avoid putting another's life at risk. Fidelity to the covenant between patient and physician does not require physicians to be oblivious or unresponsive to the overall needs of others.

Can participation of a physician in the withdrawal of life-sustaining therapy be interpreted as abandonment of the patient? As a Hastings Center task force noted,

> If explicit and ethical policies are developed by means of procedures that are open, informed, and fair, health care providers might be justified in limiting their treatments to patients in accordance with such policies. This would be in keeping with the long-standing concern of the health care professions with issues of justice and societal well-being, as well as with patient autonomy and well-being.[4]

The allocation decisions that may be made are constrained, however, by the principle of respect for autonomy and the special nature of the patient-physician relationship. The most important requirement is that patients must be aware of the conditions under which therapy may be discontinued *before* it is initiated. In other words, they must *prospectively* understand "the rules of the game." What is at issue here cannot be called "informed consent" since no meaningful choice is really being offered—the idea is, rather, that patients be forewarned. Since we currently do not inform patients or families of any restrictions on the continuation of ECMO or any other life-saving therapy, it is generally regarded as legally unacceptable to remove patients from therapy against their will, even to make room for others in need. In the example cited above, the child with the better prognosis must be denied the life-saving therapy in preference to the infant already receiving support.

The current approach, therefore, is to remove patients from life-sustaining therapy only when it is in *their* best interest, never when it is solely in the best interest of another. As noted above, however, there are compelling reasons for considering alternate methods of allocation. These would seek to maximize the benefits obtained from scarce resources by giving them to those most likely to respond to the therapy. In the case of ECMO, for example, newborns who could not be weaned from the therapy within a reasonable period (generally two weeks) would be removed from support if another child with a better prognosis needed it. Parents would be informed of this policy before being offered ECMO support. Such a policy would clearly maximize the benefits this technology has to offer.

Although ECMO is a dramatic example of a limited life-saving resource, all intensive-care therapies are fundamentally scarce, so this approach has similar relevance for virtually any form of intensive support. Adopting this strategy would therefore have a major impact on many aspects of ICU allocation. In considering these implications, it is helpful to borrow from the traditional concept of 'triage' and think of ICU patients as stratified in terms of their likelihood to benefit from ICU therapy. At one end are those patients admitted primarily for monitoring or nursing observation. These patients have a low likelihood of benefitting from ICU care since they probably will recover whether or not they are in the ICU. They have a low "benefit index," since they are too well to require all the technology and clinical skills that the ICU setting offers. At the other end of the spectrum are also patients with a low likelihood of benefitting from the ICU. In this case, however, the "benefit

index" is low because these patients are too sick and unlikely to recover no matter how much care they receive. In the middle are those patients most likely to benefit from being in the ICU—those who truly require the high level of care available and who are expected to improve and ultimately recover.

Several reports have clearly documented that physicians *do* ration ICU resources under conditions of scarcity.[5] In all cases studied, however, these resources were denied or withdrawn *exclusively* from those patients on the "too well" end of the spectrum. In no case could it be determined that a patient who would clearly die without ICU care was removed from the ICU to make room for another patient with a better prognosis. ICU care is frequently withdrawn from terminal patients when this is believed to be in *that patient's* best interest, but none of the studies indicate that dying patients are discharged from the ICU when this is necessary to benefit *another* patient.

Is our current method of allocating ICU resources the best use of this scarce and expensive technology? First we must come to an understanding of what we mean by 'best use.' While there are many possible definitions, perhaps the most compelling is that which maximizes the health benefits that can be produced. Health benefits manifest as an increase in the quality as well as the longevity of individual lives. Does a system that denies or withdraws this resource only from those on the "too well" end of the spectrum result in the "best use" of this resource?

In most instances, optimal use of a medical resource requires that access be withheld from patients with a low likelihood of benefit on *both* ends of the spectrum. Our present system of favoring those on the "too sick" end of the spectrum can be justified only when the scarce resources are *temporarily* limited. Consider the case of a battlefield physician faced with the care of a large number of casualties after a landmine explodes in the middle of his platoon. If he knows that reinforcements are on the way and that sufficient help for evacuation and care of the wounded will be available within several hours, then his best course of action is to give preferential care to some of the more severely injured soldiers. Some of those who will surely die without immediate intervention may survive with prompt care, whereas those patients who are less severely injured probably will survive at least until additional help arrives. Under conditions of temporary scarcity, the choice of which patients to treat is shifted toward the "sicker" end of the spectrum, as this strategy maximizes the number of lives saved. On the other hand, if the platoon is isolated and the physician knows that help will not arrive for several days, he should direct his attention to those patients in the middle of the spectrum, and allow to die those who will place disproportionate demands on his attention. When scarcity is not temporary, the physician should allocate the available resources symmetrically around the middle of the spectrum, as in this case favoring the "too sick" not only fails to produce the best use of the scarce resources, but unfairly places all of the burden of allocation on those who are on the "too well" side of the spectrum.

Some shortages of ICU resources *are* temporary. If several nurses are out ill for the night shift, care should be preferentially directed toward the sicker patients in anticipation of full staffing in the morning. Most ICU limitations, however (like the scarcity of ECMO beds), are not temporary. In these circumstances, rational allocation demands the option of denying or withdrawing therapy from those on the "too sick" end of the spectrum.

An analogous approach has been widely adopted by organizations regulating the allocation of another scarce resource—transplantable organs.[6] Organ banks seek to maximize the benefits obtained from the limited number of available organs by choosing from among potential recipients those who are most likely to recover and sustain long-term organ function. This strategy means that patients who will certainly die without a transplanted organ may sometimes be passed over in favor of patients with a better prognosis. While similar in principle, organ allocation differs from ICU allocation in the way patients present for treatment. Transplantation programs are able to pick a candidate for a particular organ from among a group of qualified applicants. When an ICU bed becomes available, on the other hand, there is generally not a pool of candidates waiting for the bed. ICU patients make their claims sequentially, one at a time. Ethicists who have tried to draw analogies between organ transplantation and ICU allocation have not fully appreciated this fact, and have postulated contrived scenarios (such as simultaneous cardiac arrests)[7] to draw parallels with the transplantation situation. The important implication of this difference is that ICUs cannot exclusively rely on *withholding* care to assure delivery to those most likely to benefit. Since ICUs must allocate sequentially rather than at one point in time, it is also necessary to *withdraw* care if required to accommodate an individual with a greater potential for benefit.

Successful implementation of this approach requires that we resolve several important practical problems. First, we must arrive at an understanding of what constitutes 'benefit' and then develop accurate prognostic indicators that will enable us to assign individuals a position on the "benefit spectrum." The meaning of 'benefit' varies with the medical goals to be achieved as well as with the unique values of each patient. Robert Weir has pointed out the wide variety of medical meanings of the term 'beneficial':

> (1) the treatment is "beneficial" in the sense of making the *medical management* of the patient easier for the health care providers involved in the case;
> (2) the treatment is "beneficial" in the sense of providing *immediate, short-term relief* to the patient, without any long-term benefit;
> (3) the treatment is "beneficial" in the sense of *corrective therapy*, by improving an injurious or disabling condition without being curative;

(4) the treatment is "beneficial" in the sense of *curing* a pathological condition "once and for all";
(5) the treatment is "beneficial" in the sense of *maintaining the status quo condition* of the patient for an extended period of time;
(6) the treatment is "beneficial" in the sense of *medical experimentation*, with any actual benefits of the experimental procedure occurring to other patients in the future.[8]

Weir's third definition seems most appropriate to life-sustaining ICU therapy, with perhaps a reasonable goal being survival to hospital discharge with consciousness intact. Such a goal is in accord with several prominent consensus reports, which have concluded that permanently unconscious patients should generally not receive ICU care or deprive another patient of access to a scarce medical resource.[9]

Assessing prognosis for achieving this benefit is a notoriously difficult aspect of ICU care, but nevertheless one we routinely perform every day. We prognosticate when we recommend a liver transplant based on the likelihood of survival without one; we recommend toxic antibiotics by balancing their risks against the probability that the patient will die of an infection. Our uncertainty in making predictions about outcome and survival should not paralyze our allocation decisions any more than it does our medical decisions. Prognostic indicators have been developed for many types of ICU patients, such as those with severe neurologic dysfunction, multisystem organ failure, and hematologic malignancy, or those in respiratory failure secondary to AIDS or bone marrow transplantation.[10] Severity of illness scores such as the APACHE system may further assist our ability to characterize patients in terms of their likelihood to benefit from ICU therapy.[11]

In addition, we need to choose a threshold level of benefit that would justify withdrawing care from one patient to give it to another. If a patient receiving therapy has a 59 percent probability of benefit, and a newcomer patient's probability is 60 percent, should the patient re-

ceiving therapy give it up to the newcomer? If the probabilities are reversed the following day, should the therapy once again be switched? In an effort to avoid this type of chaos, previous allocation strategies have generally not attempted to reassess entitlement after the initial allocation. When access to hemodialysis was rationed in the late 1960s, for example, committees decided which patients were allowed access to the therapy, but once a patient was accepted into the program there was no attempt made to reassess suitability or consider withdrawing the therapy.[12] A reasonable way of preventing the confusion and turmoil that could result from continual reassessment would be to honor the principle of first come, first served[13] until the probability of benefit to the person receiving the therapy declined sufficiently far to justify withdrawal of the therapy in favor of another. Although it may seem excessively arbitrary to choose a cutoff of 1, 5, or 10 percent as a threshold for the probability of benefit, in actual practice there is usually a quantum transition from a reasonable likelihood of recovery to a situation where survival would be exceedingly unlikely. In only a minority of cases is the transition gradual and continuous; but even in these cases it would be fair to choose a reasonable (albeit arbitrary) threshold for the probability of benefit, provided it was applied uniformly to all patients in similar situations. Decisions based upon these probabilities should be founded upon clear institutional guidelines or reached through the work of a committee experienced in the clinical care of the critically ill patient. The tendency to continually expand the indications for scarce therapies and progressively shrink the category of patients too sick to benefit would have to be consciously resisted, otherwise the allocation problem would not really be resolved but only shifted to all of the patients now under the same category. Decisions should be regularly reviewed by referees not involved in the allocation system, and a well-defined mechanism for appeal should be available for patients or their advocates to question these deliberations.

This raises the issue of how therapy should be withdrawn once it is agreed that a patient has a benefit index below the threshold for entitlement. One option would be to remove therapy from these patients only when another patient in need of the therapy and with a higher benefit index presented for care. The other option would be to withdraw ICU care from anyone with a benefit index below the threshold value, regardless of whether another candidate was in need of the bed. The former strategy is advantageous in permitting the most continuous use of the resource, and in giving each patient the chance to prove the system wrong by mounting an unexpected or even miraculous recovery. The principal advantage of the latter approach is that it avoids the appearance of competition between patients. One can imagine the newcomer-patient being rolled into the ICU as the patient he has bumped is being removed from the unit. Such a policy might well induce guilt in the newcomer-patient, besides generating tremendous anxiety in those resident-patients with low benefit indices as they wait for another candidate to arrive with a greater claim on the resource.

While each approach has its advantages and disadvantages, choosing a policy that withdraws care only when another patient actually requires the therapy permits our allocation decisions to be grounded in the needs of *real and particular* patients rather than in abstract considerations of probable benefit. This is crucial for preventing bedside allocation from becoming a faceless and impersonal technical task.

The model developed here is entirely dependent upon the assumption that the best use of ICU resources is that which maximizes the health benefits that can be obtained. It is plausible to argue that in matters of life and death we are seldom willing to accept an approach grounded purely in a standard of efficiency. Perhaps this is best illustrated by the fact that few

would support a policy forcing the lethal donation of the heart, liver, and kidneys from a healthy citizen to save the lives of several other people dying from single-organ failure. Such a policy would certainly be considered unacceptable even though it would promote the best use of scarce transplantable organs. Stated more generally, perhaps the ICU is simply another place where individual rights should take precedence over the pursuit of the greatest good. In evaluating this claim, we must weigh the relative value of the individual rights that may be violated against the social good that is to be gained. In the transplant example, while saving lives is certainly an important social good, the right not to have one's body forcibly violated is generally held to be more important. In the case of scarce ICU resources, we must balance the value of maximizing the benefits from this socially owned and expensive resource against the right of patients and families to demand care from which they are very unlikely to benefit. Often these demands are based on the very understandable feelings of grief and despair that frequently surround the process of death, but we must decide how much weight the community should give to these feelings when they compromise the care of others who will suffer or die without access to the resource. A strategy that seeks to maximize the health benefits available from scarce ICU resources may therefore be justified in overriding the right of individuals to demand unlimited access to resources from which they are very unlikely to benefit.

Rationing is already a reality in the ICU. Studies indicate it is being performed without a clear idea of the principles and objectives that should underlie allocation decisions. Open discussion is necessary if we are to achieve strategies for allocation that are compatible with the moral requirements and health needs of our society. If we accept the model outlined above, then we have an obligation to remove some patients from life-sustaining therapy, even when it means their unavoidably imminent death. It is certainly tragic to tell a patient that we are removing him from life support and that he will now die. It is even worse, however, to tell someone that we are denying him a life-saving therapy because another has an unquestioned claim on that resource no matter how poor his prognosis. We cannot avoid making tragic decisions, but we can make them with the knowledge that we have done our best to be compassionate and fair.

References and Notes

1. Bryan Jennett, "Inappropriate Use of Intensive Care," *British Medical Journal* 289, no. 6460 (1984): 1709–11.

2. Data from Extracorporeal Life Support Organization, April 1989.

3. Norman G. Levinsky, "The Doctor's Master," *NEJM* 311, no. 24 (1984): 1573–75.

4. The Hastings Center, *Guidelines on the Termination of Life-Sustaining Treatment and the Care of the Dying* (Bloomington: Indiana University Press, 1987), p. 120.

5. Daniel E. Singer, Phyllis L. Carr, Albert G. Mulley, et al., "Rationing Intensive Care: Physician Responses to Resource Shortage," *NEJM* 309, no. 19 (1983): 1155–60; Michael J. Strauss, James P. LoGerfo, James A. Yeltatzie, et al., "Rationing of Intensive Care Unit Services: An Everyday Occurrence," *JAMA* 255, no. 9 (1986): 1143–46; Harry P. Selker, John L. Griffith, Frederick J. Dorey, et al., "How Do Physicians Adapt When the Coronary Care Unit Is Full? A Prospective Multicenter Study," *JAMA* 257, no. 9 (1987): 1181–85; Frederic L. Sax and Mary E. Charlson, "Utilization of Critical Care Units: A Prospective Study of Physician Triage and Patient Outcome," *Archives of Internal Medicine* 147, no. 5 (1987): 929–34; Paul E. Kalb and David H. Miller, "Utilization Strategies for Intensive Care Units," *JAMA* 261, no. 16 (1989): 2389–95; Nicholas G. Smedira, Bradley H. Evans, Linda S. Grais, et al., "Withholding and Withdrawal of Life Support from the Critically Ill," *NEJM* 322, no. 5 (1990): 309–15.

6. Massachusetts Task Force on Organ Transplantation, "Patient Selection and Rationing Schemes," in *Report of the Massachusetts Task Force on Organ Transplantation* (Boston: Department of Public Health, 1984), pp. 71–86.

7. Kevin M. McIntyre, Robert C. Benfari and Margaret Pabst Battin, "Two Cardiac Arrests, One Medical Team," *Hastings Center Report* 12, no. 2 (1982): 24–25.

8. Robert F. Weir, *Abating Treatment with Critically Ill Patients: Ethical and Legal Limits to the Prolongation of Life* (New York: Oxford University Press, 1989), p. 344.

9. President's Commission for the Study of Ethical Problems in Medicine and Biomedical and Behavioral Research, *Deciding to Forego Life-Sustaining Treatment: Ethical, Medical, and Legal Issues in Treatment Decisions* (Washington, D.C.: U.S. Government Printing Office, 1983), pp. 188–89; Hastings Center, *Guidelines on the Termination of Life-Sustaining Treatment*; Task Force on Ethics of the Society of Critical Care Medicine, "Consensus Report on the Ethics of Forgoing Life-Sustaining Treatment in the Critically Ill," *Critical Care Medicine* 18 (1990): 1435–39.

10. Michael S. Berger, Lawrence H. Pitts, Mary Lovely, et al., "Outcome from Severe Head Injury in Children and Adolescents," *Journal of Neurosurgery* 62, no. 2 (1985): 194–99; William A. Knaus, Elizabeth A. Draper, Douglas P. Wagner, et al., "Prognosis in Acute Organ-System Failure," *Annals of Surgery* 202, no. 6 (1985): 685–93; Warwick Butt, Geoffrey Barker, Craig Walker, et al., "Outcome of Children with Hematologic Malignancy Who Are Admitted to an Intensive Care Unit," *Critical Care Medicine* 16, no. 18 (1988): 761–64; Roland M. Schein, Margaret A. Fischl, Arthur E. Pitchenik, et al. "ICU Survival of Patients with the Acquired Immunodeficiency Syndrome," *Critical Care Medicine* 14, no. 12 (1986): 1026–27; Scott J. Denardo, Robert K. Oye, and Paul E. Bellamy, "Efficacy of Intensive Care for Bone Marrow Transplant Patients with Respiratory Failure," *Critical Care Medicine* 17, no. 1 (1989): 4–6.

11. James A. Kruse, Mary C. Thill Baharozian, and Richard W. Carlson, "Comparison of Clinical Assessment with APACHE II for Predicting Mortality Risk in Patients Admitted to a Medical Intensive Care Unit," *JAMA* 260, no. 12 (1988): 1739–42.

12. Shana Alexander, "They Decide Who Lives, Who Dies," in *Ethical Issues in Modern Medicine*, ed. R. Hunt and John Arras (Palo Alto, Calif.: Mayfield, 1977), pp. 409–24.

13. James F. Childress, "Rationing of Medical Treatment" in *Encyclopedia of Bioethics*, vol. 4, ed. Warren T. Reich (New York: Free Press, 1978), pp. 1414–19.

⌐∞⌐

Ethical Considerations in the Allocation of Organs and Other Scarce Medical Resources Among Patients

Council on Ethical and Judicial Affairs, American Medical Association

Physicians' efforts on behalf of patients often involve the use of resources that, because of naturally limited supply or economic constraints, are not readily available to all who need them. The dilemma in such cases is how physicians may fulfill their ethical duties to "do all that (they) can for the benefit of the individual patient"[1] when the care that they can provide is constrained by the scarcity of needed resources.

In the past, scarce resources (such as organs and intensive care unit [ICU] beds) (*Wall Street Journal*. May 23, 1992:1) have been allocated according to a wide range of criteria, some appropriate and some not.[2-6] Wide variation in allocation criteria and procedures still exists,[7,8] inhibiting ethical distribution of resources according to "fair, socially acceptable, and humane criteria."[1]

In this report, the Council on Ethical and Judicial Affairs considers the ethical issues relating to the equitable allocation of organs and other scarce resources among patients, including the criteria by which scarce medical resources should be distributed and a suggested procedure for applying these criteria. In addition, the Council considers the appropriate role of physicians in allocating scarce resources.

Some argue that, in addition to such existing scarce resources as organs and ICU beds, a broader range of medical resources may become scarce in the future [7,9,10] as society rethinks its health care goals in the face of rising costs and competing social demands.[10] The debate over rationing and the setting of societal priorities in health care is beyond the scope of this report. However, should there ever be societal agreement to limit or deny medically effective care to some patients on the basis of cost, the allocation criteria discussed in this report might then be applicable to those limited resources as well.

ACCEPTABLE CRITERIA FOR RESOURCE ALLOCATION AMONG PATIENTS

Five factors relating to medical need may appropriately be taken into account when organs or other scarce medical resources, such as spaces in the ICU, are allocated. These include (1) the likelihood of benefit to the patient, (2) the impact of treatment in improving the quality of the patient's life, (3) the duration of benefit, (4) the urgency of the patient's conditions (ie, how close the patient is to death), and in some cases (5) the amount of resources required for successful treatment. Each of these criteria serves to maximize the following three primary goals of medical treatment: number of lives saved, number of years of life saved, and improvement in quality of life (ie, the criteria maximize quantity of life, quality of life, or both).

Likelihood of Benefit

Giving priority to patients with a greater likelihood of benefiting from treatment is necessary for any efficient use of medical resources.[6,11] Likelihood of benefit helps decision makers maximize the number of lives saved as well as the length and quality of life.

The major concern with a likelihood of benefit criterion is the uncertainty involved in outcome predictions. Given current knowledge

From *Archives of Internal Medicine* 155: 29–39, 1995.

and information, predictions of outcomes are necessarily imprecise. Because of this uncertainty, only very substantial differences in likelihood of benefit among patients are relevant to allocation decisions. The larger those differences are, the more relevant a likelihood of benefit criterion becomes. For example, in allocating kidneys for transplant, it would be more justified to prefer a patient with an 80% chance of graft survival over a patient with a 10% chance than it would be to prefer a 60% chance to a 40% chance. Small differences in probabilities should not be used to fine-tune allocation decisions when dealing with patients with fairly comparable chances of benefiting from treatment.

In the application of a likelihood of benefit criterion, care that has a low likelihood of benefiting the patient must be distinguished from care that is truly futile (eg, care that cannot be expected to have any physiologic benefit for the patient).[12] Patients who do have some chance of benefiting, in whatever degree, cannot be ruled out in advance as inappropriate candidates for treatment. In addition, allocation decisions that rely on nonmedical contributions to a patient's likelihood of benefit should be approached cautiously because of the risk of arbitrariness and overgeneralization. Communication or transportation problems, for instance, may be mere inconveniences rather than insurmountable obstacles. Reliance on these factors may systematically disadvantage the least well-off members of society, who, because of poverty or other reasons, may tend to experience these kinds of problems more often than others. Other criteria, such as strength of character or a supportive home environment, may contribute to likelihood of benefit[11-17] but are difficult to define or apply to individuals.

In general, if patient traits or behaviors that may adversely affect the patient's likelihood of benefit are taken into account, at least two conditions should be met. First, reasonable extra efforts on the part of physicians or others must fail to overcome the obstacles posed by the patient's traits or behaviors; and second, the traits or behaviors must

directly and substantially detract from the patient's likelihood of responding to treatment. For instance, an intravenous drug user who is a candidate for liver transplantation should not be denied consideration until the possibility of rehabilitation for drug addiction has been fully explored.

Change in Quality of Life

Benefit to patients will be maximized if treatment is provided to those who will have the greatest improvement in quality of life. The biggest difficulty in applying this criterion is deciding on a standard definition of quality of life.[18]

Conceptually, defining the benefit gained from treatment and determining its importance in a patient's life depend greatly on patients' individual, subjective values.[18-22] Prioritizing candidates for treatment on the basis of their subjective preferences, however, would be impossible in practice. It would be extremely difficult to assess patients' individual preferences, and even more difficult to make useful comparisons among patients on that basis. Some allocation systems have proposed relying on patient or public surveys to determine average quality of life ratings for different outcomes.[23] However, because an individual's quality of life depends on subjective experience and values, an individual's preferences may depart significantly from the average and yet still not be unreasonable or unworthy of respect.

While no approach is perfect, perhaps the best approach is to define quality of life in terms of functional status.[24] Improvements in quality of life would be measured for each patient by comparing functional status with treatment and functional status without treatment. Making quality of life judgments in terms of changes in functional status facilitates comparisons between patients by allowing decision makers "to assess quality of life independent of the patient's feelings."[24] Although defining quality of life as functional status precludes consideration of the nuances of individual preferences, it does allow for objective comparisons between patients that may be relevant when differences between patients are very substantial. In the context of scarcity, some idiosyncratic high valuations of very poor functional status outcomes are simply too dubious to honor at the expense of other needy patients.

In considering quality of life (as defined by functional status), the first priority should be to prevent an extremely poor outcome, such as death or a life of permanent unconsciousness or extreme pain and suffering. When patients are admitted to a crowded ICU, for instance, a patient who can be saved by treatment from entering a permanent vegetative state (and given a reasonably good outcome) should be favored over another patient who, if denied treatment, would suffer only a mild disability. Preventing an extremely poor outcome, such as a permanent vegetative state, should be given priority over preventing milder disabilities.

If none of the patients competing for spaces in the ICU faces an extremely poor outcome, or if the extremely poor outcome cannot be avoided even with treatment, then patients should be prioritized to favor those who will receive the greatest improvement in functional status, measured by the difference between functional status with treatment and functional status without treatment. However, differences in the magnitude of change in functional status among patients are ethically relevant only when they are very substantial. Measurements of change in functional status are inherently imprecise. In addition, because patients' attitudes toward a given change in functional status can differ, considering small differences in functional improvement would often fail to maximize overall benefit to patients and would be unfair to those whose preferences deviate from the norm. Consideration of only very substantial differences allows room, within reasonable limits, for expression of the range of patient valuations of a given change in functional status.

A major concern in making quality of life decisions is the possibility of discrimination against the disabled population.[23,25] The Council's approach to quality of life decisions allows resources to be directed according to where they will do the most good, without discriminating against those with preexisting disabilities. There may be occasions where disabled patients receive lower priority because their potential improvement in functional status is limited by preexisting disabilities. However, since only very substantial differences in the change in quality of life may be considered ethically relevant, a disabled patient will be given a lower priority only when doing so allows others to receive a much greater improvement in quality of life. In addition, the provision giving highest priority to those who need treatment to prevent an extremely poor outcome protects all patients, including the disabled, from receiving low priority when their need is greatest.

Duration of Benefit

The length of time a patient benefits from treatment can, in certain situations, be an appropriate consideration in maximizing overall benefit to patients.

The duration of benefit a patient receives from treatment will in many cases be limited by the patient's life expectancy. It is not always appropriate, however, to give organs or other scarce resources to the patient with the longest expected life span. There is often a lack of certainty in predicting life spans, especially at the individual level, as well as a risk of engaging in inappropriate age-based discrimination.[26] When a duration of benefit criterion is applied, patients should be assessed according to their own medical histories and prognoses, not aggregate statistics based on membership in a group.

In addition, giving priority to those who will benefit longer may not always maximize overall benefit to patients. The degree to which a longer duration of benefit actually benefits the patient depends on the patient's subjective experience and values. However, as with the quality of life criterion, some claims to treatment that will bring only a small benefit to the patient are simply too tenuous to sustain in the face of scarcity. Hence, duration of benefit can be a legitimate consideration when the differences among patients are very substantial. For example, the difference between an organ graft that lasts 8 years and one that lasts 10 years is not relevant, whereas the difference between 2 years and 10 years is relevant.

Urgency of Need

Prioritizing patients according to how long they can survive without treatment can help achieve the goal of maximizing the number of lives saved, depending on the kind of resource involved.[27] For instance, since spaces in an ICU are ordinarily scarce only intermittently, giving priority to urgent cases is generally justifiable because less urgent cases can still gain timely access to the ICU once the scarcity subsides.[11] With heart or liver transplants, however, the persistent scarcity of organs entails that some patients on the waiting list will die before an organ becomes available for them. With cases of persistent rather than temporary scarcity, then, urgency of need should be given less consideration because it would determine merely *who* will survive, rather than maximizing the *number* of survivors.[27] Furthermore, an urgency criterion can detract from length and quality of benefit. If patients with a less urgent need are set aside until their condition deteriorates to the point of dire emergency, treatment may not be as beneficial as it would have been had it been begun much earlier.

In sum, while urgency is an important criterion, it must be tempered with other considerations, including likelihood of benefit, the persistent or temporary scarcity of the resource involved, and the length of time other patients can survive without causing them irreparable harm. Preventing death (by treating urgent cases first) should generally be given priority in allocation decisions, but not if the life saved would be of extremely poor quality or extremely short duration. Also, an urgency criterion should not be used to deny resources to current patients in the expectation that others with more urgent need may soon present themselves.

Amount of Resources Required

Occasionally, assigning higher priority to patients who will need less of a scarce resource maximizes the number of lives saved. Each patient treated would require relatively little of it, making it more available for others.[28]

Conscious attempts to conserve resources in the allocation process will in general prove unnecessary. Patients who would be favored because they would require very little of a resource will often have a very high (or perhaps very low) likelihood of benefit as well, making likelihood of benefit the relevant criterion. When all else is equal, however, taking into account very substantial differences in the amount of resources required can be useful in ensuring efficient allocation. For instance, given two heart transplant candidates who are equal in all other respects, it is justified to give lower priority to the patient who would also require a liver transplant. By doing so, two lives can be saved rather than one.

This criterion should not be used to deny care to current patients in the expectation that others who will need fewer resources may soon present themselves. Rather, only when it is reasonably certain that conserving resources will have a good chance of saving more lives should this criterion be considered relevant.

INAPPROPRIATE CRITERIA FOR RESOURCE ALLOCATION AMONG PATIENTS

The Council believes that the following criteria, although often used in allocating scarce resources, are ethically unacceptable: (1) ability to pay, (2) contribution of the patient to society, (3) perceived obstacles to treatment, (4) contribution of the patient to his or her own medical condition, and (5) past use of resources. Omission from this list does not necessarily mean that a criterion is justified; the Council considers only these five because of their prevalence in the literature and in allocation decisions today.

Ability to Pay

This is perhaps the most ubiquitous allocation criterion employed today, yet from an ethical standpoint there is little to recommend it.[29] In the medical realm, consideration of ability to pay is more often considered a regrettable necessity than a positive ethical principle of distribution. If a patient cannot pay the full fee for care, many physicians will waive the fee or accept lesser payment.[30] When ability to pay does play a role in allocating scarce resources, it is usually at the point of access to health care.

Consideration of a patient's ability to pay is problematic in many areas of health care, but especially when it comes to scarce, lifesaving resources. In other areas, market mechanisms may accurately reflect individuals' different valuations of various goods and services. At present, though, income disparity across society distorts the accuracy of the market model as a fair tool for distributing scarce medical resources, for the amount an individual can spend to gain access to a needed treatment will often fall short of his or her actual valuation of it.

Physicians and institutions should continue to accept patients with limited abilities to pay and should not systematically deny needed resources to patients simply because of their lower economic status.

Social Worth

A patient's contribution to society—or social worth—should not be a factor in allocation decisions. Such judgments are usually defended as attempts to maximize the return on society's investment in medical resources.[27,31] One common use is to justify the denial of care to the elderly, who some argue no longer make a positive contribution to the social good.[6,32] The problems of age-based rationing have been discussed by the Council at length elsewhere and cannot be repeated in full here. Although age-based rationing has its supporters,[33] the Council's view is that such an approach "fails to take into account the heterogeneity within older age groups" and the "increasing proportion of the elderly population . . . still in the work force and leading active, productive lives."[26]

A social worth criterion can also be used to justify discrimination against the young and virtually any other group not actively involved in the economic productivity of society, on the grounds that those who have put the most into society are entitled to get the most back out of it.[34,35] Distinctions can be made among economic contributors as well; for instance, white collar workers with higher salaries may be favored over blue collar workers or the working poor. Social worth can also be measured by noneconomic criteria. Artists, writers, musicians, and other cultural elite may be favored over average citizens, and people with dependents may be preferred over those without families.[36]

Because of the pluralistic values of society, any single definition of social contribution or social worth is inherently suspect. Social worth judgments often reflect the preferences and values of individual decision makers rather than any objective criteria.[37] In addition, by assuming that members of a certain group make greater social contributions than others, a social worth criterion ignores diversity and the value of each individual.

Above all, a social worth criterion is a marked departure from the traditional patient-centered orientation of the medical profession. Social worth considerations would destroy public confidence in physicians' abilities to place patients' interests above broad social utility. Medicine should continue to concentrate on the best interests of patients and avoid evaluations of social worth.

Perceived Obstacles to Treatment

This criterion would give lower priority to patients whose circumstances pose special challenges to successful treatment, including patients with multiple diseases, alcohol and other drug abusers, the indigent, the uneducated, patients with transportation problems or language barriers, and patients with antisocial or aggressive personalities. Perceived obstacles to treatment may cause an unconscious prejudice in the minds of decision makers, who may think their considerations relate only to more objective medical criteria, such as likelihood of benefit.

The danger is that some patients will be given lower priority who, with a little extra effort and support, could benefit greatly from treatment. Thus, rather than downrate alcohol and other drug abusers as candidates for treatment, decision makers should consider whether rehabilitation could be successful in improving the patient's chances of benefit. Similarly, arrangements can be made to help patients with transportation problems or to provide interpreters for patients with language barriers.

Potential recipients of scarce medical resources should not be downrated prima facie because of surmountable difficulties attendant to their cases. Rather, whenever possible, physicians should encourage their patients to use additional resources, such as social workers, private charities, rehabilitation clinics, and other support networks, to facilitate their care.

Patient Contribution to Disease

This criterion assigns lower priority to patients whose past behaviors contributed significantly to their present need for scarce resources. Examples include heart transplant candidates whose high-fat diets may have contributed to their condition, or liver transplant candidates whose alcoholism led to cirrhosis of the liver.[38] The reasoning is that patients who failed to take action to prevent their illness are partially to blame for their conditions[38] and thus have forfeited the right to be given the same priority for treatment as others.

This argument is flawed in two ways. First, it is not always clear which factors actually contribute to a disease, or which are more or less to blame than other contributing factors.[38] Second, of all the possible contributors to disease, only

certain behaviors are singled out as justifications for denying treatment. Few would suggest giving lower priority to wealthy heart transplant candidates whose high-stress occupations contributed to their heart disease, or denying intensive care to sky divers or football players injured in the course of their sports. Rather, only certain socially unacceptable or morally suspect behaviors, like immoderate eating or drinking, are considered appropriate criteria for denying treatment. However, the use of judgments about patients' morals to allocate health care seems grossly inappropriate and inconsistent; physicians do not refuse to treat patients who engage in other immoral behaviors, such as adultery or tax evasion.[39]

Another problem with this criterion is its assumption that patients' past contributions to their own illnesses were voluntary actions.[39] For instance, giving alcoholics lower priority for liver transplants seems to ignore some reasons for drinking that are beyond an individual's control, such as family history of alcohol abuse or possible genetic predilections for alcoholism.[40] Some argue that it is the failure to seek treatment, rather than having the problem itself, that is morally blameworthy.[38] However, it seems unjust to punish further those who already have suffered greatly from chemical dependency, especially when many may have simply been unaware of treatment options or unable to seek out treatment. It would be fruitless and potentially devastating to allocate Medicaid resources on the basis of the perceived moral culpability of patients.

Past Use of Resources

It may be argued that patients who have had considerable access to a scarce medical resource in the past should be given lower priority than equally needy patients who have received little or none of that resource. A consequence of this view would be that some currently using a resource may be displaced by others who have not yet had access. A patient could be displaced from an ICU by another patient with the same prognosis but less past access, or a retransplant patient could be denied any chance at all of receiving additional organs.

A criterion involving past use of resources is inappropriate because it rests on a fundamentally flawed conception of equality among potential recipients of treatment. Equality does not impose an ethical requirement that equally suitable patients receive the same amount of care; indeed, scarcity makes such an obligation impossible to fulfill. The only requirement is that patients be judged equally according to their current needs, on the basis of their diagnoses and prognoses. Unlike the five ethically acceptable criteria discussed in this report—likelihood of benefit, duration of benefit, change in quality of life, urgency, and amount of resources required—past use of resources does not contribute to maximizing the number, quality, or length of lives saved. It does not contribute to maximizing overall benefit to patients.[41] In addition, the seemingly common-sense view that everyone deserves a turn at receiving scarce medical resources ignores inequalities in access to other goods that affect health, such as income, education, and access to primary care.[41] Any serious attempt to base allocation decisions on past access to medical resources would have to evaluate candidates' past access to these other goods as well,[41] a task for which medicine is ill equipped.

There may be cases in which a patient's past use of resources contributes to the patient's current likelihood of benefit, duration of benefit, or expected improvement in quality of life. For instance, a retransplant candidate will often be a poorer candidate for transplantation because of the failure of a previous graft.[41,42] If so, then the relevant allocation criteria justifying lower priority for that patient would be likelihood of benefit or perhaps duration of benefit, but not the mere fact of past access to an organ. Because past use is irrelevant to present need, it should not factor into allocation decisions.

APPLYING ALLOCATION CRITERIA

All patients who desire treatment must be assessed according to all five of the ethically appropriate criteria defined earlier: likelihood of benefit, urgency, change in quality of life, duration of benefit, and (when applicable) the amount of resources each candidate requires. All of these criteria are appropriate in certain circumstances, but only when disparities between patients are very substantial.

Once all the potential recipients have been studied, decision makers should allocate resources to maximize the number, length, and quality of lives saved. Because each of the five ethical criteria contribute to this goal in different ways, none is inherently more important than the others. However, because of the intrinsic worth of all persons, maximizing the number of lives saved should generally take priority over other goals, as long as the patients saved should not suffer an extremely poor quality of life or extremely short duration of benefit. For instance, it is better to save two patients who could each live 5 years than to save one patient who could live 10 years. In addition, preventing extremely poor outcomes should take precedence over other efforts to enhance quality of life or duration of benefit. A patient who can go from 0% (ie, death) to 50% of full functioning, for example, should be preferred over a patient who can go from 25% to 75% of full functioning.

In some cases, the five ethical criteria will not clearly identify which patients should receive highest priority for treatment. While there may be some patients who clearly should be preferred over others, there might still be a number of patients for whom there were no very substantial differences according to these criteria. When these five ethical criteria do not clearly identify the most appropriate patients for treatment, some other method must be employed that provides each appropriate candidate with an equal opportunity to receive the needed resources.

Equal opportunity would not be provided if one criterion were arbitrarily given precedence over the others or if small differences between patients were given more weight than is appropriate. Rather, equal opportunity should be provided through the use of a first-come-first-served approach. The first-come-first-served method should not be used to abdicate responsibility for making decisions when appropriate criteria can give a sound basis for preferring some patients over others. If employed only when uncertainty is too great or the differences among candidates too close to call, the first-come-first-served approach respects the equality of individuals who have equally strong claims to a scarce resource and provides each with an equal opportunity to receive scarce resources.[43]

To ensure that a first-come-first-served approach is truly equitable, all potential candidates must be able to present themselves for treatment in a timely fashion. For instance, if patients with insurance are likely to be diagnosed as having end-stage organ failure earlier that similar patients without insurance, then a first-come-first-served approach would inappropriately favor insured patients over uninsured. Appropriate safeguards are needed to ensure that differences in patient access to diagnostic services are taken into account.

There are a number of ways this general approach could be implemented. The five ethical criteria could be used to identify three groups of patients: those who are clearly good candidates for treatment, those who are clearly poor candidates, and those who do not fall into either group.[27] Within each group, patients could then be prioritized according to the first-come-first-served method or some other equal-opportunity mechanism. Alternatively, the five criteria could be used to define a minimum threshold for receiving treatment, and all potential recipients who exceed this threshold would be prioritized according to the first-come-first-served approach. Defining the boundaries of these different groups, however, is problematic. When there is a large pool of patients competing for organs, for instance, patients who fall just below the minimum threshold level or just miss entry into the group of clearly good candidates will probably not be substantially different from some patients who do make it into those groups.

To avoid drawing lines that may be arbitrary, an alternative approach would be to rank all potential organ recipients according to a weighted formula.[27] Each patient would receive a chance at treatment commensurate with his or her prognosis and need, according to the five ethical criteria discussed earlier, but no candidates would be excluded entirely. Thus, the patients who are the most deserving of treatment according to the ethical criteria would have the best chance of receiving treatment. This approach would not always generate the most efficient allocation decisions; there would inevitably be cases in which a poor candidate would beat the odds and receive the scarce resource before other patients. However, because each patient would have some chance of treatment, this approach would have the advantage of nonabandonment. All of these strategies for implementing the five ethical criteria would be ethically acceptable; no single approach is ethically mandated.

APPROPRIATE DECISION MAKERS

Physicians have an irreplaceable role in making diagnoses, determining prognoses, calculating probabilities, exploring patients' goals and values, and advocating on behalf of their patients. However, physicians of patients competing for resources are generally not in the best position to make impartial allocation decisions. Out of loyalty, physicians might feel pressured to choose their own patients over others, and any choice involving two or more of a physician's own patients would constitute a serious conflict of interest. The physician's role as patient advocate would be jeopardized, and trust between physicians and patients would be undercut.[44] Although individual physicians may have to decide which patients receive needed immediate care in some emergency triage situations, in general physicians should not be forced to make the decision to deny potentially beneficial care to their own patients.

Allocation mechanisms should be objective, flexible, and consistent. Objectivity refers to the need for decision makers not to be personally involved with patients competing for a scarce resource. Flexibility requires decision makers to weigh carefully all the relevant facts of a case, and not reflexively to apply a blanket rule, such as an age cap, to all cases. Consistency requires decision makers to consider the same (appropriate) criteria, interpreted in the same way, to ensure that all decisions are fair to the patients involved.

Centralized allocation mechanisms, such as the organ allocation formulas employed by the United Network for Organ Sharing (UNOS),[45] would probably generate the most consistent decisions. Centralized formulas, however, generally lack flexibility. The particulars of individual cases may sometimes "slip through the cracks" in the formula. In addition, formulas may gloss over uncertainty in the assignment of discrete numbers that appear objective but still only reflect our best guess as to which factors are more significant, and to what degree. These seemingly objective point values may also serve to disguise ethical decisions about the relative importance of various factors in allocation decisions. For instance, assigning points for medical urgency in organ allocation involves ethical judgments about the importance of saving those who are closest to death vs those with the best chances of long-term survival. Because of uncertainty and the need to make ethical decisions transparent, all allocation formulas should be periodically reassessed to ensure that they reflect the most current scientific and ethical consensus on allocation issues.

A more decentralized decision-making process would not overcome the inevitable uncertainties involved in allocation decisions and would probably be more difficult to apply consistently across institutional lines. However, a decentralized approach might be more flexible and would not necessarily result in unjust or arbitrary decisions. A more expansive understanding of the

ethical issues involved in resource allocation decisions can go far in encouraging reasoned, fair, and consistent choices based on careful evaluation of appropriate criteria.

The Council at this time does not advocate either centralized or decentralized approaches; further discussion of these issues will be necessary in the future.

PATIENT INFORMATION IN ALLOCATION DECISIONS

Physicians should explain the allocation criteria and procedure to their patients or designated proxies so that they understand their chances of receiving treatment and the method by which the decision is made. This is in addition to all the customary information regarding the risks, benefits, and alternatives to any medical procedure. Furthermore, patients denied access to resources should be informed by their physicians of the rationale behind such decisions.

FUTURE DIRECTIONS

The current lack of consensus on allocation decisions reflects in part deep disagreement over appropriate allocation criteria and in part a general unwillingness to face the problem of scarcity directly. More informed, public discussion of scarcity and allocation decisions will help ensure that access to scarce resources is provided equitably. The reality of scarce resources must be confronted not only by those who must make allocation decisions, but by all of society, which must live with the consequences of those decisions. Justice in this area will never be achieved until limitations imposed by scarcity are accepted by all, without attempts to circumvent the allocation process. Physicians, hospitals, and other institutions that control scarce medical resources should encourage public discussion of allocation issues. Allocation procedures should also be subject to peer review and public auditing on a regular basis. Not only will such discussion direct public attention to the problem of scarce medical resources, but it may also encourage a broader consensus on how scarce resources should be distributed.

References and Notes

1. Opinion 2.03: allocation of health resources. In: *Current Opinions of the Council on Ethical and Judicial Affairs.* Chicago, Ill: American Medical Association; 1992.

2. Kilner JF. Limited resources. In: *Who Lives? Who Dies? Ethical Criteria in Patient Selection.* New Haven, Conn: Yale University Press; 1990:chap 1.

3. Dossetor JB. Principles used in organ allocation. In: Land W, Dossetor JB, eds. *Organ Replacement Therapy: Ethics, Justice, and Commerce.* Berlin, Germany: Springer-Verlag; 1991:393–398.

4. Evans RW. Health care technology and the inevitability of resource allocation and rationing decisions: part 2. JAMA. 1983;249:2208–2219.

5. Perkins HS, Jonsen AR, Epstein WV. Providers as predictors: using outcome predictions in intensive care. Crit Care Med. 1986;14:105–110.

6. Kalb PE, Miller DH. Utilization strategies for intensive care units. JAMA. 1989; 261:2389–2395.

7. United Network for Organ Sharing. *Bylaws and Policies.* March 4, 1993. Policy 3.3.5.

8. US General Accounting Office. *Organ Transplants: increased Effort Needed to Boost Supply and Ensure Equitable Distribution of Organs.* Washington, DC: US General Accounting Office; April 1993. Publication GAO/HRD-93-56.

9. McGregor M. Technology and the allocation of resources. N Engl J Med. 1989;320:118–120.

10. Callahan D. Rationing medical progress: the way to affordable health care. N Engl J Med. 1990; 322:1810–1813.

11. Truog RD. Triage in the ICU. Hastings Cent Rep. May/June 1992;22:13–17.

12. Council on Ethical and Judicial Affairs. Guidelines for the appropriate use of do-not-resuscitate orders. JAMA. 1991;265:1868–1871.

13. Kilner JF. Psychological ability. In: *Who Lives? Who Dies? Ethical Criteria in Patient Selection.* New Haven, Conn: Yale University Press; 1990: chap 8.

14. Thompson ME. Selection of candidates for cardiac transplantation. Heart Transplant. 1983;3:65–69.

15. Leenen HJ. Selection of patients. J Med Ethics. 1982; 8:33–36.

16. Jonsen AR. Selection of recipients for cardiac transplantation. In: Evans R, ed. *National Heart Transplantation Study.* Washington, DC: Health Care Financing Administration, US Dept of Health and Human Services; 1984;4:36-1–36-8.

17. McKevitt PM, et al. The elderly on dialysis: physical and psychosocial functioning. Dialysis Transplant. 1986;15:130–137.

18. Edlund M, Tancredi LR. Quality of life: an ideological critique. Perspect Biol Med. 1985; 28:591–607.

19. Kilner JF. Quality of benefit. In: *Who Lives? Who Dies? Ethical Criteria in Patient Selection.* New Haven, Conn: Yale University Press; 1990:chap 14.

20. Lo B. Quality of life judgments in the care of the elderly. In: Monagle D, Thomasma JF, eds. *Medical Ethics: A Guide for Health Professionals.* Rockville, Md: Aspen Publishers; 1988:140–147.

21. Smith A. Qualms and QALYs. Lancet. 1987; 1:1134–1136.

22. Ferrans CE. Quality of life as a criterion for allocation of life-sustaining treatment: the case of hemodialysis. In: Anderson G, Glesnes-Anderson V, eds. *Health Care Ethics: A Guide for Decision Makers.* Rockville, Md: Aspen Publishers; 1987:109–124.

23. Menzel PT. Oregon's denial: disabilities and quality of life. Hastings Cent Rep. November/December 1992;22:21–25.

24. Dracup K, Raffin T. Withholding and withdrawing mechanical ventilation: assessing quality of life. Am Rev Respir Dis. 1989;140:S44–S46.

25. Orentlicher D. Rationing and the Americans With Disabilities Act. JAMA. 1994;271:308–314.

26. Council on Ethical and Judicial Affairs. Ethical implications of age-based rationing of health care. In: *Code of Medical Ethics: Reports.* Chicago, Ill: American Medical Association; 1992;1:53–56.

27. Brock DW. Ethical issues in recipient selection for organ transplantation. In: Mathieu D, ed. *Organ Substitution Technology: Ethical, Legal, and Public Policy Issues.* Boulder, Colo: Westview Press; 1988:86–99.

28. King TC. Ethical dilemmas of restricted resources. In: Herter F, Forde K, Mark L, De Bellis R, Kutscher A, Selder F, eds. *Human and Ethical Issues in the Surgical Care of Patients With Life-Threatening Disease.* Springfield, Ill: Charles C Thomas Publisher; 1986:169–175.

29. Callahan D. Symbols, rationality, and justice: rationing health care. *Am J Law Med.* 1992; 18:1–13.

30. Council on Ethical and Judicial Affairs. Caring for the poor. JAMA. 1993;269:2533–2537.

31. McIntyre KM, Benfari RC, Battin MP. Two cardiac arrests, one medical team. *Hastings Cent Rep.* 1982;12:24–25.

32. Kilner JF. Age. In: *Who Lives? Who Dies? Ethical Criteria in Patient Selection.* New Haven, Conn: Yale University Press; 1990:chap 7.

33. Callahan D. *Setting Limits: Medical Goals in an Aging Society.* New York, NY: Simon & Schuster; 1987.

34. Brody B. *Ethics and Its Applications.* New York, NY: Harcourt Brace Jovanovich; 1983.

35. Kilner JF. Social value. In: *Who Lives? Who Dies? Ethical Criteria in Patient Selection.* New Haven, Conn: Yale University Press; 1990:chap 3.

36. Winslow GR. *Triage and Justice.* Berkeley, Calif: University of California Press; 1982.

37. Evans RW, Blagg CR, Bryan FA Jr. Implications for health care policy: a social and demographic profile of hemodialysis patients in the United States. JAMA. 1981;245:487–491.

38. Moss AH, Siegler M. Should alcoholics compete equally for liver transplantation? JAMA. 1991; 265:1295–1298.

39. Cohen C, Benjamin M, Ethics and Social Impact Committee of the Transplant and Health Policy Center. Alcoholics and liver transplantation. JAMA. 1991; 265:1299–1301.

40. Starzl TE, Van Thiel D, Tzakis AG, et al. Orthotopic liver transplantation for alcoholic cirrhosis. JAMA. 1988;260:2542–2544.

41. Ubel PA, Arnold RM, Caplan AL. Rationing failure: the ethical lessons of the retransplantation of scarce vital organs. JAMA. 1993; 270:2469–2474.

42. Evans RW, Manninen DL, Dong FB, McLynne DA, Is retransplantation cost effective? *Transplant Proc.* 1993; 25:1694–1696.

43. Beauchamp TL, Childress JF. *Principles of Biomedical Ethics,* 3rd ed. New York, NY: Oxford University Press; 1989:290–302.

44. Levinsky NG. The doctor's master. *N. Engl J Med.* 1984;311:1573–1575.

45. United Network for Organ Sharing. *Bylaws and Policies,* March 4, 1993. Policy 3.0–3.11.3.

Cost Containment

Charles Dougherty PhD

FOUNDATIONS

There is no value named cost containment or even cost consciousness. Yet there is a value in the conceptual neighborhood of these terms that is exceptionally important in the contemporary health care arena. Whatever its proper name, its disposition is a kind of fiscal prudence. It might simply be called economics, had that term not lost its root meaning of efficient household management, an association still captured in the verb form, to economize.

The traditional moral value expressed in a desire to contain costs is thrift and under that name was long a central value for Americans.[1] It functioned as a value in several ways. Psychologically, thrift was valued as a form of puritan self-denial. It was an admired form of restraint that built character and self-sufficiency. The prizing of thrift has become such a foreign notion to contemporary Americans that both the name and the moral concept it expressed have all but disappeared from the culture in general and from

From *Back to Reform: Values, Markets, and the Health Care System.* New York: Oxford University Press, 1996.

discussions of ethics in particular. The closest contemporary expression of a value that celebrates self-denial is probably found in the areas of dieting and exercise, where restraint and self-discipline are still viewed positively, or at least seen to promote positive consequences.

Theoretically, thrift was also valued as an economic engine. At the same time that its psychology reduced demand, the financial dimensions of thrift produced savings. Americans who saved pennies put those pennies in banks. Thrift thus helped to create the capital needed for the development of modern economies, which in turn generated untold wealth. Before there was wealth, thrift also served as a practical means of coping with scarcity. In times of scarcity, the little available goes farther when all are thrifty with resources. Therefore, thrift was a value psychologically, economically, and practically.

This traditional stance began to wane in the United States after World War II. Practically, thrift was not needed in an economy of affluence and pent-up demand, nor was it the main economic engine; for individuals, corporations, and government borrowing replaced saving. The economic imperative of consumption fostered a psychological self-indulgence.

Large social trends, including the end of accelerating affluence, the increasing cost of debt, and the existential emptiness of consumerism, are beginning to move the nation back toward thrift. Americans are unlikely to embrace thrift as a moral value anytime soon, but there is an increasing moral repugnance toward waste. A move in this moral direction, away from waste and toward thrift, may introduce a greater balance in the national psyche and economy. The "golden mean" that lies between the two, at least in the arena of health care, is the value of cost containment.

The cost problem facing the American health care system has already been reviewed. The United States spends more on health care than any other nation in the world, more in dollars, more in terms of per capita spending, and more in terms of percentage of GDP. The rate of increase in spending is economically unsustainable. Projected into the near future, current rates will produce national spending of $1.7 trillion or 18.1 percent of the GDP, by the year 2000, $16 trillion or 32 percent of the GDP by 2030.[2]

This economic perspective is challenging enough on its own terms, but the need to contain costs in the health care system is also a moral issue for three reasons. First, if the health care needs of the American people can be met by spending less money, other things being equal, this should be done. Reversing the point, spending more money than necessary to address the health care needs of the population is wasteful. It is easy to be cynical on this point because what constitutes waste to one person is often income to another. Nevertheless, besides the growing cultural hostility toward it, there is a common sense moral prohibition against wastefulness. Although Americans in the second half of the twentieth century have been inclined to ignore or minimize this moral prohibition, it has become increasingly clear that the twenty-first century will be an era of limits.[3] The kind of limits that have shaped the characters of other nations and other times—limits on space, resources, financing, even opportunity—are now coming forward in the American consciousness. These limits are being reached politically by the reluctance of the public to approve new spending measures and programs, being defined in the marketplace by the increasing reluctance of payers to absorb rising health care costs, and being experienced in many households as more of the costs of health care are shifted to consumers. At the same time that limits are becoming increasingly irresistible, growth in the health care sector since World War II has made it one of the largest economic activities in the United States. In many American cities and towns, for example, hospitals are the largest employers and the largest consumers of resources. These facts have heightened awareness of the need to contain costs and given new urgency to the general moral wrongfulness of waste.

A parallel point can be made in religious terms drawn from the Judeo-Christian tradition.[4] Creation and all its multiple resources are gifts from a benevolent God, given in trust to the human species as part of a redemptive plan that is understood only "through a glass darkly." Because of the richness of the gift of nature and the incomprehensible character of the full plan for its intended use, the religious tradition has given rise, especially in modern industrial nations, to exploitative attitudes toward nature and other species. Selfishness and the drive to dominate have led to cruelties, pollution, and a generalized indifference to the issue of waste. Although these cultural expressions arose within the Judeo-Christian tradition, they do not embody its more fundamental religious insight: the duty of responsible stewardship.[5] The main intellectual thrust of the tradition is that humans are not given control over nature for purposes of domination and self-aggrandizement, but for working out a partnership in the creative work of God. In this view, waste can never simply be an economic matter. Instead, it is a profound disorientation from the basic gift of creation. Waste constitutes an act of ingratitude to God. The main thrust of the dominant religious tradition therefore supports the same conclusion as common sense: If the health care needs of the American people can be met while spending less, it should be done.

OPPORTUNITY COSTS

A second reason why cost containment is a moral issue involves the economic notion of opportunity costs. There are at least two aspects of cost to purchasing any good or service. The first cost is the money spent directly for the item. Less obvious perhaps, but nonetheless real, is the indirect cost entailed by the fact that the money spent on this item is no longer available to be spent in any other fashion. Thus a purchaser pays the direct cost for an item and pays again indirectly in lost opportunities to purchase other items. The United States now invests one-seventh of all spending in the health care sector.[6] Not only is this a staggeringly large figure in its own right (approaching one trillion dollars), but it also represents money not available for spending elsewhere, including areas in which there are significant unmet needs.[7]

The impact of these opportunity costs can be seen most graphically in state government. For a number of years, the item growing most rapidly in the budgets of most states has been the Medicaid program.[8] Total costs of the program (federal and state) more than doubled between 1989 and 1993. Medicaid costs to the states have exploded because of growing numbers of uninsured and those using the program for longterm care.

In many states this massive increase in Medicaid spending has substantially diminished discretionary spending by the state, that is, reduced the state's ability to initiate new efforts in other areas of pressing need. States have been less able, for example, to improve the lives and lots of their own citizens through initiatives in social welfare, economic development, housing, and education. There is considerable irony in this. One of the obvious goals of health care is to preserve and enhance the health of the population and individuals who constitute the population. (It must always be recalled that caring, irrespective of state of health or anticipated outcome, is also a goal of health care.) Interventions in these other areas, especially in education, housing, and economic development, can make dramatic differences in a population's health and, of course, in the health of individuals.[9] Consequently, one of the opportunity costs of an ever-expanding health care sector is the inability to improve health through non-health-care efforts.

Finally, cost containment is a moral value because waste in this arena often means the performance of unnecessary procedures. When too much money is spent on health care, too many interventions are done. A recent study, for example, suggests that twenty-three percent of procedures to place tympanostomy tubes in children (for otitis media or ear infections) are inappropriate, and another thirty-five percent are questionable.[10] Too many interventions means the creation of harms through unnecessary surgery and invasive tests. Whereas it is plainly imperative from a moral point of view to get people the health care that they need, it is also imperative for similar reasons not to provide health care people do not need, especially risky health care. Yet this obvious point can easily be lost in an overheated and intensely competitive economic sector that may soon absorb one of every five dollars in the United States economy.

RATIONING

There are, therefore, good reasons for moral concern about health care spending and for commitment to the goals of restraining cost increases and avoiding waste in the system. On the other hand, the need to create universal coverage grounded in the fundamental value of dignity is also clear. There may be other strategies for balancing the apparently incompatible demands of increasing access while restraining costs, but one is surely the rationing of health care. Debates on this subject have been extraordinarily complex and heated. Honesty demands that the ethical dimensions of this debate be treated straightforwardly and with care.[11]

Part of the reason the debate about health care rationing has been so acrimonious is because the meaning of the term is equivocal when applied to health care, and differing meanings are associated with directly antagonistic emotional evaluations.[12] One side, typically held by direct providers of care, understands rationing to be the denial of needed health care services in clinical contexts. A sinister image that typically operates behind this understanding is a scenario in which a doctor tries to help a patient whose life can be saved or whose illness can be cured by access to an available but expensive technology. Standing between the doctor and patient, however, and preventing the ability of the former to assist the latter is a government bureaucrat. This func-

tionary refuses authorization to use the machine on the basis of some estimation of the total cost of such interventions to society as a whole. Thus, the clinical point of medicine and the satisfactions of both provider and patient are frustrated by health care rationing. More importantly, the patient is harmed and may die unnecessarily or suffer a preventable loss of health. Therefore, from this perspective, rationing means denying needed care, and its emotional association is exceptionally negative. Rationing is wrong and should be resorted to only in the most grave and unusual circumstances, for example, in situations of triage caused by large-scale disasters.

There is, however, a competing interpretation of rationing, a view typically held by social workers, economists, and policy experts. In this view, rationing is an inevitable dimension of economic life, a means of allocating resources. Moreover, in some circumstances, it can be a means morally preferable to other alternatives. This view gets semantic support from dictionaries in which rationing is often defined as the *equitable* distribution of a scarce resource.[13] In this context, equitable simply means fair. Therefore, rationing means the introduction of fairness into a situation of scarcity. Because scarcity is itself an inevitable phenomena—there is rarely an unlimited amount of any desirable resource—rationing creates the opportunity to bring fairness into economic relationships. By contrast, the unhampered workings of a market system tend to drive the price of scarce commodities up, to the point that only the wealthiest can afford to buy them. This seems unfair and can be destructive of a community's sense of solidarity. Rationing assures that wealth is not the sole criteria for access to scarce commodities. It therefore makes the economic situation fairer than the pricing system on its own would be and thus prevents social discord. Rationing of health care has similar potential for creating greater fairness in the distribution of an inevitably scarce set of goods and services and for expressing national solidarity. Emotionally, this account of rationing feels good.

A DEFINITION

To move beyond this impasse in both meaning and emotional charge, it is necessary to stipulate a neutral definition of rationing. It should be one comprehensive enough to include the valid insights of both sides, yet one that does not determine by definition that all forms of rationing are inherently either good or bad. The following definition is employed here. *Health care rationing is the denial or limiting of access to needed and potentially beneficial health care because policies and practices have restricted the resources available for health care.*[14]

This neutral definition captures valid points made by both sides of the debate. On the one hand, it recognizes that rationing does mean the denial of needed health care. On the other hand, it allows that policies and practices must sometimes be shaped around the facts of scarcity. It does not, however, assume by definition that rationing as such is a good thing. This neutral definition does not entail, as many dictionary definitions do, that all schemes of rationing are fair by making equity a defining property of rationing. To reach a moral evaluation, particular schemes of rationing would have to be analyzed on their own terms. Some arrangements may be fair, others unfair. Therefore, criteria are needed by which actual or proposed rationing policies and practices can be evaluated morally. Before elaborating such criteria, one other important aspect of this definition should be detailed and more said about the general ethical challenge of rationing.

This is a broad definition. As such, it makes evident what too often escapes contemporary commentators, namely, that there is a considerable amount of rationing in the health care system at present. For the millions of uninsured, health care is limited to emergency treatment and by the charity of providers. For those in public programs, access is rationed by determination of the basic benefits package and by the eligibility standards of the programs themselves. There are, for example, very rigorous norms for financial eligibility for Medicaid in many states, and some are getting more restrictive. There is rationing, too—a peculiar form of it—in the fact that a poor sixty-four-year-old with desperate health care needs may have no health insurance in the United States, whereas every sixty-five-year-old is covered by Medicare, irrespective of need or income. There is rationing in private health plans. Limitations on services covered, maximum days of service allowed, and dollar caps all establish restrictions on access for beneficiaries.

Other features of the system also work to restrict or deny access to needed health care and thus constitute forms, however subtle, of rationing. Geography can be a significant barrier to care in many rural parts of the United States. Lack of infrastructure, difficulties in transportation, and cultural and linguistic differences create barriers for many living in American inner cities. Consequently, de facto rationing occurs in the health care system at present, much of it quite unconscious and unintended, some of it planned.[15] Hence a complete moral evaluation of any proposal to ration health care must analyze not only the details of the health care rationing proposal itself, but must also compare it with the rationing in place in the system at present. It may well be that some rationing proposals have significant moral flaws but compared with the present situation would constitute improvements. In these cases, prudence must be used to determine whether more explicit and formal kinds of rationing are preferable to the indirect and unspoken rationing that permeates the present system.

It is also important to detail the general moral problems raised by rationing health care. The most obvious problem is contained in the first portion of the definition. If health care rationing means the denial of or limitation of access to needed care, then rationing can hurt people. People may be disappointed or frustrated by the inability to obtain unnecessary or futile care, but lack of access to *needed* care means serious harms. Compared with the hypothetical possibility of a system that provides unlimited access to all needed health care, a rationed system means the acceptance of preventable death and suffering. Specific proposals to ration health care, however, must be compared not with this hypothetical ideal, but to the rationing already in place in the system. Some proposals to ration care may involve new harms or new distributions of existing harms, or they may remove or lessen existing harms. Despite the necessity for it and the other positive things that might be said in favor of a thoughtful and comprehensive plan of rationing, from the point of view of the individual denied needed health care, rationing creates real harms. It is important to stress that these harms are not equivalent to those created when commodities like gasoline or sugar are rationed, but can literally mean the difference between life and death and the difference between significant degrees of health for real individuals.

EASY RESCUE

Another significant ethical issue raised by health care rationing is the possibility that it may violate the general moral duty to come to the aid of those in need. This duty is real, but its scope must be limited.[16] Human needs are endless. Moreover, persons have fundamental liberties as well as moral duties to others. Therefore, some reasonable boundaries must exist to the duty to aid those in need. One strategy for charting boundaries here is by understanding the duty to aid as one of "easy rescue." On this account, the duty to rescue others is morally compelling only when three conditions are present. First, a substantial benefit can be conferred on those in need or a substantial harm to them avoided. Second, the risk of harm to the would-be rescuer is insignificant or at least substantially less than the benefit at stake for those in need. Finally, the would-be rescuer must be practically capable, acting alone or with others, to effect the rescue. On this account, people are not obligated, for example, to place their lives in jeopardy to secure a minor benefit for another. However, when an individual or a

group is able at a small risk to save the life of another, then it is morally incumbent on them to try, hence the notion of a moral obligation of "easy rescue."

If there is an obligation to provide easy rescue, then health care rationing may violate that duty if it denies substantial benefits to those in need when these benefits could be provided without great harm to others. Put in more general terms, there is an obligation to provide some basic level of health care to others if this can be done at a reasonable cost. Rationing could violate this duty, and surely some present forms of rationing do violate it.

Finally, depending on how a rationing scheme is designed, it may, dictionary definitions notwithstanding, create inequities in access to health care. Rationing of health care could be based on invidious or inappropriate criteria. For example, denying health care on the basis of general intelligence, strength, or membership in a given race or ethnic group would satisfy the general definition of rationing but would at the same time introduce new and substantial inequities into the distribution of health care. Moreover, certain of these inequities, especially those having to do with racial discrimination, would create with them indignities that undermine respect for persons in substantial ways. Thus, the direct harms created inevitably by rationing—denial of needed care—may under some plans be compounded by indirect harms of inequity and indignity.

With these considerations in mind, eight criteria are useful in helping to determine whether an existing or proposed system of rationing is ethically acceptable.[17] In an area so morally complex, these criteria are not meant to serve as a checklist, nor are the criteria to be thought of in quantitative terms. It would be wrong to think, for example, that a rationing scheme satisfying six of the eight criteria is acceptable, whereas one satisfying only five of the eight is not. Moral evaluation is inherently more ambiguous and difficult than that. These criteria are offered rather as eight moral considerations that should be raised in the evaluation of the ethical acceptability of a rationing plan. They must be used with practical wisdom. The first four of the eight criteria follow more or less directly from values that have already been articulated in previous chapters.

COVER EVERYONE

Rationing Should Take Place Only in a System that Provides a Basic Level of Care for Everyone

The value of human dignity and its expression in respect for persons provide the basis for this criterion. The connection to rationing is that it would be unfair and would create indignities to develop a rationing scheme for health care when some people in effect would have access to nothing more than emergency treatment. Putting the point affirmatively, it is important to bring everyone into the system and to structure a health care floor before the limitations on the system, the ceiling, can be reasonably and fairly determined.

Obviously, determination of what counts as a basic benefit package already involves rationing choices. To exclude bone marrow transplant, for example, because it is too expensive to provide to everyone who might benefit from it (or too expensive in light of serious dispute about its benefits) means that some people who might benefit, might have their lives extended meaningfully, from this procedure will face the harms of being denied it. This sort of rationing choice is inherent in any determination of a basic benefit package. The situation is therefore not as simple as creating universal coverage and then facing the need to ration. Rationing choices are made in the determination of the basic benefits to be provided to all. Nonetheless, the moral imperative is clear: Fairness requires that everyone have some before the limits are determined for all.

PRESERVE CARING AND TRUST

Health Care Rationing must Preserve the Intangibles of Caring and Trust

As argued above, caring is at the heart of the project of health care and trust in individual health care providers and in the professions in general is a significant aspect of maintaining caring relationships. Health care rationing has the potential for undermining both. The need for rationing represents a frank recognition of fiscal and political limits. It arises at a time when cost-cutting methods are becoming increasingly ruthless. Consequently, there is a possibility that explicit rationing may further undermine the climate of caring. It may make the economic dimensions of health care so insistent that the intangibles associated with altruism are driven out. Moreover, concrete expressions of care are often expensive. The ratio of nurses to hospital inpatients, for example, or the number of hospice professionals available for home care of the dying can make a significant difference in a patient's experience of care. Yet labor costs are some of the most expensive items in the health care system. Unlike the relatively fixed costs of building and equipment, labor costs are also variable, reducible by program and staff cuts. Assessment of the moral acceptability of rationing must make reference to protection of caring even as responsible limits on health care are set explicitly.

Depending on how health care rationing is organized, there is also a potential for undermining trust in providers of care, especially in doctors. Suppose, for example, that doctors were asked to become agents of rationing schemes in health care plans, perhaps by managing a given amount of resources for a number of enrolled individuals. In such a scheme, services provided to one patient could mean services not available to another. Doctors in this situation would have to consider not only whether a given patient needs a service, but also whether other potential patients in the health care plan will have a greater need for the service within the same fiscal period.

This kind of financial assessment has the potential for developing conflicts of interest in the primary fiduciary relationship between doctor and patient. It can pit an individual patient's interests against the hypothetical interests of other patients. From the patient's point of view, this introduces an element of distrust. A patient could have a reasonable worry that a doctor's advice that a procedure is unnecessary or unavailable is motivated by a desire to save the procedure for another patient, perhaps one who is more compliant or who has a more interesting case. This, of course, is an insidious concern that can erode trust in the doctor–patient relationship.

The specific role of doctors and other direct care providers in rationing health care services is a complex and controversial one, but assessment of the moral acceptability of a rationing schemes must begin with the premise that some forms of doctor involvement will be incompatible with the trust they must preserve with their patients. Doctors can provide important advice about health care rationing at the policy level and must therefore have a leading role in public debates on rationing. In clinical settings, however, it is better to have rationing imposed on doctors and patients by policymakers and administrators. In this way, doctors can remain advocates for their patients, fighting the bureaucrats who arrange and enforce the limitations.

PROTECT THE VULNERABLE

Rationing Must Protect the Most Vulnerable Among Us

As argued above, there is a special obligation to protect those who are least able to protect themselves. Health care rationing represents a conscious recognition of the struggle over scarce resources in which some will be able to bring greater influence on their own behalf, whereas some will be less able to do so. Children, the frail elderly, the mentally and physically disabled, and those subject to discrimination may find themselves disadvantaged in rationing arrangements unless their case is defended strongly by others who are able to do so.

Defending the interests of the vulnerable may have to take the form of affirmative action. If a rationing scheme were to accept the present distribution of health care resources and to place caps on it without fundamental reallocation, then inner cities, rural areas, Indian reservations, and other areas would face special additional hardships. Within the general restrictions central to the development of a rationing scheme, there must be sufficient flexibility so that additional resources can be directed to historically undeserved areas.

SERVE THE COMMON GOOD

Rationing Schemes Must Serve the Common Good

This criterion follows from the social nature of persons and of the health care system and from the general moral importance of community. It means, for example, that some expensive procedures that benefit only a few, even life-saving treatments, must be foregone in favor of health care investments that make a greater difference statistically. This is an application of the utilitarian dimension of the common good: the greatest good for the greatest number.

This criterion will not be easy to apply. Some investments in expensive medical technology, for example, may serve the overall interests of a community in the long run because the technology becomes cheaper over time or leads to discoveries that benefit all. On the other hand, explicit rationing must begin by assuring access to garden-variety health care of the sort that makes a significant difference in the community as a whole: prenatal care, pediatrics, comprehensive emergency services, and other services. Applying this simple point to the U.S. health care system would entail great change. Current tendencies favor high-tech, acute-care interventions for individuals over public health measures that could make some dramatic differences in the overall health of communities. The facts suggest that Americans prefer spending extravagantly on neonatal intensive care for low-birth-weight babies, for example, while begrudging funding for the relatively inexpensive educational and nutritional efforts that could surely reduce the incidence of low birth weight and infant mortality. Recent and proposed cuts in social programs and welfare have exacerbated this balance.

Use of this criterion also presents an occasion for detailed consideration of the opportunity costs of increased spending throughout the health care sector. If the overall health of the community could be improved by shifting some investments from health care to social services, education, housing, and economic development, then this should be done.

RATIONING MUST BE NECESSARY

Health Care Rationing Must Be Necessary

At first glance, this may seem an easy criterion to satisfy. The point has already been made that expanding access while simultaneously containing costs requires rationing. Therefore, the general necessity of rationing is easily established; but in a system as complex as the American health care system, there are many layers and cross currents of rationing. At present, for example, rationing choices are made in private insurance companies, at the federal level in the Medicare program, and at the state level in the Medicaid program. If all these choices were made consciously and explicitly, some of the rationing implications would be seen as necessary, but others would not be. For example, it may well be that federal spending on health care is approaching its political limits. It is far less clear, however, that all the states are putting adequate money into their Medicaid systems.[18] Some of the rationing by private insurers and by managed care plans is justified only by considerations of the corporate "bottom line."

To determine the necessity for any specific scheme of rationing inside the total system of American health care, difficult practical questions must be asked. Is the proper amount of money being put into that area of health care? The need for rationing in cancer care, for example, might be made more or less pressing depending on how much money is spent on AIDS research and vice versa. In addition to questions involving the internal distribution of health care resources, larger questions arise about how much is put into the entire system and by whom. Is fifteen percent of the GDP the right amount to be spending on health care? Is twenty percent? Are states paying their fair share? What is the proper role of private employers, individual taxpayers, and providers themselves? Assessment of the need for rationing must begin with examination of whether all these players contribute their appropriate share.

The issue of waste is pertinent here as well. Health care rationing, especially the kind that results in significant harms for individuals, is very hard to justify in light of the apparent waste in the system. Imagine a family being told that a rationing arrangement has disqualified their child from an expensive but potentially life-saving intervention. Heart-wrenching scenarios like this will occur in any serious rationing scheme; they occur now. Suppose, further, that after being denied this care because it is too expensive, the same family discovers the amount of money health care providers put into advertising each year, the high salaries paid to executives throughout the system, or the profits made by pharmaceutical companies. How can this hypothetical family understand and accept the life and death restrictions they face once they know the costs of the many unnecessary medical procedures performed each year, the extraordinary amount of administrative overhead in the system, or the stock market profits of investors in for-profit health care corporations?

This criterion does not require that every form of waste be removed from the system before rationing can be justified. This would be an impossible standard. It does mean, however, that it becomes more difficult to justify rationing as there is more obvious waste in the system. There can be considerable differences in opinion about what constitutes waste in health care, and these differences must be respected. One obvious benchmark is the amount of money spent outside the context of patient care. The further health care spending is from patient care, the higher the standard for justifying its use. Rationing means asking for shared sacrifice. A plausible case must be made that this level of sacrifice is indeed required. Every bit of waste makes the case that much less plausible.

KEEP THE PROCESS OPEN

Health Care Rationing Must Result from an Open Public Process

Everyone affected by rationing must have access to the process through which the limits are set. This access may occur through the political process, for example, through public hearings, legislation, and candidates for election debating explicit rationing goals and methods. This criterion also requires opening the rationing processes of private entities to public scrutiny. Enrollees should be able to know, for example, the reasons why an insurance company determines that bone marrow transplantation is not covered, why an HMO covers only thirty days of care in a rehabilitation hospital, why a managed care plan reduced its mental health care benefits. Enrollees should have some ways to shape these decisions. Many members of the public will not be able to understand the complexities of medical outcome studies and actuarial determinations of risk and service utilization. Some will have no interest in influencing coverage decisions. Nonetheless, all citizens should have access to the process that sets specific limitations on their care as a matter of rudimentary fairness. If the sacrifices of rationing are to be shared, there must be some ownership of the process that determines the specific character of the sacrifice. Fairness also requires easy access to unbiased appeals processes for individuals who are denied the health care they need.

NO DISCRIMINATION

Health Care Rationing Must Be Free of Wrongful Discrimination

Obviously, health care rationing means discriminating between covered and uncovered services and between individuals who are and are not candidates for services. Some choices may appear unfair from some individuals' points of view, especially those denied needed care. Nevertheless, this sort of discrimination is a requirement of health care rationing; it is what health care rationing means.

At the same time, however, health care rationing must be free of invidious forms of discrimination, including discrimination based on gender, race, ethnicity, religion, medical condition or disability, sexual orientation, etc. As difficult as enforcement may be on these issues, the moral point behind them is obvious to most Americans. However, there are two other areas in which consensus is more elusive.

The first area is age.[19] From one point of view, the use of age as a way to ration health care is as unacceptable as the use of race or gender. From this viewpoint, denying people medical procedures because they are elderly constitutes ageism. This view does embody a sound insight, namely, that consideration of age alone is a morally arbitrary criterion. Furthermore, it is a criterion that discriminates against a population that is generally both vulnerable because of the natural effects of aging and deserving because of a lifetime of contributions to society.

Yet age is unlike other clearly discriminatory categories in one important respect. As a rule, people do not change their gender or race. By contrast, people change their age with predictable regularity. A policy that links health care benefits to age so that certain benefits are available only after a given age (mammography, for example) and others available only before a given age (immunizations, for example) could be fair. Such a policy would affect people equally, not at the same time, but equally as they move through time. It is not unfair, broadly speaking, that more educational resources are invested on the young and more health care on the elderly because this distribution captures part of the natural rhythm of life in the contemporary world. From this perspective, age-based criteria for rationing are not inherently discriminatory. Instead, they can be reasonable patterns of social support for temporal beings.

One strategy for resolving this tension, especially as it bears on the very expensive care of the elderly and dying, is to restrict the use of age as a criterion for rationing to its relationship to prognosis. It seems discriminatory, for example, to deny seventy-year-olds heart transplantation simply because of their age, but it does seem reasonable to exclude them if patients over seventy have a demonstrably lower chance of success from such procedures. There are contexts in which this is not an easy distinction to make, nor will it be fair to all people since some seventy-year-olds will be more robust and therefore have a better individual prognosis than their age cohort. Yet the need for rationing is such that age is a reasonable consideration when it is clearly related to medical outcome, but not otherwise.

The other unsettling dimension of potential discrimination in this area is rationing based on lifestyle, especially when it involves alleged complicity in the etiology of disease. Is it fair, for example, to restrict access to certain treatments for emphysema when this condition was caused by lifelong cigarette smoking at the same time that these same treatments are available to others who have non-smoking-related emphysema?

It is important to ask individuals to assume more responsibility for their health and health care. It makes sense to use financial incentives and disincentives to encourage positive habits and discourage others. However, the use of notions of personal responsibility in the context of need for care can easily devolve into "victim-blaming."[20] This is especially so in light of the fact that the multiple variables that shape habit—genetics, environment, personal choice—are so interwoven as to make assessment of degree of responsibility a practically impossible task. Moreover, using personal responsibility to determine access to care could undermine the caring attitude so necessary for health care professionals and institutions.

On balance, then, individuals should be presumed responsible when prevention and health education efforts are mounted. Some financial incentives can be acceptable. In clinical context, however, it is inappropriate to use lifestyle or personal responsibility for health in making rationing decisions. Here a caring response to patient need is the right attitude, not judgmental and debatable assessments of responsibility.

RATIONING FOR ALL

Those Who Ration Health Care Should Be Subject to Rationing Themselves

This is at once the most obvious and the most challenging criterion. It is the most obvious because of the evident unfairness in allowing a system in which some people ration health care for others and yet remain free of the same restrictions that they create. The state legislators who vote to restrict access to Medicaid, but who have comprehensive coverage for themselves, are a case in point. So is the case of the U.S. Senator who opposes universal health care coverage but receives publicly funded comprehensive care. The Golden Rule, an insight at the core of many religious and ethical codes, mandates that one adopt the same standards of conduct toward others that one would want were roles reversed. The Golden Rule insight demands moral reciprocity. It disallows making exceptions for oneself, rejecting as immoral, for example, an insistence on honesty from others but on freedom to lie for oneself. Yet this is the same kind of moral exception claimed, in effect, by "unrationed rationers." These people and their families enjoy access to all that contemporary health care can offer, while at the same time they limit—actively or passively—access for others. On the face of it, this is inequitable. It creates a kind of medical class system.

On the other hand, the reason this principle is so difficult to accept and apply has to do with the plural character of the U.S. health care system. The state legislator, for example, who votes to restrict access to services in the Medicaid program may have Blue Cross insurance coverage provided by a private employer. As a state legislator, this person is placing restrictions on the spending of public funds; as a private citizen, this same person is accepting a fringe benefit in a private employment contract.

Demanding that those who ration be subject to the rationing they impose would be more feasible were the system more unitary. For example, if there were a national health board that determined the basic benefit package for all Americans, it would be a reasonable demand that the individuals who determine that package live with it themselves. The practical expectation is that the standards for acceptable rationing would rise when rationing is also applied to the rationers and their families, not simply to "the other." Yet this anticipates large and complex changes in the health care system.

Moreover, this criterion runs into another fundamental American value, the freedom to accumulate and dispose of wealth. Suppose some member of the national commission that determines the basic benefit package to be provided to all is a corporate leader and a millionaire. It would violate fundamental assumptions in American culture to forbid this individual from using some personal wealth to purchase additional health care beyond the minimal package designed by the board. It certainly seems problematic to hold that a millionaire can own multiple homes, cars, and endless luxury items but cannot buy more dialysis or better long-term care.

For these reasons, a more pragmatic version of the same principle would require movement toward a health care system that has such a comprehensive basic benefit package that even well-off citizens (though perhaps not the truly wealthy) would have little inclination to buy more, or at least those who did would be few. These considerations raise the problem of a two-tiered or multitiered health care system. A strict interpretation of the principle that those who ration must be subject to rationing anticipates a unitary system with one tier of care for all. This may never be the case in the United States. If one tier is never to be, the nature of the tiers that are probable must be assessed because some tier arrangements are morally preferable to others.

A system with fewer people in a second, more comprehensive tier of care is morally better than one with a large percentage of the population in a second, better tier. For example, a situation in which ten percent of the population buys more than the basic benefit package is morally preferable to a situation in which seventy-five percent of the population buys more. In the second scenario, there is good reason to think that what is defined as basic in the benefit package is inadequate; certainly the majority behaves as if they believe it is so. Moreover, with so many people buying more or relying on a different system entirely, there would be little political support to keep the quality high and the benefit package adequate in the publicly defined system. Consequently, a practical compromise with the realities of the American health care system now and in the foreseeable future requires a moral strategy that seeks to keep as many of the powerful and influential rationers, especially middle class voters, in a single system of rationing. Inevitably, some Americans will have the desire and ability to escape health care restrictions by using their own private funds. As troubling as this compromise is from the Golden Rule perspective, it is built around presently irreducible facts about the nation's political culture.

The logic of recent debates on health care rationing has been disingenuous on both sides. Progressives who demand universal access insist at the same time that expansion of access has no connection to the need for health care rationing; this is false. Health care rationing is probably the only tool available for achieving the twin goals of expanded access and cost constraint. At the same time, conservatives who resist demands for universal access invoke the specter of health care rationing as if restrictions would occur only under some new scheme for universal coverage, as if there were no rationing in the present system; this is also false. The health care system rations now. Issues of rationing are unavoidable either way. There is rationing in American health care now. There will be rationing in American health care in any conceivable future. The real question is whether ethical criteria will be used to guide it.

References and Notes

1. David M. Tucker, *The Decline of Thrift in America* (New York: Praeger, 1991).

2. Sally Burner, Daniel Waldo, and David McKusick, "National Health Expenditures Projections Through 2030," *Health Care Financing Review* 14, no. 1 (1992): 1–30.

3. Callahan, *Setting Limits*.

4. On Christianity and the environment, see John Carmody, *Ecology and Religion: Toward a New Christian Theology of Nature* (New York: Paulist Press, 1983); and James M. Gustafson, *A Sense of the Divine: The Natural Environment from a Theocentric Perspective* (Cleveland, Ohio: Pilgrim Press, 1994).

5. Prentiss Pemberton, *Toward a Christian Economic Ethic: Stewardship and Social Power* (Minneapolis: Winston Press, 1985); and Mary Evelyn Jegen and Bruno Manno, eds., *The Earth is the Lord's: Essays on Stewardship* (New York: Paulist Press, 1978).

6. Eckholm, *New York Times*, pp. 1 and 20.

7. Ibid.

8. Iglehart, "Medicaid," pp. 896–900.

9. See, e.g., E. Rogot P. Sorlie, N. Johnson, "Life Expectancy by Employment Status, Income, and Education in the National Longitudinal Mortality Study," *Public Health Reporter* 107, no. 4 (1992): 457–61.

10. L. Kleinman, et al., "The Medical Appropriateness of Tympanostomy Tubes Proposed for Children Younger Than 16 Years in the United States," *JAMA* 271, no. 16 (1994): 1250–55.

11. Charles J. Dougherty, *Ethical Dimensions of Healthcare Rationing*, (St. Louis, Catholic Health Association, 1994), 1–13.

12. Larry Churchill, *Self Interest and Universal Health Care* (Cambridge, Mass.: Harvard University Press, 1994), 6–23.

13. See, e.g., *Webster's Ninth New Collegiate Dictionary* (Springfield, Mass.: Merriam-Webster, 1983), 977.

14. Dougherty, "Ethical Dimensions of Healthcare Rationing," p. 3.

15. Larry R. Churchill, *Rationing Health Care in America* (Notre Dame, Ind.: University of Notre Dame Press, 1987), 5–19.

16. Beauchamp and Childress, *Principles of Biomedical Ethics*, pp. 266–71.

17. Dougherty, "Ethical Dimensions of Healthcare Rationing," pp. 8–13.

18. Marilyn Bach et al., "Ethics and Medicaid: A New Look at an Old Problem," *Journal of Health Care for the Poor and Underserved* 2, no. 4 (1992), pp. 427–47.

19. See, generally, Norman Daniels, *Am I My Parents' Keeper?* (New York: Oxford University Press, 1988), esp. pp. 83–102.

20. Charles J. Dougherty, "Bad Faith and Victim-Blaming: The Limits of Health Promotion," *Health Care Analysis* 1, no. 3, (1993): 111–19.

QUESTIONS FOR DISCUSSION

1. Given that human organs are scarce, if an individual has received an organ transplant that has failed and needs another transplant to save his life, should his claim to receive a second transplant be equal to the claim of others in need of a first transplant? What would fairness require in such a case?

2. Some argue that denying life-extending treatment to the elderly beyond a certain age discriminates against them and thus is unfair. Others argue that giving

priority to such treatment over preventive care early in life discriminates against and is unfair to the young because it makes it more difficult for them to achieve the same number of life-years and experiences that the elderly already have had. Assess the comparative strengths and weaknesses of these two arguments.

3. When the availability of a given resource is such that we can use all of it to save one person or else divide it up to save three other people, should we allocate it by a lottery that gives an equal chance to all four, or should we give it to the three in order to save the greater number? Are numbers all that count here?

4. The concept of quality adjusted life-years (QALYs) as a measure of cost-effectiveness in health care has been criticized on the ground that it discriminates against the elderly, the disabled, and other social groups. Is there an alternative method of allocating care that can be both cost-effective and fair at the same time?

5. Some have advocated a two-tiered health care system as a way of rationing health care. The lower tier would guarantee that everyone had access to a decent minimum of care, while the higher tier would allow those who wanted to pay for supplementary or expedited care to receive it. Would this be unfair to those who could not afford to pay for care in the higher tier, even if access to the lower tier ensured a decent minimum level of health and well-being? Explain.

CASES

Strunk v. Strunk. Court of Appeals of Kentucky, 455 S.W. 2d 145 (1969). Tommy Strunk, aged 28, suffered from a fatal kidney disease and was being kept alive temporarily by dialysis. His brother, Jerry, 27, had the mental capacity of approximately a six-year-old and was considered incompetent. Jerry was the only potential donor whose blood and tissue type were compatible with Tommy's. Their mother, Ava Strunk, petitioned the court to proceed with an operation in which one of Jerry's kidneys would be transplanted into his brother. She argued that the transplant would be beneficial not only to Tommy but to Jerry as well, since he was so emotionally dependent on his brother. The loss of Tommy through death as a consequence of not having the transplant would have a more adverse impact on Jerry's well-being than would going through with the transplant. On this basis, as well as the mother's legitimate substituted judgment, the court authorized the operation.

Head v. Colloton. Supreme Court of Iowa, 331 N.W. 2d 870 (1983). In 1982, the plaintiff (Head) phoned the transplant unit of the University of Iowa Hospitals and Clinics and learned that the hospital bone marrow transplant registry included the name of a woman who, upon further testing, might have proven to be a suitable donor to him. The hospital had placed her name in the bone marrow registry without her consent. The defendants (Colloton and Filer) were hospital employees with access to the registry. Head asked for a mandatory injunction to require the defendants to disclose the identity of the potential donor either to the court or to his attorney. But the defendants refused on the ground that the registry must be